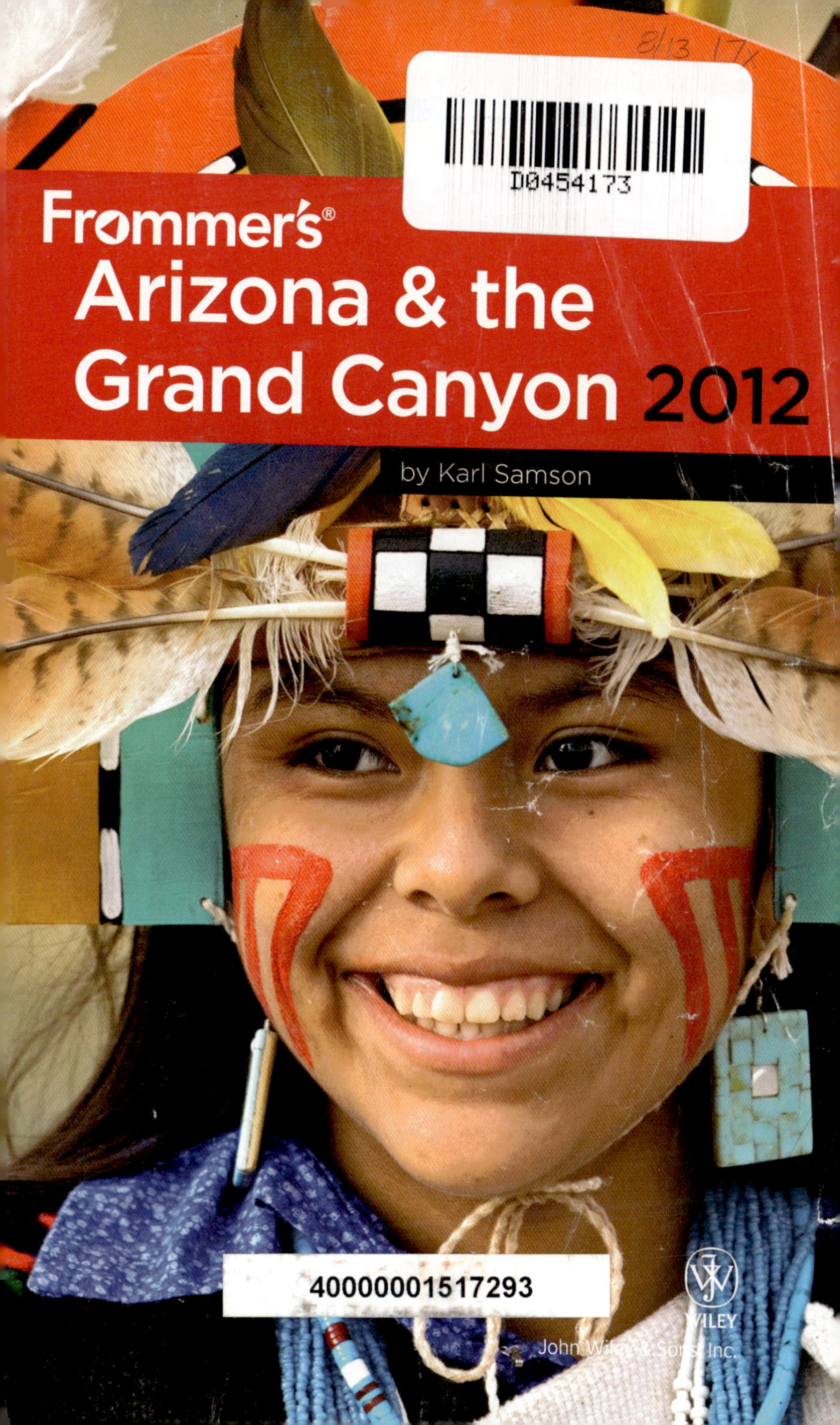
8/13 17x
D0454173
Frommer's®
Arizona & the
Grand Canyon 2012
by Karl Samson
40000001517293
WILEY
John Wiley & Sons, Inc.

Published by:
John Wiley & Sons, Inc.
111 River St.
Hoboken, NJ 07030-5774

ISBN 978-1-118-01727-2 (paper); ISBN 978-1-118-12151-1 (ebk);
ISBN 978-1-118-12152-8 (ebk); ISBN 978-1-118-12153-5 (ebk)

Editor: Cate Latting
Production Editor: Erin Amick
Cartographer: Roberta Stockwell
Photo Editor: Richard H. Fox
Production by Wiley Indianapolis Composition Services

Front cover photo: Havasu Falls, Havasupai, Arizona ©Peter Mukherjee / Vetta / Getty Images
Back cover photos: *Left:* A man in a slot canyon, Navajo Nation, Arizona ©Whit Richardson / Aurora / Getty Images; *Middle:* Rafters brave rapids on the Colorado River in Grand Canyon NP ©Blickwinkel / Alamy Images; *Right:* Route 66 memorabilia ©Jeremy Woodhouse / Getty Images.

For information on our other products and services or to obtain technical support, please contact our Customer Care Department within the U.S. at 877/762-2974, outside the U.S. at 317/572-3993 or fax 317/572-4002.

Wiley also publishes its books in a variety of electronic formats. Some content that appears in print may not be available in electronic formats.

Manufactured in China

5 4 3 2 1

CONTENTS

8 EASTERN ARIZONA'S HIGH COUNTRY 373

9 TUCSON 391

10 SOUTHERN ARIZONA 465

11 ARIZONA'S "WEST COAST" 512

12 PLANNING YOUR TRIP TO ARIZONA 539

INDEX 556

LIST OF MAPS

HOW TO CONTACT US

In researching this book, we discovered many wonderful places—hotels, restaurants, shops, and more. We're sure you'll find others. Please tell us about them, so we can share the information with your fellow travelers in upcoming editions. If you were disappointed with a recommendation, we'd love to know that, too. Please write to:

Frommer's Arizona & the Grand Canyon 2012
John Wiley & Sons, Inc. • 111 River St. • Hoboken, NJ 07030-5774
frommersfeedback@wiley.com

ADVISORY & DISCLAIMER

Travel information can change quickly and unexpectedly, and we strongly advise you to confirm important details locally before traveling, including information on visas, health and safety, traffic and transport, accommodations, shopping, and eating out. We also encourage you to stay alert while traveling and to remain aware of your surroundings. Avoid civil disturbances, and keep a close eye on cameras, purses, wallets, and other valuables.

While we have endeavored to ensure that the information contained within this guide is accurate and up-to-date at the time of publication, we make no representations or warranties with respect to the accuracy or completeness of the contents of this work and specifically disclaim all warranties, including without limitation warranties of fitness for a particular purpose. We accept no responsibility or liability for any inaccuracy or errors or omissions, or for any inconvenience, loss, damage, costs, or expenses of any nature whatsoever incurred or suffered by anyone as a result of any advice or information contained in this guide.

The inclusion of a company, organization, or website in this guide as a service provider and/or potential source of further information does not mean that we endorse them or the information they provide. Be aware that information provided through some websites may be unreliable and can change without notice. Neither the publisher nor author shall be liable for any damages arising herefrom.

ABOUT THE AUTHOR

Karl Samson lives in Oregon, where he spends his time juggling his obsessions with traveling, gardening, outdoor sports, and wine. Each winter, to dry out his webbed feet, he flees the soggy Northwest and heads to Arizona, where he updates *Frommer's Arizona & the Grand Canyon.* Karl is also the author of *Frommer's Seattle* and *Frommer's Washington State.*

FROMMER'S STAR RATINGS, ICONS & ABBREVIATIONS

Every hotel, restaurant, and attraction listing in this guide has been ranked for quality, value, service, amenities, and special features using a **star-rating system.** In country, state, and regional guides, we also rate towns and regions to help you narrow down your choices and budget your time accordingly. Hotels and restaurants are rated on a scale of zero (recommended) to three stars (exceptional). Attractions, shopping, nightlife, towns, and regions are rated according to the following scale: zero stars (recommended), one star (highly recommended), two stars (very highly recommended), and three stars (must-see).

In addition to the star-rating system, we also use **seven feature icons** that point you to the great deals, in-the-know advice, and unique experiences that separate travelers from tourists. Throughout the book, look for:

special finds—those places only insiders know about

fun facts—details that make travelers more informed and their trips more fun

kids—best bets for kids and advice for the whole family

special moments—those experiences that memories are made of

overrated—places or experiences not worth your time or money

insider tips—great ways to save time and money

great values—where to get the best deals

The following **abbreviations** are used for credit cards:

AE American Express

DISC Discover

V Visa

DC Diners Club

MC MasterCard

TRAVEL RESOURCES AT FROMMERS.COM

Frommer's travel resources don't end with this guide. Frommer's website, **www.frommers.com**, has travel information on more than 4,000 destinations. We update features regularly, giving you access to the most current trip-planning information and the best airfare, lodging, and car-rental bargains. You can also listen to podcasts, connect with other Frommers.com members through our active-reader forums, share your travel photos, read blogs from guidebook editors and fellow travelers, and much more.

1

THE BEST OF ARIZONA

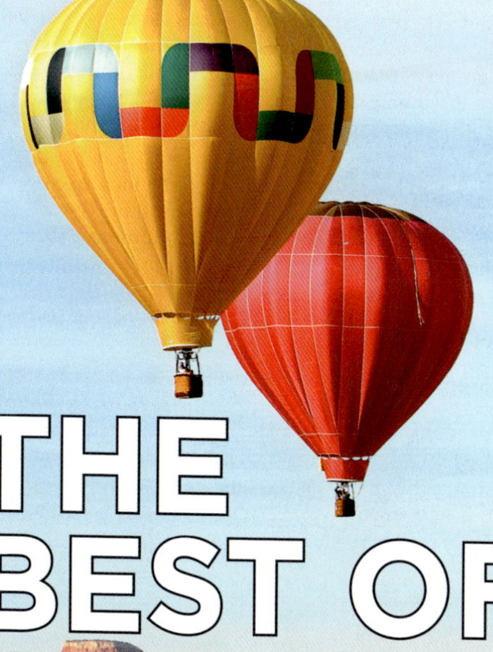

It's easy to be smug when you're home to one of the seven natural wonders of the world, and Arizona's license plate succinctly sums it up: Grand Canyon State. However, there is more to this Southwestern state than the vast canyon of the Colorado River. Stately saguaro cacti and rugged red-rock landscapes have served as backdrop both for Western history and Western movies. Cowboys and Indians are still at home on the range here in Arizona, but it is as a seller of sunshine to the winter-weary that Arizona has made its fortune.

Cities In **Phoenix,** the nation's fifth largest city, Ford Mustangs far outnumber wild mustangs and the golf course greens of luxury resorts have long since tamed the desert. Set against a craggy mountain backdrop, **Tucson** strives to preserve both its Hispanic heritage and its forests of saguaro cacti. College-town character and a historic downtown make **Flagstaff** a lively gateway to the Grand Canyon. **Jerome** and **Bisbee,** once booming mining towns, have once again struck pay dirt, this time in the guise of galleries and boutiques.

The Great Outdoors Take a hike, ride a mule, or hang on for a rip-roarin' raft ride. No matter how you approach it, a **Grand Canyon** adventure is world class. In the state's northeast corner, the buttes and mesas of **Monument Valley** compete with the canyon for the title of the state's most astonishing landscape. In southern Arizona, explore the **Sonoran Desert,** one of the greenest deserts on earth. In scenic **Sedona,** rumble through the red rocks in a Jeep, or search out some quiet on a hike or mountain-bike ride.

Eating & Drinking With Mexico for a neighbor, it should come as no surprise that Arizona relishes south-of-the-border flavors. From **street tacos, Sonoran hot dogs,** and air-dried ***carne seca*** to the complex Southwestern and Nuevo Latino dishes served at such celebrated restaurants as **Janos, Kai, Poca Cosa,** and the **Turquoise Room,** there's a regional dish for every palate. Native American **fry bread tacos** are a local guilty pleasure not to be missed. Wash it all down with a **margarita, microbrew,** or even an **Arizona wine.**

National Parks While millions of people come to Arizona each year to visit **Grand Canyon National Park,** the state is also home to more than a dozen other national parks and monuments. Massive saguaro cacti are preserved in Tucson's two units of **Saguaro National Park,** while to the west of Tucson, more cacti are preserved in **Organ Pipe Cactus National Monument.** In such national monuments as **Canyon de Chelly, Montezuma Castle, Navajo, Wupatki,** and **Tonto,** cliff dwellings and ancient pueblo ruins can be explored.

PREVIOUS PAGE: The Lake Powell Balloon Regatta in Page.

THE best PLACES TO COMMUNE WITH CACTUS

- **Desert Botanical Garden** (Phoenix): There's no better place in the state to learn about the plants of Arizona's Sonoran Desert and the many other deserts of the world. Displays at this Phoenix botanical garden explain plant adaptations and how indigenous tribes once used many of this region's wild plants. See p. 140.
- **Boyce Thompson Arboretum** (east of Phoenix): Just outside the town of Superior, this was the nation's first botanical garden established in a desert environment. It's set in a small canyon framed by cliffs and has desert plantings from all over the world—a fascinating educational stroll in the desert. See p. 194.
- **Arizona-Sonora Desert Museum** (Tucson): The name is misleading—this is actually more a zoo and botanical garden than a museum. Naturalistic settings house dozens of species of desert animals, including a number of critters you probably wouldn't want to meet in the wild (rattlesnakes, tarantulas, scorpions, black widows, and Gila monsters). See p. 431.
- **Saguaro National Park** (Tucson): With units both east and west of Tucson, this national park preserves "forests" of saguaro cacti and is the very essence of the desert that so many imagine it to be. You can hike it, bike it, or drive it. See p. 435.
- **Tohono Chul Park** (Tucson): Although this park is not that large, it packs a lot of desert scenery into its modest space. Impressive plantings of cacti are the star attractions, but there are also good wildflower displays in the spring. See p. 444.

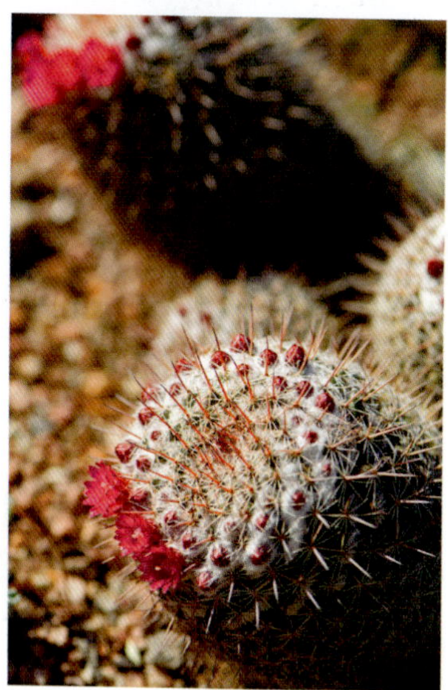

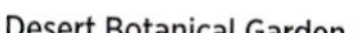
Desert Botanical Garden.

Saguaro National Park.

- **Organ Pipe Cactus National Monument** (west of Tucson): The organ pipe cactus is a smaller, multitrunked relative of the giant saguaro and lives only along the Mexican border about 100 miles west of Tucson. This remote national monument has hiking trails and a couple of scenic drives. See p. 467.

THE best ACTIVE VACATIONS

- **Rafting the Grand Canyon:** Whether you go for 3 days or 2 weeks, nothing comes even remotely close to matching the excitement of a rafting trip through the Grand Canyon. Sure, the river is crowded with groups in the summer, but the grandeur of the canyon is more than enough to make up for such a small inconvenience. See p. 279.
- **Hiking into the Grand Canyon or Havasu Canyon:** Not for the unfit or the faint of heart, a hike down into the Grand Canyon or Havasu Canyon is a journey through millions of years set in stone. This trip takes plenty of advance planning and requires some very strenuous hiking. With both a campground and a lodge at the bottom of each canyon, you can choose to make this trip with either a fully loaded backpack or just a light daypack. See p. 271 and 313.
- **Riding the Range at a Guest Ranch:** Yes, there are still cowboys in Arizona. They ride ranges all over the state, and so can you if you book a stay at one of Arizona's many guest ranches (once known as dude ranches). You might even get to drive some cattle down the trail. After a long (or short) day in the saddle, you can often opt to soak in a hot tub, go for a swim, or play a game of tennis before chowing down. See chapters 5, 8, 9, and 10.
- **Staying at a Golf or Tennis Resort:** If horseback riding and cowboy cookouts aren't your thing, how about as much golf or tennis as your shoulders can handle? The Phoenix/Scottsdale area has one of the nation's greatest concentrations of resorts, and Sedona and Tucson add many more options to the mix. There's something very satisfying about swinging a racket or club with the state's spectacular scenery in the background, and the climate means you can play practically year-round. See chapters 4, 5, and 9.
- **Mountain Biking in Sedona:** Forget Moab—there are too many other hardcore mountain bikers. Among the red rocks of Sedona, you can escape the crowds and pedal through awesome scenery on some of the most memorable single-track trails in the Southwest. There's even plenty of slickrock for that Canyonlands experience. See p. 238.
- **Bird-Watching in Southeastern Arizona:** As an avid bird-watcher, I know

Rafting in the Grand Canyon.

Biking in Sedona's red rocks.

that this isn't the most active of sports, but a birder can get in a bit of walking when it's necessary (for instance, to get to the nesting tree of an elegant trogon). The southeast corner of the state is one of the best birding regions in the entire country. See "The Best Bird-Watching Spots" later in this chapter and the map "Arizona Birding Guide" on p. 56.

THE best DAY HIKES & NATURE WALKS

- **Camelback Mountain** (Phoenix): For many Phoenicians, the trail to the top of Camelback Mountain is a ritual, a Phoenix institution. Sure, there are those who make this a casual but strenuous hike, but many more turn it into a serious workout by jogging to the top and back down. I prefer a more leisurely approach so that I can enjoy the views. See p. 166.
- **Peralta Trail** (east of Phoenix in the Superstition Mountains): This moderately difficult trail through the rugged Superstition Mountains will lead you to one of the most astonishing views in the state. Hike the trail on a weekday to avoid the crowds. See p. 168.
- **Picacho Peak State Park** (south of Casa Grande): The hike up this central Arizona landmark is short but strenuous, and from the top there are superb views out over the desert. The best time of year to make the hike is in spring, when the peak is painted with wildflowers. Picacho Peak is between Casa Grande and Tucson just off I-10. See p. 195.
- **Bell Rock/Courthouse Butte Loop Trail** (Sedona): There simply is no better introduction to Sedona's myriad red-rock hiking opportunities than this easy 4-mile loop hike. The trail begins right on Ariz. 179 in the Village of Oak

Betatakin cliff dwellings at Navajo National Monument.

Creek, which is a few miles south of Sedona. Views, views, views! Unfortunately, though, there are plenty of other hikers, too. See p. 237.

- **The South Kaibab Trail** (Grand Canyon South Rim): Forget the popular Bright Angel Trail, which, near its start, is a human highway. The South Kaibab Trail offers better views to day hikers and is the preferred downhill route for anyone heading to Phantom Ranch for the night. This is a strenuous hike even if you go only a mile or so down the trail. Remember, the trip back is all uphill. See p. 273.
- **The White House Ruins Trail** (Canyon de Chelly National Monument): There's only one Canyon de Chelly hike that the general public can take without a Navajo guide, and that's the 2.5-mile trail to White House Ruins, a small site once inhabited by Ancestral Puebloans (formerly called Anasazis). The trail leads from the canyon rim across bare sandstone, through a tunnel, and down to the floor of the canyon. See p. 351.
- **The Wildcat Trail** (Monument Valley Navajo Tribal Park): As at Canyon de Chelly, there's only one trail at Monument Valley that you can hike without a guide. This easy 3.2-mile trail loops around West Mitten Butte, providing a close-up look at one of the most photographed rock formations in the West. Don't miss this hike. See p. 359.
- **Betatakin** (Navajo National Monument): Betatakin is one of the most impressive cliff dwellings in the Southwest, and while most people just marvel at it from a distance, it's possible to take a ranger-led 5-mile hike to the ruins. After hiking through remote Tsegi Canyon, you'll have a

Heart of Rocks Trail.

better understanding of the Ancestral Puebloan people who once lived here. See p. 356.

- **Antelope Canyon** (Page): More a slow walk of reverence than a hike, this short trail lets you see the amazing beauty that can result when water and rock battle each other in the Southwest. The trail leads through a picture-perfect sandstone slot canyon, which is only a few feet wide in some places. See p. 365.
- **The Seven Falls Trail** (Tucson): There is something irresistible about waterfalls in the desert, and on this trail you get more than enough falls to satisfy any craving to cool off on a hot desert day. The Seven Falls Trail is in the Sabino Canyon Recreation Area in northeast Tucson. See p. 450.
- **The Heart of Rocks Trail** (Cochise County): While the national parks and monuments in northern Arizona get all the publicity, Chiricahua National Monument, down in the southeast corner of the state, quietly lays claim to some of the most spectacular scenery in Arizona. On this trail, you'll hike through a wonderland of rocks. See p. 505.

THE best SCENIC DRIVES

- **The Apache Trail** (east of Phoenix): Much of this winding road, which passes just north of the Superstition Mountains, is unpaved and follows a rugged route once traveled by Apaches. This is some of the most remote country in the Phoenix area, with far-reaching desert vistas and lots to see and do along the way. See p. 192.
- **Oak Creek Canyon** (Sedona): Slicing down from the pine country outside Flagstaff to the red rocks of Sedona, Oak Creek Canyon is a cool oasis. From the scenic overlook at the top of the canyon to the swimming holes and hiking

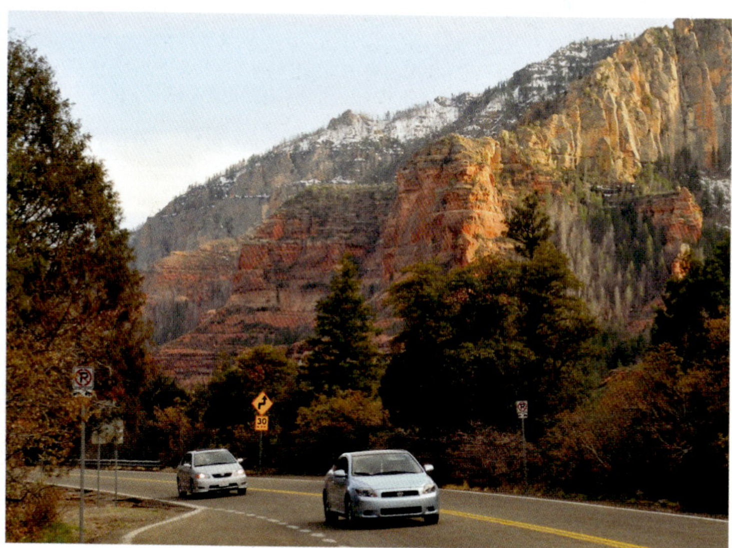

A drive along Oak Creek Canyon showcases the region's diverse scenery.

The snow-covered Mount Lemmon in Tucson.

trails at the bottom, this canyon road provides a rapid (and scenic) change in climate and landscape. See p. 225.

- **Canyon de Chelly National Monument** (Chinle): This fascinating complex of canyons on the Navajo Indian Reservation has limited public access because it is still home to numerous Navajo families. However, roads that parallel the north and south rims of the canyon provide lots of scenic overlooks. See p. 347.
- **Monument Valley Navajo Tribal Park** (north of Kayenta): This valley of sandstone buttes and mesas is one of the most photographed spots in America and, because of the countless movies, TV shows, and commercials that have been shot here, is familiar to people all over the world. A 17-mile dirt road winds through the park, giving visitors close-up views of such landmarks as Elephant Butte, the Mittens, and Totem Pole. See p. 356.
- **Mount Lemmon** (Tucson): Sure, the views of Tucson from the city's northern foothills are great, but the vistas from Mount Lemmon are even better. This mountain rises up from the desert like an island rising from the sea, and the road up the mountain climbs from cactus country to cool pine forests. See p. 451.

THE best GOLF COURSES

- **The Boulders' South Course** (Carefree, near Phoenix; ✆ **480/488-9028**): If you've ever seen a photo of someone teeing off beside a massive balancing rock and longed to play that same hole, then you've dreamed about playing the Boulders' South Course. Jay Morrish's desert-style design plays around and through the jumble of massive boulders for which the resort is named. See p. 163.
- **The Gold Course at the Wigwam Golf Resort & Spa** (Litchfield Park, near Phoenix; ✆ **800/909-4224**): If you're a traditionalist who eschews those cactus- and rattlesnake-filled desert target courses, be sure to reserve a tee time on the Wigwam's Gold Course. This 7,100-yard resort course has long been an Arizona legend. See p. 163.

- **Gold Canyon Golf Resort** (Apache Junction, near Phoenix; ✆ **480/982-9449**): This resort east of Phoenix offers superb golf at the foot of the Superstition Mountains. The 2nd, 3rd, and 4th holes on the Dinosaur Mountain Course are truly memorable. They play across the foot of Dinosaur Mountain and are among the top holes in the state. See p. 163.
- **Troon North Golf Club** (Scottsdale; ✆ **480/585-7700**): Designed by Tom Weiskopf and Jay Morrish, this semiprivate, desert-style course is named for the famous Scottish links that overlook the Firth of Forth and the Firth of Clyde—but that's where the similarities end. Troon North has two 18-hole courses, but the original, known as the Monument Course, is still the favorite. See p. 164.
- **Tournament Players Club (TPC) of Scottsdale** (Scottsdale; ✆ **888/400-4001**): If you've dreamed of playing where the pros play, then plan a visit to the Fairmont Scottsdale Princess. Book a tee time on the resort's Stadium Course, and you can play on the course that hosts the PGA Tour's Phoenix Open. See p. 164.
- **We-Ko-Pa Golf Club** (✆ **866/660-7700**): Located on the Yavapai Nation northeast of Scottsdale, this golf club includes two challenging 18-hole courses that are bounded by open desert and stupendous views. See p. 164.
- **Sedona Golf Resort** (Sedona; ✆ **877/733-6630**): It's easy to assume that all of Arizona's best courses are in the Phoenix and Tucson areas, but it just isn't so. Up in red-rock country, at the mouth of Oak Creek Canyon, the Sedona Golf Resort boasts a traditional course with terrific red-rock views. See p. 238.

The Boulders' South Course.

Lake Powell National Golf Course.

- **Lake Powell National Golf Course** (Page; ✆ **928/645-2023**): With fairways that wrap around the base of the red sandstone bluff atop which sits the town of Page, this is one of the most scenic golf courses in the state. Walls of eroded sandstone come right down to the greens, and one tee box is on top of the bluff. See p. 369.
- **Ventana Canyon Golf and Racquet Club** (Tucson; ✆ **520/577-4015**): Two Tom Fazio–designed courses, the Canyon and the Mountain, are shared by two of the city's finest resorts. Both desert-style courses play through some of the most stunning scenery in the state. If I had to choose between them, I'd play the Mountain Course. See p. 448.
- **Omni Tucson National Resort** (Tucson; ✆ **520/575-7540**): With its wide expanses of grass on 18 holes and its additional 9 holes of desert-style golf, this course, once the site of the PGA Tour's Tucson Open, is both challenging and forgiving. The 18th hole of the combined Orange and Gold courses was considered one of the toughest finishing holes on the tour. See p. 449.

THE best BIRD-WATCHING SPOTS

- **Vermilion Cliffs National Monument:** Although it is often possible to see California condors on the South Rim of the Grand Canyon, the condor release site viewing area at the base of the Vermilion Cliffs is the most reliable spot to cross these giant birds off your life list. See p. 290.
- **Madera Canyon:** The mountain canyons of southern Arizona attract an impressive variety of bird life, from species common in lowland desert to those that prefer forest settings. Madera Canyon is a good place to see birds that prefer both habitats. See p. 448.
- **Buenos Aires National Wildlife Refuge:** Gray hawks and masked bobwhite quails are among the refuge's rarer birds, but a *cienega* (wetland), lake, and stream attract plenty of others. See p. 470.

- **Patagonia:** With a year-round stream, a Nature Conservancy preserve on the edge of town, and Sonoita Creek State Natural Area, Patagonia is one of the best spots in the state for sighting various flycatcher species. See p. 479.
- **Ramsey Canyon Preserve:** Nearly 200 species of birds, including 14 species of hummingbirds, frequent this canyon, one of the top birding spots in the country. Also nearby are a couple of privately owned birding hot spots. See p. 487.
- **San Pedro Riparian National Conservation Area:** Water is a scarce commodity in the desert, so it isn't surprising that the San Pedro River attracts a lot of animal life, including more than 300 bird species. This is a life-list bonanza spot. See p. 488.
- **Cave Creek Canyon:** Although other rare birds can be seen in this remote canyon, most people come in hopes of spotting the elegant trogon, which reaches the northernmost limit of its range here. See p. 506.
- **Cochise Lakes** (Willcox Ponds): Wading birds in the middle of the desert? You'll find them at the Willcox sewage-treatment ponds south of town. Avocets, sandhill cranes, and a variety of waterfowl all frequent these shallow bodies of water. See p. 507.

THE most offbeat TRAVEL EXPERIENCES

- **Taking a Vortex Tour in Sedona:** Crystals and pyramids are nothing compared to the power of the Sedona vortexes, which just happen to be in the middle of some very beautiful scenery. Organized tours shuttle believers from one vortex to the next. If you offer it, they will come. See p. 229.
- **Gazing at the Stars:** Insomniacs and stargazers will find plenty to keep them sleepless in the desert as they peer at the stars through telescopes at Lowell

Fourteen species of hummingbirds can be found in Ramsey Canyon Preserve.

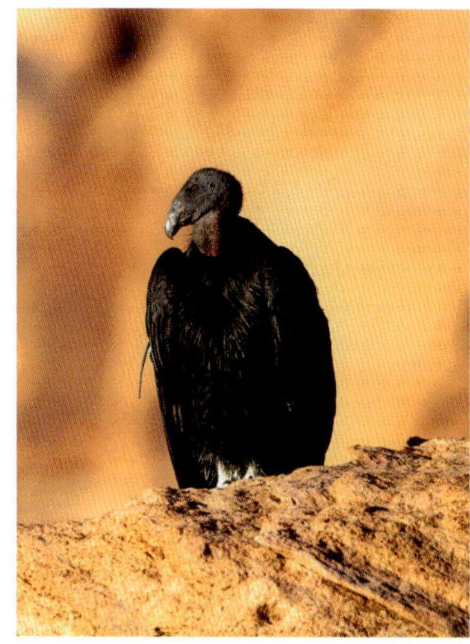

Catch a glimpse of condors at Vermilion Cliffs National Park.

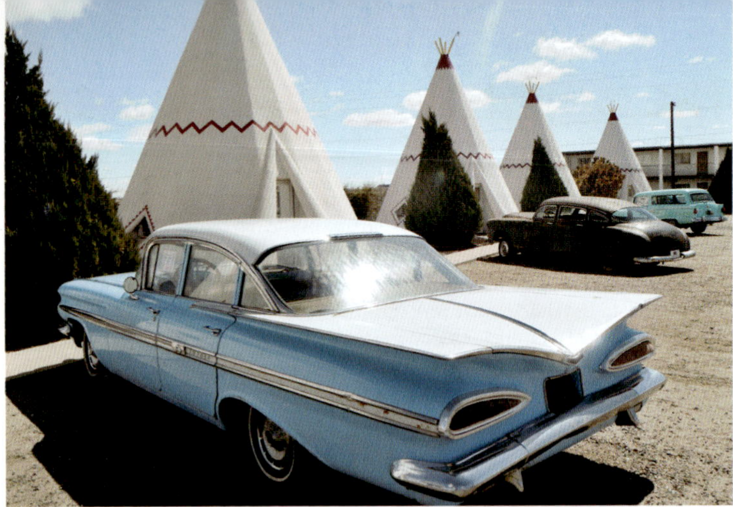

Observatory in Flagstaff or Kitt Peak National Observatory near Tucson. North of Flagstaff, you can even stay at a B&B that doubles as an astronomical observatory. See p. 298.

- **Touring Walpi Village:** It is said that the Hopi village of Walpi, built atop a narrow promontory-like mesa in northeastern Arizona, has been occupied for more than 1,000 years. Guided tours of this ancient, stone-walled village provide a glimpse into the history of the village and the Hopi culture. See p. 332.
- **Marveling at a Meteorite Crater:** East of the town of Winslow, you can visit the best-preserved meteorite impact crater in the world. The crater is 2½ miles in circumference and 550 feet deep. In the 1960s, NASA even used the crater to train moon-bound astronauts. See p. 328.

FROM TOP: **Guests sleep in tepees at the Wigwam Motel in Holbrook; catch live cowboy action at Old Tucson Studios.**

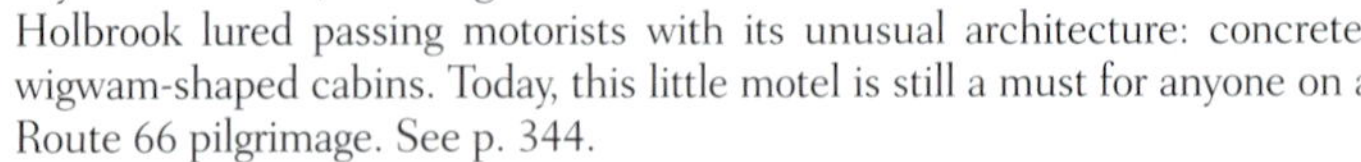

- **Sleeping in a Wigwam:** Back in the heyday of Route 66, the Wigwam Motel in Holbrook lured passing motorists with its unusual architecture: concrete, wigwam-shaped cabins. Today, this little motel is still a must for anyone on a Route 66 pilgrimage. See p. 344.

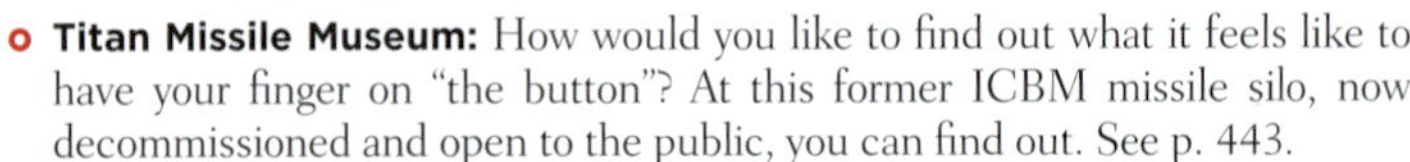

- **Titan Missile Museum:** How would you like to find out what it feels like to have your finger on "the button"? At this former ICBM missile silo, now decommissioned and open to the public, you can find out. See p. 443.
- **Stopping to Smell the Roses of the World's Largest Rose Plant:** The town of Tombstone in southeastern Arizona is best known as the site of the shootout at the O.K. Corral, but the "town too tough to die" is also home to the world's largest rose tree. See p. 494.

THE best FAMILY EXPERIENCES

- **Cowboy Steakhouses:** No family should visit Arizona without spending an evening at a "genuine" cowboy steakhouse. With false-fronted buildings, country bands, gunslingers, and gimmicks (one place cuts off your necktie, another has a slide from the bar to the dining room), these eateries are all entertainment and loads of fun. See p. 135 and 429.
- **Rawhide at Wild Horse Pass** (Phoenix): Your kids can climb atop a mechanical bull, catch a stunt show, watch a real gunslinger, or ride in a stagecoach or train. After all this activity, you'll want to head to Rawhide's steakhouse. See p. 150.
- **Goldfield Ghost Town** (Apache Junction): Although it may look a little too contrived these days, Goldfield really was a mining town at one time. Today, you can take a tour of the old mine, learn about the legend of the Lost Dutchman Mine, and otherwise have a thoroughly Wild West experience. See p. 150.
- **Grand Canyon Railway:** Not only is this train excursion a fun way to get to the Grand Canyon, but it also lets you avoid the parking problems and congestion that can be so wearisome. Shootouts and train robberies are to be expected in this corner of the Wild West. See p. 277.
- **Arizona-Sonora Desert Museum** (Tucson): This is actually a zoo featuring the animals of the Sonoran Desert. Exhibits include rooms full of snakes, a prairie-dog town, enclosures that are home to bighorn sheep and mountain lions, and an aviary full of hummingbirds. Kids and adults love this place. See p. 431.
- **Old Tucson Studios** (Tucson): Cowboy shootouts, cancan girls, and horseback rides make this old movie-studio set loads of fun for the family. You might even get to see a movie or commercial being filmed. See p. 437.
- **Shootouts at the O.K. Corral** (Tombstone): Tombstone may be "the town too tough to die," but poor Ike Clanton and his buddies the McLaury boys have to die over and over again at the frequent reenactments of Tombstone's famous gunfight. See p. 492.

THE best FAMILY VACATIONS

- **Saddling Up on a Dude Ranch:** Ride off into the sunset with your family at one of Arizona's many dude ranches (now called guest ranches). Most ranches have lots of special programs for kids. See "Where to Stay" choices throughout this book.
- **Floating on a Houseboat:** Renting a floating vacation home on lakes Powell, Mead, or Mohave is a summer tradition for many Arizona families. With a houseboat, you aren't tied to one spot and can cruise from one scenic beach to the next. See p. 370.
- **Lounging by the Pool:** While most Arizona resorts are geared primarily toward adults, there are a handful in Phoenix and Tucson that have extensive pool complexes. The kids can play in the sand, shoot down a water slide, or even float down an artificial river in an inner tube. See "The Best Swimming Pools," later in this chapter.

- **Having a Grand Vacation:** You can spend the better part of a week exploring Grand Canyon National Park, with trails to hike, mules to ride down into the canyon (if your kids are old enough), air tours by plane or helicopter, rafting trips both wild and tame, and even a train ride to and from the canyon. See chapter 6.

THE best MUSEUMS

- **Heard Museum** (Phoenix): This is one of the nation's premier museums devoted to Native American cultures. In addition to historical exhibits, a huge kachina doll collection, and an excellent museum store, there are annual exhibits of contemporary Native American art as well as dance performances and demonstrations of traditional skills. See p. 140.
- **Musical Instrument Museum** (Phoenix): This huge museum houses thousands of musical instruments from all over the world. There are galleries organized by countries and continents, as well as exhibits of such rare instruments as the first Steinway piano ever made and the Steinway piano on which John Lennon composed "Imagine." See p. 147.
- **Phoenix Art Museum** (Phoenix): This large art museum has acres of wall space and houses an outstanding collection of contemporary art as well as a fascinating exhibit of miniature rooms. See p. 142.
- **Scottsdale Museum of Contemporary Art** (Scottsdale): The Phoenix area's largest museum of contemporary art is noteworthy as much for its bold architecture as for its wide variety of exhibits. Unlike most other art galleries in Scottsdale, this museum eschews cowboy art. See p. 143.
- **Desert Caballeros Western Museum** (Wickenburg): This museum in the Wild West town of Wickenburg is a celebration of all things Western, including Western (or cowboy) art and the trappings of the American West. See p. 203.

The Heard Museum's large kachina doll collection.

The Scottsdale Museum of Contemporary Art.

- **Phippen Museum** (Prescott): This museum is devoted exclusively to Western art and features works by members of the prestigious Cowboy Artists of America. See p. 207.
- **Museum of Northern Arizona** (Flagstaff): The geology, ethnography, and archaeology of this region are all explored in fascinating detail at this Flagstaff museum. Throughout the year, excellent special exhibits and festivals focus on the region's tribes. See p. 299.
- **The University of Arizona Museum of Art** (Tucson): This collection ranges from the Renaissance to the present. Georgia O'Keeffe and Pablo Picasso are among the artists whose works are on display here. See p. 439.
- **Amerind Foundation Museum** (west of Willcox): Located in the remote southeastern corner of the state, this museum and research center houses a superb collection of Native American artifacts. Displays focus on tribes of the Southwest, but other tribes are also represented. See p. 504.

THE best PLACES TO DISCOVER THE OLD WEST

- **Rodeos:** Any rodeo, and this state has plenty, will give you a glimpse of the Old West, but the rodeos in Prescott and Payson both claim to be the oldest in the country. Whichever rodeo you attend, you'll see plenty of bronco busting, bull riding, and beer drinking. See p. 202 and 375.
- **Guest Ranches:** On guest ranches all over the state, the Old West lives on, and wranglers lead city slickers on horseback rides through desert scrub and mountain meadows. Campfires, cookouts, and cattle are all part of the experience. See "Where to Stay" choices throughout this book.
- **Monument Valley** (north of Kayenta): John Ford made it the hallmark of his Western movies, and no wonder: The starkly beautiful and fantastically shaped buttes and mesas of this valley are the quintessential Western landscape. You'll recognize Monument Valley the moment you see it. See p. 356.

Monument Valley.

- **Old Tucson Studios** (Tucson): Originally constructed as a movie set, this back lot and amusement park provides visitors with a glimpse of the most familiar Old West—the Hollywood West. Sure, the shootouts and cancan revues are silly, but it's all in good fun, and everyone gets a thrill out of seeing the occasional film crew in action. See p. 437.
- **Cowboy Poetry Festivals:** From heroes on horseback to poets on the prairie, it's been a long, lonesome ride for the American cowboy. At several events around the state, you can hear how some cowboys deal with the hardships and happiness of the cowboy life. See "Arizona Calendar of Events" in chapter 2.
- **Tombstone:** Unlike Old Tucson, which is the *reel* Old West, Tombstone is a genuine historic town—the *real* Old West. However, "the town too tough to die" was reincarnated long ago as a major tourist attraction with gunslingers in the streets, stagecoach rides, and shootouts at the O.K. Corral. See p. 492.

THE best PLACES TO SEE INDIAN RUINS

- **Tonto National Monument** (east of Phoenix): Reached via the Apache Trail scenic road, this archaeological site has one of Arizona's only easily accessible cliff dwellings where visitors are allowed to walk around inside the ruins, albeit under the watchful eye of a ranger. See p. 193.
- **Besh-Ba-Gowah Archaeological Park** (Globe): These reconstructed ruins have been set up to look the way they might have appeared 700 years ago. Consequently, this park provides a bit more cultural context than is to be found at other ruins in the state. See p. 194.
- **Casa Grande Ruins National Monument** (west of Florence): Unlike most of Arizona's other ruins, which are constructed primarily of stone, this large and unusual structure is built of packed desert soil. Inscrutable and perplexing, Casa Grande seems to rise from nowhere. See p. 195.
- **Montezuma Castle National Monument** (north of Camp Verde): Located just off I-17, this is the most easily accessible cliff dwelling in Arizona, although it cannot be entered. Nearby Montezuma Well also has some small ruins. See p. 222.

- **Wupatki National Monument** (north of Flagstaff): Not nearly as well known as the region's Ancestral Puebloan cliff dwellings, these ruins are set on a wide plain. A ball court similar to those found in Mexico and Central America hints at cultural ties with Mesoamerican cultures such as the Aztecs. See p. 301.
- **Canyon de Chelly National Monument:** Small cliff dwellings up and down the length of Canyon de Chelly can be seen from overlooks, and a trip into the canyon itself offers a chance to see some of these ruins up close. See p. 347.
- **Navajo National Monument** (west of Kayenta): Keet Seel and Betatakin, the two main ruins here, are some of the finest examples of Ancestral Puebloan cliff dwellings in the state. Although the ruins are at the end of long hikes, their size and state of preservation make them well worth the effort. See p. 354.

THE best PLACES TO SEE PETROGLYPHS & PICTOGRAPHS

- **Deer Valley Rock Art Center** (Phoenix): This park, northwest of Phoenix, not only preserves a rock-strewn hillside covered with petroglyphs, but is also the best place in the state to learn about rock art. See p. 137.
- **Palatki Heritage Site** (Sedona): This small Sinagua cliff dwelling west of Sedona preserves not only ruins but also quite a few pictographs (paintings). Such paintings survive in only a few well-protected spots in the state. See p. 231.
- **V Bar V Heritage Site** (Sedona): Not only are the petroglyphs at this national forest site extensive, but they also have been linked to a variety of solar events. At different times of the year, shadows fall on different images on the rock wall here. See p. 232.

Casa Grande Ruins National Monument.

- **Rock Art Ranch** (southeast of Winslow): Set in a remote little canyon, this private historic site preserves one of the most extensive collections of petroglyphs in the state. You can visit only by reservation, and if you're lucky, you might have the place all to yourself. See p. 328.
- **Saguaro National Park** (Tucson): Signal Hill, in the west unit of Saguaro National Park, has a large petroglyph spiral that often catches the light of the setting sun just right. Although this spot doesn't have a lot of petroglyphs, a sunset visit can be a magical experience. See p. 435.

THE best LUXURY HOTELS & RESORTS

- **Hyatt Regency Scottsdale Resort & Spa at Gainey Ranch** (Scottsdale; www.scottsdale.hyatt.com; ✆ **800/554-9288**): Contemporary architecture, dramatic landscaping, a water playground with its own beach, a staff that's always ready to assist you, good restaurants, and even gondola rides—it all adds up to a lot of fun at one of the most smoothly run resorts in Arizona. See p. 100.
- **Camelback Inn, a JW Marriott Resort & Spa** (Scottsdale; www.camelback inn.com; ✆ **800/242-2635**): The Camelback Inn, opened in 1936 and kept up-to-date with regular renovations, is today one of the few Scottsdale resorts that retains an Old Arizona atmosphere while at the same time offering a wide range of modern amenities. See p. 101.
- **The Phoenician** (Scottsdale; www.thephoenician.com; ✆ **800/888-8234**): This Xanadu of the resort world is brimming with marble, crystal, and works

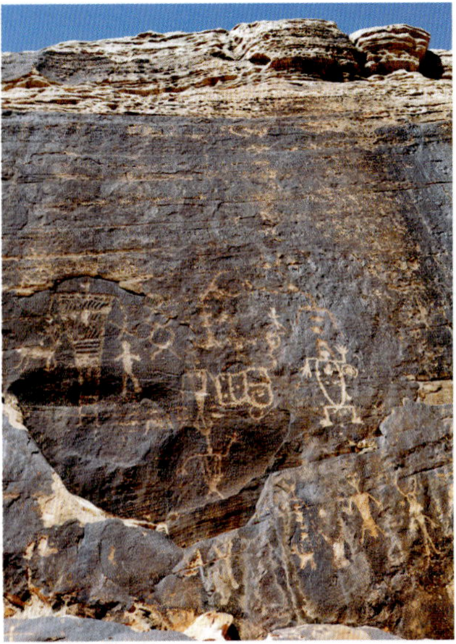

Petroglyphs at the Rock Art Ranch outside Winslow.

Frank Lloyd Wright's design is evident throughout the Arizona Biltmore.

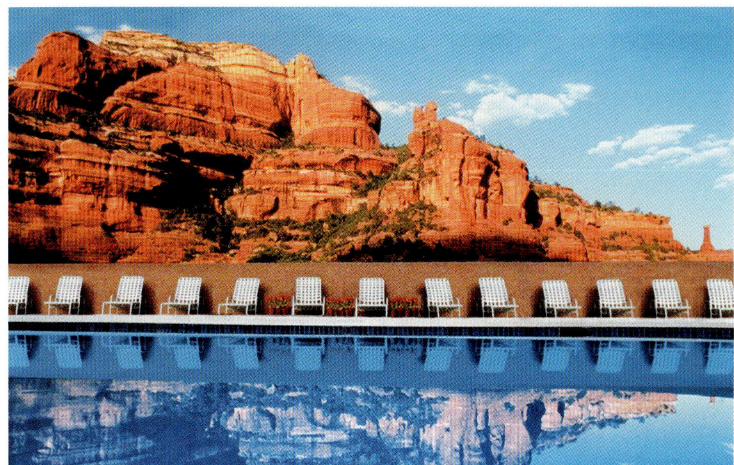

The Enchantment Resort is nestled amidst Sedona's red rocks.

of art, and with staff seemingly around every corner, the hotel offers guests impeccable service. Camelback Mountain looms above the resort's lush grounds. See p. 101.

- **Fairmont Scottsdale** (Scottsdale; www.fairmont.com/scottsdale; ✆ **800/344-4758**): The Moorish styling and numerous fountains and waterfalls of this resort create a setting made for romance. A beautiful spa, a challenging golf course, and a superb modern steakhouse top it off. See p. 105.
- **Four Seasons Resort Scottsdale at Troon North** (Scottsdale; www.fourseasons.com/scottsdale; ✆ **888/207-9696**): Located in north Scottsdale amid a jumble of giant granite boulders, this is the most luxurious resort in the Phoenix area. The setting is dramatic, the accommodations are spacious, and one of Arizona's top golf courses is next door. See p. 106.
- **Arizona Biltmore** (Phoenix; www.arizonabiltmore.com; ✆ **800/950-0086**): Combining discreet service and the architectural styling of Frank Lloyd Wright, the Biltmore has long been one of the most prestigious resorts in the state. This is a thoroughly old-money sort of place, though it continues to keep pace with the times. See p. 107.
- **InterContinental Montelucia Resort & Spa** (Paradise Valley; www.icmontelucia.com; ✆ **888/627-3010**): Set at the foot of Camelback Mountain, this compact boutique resort draws on Spain's famed Alhambra for architectural inspiration and feels exceedingly exotic. The location is convenient to both Phoenix and Scottsdale. See p. 100.
- **Enchantment Resort** (Sedona; www.enchantmentresort.com; ✆ **800/826-4180**): A breathtaking setting in a red-rock canyon makes this the most unforgettable resort in Arizona. If you want to feel as though you're truly vacationing in the desert, this place fits the bill. Guest rooms are constructed in a pueblo architectural style, and the spa is one of the finest in the state. See p. 241.

- **The Ritz-Carlton, Dove Mountain** (Marana; www.ritzcarlton.com/dove mountain; ✆ **800/241-3333**): Set amid saguaro-covered hills, this luxury resort 45 minutes outside Tucson feels as though it is in a national park. The resort's Western ranch styling, desert landscaping, and access to miles of hiking trails make it a superb place to experience the desert. See p. 410.
- **Loews Ventana Canyon Resort** (Tucson; www.loewshotels.com/hotels/tucson; ✆ **800/234-5117**): With the Santa Catalina Mountains rising in the backyard and a little waterfall steps away from the lobby, this is Tucson's most dramatic resort. Contemporary styling throughout makes constant reference to the desert setting. See p. 408.

THE best FAMILY RESORTS

- **Hyatt Regency Scottsdale Resort & Spa at Gainey Ranch** (Scottsdale; www.scottsdale.hyatt.com; ✆ **800/554-9288**): With children's programs, gondola rides, and a 10-pool, 2½-acre water playground complete with sand beach and waterfalls, this place is a kid's dream come true. See p. 100.
- **Pointe Hilton Squaw Peak Resort** (Phoenix; www.pointehilton.com; ✆ **800/876-4683**): A water slide, tubing river, and waterfall make the water park here one of the most family-oriented at any resort in the Valley. Throw in some fun children's programs, and you can be sure your kids will beg to come back. See p. 110.
- **Arizona Grand Resort** (Phoenix; www.arizonagrandresort.com; ✆ **866/267-1321**): Let's see . . . water slides that drop nearly 70 feet, a wave pool, a water play area for the youngest ones, a tubing river, even spa treatments for kids and teens. Can you say "fun for the whole family"? See p. 111.
- **Enchantment Resort** (Sedona; www.enchantmentresort.com; ✆ **800/826-4180**): This remote red-rock resort may not have a water slide or kid-oriented pool area, but it does have a really cool location in a cliff-walled canyon. There are also fun children's programs and suites that are ideal for families. See p. 241.
- **Loews Ventana Canyon Resort** (Tucson; www.loewshotels.com/hotels/tucson; ✆ **800/234-5117**): With a playground, a kids' club, and its own waterfall, this resort has plenty to keep the kids busy. A hiking trail starts from the edge of the property, and Sabino Canyon Recreation Area is nearby. See p. 408.
- **The Ritz-Carlton, Dove Mountain** (Marana; www.ritzcarlton.com/dove mountain; ✆ **800/241-3333**): With the longest water slide in Tucson, a play fountain for the kids, children's programs, hiking trails, jeep tours, and horseback riding, this luxury resort has more than enough to keep the kids entertained throughout the day. See p. 410.
- **The Westin La Paloma Resort & Spa** (Tucson; www.westinlapalomaresort.com; ✆ **800/937-8461**): Kids get their own lounge and game room here, and the pool area has a great water slide. In summer and during holiday periods, special programs for the kids allow their parents a little free time. See p. 408.

THE best HOTELS FOR OLD ARIZONA CHARACTER

- **The Hermosa Inn** (Paradise Valley; www.hermosainn.com; ✆ **800/241-1210**): The main building here dates from 1930 and was once the home of Western artist Lon Megargee. Today, the old adobe house is surrounded by beautiful gardens and has become a tranquil boutique hotel with luxurious Southwestern-style rooms and a beautiful restaurant terrace. See p. 108.
- **Royal Palms Resort and Spa** (Phoenix; www.royalpalmsresortandspa.com; ✆ **800/672-6011**): With Mediterranean styling and towering palm trees, this place seems far removed from the glitz that prevails at most area resorts. The Royal Palms is a classic, perfect for romantic getaways, and its designer showcase rooms are among the most dramatic in the Valley. See p. 107.
- **El Portal Sedona** (Sedona; www.elportalsedona.com; ✆ **800/313-0017**): Built of hand-cast adobe blocks and incorporating huge wooden beams salvaged from a railroad trestle, this inn is a work of art both inside and out. The mix of Arts and Crafts and Santa Fe styling conjures up haciendas of old. See p. 243.
- **El Tovar Hotel** (Grand Canyon Village; www.grandcanyonlodges.com; ✆ **888/297-2757**): This classic log-and-stone mountain lodge stands in Grand Canyon Village only feet from the South Rim and is utterly timeless. The lobby may not be very big, but it has the requisite trophy animal heads and a stone fireplace. See p. 281.
- **Grand Canyon Lodge** (Grand Canyon North Rim; www.grandcanyonlodgenorth.com; ✆ **877/386-4383**): This, the Grand Canyon's other grand lodge, sits right on the North Rim of the canyon. Rooms are primarily in

The ballroom at La Posada.

cabins, which aren't quite as impressive as the main building, but guests tend to spend a lot of time sitting on the lodge's two viewing terraces or in the sunroom. See p. 292.

- **La Posada** (Winslow; www.laposada.org; ✆ **928/289-4366**): Designed by Mary Elizabeth Jane Colter, who also designed many of the buildings on the South Rim of the Grand Canyon, La Posada first opened in 1930 and was the last of the great Santa Fe Railroad hotels. Today, La Posada has been restored to its former glory and is again one of the finest hotels in the West. See p. 330.
- **Arizona Inn** (Tucson; www.arizonainn.com; ✆ **800/933-1093**): With its pink-stucco walls and colorful, fragrant gardens, this small Tucson resort dates from Arizona's earliest days as a vacation destination and epitomizes slower times, when guests came for the winter, not just a quick weekend getaway. See p. 404.

THE best BED & BREAKFASTS

- **Rocamadour Bed & Breakfast for (Rock) Lovers** (Prescott; ✆ **928/771-1933**): Set amid the rounded boulders of the Granite Dells on the north side of Prescott, this inn combines a spectacular setting with French antiques and very luxurious accommodations. You won't find a more memorable setting anywhere in the state. See p. 212.
- **Briar Patch Inn** (Sedona; www.briarpatchinn.com; ✆ **888/809-3030**): This collection of luxurious cottages is located in tree-shaded Oak Creek Canyon, a few miles north of Sedona. Few experiences are more restorative than breakfast on the shady banks of the creek. See p. 243.
- **England House Bed & Breakfast** (Flagstaff; www.englandhousebandb.com; ✆ **877/214-7350**): Set behind a stone wall and built of sandstone blocks, this Victorian house is only blocks from downtown Flagstaff. Guest rooms are filled with beautiful antiques, and breakfasts are served in a sunroom just off the big kitchen where guests often gather in the morning. See p. 302.
- **The Inn at 410** (Flagstaff; www.inn410.com; ✆ **800/774-2008**): This restored 1907 bungalow offers a convenient location in downtown Flagstaff, pleasant surroundings, comfortable rooms, and delicious breakfasts. Rooms all feature different, distinctive themes. See p. 303.
- **The Royal Elizabeth** (Tucson; www.royalelizabeth.com; ✆ **877/670-9022**): In downtown Tucson just a block from the Temple of Music and Art, this territorial-style historic home is filled with beautiful Victorian antiques and architectural details. Guest rooms have lots of touches not often seen in historic B&Bs, including TVs, fridges, and safes. See p. 405.
- **El Rancho Merlita** (Tucson; www.bedbreakfasttucsonaz.com; ✆ **888/218-8418**): Once the home of cosmetics queen Merle Norman, this sprawling ranch house has been lovingly restored and decorated by some of Tucson's top interior designers. The B&B has a gorgeous view of the Santa Catalina Mountains and is surrounded by green lawns and desert landscaping. See p. 406.
- **Across the Creek at Aravaipa Farms** (Winkelman; www.aravaipafarms.com; ✆ **520/357-6901**): This is the quintessential desert B&B experience, though it isn't for everyone. To reach this inn, you have to drive *through* Aravaipa Creek (or have the innkeeper shuttle you across). Relaxing and,

alternatively, exploring the nearby wilderness area are the main activities in this remote locale. See p. 413.

- **Cochise Stronghold B&B** (Cochise County; www.cochisestrongholdbb.com; ✆ **877/426-4141**): Surrounded by the national forest and mountainsides strewn with giant boulders, this is another of the state's remote inns. The passive-solar building was constructed from straw bales and is not only energy-efficient, but also quite beautiful. See p. 508.

THE best SWIMMING POOLS

- **Hyatt Regency Scottsdale Resort & Spa at Gainey Ranch** (Scottsdale; ✆ **800/554-9288**): This Scottsdale resort boasts a 10-pool, 2½-acre water playground complete with sand beach, sports pool, lap pool, adult pool, three-story water slide, giant whirlpool, and lots of waterfalls. See p. 100.
- **The Phoenician** (Scottsdale; ✆ **800/888-8234**): This resort's seven pools are as impressive as the Hyatt's, but they have a much more sophisticated air. Waterfalls, a water slide, play pools, a lap pool, and the crown jewel—a mother-of-pearl pool (actually, opalescent tile)—add up to plenty of aquatic fun. See p. 101.
- **Pointe Hilton Squaw Peak Resort** (Phoenix; ✆ **800/876-4683**): There's not just a pool here, there's a River Ranch, with an artificial tubing river, a water slide, and a waterfall pouring into the large free-form main pool. See p. 110.
- **Pointe Hilton Tapatio Cliffs Resort** (Phoenix; ✆ **800/876-4683**): The Falls, a slightly more adult-oriented pool complex than that at sister property

Pools and gorgeous landscaping at the Hyatt Regency Scottsdale.

Pointe Hilton Squaw Peak Resort, includes two lagoon pools, a 40-foot waterfall, a 138-foot water slide, and rental cabanas. See p. 110.

- **Arizona Grand Resort** (Phoenix; ✆ **866/267-1321**): The Oasis Water Park here leaves other area resort pools high and dry. The wave pool, tubing river, and two terrifyingly steep water slides are enough to make summer in the desert almost bearable. See p. 111.
- **The Buttes, a Marriott Resort** (Tempe; ✆ **888/867-7492**): A lush stream cascading over desert rocks seems to feed this free-form pool, a desert-oasis fantasy world you won't want to leave. A narrow canal connects the two halves of the pool, and tucked in among the rocks are several whirlpools. See p. 112.
- **The Westin La Paloma Resort & Spa** (Tucson; ✆ **800/937-8461**): With a 177-foot-long water slide and enough poolside lounge chairs to put a cruise ship to shame, the pool at this Tucson foothills resort is a fabulous place to while away an afternoon. See p. 408.

THE best PLACES TO SAVOR SOUTHWEST FLAVORS

- **Cowboy Ciao** (Scottsdale; ✆ **480/946-3111**): Scottsdale may not have many real cowboys anymore, but it has great cowboy chow. Forget burned steaks and chili; this place serves the likes of buffalo carpaccio and wild-boar meatballs. See p. 115.
- **Vincent on Camelback** (Phoenix; ✆ **602/224-0225**): Chef Vincent Guerithault has made a career of merging classic French culinary techniques with the robust flavors of the Southwest. The results, for many years, have been absolutely unforgettable. See p. 126.
- **Fry Bread House** (Phoenix; ✆ **602/351-2345**): Unless you've traveled in the Southwest before, you've probably never had a fry-bread taco. This stick-to-your-ribs dish is a staple on Indian reservations throughout Arizona, but the fry-bread tacos at this Phoenix restaurant are among the best I've had anywhere in the state. See p. 131.
- **Blue Adobe Grille** (Mesa; ✆ **480/962-1000**): This nondescript restaurant in an otherwise forgettable area of Mesa serves some of the best Southwestern fare in the state. Meals are flavorful (without being too spicy), prices are great, and there's even a good wine list. See p. 132.
- **The Turquoise Room** (Winslow; ✆ **928/289-2888**): This restaurant serves dishes that incorporate both Mexican and Native American influences and conjures up the days when the wealthy still traveled by railroad. Rarely will you find such superb meals in such an off-the-beaten-path locale. See p. 330.

The best fry-bread tacos in the state are at Fry Bread House in Phoenix.

Beef, air-dried on the restaurant's roof, goes into El Charro Café's *carne seca.*

- **Café Poca Cosa** (Tucson; ✆ **520/622-6400**): Forget the gloppy melted cheese and flavorless red sauces. This place treats south-of-the-border ingredients with the respect they deserve. It's Mexican food the likes of which you'll never find at your local Mexican joint. See p. 418.
- **El Charro Café** (Tucson; ✆ **520/622-1922**): Nothing sums up Tucson-style Mexican food quite like the *carne seca* at this, the oldest family-run Mexican restaurant in Tucson. *Carne seca,* which is a bit like shredded beef jerky in a spicy sauce, is made from strips of beef that air-dry on the roof of this restaurant. See p. 419.
- **El Guero Canelo** (Tucson; ✆ **520/882-8977**): Ever had a Mexican hot dog? No? Well, here's your chance. Wrapped in bacon, topped with beans and salsa, and known locally as Sonoran dogs, the pups served at this big Mexican fast-food joint are legendary. See p. 421.
- **Janos/J Bar** (Tucson; ✆ **520/615-6100**): Serving a combination of French-inspired regional and Southwestern dishes, Janos has long been one of Tucson's premier restaurants. While Janos is as formal a place as you'll find in this city, J Bar is a more casual bar and grill. See p. 424 and 426.
- **Desert Rain Café** (Sells; ✆ **520/383-4918**): This little cafe an hour west of Tucson on the Tohono O'odham reservation serves simple dishes made with traditional ingredients such as tepary beans, cholla cactus buds, and prickly-pear syrup. If you happen to be passing through the area, Desert Rain should not be missed. See p. 468.
- **Canela** (Sonoita; ✆ **520/455-5873**): This little roadside bistro in southern Arizona's wine country is one of the best restaurants in the region and is a good place to sample the likes of quail stuffed with chorizo sausage–cornbread stuffing. Whether or not you're in the area to taste wine, you should be sure to fit Canela into your itinerary. See p. 484.

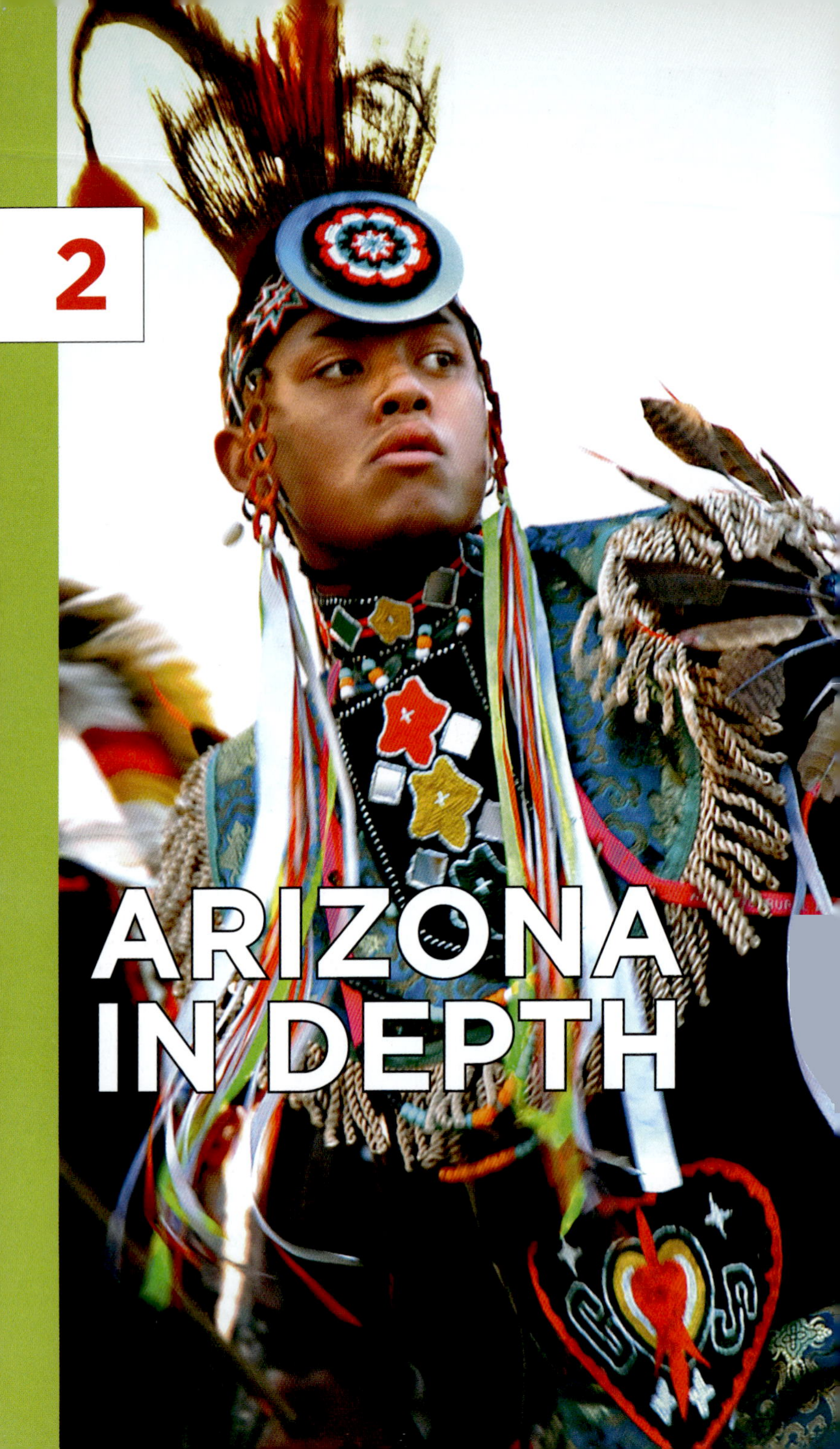

2

ARIZONA IN DEPTH

Despite the searing summer temperatures, the desolate deserts, and the lack of water, people have been drawn to Arizona for hundreds of years. In the 16th century, the Spanish came looking for gold, but settled on saving souls. In the 19th century, despite frightful tales of spiny cactus forests, ranchers drove their cattle into the region and discovered that a few corners of the state actually had lush grasslands. At the same time, sidetracked forty-niners were scouring the hills for gold (and found more than the Spanish did). However, boomtowns—both cattle and mining—soon went bust. Despite occasional big strikes, mining didn't prove itself until the early 20th century, and even then, the mother lode was neither gold nor silver, but copper, which Arizona has in such abundance that it is known as the Copper State.

In the 1920s and 1930s, Arizona struck a new source of gold: sunshine. The railroads had made travel to the state easy, and word of the mild winter climate spread to colder corners of the nation. Among the first "vacationers" were people suffering from tuberculosis. These "lungers," as they were known, rested and recuperated in the dry desert air. It didn't take long for the perfectly healthy to realize that they, too, could avail themselves of Arizona's sunshine, and wintering in the desert soon became fashionable with wealthy Northerners.

Today, it's still the golden sun that lures people to Arizona, and Scottsdale, Phoenix, Tucson, and Sedona are home to some of the most luxurious and expensive resorts in the country. Then there are those who come to Arizona on vacation and decide to make the move permanent. In the past half-century, the state has seen a massive influx of retirees, many of whom have found the few pockets of Arizona where the climate is absolutely perfect—not too hot, not too cold, and with plenty of sunshine.

While the weather is a big draw, it's the Grand Canyon that attracts the most visitors to Arizona. However, the state has plenty of other natural wonders as well. The earth's best-preserved meteorite crater, the Painted Desert, the spectacular red-rock country of Sedona, the sandstone buttes of Monument Valley, and "forests" of saguaro cacti are just a few examples.

The human hand has also left its mark on Arizona. More than 1,000 years ago, the Ancestral Puebloans (formerly called Anasazis), Sinagua, and Hohokam tribes built villages on mesas, in valleys, and in the steep cliff walls of deep canyons. In more recent years, much larger structures have risen in canyons across the state. The Hoover and Glen Canyon dams on the Colorado River are among the largest dams in the country and have created the nation's largest and most spectacular reservoirs, although at the expense of the rich riparian areas that

FACING PAGE: **A Native American man participates in a dance at a powwow.**

once thrived in the now-flooded desert canyons. Today, these reservoirs are among the state's most popular destinations, especially with Arizonans.

Just as compelling as Arizona's sunshine, resorts, and reservoirs are the tall tales of the state's fascinating history. This is the Wild West, the land of cowboys and Indians, of prospectors and ghost towns, coyotes and rattlesnakes. Scratch the glossy surface of modern, urbanized Arizona, and you'll strike real gold—the story of the American West.

ARIZONA TODAY

Just as the promise of silver and gold once lured prospectors, just as the promise of vast grasslands once lured cowboys, just as dry desert air once lured tuberculosis sufferers, the sun lures the winter-weary to Arizona. This state is solidly a part of the Sunbelt, the region of the southern United States that stretches from coast to coast and is characterized by sunshine and warm temperatures for much of the year. Before the current recession hit, when the economy was booming, Phoenix was one of the fastest-growing cities in America. Vast tracts of desert sprouted housing developments and shopping malls. However, just as mining towns such as Tombstone, Bisbee, and Jerome went bust, Arizona's economic forecast turned from sunny to gray and gloomy with the collapse of the housing market.

Because Arizona built so much of its recent economic wealth on the construction of new homes, when the housing and lending markets crashed, the state saw its tax revenues plummet. By 2010, Arizona was struggling to stay solvent. With high unemployment, high mortgage foreclosure rates, high taxes, and cuts in state services, it isn't surprising that Arizona citizens would look around for someone on whom to blame the state's woes. Illegal immigrants felt the brunt of the anger and frustration when, in April 2010, the Arizona state legislature passed the toughest immigration law in the nation. The new law made it a crime for illegal immigrants to be in the state and required law-enforcement officers to ask suspected illegal immigrants for documentation proving they have a right to

Casinos help bring money into Arizona's Indian reservations.

The state's landscape is dwindling due to rapid development.

be in the United States. Proponents of the law say the federal government isn't doing enough to secure the U.S. border. Critics say that the law will lead to racial profiling and that anyone who looks Hispanic will be targeted by law-enforcement officers. By July 2010, the law was already being challenged in court. However, although the law was criticized across the nation and across the globe, it was popular enough among Arizona citizens that, in the wake of its passage, the state reelected Gov. Jan Brewer, who had signed the legislation into law. In that same 2010 election, conservative candidates, including several supported by the controversial Tea Party, won enough races to give Arizona one of the most conservative legislatures in the country.

The international news spotlight once again focused on Arizona when, on January 8, 2011, a gunman killed 6 people and wounded 13 others, including congresswoman Gabrielle Giffords, in front of a grocery store in Tucson. This tragic shooting, which some linked to heated and contentious political rhetoric, brought renewed attention to Arizona and its lenient gun laws. Carrying an openly displayed firearm in public is legal in Arizona, and, as of 2010, a license is no longer required for carrying a concealed weapon. In early 2011, the recently elected (Nov 2010) conservative legislature proposed loosening the state's already liberal gun laws even more. Some people believe these laws make Arizona safer, while others contend it is just the opposite.

If all this has you wondering if this state is big enough for both you and the state's highly vocal gun advocates, don't worry, you won't have to get out of town before sundown. It's okay. Corral your apprehensions. Chances are the only guns you'll see will be on actors performing staged shootouts in the streets of Tombstone or Old Tucson Studios. You are likely, however, to see a few modern-day outlaw wannabes. As glorified in countless Hollywood westerns, the cowboy and the outlaw are iconic images of the Wild West. While most people the world over associate these characters with the 19th century, in Arizona they are alive and well. Visit one of the state's resuscitated ghost towns on any weekend, and you will see ranks of Harley-Davidson's (today's trusty steed of choice) lined up in front of one bar or another. However, take a look at the motorcycle riders, and what you'll see are mostly old gray-haired guys, often highly paid professionals, who are busy living out their fantasies of being real outlaws, at least until Monday when they have to go back to the office.

Obviously, Arizona is still struggling to strike a balance between the new West and the old West. Hopis still perform their age-old dances atop their mesas, while in Phoenix and Tucson, hipsters dance to the latest techno beats. Stoic wranglers are still at home on the range, but they're as likely to be leading city slickers on a staged cattle drive as to be scouring the scrublands for wayward longhorn steers. There are still working cattle ranches all over the state, but the word "ranch" is just as likely to show up in the name of a new subdivision full of multimillion-dollar winter homes for wealthy retirees from colder climes.

This struggle between the old and new has been going on in one way or another since the Spanish first arrived in the region in the 16th century. Then, and for more than 300 years after the arrival of the Spanish, the struggle was between settlers and Native Americans. For Arizona's Native Americans, the days of the Wild West were days of hardship and misery, and today the state's many tribes continue to strive for the sort of economic well-being enjoyed by the state's non-native population. Traditional ways still survive, but tribes are struggling to preserve their unique cultures—languages, religious beliefs, ceremonies, livelihoods, and architecture.

Arizona is home to the largest Indian reservation in the country—the Navajo Nation—as well as nearly two dozen smaller reservations. Poverty, unemployment, and alcoholism are major problems on many of these reservations. However, several of the state's tribes have, through their arts and crafts, managed to both preserve some of their traditional culture and share it with non-natives.

Today, however, many non-natives visit reservations not out of an interest in learning about another culture, but rather to gamble. Throughout the state, there are numerous tribal casinos, and despite the controversies surrounding such enterprises, many Native peoples are finally seeing some income on their once-impoverished reservations.

Many of the people who visit these new casinos are retirees, who are among the fastest-growing segment of Arizona's population. Each winter, the state's mild climate attracts hundreds of thousands of retirees from colder parts of the United States and Canada. Many of these winter residents, known as snowbirds, park their RVs outside such warm spots as Yuma and Quartzsite. Others have winter homes in the state, and still others have settled permanently in retirement communities such as Sun City and Green Valley.

This graying of the population, combined with strong ranching and mining industries, has made Arizona one of the most conservative states. Although by today's standards Barry Goldwater could almost be considered a liberal, his conservative politics were so much a part of the Arizona mind-set that the state kept him in the Senate for 30 years. The town of Paradise Valley even has a small park dedicated to him.

Arizona's environmental politics are some of the most contentious in the country and have been for decades. There are heated debates going on over managed flooding of the Colorado River within Grand Canyon National Park, uranium mining adjacent to the Grand Canyon, and the ongoing destruction of desert habitat as the Phoenix and Tucson metropolitan areas continue to sprawl. Although many people think of the desert as a wasteland in need of transformation, others see it as a fragile ecosystem that has been endangered by the encroachment of civilization. Saguaro cacti throughout the state are protected by law, but the deserts they grow in are not.

In many parts of the Tucson metropolitan area, houses have

> **Teddy's Tip**
>
> ***Do nothing to mar its grandeur . . . keep it for your children, your children's children, all who come after you, as the one great sight which every American should see.***
>
> **—President Theodore Roosevelt, after visiting the Grand Canyon in 1903**

Happy Birthday, Arizona!

On February 14, 2012, the state of Arizona will turn 100. Unfortunately, the state's ongoing economic troubles have prevented Arizona from planning the sort of big centennial celebration you might expect. However, smaller events around the state are playing up the state's centennial. For information on festivities, contact the Arizona Centennial Commission (✆ 602/364-4157; www.arizona100.org).

been built right up to the edge of national forest lands. The consequences of creating such a stark line between wild and developed lands came to the forefront of the news in 2004, when mountain lions moved into the popular Sabino Canyon recreation area and were even seen on the grounds of a public school. The presence of the big cats caused the immediate closure of Sabino Canyon and other nearby trails into the national forest. Today, when you visit Sabino Canyon and other natural areas around the state, you'll be warned repeatedly about the presence of mountain lions in the area.

Way up at the north end of the state, remote Grand Canyon National Park has long suffered from its own popularity. With more than four million visitors a year, the park has for many years seen summer traffic jams and parking problems that often made a visit an exercise in patience. To help alleviate congestion and air pollution, the national park now uses alternative-fuel buses to transport visitors to and around the South Rim and Grand Canyon Village. With the addition in 2009 of three large parking lots, the park has in recent years become a little more user-friendly.

Efforts at preserving the state's environment make it clear that Arizonans value the outdoors, but a ski boat in every driveway doesn't mean the arts are ignored. Although it hasn't been too many years since evening entertainment in Arizona meant dance-hall girls or a harmonica by the campfire, Phoenix and Tucson have become centers for the performing arts. The two cities share an opera company, a ballet company, and a theater company, and the Valley of the Sun is home to several symphony orchestras and numerous theater companies.

The arts, though, are often overshadowed by the Phoenix area's obsession with professional sports. Downtown Phoenix has positioned itself as the state's primary sports and entertainment mecca, with Chase Field, US Airways Center, and numerous sports bars and nightclubs. However, it isn't just downtown Phoenix that is big on professional sports. The city of Glendale, west of Phoenix, is now home to both University of Phoenix Stadium, where the NFL's Arizona Cardinals play football, and the Jobing.com Arena, where the NHL's Phoenix Coyotes play professional hockey. In addition, more than a dozen professional baseball teams have their spring training camps in the Phoenix area.

Suburban sprawl has long been a fact of life in the Phoenix area, but there are signs that even Phoenicians are tiring of the metro area's never-ending expansion. Inner-city Phoenix neighborhoods have been rediscovered, and many old homes have now been restored. Although construction has been slow since 2009, hip loft-style condominiums have been built near downtown Phoenix, and a trendy, urban art scene now flourishes in long-abandoned commercial and industrial neighborhoods in downtown Phoenix. The city even has a light-rail line.

The new urban vibe that is taking hold in the Phoenix metro area is most evident in downtown Scottsdale, which is home to several hip hotels, including a

W Hotel. Scottsdale also has one of the hottest nightlife scenes between Miami and Los Angeles, and high-style bars and clubs attempt to outdo each other with their daring interior decors.

It isn't just in Phoenix that Arizona style is changing. There are chic hotels in Sedona and even Lake Havasu City. Espresso bars are proliferating in Phoenix, Tucson, and Sedona. Flagstaff, a high-country college town, has several gourmet restaurants, and Prescott, a classic small-town-America sort of place, even has a jazz club. What's a cowboy to do?

LOOKING BACK AT ARIZONA

EARLY HISTORY Arizona is the site of North America's oldest cultures and one of the two longest continuously inhabited settlements in the United States—the Hopi village of Oraibi, which has had inhabitants for roughly 1,000 years. However, the region's human habitation dates back more than 11,000 years, to the time when Paleo-Indians known as the Clovis people inhabited southeastern Arizona. Stone tools and arrowheads of the type credited to the Clovis have been found in southeastern Arizona, and a mammoth-kill site has become an important source of information about these people, who were among the earliest inhabitants of North America.

Few records exist of the next 9,000 years of Arizona's prehistory, but by about A.D. 200, wandering bands of hunter-gatherers took up residence in Canyon de Chelly in the northern part of the state. Today these early Arizonans are known as the Ancestral Puebloans. The earliest Ancestral Puebloan period, stretching from A.D. 200 to 700, is defined as the Basket Maker period because of the large number of baskets that have been found in ruins from this time. During the Basket Maker period, the Ancestral Puebloans gave up hunting and gathering and took up agriculture, growing corn, beans, squash, and cotton on the canyon floors in northeastern Arizona.

During the Pueblo period, which spanned from 700 to 1300, the Ancestral Puebloans began building multistory pueblos and cliff dwellings. However, despite decades of research, it is still not clear why the Ancestral Puebloans began living in niches and caves high on the cliff walls of the region's canyons. It may have been to conserve farmland as their population grew and required larger harvests or for protection from flash floods. Whatever the reason the cliff dwellings were originally constructed, they were all abandoned by 1300. It's unclear why the villages were abandoned, but a study of tree rings indicates that the region experienced a severe drought between 1276 and 1299, which suggests the Ancestral Puebloans may have left in search of more fertile farmland. Keet Seel and Betatakin, at Navajo National Monument, as well as the many ruins in Canyon de Chelly, are Arizona's best-preserved Ancestral Puebloan sites.

During the Ancestral Puebloan Basket Maker period, the Sinagua culture began to develop in the fertile plateau northeast of present-day Flagstaff and southward into the Verde River valley. The Sinagua, whose name is Spanish for "without water," built their stone pueblos primarily on hills and mesas such as those at Tuzigoot near Clarkdale and Wupatki near Flagstaff, both now preserved as national monuments. They also built cliff dwellings in places such as Walnut Canyon and Montezuma Castle, both also national monuments. By the mid–13th century, Wupatki had been

Hopi girls weaving in Shipaulovi in 1903.

abandoned, and by the early 15th century, Walnut Canyon and pueblos in the lower Verde Valley region had also been deserted.

As early as A.D. 450, the Hohokam culture, from which the Sinagua most likely learned irrigation, had begun to farm the Gila and Salt River valleys between Phoenix and Casa Grande. Over a period of 1,000 years, they constructed a 600-mile network of irrigation canals, some of which can still be seen today. However, because the Hohokam built their homes of earth, few structures exist from this period. One exception is the Casa Grande ruin, a massive earth-walled building that has been well preserved and is now a national monument. There are also many Hohokam petroglyph (rock art) sites that are a lasting reminder of the people who first made the desert flourish. By the 1450s, however, the Hohokam had abandoned their villages, and today many archaeologists believe that the irrigation of desert soil for hundreds of years may have left a thick crust of alkali in farm fields, which would have made further farming impossible. The disappearance of the Hohokam is commemorated in the tribe's name, which, in the language of today's Tohono O'odham people, means "the people who have vanished."

HISPANIC HERITAGE The first Europeans to visit the region may have been a motley crew of shipwrecked Spaniards, among whom was a black man named Estévan de Dorantes. This unfortunate group spent 8 years wandering across the Southwest, and when they arrived back in Spanish territory, they told a fantastic story of having seen seven cities so rich that the inhabitants even decorated their doorways with jewels. No one is sure whether they actually passed through Arizona, but in 1539 their story convinced the viceroy of New Spain (Mexico) to send a small expedition, led by Father Marcos de Niza and Estévan de Dorantes, into the region. Father de Niza's report of finding the fabled Seven Cities of Cíbola inspired Don Francisco Vásquez de Coronado to set off in search of wealth in 1540. Instead of fabulously wealthy cities, however, Coronado found only pueblos of stone and mud. A subordinate expedition led by Garcia Lopez de Cárdenas stumbled upon the Grand Canyon, while another group of Coronado's men, led by Don Pedro de Tovar, visited the Hopi mesas.

In the 150 years that followed, only a handful of Spanish explorers, friars, and settlers visited Arizona. In the 1580s and 1600s, Antonio de Espejo and Juan de Oñate explored northern and central Arizona and found indications that there were mineral riches in the region. In the 1670s, the Franciscans founded several missions among the Hopi pueblos, but the Pueblo Revolt of 1680 obliterated this small Spanish presence.

In 1687, Father Eusebio Francisco Kino, a German-educated Italian Jesuit, began establishing missions in the Sonoran Desert region of northern New Spain. In 1691, he visited the Pima village of Tumacácori. Father Kino taught the inhabitants European farming techniques, planted fruit trees, and gave the Natives cattle, sheep, and goats to raise. However, it was not until 1751, in response to a Pima rebellion, that the permanent mission of Tumacácori and the nearby presidio (military post) of Tubac were built. Together these two Spanish outposts became the first permanent European settlements in what is today Arizona.

Spanish explorer Don Francisco Vásquez de Coronado.

In 1775, a group of settlers led by Juan Bautista de Anza set out from Tubac to find an overland route to California, and in 1776, this group founded the city of San Francisco. That same year, the Tubac presidio was moved to Tucson. As early as 1692, Father Kino had visited the Tucson area and by 1700 had laid out the foundations for the first church at the mission of San Xavier del Bac. However, it was not until some time around 1783 that construction of the present church, known as the White Dove of the Desert, began.

In 1821, Mexico won its independence from Spain, and Tucson, with only 65 inhabitants, became part of Mexico. Mexico at that time extended all the way to Northern California, but in 1848, most of this land, except for a small section of southern Arizona that included Tucson, became U.S. territory in the wake of the Mexican-American War. Five years later, in 1853, Mexico sold the remainder of what is today southern Arizona to the United States in a transaction known as the Gadsden Purchase.

INDIAN CONFLICTS At the time the Spanish arrived in Arizona, the tribes living in the southern lowland deserts were peaceful farmers, but in the mountains of the east lived the Apache, a hunting-and-gathering tribe that frequently raided neighboring tribes. In the north, the Navajo, relatively recent immigrants to the region, fought over land with the neighboring Ute and Hopi (who were also fighting among themselves).

Coronado's expedition through Arizona and into New Mexico and Kansas was to seek gold. To that end he attacked one pueblo, killed the inhabitants of another, and forced still others to abandon their villages. Spanish-Indian relations were never to improve, and the Spanish were forced to occupy their new lands with a strong military presence. Around 1600, 300 Spanish settlers moved into the Four Corners region, which at the

Far from Heaven

Oh yes, I have heard of that country. It is just like hell. All it lacks is water and good society.

—A 19th-century senator from Ohio

time supported a large population of Navajos. The Spanish raided Navajo villages to take slaves, and angry Navajos responded by stealing Spanish horses and cattle.

For several decades in the mid-1600s, missionaries were tolerated in the Hopi pueblos, but the Pueblo tribes revolted in 1680, killing the missionaries and destroying the missions. Encroachment by farmers and miners moving into the Santa Cruz Valley in the south caused the Pima people to stage a similar uprising in 1751, attacking and burning the mission at Tubac. This revolt led to the establishment of the presidio at Tubac that same year. When the military garrison moved to Tucson, Tubac was quickly abandoned because of frequent raids by Apaches. In 1781, the Yuman tribe, whose land at the confluence of the Colorado and Gila rivers had become a Spanish settlement, staged a similar uprising that wiped out the settlement at Yuma.

By the time Arizona became part of the United States, it was the Navajo and Apaches who were proving most resistant to white settlers. In 1863, the U.S. Army, under the leadership of Col. Kit Carson, forced the Navajo to surrender by destroying their winter food supplies. The survivors were marched to an internment camp in New Mexico; the Navajo refer to this as the Long Walk. Conditions at the camp in New Mexico were deplorable, and within 5 years the Navajos were returned to their land, although they were forced to live on a reservation.

The Apaches resisted white settlement 20 years longer than the Navajo did. Skillful guerrilla fighters, the Apaches, under the leadership of Geronimo and Cochise, attacked settlers, forts, and towns despite the presence of U.S. Army troops sent to protect the settlers. Geronimo and Cochise were the leaders of the last resistant bands of rebellious Apaches. Cochise eventually died in his Chiricahua Mountains homeland. Geronimo finally surrendered in 1886, and he and many of his followers were relocated to Florida by the U.S. government. Open conflicts between whites and Indians finally came to an end.

TERRITORIAL DAYS In 1846, the United States went to war with Mexico, which at the time extended all the way to Northern California and included parts of Colorado, Wyoming, and New Mexico. When the war ended, the United States claimed almost all the land extending from Texas to Northern California. This newly acquired land, called the New Mexico Territory, had its capital at Santa Fe. The land south of the Gila River, which included Tucson, was still part of Mexico, but when surveys determined that this land was the best route for a railroad from Mississippi to California, the U.S. government negotiated the Gadsden Purchase. In 1853, this land purchase established the current Arizona-Mexico border.

When the California gold rush began in 1849, many hopeful miners from the east crossed Arizona en route to the gold fields, and some stayed to seek mineral riches in Arizona. However, despite the ever-increasing numbers of settlers, the U.S. Congress refused to create a separate Arizona Territory. When the Civil War broke out, Arizonans, angered by Congress's inaction on their request to become a separate territory, sided with the Confederacy, and in 1862, Arizona was proclaimed the Confederate Territory of Arizona. Although Union troops easily defeated the Confederate troops who had occupied Tucson, this dissension convinced Congress, in 1863, to create the Arizona Territory.

Miners discovered copper, which became the source of Arizona's wealth.

The capital of the new territory was temporarily established at Fort Whipple near Prescott, but later the same year was moved to Prescott itself. In 1867 the capital moved again, this time to Tucson. Ten years later, Prescott again became the capital, which it remained for another 12 years before the seat of government finally moved to Phoenix, which remains Arizona's capital to this day.

During this period, mining flourished, and although small amounts of gold and silver were discovered, copper became the source of Arizona's economic wealth. With each mineral strike, a new mining town would boom, and when the ore ran out, the town would be abandoned. These towns were infamous for their gambling halls, bordellos, saloons, and shootouts. Tombstone and Bisbee became the largest towns in the state and were known as the wildest towns between New Orleans and San Francisco.

In 1867, farmers in the newly founded town of Phoenix began irrigating their fields using canals that had been dug centuries earlier by the Hohokam. In the 1870s, ranching became another important source of revenue in the territory, particularly in the southeastern and northwestern parts of the state. In the 1880s, the railroads finally arrived, and life in Arizona changed drastically. Suddenly the region's mineral resources and cattle were accessible to the east.

Name Game

As the mythical phoenix rose reborn from its ashes, so shall a great civilization rise here on the ashes of a past civilization. I name thee Phoenix.

—"Lord" Bryan Phillip Darrell Duppa, the British settler who named Phoenix

STATEHOOD & THE 20TH CENTURY By the beginning of the 20th century, Arizonans were trying to convince Congress to make the territory a state. Congress balked at the requests, but finally in 1910 allowed the territorial government to draw up a state constitution. Territorial legislators were progressive thinkers, and the draft of Arizona's state constitution included clauses for the recall of elected officials. President William Howard Taft vetoed the bill that would have made Arizona a state because he opposed the recall of judges. Arizona politicians removed the controversial clause, and on February 14, 1912, Arizona became the 48th state. One of the new state legislature's first acts was to reinstate the clause providing for the recall of judges.

Much of Washington's opposition to Arizona's statehood had been based on the belief that Arizona could never support economic development. This belief was changed in 1911 by one of the most important events in state history—the completion of the Salt River's Roosevelt Dam (later to be renamed the Theodore Roosevelt Dam). The dam provided irrigation water to the Phoenix area and tamed the violent floods of the river. The introduction of water to the heart of Arizona's vast desert enabled large-scale agriculture and industry. Over the next decades, more dams were built throughout Arizona, and, in 1936, the Hoover Dam on the Colorado River became the largest concrete dam in the Western Hemisphere. This dam also created the largest man-made reservoir in North America. Arizona's dams would eventually provide not only water and electricity but also the state's most popular recreation areas.

Despite labor problems, copper mining increased throughout the 1920s and 1930s, and with the onset of World War II, the mines boomed as military munitions manufacturing increased the demand for copper. However, within a few years after the war, many mines were shut down. Today, Arizona is littered with old mining ghost towns that boomed and then went bust. A few towns, such as Jerome and Bisbee, managed to hang on after the mines shut down and were eventually rediscovered by artists, writers, and retirees. Today, both Bisbee and Jerome are major tourist attractions known for their many art galleries, interesting shops, and boomtown atmosphere.

World War II created a demand for beef, leather, and cotton, and Arizona farmers and ranchers stepped in to meet the need. Cotton, which was used in the manufacture of tires, quickly became the state's most important

The Theodore Roosevelt Dam.

crop. Goodyear planted huge fields of the crop and even built the company town of Goodyear, which today is home to one of Arizona's oldest and most prestigious resorts. During the war, Arizona's clear desert skies also provided ideal conditions for training pilots, and several military bases were established in the state. Phoenix's population doubled during the war years, and, when peace finally arrived, many veterans returned with their families. However, it would take the invention of air-conditioning to truly open up the desert to major population growth.

During the postwar years, Arizona attracted a number of large manufacturing industries and slowly moved away from its agricultural economic base. Today, electronics manufacturing, aerospace engineering, and other high-tech industries provide employment for thousands of Arizonans. The largest economic segment, however, is now the service industries, with tourism playing a crucial role.

Even by the 1920s, Arizona had become a winter destination for the wealthy, and the Grand Canyon, declared a national park in 1919, was luring visitors even when they had to get there by stagecoach. The clear, dry air also attracted people suffering from allergies and lung ailments, and Arizona became known as a healthful place. With Hollywood Westerns enjoying immense popularity, dude ranches began to spring up across the state. Eventually the rustic guest ranches of the 1930s gave way to luxurious golf resorts. Today, Scottsdale, Phoenix, and Tucson boast dozens of luxury resorts. In addition, tens of thousands of retirees from as far north as Canada make Arizona their winter home and play a substantial role in the state's economy.

Continued population growth throughout the 20th century resulted in an ever-increasing demand for water. Yet, despite the damming of nearly all of Arizona's rivers, the state still suffered from insufficient water supplies in the south-central population centers of Phoenix and Tucson. It took the construction of the controversial and expensive Central Arizona Project (CAP) aqueduct to carry water from the Colorado River over mountains and deserts, and deliver it where it was wanted. Construction on the CAP began in 1974, and in 1985 water from the project finally began irrigating fields near Phoenix. In 1992, the CAP reached Tucson. However, a drought that began in the mid-1990s has left Phoenix and Tucson once again pondering where they will come up with the water to fuel future growth.

By the 1960s, Arizona had become an urban state with all the problems confronting other areas around the nation. The once-healthful air of Phoenix now rivals that of Los Angeles for the thickness of its smog. Allergy sufferers are plagued by pollen from the nondesert plants that have been introduced to make this desert region look more lush and inviting. However, until the recent economic downturn, the state's economy was still growing quite rapidly. High-tech companies had been locating within Arizona, and a steady influx of retirees, as well as Californians fleeing earthquakes and urban problems, had given the state new energy and new ideas. Things slowed considerably in 2009, but, of course, the sun still shines here, even in January and February when much of the rest of the country is locked in a deep freeze, and that is a powerful lure. As long as winters in Arizona continue to be sunny and warm, you can bet that the state will continue to boom.

ARIZONA IN POP CULTURE

Books

HISTORY Marshall Trimble's *Roadside History of Arizona* is an ideal book to take along on a driving tour of the state. It goes road by road and discusses events that happened in the area. If you're interested in learning more about the infamous shootout at the O.K. Corral, read Paula Mitchell Marks's *And Die in the West: The Story of the O.K. Corral Gunfight,* an objective, non-Hollywood look at the most glorified and glamorized shootout in Western history.

THE GRAND CANYON & THE COLORADO RIVER John Wesley Powell's diary produced the first published account (1869) of traveling through the Grand Canyon. Today, his writings still provide a fascinating glimpse into the canyon. *Exploration of the Colorado River and Its Canyons,* with an introduction by Wallace Stegner, is a republishing of Powell's writings. Alternatively, read Stegner's *Beyond the Hundredth Meridian: John Wesley Powell and the Second Opening of the West,* an in-depth biography of Powell.

For an interesting account of the recent human history of the canyon, read Stephen J. Pyne's *How the Canyon Became Grand.* Colin Fletcher's *The Man Who Walked Through Time* is a narrative of one man's hike through the rugged inner canyon. In *Down the River,* Western environmentalist Edward Abbey chronicles many of his trips down the Colorado and other Southwest rivers. *Grand Canyon: True Stories of Life Below the Rim* (Travelers' Tales Guides) provides a wide range of perspectives on the Grand Canyon experience, with essays by Edward Abbey, Colin Fletcher, Barry Lopez, and many others. For a slightly macabre look at the canyon, read *Over the Edge: Death in Grand Canyon,* by Thomas M. Myers and Michael P. Ghiglieri. As the title implies, this book looks at the many ways people have died in the Grand Canyon. For an equally offbeat read, pick up *Sunk Without a Sound: The Tragic Colorado River Honeymoon of Glen and Bessie Hyde,* by Brad Dimock. The book title says it all.

Water rights and human impact on the deserts of the Southwest raised many controversies in the 20th century. *Cadillac Desert: The American West and Its Disappearing Water,* by Marc Reisner, focuses on the West's insatiable need for water. *A River No More: The Colorado River and the West,* by Philip L. Fradkin, addresses the fate of the Colorado River.

NATURAL HISTORY & THE OUTDOORS Anyone curious about the plants and animals of the Sonoran Desert should be sure to acquire *A Natural History of the Sonoran Desert.* Cacti, wildflowers, tarantulas, roadrunners—they're all here and described in very readable detail. Halka Chronic's *Roadside Geology of Arizona* is another handy book to keep in the car, as is *Geology Underfoot in Northern Arizona,* by Lon Abbott and Terri Cook. If you're a hiker, you'll find Scott S. Warren's *100 Classic Hikes in Arizona* to be an invaluable traveling companion.

FICTION Tony Hillerman's murder mysteries are almost all set on the Navajo Reservation in the Four Corners area of the state and include many references to locations you can visit on a vacation in the area. Among Hillerman's many Navajo mysteries are *Skeleton Man, Sacred Clowns, A Thief of Time,* and *The Ghostway.*

Author J. A. Jance sets many of her murder mysteries in southeast Arizona's Cochise County, where she grew up. The protagonist of the series is

Sheriff Joanna Brady. Titles include *Devil's Claw, Dead to Rights, Rattlesnake Crossing, Outlaw Mountain,* and *Tombstone Courage.*

Barbara Kingsolver, a biologist and social activist, has set several of her novels either partly or entirely in Arizona. *The Bean Trees, Pigs in Heaven,* and *Animal Dreams* are peopled by Anglo, Indian, and Hispanic characters, allowing for quirky, humorous narratives with social and political overtones that provide insights into Arizona's cultural mélange. Kingsolver's nonfiction works include *High Tide in Tucson* and *Holding the Line: Women in the Great Arizona Mine Strike of 1983.* The former is a collection of essays, many of which focus on the author's life in Tucson, while the latter is an account of a copper-mine strike.

Edward Abbey's *The Monkey Wrench Gang* and *Hayduke Lives!* are tales of an unlikely gang of eco-terrorists determined to preserve the wildernesses of the Southwest, including parts of northern Arizona.

Zane Grey spent many years living in north-central Arizona and based many of his Western novels on life in this region of the state. Among his books are *Riders of the Purple Sage, The Vanishing American, Call of the Canyon, The Arizona Clan,* and *To the Last Man.*

TRAVEL If you're particularly interested in Native American art and crafts, you may want to seek out a copy of *Trading Post Guidebook,* by Patrick Eddington and Susan Makov. It's an invaluable guide to trading posts, artists' studios, galleries, and museums in the Four Corners region.

Film

Spectacular landscapes, rugged deserts, ghost towns, and its cowboy mystique have, over the years, made Arizona the location for hundreds of films, from obscure B Westerns starring long-forgotten singing cowboys to the seminal works of John Ford. This state has become so associated with the Old West that fans come from halfway around the world to walk in the footsteps of John Wayne and Clint Eastwood.

Production companies working on movies, television shows, and commercials have over the years traveled to every corner of Arizona to find just the right setting for their work. The state has represented the past, the present, and the future, and the state's landscape is so varied that it has doubled for Texas, Kansas, Mexico, foreign planets, a postapocalyptic earth, and even New York.

In 1939, a set was built in Tucson for the filming of the movie *Arizona,* and when the shooting was done, the set was left to be used in other productions. Today, this mock-Western town is known as Old Tucson Studios and is still used for film and video productions. Movies that have been filmed here include *Tombstone;* John Wayne's *Rio Lobo, Rio Bravo,* and *El Dorado;* Clint Eastwood's *The Outlaw Josey Wales;* Kirk Douglas's *Gunfight at the O.K. Corral;* and Paul Newman's *The Life and Times of Judge Roy Bean.*

John Ford made the otherworldly landscape of Monument Valley a trademark of his filmmaking, using it as the backdrop for such movies as *Stagecoach, She Wore a Yellow Ribbon, My Darling Clementine, Rio Grande,* and *The Searchers.* Other Westerns filmed here have included *How the West Was Won, The Legend of the Lone Ranger,* and *Mackenna's Gold.* The valley has also shown up in such non-Western films as *Back to the Future III, 2001: A Space Odyssey, Thelma and Louise,* and *Forrest Gump.*

The red rocks of Sedona have also attracted many filmmakers over the years. The original 1957 version of *3:10 to Yuma, The Riders of the Purple Sage,* and *The Call of the Canyon* were all filmed in Sedona and nearby Oak Creek Canyon.

The area around the small town of Patagonia, in southeastern Arizona, has also served as a backdrop for quite a few films, including *Oklahoma!, Red River, McClintock, Broken Lance, David and Bathsheba,* and *A Star Is Born.* Television programs such as *Little House on the Prairie, The Young Riders,* and *Red Badge of Courage* have been filmed in this part of southern Arizona, too.

In 1987, the Coen Brothers produced one of the most offbeat films to have been shot in Arizona. *Raising Arizona,* starring Nicolas Cage, Holly Hunter, John Goodman, and Frances McDormand, is a bizarre story of a childless couple who kidnap a baby. Other offbeat and non-Western films that have been filmed in the state include *Broken Arrow* (starring John Travolta), *Nurse Betty* (starring Morgan Freeman and Renée Zellweger), *Days of Thunder* (starring Tom Cruise, Nicole Kidman, and Robert Duvall), *Traffic* (starring Michael Douglas and Catherine Zeta-Jones), and, most recently, *Transformers,* a science-fiction film based on a line of toys. The movie includes scenes shot at Hoover Dam.

Music

Arizona has a soundtrack. You hear it in hotel lobbies and gift shops, in restaurants and national park visitor centers. It is the sound of Native American flute music. The haunting melodies of this music are the perfect accompaniment to a long drive across the wide-open spaces of Arizona. R. Carlos Nakai, who was born in Flagstaff and is of Navajo and Ute heritage, is considered the preeminent Native American flutist, and you'll find his music for sale in gift shops all over the state. Keep an eye out for some, and you can start the soundtrack of your trip.

Tucson, home to April's annual Tucson International Mariachi Conference, is called the mariachi capital of America, and year-round you can hear this lively south-of-the-border music in Mexican restaurants. Also in Tucson, you can sometimes catch a bit of indigenous *waila* music. This is the music of southern Arizona's Tohono O'odham tribe and is a mix of polka, waltz, and various Mexican influences.

EATING & DRINKING IN ARIZONA

Because Arizona is a mélange of cultures—Anglo, Hispanic, Native American—the state's culinary scene is equally diverse. Of course, you'll find plenty of fast-food restaurants as well as restaurants following the latest trends, but you'll also find Native American foods little changed in hundreds of years and an astonishingly wide variety of Mexican food, from Baja-style fish tacos to Nuevo Latino preparations that seem lifted from the pages of *Like Water for Chocolate.*

If you have an adventurous palate, be sure to search out some of the state's Southwestern restaurants. Although many of these can be rather expensive, the flavors, which combine the spices of Mexico with the fruit-and-meat pairings of nouvelle cuisine, are so distinctive that you'll likely find yourself soon craving more. Don't worry, Southwestern cooking is not all about fiery peppers. Expect pistachio-crusted meats, fruit salsas, cream sauces made with smoky chipotle peppers, and the likes of duck tamales and cassoulet made with indigenous tepary beans. Among my favorite Southwestern restaurants in Arizona are Janos (and its affiliated and less expensive J Bar; see p. 424 and 426) in Tucson; Vincent on Camelback (p. 126), Cowboy Ciao (p. 115), and Kai (p. 133) in the Phoenix area; and the Turquoise Room (p. 330) at La Posada hotel in Winslow.

At the other end of the culinary spectrum is the simple fare favored by Arizona's Native Americans. On reservations throughout the state, you'll usually find fry bread on the menu. These deep-fried disks of dough are similar to that county-fair staple, the elephant ear (only without the sugar and cinnamon). Fry bread is eaten as a side or is used to make fry-bread tacos (called Navajo tacos on the Navajo Reservation). These tacos are made by piling shredded lettuce, ground beef, pinto beans, and cheese on top of a circle of fry bread. The best fry-bread tacos I've had in Arizona are in Phoenix at the Fry Bread House (p. 131) and Sacred Hogan Navajo Frybread (p. 132). The biggest are at the Cameron Trading Post restaurant (p. 281) near the east entrance to Grand Canyon National Park. One regular fry-bread taco here is enough for two people.

Southwestern-inspired fare at Scottsdale's Cowboy Ciao.

Other than fry-bread tacos, authentic Native American fare is hard to come by in Arizona. At the Ch'ihootso Indian Market (p. 347), in the Navajo Nation capital of Window Rock, you can sample such traditional dishes as mutton stew and steam corn (a soup made with whole corn kernels). Also, if you should happen to see a roadside sign for kneel-down bread, be sure to buy some. This traditional Navajo corn bread is similar to a tamale, only sweeter. Wherever you should happen to sample Navajo food, ask whether Navajo tea is available. This is a mild herbal tea made from a plant that grows in northern Arizona.

On the Hopi Reservation, at the Hopi Cultural Center (p. 337), you can sample traditional Hopi stew (made with hominy, green chilies, and lamb). In the southern part of the state, you can often sample Native foods at stalls in the parking lot of Mission San Xavier del Bac (p. 436) south of Tucson. If you'd like to take home some Native American ingredients, stop by Native Seeds/SEARCH (p. 456), a Tucson nonprofit organization involved in preserving the indigenous crops of the Southwest.

No discussion of Arizona cuisine would be complete without mentioning Mexican food. Yes, I know that Mexican food is ubiquitous all over the U.S., but Arizona Mexican restaurants have far more to offer than deep-fried chalupas, flavorless burritos, and plates of unidentifiable stuff covered under a dense layer of molten yellow cheese. How about a Sonoran hot dog? I bet you can't get one of those at your local gringo-mex joint. Sonoran dogs, available at El Guero Canelo (p. 421) in Tucson, are hot dogs wrapped in bacon and slathered with beans and salsa. For another distinctive Sonoran dish, sample the *carne seca* at Tucson's El Charro Café (p. 419). The English translation of this dish (dry meat) may not sound too appetizing, but, trust me, this stuff is great. At the other end of the Mexican spectrum are the flavorful and creative dishes concocted by chef Suzana Davila at her Tucson restaurant Café Poca Cosa (p. 418).

Because of the heat and proximity to Mexico, margaritas are among the most popular cocktails in the state, and they come in a wide range of flavors. Although I am a traditional on-the-rocks-with-salt person, I can never resist a prickly-pear margarita. These cocktails, prepared with a syrup made from the fruit of the prickly pear cactus, are shockingly pink and surprisingly good.

You may never have thought of the desert as wine country, but Arizona is actually producing some decent wines. Wineries can be found both in southern Arizona in and near the small town of Sonoita, and in central Arizona near Sedona and Cottonwood. Big reds are the focus of most of the state's wineries. My favorite wine producers include Callaghan Vineyards (p. 482), Alcantara Vineyards (p. 224), and Page Springs Cellars (p. 235).

WHEN TO GO

Arizona is a year-round destination, although people head to different parts of the state at different times of the year. In Phoenix, Tucson, and other parts of the desert, the high season runs from October to mid-May, with the highest hotel rates from January to April. At the Grand Canyon, summer is the busy season.

The all-around best times to visit are spring and autumn, when temperatures are cool in the mountains and warm in the desert, but without extremes (although you shouldn't be surprised to get a bit of snow as late as Memorial Day in the mountains and thunderstorms in the desert Aug–Sept). Late spring and early autumn (specifically May and Sept) are also good times to save money—low summer rates are still in effect at the desert resorts—and to see the Grand Canyon when it's not its most crowded. In spring, you might also catch great wildflower displays, which begin in March and last until May, when the tops of saguaro cacti are covered with waxy white blooms.

If for some reason you happen to be visiting the desert in July or August, be prepared for sudden thunderstorms. These storms often cause flash floods that make many roads briefly impassable. Signs warning motorists not to enter low areas when flooded should be taken very seriously.

Also, don't even think about venturing into narrow slot canyons, such as Antelope Canyon near Page or the West Fork of Oak Creek Canyon, if there's any chance of a storm anywhere in the region. Rain falling miles away can send flash floods roaring down narrow canyons with no warning. In 1997, several hikers died when they were caught in a flash flood in Antelope Canyon, and in 2009, a flash flood inundated the parking lot at Sedona's Tlaquepaque shopping center.

One more thing to keep in mind: Sedona is just high enough that it actually gets cold in the winter—sometimes it even snows. So if you're looking for sunshine and time by the pool, book your Sedona vacation for a time other than the winter.

Weather

The first thing you should know is that the desert can be cold as well as hot. Although winter is the prime tourist season in Phoenix and Tucson, night temperatures can be below freezing and days can sometimes be too cold for sunning or swimming. However, although there can be several days in a row of cool, cloudy, and even rainy weather in January and February, on the whole, winters in Arizona are positively delightful.

In the winter, sun seekers flock to the deserts, where temperatures average in the high 60s (low 20s Celsius) by day. In the summer, when desert temperatures top 110°F (43°C), the mountains of eastern and northern Arizona are pleasantly warm, with daytime averages in the low 80s (high 20s Celsius). Yuma is one of the desert communities where winter temperatures are the highest in the state, while Prescott and Sierra Vista, in the 4,000- to 6,000-foot elevation range, claim temperate climates that are just about ideal.

Average Temperatures & Days of Rain

PHOENIX	JAN	FEB	MAR	APR	MAY	JUNE	JULY	AUG	SEPT	OCT	NOV	DEC
AVG. HIGH (°F)	66	70	75	84	93	103	105	103	99	88	75	66
AVG. HIGH (°C)	19	21	24	29	34	39	41	39	37	31	24	19
AVG. LOW (°F)	41	44	49	55	64	72	80	79	72	61	48	42
AVG. LOW (°C)	5	7	9	13	18	22	27	26	22	16	9	6
DAYS OF RAIN	4	4	4	2	1	1	4	5	3	3	3	4

FLAGSTAFF	JAN	FEB	MAR	APR	MAY	JUNE	JULY	AUG	SEPT	OCT	NOV	DEC
AVG. HIGH (°F)	42	45	49	58	67	78	82	79	74	64	51	44
AVG. HIGH (°C)	6	7	9	14	19	26	28	26	23	18	11	7
AVG. LOW (°F)	15	18	22	27	34	41	50	49	41	31	22	16
AVG. LOW (°C)	-9	-8	-6	-3	1	5	10	9	5	-1	-6	-9
DAYS OF RAIN	8	7	9	6	5	3	11	11	6	5	5	6

Holidays

Banks, government offices, post offices, and many stores, restaurants, and museums are closed on the following legal national holidays: January 1 (New Year's Day), the third Monday in January (Martin Luther King, Jr., Day), the third Monday in February (Presidents' Day), the last Monday in May (Memorial Day), July 4 (Independence Day), the first Monday in September (Labor Day), the second Monday in October (Columbus Day), November 11 (Veterans' Day/Armistice Day), the fourth Thursday in November (Thanksgiving Day), and December 25 (Christmas). The Tuesday after the first Monday in November is Election Day, a federal government holiday in presidential-election years (held every 4 years, and next in 2012).

Arizona Calendar of Events

For an exhaustive list of events beyond those listed here, check http://events.frommers.com, where you'll find a searchable, up-to-the-minute roster of what's happening in cities all over the world.

JANUARY

Tostitos Fiesta Bowl, University of Phoenix Stadium, Glendale. This college bowl game usually sells out nearly a year in advance. There's also an associated parade. Call ✆ **800/635-5748** or 480/350-0911, or go to www.fiestabowl.org. Early January.

Barrett-Jackson Collector Car Auction, Scottsdale. More than 1,000 immaculately restored classic cars are auctioned off in an event attended by more than 250,000 people. Call ✆ **480/663-6255,** or go to www.barrett-jackson.com. Mid-January.

Wings over Willcox, Willcox. You can take part in birding tours, workshops, and, of course, watching the tens of thousands of sandhill cranes that gather in the Sulphur Springs Valley near Willcox. Call ✆ **800/200-2272,** or go to www.wingsoverwillcox.com. Mid-January.

Tucson Gem and Mineral Show, Tucson. This huge show at the Tucson Convention Center offers seminars, museum displays from around the world, and hundreds of dealers selling just about any kind of rock you can imagine. In addition, there are more than 30 other smaller shows in the weeks prior to the main show; for information on these smaller shows, visit www.tucsonshowguide.com. Call ✆ **520/322-5773,** or go to www.tgms.org. Late January to mid-February.

Waste Management Phoenix Open Golf Tournament, Scottsdale. Prestigious PGA golf tournament at the Tournament Players Club. Call ✆ **602/870-0163,** or go to www.wastemanagementphoenixopen.com. Late January to early February.

FEBRUARY

Arizona Renaissance Festival, Apache Junction. Patterned after a 16th-century English country fair, this festival features costumed participants and tournament jousting. Call ✆ **520/463-200,** or go to www.royalfaires.com/arizona. Weekends from mid-February to early April.

Tubac Festival of the Arts, Tubac. Exhibits by North American artists and craftspeople. Call ✆ **520/398-2704,** or go to www.tubacaz.com/festival.asp. Early February.

World Championship Hoop Dance Contest, Phoenix. Native American dancers from around the nation take part in this colorful competition held at the Heard Museum. Call ✆ **602/252-8848,** or go to www.heard.org. Early February.

Cochise Cowboy Poetry & Music Gathering, Sierra Vista. More than 50 cowboy poets, singers, and musicians gather in Sierra Vista for a weekend of Wild West poetry and music. Call ✆ **520/678-9952,** or go to www.cowboypoets.com. Mid-February.

O'odham Tash, Casa Grande. This is one of the largest annual Native American festivals in the country, attracting dozens of tribes that participate in rodeos, arts-and-crafts exhibits, and dance performances. Call ✆ **520/836-4723.** Mid-February.

Scottsdale Arabian Horse Show, Scottsdale. This celebration of the Arabian horse is said to be the largest Arabian horse show in the world. Call ✆ **480/515-1500,** or go to www.scottsdaleshow.com. Mid- to late February.

La Fiesta de los Vaqueros, Tucson. This cowboy festival and rodeo at the Tucson Rodeo Grounds includes the Tucson Rodeo Parade, which claims to be the world's longest nonmotorized parade. Call ✆ **800/964-5662** or 520/741-2233, or go to www.tucsonrodeo.com. Late February.

Parada del Sol Parade and Rodeo, Scottsdale. The state's largest horse-drawn parade includes a street dance and rodeo. Call ✆ **480/990-3179,** or go to www.paradadelsol.org. Late February.

Sedona International Film Festival, Sedona. View various new indie features, documentaries, and animated films before they (it is hoped) get picked up for wider distribution. Call ✆ **928/282-1177,** or go to www.sedonafilmfestival.com. Late February.

MARCH

Heard Museum Guild Indian Fair & Market, Phoenix. Indian cultural and dance presentations and one of the largest selections of Native American crafts in the Southwest make this a fascinating festival. Go early to avoid the crowds. Call ✆ **602/252-8848,** or go to www.heard.org. First weekend in March.

Festival of the West, Chandler. A celebration of all things cowboy, from cowboy poetry to Western music and movies. There's also a chuck-wagon cook-off and a mountain-man rendezvous. Call ✆ **602/996-4387,** or go to www.festivalofthewest.com. Mid-March.

Ostrich Festival, Chandler. Give the carnival a miss and head straight for the ostrich races. Although brief, these unusual races are something you ought to see at least once in your lifetime. Call ✆ **480/963-4571,** or go to www.ostrich festival.com. Mid-March.

Scottsdale Arts Festival, Scottsdale Mall. This visual and performing arts festival includes concerts, an art fair, and children's events. Call ✆ **480/994-2787,** or go to www.scottsdaleartsfestival.org. Mid-March.

Wa:k Pow Wow, Tucson. Tohono O'odham celebration at Mission San Xavier del Bac, featuring many Southwestern Native American groups. Call ✆ **520/573-4000.** Second weekend in March.

Welcome Back Buzzards, Superior. A flock of turkey vultures (buzzards) arrives annually at the Boyce Thompson Arboretum to roost in eucalyptus trees and on volcanic cliffs, and this festival celebrates their arrival. Call ✆ **520/689-2811,** or go to http://arboretum.ag.arizona.edu. Mid- to late March.

APRIL

Tucson International Mariachi Conference. Mariachi bands from all over the world come to compete before standing-room-only crowds. Call ✆ **520/838-3908,** or go to www.tucsonmariachi.org. Late April.

MAY

Cinco de Mayo, Phoenix and other cities. Celebration of the Mexican victory over the French in a famous 1862 battle comes complete with food, music, and dancing. Check local newspapers for area festivities. Around May 5.

Route 66 Fun Run, Kingman area. Classic hot rods hit the road for 3 days of roaring up and down historic Route 66. Call ✆ **928/753-5001,** or go to www.azrt66.com. First weekend in May.

Phippen Museum Western Art Show & Sale, Prescott. This is the state's premier Western-art sale. Call ✆ **928/778-1385,** or go to www.phippenartmuseum.org. Memorial Day weekend.

Wyatt Earp Days, Tombstone. Gunfights are reenacted in memory of the shootout at the O.K. Corral. Call ✆ **888/457-3929** or 520/457-3929, or go to www.wyattearpdays.com. Memorial Day weekend.

JUNE

Prescott Frontier Days/World's Oldest Rodeo, Prescott. This is one of the state's two rodeos that claim to be the nation's oldest. Call ✆ **800/358-1888** or 928/445-3103, or go to www.worlds oldestrodeo.com. Late June to July 4.

JULY

Hopi Festival of Arts and Culture, Flagstaff. This exhibition and sale is held at the Museum of Northern Arizona and includes crafts vendors and demonstrations, music, dancing, Hopi foods, and various cultural events. Call ✆ **928/774-5213,** or go to www.musnaz.org. Early July.

Sidewalk Egg Fry Contest, Oatman. In the ghost town of Oatman, located near one of the hottest places on earth, contestants use their own devices, such as mirrors, to fry an egg in 15 minutes. Call ✆ **928/768-6222,** or go to www.oatman goldroad.org. July 4 at high noon.

Independence Day. For information on fireworks displays in Phoenix, call ✆ **602/534-3378;** for Tucson, phone ✆ **800/638-8350** or 520/624-1817. For other areas, contact the local chamber of commerce. July 4.

AUGUST

Navajo Festival of Arts and Culture, Flagstaff. This exhibition and sale at the Museum of Northern Arizona includes rug-weaving demonstrations, hoop dances, crafts vendors, and cultural events. Call ✆ **928/774-5213,** or go to www.musnaz.org. Early August.

Southwest Wings Birding and Nature Festival, Sierra Vista. Spotting hummingbirds and looking for owls and bats keep participants busy. Includes lectures and field trips throughout southeastern Arizona. Go to www.swwings.org. Early August.

August Doins Rodeo, Payson. This is the second of Arizona's rodeos claiming to be the country's oldest. Call ✆ **800/672-9766** or 928/474-4515, or go to www.paysonrimcountry.com/augustdoins. Third weekend in August.

Grand Canyon Music Festival, Grand Canyon Village. For more than a quarter of a century, this festival has been bringing classical music to the South Rim of the Grand Canyon. Call ✆ **800/997-8285** or 928/638-9215, or go to www.grandcanyonmusicfest.org. Late August to early September.

SEPTEMBER

Navajo Nation Fair, Window Rock. This fair features traditional music and dancing, a Miss Navajo contest, and more. Call ✆ **928/871-6478,** or go to www.navajonationfair.com. Early September.

OCTOBER

Sedona Arts Festival, Sedona. One of the top arts festivals in the state. Call ✆ **928/204-9456,** or go to www.sedonaartsfestival.org. Early to mid-October.

Arizona Exposition & State Fair, Phoenix. Featured are rodeos, top-name entertainment, demolition derbies, ethnic food, and lots of activities for kids. Call ✆ **602/252-6771,** or go to www.azstatefair.com. Mid-October to early November.

Bisbee 1000, Bisbee. This foot race sends runners up and down 1,000 steps in the old mining town of Bisbee. Go to www.bisbee1000.org. Third weekend in October.

Helldorado Days, Tombstone. Attendants of this festival can check out an 1880s fashion show, beard contest, reenactments, and street entertainment. Call ✆ **888/457-3929** or 520/457-3929, or go to www.helldoradodays.com. Third full weekend in October.

Cowboy Artists of America Annual Exhibition and Sale, Phoenix. The Phoenix Art Museum hosts the most prestigious and best-known Western-art show in the region. Call ✆ **602/257-1222,** or go to www.phxart.org. Late October to mid-November.

DECEMBER

Festival of Lights, Sedona. Thousands of *luminarias* are lit at dusk at the Tlaquepaque Arts and Crafts Village. Call ✆ **928/282-4838,** or go to www.tlaq.com. Mid-December.

Pueblo Grande Museum Indian Market, Phoenix. This is the largest market of its kind in the state, with more than 250 Native American artisans. Call ✆ **877/706-4408** or 602/495-0900, or go to www.pueblogrande.com. Second full weekend in December.

THE LAY OF THE LAND

Although the very mention of Arizona may cause some people to turn the air-conditioning on full blast, this state is much more than a searing landscape of cacti and mesquite trees. From the baking shores of the lower Colorado River to the snowcapped heights of the San Francisco Peaks, Arizona encompasses virtually every North American climatic zone. Cactus flowers bloom in spring, and mountain wildflowers have their turn in summer. In autumn, the aspens color the White Mountains golden, and in winter, snows blanket the higher elevations from the Grand Canyon's North Rim to the Mexican border.

The River Wild

We are three-quarters of a mile in the depths of the earth, and the great river shrinks into insignificance as it dashes its angry waves against the walls and cliffs that rise to the world above.

—John Wesley Powell, leader of the first river trip through the Grand Canyon

But it's the Sonoran Desert, with its massive saguaro cacti, that most people associate with Arizona, and it is here in the desert that the state's two largest cities—Phoenix and Tucson—are found. Due in large part to the relatively plentiful rains in the region, the Sonoran Desert is one of the world's greenest and most biologically diverse deserts. In Arizona, rain falls during both the winter and the late summer. This latter rainy season, when clamorous thunderstorms send flash floods surging down arroyos, is known as the monsoon season and is the most dramatic time of year in the desert. The sunsets are unforgettable, but so, too, are the heat and humidity.

Before the introduction of dams and deep wells, many Arizona rivers and streams flowed year-round and nurtured a surprising variety of plants and animals. Today, however, only a few rivers and creeks still flow unaltered through the desert. They include Sonoita and Aravaipa creeks and the San Pedro, Verde, and Hassayampa rivers. The green riparian areas along these watercourses are characterized by rare cottonwood-willow forests and serve as magnets for wildlife, harboring rare birds as well as fish species unique to Arizona.

Outside the desert regions, there is great diversity as well. In the southern part of the state, small mountain ranges rise abruptly from the desert floor, creating refuges for plants and animals that require cooler climates. It is these so-called sky islands that harbor the greatest varieties of bird species in the continental United States. Birds from both warm and cold climates find homes in such oases as Ramsey, Madera, and Cave Creek canyons.

Although rugged mountain ranges crisscross the state, only a few rise to such heights that they support actual forests. Among these are the Santa Catalinas outside Tucson, the White Mountains along the state's eastern border, and the San Francisco Peaks north of Flagstaff. However, it's atop the Mogollon Rim and the Kaibab Plateau that the ponderosa pine forests cover the greatest areas. The Mogollon Rim is a 2,000-foot-high escarpment that stretches from central Arizona all the way into New Mexico. The ponderosa pine forest here is the largest in the world and is dotted with lakes well known for their fishing. The Mogollon Rim area is also home to large herds of elk. At more than 8,000 feet in elevation, the Kaibab Plateau is even higher than the Mogollon Rim, yet it is through the Kaibab Plateau that the Grand Canyon cuts its mighty chasm.

Arizona, though a desert, still gets snow in its northern regions.

Arizona's violent monsoons can sometimes result in colorful sunsets.

Arizona Flora & Fauna

SAGUAROS & THEIR SPINY FRIENDS

From the diminutive hedgehog to the stately saguaro, the cacti of the Sonoran Desert display a fascinating variety of shapes and sizes. While your first thought is usually to give them a wide berth, Arizona's cacti are worth a closer inspection, especially in the spring, when their large, waxy flowers paint the desert with splashes of color. May is probably the best all-around month for seeing cactus flowers, but you can see them in April and June as well.

The best natural areas to see cacti (it's okay to say cactuses, too) are Saguaro National Park (outside Tucson), Organ Pipe Cactus National Monument (100 miles west of Tucson), Sabino Canyon Recreation Area (in Tucson), Picacho Peak State Park (near Casa Grande), and South Mountain Park (in Phoenix). To learn more about cacti, visit the Desert Botanical Garden in Phoenix, Boyce Thompson Southwestern Arboretum in Superior, or Tucson's Arizona–Sonora Desert Museum.

SAGUARO CACTUS The saguaro (pronounced sa-*hwah*-ro) is the largest cactus of Arizona's Sonoran Desert and grows nowhere else on earth. (Saguaro throughout the state are protected by law.) Reaching heights of as much as 50 feet, saguaros are the redwoods of the desert, and often grow in dense stands that resemble forests. Saguaros are a slow-growing cactus; a 6-inch-tall cactus might be 10 years old, and it can take 75 years for a saguaro to sprout its first branch. The oldest-known saguaros are around 200 years old, and some have more than 40 arms.

To support their great size in such an arid environment, saguaros have a highly efficient root system that can be as large as 100 feet in diameter. These roots soak up water quickly and store it in the spongy interior of the cactus. After a rainstorm, a mature saguaro can weigh as much as 7 tons and survive for up to 2 years without another drop of water. Supporting this great mass is an internal framework of sturdy ribs, while the exterior of the cactus is pleated so that it can expand and contract as it takes up and loses water.

Each spring, waxy white flowers sprout from the tips of saguaro arms. These flowers are pollinated by white-winged doves and lesser long-nosed bats that come from hundreds of miles away in Mexico just for saguaro flowering season. Other animals that rely on saguaros include Gila woodpeckers and elf owls that nest in holes in saguaro trunks.

The Tohono O'odham people, natives of the Sonoran Desert, have long relied on saguaro cactus fruit as an important food source, even making a traditional ceremonial wine from the red, seedy pulp. So important has the saguaro harvest been in the past that the Tohono O'odham consider the saguaro harvest the start of the new year.

ORGAN PIPE CACTUS This close relative of the saguaro takes its name from its many trunks, which give it the appearance of an old pipe organ. The organ pipe cactus is even more frost-sensitive than the saguaro and lives only in an area 100 miles west of Tucson on both sides of the Mexican border. This population of stately cacti has been preserved in Organ Pipe Cactus National Monument.

BARREL CACTUS When mature, these cacti look much as their name implies and can be confused with young saguaros. However, the barrel cactus can be distinguished by its fishhook-shaped spines, which are usually yellow or red. This is the cactus that for years has been touted as a source of life-giving water to anyone lost in the desert. The liquid in this cactus's spongy interior is actually quite bitter and foul-tasting. However, the same spongy pulp, when cooked in sugar water, becomes very tasty.

CHOLLA CACTUS The cholla (pronounced *choi*-yah) is the most dreaded of all the Arizona cacti. Its spines are long, plentiful, sharp, and brittle. To brush up against a cholla is to experience certain pain. Here in Arizona, there are several species of cholla, most of which resemble small trees. They go by such graphic names as jumping cholla, which is said to throw pieces of its spiny branches at unwary passersby; teddy bear cholla, which is so covered with spines that it looks fuzzy; and chain fruit cholla, on which fruit hang in fragile, spiny chains. The chollas are favored nesting spots of cactus wrens and doves. Give chollas a wide berth.

PRICKLY PEAR CACTUS This is one of the largest and most widespread families of cacti and can be found throughout the United States, not just in the desert. They are also among the most commercially important cacti. The flat stems or pads (known as *nopales* in Spanish) of one species are used in Mexican cooking and can be found both fresh and canned in markets in Arizona. The fruit of the prickly pear is also edible and is relished by both humans and animals. Here in Arizona, it's possible to find prickly-pear jams and jellies, as well as prickly-pear ice cream and margaritas.

ROADRUNNER, COYOTE & OTHER DESERT DENIZENS

Just as cacti have adapted to the desert, so too, have the animals that live here. Many desert animals spend the sweltering daytime in burrows and venture out only in the cool of the night. Under cover of darkness, coyotes howl, rattlesnakes and great horned owls hunt kangaroo rats, and javelinas root about for anything edible. Gila monsters drag their ungainly bodies through the dust, while tarantulas tiptoe silently in search of unwary insects.

GREATER ROADRUNNER "Roadrunner, if he catches you, you're through." Now, I know that the words from the cartoon theme song were meant as a warning to the roadrunner that the wily coyote was after him, but, if you

Prickly pear cactus.

Roadrunner.

happen to be a snake or a lizard and a roadrunner catches you, you are definitely through. Real roadrunners, which prey on snakes and lizards, are the largest North American member of the cuckoo family and can run 15 mph. Although they are able to fly, they rarely do. Roadrunners are curious creatures; I once saw one running around in a Tucson brewpub parking lot checking out new customers as they got out of their cars.

COYOTE No other creature better symbolizes the desert Southwest than the coyote. Celebrated as the Trickster in Native American stories, coyotes are curious animals that have adapted well to life amid the ever-expanding cities and towns of Arizona. They are often seen boldly strolling across not just remote stretches of highway, but suburban streets as well. I once watched a coyote curiously following a foursome on a golf course in Scottsdale. Nothing captures the essence of the desert quite like the crazy cackling of coyotes at sunset.

GILA MONSTER Despite the fearful name, this is actually just a lizard, albeit a large, ugly, and poisonous lizard. In fact, Gila monsters are one of only two poisonous lizards in the world. With their mottled black-and-pink coloring, their warty-looking scales, and their fat, stubby tails, these slow-moving lizards are indeed a monstrous sight. However, because they are relatively uncommon, your chances of encountering one in the wild are slight. By the way, the Gila monster's warty appearance is caused by osteoderms, bony plates that were common among dinosaurs but are rare in modern reptiles.

CALIFORNIA CONDOR Although they are certainly ugly, California condors can have a wingspan of 9 feet, which gives them the largest wingspan of any North American bird. In 1987, there were only 22 California condors left on earth. At that point, all of them were captured so that they could be bred in captivity. Today, there are nearly 300 of the huge birds, and many of them live in Grand Canyon National Park and Vermilion Cliffs National Monument, where a release site is located. Condors are also often seen in the vicinity of Grand Canyon Village on the South Rim of the Grand Canyon.

COLLARED PECCARY Known in Arizona as javelinas (pronounced hav-uh-*lee*-nuhs), these strange-looking creatures look a bit like long-haired, neckless pigs. Javelinas are very well adapted to life in the desert; they can even eat prickly pear cactus—spines and all. While not normally aggressive, they are so nearsighted that in their hurry to get away from you, they might run straight at you, not realizing where you're standing. Several times over the years I have spooked javelinas on trails in the Tucson area. I've always been just as startled by them as they have been by me.

Javelinas are well adapted to desert life.

TARANTULA Okay, I know these giant arachnids are about as creepy as a crawly thing can be, but actually they're neither aggressive nor particularly poisonous. However, with their 2-inch bodies, 4-inch legs, and Hollywood horror-movie reputation, they often inspire terror in Arizona visitors. After late-summer rainstorms, male tarantulas can often be seen wandering across roads. They're wandering in search of a mate, and after mating, the male usually dies within a few months. Female tarantulas, however, can live for 25 years or more.

RESPONSIBLE TRAVEL

Let's face it: It's hard to be green in the desert. The desert simply is not a very sustainable place to build major cities. High temperatures and lack of water long precluded the development of arid landscapes. However, with the advent of air-conditioning, giant dams, and canals that can transport huge amounts of water hundreds of miles across the desert, cities such as Phoenix and Tucson have been able to grow into the sprawling metropolises of today. Unfortunately, in places where it often tops 120°F (49°C) in the summer, massive amounts of energy must be used to keep cool. Likewise, the scarcity of water in the desert Southwest would suggest that perhaps the Sonoran Desert is not the best place to locate large metropolitan areas.

For decades, resort hotels in Phoenix and Tucson have been criticized for their profligate water usage, and such criticism has yet to eliminate the vast acres of lawns that surround some of the state's resorts. Arizona is well known for its hundreds of golf courses, but those courses use up an inordinate amount of water. The state's guest ranches make great family destinations, but cattle ranching can be very damaging to the desert environment.

Slowly but surely, however, resorts, hotels, inns, and other businesses across the state are showing signs of turning green. In Phoenix, the Hyatt Regency Scottsdale Resort & Spa at Gainey Ranch has a solar hot-water system. The U.S. Green Building Council has given LEED certification to Tempe's hip Aloft hotel where, among other green features, drivers of hybrid cars get preferred parking spaces. In Tucson, there's a solar-powered pizza place and even a solar-powered bar, and in Flagstaff, there's a burger joint that uses beef from a local ranch. You'll find information on these and other eco-friendly restaurants and accommodations throughout this book.

While the desert, by definition, may not be very green, there are some things you can do to make your Arizona vacation a little bit more sustainable. Stay at a resort that uses native desert landscaping rather than one surrounded by thirsty lawns. Play golf on a water-conserving "desert-style" course; while these courses can be very challenging, they preserve the natural desert environment and save water. Some courses have even been certified by the Audubon Society as wildlife sanctuaries. See the **Golf & the Environment** website (www.golfandenvironment.com) for details. If you're heading to Grand Canyon National Park, take the train and then use the park's free, environmentally friendly compressed-natural-gas buses to get around.

To find out about a few other options for greening your Arizona vacation, visit the **Arizona Office of Tourism's** website (www.arizonaguide.com) and click on "Things to Do" and then "Nature." This will take you to a page with links to sites focused on ecotourism and volunteer tourism.

Volunteer travel has become increasingly popular among those who want to venture beyond the standard group-tour experience to learn languages, interact with locals, and make a positive difference while on vacation. Volunteer travel usually doesn't require special skills—just a willingness to work hard—and programs vary in length from a few days to a number of weeks. Some programs provide free housing and food, but many require volunteers to pay for travel expenses, which can add up quickly. For some volunteer opportunities in Arizona, see "Volunteer & Working Trips" below.

In addition to the resources for Arizona listed above, see frommers.com/planning for more tips on responsible travel.

TOURS

Academic Trips

If you'd like to turn a trip to the Grand Canyon into an educational experience, the **Grand Canyon Field Institute,** P.O. Box 399, Grand Canyon, AZ 86023 (✆ **866/471-4435** or 928/638-2485; www.grandcanyon.org/fieldinstitute), offers a variety of programs throughout the year, but primarily from early spring to late fall. Examples include guided hikes and backpacking trips (some for women only) with a natural-history or ecological slant, photography classes, mule-assisted treks, rafting trips, and hands-on archaeology trips.

Learning Expeditions, a program run by the **Arizona State Museum,** occasionally offers scholar-led archaeological tours, including a trip to Navajo and Hopi country. For information, contact the marketing department at the **Arizona State Museum,** P.O. Box 210026, Tucson, AZ 85721-0026 (✆ **520/626-8381;** www.statemuseum.arizona.edu).

Through its Ventures program, the **Museum of Northern Arizona,** 3101 N. Fort Valley Rd., Flagstaff, AZ 86001 (✆ **928/774-5213;** www.mnaventures.org), offers educational camping, backpacking, and hotel-based tours primarily in the Colorado Plateau region of northern Arizona. Trips range in length from 1 to 6 days.

Old Pueblo Archaeology Center, P.O. Box 40577, Tucson, AZ 85717-0577 (✆ **520/798-1201;** www.oldpueblo.org), is a nonprofit educational and

Arizona the Beautiful

If you're planning on visiting Grand Canyon National Park, some of the state's other national parks and monuments, and perhaps some of the national parks in southern Utah, New Mexico, or Colorado, you should consider getting an **America the Beautiful—National Park and Federal Recreational Lands Pass.** This pass costs $80 and is valid for 1 year. In Arizona, the pass will get you into Grand Canyon National Park, Saguaro National Park, Petrified Forest National Park, Organ Pipe Cactus National Monument, Montezuma Castle National Monument, Wupatki National Monument, Casa Grande Ruins National Monument, Tonto National Monument, Tumacácori National Historical Park, and a handful of other sites. A pass can be purchased at any national park or national monument that charges an admission fee. For more information, go to www.nps.gov/fees_passes.htm, or call the United States Geological Survey/ USGS (✆ **888/275-8747**), which issues the passes. For information on America the Beautiful passes for seniors and people with disabilities, see chapter 12.

scientific organization that throughout the years has led numerous archaeology-oriented trips around Arizona.

If you have an interest in the Native American cultures of Arizona, contact **Crossing Worlds Journeys & Retreats,** P.O. Box 3288, Sedona, AZ 86340 (✆ **800/350-2693** or 928/282-0846; www.crossingworlds.com), which offers tours throughout the Four Corners region. Trips visit the Hopi mesas as well as the Navajo Reservation. Journeys of self-discovery are a specialty of this company.

Finally, if you're interested in architecture or the ecology of urban design, you may want to help out on the continued construction of **Arcosanti,** the slow realization of Paolo Soleri's dream of a city that merges architecture and ecology. Located 70 miles north of Phoenix, Arcosanti offers 5-week learning-by-doing workshops ($1,350 per person) and 1-week seminars ($485 per person). Contact Arcosanti Workshop Coordinator, H.C. 74, Box 4136, Mayer, AZ 86333 (✆ **928/632-6233;** www.arcosanti.org).

Adventure Trips

Because Arizona is home to the Grand Canyon—the most widely known white-water-rafting spot in the world and also one of the world's premier backpacking destinations—the state is known for active, adventure-oriented vacations. For others, Arizona is synonymous with winter golf and tennis. Whichever category of active vacationer you fall into, you'll find information below to help you plan your trip.

Twice a year, **Canyon Calling, Adventures for Women,** 200 Carol Canyon Dr., Sedona, AZ 86336 (✆ **928/282-0916;** www.canyoncalling.com), offers a 7-day women-only tour that visits the Grand Canyon, Sedona, the Hopi mesas, Canyon de Chelly, Lake Powell, Rainbow Bridge, and Havasu Canyon. The cost is $1,895 per person. There are also twice-yearly 5-day tours of the Sedona area for $1,595.

BICYCLING

With its wide range of climates, Arizona offers good biking somewhere in the state every month of the year. In winter, there's good road biking around Phoenix and Tucson, while from spring to fall, the southeastern corner of the state offers good routes. In summer, the White Mountains (in the eastern part of the state) and Kaibab National Forest (btw. Flagstaff and Grand Canyon National Park) offer good mountain biking. There's also excellent mountain biking at several Phoenix parks, and Tucson is one of the most bicycle-friendly cities in the country.

Backroads, 801 Cedar St., Berkeley, CA 94710-1800 (✆ **800/462-2848** or 510/527-1555; www.backroads.com), offers 6-day multisport and family trips that take in southern Utah and the Grand Canyon. These trips range in price from $1,898 to $2,698. **Sojourn Bicycling & Active Vacations,** 939 Ferry Rd., Charlotte, VT 05445 (✆ **800/730-4771** or 802/425-4771; www.gosojourn.com), offers weeklong bike tours of the Sonoran Desert near Tucson. Tours are $2,395. **Western Spirit Cycling Adventures,** 478 Mill Creek Dr., Moab, UT 84532 (✆ **800/845-2453** or 435/259-8732; www.westernspirit.com), has a number of interesting mountain-bike tours, including trips to both the North and South rims of the Grand Canyon and through the desert south of Tucson. This company also offsets its carbon emissions and consequently is a carbon-neutral company. Each trip lasts 5 days and costs $1,185.

Arizona Outback Adventures, 16447 N. 91st St., Ste. 101, Scottsdale, AZ 85260 (✆ **866/455-1601** or 480/945-2881; www.aoa-adventures.com), does 3-day trips in the Sonoran Desert for $599.

WomanTours, 2340 Elmwood Ave., Rochester, NY 14618 (✆ **800/247-1444** or 585/256-9807; www.womantours.com), offers a couple of different Arizona bike tours that are exclusively for women. You'll pay $1,790 for a 7-day tour.

For information on mountain-bike tours and recommended rides in Phoenix and Tucson, see "Outdoor Pursuits" in chapters 4 and 9. You'll also find recommended rides in the Sedona and Prescott sections of chapter 5. If you plan to do much mountain biking around the state, pick up a copy of *Fat Tire Tales and Trails,* by Cosmic Ray. This little book of rides is both fun to read and fun to use; it's available in bike shops around the state.

BIRD-WATCHING

Arizona is a birder's bonanza. In the southeastern corner of the state, many species found primarily south of the border reach the northern limits of their ranges. Combine this with several mountains that rise like islands from the desert and provide appropriate habitat for hundreds of species, and you have some of the best bird-watching in the country.

Birding hot spots include Ramsey Canyon Preserve (known for its many species of hummingbirds); Cave Creek Canyon (nesting site for elegant trogons); Patagonia–Sonoita Creek Sanctuary (home to 22 species of flycatchers, kingbirds, and phoebes, as well as Montezuma quails); Madera Canyon (another "mountain island" hot spot that attracts many of the same species seen at Ramsey Canyon and Sonoita Creek); Buenos Aires National Wildlife Refuge (home to masked bobwhite quails and gray hawks); and the sewage ponds outside the town of Willcox (known for avocets and sandhill cranes). For further information on these birding spots, see chapter 10. To find out which birds have been spotted lately or to join a bird-watching field trip, call the **Tucson Audubon Society's Rare Bird Alert line** (✆ **520/629-0510,** ext. 3; www.tucsonaudubon.org).

Serious birders eager to add lots of rare birds to their life lists may want to visit southeastern Arizona on a guided tour. These are available through **High Lonesome Birdtours,** 570 S. Little Bear Trail, Sierra Vista, AZ 85635

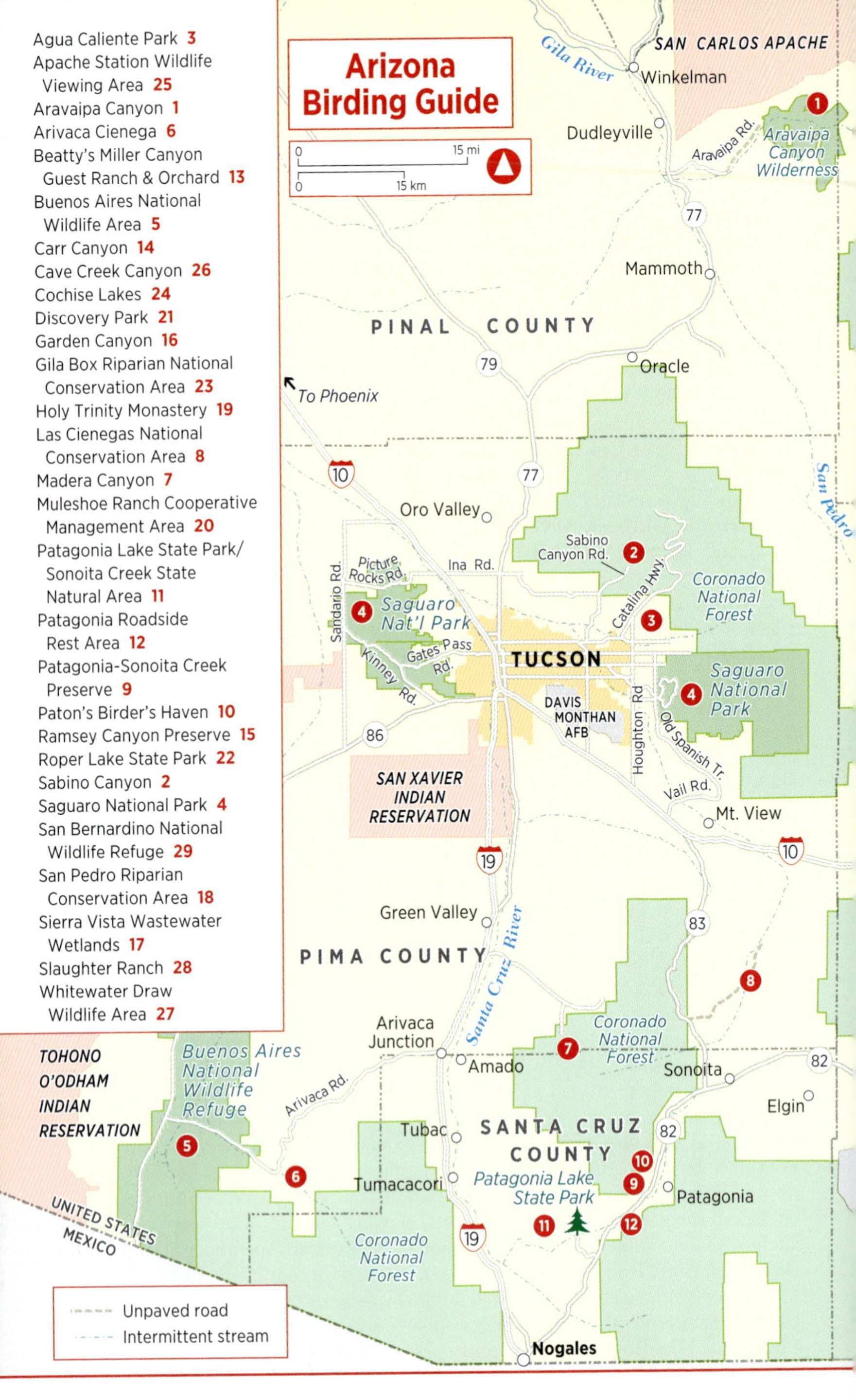

Agua Caliente Park 3
Apache Station Wildlife Viewing Area 25
Aravaipa Canyon 1
Arivaca Cienega 6
Beatty's Miller Canyon Guest Ranch & Orchard 13
Buenos Aires National Wildlife Area 5
Carr Canyon 14
Cave Creek Canyon 26
Cochise Lakes 24
Discovery Park 21
Garden Canyon 16
Gila Box Riparian National Conservation Area 23
Holy Trinity Monastery 19
Las Cienegas National Conservation Area 8
Madera Canyon 7
Muleshoe Ranch Cooperative Management Area 20
Patagonia Lake State Park/ Sonoita Creek State Natural Area 11
Patagonia Roadside Rest Area 12
Patagonia-Sonoita Creek Preserve 9
Paton's Birder's Haven 10
Ramsey Canyon Preserve 15
Roper Lake State Park 22
Sabino Canyon 2
Saguaro National Park 4
San Bernardino National Wildlife Refuge 29
San Pedro Riparian Conservation Area 18
Sierra Vista Wastewater Wetlands 17
Slaughter Ranch 28
Whitewater Draw Wildlife Area 27
Arizona Birding Guide
0 15 mi
0 15 km
Gila River
SAN CARLOS APACHE
Winkelman
Dudleyville
Aravaipa Rd.
Aravaipa Canyon Wilderness
77
Mammoth
PINAL COUNTY
79
Oracle
To Phoenix
10
77
San Pedro
Oro Valley
Sabino Canyon Rd.
Picture Rocks Rd.
Ina Rd.
Catalina Hwy.
Coronado National Forest
Sandario Rd.
Saguaro Nat'l Park
Gates Pass Rd.
Kinney Rd.
TUCSON
Saguaro National Park
DAVIS MONTHAN AFB
Houghton Rd
Old Spanish Tr.
86
SAN XAVIER INDIAN RESERVATION
Vail Rd.
Mt. View
10
19
Green Valley
Santa Cruz River
PIMA COUNTY
83
Arivaca Junction
Amado
Coronado National Forest
Sonoita
82
Elgin
TOHONO O'ODHAM INDIAN RESERVATION
Buenos Aires National Wildlife Refuge
Arivaca Rd.
Tubac
SANTA CRUZ COUNTY
82
Tumacacori
Patagonia Lake State Park
Patagonia
UNITED STATES
MEXICO
19
Coronado National Forest
Unpaved road
Intermittent stream
Nogales

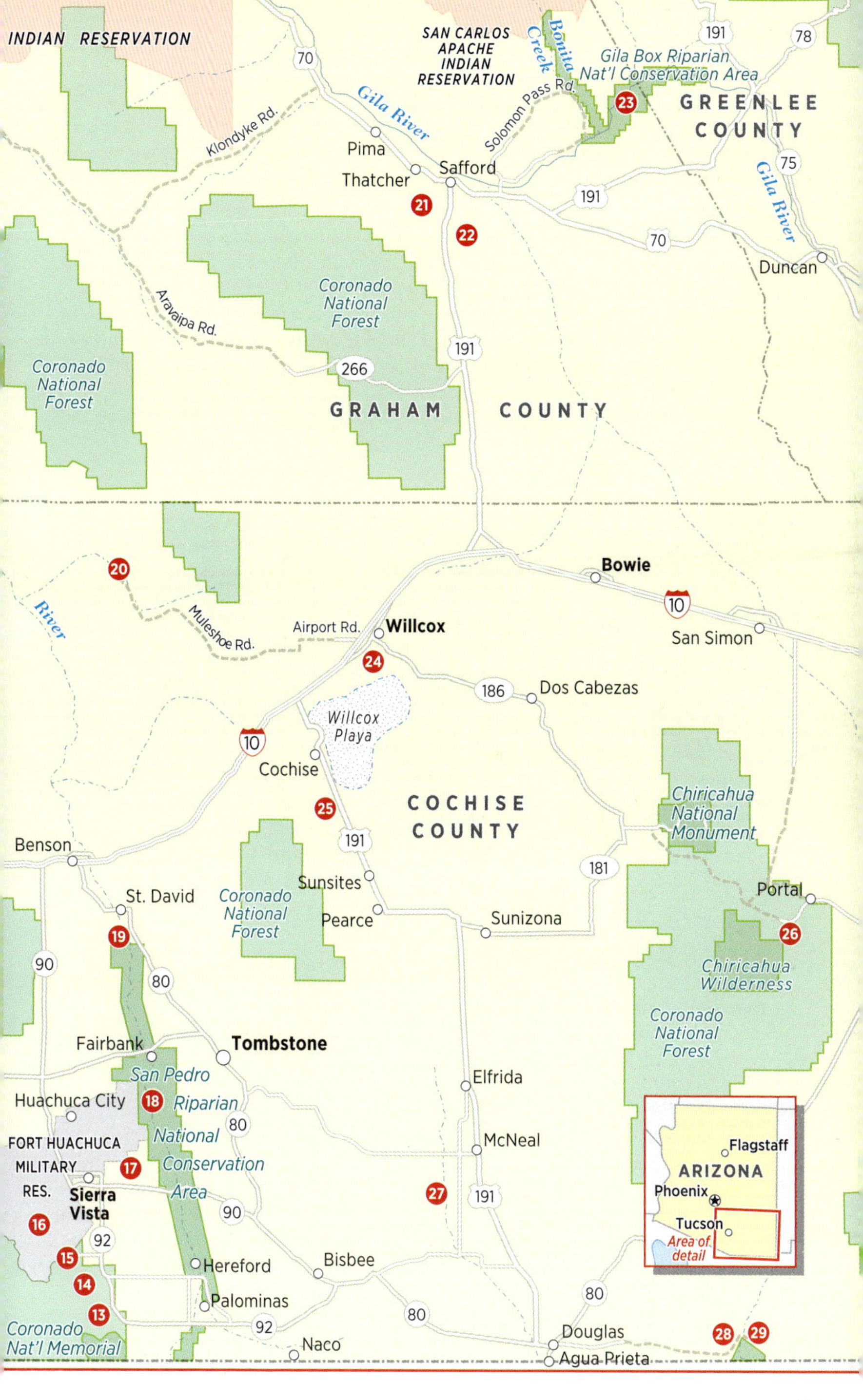
INDIAN RESERVATION
SAN CARLOS APACHE INDIAN RESERVATION
Gila River
Bonita Creek
Gila Box Riparian Nat'l Conservation Area
GREENLEE COUNTY
Klondyke Rd.
Solomon Pass Rd.
Pima
Thatcher
Safford
Gila River
Duncan
Aravaipa Rd.
Coronado National Forest
Coronado National Forest
GRAHAM COUNTY
Bowie
River
Muleshoe Rd.
Airport Rd.
Willcox
San Simon
Dos Cabezas
Willcox Playa
Cochise
COCHISE COUNTY
Chiricahua National Monument
Benson
St. David
Coronado National Forest
Sunsites
Pearce
Sunizona
Portal
Chiricahua Wilderness
Coronado National Forest
Fairbank
Tombstone
San Pedro Riparian National Conservation Area
Huachuca City
FORT HUACHUCA MILITARY RES.
Sierra Vista
Elfrida
McNeal
Flagstaff
ARIZONA
Phoenix
Tucson
Area of detail
Hereford
Palominas
Bisbee
Naco
Douglas
Agua Prieta
Coronado Nat'l Memorial

(✆ **443/838-6589;** www.hilonesometours.com), which charges $1,150 per person for a 5-day trip, $1,475 for a 6-day trip, and $2,450 for an 8-day trip.

CANOEING/KAYAKING

Okay, so maybe these sports don't jump to mind when you think of the desert, but there are indeed rivers and lakes here (and they happen to be some of the best places to see wildlife). By far the most memorable place for a flat-water kayak tour is Lake Powell. Multiday kayak tours are offered by **Hidden Canyon Kayak,** P.O. Box 2526, Page, AZ 86040-2526 (✆ **800/343-3121** or 928/645-8866; www.diamondriver.com/kayak), which charges $760 to $1,000 for 4- to 6-day trips. Guided kayak trips are also offered by **Kayak Powell** (✆ **888/854-7862;** www.kayaklakepowell.com), which charges $495 for a 2-day tour, $695 for a 3-day tour, $795 for a 4-day tour, and $895 for a 5-day tour.

There are also a couple of companies that rent canoes and offer trips on the Colorado River south of Lake Mead. See chapter 11 for details.

FISHING

The fishing scene in Arizona is as diverse as the landscape. Large and small lakes around the state offer excellent fishing for warm-water game fish such as largemouth, smallmouth, and striped bass. Good trout fishing can be found in lakes atop the Mogollon Rim and in the White Mountains, as well as in the easily accessible section of the free-running Colorado River between Glen Canyon Dam and Lees Ferry just upstream from the Grand Canyon. In fact, this latter area is among the country's most fabled stretches of trout water.

Fishing licenses for nonresidents are available for 1 day, 5 days, 4 months, and 1 year. Various special stamps and licenses may also apply. Nonresident fees range from $17 for a 1-day license (valid for trout) to $70 for a 1-year license ($58 additional for a trout stamp). A separate license ($49) is available for fishing just the Colorado River. Keep in mind that if you're heading for an Indian reservation, you'll have to get a special permit for that reservation. For information on Arizona state fishing licenses, contact the **Arizona Game and Fish Dept.,** 5000 W. Carefree Hwy., Phoenix, AZ 85086-5000 (✆ **602/942-3000;** www.azgfd.com).

GOLF

For many of Arizona's winter visitors, golf is the main attraction. The state's hundreds of golf courses range from easy public courses to PGA championship links that have challenged the pros.

In Phoenix and Tucson, greens fees, like room rates, are seasonal. In the popular winter months, greens fees at resort courses generally range from about $150 to $250 for 18 holes, although this usually includes a golf cart. In summer, fees often drop to less than half this amount. Almost all resorts offer special golf packages as well.

For information on some of the state's top courses, see "Hot Links," below. For more information on golfing in Arizona, contact the **Arizona Golf Association,** 7226 N. 16th St., Ste. 200, Phoenix, AZ 85020 (✆ **800/458-8484** in Arizona, or 602/944-3035; www.azgolf.org), which publishes a directory listing all the courses in the state. You can also access the directory online. In addition, you can pick up the *Arizona Golf Guide* (www.azgolfguides.com) at visitor centers, golf courses, and many hotels and resorts.

HIKING/BACKPACKING

Arizona offers some of the most fascinating and challenging hiking in the country. All across the state's lowland deserts, parks and other public lands are laced with trails that lead past saguaro cacti, to the tops of desert peaks, and deep into rugged canyons. The state also has vast forests, many of which are protected in wilderness areas, which have many more miles of hiking trails. In northern Arizona, there are good day hikes in Grand Canyon National Park, in the San Francisco Peaks north of Flagstaff, near Lake Powell, and in Navajo National Monument. In the Phoenix area, popular day hikes include the trails up Camelback Mountain and Piestewa Peak, and the many trails in South Mountain Park. In the Tucson area, there are good hikes in Saguaro National Park, Coronado National Forest, Sabino Canyon, and Catalina State Park. In the southern part of the state, there are good day hikes in Chiricahua National Monument, Coronado National Forest, Cochise Stronghold, Organ Pipe Cactus National Monument, and the Nature Conservancy's Ramsey Canyon Preserve and its Patagonia–Sonoita Creek Sanctuary.

The state's two most unforgettable overnight backpack trips are the hike down to Phantom Ranch at the bottom of the Grand Canyon and the hike into Havasu Canyon, a side canyon of the Grand Canyon. A third popular backpacking trip is through Paria Canyon, a narrow slot canyon that originates in Utah and terminates in Arizona at Lees Ferry. There are also many overnight opportunities in the San Francisco Peaks north of Flagstaff and in the White Mountains of eastern Arizona.

Guided backpacking trips of different durations and difficulty levels are offered by the **Grand Canyon Field Institute,** P.O. Box 399, Grand Canyon, AZ 86023 (© **866/471-4435** or 928/638-2485; www.grandcanyon.org/fieldinstitute), and by **Discovery Treks,** 28248 N. Tatum Blvd., Ste. B1, no. 414, Cave Creek, AZ 85331 (© **888/256-8731;** www.discoverytreks.com).

Backroads, 801 Cedar St., Berkeley, CA 94710-1800 (© **800/462-2848** or 510/527-1555; www.backroads.com), better known for its bike trips, also offers a 6-day hiking/biking trip to Grand Canyon, Bryce Canyon, and Zion national parks for between $1,898 and $2,698.

Vermont-based **Country Walkers,** P.O. Box 180, Waterbury, VT 05676 (© **800/464-9255** or 802/244-1387; www.countrywalkers.com), has a 6-day hiking-oriented trip that takes in the Grand Canyon and Sedona and costs $2,998.

HORSEBACK RIDING/WESTERN ADVENTURES

Saddle up that palomino, pardner, and let's ride. Arizona is a city slicker's dream come true. All over Arizona there are stables where you can climb into the saddle of a sure-footed trail horse and ride off into the sunset. Among the more scenic spots for riding are Grand Canyon National Park, Monument Valley Navajo Tribal Park, Canyon de Chelly National Monument, the red-rock country around Sedona, Phoenix's South Mountain Park, the foot of the Superstition Mountains east of Phoenix, and the foot of the Santa Catalina Mountains outside Tucson. See the individual chapters that follow for listings of riding stables.

Among the most popular guided adventures in Arizona are the mule rides down into the Grand Canyon. These trips vary in length from 1 to 2 days; for reservations and more information, contact **Grand Canyon National Park Lodges/Xanterra Parks & Resorts** (© **888/297-2757,** 303/297-2757, or, for last-minute reservations, 928/638-2631; www.grandcanyonlodges.com). You'll

HOT links

You don't have to be a hotshot golfer to get all heated up over the prospect of a few rounds of golf in Arizona. Combine near-perfect golf weather most of the year with great views and some unique challenges, and you've got all the makings of a great game. Phoenix and Tucson are known as winter golf destinations, but the state also offers golf throughout the year at higher-altitude courses in such places as Prescott, Flagstaff, and the White Mountains.

State water-conservation legislation limits the acreage that new Arizona golf courses can irrigate, which has given the state some of the most distinctive and difficult courses in the country. These desert or "target" courses are characterized by minimal fairways surrounded by natural desert landscapes. You might find yourself teeing off over the tops of cacti or searching for your ball amid boulders and mesquite. If your ball comes to rest in the desert, you can play the ball where it lies or, with a one-stroke penalty, drop it within two club lengths of the nearest point of grass (but no nearer the hole).

With more than 200 golf courses, the Phoenix metropolitan area has the greatest concentration of fairways in the state. Whether you're looking to play one of the area's challenging top-rated resort courses or an economical-but-fun municipal course, you'll find plenty of choices.

For spectacular scenery at a resort course, it's just plain impossible to beat the **Boulders** (✆ **480/488-9028**), north of Scottsdale in the town of Carefree. Elevated tee boxes beside giant balanced boulders are enough to distract anyone. East of here, near the town of Fountain Hills, you can play amid spectacular desert scenery at the **We-Ko-Pa Golf Club** (✆ **866/660-7700**), which is on the Fort McDowell Yavapai Nation. Also on the east side of the valley in Apache Junction, the **Gold Canyon Golf Resort** (✆ **480/982-9449**) has what have been rated as three of the best holes in the state: the 2nd, 3rd, and 4th holes on the Dinosaur Mountain course. Jumping over to Litchfield Park, on the far west side of the valley, you'll find the **Wigwam Golf Resort & Spa** (✆ **800/909-4224** or 623/935-9414) and its three traditional 18-hole courses; the Gold Course here is legendary. The **Phoenician Golf Club** (✆ **800/888-8234** or 480/423-2449) is another noteworthy resort course in the area. It has a mix of traditional and desert-style holes. The semiprivate **Troon North Golf Club** (✆ **480/585-7700**), a course that seems only barely carved out of raw desert, garners the most local accolades

need to make mule-ride reservations many months in advance. However, if at the last minute (1 or 2 days before you want to ride) you decide you want to go on a mule trip into the Grand Canyon, contact Grand Canyon National Park Lodges at its last-minute reservations phone number (see above), or stop by the **Bright Angel Transportation Desk,** in Grand Canyon Village. Spaces sometimes open up when there are sudden cancellations.

It's also possible to do overnight horseback rides in various locations around the state. For information on overnight rides into the Superstition Mountains east of Phoenix, contact **Don Donnelly's D-Spur Ranch & Riding Stables** (✆ **602/810-7029;** www.dondonnelly.com).

Want to kick it up a notch? At the **Arizona Cowboy College,** Lorill Equestrian Center, 30208 N. 152nd St., Scottsdale, AZ 85262 (✆ **888/330-8070** or (and charges some of the highest greens fees in the state). If you want to swing where the pros do, beg, borrow, or steal a tee time on the Stadium Course at the **Tournament Players Club (TPC) of Scottsdale** (✆ **888/400-4001** or 480/585-4334). The area's favorite municipal course is Phoenix's **Papago Golf Course** (✆ **602/275-8428**), which has a killer 17th hole.

Tucson may not have as many golf courses as the Valley of the Sun, but the courses here are every bit as challenging and memorable. Among the city's resort courses, the Mountain Course at the **Ventana Canyon Golf and Racquet Club** (✆ **520/577-4015**) is legendary, especially the spectacular 107-yard, par-3 hole 3. The 8th hole on the Sunrise Course at **El Conquistador Country Club** (✆ **520/544-1801**) is another of the area's more memorable par-3 holes. If you want to play where the pros have played, reserve a tee time at the **Omni Tucson National Resort** (✆ **520/575-7540**), which for many years was home to the Tucson Open. **Randolph Golf Course** (✆ **520/791-4161**), Tucson's best municipal course, has been the site of the city's annual LPGA tournament. The **Silverbell Golf Course** (✆ **520/791-5235**) boasts a bear of a par-5 17th hole, and at **Fred Enke Golf Course** (✆ **520/791-2539**), you'll find the city's only desert-style municipal golf course.

Courses worth trying in other parts of the state include **Los Caballeros Golf Club** (✆ **928/684-2704**), which is part of a luxury guest ranch outside Wickenburg. *Golf Digest* has rated this course one of Arizona's top ten. For concentration-taxing scenery, few courses compare with the **Sedona Golf Resort** (✆ **877/733-6630**), which has good views of the red rocks; try to get a sunrise or twilight tee time. Way up in the Four Corners region, in the town of Page, you'll find the 27-hole **Lake Powell National Golf Course** (✆ **928/645-2023**), which is one of the most spectacular in the state. The fairways here wrap around the base of the red-sandstone bluff atop which Page is built. South of Tucson, the **Tubac Golf Resort** (✆ **520/398-2021**) has cows grazing along its fairways for a classic Wild West feel. For dramatic views near the Colorado River in western Arizona, check out the **Emerald Canyon Golf Course** (✆ **928/667-3366**), a municipal course in Parker that plays up and down small canyons and offers the sort of scenery usually associated only with the most expensive desert resort courses.

480/471-3151; www.cowboycollege.com), you can literally learn the ropes and the brands and how to say "Git along little doggie!" like you really mean it. This is no city slicker's staged roundup; this is the real thing. You actually learn how to be a real cowboy. Six-day programs cost $2,250.

HOT-AIR BALLOONING

For much of the year, the desert has the perfect environment for hot-air ballooning—cool, still air and wide-open spaces. Consequently, dozens of ballooning companies operate across the state. Most are in Phoenix and Tucson, but several others operate near Sedona, which is by far the most picturesque spot in the state for a balloon ride. See the individual chapters for specific information.

HOUSEBOATING

With the Colorado River turned into a string of long lakes, houseboat vacations are a natural in Arizona. Although this doesn't have to be an active vacation, fishing, hiking, and swimming are usually an essential part of spending time on a houseboat. Rentals are available on Lake Powell, Lake Mead, and Lake Mohave; however, the canyon scenery of Lake Powell makes it the hands-down best spot for a houseboat vacation. Make reservations well in advance for a summer trip. No prior experience (or license) is necessary, and plenty of hands-on instruction is provided before you leave the marina. See chapters 7 and 11 for more information on houseboat rentals.

SKIING

Although Arizona is better known as a desert state, it also has snow-capped mountains and even a few ski areas. The two biggest and best ski areas are **Arizona Snowbowl** (✆ **928/779-1951;** www.arizonasnowbowl.com), outside Flagstaff, and **Sunrise Park Resort** (✆ **800/772-7669** or 928/735-7669; www.sunriseskipark.com), on the White Mountain Apache Reservation outside the town of McNary in the White Mountains. Snowbowl is more popular because of the ease of the drive from Phoenix and the proximity to good lodging and dining options in Flagstaff. However, despite the convenience and the fact that Snowbowl has more vertical feet of skiing, Sunrise is my favorite Arizona ski area because it offers almost twice as many runs. Both ski areas offer rentals and lessons.

When it's a good snow year, Tucsonans head up to **Mount Lemmon Ski Valley** (✆ **520/576-1321;** www.skithelemmon.com), the southernmost ski area in the U.S. Snows here aren't as reliable as they are farther north, so be sure to call first to make sure the ski area is operating.

During snow-blessed winters, cross-country skiers can find plenty of snow-covered forest roads outside Flagstaff, at Sunrise Park outside the town of McNary, at the South Rim of the Grand Canyon, in the White Mountains around Greer and Alpine, and on Mount Lemmon outside Tucson.

TENNIS

After golf, tennis is probably the most popular winter sport in the desert, and resorts all over Arizona have tennis courts. Keep in mind that many resorts require you to wear traditional tennis attire and don't include court time in the room rates. No courts anywhere in the state can match the views you'll have from those at Enchantment Resort, outside Sedona. Other noteworthy tennis-oriented resorts include, in the Phoenix/Scottsdale area, the Phoenician, the Fairmont Scottsdale, the Arizona Grand Resort, and the Pointe Hilton Tapatio Cliffs Resort; and, in Tucson, the Lodge at Ventana Canyon, the Hilton Tucson El Conquistador Golf & Tennis Resort, the Westin La Paloma Resort & Spa, the Westward Look Resort, and the Omni Tucson National Resort.

WHITE-WATER RAFTING

The desert doesn't support a lot of roaring rivers, but with the white water in the Grand Canyon, you don't need too many other choices. Rafting the Grand Canyon is the dream of nearly every white-water enthusiast—if it's one of yours as well, plan well ahead. Companies and trips are limited, and they tend to fill up early. For a discussion and list of companies that run trips down the canyon, see chapter 6.

For 1-day rafting trips on the Colorado below the main section of the Grand Canyon, contact **Hualapai River Runners** (✆ **888/868-9378;** www.grandcanyonwest.com). For a half-day float on the Colorado above the Grand Canyon, contact **Colorado River Discovery** (✆ **888/522-6644** or 928/645-9175; www.raftthecanyon.com), which runs trips between Glen Canyon Dam and Lees Ferry.

Rafting trips are also available on the upper Salt River east of Phoenix. **Wilderness Aware Rafting** (✆ **800/462-7238;** www.inaraft.com), **Canyon Rio Rafting** (✆ **800/272-3353;** www.canyonrio.com), and **Mild to Wild Rafting** (✆ **800/567-6745;** www.mild2wildrafting.com) all run trips of varying lengths down this river (conditions permitting).

Food & Wine Trips

If you'd like to learn how to cook Southwestern cuisine while you're in Arizona, you have a couple of options around the state. In Tucson, celebrated local chef Janos Wilder offers 2-hour classes ($50 per person) at his eponymously named restaurant at the Westin La Paloma Resort. See p. 424 for information on **Janos** restaurant. At Sedona's luxurious **Enchantment Resort** (p. 241), there are cooking demonstrations offered several days a week.

The desert may not seem like wine country, but Arizona has such a diversity of climates that it actually has several separate wine regions. Tours to the central Arizona wine country near Sedona, the Elgin/Sonoita region, and to southeastern Arizona are offered by **AZ Wine Tours** (✆ **480/528-2834;** www.azwinetours.com). See chapters 5 and 9 for information on touring Arizona wine country.

Guided & Package Tours

If you want to see the best of Arizona, but would rather not do all the logistical planning or driving, then you might want to consider a guided tour. **Detours** (✆ **866/438-6877;** www.detoursaz.com) specializes in small-group tours throughout Arizona and other parts of the Southwest. One of its tours, **Hillerman Country,** is a 5-day journey through northern Arizona with a focus on spots that have been mentioned in Tony Hillerman novels about Navajo Tribal Police officers Jim Chee and Joe Leaphorn. **Open Road Tours** (✆ **800/766-7117** or 602/997-6474; www.openroadtours.com) offers a variety of 1- to 4-day tours around the state. Most of these focus on the Grand Canyon. The British tour company **Trek America** (✆ **800/873-5872** or 844/576-1400 in the U.K.; www.trekamerica.com) specializes in off-the-beaten-path small-group adventure travel and offers tours of the American Southwest; most include stops at the Grand Canyon and other scenic locations in Arizona. For a tour of some of Arizona's and Utah's most spectacular scenery, check out the Southwest Splendor tour offered each year by **High Point Tours** (✆ **928/445-2639;** www.ilivehistory.com). Company co-owner and guide Todd Weber, an experienced living-history presenter, highlights not only the area's fascinating geology but also its more colorful historical characters.

One great place to shop for Arizona vacation packages is at **www.arizonavacationvalues.com**, a website sponsored by the Arizona Office of Tourism (✆ **866/275-5816**). This website is a clearinghouse for a wide variety of packages.

If you're coming to Arizona specifically to play golf, you might want to let a golf packager arrange your trip for you. For vacations in Scottsdale, contact **Arizona Golf Packages** (✆ **866/444-0992** or 602/910-6821; www.arizonagolfpackages.com). For vacations in Tucson, contact **Tucson Golf Tours** (✆ **866/444-0992;** www.tucsongolftours.com).

Volunteer & Working Trips

If you enjoy the wilderness and want to get more involved in its preservation, consider a Sierra Club service trip. These trips are for building, restoring, and maintaining hiking trails in wilderness areas. Contact the **Sierra Club Outings Dept.,** 85 Second St., 2nd Floor, San Francisco, CA 94105 (✆ **415/977-5522;** www.sierraclub.org). The Sierra Club also offers hiking, camping, and other adventure trips to various destinations in Arizona.

You can also join a work crew organized by the **Arizona Trail Association,** P.O. Box 36736, Phoenix, AZ 85067-6736 (✆ **602/252-4794;** www.aztrail.org). These crews spend 1 to 2 days building and maintaining various portions of the Arizona Trail, which stretches from the Utah state line to the Mexico border.

Another sort of service trip is offered by the National Park Service. It accepts volunteers to pick up garbage left by thoughtless visitors to Glen Canyon National Recreation Area. In exchange for picking up trash, you'll get to spend 5 or 7 days on a houseboat called the Trash Tracker, cruising through the gorgeous canyonlands of Lake Powell. Volunteers must be at least 18 years old and in good physical condition, and must provide their own food, sleeping bag, and transportation to the marina. For information, contact **Glen Canyon National Recreation Area,** Attn: Trash Tracker, P.O. Box 1507, Page, AZ 86040 (✆ **928/608-6350;** www.nps.gov/glca/supportyourpark/trashtracker.htm).

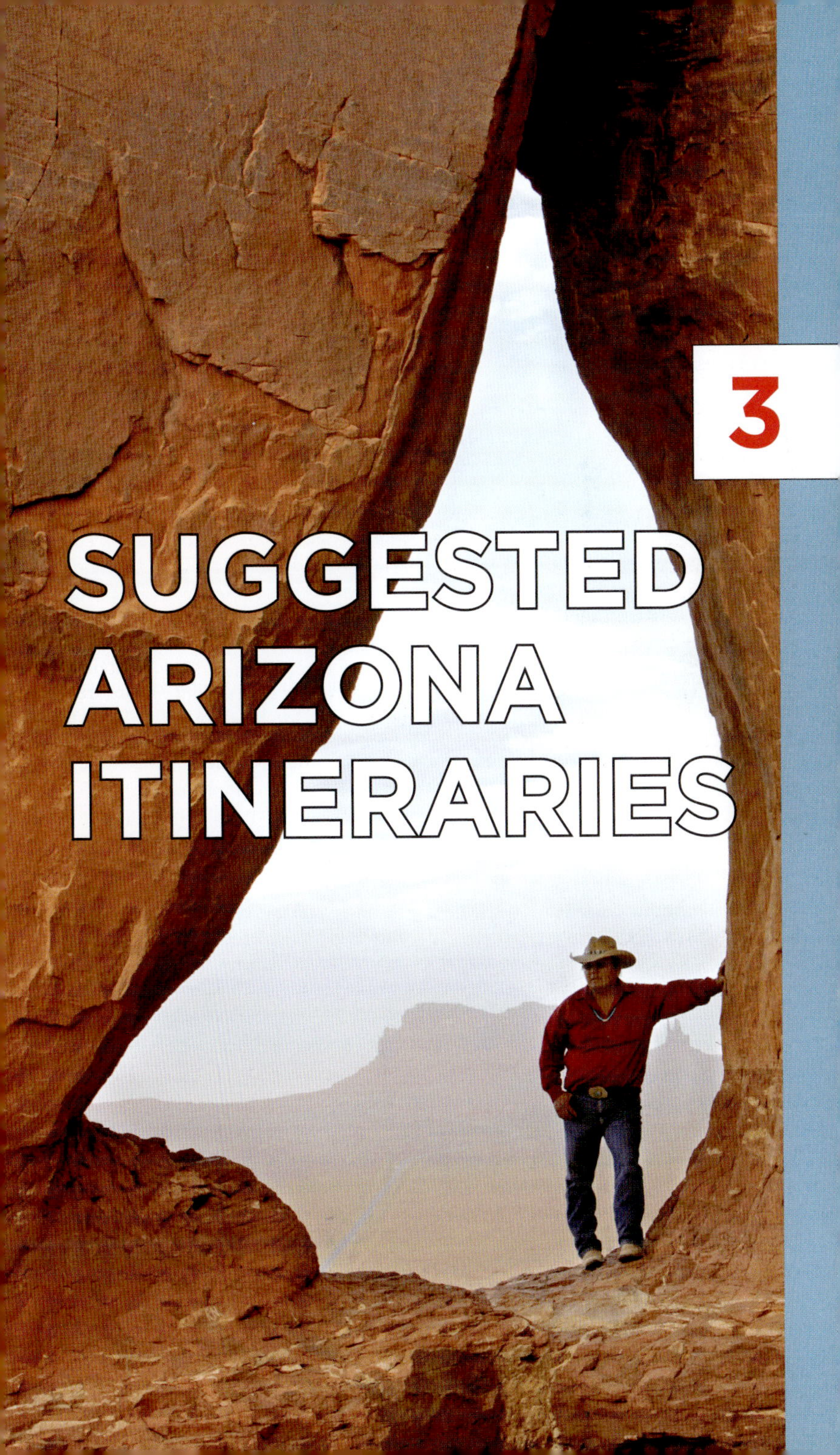

3 SUGGESTED ARIZONA ITINERARIES

Y ou could spend a lifetime exploring Arizona—an important fact to keep in mind when planning a trip to this vast and incredibly diverse region of the American Southwest. Maps just don't give you a clear picture of how big this state is. It's roughly 400 miles from north to south (about as far as from New York City to Raleigh, North Carolina, or Brussels, Belgium, to Bern, Switzerland) and 300 miles from east to west (think New York to Richmond, Virginia, or Paris, France, to Bonn, Germany). It could easily take you 9 hours to drive from one end of the state to the other, and if you want to see it all, you'll be doing just that—driving for hours and hours. Even if you just want to hit the highlights, reconcile yourself to doing a lot of driving. Luckily, the speed limit on interstate highways here can be as high as 75 mph.

Where should you go? What should you see? What's the best route? How do you maximize your time? I know all these questions well. I've asked them myself when I've been planning research trips around the state, and I've been asked them countless times by friends, family, and total strangers planning trips to Arizona. This chapter helps you answer those questions. I'm not going to get down to the nitty-gritty details such as where to get gas (just keep that tank topped off; it can often be 60 miles to the next gas station), but I do mention the occasional not-to-be-missed or out-of-the-way restaurant.

If you read through all these itineraries, you'll notice a bit of overlap. There are some attractions that just should not be missed on any visit to the state. Also, try to think of these as general ideas. Because Phoenix and Tucson are less than 2 hours apart, you could easily swap days I mention for Phoenix for time spent in Tucson (or vice versa) and not add too much extra driving to your vacation. Personally, I prefer Tucson's more low-key character to the congested streets of Phoenix and Scottsdale. However, because these two cities have the state's two main airports, you'll likely end up starting and/or ending your trip at one or the other.

REGIONS IN BRIEF

PHOENIX, SCOTTSDALE & THE VALLEY OF THE SUN This region encompasses the sprawling metropolitan Phoenix area, which covers more than 400 square miles and includes more than 20 cities and communities surrounded by several distinct mountain ranges. It's the economic and population center of the state, and is Arizona's main winter- and spring-vacation destination. It is here that you'll find the greatest concentrations of resorts and golf courses. It is also where you'll find the worst traffic congestion and highest resort rates.

PREVIOUS PAGE: **Monument Valley's rock formations are the subject of numerous photos and films.**

Minerals create the colors of the Painted Desert.

CENTRAL ARIZONA This region lies between Phoenix and the high country of northern Arizona and includes the red-rock country around the town of Sedona, which is one of the state's most popular tourist destinations. The rugged scenery around Sedona played many a role in old Western movies and has long attracted artists. Today, Sedona abounds in art galleries, recreational opportunities, and excellent lodging choices. Also within this region are historic Prescott (the former territorial capital of Arizona); the old mining town of Jerome, now an artists' community; and several Indian ruins and petroglyph sites that are open to the public.

THE GRAND CANYON & NORTHERN ARIZONA Home to the Grand Canyon, one of the natural wonders of the world, northern Arizona is a vast and sparsely populated region comprised primarily of public lands and Indian reservations. Because Grand Canyon National Park attracts millions of visitors each year, the city of Flagstaff and the towns of Williams and Tusayan abound in accommodations and restaurants catering to canyon-bound travelers. North of the Grand Canyon and bordering on southern Utah lies a region known as the Arizona Strip. This is the most remote and untraveled region of the state. The Grand Canyon acts as a natural boundary between the Arizona Strip and the rest of the state, and the lack of paved roads and towns keeps away all but the most dedicated explorers. Vermilion Cliffs National Monument is at the eastern end of the Arizona Strip, and the inaccessible Grand Canyon–Parashant National Monument lies at the western end.

THE FOUR CORNERS The point where Arizona, Utah, Colorado, and New Mexico come together is the only place in the U.S. where four states share a common boundary. The region is also almost entirely composed of Hopi and Navajo reservation land. This region of spectacular canyons and towering mesas and buttes includes Canyon de Chelly, the Painted Desert, the Petrified Forest, and Monument Valley.

EASTERN ARIZONA'S HIGH COUNTRY This area, which comprises the Mogollon Rim region and the White Mountains, is a summertime escape for residents of the lowland desert areas, and abounds with mountain cabins and summer homes. Most of this high country is covered with ponderosa pine

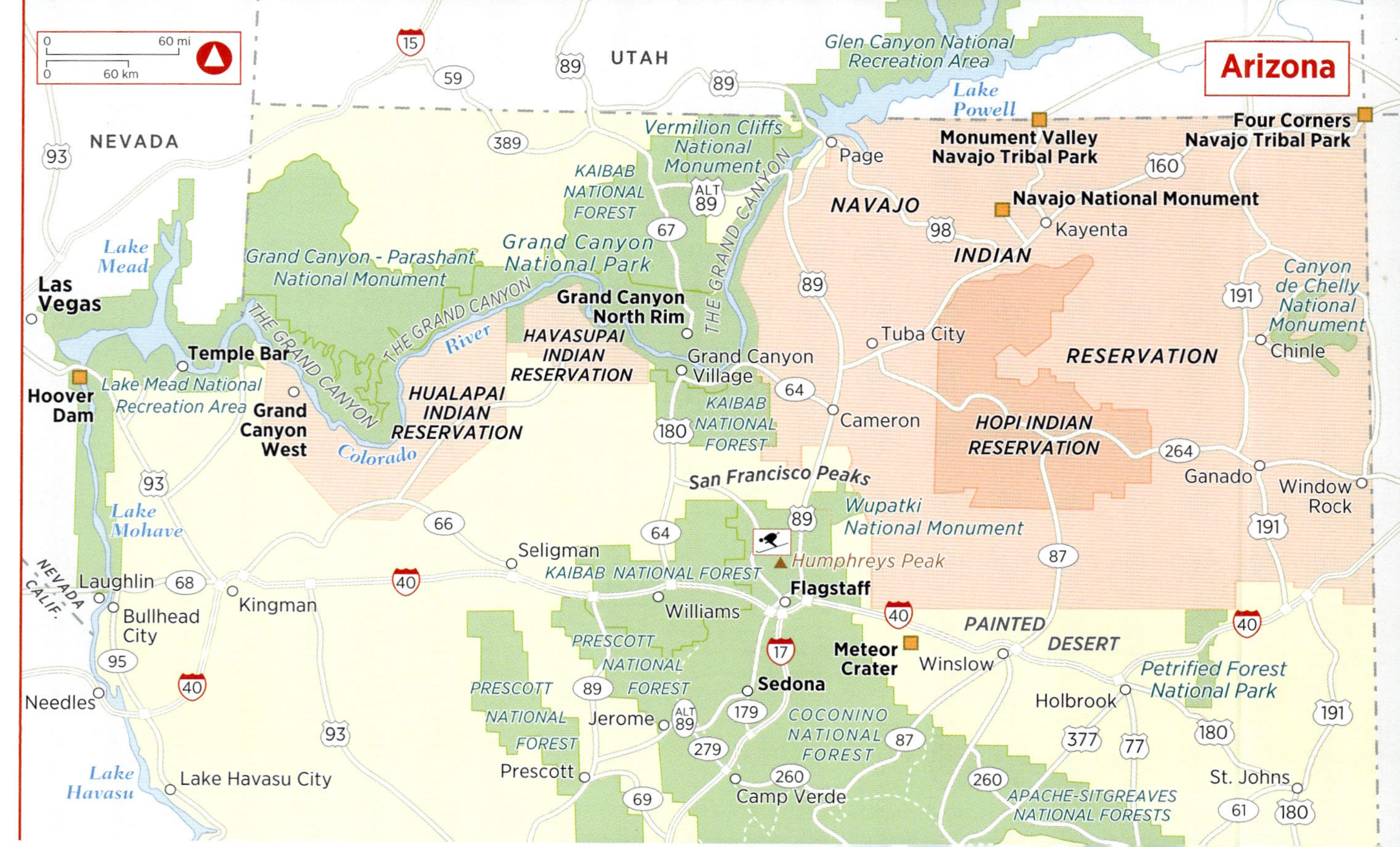
Arizona
0 60 mi
0 60 km
UTAH
NEVADA
NEVADA
CALIF.
Glen Canyon National Recreation Area
Lake Powell
Four Corners Navajo Tribal Park
Monument Valley Navajo Tribal Park
Navajo National Monument
Kayenta
Page
NAVAJO
INDIAN
RESERVATION
Canyon de Chelly National Monument
Chinle
Tuba City
HOPI INDIAN RESERVATION
Cameron
Ganado
Window Rock
Vermilion Cliffs National Monument
KAIBAB NATIONAL FOREST
Grand Canyon National Park
THE GRAND CANYON
Grand Canyon - Parashant National Monument
Grand Canyon North Rim
HAVASUPAI INDIAN RESERVATION
Grand Canyon Village
KAIBAB NATIONAL FOREST
Lake Mead
Las Vegas
Temple Bar
River
Hoover Dam
Lake Mead National Recreation Area
Grand Canyon West
HUALAPAI INDIAN RESERVATION
Colorado
San Francisco Peaks
Wupatki National Monument
Humphreys Peak
Lake Mohave
Seligman
KAIBAB NATIONAL FOREST
Flagstaff
Laughlin
Bullhead City
Kingman
Williams
PAINTED DESERT
PRESCOTT NATIONAL FOREST
Meteor Crater
Winslow
Petrified Forest National Park
Sedona
Holbrook
Needles
PRESCOTT NATIONAL FOREST
Jerome
COCONINO NATIONAL FOREST
Prescott
Camp Verde
Lake Havasu
Lake Havasu City
St. Johns
APACHE-SITGREAVES NATIONAL FORESTS
15
59
89
89
93
389
ALT 89
67
160
98
89
191
64
180
264
89
64
66
93
87
68
40
40
40
17
95
40
89
ALT 89
179
87
377
77
180
191
93
279
260
260
69
61
180

CALIFORNIA
Colorado River
Parker
Quartzsite
Yuma
Kofa National Wildlife Refuge
Wickenburg
Agua Fria National Monument
PHOENIX
Gila Bend
Ajo
Cabeza Prieta National Wildlife Refuge
Organ Pipe Cactus National Monument
GILA RIVER INDIAN RESERVATION
Casa Grande
TOHONO O'ODHAM INDIAN RESERVATION
Picacho Peak
Ironwood National Monument
Saguaro National Park
Buenos Aires National Wildlife Refuge
MEXICO
Carefree/ Cave Creek
Scottsdale
Tempe
Mesa
Apache Junction
Florence
Payson
TONTO NATIONAL FOREST
Superior
Globe
SAN CARLOS APACHE INDIAN RESERVATION
FORT APACHE INDIAN RESERVATION
Show Low
Pinetop-Lakeside
McNary
Springerville
Eagar
Greer
Alpine
White Mountains
Mt. Baldy
APACHE-SITGREAVES NATIONAL FORESTS
Safford
CORONADO NATIONAL FOREST
Mt. Lemmon
Tucson
SAN XAVIER INDIAN RESERVATION
Arivaca Jct.
Arivaca
Tubac
Nogales
Patagonia
Sonoita
Sierra Vista
Benson
Tombstone
Bisbee
Willcox
Chiricahua National Monument
Portal
Douglas
Ski Area
Arizona
UNITED STATES

Watersports, including kayaking, are popular on western Arizona's miles of lakeshore.

forests, laced with trout streams, and dotted with fishing lakes. Although this region comes into its own in summer, it also sees some winter visitation because it has the best ski area in the state: Sunrise Park Resort, on the White Mountain Apache Indian Reservation. Because the area lacks national parks, monuments, and other major geographical attractions, it is not much of a destination for out-of-state visitors.

TUCSON Located a bit more than 100 miles south of Phoenix, Tucson is Arizona's second-most populous metropolitan area and is home to numerous resorts and golf courses. The main attractions include Saguaro National Park and the Arizona–Sonora Desert Museum. With mountain ranges rising in all directions, this city seems more in touch with its natural surroundings than Phoenix, though traffic congestion and sprawl also plague Tucson. If you prefer Boston to New York, San Francisco to Los Angeles, or Portland to Seattle, you'll likely prefer Tucson to Phoenix.

SOUTHERN ARIZONA Southern Arizona is a region of great contrasts, from desert lowlands to mountain "islands" to vast grassy plains. Mile-high elevations also account for southeastern Arizona having one of the most temperate climates in the world. The mild climate has attracted lots of retirees, and it also brings in rare birds (and birders) and helps support a small wine industry. The western part of southern Arizona is lower in elevation and much hotter than the southeastern corner of the state and, because much of this area is a U.S. Air Force bombing range, is one of the least-visited corners of the state. Organ Pipe Cactus National Monument, wedged between the vast Cabeza Prieta National Wildlife Refuge and the Tohono O'odham Indian Reservation, preserves some of the most spectacular desert scenery in this region. Other than the Tucson metropolitan area, there are few communities of any size. However, a couple of interesting historic towns—Bisbee and Tubac—have become artists' communities.

WESTERN ARIZONA Although Arizona is a landlocked state, its western region is bordered by hundreds of miles of lakeshore that were created by the damming of the Colorado River. Consequently, the area has come to be known as Arizona's West Coast. Despite the fact that the low-lying lands of this region are among the hottest places in the state during the summer (and the warmest in winter), Arizona's West Coast is a popular summer destination for budget-conscious desert denizens. College students and families visit for the water-skiing, fishing, and other watersports.

ARIZONA IN 1 WEEK

Arizona is a big state, so don't expect to see it all in 7 days. If you want to take in some of my favorite spots in just a week, you'll need to do a lot of driving and get up early most mornings. (As an added incentive for early rising, let me tell you that sunrises at most of the destinations listed in this itinerary are absolutely awe-inspiring.) This itinerary is best from fall through spring. During the summer, Phoenix is just too hot for hanging out or playing golf (unless you do your swimming at night and tee off at dawn). In the hot months, you may want to head straight to Sedona after touching down in Phoenix, and, if your return flight isn't too early, it's possible to spend your last night in Sedona or Prescott and still have a fairly short drive to the airport in Phoenix.

DAY 1: Phoenix ★★

Head straight for the pool at your resort—after all, lounging in the sun is one of the main reasons to be here. If you've got time, visit the **Desert Botanical Garden** (p. 140) around sunset. This garden has an amazing variety of cacti and is an excellent introduction to the Arizona desert. Head to Scottsdale for dinner, and, if it happens to be a Thursday night, check out some of the art galleries, many of which stay open late on Thursday. The next morning, visit the **Heard Museum** (p. 140), which is one of the nation's premier museums of Native American art and culture. Grab a bite to eat at the museum's excellent cafe or nearby at the **Sacred Hogan Navajo Frybread** (p. 132), where you can try a fry-bread taco. These filling

The historic town of Jerome has become a haven for artists.

meals are a standard on Indian reservations across the state. After lunch head north to Sedona, and, if you leave Phoenix early enough, take the scenic route through Wickenburg, Prescott, and Jerome. If you take this route, stop in Wickenburg at the **Desert Caballeros Western Museum** (p. 203) or in Prescott at the **Phippen Museum** (p. 207). If you time it just right, you can catch the sunset over the Verde Valley from the artsy historic town of **Jerome** (p. 216), which is perched high on the slopes of Mingus Mountain.

DAY 2: Sedona ★★★

Sedona may be touristy, but the red-rock cliffs, buttes, and mesas that surround the city make this one of the most beautiful places in America. To get out amid the red rocks, take a **jeep tour** (p. 235) or hike the 4- to 5-mile loop trail around **Bell Rock** and **Courthouse Butte.** Although this trail sees a lot of hikers, it is just about the best introduction to the amazing hiking that can be done in the Sedona area. Head to **Crescent Moon Recreation Area** or **Airport Mesa** for the sunset. If you don't do a jeep tour this day, plan to do one the next morning.

DAY 3: Grand Canyon ★★★

Drive north to the Grand Canyon by way of scenic **Oak Creek Canyon** (p. 225). Take U.S. 89 from Flagstaff to the east entrance of Grand Canyon National Park. It's worthwhile to make the short detour to see the Sinagua pueblo ruins at **Wupatki National Monument** (p. 301). Also be sure to stop at the **Cameron Trading Post** (p. 281) to see the gallery of Native American artifacts in the historic stone building across the parking lot from the main trading post. If you've developed a taste for fry-bread tacos, be sure to have lunch here. Stop at **Desert View,** just inside the park entrance, and also **Lipan Point,** and catch the sunset over the Grand Canyon. Check into your hotel. The next day, get up early to catch the sunrise, and then do a half-day hike down into the canyon.

Desert View is one of the first stops within the Grand Canyon.

Arizona in 1 Week

Arizona in 2 Weeks

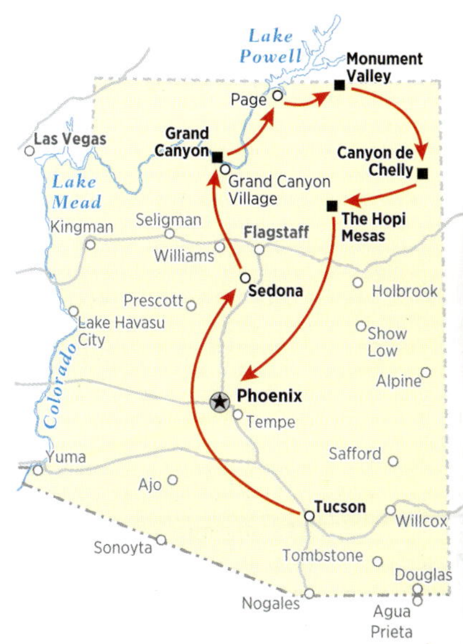

Arizona for Families

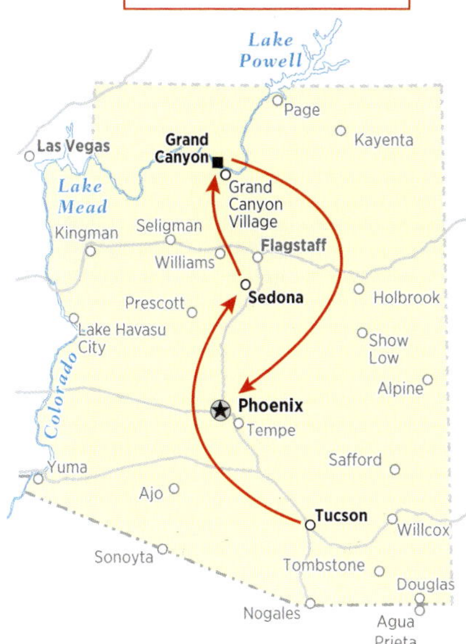

A Sojourn in Southeastern Arizona

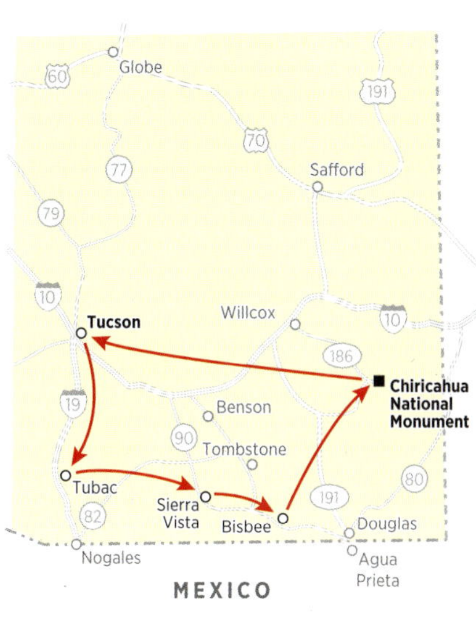

DAY 4: Monument Valley ★★★

It's a long drive from the Grand Canyon to **Monument Valley Navajo Tribal Park** (p. 356), but it's worth it. Arrive in time to take an afternoon jeep tour of the valley with a Navajo guide, and stick around to take pictures of the sunset on the Mitten Buttes.

A truck tour is the best way to see Canyon de Chelly.

DAY 5: Canyon de Chelly ★★★

Even if you're not an early riser, I highly recommend getting up for sunrise on the buttes and mesas of Monument Valley. Next, drive to **Canyon de Chelly National Monument** (p. 347), which is still inhabited in summer by Navajo families who farm and raise sheep much the same way that their ancestors did hundreds of years ago. Make reservations in advance for one of the **truck tours** (p. 352) of the canyon. If you don't have reservations, you may be able to hire a Navajo guide to take you into the canyon by jeep or on horseback. Alternatively, drive one of the rim drives. I recommend the **South Rim Drive** (p. 350) because it provides an opportunity to hike down into the canyon on the **White House Ruins Trail** (p. 351).

DAY 6: The Painted Desert & Petrified Forest ★

The next day, head west across the Hopi Reservation and stop in the village of **Walpi** (p. 332), where you can do a guided tour of this ancient mesa-top pueblo. Also be sure to stop at **Tsakurshovi** (p. 336), a tiny crafts shop that specializes in traditional Hopi kachina dolls. Have lunch at the **Hopi Cultural Center** (p. 333). Continue south to Holbrook and **Petrified Forest National Park** (p. 340), which preserves both the petrified forest and parts of the Painted Desert. End your day in Winslow at the historic **La Posada** hotel (p. 330).

DAY 7: Phoenix ★★

On the way back to Phoenix, stop to see the cliff dwellings at **Montezuma Castle National Monument** (p. 222) near Camp Verde. If you've got a sweet tooth, also stop at the **Rock Springs Café** (p. 196) for some of the best pie in the state. After this whirlwind tour of Arizona's highlights, you'll probably want to park yourself by the pool for the rest of the day.

ARIZONA IN 2 WEEKS

Plan on spending 2 weeks in Arizona, and you'll get a much better sense of this state's diverse landscapes. You can spend more time at the Grand Canyon, marvel at massive saguaro cacti in the desert lowlands, spend a bit more time lounging at a resort, and visit one or more of the state's picturesque artists' communities. Just remember that Arizona's size makes occasional long drives a necessity.

DAYS 1, 2 & 3: Tucson ★★

To get yourself in vacation mode, head straight for the pool at your resort. If you're a hiker, try one of the trails in the foothills of the Santa Catalina Mountains. **Sabino Canyon** (p. 434), with its trams and network of trails, is just about the best place in the city for a quick hike. The next day, go west to the **Arizona–Sonora Desert Museum** (p. 431), the state's single-best introduction to the Sonoran Desert. Despite the name, this is more zoo than museum. By the way, there's a great cafe here.

After you've hung out with the hummingbirds and communed with the coatis, drive a few miles farther west to **Saguaro National Park** (p. 435). This park has units on both the east and west sides of Tucson, but this western unit has the most impressive stands of the saguaro cacti for which the park is named. Be sure to check out the petroglyphs at Signal Hill. On your third day, drive south to the historic arts community of **Tubac** (p. 470). En route, stop at **Mission San Xavier del Bac** (p. 436), a Spanish mission church that is known as the "White Dove of the Desert." In Tubac, check out the galleries, **Tubac Center of the Arts,** and **Tubac Presidio State Historic Park** (p. 471), and then head a few miles south to **Tumacácori National Historical Park** (p. 471), which preserves the ruins of another Spanish mission church.

DAYS 4 & 5: Sedona ★★★

En route north to Sedona from Tucson, be sure to stop in Phoenix to visit the **Heard Museum** (p. 140). This is the state's best introduction to the Native American cultures of the region. After lunch, take the scenic route to Sedona via Wickenburg and Prescott. This will allow you to stop at

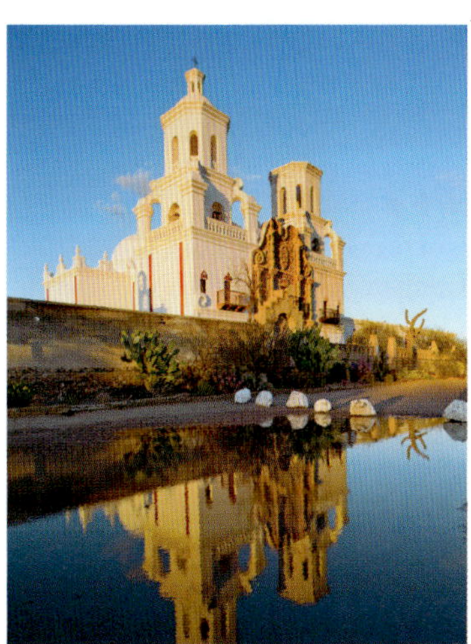

The Spanish Mission San Xavier del Bac.

Hermit's Rest blends in well with its surroundings at the Grand Canyon.

Wickenburg's **Desert Caballeros Western Museum** (p. 203) for the cowboy perspective on the Wild West. Alternatively, you could stop at Prescott's **Phippen Museum** (p. 207), which showcases artworks by members of the Cowboy Artists of America. If you time things right, you should be in the historic artists' community of Jerome just in time to catch the sunset on Sedona's distant red rocks.

To get out amid the red rocks of Sedona, take a **jeep tour** (p. 235) or hike the 4- to 5-mile loop trail around **Bell Rock** and **Courthouse Butte** (p. 230). In the afternoon, visit either the petroglyphs at **V Bar V Heritage Site** (p. 232) or the Sinagua ruins at **Palatki Heritage Site** (p. 231). When the sun sets, be sure you're either at the **Crescent Moon Picnic Area** (p. 231) or atop **Airport Mesa.**

DAYS 6 & 7: Grand Canyon ★★★

For **DAY 6,** follow my suggestions for **DAY 3** in the "Arizona in 1 Week" itinerary above.

The next day, get up early to catch the sunrise, and then do a day hike or mule ride down into the canyon. If you plan ahead, you can even spend the night down in the canyon at Phantom Ranch. If you're not a hiker, spend the day exploring along Hermit Drive, where there are numerous overlooks. Whenever I'm out this way, I like to spend time sitting by the fire at **Hermit's Rest,** a fascinating little building designed by Mary Elizabeth Jane Colter, who designed several of the most interesting and attractive buildings on the South Rim.

DAYS 8 & 9: Page & Lake Powell ★★

From the Grand Canyon, go northeast to the town of Page. En route, you may want to make a short detour to Tuba City, where you can see **dinosaur tracks** (p. 337) in sedimentary stone west of town. Page sits atop a mesa overlooking **Glen Canyon National Recreation Area** (p. 362) and **Lake Powell,** the reservoir created by Glen Canyon Dam. This reservoir is the most astonishing body of water in the West. The vast mirage-like lake is flanked by red-rock canyon walls similar to those of the Grand Canyon. You can tour the massive dam and rent a variety of boats for exploring the lake. The morning after you arrive, take the boat tour up the lake to **Rainbow Bridge National Monument** (p. 364).

DAY 10: Monument Valley ★★★

From Page, head to **Monument Valley Navajo Tribal Park** (p. 356). On the way, be sure to visit **Antelope Canyon** (p. 365), which is one of the most accessible slot canyons in the Southwest. If you get an early enough start, you should also have time to visit **Navajo National Monument** (p. 354) and take a look at the Betatakin cliff dwellings. Just be sure you arrive at Monument Valley early enough in the afternoon to do a jeep tour of the valley with a Navajo guide. Stick around to take pictures of the sunset on the Mitten Buttes. Also, the unforgettable landscape here makes Monument Valley the best place in Arizona to go for a horseback ride.

DAYS 11 & 12: Canyon de Chelly ★★★

The next day, perhaps after a horseback ride or jeep tour (whichever you didn't do the day before), drive to **Canyon de Chelly National**

Meteor Crater, east of Winslow.

Monument (p. 347). The following day, do one of the **truck tours** (p. 352) of the canyon, or hire a Navajo guide to take you into the canyon by jeep or on horseback. Alternatively, drive the rim drives. The **South Rim Drive** (p. 350) is my favorite of the two because it provides the opportunity to hike down into the canyon on the **White House Ruins Trail** (p. 351).

DAY 13: The Hopi Mesas

After leaving Canyon de Chelly, drive south to Ganado and visit the historic **Hubbell Trading Post National Historic Site** (p. 345). Then head west across the Hopi Reservation and stop in the village of **Walpi** (p. 332), where you can take a guided tour of this ancient mesa-top pueblo. Be sure to stop at **Tsakurshovi** (p. 336), a tiny crafts shop that specializes in traditional Hopi kachina dolls. Continue south to Winslow and stay at the historic **La Posada** hotel (p. 330).

DAY 14: Phoenix ★★

On your way back to Phoenix to catch a plane home, stop at **Meteor Crater** (p. 328), which is 20 miles east of Winslow. You may want to have lunch in Flagstaff. Once you get back to Phoenix, lie by the pool and chill out for a few hours.

ARIZONA FOR FAMILIES

With the exception of the Grand Canyon and a few other mountainous areas of the state, Arizona is just too darn hot in the summer for an enjoyable family vacation. Arizonans all head for the hills or San Diego when the temperatures hit triple digits, so you'd have to be crazy to want to spend summer vacation in the middle of the desert. However, spring break is a completely different matter. The weather is usually just warm enough in Tucson and Phoenix, and not too cold or snowy at the Grand Canyon. So, if you're looking for a fun family vacation for the kids' annual spring break, consider the following itinerary. A bit of time by the pool, a little culture, the grandest of canyons—this one should keep everyone happy.

DAYS 1, 2 & 3: Tucson ★★

In Tucson you can learn about the desert and the kids can pet snakes and tarantulas at the **Arizona–Sonora Desert Museum** (p. 431). Spend the entire morning at this amazing place, which is actually more of a zoo than a museum. After lunch, explore the cactus forests of **Saguaro National Park** (p. 435). The next day, head back to this same area to visit **Old Tucson Studios** (p. 437), a one-time movie set that is now a sort of Wild West amusement park with plenty to keep kids and adults entertained (although there aren't any Disneyland-style thrill rides). Your kids might also enjoy visiting the **Mini-Time Machine Museum of Miniatures** (p. 446). On one of your nights in town, have dinner at **Pinnacle Peak Steakhouse** (p. 429), a family-oriented cowboy steakhouse. Alternatively, spend a couple of days at one of Tucson's guest ranches. On your third day in Tucson, do a day trip to **Tombstone** (p. 492). Yes, there is a Tombstone, and it's where Wyatt Earp and Doc Holliday once shot it out with the bad guys at the O.K. Corral. On the way to or from Tombstone, you should be sure to head underground at **Kartchner Caverns State Park®** (p. 485). The caverns here are comparable to the much better known Carlsbad Caverns in New Mexico.

DAY 4: Sedona ★★★

From Tucson, drive north to Sedona. It's a long drive (about 4 hr.), so get an early start. In the town of Picacho, not far north of Tucson, you can let the kids feed the ostriches at the **Rooster Cogburn Ostrich Ranch** (p. 195). North of Phoenix in the town of Rock Springs, stop for lunch (and great pie) at the **Rock Springs Café** (p. 196). If you get to Sedona early enough, take the kids on the **Pink Jeep Tours'** (p. 236) gnarly Broken Arrow tour. This is four-wheeling at its most rugged. If you arrive too late, schedule the tour for the next morning. At sunset, head to **Crescent Moon Picnic Area** (p. 231), where the kids can splash in Oak Creek while you marvel at the sunset light show on Cathedral Rock.

DAYS 5 & 6: Grand Canyon ★★★

Leave Sedona and head up scenic **Oak Creek Canyon** (p. 225) to Flagstaff. If it's a hot day, be sure to stop at **Slide Rock State Park** (p. 233).

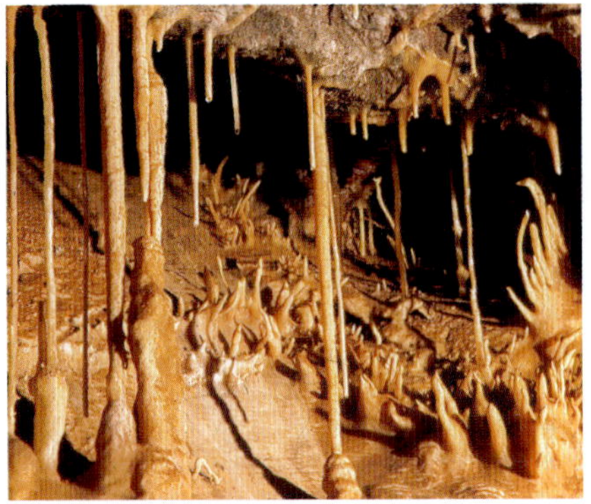
Kids will be fascinated by the rock formations at Kartchner Caverns®.

Pink Jeep Tours take you four-wheeling through Sedona's red rocks.

From Flagstaff, continue north on U.S. 89 to the east entrance of **Grand Canyon National Park** (p. 255). Check out the views from the many overlooks as you make your way west to Grand Canyon Village and its many hotels. You can dawdle along the way, but be sure you make it to the Grand Canyon in time for sunset. Spend the next day hiking into the canyon, riding a mule along the rim, or exploring along Hermit Road. The historic little Hermit's Rest is a good place to get cocoa and hang out by a fire.

DAYS 7 & 8: Phoenix ★★

From the Grand Canyon, head back south to **Phoenix.** If you head south from the canyon on Ariz. 64, there are some fun places to stop near Williams, including **Grand Canyon Deer Farm** (p. 310) and **Bearizona** (p. 309). Once back in Phoenix, spend a couple of days chilling out at one of the city's big resorts. Many resorts in the area have water parks with slides and other features aimed specifically at keeping kids happy. If you can pry the kids away from the pool area, take them to the **Heard Museum** (p. 140) to expose them to a little Native American culture. If you haven't yet had enough of Wild West towns, head east of the city to **Goldfield Ghost Town** (p. 150), which is a bit too lively to really be a ghost town but is loads of fun, or south to **Rawhide** (p. 150), a mock-up of an old cow town.

A SOJOURN IN SOUTHEASTERN ARIZONA

Tombstone, Wyatt Earp, Doc Holliday, Geronimo, Cochise, the O.K. Corral. The names are familiar, but what you might not know is that these are all names from southeastern Arizona. This corner of the state may not have the major natural attractions that northern Arizona has, but it does have loads of Wild West history; plenty of natural beauty; and great resorts, restaurants, and museums in and around Tucson. With the exception of the Tucson area, the climate here is mild year-round, so you'll be comfortable whether you visit in summer or winter. Southeastern Arizona is also one of the best bird-watching regions in the country. Many bird species reach the northern limits of their ranges in this area.

DAYS 1, 2 & 3: Tucson ★★

Spend your first few days exploring Tucson and, if the weather is warm, lounging by the pool. On your first full day in town, head first to the **Arizona–Sonora Desert Museum** (p. 431), which is more zoo than museum and is the state's best introduction to the flora and fauna of the Sonoran Desert. The museum is just a few miles down the road from the west unit of **Saguaro National Park** (p. 435), so once you've gotten familiar with life in the desert, strike out on the trail or on a scenic drive to get up close and personal with some gigantic saguaro cacti. If you're in good shape, I recommend hiking the **Hugh Morris Trail** to the summit of **Wasson Peak,** which has superb views across miles of desert. Try to stick around until sunset so that you can watch the light of the setting sun on the petroglyphs at **Signal Hill,** which is within the national park. The next day, visit the **Tucson Museum of Art** and wander around downtown Tucson's historic neighborhoods to get a feel for the city's mix of Spanish, Mexican, and

Anglo history. If your timing is right, take a guided tour of one of the museum's historic homes. In the afternoon, visit **Tohono Chul Park** and **Sabino Canyon.**

DAY 4: Tubac ★★

After you've gotten a feel for Tucson, take a day trip south toward Mexico. Just south of Tucson, you'll come to **Mission San Xavier del Bac** (p. 436), a historic Spanish mission church that is known as the "White Dove of the Desert." If you're hungry, this is a good place to try Indian fry-bread tacos; there's a little walk-up food window in the plaza across the parking lot from the church, and Native Americans often set up grills and sell food from stalls in the parking lot. Continue south to the historic town of **Tubac,** which was founded by the Spanish and is now filled with art galleries. Just south of Tubac is **Tumacácori National Historical Park** (p. 471), where you can see the ruins of another mission church. Spend the night at the **Tubac Golf Resort & Spa** (p. 474).

DAYS 5 & 6: Bisbee or Sierra Vista ★★

From Tubac, drive down to the border town of **Nogales** and then head east to **Patagonia,** a small town best known for its great bird-watching, and **Sonoita,** which is both wide-open ranch country and Arizona's own little wine country (Callaghan Vineyards is my favorite area winery, but there are several other good places to sample local wines). Birders should be sure to stop at **Patagonia Lake State Park/Sonoita Creek State Natural Area** (p. 481), the Nature Conservancy's **Patagonia–Sonoita Creek Preserve** (p. 480), and **Paton's Birder's Haven** (p. 480). Try to time things so that you can have lunch at Patagonia's **Velvet Elvis Pizza Company** (p. 483). If you're a birder, you'll want to stay a couple of nights at one of the inns south of Sierra Vista. Several inns cater specifically to the birders who flock to the area to see hummingbirds at **Ramsey Canyon Preserve** (p. 487) and a wide variety of other birds at area birding hot spots such as the **San Pedro Riparian National Conservation Area** (p. 488). If you're not a birder, continue to the funky historic town of Bisbee, which is full of countercultural types who have turned this former copper-mining town into the most interesting small town in Arizona. Be sure to eat dinner at **Cafe Roka** (p. 501). While you're in the area, visit **Coronado National Memorial** (p. 487) to learn about the Spanish explorer who passed through this region between 1540 and 1542. And, of course,

The Arizona-Sonora Desert Museum is a good intro to indigenous flora and fauna.

Sonoita is home to several wineries, including Callaghan Vineyards.

you shouldn't miss **Tombstone** (p. 492), home of the famous shootout at the O.K. Corral.

DAYS 7 & 8: The Chiricahuas ★★

From Bisbee or Sierra Vista, head northeast to **Chiricahua National Monument** (p. 505) and **Cochise Stronghold** (p. 504). At the former, hike part or all of the **Heart of Rocks Trail,** which is one of the most memorable hikes in the state. If you have an interest in Western history, save time for the 3-mile round-trip hike to **Fort Bowie National Historic Site** (p. 505). You'll be hiking with the ghosts of Apaches, soldiers, and stagecoach travelers. On your last day in the area, visit the remote **Amerind Foundation Museum** (p. 504), which has an outstanding collection of Native American artifacts and is set amid huge granite boulders in Texas Canyon. On your way back to Tucson, be sure to detour south from Benson to **Kartchner Caverns State Park**® (p. 485). The caverns here are among the most spectacular in the country.

NATIVE TRAILS OF ARIZONA

You may think you're venturing off into the great unknown when you take off across Arizona, but believe me, others have been here before you. Down in the southeastern part of the state near the present-day San Pedro River, archaeologists discovered a mammoth kill site that proves humans were living in Arizona more than 10,000 years ago. All across Arizona you'll find signs of those who have come before. Cliff dwellings, pueblo ruins, and petroglyphs abound in the desert. This itinerary will help you search out the outstanding remains of Arizona's Native American cultures both past and present. Along the way, you can also learn about the state's Native cultures at museums that focus on Native American art, artifacts, and heritage. Of course, you'll also have plenty of opportunities to meet today's Navajos, Hopis, and Apaches, as well as members of other tribes.

DAYS 1, 2 & 3: Phoenix ★★

The best "trail head" for an exploration of Arizona's Native trails is Phoenix. Here you should visit the superb **Heard Museum** (p. 140) to learn all about the tribes of the region and see samples of their traditional arts and crafts. Right in Phoenix, at **Pueblo Grande Museum and Archaeological Park** (p. 141), you can visit the remains of a Hohokam village and learn about the people who once built an extensive network of canals here in the middle of the desert. When you visit the Heard Museum, be sure to have lunch at the nearby **Fry Bread House** (p. 131) or **Sacred Hogan Navajo Frybread** (p. 132), where you can try fry-bread tacos, which are a staple on reservations across the state. Visit the **Deer Valley Rock Art Center** (p. 137) to see a dense concentration of petroglyphs and then, late in the day, go to the **Desert Botanical Garden** (p. 140). In addition to having lots of cacti on display, this attraction has an ethnobotanical garden where you can learn about the desert plants traditionally utilized by the Native inhabitants of the Sonoran Desert. On your third day, do a day trip out of the city. If you head south to Coolidge, you can visit **Casa Grande Ruins National Monument** (p. 195), and then drive northeast to Globe to see the reconstructed **Besh-Ba-Gowah Archaeological Park** (p. 194). After lunch, continue to **Tonto National Monument** (p. 193), which is the southernmost cliff dwelling in the state. Return to Phoenix on the winding, gravel Apache Trail route.

DAYS 4 & 5: Sedona ★★★

From Phoenix, journey north to Sedona. En route, there are three stops you should make. At Camp Verde, detour to Cottonwood to visit the reconstructed hilltop ruins of **Tuzigoot National Monument** (p. 223). Head back to I-17 and continue north to **Montezuma Castle National Monument** (p. 222), another well-preserved cliff dwelling. At the Ariz. 179 exit for Sedona, get off I-17, but turn away from Sedona, not toward it. A few miles down this road is the **V Bar V Heritage Site** (p. 232), which

The ball court at Wupatki National Monument.

Native Trails of Arizona

Arizona in the Winter

preserves one of the most impressive petroglyph sites in the state. The next day, after you've spent some time ogling the red rocks, head west of town to **Palatki Heritage Site** (p. 231), where you can see the ruins of Sinagua cliff dwellings. While you're out this way, hike up **Boynton Canyon,** where you may spot some of the canyon's small ruin sites.

DAY 6: Flagstaff ★★

It's barely an hour's drive from Sedona to Flagstaff, and the first place to visit there is the **Museum of Northern Arizona** (p. 299). This museum has outstanding exhibits on the Native cultures of the Colorado Plateau. Outside of town, you'll find two national monuments that preserve old ruin sites. **Wupatki National Monument** (p. 301) is, in my opinion, the more impressive of the two. Not only can you wander around several Sinagua pueblo sites, but at the main pueblo of Wupatki, you'll also find both a ball court similar to those found in Mexico and a fascinating "blowhole" that either blows or sucks air, depending on temperature and barometric pressure. Closer to Flagstaff, you can explore small cliff dwellings at **Walnut Canyon National Monument** (p. 300). The small rooms wedged into the cliffs at this monument were also built by the Sinagua. Be sure to stop in at **Jonathan Day's Indian Arts** (p. 297) before you leave town. This shop specializes in traditional Hopi kachinas and old Indian trade blankets.

DAY 7: The Hopi Mesas ★★

From Flagstaff, head east to the villages of the Hopi mesas. Along the way, you'll pass numerous shops selling Hopi silver overlay jewelry, as well as kachina dolls, pottery, and baskets. Stop at the **Hopi Cultural Center** (p. 333) to tour the small museum and have a lunch of traditional Hopi stew. At First Mesa, you can take a guided tour of the ancient cliff-top village of **Walpi** (p. 332). Continue east to the Navajo community of Ganado, where you can tour the historic **Hubbell Trading Post** (p. 345), and then backtrack a few miles to head north to **Canyon de Chelly National Monument** (p. 347).

DAY 8: Canyon de Chelly National Monument ★★★

Do a "shake-and-bake" truck tour of Canyon de Chelly. These tours, which are in rugged military surplus trucks outfitted with bench seats, head deep into the canyon to places you're not allowed to visit without a Navajo guide. You'll stop at numerous ruin sites and see well-preserved pictographs. You may even encounter Navajo farmers and shepherds who still live in the canyon during the summer months. See p. 352.

DAY 9: Monument Valley Navajo Tribal Park ★★★

Monument Valley Navajo Tribal Park (p. 356) is really a landscape attraction and not a cultural attraction, but you can't visit this park without meeting a few Navajos. Local families operate jeep tours, horseback tours, and hiking tours. Take a **jeep tour** (p. 358), and you'll not only get to see some interesting petroglyphs, but you might also encounter a Navajo gazing off into the distance as he sits astride his noble steed. (I'm not kidding; there really are people who pose on horseback for photos.)

DAYS 10 & 11: Grand Canyon ★★★

Okay, so the **Grand Canyon** (p. 255) isn't known for its cultural heritage, but for many centuries, Native Americans lived in and near the canyon. All through the canyon there are caves, cliff dwellings, and pueblo sites. However, most of them are way off the beaten track and hard to get to. Besides that, the park service doesn't even want you to know most of these sites exist, for fear you might vandalize them. That said, you should be sure to visit the **Tusayan Museum** (p. 266), which is built on the site of an Ancestral Puebloan (Anasazi) ruin. En route to the Grand Canyon from Monument Valley, be sure to visit **Navajo National Monument** (p. 354), where you can take a 1-mile walk to a viewpoint

You'll likely interact with Navajos at Monument Valley Navajo Tribal Park.

overlooking the large Betatakin cliff dwelling. If you have an extra day to spare and can be here at the monument early in the morning, you can try to get a space on one of the guided hikes to the Betatakin ruins. Spend a second day in Grand Canyon National Park exploring along the park's rim drives or hiking down into the canyon.

DAY 12: Phoenix ★★

Head back to Phoenix by taking Ariz. 64 south to U.S. 180 to Flagstaff, where you'll pick up I-17. Once you reach Phoenix, check into your hotel, pull up a lounge chair by the pool, and meditate on all that you've seen as you've followed the Native trails of Arizona.

ARIZONA IN THE WINTER

Arizona in the winter means golf, desert explorations, and enough sunshine to help you forget all about shoveling the snow out of your driveway back home. Sure, you can go to the Grand Canyon (and even avoid the crowds), but it will be very cold, and snow often makes the area's roads impassable. So think of this as an escape from the cold up north, not just as a once-in-a-lifetime trip to see the Grand Canyon. Although I have written this itinerary with the emphasis on Phoenix, you could just as easily spend the bulk of your week in Tucson. You'd just have a longer drive north to Sedona.

DAYS 1, 2 & 3: Phoenix ★★

I know I've said it before, but when I get to the sunshine and warmth of the desert, I always make the resort pool my very first stop. Order a froufrou cocktail, grab a lounge chair, and say, "Aaaahhh." Repeat when necessary for the next 3 days. Once you've relaxed for a bit, it's time to get to know this city, and the best way I can think of is a bit strenuous but, for anyone in good shape, exhilarating. What I'm talking about is a little peak bagging. If you've got lots of energy, hike up **Camelback Mountain** (p. 166) or **Piestewa Peak** (p. 166) for incomparable views of the valley. While you're up here with all the other buff hikers, get your bearings. After a shower (you'll need it), head to Scottsdale for dinner and check out some of the great nightlife. On your second day, play a round of golf or some tennis in the morning, or, if you're more interested in culture, visit the **Heard Museum** (p. 140) and the **Phoenix Art Museum** (p. 142). In the afternoon, get in another swim, and then, around sunset, visit the **Desert Botanical Garden** (p. 140). Phoenix is a huge metropolitan area, so to see what the desert is really like, drive the **Apache Trail** (p. 192), east of the city, on **DAY 3.** This drive will take all day, so get an early start.

DAYS 4 & 5: Sedona ★★★

Maybe you've never heard of Sedona before, but once you see the red-rock cliffs, buttes, and mesas that frame this wealthy community, you'll probably start scheming ways to move here. Sedona quite simply has the most beautiful setting of any town in the West. On your way north from Phoenix, be sure to stop at **Montezuma Castle National Monument** (p. 222). Once in Sedona, your best introduction to the area is a **jeep tour** (p. 228). Just make sure that by sunset you're atop **Airport Mesa** (p. 238) to take in the

Camelback Mountain is a popular spot for hikers, especially in winter.

natural light show. The next day, in the morning, visit the **V Bar V Heritage Site** (p. 232), which is one of the most impressive petroglyph sites in the state and is at its photogenic best before the sun hits the rocks in the early afternoon. After you've marveled at these ancient symbols, do some hiking or mountain biking. Sedona is surrounded by national forest, and there are dozens of miles of easily accessed trails. I recommend any of the trails to the west of the city. Hiking the **Boynton Canyon Trail** (p. 231) or the **Vultee Arch Trail** (p. 238) will put you close to **Palatki Heritage Site** (p. 231), a small Sinagua cliff dwelling. You'll also end the day not far from **Crescent Moon Recreation Area** (p. 231), where you can watch the sunset light up Cathedral Rock as the waters of Oak Creek flow by in the foreground. If you're a golfer, be sure to get in a round amid the red rocks while you're in town.

DAY 6: Grand Canyon ★★★

This is a tough one; if you plan this day in advance, you may be disappointed. The road to the **Grand Canyon** (p. 255) is sometimes closed by snow in winter, though usually only for a short time. Still, you came to Arizona to get away from snow, right? So, who wants to head back into subfreezing temperatures? But as long as you're this close, you might as well try to see the canyon, so if the weather is good, make a mad dash up to the canyon and snap some photos before your fingers freeze. Either spend the night at the canyon or drive back to Sedona the same day. Your best route for this quick visit is to drive north to Flagstaff and then take U.S. 89 north to Ariz. 64, which leads west to the east entrance of Grand Canyon National Park. Return via U.S. 180 to Flagstaff.

DAY 7: Phoenix ★★

Head back to Phoenix by way of **Jerome** (p. 216), a former mining town that is now an artists' community. Peruse the galleries and tour the ghost town and mine on the edge of town. If you have time, schedule a ride on the **Verde Canyon Railroad** (p. 221). Try to get in one last swim when you get back to your resort in Phoenix.

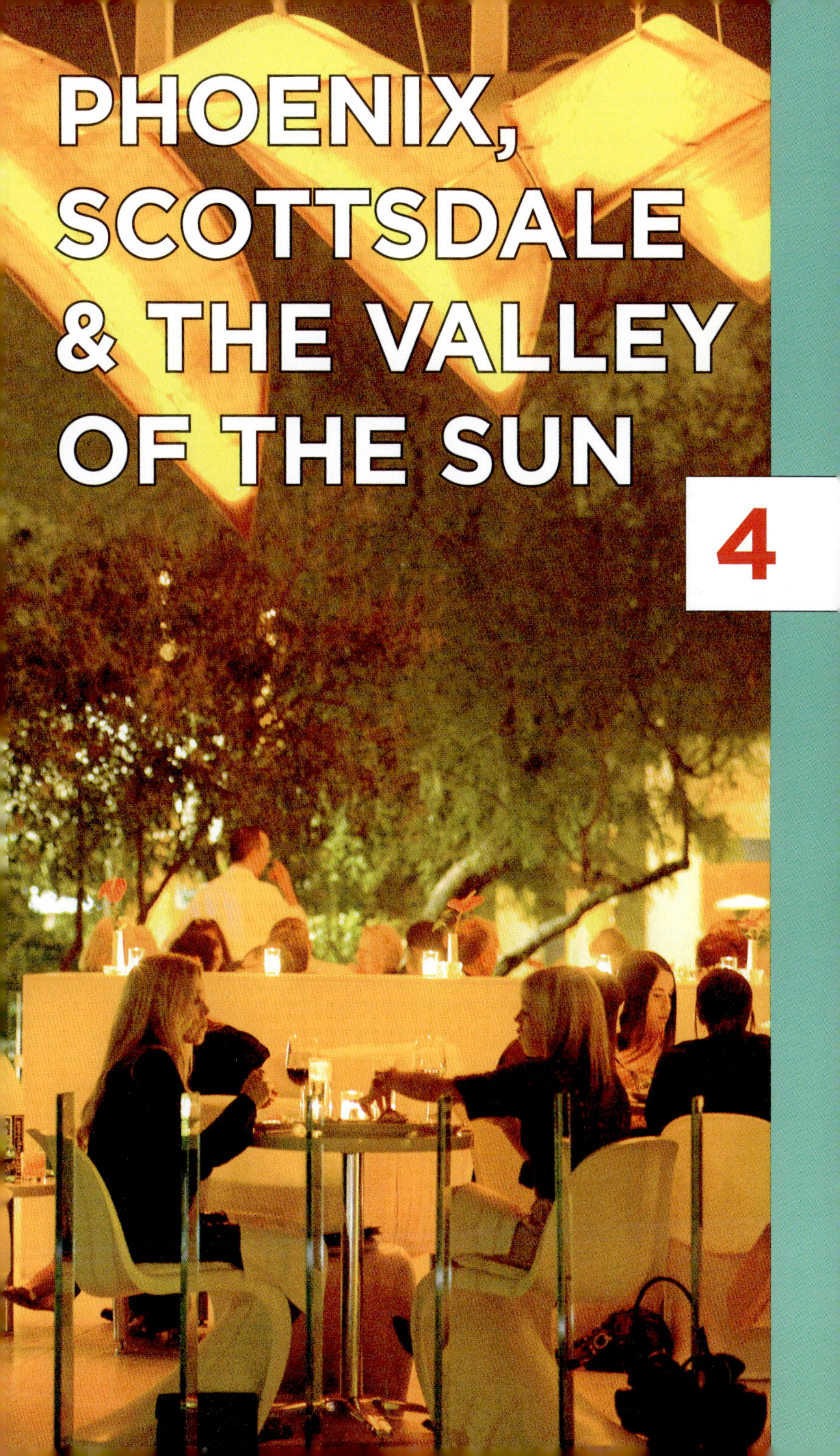

PHOENIX, SCOTTSDALE & THE VALLEY OF THE SUN

4

Forget the spiny cacti and the cowboys on their trusty steeds. Think Los Angeles without the Pacific. Sprawling across more than 500 square miles of what once was cactus and creosote bushes, the greater Phoenix metropolitan area, also known as the Valley of the Sun, is home to dozens of resorts, hundreds of golf courses, countless great restaurants, fascinating museums, and a red-hot nightlife scene. However, in the end, it is the sunshine and winter warmth that are the city's biggest attractions.

Things to Do Although it's known for its furnacelike summers, actually finding the desert in Phoenix can be a challenge. At the **Desert Botanical Garden,** marvel at bizarre desert plants from around the world. Hike **South Mountain Park** or **Camelback Mountain** to experience Arizona's own Sonoran Desert. For a superb introduction to Native American cultures, visit the **Heard Museum,** and for a glimpse of the Wild West visit **Goldfield Ghost Town, Rawhide,** or **Cave Creek.** March's baseball spring-training camps bring the boys of summer (and their fans) to town.

Active Pursuits Ample winter sunshine and more than 200 golf courses mean golfers vacationing in the Valley have plenty of opportunities to improve their handicaps. For wide, forgiving greens, head to such classics as the **Wigwam Golf Resort & Spa** or the **Arizona Biltmore Golf Club.** Once you're up to par, tee off at a challenging desert course such as **Troon North Golf Club** or the **Boulders.** If you're not a golfer, go take a **hike** or redefine lounging by the pool as an active pursuit.

Restaurants & Dining Beans and black coffee may once have kept cowboys contented, but today, Phoenicians are a bit more discriminating. Savor the flavor combinations of James Beard–award-winning chefs, or troll for dinner at one of the many restaurants along the **Scottsdale Waterfront.** Wake up your taste buds at **Mexican** and **Southwestern** restaurants serving up bold flavors, with or without fire. **Cowboy steakhouses** offer up both hefty steaks and family fun.

Nightlife & Entertainment It wasn't that long ago that a harmonica by the campfire constituted nightlife in these parts, but today, the Valley of the Sun club scene is as hot as, well, Arizona in the summer. Swanky Scottsdale bars and night clubs, such as **AZ88, Myst,** and **Axis/Radius** lure the city's hip fashionistas and the occasional Hollywood celebrity. Cowboys, urban and otherwise, can ride off into the sunset and do a bit of **boot scootin'** at bars such as the **Rusty Spur** and the **Buffalo Chip Saloon.**

PREVIOUS PAGE: **Outdoor dining at Scottsdale's AZ88.**

Downtown Phoenix's skyline.

ORIENTATION

Arriving

BY PLANE Centrally located 3 miles east of downtown Phoenix, **Sky Harbor International Airport,** 3400 E. Sky Harbor Blvd. (✆ **602/273-3300;** www.phxskyharbor.com), has three terminals, with a free 24-hour shuttle bus offering frequent service between them. For information on airlines serving Phoenix, see chapter 12.

There are two entrances to the airport. The west entrance can be accessed from either the Papago Freeway (I-10) or 24th Street, while the east entrance can be accessed from the Hohokam Expressway (Ariz. 143) or the Sky Harbor Expressway (Ariz. 153), which is an extension of 44th Street. If you're headed to downtown Phoenix, leave by way of the 24th Street exit and continue west on Washington Street. If you're headed to Scottsdale, Tempe, or Mesa, head east out of the airport and follow signs for Ariz. 202 Loop.

There is also now an alternative airport on the east side of the Valley. The **Phoenix-Mesa Gateway Airport (AZA),** 6033 S. Sossaman Rd., Mesa (✆ **480/988-7600;** www.phxmesagateway.org), is served by **Allegiant Airlines** (✆ **702/505-8888;** www.allegiantair.com), which has service from small cities in the Northwest and Midwest. This airport is south of Ariz. 202 Loop at the Power Road exit.

SuperShuttle (✆ **800/258-3826** or 602/244-9000; www.supershuttle.com) offers 24-hour door-to-door van service between Sky Harbor Airport and resorts, hotels, and homes throughout the Valley. Per-person shared-ride fares average $12 to $14 to the downtown and Tempe area, $16 to downtown Scottsdale, and $24 to $31 to north Scottsdale.

A Name Change

In 2003, the official name of Phoenix's Squaw Peak was changed to Piestewa Peak (pronounced Pie-ess-too-uh) to honor Pfc. Lori Ann Piestewa, a member of the Hopi tribe and the first female soldier killed in the Iraq War. The peak in north Phoenix has long been a popular hiking destination. If you hear people referring to both Squaw Peak and Piestewa Peak, it's one and the same place. Ditto for the Squaw Peak Parkway, which is now Piestewa Freeway.

The light-rail is a good way to explore downtown Phoenix.

Taxis can be found outside all three terminals and cost only slightly more than shuttle vans. You can also call **AAA/Yellow Cab** (✆ **602/888-8888**), **Apache Taxi** (✆ **480/557-7000**), or **Mayflower Cab** (✆ **602/955-1355;** www.discountcab.com). Taxis from the airport charge $5 for turning on the meter, a $1 airport surcharge, $2.10 per mile, and a minimum fare of $15. A taxi from the airport to downtown Phoenix will cost around $16; to Scottsdale, between $21 and $36.

Metro (✆ **602/253-5000;** www.valleymetro.org), the valley's light-rail line, connects Phoenix Sky Harbor Airport with the cities of Phoenix, Tempe, and Mesa. Metro runs daily every 12 to 20 minutes, between 4am and 11:50pm (until 2:40am or later on weekends). To take the light-rail, you'll first need to ride the free airport shuttle to the light-rail station at the corner of Washington and 44th streets. The ride from the light-rail station to downtown takes about 15 minutes and costs $1.75. There is no Metro service to Scottsdale, so you'll first need to go to Tempe and then transfer to a northbound Valley Metro bus.

BY CAR Phoenix is connected to Los Angeles and Tucson by I-10 and to Flagstaff via I-17. If you're headed to Scottsdale, the easiest route is to take the Red Mountain Freeway (Ariz. 202) east to U.S. 101 N. This latter freeway loops all the way around the east, north, and west sides of the Valley. The Superstition Freeway (U.S. 60) leads to Tempe, Mesa, and Chandler.

BY TRAIN There is no passenger rail service to Phoenix. **Amtrak** (✆ **800/872-7245;** www.amtrak.com) will sell you a ticket to Phoenix, but you'll have to take a shuttle bus from either Flagstaff or Tucson. The scheduling is so horrible on these routes that you'd have to be a total masochist to opt for Amtrak service to Phoenix. There is a closer stop to Phoenix, in the community of Maricopa, but there is no public transportation option to get you from there to Phoenix.

Visitor Information

You'll find **tourist information desks** in all three terminals at Sky Harbor Airport. The city's main visitor center is the **Greater Phoenix Convention & Visitors Bureau,** 125 N. Second St., Ste. 120 (✆ **877/225-5749** or 602/254-6500; www.visitphoenix.com; Mon–Fri 8am–5pm), across from the main entrance of the Hyatt Regency in downtown Phoenix.

The **Visitor Information Line** (✆ **602/252-5588**) has recorded information about current events in Phoenix and is updated weekly.

If you're staying in Scottsdale, you can get information at the **Scottsdale Convention & Visitors Bureau Visitor Center,** Galleria Corporate Center, 4343 N. Scottsdale Rd., Ste. 170 (✆ **800/782-1117;** www.scottsdalecvb.com; Mon–Fri 8am–5pm).

MAIN ARTERIES & STREETS **U.S. Loop 101** forms a loop around the east, north, and west sides of the Valley, providing freeway access to Scottsdale from I-17 on the north side of Phoenix and from U.S. 60 in Tempe.

I-17 (Black Canyon Fwy.), which connects Phoenix with Flagstaff, is the city's main north-south freeway. This freeway curves to the east just south of downtown (where it is renamed the **Maricopa Fwy.** and merges with I-10). **I-10,** which connects Phoenix with Los Angeles and Tucson, is called the **Papago Freeway** on the west side of the Valley and as it passes north of downtown; as it curves around to pass to the west and south of the airport, it merges with I-17 and is renamed the Maricopa Freeway. At Tempe, this freeway curves to the south and heads out of the Valley.

North of the airport, **Ariz. 202 (Red Mountain Fwy.)** heads east from I-10 and passes along the north side of Tempe, providing access to downtown Tempe, Arizona State University, Mesa, and Scottsdale (via U.S. Loop 101). On the east side of the airport, **Ariz. 143 (Hohokam Expwy.)** connects Ariz. 202 with I-10.

At the interchange of I-10 and Ariz. 202, northwest of Sky Harbor Airport, **Ariz. 51 (Piestewa Fwy.)** heads north through the center of Phoenix to U.S. Loop 101 and is the best north-south route in the city.

South of the airport off I-10, **U.S. 60 (Superstition Fwy.)** heads east to Tempe, Chandler, Mesa, and Gilbert. **U.S. Loop 101** leads north from U.S. 60 (and Ariz. 202) through Scottsdale and across the north side of Phoenix to connect with I-17. U.S. 60 and U.S. Loop 101 provide the best route from the airport to the Scottsdale resorts. U.S. Loop 101 also heads south through Chandler to connect with I-10. This section is called the Price Freeway. The section of this freeway north through Scottsdale is called the Pima Freeway.

Secondary highways in the Valley include the **Beeline Highway (Ariz. 87),** which starts at the east end of Ariz. 202 (Red Mountain Fwy.) in Mesa and leads to Payson, and **Grand Avenue (U.S. 60),** which starts downtown and leads west to Sun City and Wickenburg.

Phoenix and the surrounding cities of Mesa, Tempe, Scottsdale, and Chandler, and even those cities farther out in the Valley, are laid out in a grid pattern with major avenues and roads about every mile. For traveling east to west across Phoenix, your best choices (other than the above-mentioned freeways) are Camelback, Indian School, and McDowell roads. For traveling north and south, 44th Street, 24th Street, and Central Avenue are good choices. Hayden Road is a north-south alternative to Scottsdale Road, which gets jammed at rush hours.

FINDING AN ADDRESS **Central Avenue,** which runs north to south through downtown Phoenix, is the starting point for all east-and-west street numbering. **Washington Street** is the starting point for north and south numbering. North-to-south numbered *streets* are to be found on the east side of the city, while north-to-south numbered *avenues* will be found on the west.

For the most part, street numbers advance by 100 with each block. Odd-numbered addresses are on the south and east sides of streets, while even-numbered addresses are on the north and west sides of streets.

For example, if you're looking for 4454 E. Camelback Rd., you'll find it 44 blocks east of Central Avenue between 44th and 45th streets on the north side of the street. If you're looking for 2905 N. 35th Ave., you'll find it 35 blocks west of Central Avenue and 29 blocks north of Washington Street on the east side of the street. Just for general reference, Camelback Road marks the 5000 block north. Also, whenever you're getting directions, ask for the cross street closest to where you're going. Street numbers can be hard to spot when you're driving past at 45 mph.

STREET MAPS The street maps handed out by rental-car companies may be good for general navigation around the city, but they are almost useless for finding a particular address if it is not on a major arterial; so as soon as you can, stop at a minimart and buy a Phoenix map. Unfortunately, you'll probably also have to buy a separate Scottsdale map. Alternatively, if you are a member of AAA, you can get a good Phoenix map before you leave home. You can also get a simple map at the airport tourist information desks or at the downtown visitor center. However, your best bet these days is to rent a car with a navigation system, or bring your own with you.

Neighborhoods in Brief

Because of urban sprawl, Phoenix has yielded its importance to an area known as the Valley of the Sun (or just "the Valley"), an area encompassing Phoenix and its metropolitan area of more than 20 cities. Consequently, as outlying cities have taken on regional importance, neighborhoods per se have lost much of their significance. Think of the Valley's many cities as automobile-oriented neighborhoods. That said, there are also some actual neighborhoods worth noting.

DOWNTOWN PHOENIX Roughly bordered by Thomas Road on the north, Buckeye Road on the south, 19th Avenue on the west, and Seventh Street on the east, downtown is primarily a business, financial, and government district, where both the city hall and the state capitol are located. Downtown Phoenix is also the Valley's prime sports, entertainment, and museum district. The Arizona Diamondbacks play big-league baseball at **Chase Field,** while the Phoenix Suns shoot hoops at the **US Airways Center.** Of course, there are also lots of sports bars in the area. Three major performing arts venues—the historic **Orpheum Theatre, Symphony Hall,** and the **Herberger Theater Center**—are located here. Downtown museums and attractions include the **Arizona Science Center, Heritage Square** (historic homes), the **Arizona Capitol Museum,** and the **Arizona Mining & Mineral Museum.** On the northern edge of downtown are the **Heard Museum,** the **Phoenix Central Library** (an architectural gem), and the **Phoenix Art Museum.** Downtown Phoenix is also an art-gallery district featuring cutting-edge contemporary art. In recent years, condominiums have been proliferating downtown and have infused the area with new life.

BILTMORE DISTRICT The Biltmore District, also known as the **Camelback Corridor,** centers on Camelback Road between 24th and 44th streets and is Phoenix's upscale shopping, residential, and business district. The area is characterized by modern office buildings and is anchored by the Arizona Biltmore Hotel and Biltmore Fashion Park shopping mall.

SCOTTSDALE A separate city of more than 200,000 people, Scottsdale extends from Tempe in the south to Carefree in the north, a distance of more than 20 miles. Scottsdale Road between Indian School Road and Shea Boulevard was once known as **Resort Row** and was home to more than a dozen major resorts. However, as Scottsdale has sprawled ever northward, so, too, have the resorts. North Scottsdale has now become the center of the resort, shopping, and restaurant scene. Downtown Scottsdale—which is made up of Old Town, the Main Street Arts and Antiques District, the Marshall Way Contemporary Arts District, the Fifth Avenue Shops, and the Scottsdale Waterfront—is filled with tourist shops, galleries, boutiques, Native American crafts stores, and restaurants.

TEMPE Tempe is the home of Arizona State University and has lots of nightclubs and bars as well as all the other trappings of a university town. **Mill Avenue,** which has dozens of interesting shops along a stretch of about 4 blocks, is the center of activity both day and night. This is one of the few areas in the Valley where locals actually walk the streets and hang out at sidewalk cafes. (Old Town Scottsdale always has people on its streets, but few are locals.)

PARADISE VALLEY If Scottsdale is Phoenix's Beverly Hills, then Paradise Valley is its Bel-Air. This is the most exclusive community in the Valley and is almost entirely residential, but you won't see too many of the more lavish homes because they're set on large tracts of land.

MESA This eastern suburb of Phoenix is the Valley's main high-tech area. Large shopping malls, numerous inexpensive chain motels, a couple of small museums, and the beautiful Mesa Arts Center attract both locals and visitors to Mesa.

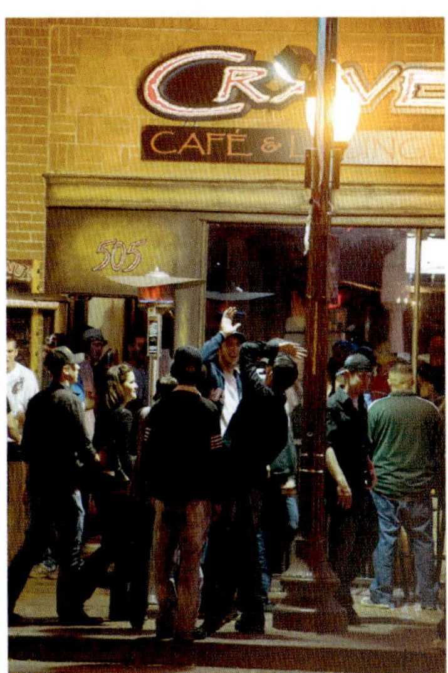

Mill Avenue buzzes on weekends with students from nearby Arizona State University.

Antiques shops line the streets of downtown Glendale.

CHANDLER Lying to the south of Tempe, this city has been booming over the past decade. New restaurants have opened, and the old downtown has had a bit of a face-lift. This area is of interest primarily to east Valley residents, but there is an attractive older resort right in downtown Chandler.

GLENDALE Located northwest of downtown Phoenix, Glendale has numerous historic buildings in its downtown, and with its dozens of antiques and collectibles stores, it has become the antiques capital of the Valley. The city is home to the Bead Museum, an interesting little specialty museum. This is also where you'll find the Arizona Cardinals' University of Phoenix Stadium and the Jobing.com Arena, home of the Phoenix Coyotes hockey team.

CAREFREE & CAVE CREEK About 20 miles north of Old Scottsdale, these two communities represent the Old West and the New West. Carefree is a planned community and home to the prestigious Boulders Resort and el Pedregal shopping center. Neighboring Cave Creek, on the other hand, plays up its Western heritage with contemporary cow-town architecture and a preponderance of saloons, steakhouses, and shops selling Western crafts and other gifts.

GETTING AROUND

By Car

Phoenix and the surrounding cities that together make up the Valley of the Sun sprawl across more than 400 square miles, so if you want to make the best use of your time, it's essential to have a car. Outside downtown Phoenix, there's almost always plenty of free parking wherever you go (although finding a parking space can be time-consuming in Old Scottsdale and at some of the more popular malls and shopping plazas). If you want to feel like a local, opt for the ubiquitous valet parking (just be sure to keep plenty of small bills on hand for tipping the parking attendants).

For the past few years Phoenix has had some of the highest car-rental rates in the country, and with taxes and surcharges at Sky Harbor Airport adding up to 50% or more, be prepared for sticker shock when you see what a 1-week car rental is going to run you. Expect to pay anywhere from $250 to $400 per week ($400–$600 with taxes) for a compact car in the high season. See chapter 12 for general tips on car rentals.

All major rental-car companies have desks at Sky Harbor Airport's Rental Car Center, which is separate from the airport terminals and is served by a free shuttle bus. Be sure to leave time in your schedule to get from the Rental Car Center to the correct terminal for your flight. There are also plenty of other car-rental offices in Phoenix and Scottsdale and you can sometimes save a bit on your rental by picking up your car someplace other than the airport. Rental-car companies at the airport include the following: **Advantage** (✆ 800/777-5500 or 602/252-2811; www.advantage.com), **Alamo** (✆ 877/222-9075 or 602/244-0897; www.alamo.com), **Avis** (✆ 800/331-1212 or 602/261-5900; www.avis.com), **Budget** (✆ 800/527-0700 or 602/261-5950; www.budget.com), **Dollar** (✆ 800/800-3665 or 866/434-2226; www.dollar.com), **Enterprise** (✆ 800/261-7331 or 602/225-0588; www.enterprise.com), **Fox** (✆ 800/225-4369; www.foxrentacar.com), **Hertz** (✆ 800/654-3131 or 602/267-8822; www.hertz.com), **National** (✆ 877/222-9058 or 602/275-4771; www.nationalcar.com), **Payless**

(✆ 800/729-5377 or 602/681-9589; www.paylesscar.com), and **Thrifty** (✆ 800/847-4389 or 877/283-0898; www.thrifty.com).

For a bit more style while you cruise from resort to golf course to nightclub, **Rent-a-Vette,** 1215 N. Scottsdale Rd., Scottsdale (✆ **888/308-5995** or 480/941-3001; www.exoticcarrentalsphoenix.com), charges $299 per day for a Corvette. It also rents Porsches, Mustangs, Camaros, Hummers, and a variety of Mercedes.

By Public Transportation

Unfortunately, **Valley Metro** (✆ **602/253-5000;** www.valleymetro.org), the Phoenix public bus system, is not very useful to tourists. It's primarily meant to be used by commuters. However, if you decide you want to take the bus, pick up a copy of the *Transit Book* at one of the tourist information desks in the airport (where it's sometimes available), at Central Station at the corner of Central Avenue and Van Buren Street, or at any Fry's supermarket. Local bus fare is $1.75; express bus fare is $2.75. Also available are 1-, 3-, and 7-day passes, and a monthly pass.

Of slightly more value to visitors is the free **Downtown Area Circulator (DASH),** which provides bus service within the downtown area Monday through Friday from 6:30am to 6:30pm. These buses serve regular stops every 12 minutes; they're primarily for downtown workers, but attractions along the route include the state capitol and Heritage and Science Park. In Tempe, **FLASH** buses provide a similar service on a loop around Arizona State University, including Mill Avenue and Sun Devil Stadium, Monday through Friday from 7am to 6pm; another loop operates Monday through Thursday from 7am to 1am and Friday from 7am to 10pm. For information on both DASH and FLASH, call ✆ **602/253-5000.**

In Scottsdale, the **Scottsdale Trolley** (✆ **480/421-1004;** www.scottsdaletrolley.com) shuttle buses run between Scottsdale Fashion Square, the Fifth Avenue shops, the Main Street Arts district, and the Old Town district. These buses run daily from 11am to 6pm (until 9pm on Thurs), with service every 15 minutes. Between early January and early April, free shuttles serve many of the area's resorts, including, among others, Camelback Inn, Sanctuary on Camelback, and the InterContinental Montelucia Resort & Spa. These trolleys operate Wednesday to Sunday from 11am to 4pm, with hourly service, and will take you to Scottsdale Fashion Square. From there you can take the Scottsdale Trolley to other shopping districts.

The area's most useful public-transit alternative is Valley Metro's **METRO light-rail system,** which runs along Central Avenue, through downtown Phoenix, and east to Tempe and Mesa. Attractions along or close to the line include the Heard Museum, Phoenix Art Museum, Historic Heritage Square, Phoenix Museum of History, Arizona Science Center, Pueblo Grande Museum and Archaeological Park, Desert Botanical Garden, Phoenix Zoo, Hall of Flame Firefighting Museum, Tempe's Mill Avenue shopping district, and the Arizona State University Art Museum. There is also a free airport shuttle that connects the 44th Street/Washington Street stop to the airport. For more information, contact Valley Metro (✆ **602/253-5000;** www.valleymetro.org).

By Taxi

Because distances in Phoenix are so great, the price of an ordinary taxi ride can be quite high. However, if you don't have your own wheels or had too much to drink and the bus isn't running because it's late at night or the weekend, you won't have any choice but to call a cab. **AAA Yellow Cab** (✆ **602/252-5252;** www.aaayellowaz.com) charges $2.50 for the first mile and $2 per mile thereafter. **Discount Cab** (✆ **602/200-2000;** www.discountcab.com) charges $2.95 for the first mile and $1.95 per mile after that. This latter company has a large fleet of hybrid vehicles, so if you want to go green when you call a cab, contact Discount.

[Fast FACTS] PHOENIX

American Express There's an American Express office at 2201 E. Camelback Rd. (✆ **602/468-1199;** www.amextravelresources.com). It's open Monday through Friday from 10am to 6pm and Saturday from 10am to 4pm.

Car Rentals See "Getting Around," above.

Dentist Call the **Dental Referral Service** (✆ **866/639-7444;** www.dentalreferral.com).

Doctor Call the **Banner Health Physician & Resource Line** (✆ **602/230-2273;** www.bannerhealth.com) for doctor referrals.

Emergencies For police, fire, or medical emergencies, phone ✆ **911.**

Eyeglass Repair **Nationwide Vision Centers** (www.nationwidevision.com) has locations around the Valley, including 7904 E. Chaparral Rd., Ste. A-108, Scottsdale (✆ **480/874-2543**); 4280 E. Indian School Rd., Ste. 107, Phoenix (✆ **602/952-8667**); and 2040 E. Rio Salado Pkwy., Ste. 120, Tempe (✆ **480/966-4992**).

Hospitals The **Banner Good Samaritan Medical Center,** 1111 E. McDowell Rd., Phoenix (✆ **602/839-2000;** www.bannerhealth.com), is one of the largest hospitals in the Valley.

Hot Lines The **Visitor Information Line** (✆ **602/252-5588**) has recorded tourist information on events in Phoenix and the Valley of the Sun.

Information See "Visitor Information," earlier in this chapter.

Internet Access If your hotel doesn't provide Internet access, your next best bet, if you aren't traveling with your own laptop, is to visit one of the **FedEx Offices** in the area. There are locations in downtown Phoenix at 201 E. Washington St. (✆ **602/252-4055**); off the Camelback Corridor at 3801 N. Central Ave. (✆ **602/241-9440**); and in Scottsdale just off Camelback Road at 4513 N. Scottsdale Rd. (✆ **480/946-0500**).

Lost Property If you lose something at the airport, call ✆ **602/273-3333;** for anything that was lost on a Valley Metro bus or the light rail, call ✆ **602/534-5053.**

Newspapers & Magazines The *Arizona Republic* (www.azcentral.com) is Phoenix's daily newspaper. The Thursday edition has a special section with schedules of the upcoming week's movie, music, and cultural performances. *New Times* is a free weekly journal with comprehensive listings of cultural events, films, clubs, and concert schedules. The best place to find *New Times* is at corner newspaper boxes in downtown Phoenix, Scottsdale, or Tempe.

Pharmacies Contact **Walgreens** (✆ **800/925-4733;** www.walgreens.com) for the Walgreens pharmacy that's nearest you; some are open 24 hours a day.

Police For police emergencies, phone ✆ **911.**

Post Office The **Phoenix Downtown Post Office,** 522 N. Central Ave. (✆ **602/253-9648**), is open Monday through Friday from 9am to 5:30pm. In Scottsdale, the **Scottsdale Post Office,** 1776 N. Scottsdale Rd.

(✆ **480/948-1448**), is open Monday through Friday from 8am to 5pm and Saturday from 9am to 4pm. For other locations, contact the **United States Postal Service** (✆ **800/ 275-8777;** www.usps.com).

Safety Don't leave valuables in view in your car, especially when parking in downtown Phoenix or at trail heads. Put anything of value in the trunk or under the seat. Take extra precautions after dark in the south-central Phoenix area and downtown. Violent acts of road rage have been all too common in Phoenix in the past, so it's a good idea to be polite when driving. Aggressive drivers should be given plenty of room.

Taxes State sales tax is 6.6% (plus variable local taxes, so expect to pay around 9%). Hotel room taxes vary considerably by city but are mostly between 12% and 15%. It's in renting a car that you really get pounded. The total taxes and surcharges when renting a car at Sky Harbor Airport add up to more than 50%.

Taxis See "Getting Around," above.

Weather For weather information, call ✆ **800/ 555-8355,** and say "weather."

WHERE TO STAY

Because the Phoenix area has long been popular as a winter refuge from cold and snow, it now has one of the greatest concentrations of resorts in the continental United States. However, even with all the hotel rooms here, sunshine and baseball's spring training combine to make it hard to find a room on short notice between February and April. If you plan to visit during these months, make your reservations as far in advance as possible. Also keep in mind that in late winter and early spring, the Phoenix metro area has some of the highest room rates in the country.

Most resorts offer a variety of weekend, golf, and tennis packages, as well as off-season discounts and corporate rates (which you can often get just by asking). I've given the official "rack rates," or walk-in rates, below, but it always pays to ask about special discounts or packages. Sometimes you can get a lower rate just by asking. If a hotel isn't full and isn't expected to be, you should be able to get a lower rate. Also, don't forget your AAA or AARP discounts if you belong to one of these organizations. Remember that business hotels downtown and near the airport often lower their rates on weekends. Also, don't forget to check hotel websites for special deals.

If you're looking to save even more money, consider traveling during the shoulder seasons of late spring and early fall. Temperatures are not at their midsummer highs, and room rates are often only slightly higher than they are during the summer slow season. If you'll be traveling with children, always ask whether your child will be able to stay free in your room, and whether there's a limit on the number of children who can stay free.

I prefer to request a room with a view of the mountains whenever possible. You can overlook a swimming pool anywhere, but some of the main selling points of Phoenix and Scottsdale hotels are the views of Mummy Mountain, Camelback Mountain, and Piestewa Peak.

With the exception of valet-parking services and parking garages at downtown convention hotels, parking is free at most Phoenix hotels. If there is a parking charge, I have noted it. You'll find that all hotels have nonsmoking rooms and all but the cheapest have wheelchair-accessible rooms.

BED & BREAKFASTS While most people dreaming of a Phoenix vacation have visions of luxury resorts dancing in their heads, there are some

Arizona Biltmore Resort & Spa **8**
Arizona Grand Resort **30**
Best Western Dobson Ranch Inn & Resort **29**
Best Western InnSuites Phoenix Biltmore/Scottsdale **2**
Best Western Papago Inn & Resort **25**
Best Western Sundial Resort **22**
The Buttes, a Marriott Resort **28**
Camelback Inn, a JW Marriott Resort & Spa **14**
Clarendon Hotel & Suites **4**
Clarion Hotel Scottsdale **20**
Crowne Plaza San Marcos Golf Resort **32**
Days Inn Scottsdale Resort at Fashion Square Mall **18**
Embassy Suites Biltmore **6**
Extended Stay Deluxe Phoenix-Biltmore **5**
Fairmont Scottsdale **11**
Fiesta Resort Conference Center **27**
FireSky Resort & Spa **21**
The Hermosa Inn **7**
Hotel Valley Ho **24**
Hyatt Place Scottsdale Old Town **23**
Hyatt Regency Scottsdale Resort & Spa at Gainey Ranch **12**
InterContinental Montelucia Resort & Spa **15**
Maricopa Manor **2**
The Phoenician **18**
Pointe Hilton Squaw Peak Resort **9**
Pointe Hilton Tapatio Cliffs Resort **1**
Royal Palms Resort and Spa **17**
Sanctuary on Camelback Mountain **16**
Scottsdale Resort & Athletic Club **13**
Sheraton Wild Horse Pass Resort & Spa **31**
Tempe Mission Palms Hotel **26**
Westin Kierland Resort & Spa **10**

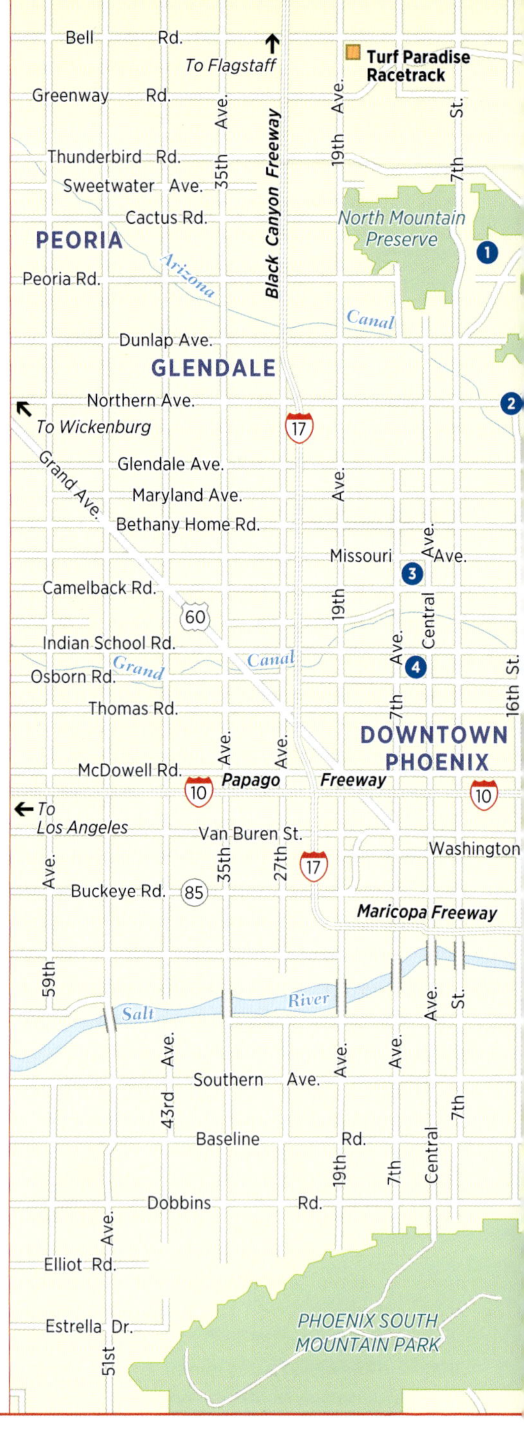

Hotels in Phoenix, Scottsdale & the Valley of the Sun
0
3 mi
0
3 km
Flagstaff
ARIZONA
Phoenix
Tucson
Bell Rd.
Greenway Rd.
Thunderbird Rd.
Sweetwater Ave.
Cactus Rd.
Shea Blvd.
Doubletree Ranch Rd.
Frank Lloyd Wright Blvd.
Cave Creek Rd.
32nd St.
Tatum Rd.
56th St.
Invergordon Rd.
Scottsdale Rd.
Hayden Rd.
Dreamy Draw Park
Phoenix Mountains Preserve
Piestewa Peak Park
Piestewa Freeway
PARADISE VALLEY
Indian Bend Rd.
Lincoln Dr.
McDonald Dr.
Camelback Mountain/ Echo Canyon Recreation Area
Pima Rd.
Pima Freeway
Camelback Rd.
Indian School Rd.
To Payson
Osborn Rd.
Thomas Rd.
SCOTTSDALE
Dobson Rd.
Beeline Hwy.
McDowell Rd.
Red Mountain Freeway
Papago Park
Van Buren St.
McKellips Rd.
MESA
Sky Harbor International Airport
Salt River
Hohokam Expy.
TEMPE
University Dr.
Apache Blvd.
Broadway Rd.
Main St.
Country Club Dr.
Mesa Dr.
Stapley Dr.
Priest Dr.
Mill Ave.
Southern Ave.
Superstition Freeway
Baseline Rd.
Guadalupe Rd.
Elliot Rd.
Warner Rd.
Ray Rd.
Rural Rd.
McClintock Dr.
Price Rd.
Price Freeway
Dobson Rd.
Alma School Rd.
Arizona Ave.
McQueen Rd.
Cooper Rd.
Maricopa Freeway
To Tucson
24th St.
40th St.
44th St.
48th St.
52nd St.
64th St.
68th St.
Miller Rd.
Hayden Rd.

bed-and-breakfasts around the Valley. **Mi Casa Su Casa** (✆ **800/456-0682** or 480/990-0682; www.azres.com) can book you into dozens of different homes in the Valley of the Sun, as can **Arizona Trails Travel Services** (✆ **888/799-4284** or 480/837-4284; www.arizonatrails.com), which also books tour and hotel reservations.

Scottsdale

With half a dozen or so resorts lined up along Scottsdale Road, the city of Scottsdale is the center of the Valley's resort scene. And because Scottsdale is also the Valley's main shopping and dining district, this is the most convenient place to stay if you're here to eat and shop. However, traffic in Scottsdale is bad, the landscape at most resorts is flat (compared with the hillside settings in north Scottsdale), and you don't get much of a feel for the desert.

VERY EXPENSIVE

Hyatt Regency Scottsdale Resort & Spa at Gainey Ranch ★★★ ☺ From the colonnades of palm trees to the lobby walls that slide away, this luxurious resort is designed to impress and continues to be my favorite Scottsdale resort. It's relatively close to downtown Scottsdale and has interesting architecture, beautiful grounds, and a large spa. What's not to love? A 2½-acre water playground serves as the resort's focal point, and the extravagant complex of 10 swimming pools includes a water slide, sand beach, and a huge whirlpool spa. Guest rooms are just as luxurious as the surroundings would suggest. The resort's Alto ristorante e bar features after-dinner gondola rides. The resort's Native American and Environmental Learning Center provides a glimpse into Sonoran Desert culture and ecology. Children's programs make this a super choice for families.

7500 E. Doubletree Ranch Rd., Scottsdale, AZ 85258. www.scottsdale.hyatt.com. ✆ **800/554-9288** or 480/444-1234. Fax 480/483-5550. 493 units. Jan to mid-May $399 double, from $900 suite and casita; mid-May to mid-Sept $129 double, from $500 suite and casita; mid-Sept to Dec $289 double, from $900 suite and casita. Rates do not include $20 resort fee. Children 18 and under stay free in parent's room. AE, DC, DISC, MC, V. Valet parking $27. Pets accepted ($50 fee). **Amenities:** 5 restaurants; 3 lounges; babysitting; bikes; children's programs; concierge; executive-level rooms; 27-hole golf course; health club & spa; 4 Jacuzzis; 10 pools; room service; 4 tennis courts. *In room:* A/C, TV, fridge, hair dryer, MP3 docking station, Wi-Fi (included in resort fee).

InterContinental Montelucia Resort & Spa ★★★ With the red rocks of Camelback Mountain looming overhead and architecture inspired by Spain's fabled Alhambra, this resort is one of Arizona's prettiest getaways. There are splashing fountains, a restaurant serving excellent Mediterranean cuisine, and a spa inspired by the *hammams* (public baths) of Morocco. Guest rooms continue the Spanish/Moroccan themes and are divided into five different "villages." If you like peace and quiet, ask for a room in the Bocce Garden Village (and have a bocce court right outside your door). Night owls should opt for a room in the Kasbah Village, which is close to the open-air lounge and the main pool. Throughout the property, you'll see fascinating Spanish antiquities, including two giant amphorae in the entry courtyard and huge wooden doors that lead to the resort's ballroom. Not too big, not too small, Montelucia is just right.

4949 E. Lincoln Dr., Paradise Valley, AZ 85253. www.icmontelucia.com. ✆ **888/627-3010** or 480/627-3200. 293 units. Jan–Apr $395–$845 double, $695–$4,000 suite; May to mid-June and mid-Sept to Dec $245–$625 double, $545–$3,000 suite; mid-June to mid-Sept $145–$425 double, $345–$2,000 suite. Rates do not include $24 daily resort fee. Children 18 and under stay free in parent's room. AE, DC, DISC, MC, V. Valet parking $19. Pets accepted ($100 fee). **Amenities:** 5 restaurants; snack bar; 2 lounges; babysitting; bikes; children's programs; concierge; exercise room and access to nearby health club; 2 Jacuzzis; 3 pools; room service; full-service spa. *In room:* A/C, TV, CD player, hair dryer, minibar, MP3 docking station, Wi-Fi ($13 per day).

JW Marriott Camelback Inn Resort & Spa ★★★ ☺ Set at the foot of Mummy Mountain and overlooking Camelback Mountain, the Camelback Inn, which opened in 1936, is one of the grande dames of the Phoenix hotel scene and abounds in traditional Southwestern character. Forget the glitz of the Phoenician (see below); this legendary retreat gives you old-school luxury with 21st-century enhancements. The two 18-hole golf courses are a magnet for golfers, and the spa is among the finest in the state. An extensive pool complex appeals to families. Guest rooms, which are spread over the sloping grounds, are decorated with Southwestern furnishings and art, and all have balconies or patios. Some rooms even have private pools. This is an old-money getaway that seamlessly melds tradition with modern amenities.

5402 E. Lincoln Dr., Scottsdale, AZ 85253. www.camelbackinn.com. ✆ **800/242-2635** or 480/948-1700. Fax 480/951-8469. 453 units. Jan to early June $299–$549 double, $570–$2,500 suite; early June to early Sept $179–$199 double, $260–$900 suite; early Sept to Dec $349–$459 double, $595–$1,700 suite. Rates do not include $13 daily resort fee. Children 17 and under stay free in parent's room. AE, DC, DISC, MC, V. Small pets accepted (fee varies). **Amenities:** 7 restaurants; 3 lounges; babysitting; bikes; children's programs; concierge; two 18-hole golf courses; health club; 3 Jacuzzis; 2 pools; room service; full-service spa; 6 tennis courts. *In room:* A/C, TV, CD player, hair dryer, kitchenette, minibar, MP3 docking station, Wi-Fi (included in resort fee).

The Phoenician ★★★ ☺ Situated on 250 acres at the foot of Camelback Mountain, this palatial getaway is one of the world's finest resorts. So, if you must stay at the very best, this is it. Polished marble and sparkling crystal abound in the lobby, but the view through a wall of glass is what commands most guests' attention when they first arrive. The resort has a classic, international character, and service is second to none. The pool complex, with its water slide for the kids, is irresistibly seductive, and the resort's Centre for Well Being offers all the spa pampering anyone could ever want. There are also 27 holes of golf. The luxurious guest rooms have large patios and sunken tubs for two. For the ultimate in luxury, book a room in the Canyon Suites, a separate boutique hotel within the resort. J&G Steakhouse is operated by Jean-Georges Vongerichten.

6000 E. Camelback Rd., Scottsdale, AZ 85251. www.thephoenician.com. ✆ **800/888-8234** or 480/941-8200. Fax 480/947-4311. 643 units. Jan–May from $469 double, from $869 suite; June to mid-Sept from $179 double, from $479 suite; mid-Sept to Dec from $349 double, from $749 suite. Children 17 and under stay free in parent's room. AE, DC, DISC, MC, V. Valet parking $29. Pets accepted ($150 deposit). **Amenities:** 3 restaurants; 4 snack bars/cafes; 5 lounges; babysitting; bikes; children's programs; concierge; executive-level rooms; 27-hole golf course; health club and spa; 2 Jacuzzis; 9 pools; room service; 11 tennis courts. *In room:* A/C, TV, CD player, hair dryer, minibar, Wi-Fi ($13 per day).

Sanctuary on Camelback Mountain ★★★ This visually breathtaking place was the Valley's first hip resort, and I still like the contemporary rooms here better than those at other hip hotels around town. Located high on the northern flanks of Camelback Mountain, the lushly landscaped property has unforgettable views across the Valley, especially from its restaurant and two bars. The extremely spacious guest rooms are divided between the more conservative deluxe casitas and the boldly contemporary spa casitas. With their dyed-cement floors, L-shaped couches, and streamline-modern cabinetry, these latter units are absolutely stunning. Bathrooms are huge, and some have private outdoor soaking tubs. The resort's spa is gorgeous. So seductive is this resort that it has become a favorite of celebrities.

5700 E. McDonald Dr., Paradise Valley, AZ 85253. www.sanctuaryaz.com. ✆ **800/245-2051** or 480/948-2100. 111 units. Jan to mid-May and late Dec $520–$725 double, $650–$1,580 suite; mid-May to mid-Sept $235–$415 double, $340–$935 suite; mid-Sept to mid-Dec $415–$620 double, $545–$1,370 suite. Rates do not include $18 daily resort fee. Children 17 and under stay free in parent's room. AE, DC, DISC, MC, V. Pets accepted ($100 fee). **Amenities:** Restaurant, elements (review, p. 134); 1 lounge; bikes; concierge; exercise room and access to nearby health club; 2 Jacuzzis; 4 pools; room service; sauna; full-service spa; 5 tennis courts. *In room:* A/C, TV/DVD, hair dryer, minibar, Wi-Fi (included in resort fee).

EXPENSIVE

Hotel Valley Ho ★★ This Scottsdale hotel dates back to the 1950s, but in 2005, it got a complete face-lift. What a looker it is now. The Valley Ho is one of my favorite Scottsdale hotels; it's hip and convenient, and has loads of outdoor space for soaking up the sun. I love the big rooms, which are done in a bold contemporary style. The studio rooms are my favorites; they have curtains to partition off the vanity area and an ultracool free-standing tub. Big balconies and patios provide plenty of space for lounging outdoors. When it's time to get even more relaxed, grab one of the plush, circular lounge chairs at the pool. For a totally retro experience, there's even a Trader Vic's Polynesian restaurant here.

6850 E. Main St., Scottsdale, AZ 85251. www.hotelvalleyho.com. ✆ **866/882-4484** or 480/248-2000. Fax 480/248-2002. 231 units. Jan–Apr $229–$309 double, $399–$999 suite; May and Sept $159–$259 double, $289–$689 suite; June–Aug $99–$179 double, $199–$399 suite; Oct–Dec $189–$299 double, $329–$729 suite. Children 17 and under stay free in parent's room. AE, DC, DISC, MC, V. Valet parking $14. Pets accepted. **Amenities:** 3 restaurants; 3 lounges; babysitting; bikes; concierge; executive-level rooms; exercise room and access to nearby health club; 2 Jacuzzis; pool; room service; full-service spa. *In room:* A/C, TV, hair dryer, minibar, Wi-Fi ($15 per day).

Hyatt Place Scottsdale/Old Town ★ With a great location in the heart of downtown Scottsdale, this hip business hotel is well worth choosing even if you're in town on vacation. The guest rooms are all spacious suites done in a homey, contemporary style with separate sitting and sleeping areas and 42-inch wall-hung flat-panel TVs that can be angled to either area. Unusual features include electronic self-service check-in kiosks, continental (free) or hot (charge) breakfasts, and a tiny lounge area to one side of the lobby. You can even get a light meal here if you don't feel like going out to a restaurant for dinner.

7300 E. 3rd Ave., Scottsdale, AZ 85251. www.hyattplace.com. ✆ **888/492-8847** or 480/423-9944. Fax 480/423-2991. 127 units. $99–$329 double. Rates include continental breakfast. Children 17 and under stay free in parent's room. AE, DC, DISC, MC, V. **Amenities:** Restaurant; lounge; exercise room and access to nearby health club; outdoor pool. *In room:* A/C, TV, fridge, hair dryer, free Wi-Fi.

Westin Kierland Resort & Spa ★★★ ☺ A convenient location and a distinct sense of place make this one of my favorite Phoenix-area resorts. Located just off Scottsdale Road adjacent to the Kierland Commons shopping center, the resort features artwork by Arizona artists, numerous interpretive plaques, and historical photos that provide insight into Arizona's cultural and natural history.

Guest rooms all have balconies or patios, and you should be sure to request a room overlooking the golf course. Of course, there are also Westin's incredibly comfortable pillow-top mattresses. Excellent Nuevo Latino cuisine is served at deseo (p. 118), and there's a great cowboy-style bar as well. The main pool area includes a long tubing river, a water slide, and a beach area. The bagpiper at sunset is not to be missed.

6902 E. Greenway Pkwy., Scottsdale, AZ 85254. www.kierlandresort.com. ✆ **800/937-8461** or 480/624-1000. Fax 480/624-1001. 732 units. Jan–Mar $289–$699 double; Apr–June $239–$489 double; July to mid-Sept $149–$349 double; mid-Sept to Dec $239–$529 double. Rates do not include $19 daily resort fee. Children 18 and under stay free in parent's room. AE, DISC, MC, V. Valet parking $27. Pets accepted. **Amenities:** 8 restaurants, including deseo (review, p. 118); 4 lounges; babysitting; children's programs; concierge; executive-level rooms; 27-hole golf course; health club and full-service spa; 3 Jacuzzis; 4 pools; room service; 2 tennis courts. *In room:* A/C, TV, hair dryer, minibar, Wi-Fi (included in resort fee).

MODERATE

Best Western Plus Sundial Resort ★ Throw away any preconceived ideas you have about Best Western hotels; this conveniently located little resort boasts boldly contemporary styling in its guest rooms. There are black granite counters and wall-hung TVs. A wide variety of room types provide plenty of options. Twelve rooms use signs of the zodiac for their theme, and other rooms have in-room whirlpool tubs set under walls of glass block. There are suites with sunrooms and large patios and high-ceilinged "bungalow"-style rooms. Old Town Scottsdale is about a 20-minute walk away, and the Waterfront, the gallery district, and Scottsdale Fashion Square are even closer.

7320 E. Camelback Rd., Scottsdale, AZ 85251. www.bestwesternarizona.com. ✆ **800/937-8376** or 480/994-4170. Fax 480/659-3925. 54 units. Oct–Apr $150–$230 double, $210–$310 suite; May–Sept $80–$130 double, $150–$200 suite. Rates include full breakfast. Children 16 and under stay free in parent's room. AE, DC, DISC, MC, V. Pets accepted ($25 per night). **Amenities:** Concierge; exercise room and access to nearby health club; Jacuzzi; outdoor pool. *In room:* A/C, TV, fridge, hair dryer, MP3 docking station, free Wi-Fi.

FireSky Resort & Spa ★★ An exceptional location in the heart of the Scottsdale shopping district, a dramatic Southwestern contemporary styling (the focal point of the lobby is an impressive sandstone fireplace), and a small but well-designed pool area are the main reasons I like this little resort. Set in a lushly planted courtyard are a small lagoon-style pool, complete with sand beach and waterfall, and a second pool with flame-topped columnar waterfalls. An artificial stream and faux sandstone ruins add up to a lush desert fantasy landscape (although not on the grand scale to be found at some area resorts). The guest rooms are quite comfortable, and there's a pretty little spa on the premises.

4925 N. Scottsdale Rd., Scottsdale, AZ 85251. www.fireskyresort.com. ✆ **800/528-7867** or 480/945-7666. Fax 480/946-4056. 204 units. Jan to mid-Apr $189 double, $599 suite; mid-Apr to May $159 double, $499 suite; June–Aug $109 double, $325 suite; Sept–Dec $159 double, $499 suite. Children 18 and under stay free in parent's room. AE, DISC, MC, V. Pets accepted. **Amenities:** Restaurant; lounge; concierge; exercise room and access to nearby health club; Jacuzzi; 2 pools; room service; full-service spa. *In room:* A/C, TV, hair dryer, minibar, MP3 docking station, Wi-Fi ($10 per day).

Scottsdale Resort & Athletic Club ★★ Fitness fanatics, rejoice; this club's for you. If you can't stand the thought of giving up your workout just because you're on vacation, book a stay at this little boutique hotel (and timeshare resort) just off busy Scottsdale Road and adjacent to the Silverado Golf Course. With standard rooms and huge one-, two-, and three-bedroom "villas," this place is plenty comfortable, but the main reason I like this hotel is that it's affiliated with the Scottsdale Athletic Club, a large workout facility that emphasizes its tennis program. The basic rooms are a real steal for Scottsdale, and while the villas are quite a bit more expensive, they're gigantic and have fireplaces, DVD players, full kitchens, and washers and dryers. On top of all this, you get a view of Camelback Mountain.

8235 E. Indian Bend Rd., Scottsdale, AZ 85250. www.scottsdaleresortandathleticclub.com. ✆ **877/343-0033** or 480/344-0600. Fax 480/344-0650. 85 units. Late Dec to mid-Apr $159 double, $189–$609 suite or villa; mid-Apr to May and mid-Sept to late Dec $139 double, $169–$579 suite or villa; June to mid-Sept $89 double, $109–$259 suite or villa. Rates include continental breakfast. Children 11 and under stay free in parent's room. AE, DISC, MC, V. Pets accepted ($100 deposit). **Amenities:** Restaurant; lounge; babysitting; children's programs; concierge; health club; 2 Jacuzzis; 3 pools; room service; sauna; full-service spa; 11 tennis courts. *In room:* A/C, TV/DVD, CD player, fridge, hair dryer, free Wi-Fi.

INEXPENSIVE

Despite the high-priced real estate, Scottsdale does have a few relatively inexpensive chain motels, although during the winter season, prices are higher than you might expect. For location alone, your best choice would be the **Motel 6–Scottsdale,** 6848 E. Camelback Rd. (✆ **480/946-2280**), which has doubles for $76 to $79 during the high season.

Best Western Papago Inn & Resort Located just east of Scottsdale Road, adjacent to a shopping center with a distinctive contemporary Santa Fe styling, this older hotel may not be fancy, but it has a pretty courtyard with green lawns and a large aviary full of parakeets and other species of birds. The courtyard layout gives the hotel a somewhat secluded feeling; you'd never know there's a busy four-lane road out front. Guest rooms have been remodeled in recent years and have modern furnishings and pillow-top mattresses. Both downtown Tempe and Papago Park, which is home to the Desert Botanical Garden and Phoenix Zoo, are only a mile away.

7017 E. McDowell Rd., Scottsdale, AZ 85257-3313. www.bestwestern.com. ✆ **866/806-4400** or 480/947-7335. Fax 480/994-0692. 58 units. $60–$130 double. Children 17 and under stay free in parent's room. AE, DC, DISC, MC, V. **Amenities:** Restaurant; lounge; exercise room; outdoor pool. *In room:* A/C, TV, hair dryer, free Wi-Fi.

Clarion Hotel Scottsdale ★ With a very pleasant pool area in a palm-shaded courtyard and rooms that were redone in a sort of Spanish colonial style a few years ago, this renovated hotel is a good choice close to Old Town Scottsdale. The courtyard, with its palm and olive trees, is the main reason to stay here, but the stylish lounge and restaurant also add to the appeal. Although they cost a bit extra, the pool-view rooms are worth requesting.

5101 N. Scottsdale Rd., Scottsdale, AZ 85250. www.clarionhotel.com. ✆ **877/424-6423** or 480/945-4392. Fax 480/947-3044. 211 units. Jan–Apr $100–$200 double, $180–$230 suite; May–Dec $55–$120 double, $110–$150 suite. Children 17 and under stay free in parent's room. AE, DC, DISC, MC, V. Pets accepted ($250 deposit plus $25 per night). **Amenities:** Restaurant; lounge; exercise room; Jacuzzi; small outdoor pool; room service. *In room:* A/C, TV, hair dryer, MP3 docking station, free Wi-Fi.

Days Inn Scottsdale Resort at Fashion Square Mall This is one of the last economical hotels in the Old Town Scottsdale area, and its location adjacent to the Scottsdale Fashion Square Mall makes it a great choice for shopaholics. The Days Inn may be just an aging chain motel, but its green lawns, pool, tall palm trees, and a convenient downtown location all make it worth recommending, particularly for families.

4710 N. Scottsdale Rd., Scottsdale, AZ 85251. www.daysinn.com. ✆ **800/544-8313** or 480/947-5411. Fax 480/946-1324. 167 units. Jan–Mar $90–$110 double; Apr–Dec $60–$90 double. Rates include continental breakfast. Children 17 and under stay free in parent's room. AE, DC, DISC, MC, V. Pets accepted ($25 fee). **Amenities:** Seasonal poolside bar; Jacuzzi; small outdoor pool. *In room:* A/C, TV, fridge, hair dryer, free Wi-Fi.

North Scottsdale, Carefree & Cave Creek

With great golf courses, superb restaurants, rugged desert scenery, and a bit of Western character, this area gets my vote for best place to get away from it all, soak up some sun, and get to know the desert. The one caveat is that the resorts in this area are a 30-minute drive from downtown Scottsdale (longer during rush hour).

VERY EXPENSIVE

The Boulders Resort ★★★ Set amid a jumble of giant boulders 45 minutes north of downtown Scottsdale, this was the first luxury golf resort in the north Valley's rugged foothills. The adobe buildings blend unobtrusively into the desert, and the two golf courses epitomize the desert golf course experience. When not golfing, you can lounge by the small pool, play tennis, relax at the resort's Golden Door Spa, or even try rock climbing. The lobby is in a Santa Fe–style building with tree-trunk pillars and a flagstone floor, and the guest rooms continue the pueblo styling with beehive fireplaces and beamed ceilings. For the best views, ask for one of the second-floor units. Bathrooms are large and luxuriously appointed, with tubs for two and separate showers. The Boulders emphasizes organic ingredients in its restaurants.

34631 N. Tom Darlington Dr. (P.O. Box 2090), Carefree, AZ 85377. www.theboulders.com. ✆ **888/579-2631** or 480/488-9009. Fax 480/488-4118. 215 units. Late Dec to May from $259 double, from $599 villa; May to early Sept from $129 double, from $399 villa; early Sept to late Dec from $199 double, from $499 villa. Rates do not include $30 daily service charge. Children 18 and under stay free in parent's room. AE, DC, DISC, MC, V. Pets accepted ($100 fee). **Amenities:** 6 restaurants; 2 lounges; babysitting; bikes; concierge; two 18-hole golf courses; health club and full-service spa; 4 Jacuzzis; 4 pools; room service; 8 tennis courts. *In room:* A/C, TV/DVD, CD player, hair dryer, minibar, MP3 docking station, Wi-Fi (included in service charge).

Fairmont Scottsdale ★★★ I know this faux Moorish palace belongs in Spain, not Arizona, but I still love it. With its royal palms, tiled fountains, and waterfalls, the Fairmont offers an exotic atmosphere that will delight anyone in search of a getaway that doesn't entail learning Spanish or spending euros. A water playground (with two water slides) and a kids' fishing pond also make this resort a hit with families. The resort, a 20-minute drive from Old Town Scottsdale, is home to the Waste Management Phoenix Open golf tournament, which means the fairways here are top-notch. Guest rooms are done in contemporary Southwestern style, and bathrooms have double vanities and separate showers and tubs. All units have private balconies. For stepped-up amenities, opt for a room in the Gold wing. There's also the Willow Stream spa (p. 174), and the resort offers an eco-education program that includes guided hikes.

7575 E. Princess Dr., Scottsdale, AZ 85255. www.fairmont.com/scottsdale. ✆ **800/344-4758** or 480/585-4848. Fax 480/585-0091. 649 units. $149–$499 double; $349–$2,999 suite. Children 17 and under stay free in parent's room. AE, DISC, MC, V. Valet parking $20; self-parking $10. Pets accepted ($25 per night). **Amenities:** 4 restaurants; 4 lounges; babysitting; bikes; children's programs; concierge; executive-level rooms; two 18-hole golf courses; exercise room; 3 Jacuzzis; 5 pools; room service; full-service spa; 7 tennis courts. *In room:* A/C, TV, hair dryer, minibar, MP3 docking station, Wi-Fi ($15 per day).

Four Seasons Resort Scottsdale at Troon North ★★★ In the foothills of north Scottsdale adjacent to (and with privileges at) the legendary Troon North golf course, the Four Seasons is even more impressive than the nearby Boulders Resort. This superluxurious resort may not feel as expansive as the Boulders, but in every other aspect it is superior. With casita accommodations scattered across a boulder-strewn hillside, the Four Seasons boasts one of the Valley's most dramatic settings, and with a hiking trail to nearby Pinnacle Peak Park, the resort is a good choice for anyone who wants to explore the desert on foot. Guest rooms and suites are among the most lavish you'll find in Arizona. If you can afford it, opt for one with a private plunge pool and an outdoor shower—a luxury usually found only in tropical resorts.

10600 E. Crescent Moon Dr., Scottsdale, AZ 85262. www.fourseasons.com/scottsdale. ✆ **888/207-9696** or 480/515-5700. Fax 480/515-5599. 210 units. Jan–May $325–$645 double, $875–$5,800 suite; June–Aug $205–$280 double, $530–$3,200 suite; Sept–Dec $225–$395 double, $530–$3,200 suite. Children 18 and under stay free in parent's room. AE, DC, DISC, MC, V. Valet parking $27; self-parking $10. Small pets accepted. **Amenities:** 3 restaurants; 2 lounges; babysitting; children's programs; concierge; two 18-hole golf courses; health club and spa; Jacuzzi; 3 pools (including large 2-level pool); room service; 2 tennis courts. *In room:* A/C, TV/DVD, CD player, hair dryer, minibar, MP3 docking station, Wi-Fi ($10 per day).

EXPENSIVE

Radisson Fort McDowell Resort & Casino ★★ In the Scottsdale area, you just can't stay any closer to the desert than at this beautiful resort northeast of Fountain Hills. Although the Radisson is a 30-minute drive from downtown Scottsdale, the location is hard to beat if you've come to the area to experience the desert. The resort is on the Fort McDowell Yavapai Nation, and the tribe's Fort McDowell Casino is a big draw for many guests. However, the two 18-hole courses at the adjacent We-Ko-Pa Golf Club are also major draws here. Personally, I like the resort best for its creative Native American styling and its great desert and mountain views. For families, there's a children's water-play area and horseback riding, and, in summer, float trips down the nearby Verde River can be arranged.

10438 N. Fort McDowell Rd., Fountain Hills, AZ 85264. www.radisson.com/ftmcdowellaz. ✆ **800/333-3333** or 480/789-5300. Fax 480/789-5333. 248 units. Jan–Mar $269–$299 double; Apr $199–$210 double; May, Sept, and Dec $139–$159 double; June–Aug $109–$139 double; Oct–Nov $219–$239 double. Children 11 and under stay free in parent's room. AE, DC, DISC, MC, V. Pets accepted. **Amenities:** Restaurant; snack bar; lounge; babysitting; concierge; two 18-hole golf courses; health club; 2 Jacuzzis; 2 outdoor pools; room service; full-service spa. *In room:* A/C, TV, hair dryer, minibar, free Wi-Fi.

MODERATE

Inn at Eagle Mountain ★ This secluded, residential-style hotel is 15 minutes east of U.S. 101 and just off Shea Boulevard near the town of Fountain Hills, and while the location is a bit out of the way, the hillside setting, valley views, spacious accommodations, and adjacent golf course make this a good choice. Rooms, of which there are several styles and sizes, have simple Southwestern-inspired furniture. All the rooms have gas fireplaces and large bathrooms with Jacuzzi tubs. There are also balconies and patios. The pool overlooks a small lake on the golf course. There's a desert preserve with hiking trails nearby, but it's at least a 15-minute drive to good restaurants.

9800 N. Summer Hill Blvd., Fountain Hills, AZ 85268. www.innateaglemountain.com. ✆ **800/992-8083** or 480/816-3000. Fax 480/816-3090. 43 units. Jan, Apr, and Oct–Nov $129–$209 double; Feb–Mar $149–$239 double; June–Aug $69–$159 double; May, Sept, and Dec $89–$179 double. Children 17 and under stay free in parent's room. AE, DC, DISC, MC, V. **Amenities:** Restaurant; lounge; concierge; 18-hole golf course; access to nearby health club; Jacuzzi; outdoor pool. *In room:* A/C, TV/VCR, fridge, hair dryer, free Wi-Fi.

Central Phoenix & the Camelback Corridor

This area is the heart of the upscale Phoenix shopping and restaurant scene and is home to the prestigious Arizona Biltmore resort. Old money and new money rub shoulders along the avenues here, and valet parking is de rigueur. Located roughly midway between Old Scottsdale and downtown Phoenix, this area is a good bet for those intending to split their time between the downtown Phoenix cultural and sports district and the world-class shopping and dining in Scottsdale.

VERY EXPENSIVE

Arizona Biltmore ★★★ ☺ For more than 80 years, this resort has been the favored Phoenix address of celebrities, politicians, and old money, and the distinctive cast-cement blocks inspired by a Frank Lloyd Wright design make it a unique architectural gem. However, it's the historical character and timeless elegance that really set this place apart. With wide lawns, colorful flower gardens, and views of Piestewa Peak, this is a resort for outdoor lounging. While the two golf courses and expansive spa are the main draws, the children's activities center and lawn games make this a popular choice for families. Of the several different styles of accommodations, the "resort rooms" are quite comfortable and have balconies or patios. Those rooms in the Paradise Wing are also good choices. Afternoon tea is served in the lobby Thursday through Sunday.

2400 E. Missouri Ave., Phoenix, AZ 85016. www.arizonabiltmore.com. ✆ **800/950-0086** or 602/955-6600. Fax 602/381-7600. 738 units. Jan to mid-May $499–$639 double, from $679 suite; mid-May to early Sept $259–$359 double, from $389 suite; early Sept to Dec $399–$559 double, from $589 suite. Rates do not include $28 daily service fee. Children 18 and under stay free in parent's room. AE, DC, DISC, MC, V. Valet parking $27; self-parking $12. Pets under 50 lb. accepted in cottage rooms ($100 deposit, $50 nonrefundable). **Amenities:** 4 restaurants; 3 lounges; bikes; children's programs; concierge; executive-level rooms; two 18-hole golf courses; health club and full-service spa; 6 Jacuzzis; 8 pools; room service; saunas; 7 tennis courts. *In room:* A/C, TV, fridge, hair dryer, free Internet, minibar, MP3 docking station.

Royal Palms Resort and Spa ★★ This gorgeous little hideaway has the feel of a Spanish villa and is so romantic and beautiful that the moment you set foot in the first cloistered garden, you might imagine that you hear flamenco music. Located midway between Old Town Scottsdale and Biltmore Fashion Park, the Royal Palms was constructed more than 80 years ago by Cunard Steamship executive Delos Cooke and is done in Spanish mission style. Giving the resort the tranquil feel of a Mediterranean monastery are lush walled gardens where antique water fountains splash. The most memorable guest rooms are the designer casitas, each with a distinctive decor ranging from opulent contemporary to classic European. However, all the rooms are beautiful and have super-plush beds. T. Cook's restaurant is one of the city's most romantic restaurants (see "Where to Eat," later in this chapter).

5200 E. Camelback Rd., Phoenix, AZ 85018. www.royalpalmsresortandspa.com. ✆ **800/672-6011** or 602/840-3610. Fax 602/840-6927. 119 units. Jan–May $359–$549 double, $409–$2,549 suite; June to mid-Sept $169–$329 double, $179–$2,329 suite; mid-Sept to Dec $239–$499 double, $239–$2,499 suite. Rates do not include $25 daily service fee. Children 17 and under stay free in parent's room. AE, DC, DISC, MC, V. Pets accepted ($300 deposit, $100 nonrefundable). **Amenities:** 2 restaurants, including T. Cook's (see review, p. 126); 2 lounges; babysitting; concierge; exercise room; Jacuzzi; outdoor pool w/cabanas; room service; full-service spa. *In room:* A/C, TV/VCR, CD player, hair dryer, minibar, free Wi-Fi.

EXPENSIVE

Embassy Suites Biltmore ★ Located across the parking lot from the Biltmore Fashion Park shopping center, this hotel makes a great base if you want to be within walking distance of half a dozen good restaurants. The atrium is filled with interesting tile work, tropical greenery, waterfalls, and ponds filled with koi (colorful Japanese carp). In the atrium, you'll also find a romantic lounge with huge banquettes shaded by palm trees. All in all, this hotel is a good value, especially when you consider that rates include both breakfast and afternoon drinks.

2630 E. Camelback Rd., Phoenix, AZ 85016. www.phoenixbiltmore.embassysuites.com. ✆ **800/362-2779** or 602/955-3992. Fax 602/955-6479. 232 units. Jan–Mar $289 double; Apr to late May $239 double; late May to mid-Sept $199 double; mid-Sept to Dec $269 double. Rates include full breakfast and afternoon drinks. Children 18 and under stay free in parent's room. AE, DC, DISC, MC, V. Parking $8. Pets accepted ($45 fee). **Amenities:** Restaurant; lounge; babysitting; bikes; concierge; exercise room; Jacuzzi; outdoor pool; room service. *In room:* A/C, TV, fridge, hair dryer, Wi-Fi ($15 per day).

The Hermosa Inn ★★ With cactus gardens, tall palms, mesquite trees, green lawns, and colorful flower gardens, this luxurious boutique hideaway is one of the few hotels in the Valley to offer any Old Arizona atmosphere. Set on 6 acres in the wealthy residential community of Paradise Valley, the Hermosa Inn is built around the 1930s adobe home of cowboy artist Lon Megargee. The rooms, most of which are quite large, have a luxurious modern ranch feeling. Huge bathrooms, with large walk-in showers and deep bathtubs, are a highlight. Most rooms also have gas fireplaces and big patios for enjoying the garden setting. With its quiet, laid-back feeling, great restaurant, and pretty gardens, the Hermosa Inn is a sure bet for a relaxing getaway.

5532 N. Palo Cristi Rd., Paradise Valley, AZ 85253. www.hermosainn.com. ✆ **800/241-1210** or 602/955-8614. Fax 602/955-8299. 34 units. Jan to May $239–$459 double; June–Aug $189–$369 double; Sept–Dec $239–$459 double. Children 12 and under stay free in parent's room. AE, DISC, MC, V. Take 32nd St. north from Camelback Rd., turn right on Stanford Rd., and turn left on N. Palo Cristi Rd. From Lincoln Dr., turn south on N. Palo Cristi Rd. (east of 32nd St.). Pets accepted ($100 fee). **Amenities:** Restaurant, LON's at the Hermosa (see review, p. 126); lounge; babysitting; bikes; concierge; access to nearby health club; 2 Jacuzzis; outdoor pool; room service; spa. *In room:* A/C, TV, CD player, fridge, hair dryer, free Wi-Fi.

Maricopa Manor Centrally located between downtown Phoenix and Scottsdale, Maricopa Manor, which has long been Phoenix's best B&B, is just a block from both Camelback Road and a light-rail station. The inn's main building, designed to resemble a Spanish manor house, was built in 1928, and the orange trees, palms, and large yard all lend an Old Phoenix atmosphere. All guest rooms are large, comfortable suites, and some have gas fireplaces, jetted tubs, and Arts and Crafts touches. All the suites have kitchenettes, and some have two separate sleeping areas. Breakfast is delivered to your door, and you can eat in your room or at tables in the garden.

15 W. Pasadena Ave., Phoenix, AZ 85013. www.maricopamanor.com. ✆ **800/292-6403** or 602/264-9204. Fax 602/264-9204. 6 units. Mid-Dec to mid-Apr $189–$239 double; mid-Apr to mid-June and Nov to mid-Dec $149–$189 double; mid-Sept to Oct $139–$169 double; mid-June to mid-Sept $129 double. Rates include full breakfast. Children 12 and under stay free in parent's room. AE, DC, DISC, MC, V. Pets accepted. **Amenities:** Access to nearby health club; Jacuzzi; seasonal outdoor pool. *In room:* A/C, TV/VCR/DVD, CD player, hair dryer, kitchenette, free Wi-Fi.

INEXPENSIVE

Extended Stay Deluxe Phoenix-Biltmore Billing itself as a temporary residence and located just north of Camelback Road not far from Biltmore Fashion Park, this hotel consists of studio-style apartments and offers discounts for stays of 7 days or more. Although designed primarily for corporate business travelers on temporary assignment in the area, this lodging makes a good choice for families as well. All units have full kitchens, big bathrooms, and separate sitting areas. Keep in mind that you only get maid service if you pay $5 to $10 extra per day or stay for a week or more.

5235 N. 16th St., Phoenix, AZ 85016. www.extendedstaydeluxe.com. ✆ **800/804-3724** or 602/265-6800. Fax 602/265-1114. 112 units. $63–$78 double. Rates include continental breakfast. Children 16 and under stay free in parent's room. AE, DC, DISC, MC, V. Pets accepted ($25 per night, $150 maximum). **Amenities:** Exercise room; Jacuzzi; small outdoor pool. *In room:* A/C, TV, hair dryer, kitchen, MP3 docking station, Wi-Fi ($5 per stay).

North Phoenix

Some of the Valley's best scenery is in north Phoenix, where several small mountains have been protected as parks and preserves; the two Pointe Hilton resorts claim great locations close to these parks. So, if you're looking for quick access to desert trails, the resorts here are good choices. However, the Valley's best shopping and dining, as well as most major attractions, are all at least a 30-minute drive away.

VERY EXPENSIVE

JW Marriott Desert Ridge Resort & Spa ★★ This is the largest resort in the state and stays crowded with conference and convention groups. Because it is miles from any other resorts, high-end shopping areas, or concentrations of good restaurants, Desert Ridge is primarily a place to stay put and spend your days sitting in the sun drinking margaritas by the pool. To this end, there are 4 acres of water features and pools (including a tubing "river"). At the grand entrance, desert landscaping and rows of palm trees give the resort a sense of place, and the lobby's roll-up walls let plenty of balmy desert air in during the cooler months. Guest rooms have balconies and hints of Mediterranean styling. Be sure to ask for a room with a view to the south; these rooms look out to several of Phoenix's mountain preserves.

5350 E. Marriott Blvd., Phoenix, AZ 85054. www.jwdesertridgeresort.com. ✆ **800/835-6206** or 480/293-5000. Fax 480/293-3600. 950 units. Jan–Apr $369–$429 double; May to mid-Sept $189–$309 double; mid-Sept to Dec $299–$369 double. Rates do not include $25 resort fee. Children 17 and under stay free in parent's room. AE, DC, DISC, MC, V. Valet parking $25; self-parking $10. **Amenities:** 5 restaurants; 2 snack bars/cafes; 5 lounges; babysitting; bikes; children's programs; concierge; executive-level rooms; two 18-hole golf courses; health club and full-service spa; 5 Jacuzzis; 5 pools; room service; 8 tennis courts. *In room:* A/C, TV, hair dryer, minibar, Wi-Fi ($13 per day).

MODERATE

Pointe Hilton Squaw Peak Resort ★★ ☺ At the foot of the Phoenix Mountains, this lushly landscaped resort makes a big splash with its 4-acre Hole-in-the-Wall River Ranch aquatic playground, which features a tubing "river," water slide, waterfall, sports pool, and lagoon pool. This pool area alone would make this resort a great spot for a family vacation, but there are also children's programs. The resort is done in the Spanish villa style, and most of the accommodations are large two-room suites. For a family vacation, this place is hard to beat. However, I prefer the nearby Pointe Hilton Tapatio Cliffs Resort for its dramatic hillside setting and location adjacent to the hiking trails of the North Mountain Recreation Area.

7677 N. 16th St., Phoenix, AZ 85020. www.pointehilton.com. ✆ **800/876-4683** or 602/997-2626. Fax 602/997-2391. 563 units. Jan to mid-May $159–$399 double; mid-May to mid-Sept $99–$199 double; mid-Sept to Dec $139–$299 double; year-round $1,500 grande or palacio suite. Children 18 and under stay free in parent's room. AE, DC, DISC, MC, V. Pets accepted ($75 fee). **Amenities:** 3 restaurants; 2 snack bars; 5 lounges; babysitting; children's programs; concierge; health club and small full-service spa; 7 Jacuzzis; 8 pools; room service; 3 tennis courts. *In room:* A/C, TV, fridge, hair dryer, Internet ($12 per day), MP3 docking station.

Pointe Hilton Tapatio Cliffs Resort ★★ If you love to lounge by the pool, then this resort is a great choice. The Falls, a 3½-acre water playground, includes two pools, a 138-foot water slide, 40-foot cascades, a whirlpool tucked into an artificial grotto, and rental cabanas. If you're a hiker, you can head out on the trails of the adjacent North Mountain Recreation Area. All rooms are spacious suites with Southwest-inspired furnishings; corner units are particularly bright. This resort has steep walkways, so you need to be in good shape to stay here. At the top of the property is Different Pointe of View, a continental restaurant with one of the finest views in the city. This resort is more adult-oriented than the Pointe Hilton Squaw Peak Resort, but otherwise is similar.

11111 N. 7th St., Phoenix, AZ 85020. www.pointehilton.com. ✆ **800/876-4683** or 602/866-7500. Fax 602/993-0276. 584 units. Jan to mid-May $159–$299 double; mid-May to mid-Sept $99–$199 double; mid-Sept to Dec $139–$299 double; year-round $1,500 grande suite. Children 18 and under stay free in parent's room. AE, DC, DISC, MC, V. Pets accepted ($75 fee). **Amenities:** 4 restaurants; poolside cafe; 4 lounges; babysitting; children's programs; concierge; golf course; exercise room; 8 Jacuzzis; 8 pools; room service; small full-service spa; 2 tennis courts. *In room:* A/C, TV, hair dryer, Internet ($12 per day), minibar, MP3 docking station.

INEXPENSIVE

Best Western InnSuites Phoenix Biltmore/Scottsdale ★ ☺ Just off Ariz. 51 and not far from the miles of desert trails at Dreamy Draw Recreation Area and Piestewa Peak, this hotel is both convenient and economical. This hotel provides not only easy access to desert trails, but also easy freeway access to both downtown Phoenix and north Scottsdale. Rooms are surprisingly modern, attractively furnished, and have plush, pillow-top beds. After a hot hike, you can cool off in the pool or soak sore muscles in the hot tub. With its breakfast buffet, evening snacks, and large rooms, this is also an excellent and economical place to stay with the kids.

1615 E. Northern Ave., Phoenix, AZ 85020. www.innsuites.com/phoenix. ✆ **800/752-2204** or 602/997-6285. Fax 602/943-1407. 111 units. $96–$124 double. Rates include full breakfast and evening social hour. Children 17 and under stay free in parent's room. AE, DC, DISC, MC, V. Pets accepted ($20 per night). **Amenities:** Exercise room; Jacuzzi; outdoor pool. *In room:* A/C, TV, fridge, hair dryer, MP3 docking station, free Wi-Fi.

Downtown, South Phoenix & the Airport Area

Unless you're a sports fan or are in town for a convention, there's not much to recommend downtown Phoenix. Primarily a 9-to-5 neighborhood, downtown can feel like a ghost town at night. Even less recommendable, south Phoenix is one of the poorest parts of the city. However, it does have a couple of wealthy enclaves that are home to exceptional resorts, and Phoenix South Mountain Park is one of the best places in the city to experience the desert.

VERY EXPENSIVE

Sheraton Wild Horse Pass Resort & Spa ★★★ Named for the area's wild horses, this resort is located 20 minutes south of Phoenix Sky Harbor International Airport on the Gila River Indian Reservation, and because the resort looks out across miles of desert, it has a surprisingly remote feel. Throw in horseback riding, a full-service spa featuring desert-inspired treatments, two golf courses, a nature trail along a 2½-mile-long artificial river, a pool with a water slide, the Rawhide Wild West theme park, and a nearby casino, and you'll find plenty to keep you busy. The resort is owned by the Maricopa and Pima tribes, who go out of their way to share their culture with resort guests. Guest rooms have great beds, small patios, and large bathrooms and underwent extensive updating in 2010. The menu in Kai (p. 133), the main dining room, focuses on indigenous Southwestern flavors.

5594 W. Wild Horse Pass Blvd., Chandler, AZ 85226. www.wildhorsepassresort.com. ✆ **888/218-8989** or 602/225-0100. Fax 602/225-0300. 500 units. Early Jan to late May $329–$495 double, $650–$1,400 suite; late May to mid-Sept $189–$289 double, $600–$950 suite; mid-Sept to early Jan $289–$495 double, $650–$1,400 suite. Children 17 and under stay free in parent's room. AE, DC, DISC, MC, V. Valet parking $22. Pets accepted. **Amenities:** 5 restaurants, including Kai (see review, p. 133); 4 lounges; children's programs; concierge; executive-level rooms; two 18-hole golf courses; health club and full-service spa; 5 Jacuzzis; 4 outdoor pools; room service; 2 tennis courts. *In room:* A/C, TV/DVD, CD player, hair dryer, minibar, MP3 docking station, Wi-Fi ($12 per day).

EXPENSIVE

Arizona Grand Resort ★★ ☺ This sprawling resort, which underwent a $52-million makeover a few years ago, abuts the 17,000-acre South Mountain Park and is one of the best choices in the Valley for families. If I were a 12-year-old, I would beg my parents to stay here and spend every day playing in the wave pool, tubing "river," twisty water slide, and two free-fall-style water slides. There are also numerous children's programs. The guest rooms, all suites, feature contemporary Southwestern furnishings and lots of space. Rustler's Rooste, the resort's fun cowboy steakhouse, serves rattlesnake appetizers (see "Where to Eat," below) and is a favorite with families.

8000 S. Arizona Grand Pkwy., Phoenix, AZ 85044. www.arizonagrandresort.com. ✆ **866/267-1321** or 602/438-9000. Fax 602/431-6535. 740 units. Jan–Apr $199–$399 double; May to early Sept $119–$199 double; early Sept to Dec $179–$299 double. Rates do not include $30 daily resort fee. Children 17 and under stay free in parent's room. AE, DC, DISC, MC, V. **Amenities:** 5 restaurants, including Rustler's Rooste (see review, p. 135); 3 lounges; babysitting; bikes; children's programs; concierge; executive-level rooms; 18-hole golf course; health club and full-service spa; 9 Jacuzzis; 7 outdoor pools (including 7-acre water park); room service. *In room:* A/C, TV, hair dryer, minibar, Wi-Fi (included in resort fee).

The Buttes, a Marriott Resort ★★ Just 3 miles from Sky Harbor Airport and adjacent to Tempe Diablo Stadium (where the L.A. Angels hold spring training), this resort makes the most of its craggy hilltop location, and although some people complain that the nearby freeway ruins the view, the rocky setting is quintessentially Southwestern. The only other resorts in the area with as much desert character are the far more expensive Boulders and Four Seasons. From the cactus garden and waterfall *inside* the lobby to the circular restaurant and free-form swimming pools, this resort is calculated to take your breath away. Guest rooms are stylishly elegant. The city-view rooms are a bit larger than the hillside-view rooms, but second-floor hillside-view rooms have patios. Most bathrooms have walk-in showers. The Top of the Rock restaurant has great views.

2000 Westcourt Way, Tempe, AZ 85282. www.marriott.com/phxtm. ✆ **888/867-7492** or 602/225-9000. Fax 602/438-8622. 353 units. Jan–Apr $240–$356 double, from $475 suite; May–Aug $120–$240 double, from $375 suite; Sept–Dec $210–$310 double, from $475 suite. Children 17 and under stay free in parent's room. AE, DC, DISC, MC, V. Parking $10. **Amenities:** 3 restaurants; 2 lounges; bikes; concierge; exercise room; 4 Jacuzzis; 2 large pools; room service; full-service spa; 2 tennis courts. *In room:* A/C, TV, hair dryer, minibar, Wi-Fi ($15 per day).

INEXPENSIVE

The Clarendon Hotel ★ 🎁 If you're looking for a stylish yet casual place in downtown Phoenix, the Clarendon is a great choice. Having had an extreme makeover, it's now a hip hangout for young, style-conscious travelers and attracts a surprising number of celebrities. Guest rooms are done in a sort of budget contemporary that will appeal to young and artistic travelers. In the hotel's central courtyard, there's a 50-person hot tub and a gorgeous pool with gold- and platinum-coated tiles, dozens of fountains that spray water into the pool, and underwater speakers. Definitely a see-and-be-seen pool scene. The restaurant and cocktail bar are designed to appeal to young nightclubbers and fashionistas, and there's a rooftop lounge for sunset cocktails.

401 W. Clarendon Ave., Phoenix, AZ 85013. www.goclarendon.com. ✆ **602/252-7363.** 105 units. Oct–May $89–$289 double; June–Sept $59–$169 double. Rates do not include $15 daily service charge. Children 17 and under stay free in parent's room. AE, DC, DISC, MC, V. Pets accepted ($50 fee). **Amenities:** Restaurant; lounge; concierge; exercise room; Jacuzzi; outdoor pool; room service. *In room:* A/C, TV, fridge, hair dryer, MP3 docking station, Wi-Fi (cost included in daily service charge).

Tempe, Mesa & the East Valley

Tempe, which lies just a few miles east of the airport, is home to Arizona State University and consequently supports a lively nightlife scene. Along Tempe's Mill

Avenue, you'll find one of the only neighborhoods in the Valley where locals actually get out of their cars and walk the streets. Tempe is also convenient to Papago Park, which is home to the Phoenix Zoo, the Desert Botanical Garden, a municipal golf course, and hiking and mountain-biking trails.

EXPENSIVE

Tempe Mission Palms Hotel ★ With a great location on Tempe's lively Mill Avenue and guest rooms decorated in shades of beige and brown, this is the perfect choice for a fun-filled weekend in Tempe. Sure, this is a business hotel (ergonomic desk chairs), but with a rooftop pool, tennis court, and Mill Avenue's nightlife right out the front door, it's also a great choice for active travelers. Come in the spring and you won't want to leave the courtyard, which is scented by the flowers of citrus trees.

60 E. 5th St., Tempe, AZ 85281. www.missionpalms.com. ✆ **800/547-8705** or 480/894-1400. Fax 480/968-7677. 303 units. Jan–Apr $199–$299 double, $399 suite; May–June $139–$179 double, $279 suite; July–Aug $99–$169 double, $269 suite; Sept–Dec $159–$229 double, $339 suite. Rates do not include $11 daily hospitality fee. Children 17 and under stay free in parent's room. AE, DC, DISC, MC, V. Pets accepted ($100 deposit, $25 fee). **Amenities:** 2 restaurants; lounge; free airport transfers; bikes; concierge; exercise room and access to nearby health club; 2 Jacuzzis; outdoor pool; room service; tennis court. *In room:* A/C, TV, CD player, fridge, hair dryer, free Wi-Fi.

MODERATE

Aloft Tempe ★ Ever wished you had a loft in the city? At this hotel near the shores of Tempe Town Lake, you'll have just that—a high-ceilinged room with big windows and hip decor. Aloft hotels are affiliated with the über-hip W hotels, but are much less aggressive about their hipness quotient. Bright colors, modern furniture, a 24-hour "pantry," and a cool lobby bar that even has a pool table make for a setting that will appeal to young travelers. With their platform beds and big bathrooms, guest rooms depart from the familiar styling of most corporate hotels. Throw in a LEED certification and you have a hotel that's not only hip but green, too. There are even special amenities for kids (goodie bags, special kid bedding, a splash pool). How cool is that?

951 E. Playa del Norte Dr., Tempe, AZ 85281. www.alofthotels.com/tempe. ✆ **877/462-5638** or 480/621-3300. 136 units. Feb to mid-May $149–$219 double; mid-May to mid-Sept $119–$139 double; mid-Sept to Jan $149–$169 double. Children 17 and under stay free in parent's room. AE, DC, DISC, MC, V. Pets accepted. **Amenities:** Concierge; exercise room; outdoor pool. *In room:* A/C, TV, hair dryer, free Wi-Fi.

Gold Canyon Golf Resort ★ Golfers willing to stay way out on the eastern outskirts of the Valley of the Sun (a 30- to 45-min. drive from the airport) will be thrilled by the economical room rates and great golf at this resort. At the foot of the Superstition Mountains, Gold Canyon is a favorite of golfers for its exceedingly scenic holes. The spacious guest rooms are housed in pueblo-inspired buildings; some have fireplaces, while others have whirlpools. The deluxe golf-course rooms are definitely worth the higher rates. If you're here primarily to play golf and don't have a fortune to spend, this is *the* place to stay.

6100 S. Kings Ranch Rd., Gold Canyon, AZ 85218. www.gcgr.com. ✆ **800/827-5281** or 480/982-9090. Fax 480/983-9554. 85 units. $115–$260 double. Rates do not include $10 daily resort fee. Children 18 and under stay free in parent's room. AE, DC, DISC, MC, V. Pets accepted

($55 fee). **Amenities:** Restaurant; lounge; concierge; executive-level rooms; two 18-hole golf courses; exercise room; Jacuzzi; pool; small full-service spa. *In room:* A/C, TV, hair dryer, minibar, Wi-Fi (included in resort fee).

INEXPENSIVE

Apache Boulevard in Tempe becomes Main Street in Mesa, and along this stretch of road there are numerous old motels charging some of the lowest rates in the Valley. However, these motels are very hit-or-miss. If you're used to staying at nonchain motels, you might want to cruise this strip and check out a few places. Otherwise, try the chain motels in the area (which tend to charge $20–$40 more per night than nonchain motels).

Best Western Dobson Ranch Inn & Resort This aging budget resort may not be very luxurious, but it has just about everything a sun-starved winter visitor could ask for—green lawns, flower gardens, palm trees, and a big pool surrounded by lounge chairs. The location, right off U.S. 60 at the junction with U.S. 101, also makes this resort relatively convenient for exploring the Valley. Guest rooms are simply furnished, yet quite modern, and although they are more functional than fancy, the grounds more than make up for the unremarkable rooms.

1666 S. Dobson Rd., Mesa, AZ 85202-5699. www.dobsonranchinn.com. ✆ **800/528-1356** or 480/831-7000. Fax 480/831-7000. 213 units. $64–$130 double. Rates include full breakfast. Children 12 and under stay free in parent's room. AE, DC, DISC, MC, V. Pets accepted ($50 deposit). **Amenities:** Restaurant; lounge; exercise room; 2 Jacuzzis; large outdoor pool; room service; free Wi-Fi. *In room:* A/C, TV, fridge, hair dryer, free Internet.

Crowne Plaza San Marcos Golf Resort ★ Built in 1912, the San Marcos is the oldest golf resort in Arizona and has a classic mission-revival styling. I love the timeless feel of this resort's palm-shaded courtyards, and I'm sure you will, too. Guest rooms are simply furnished and nothing special, but they've been kept up-to-date. You'll want to spend your time splashing around in the pool when you aren't playing tennis or golf. Downtown Chandler, where the San Marcos is located, has been undergoing a renaissance in recent years. There are now art galleries and some decent restaurants on the plaza just outside the resort's front door. Although the San Marcos is out of the tourist mainstream, the rates make it a real bargain.

1 San Marcos Place, Chandler, AZ 85225. www.sanmarcosresort.com. ✆ **800/528-8071** or 480/812-0900. Fax 480/963-6777. 263 units. $95–$144 double; $142–$189 suite (lower rates in summer). Rates do not include $8 daily service charge. Children 17 and under stay free in parent's room. AE, DC, DISC, MC, V. Pets accepted ($50 fee). **Amenities:** 2 restaurants; 2 lounges; concierge; 18-hole golf course; exercise room; Jacuzzi; outdoor pool; room service; 2 tennis courts. *In room:* A/C, TV, CD player, hair dryer, free Internet.

Fiesta Resort Conference Center ★ Reasonable rates, green lawns, palm- and eucalyptus-shaded grounds, and a location close to the airport, ASU, and Tempe's Mill Avenue make this older, casual resort one of the best deals in the Valley. Okay, so it doesn't have the desert character of the Buttes resort across the freeway, and it isn't as stylish as the resorts in Scottsdale, but you can't argue with the rates. The large guest rooms have pillow-top mattresses on the beds. You may not feel like you're in the desert when you stay here (due to the lawns and shade trees), but you'll certainly get a lot more for your money than at other area hotels in this price range.

2100 S. Priest Dr., Tempe, AZ 85282. www.fiestainnresort.com. ✆ **800/528-6481** or 480/967-1441. 270 units. $80–$152 double. Children 17 and under stay free in parent's room. AE, DC, DISC,

MC, V. Pets accepted ($25). **Amenities:** Restaurant; lounge; free airport transfer; concierge; exercise room; Jacuzzi; pool; room service. *In room:* A/C, TV, fridge, hair dryer, free Internet.

West Valley

EXPENSIVE

The Wigwam Golf Resort & Spa ★★ Located 20 minutes west of downtown Phoenix and more than twice that far from Scottsdale, this property, which opened its doors to the public in 1929, is one of the nation's premier golf resorts. It's a classic, old-money sort of place that makes a great golf getaway, but it's a bit inconveniently located for anyone planning on visiting museums and galleries or eating out. With its green lawns, tall palms, flower gardens, and Santa Fe–style buildings, the resort is a neatly manicured world unto itself. Guest rooms are spacious and feature Southwestern furniture and plush beds, and some units have fireplaces. The traditional-style golf courses here are the main attraction, and the rooms to request are those along the fairways. In addition to the golf courses, the resort is noted for its Elizabeth Arden Red Door Spa.

300 E. Wigwam Blvd., Litchfield Park, AZ 85340. www.wigwamresort.com. ✆ **800/327-0396** or 623/935-3811. Fax 623/935-3737. 331 units. Early Jan to mid-Apr $219–$309 double, $239–$329 suite; mid-Apr to May and Sept to early Jan $159–$209 double, $179–$259 suite; June–Sept $79–$129 double, $99–$179 suite. AE, DC, MC, V. Valet parking $15. Pets accepted ($25 deposit). **Amenities:** 3 restaurants; poolside snack bar; 4 lounges; babysitting; children's programs; concierge; executive-level rooms; three 18-hole golf courses; health club and full-service spa; 3 Jacuzzis; 3 pools; room service; 9 tennis courts. *In room:* A/C, TV, CD player, hair dryer, minibar, Wi-Fi ($8 per day).

WHERE TO EAT

As you would expect of any major metropolitan area with a population running into the millions, the Valley of the Sun boasts countless excellent restaurants. While there is hardly a corner of the Valley that doesn't have someplace good to eat, many of the best restaurants are concentrated in the Scottsdale Road, north Scottsdale, and Biltmore Corridor areas. If you want to splurge on only one expensive meal while you're here, consider a resort restaurant or a place that offers a view of the city lights. If you've got the kids with you, you'll want to be sure to have dinner at one of the Valley's "cowboy" steakhouses. These family-oriented restaurants feature Wild West decor, live cowboy music, and lots of other fun entertainment.

Good places to go trolling for a place to eat include the trendy Biltmore Fashion Park shopping center, at Camelback Road and 24th Street (✆ **602/955-1963**), and Old Town Scottsdale. At the former, you'll find nearly a dozen restaurants, while in the latter, you'll find twice that many.

Phoenix is a sprawling city, and it can be a real pain to have to drive around in search of a good lunch spot. If you happen to be visiting the Phoenix Art Museum, the Heard Museum, or the Desert Botanical Garden anytime around lunch, stay put for your noon meal. All three of these attractions have cafes serving decent, if limited, menus.

Scottsdale

EXPENSIVE

Cowboy Ciao ★★ SOUTHWESTERN/NEW AMERICAN Yee-ha, bambino, the food at this place beats the heck out of cowboy beans and deep-fried

Alice Cooper'stown **11**
America's Taco Shop **8**
Arcadia Farms **34**
Bandera **33**
Beckett's Table **26**
Bloom **16**
Bourbon Steak **13**
Café Lalibela **42**
Carlsbad Tavern **36**
Carolina's **12**
Chelsea's Kitchen **21**
Coup des Tartes **2**
Cowboy Ciao Wine Bar & Grill **30**
Delux **23**
deseo **15**
Eddie's House **34**
El Chorro Lodge **27**
El Molino Mexican Café **37**
Elements **17**
The Farm at South Mountain/ Morning Glory Café & Bakery **42**
5th and Wine **32**
FnB **29**
Frank & Lupe's **33**
Fry Bread House **5**
Grazie **35**
The Grind 25
Guedo's Cantina Grille **49**
House of Tricks **40**
Humble Pie **29**
Kai **44**
La Grande Orange Pizzeria **19**
LON's at the Hermosa **22**
Los Sombreros **38**
MacAlpine's Restaurant and Soda Fountain **7**
Malee's Thai Bistro **32**
The Mission **32**
Monti's La Casa Vieja **41**
Nobuo at Teeter House **10**
noca **23**
Old Town Tortilla Factory **34**
Organ Stop Pizza **48**
The Original Blue Adobe Grille **47**
Pane Bianco **4**
The Parlor **24**
Petite Maison **31**
Pizzeria Bianco **10**
Quiessence **43**
Rancho Pinot **28**
Rawhide **45**
Roaring Fork **30**
Rustler's Rooste **44**
Sacred Hogan Navajo Frybread **6**
Sierra Bonita Grill **1**
Stax **31**
St. Francis **3**
The Stockyards Restaurant & 1889 Saloon **39**
T. Cook's **18**
Ted's Hot Dogs **46**
Tuck Shop **9**
Veneto Trattoria Italiana **28**
Vincent on Camelback **20**
Vincent Market Bistro **20**
Zinc Bistro **14**

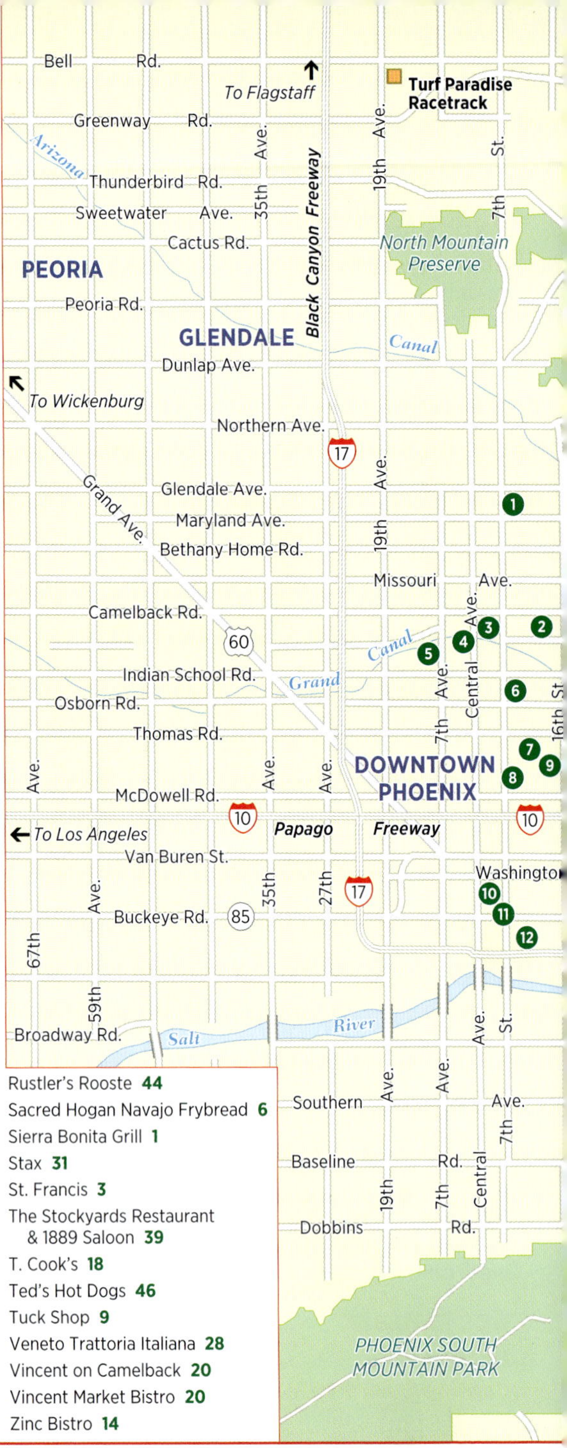

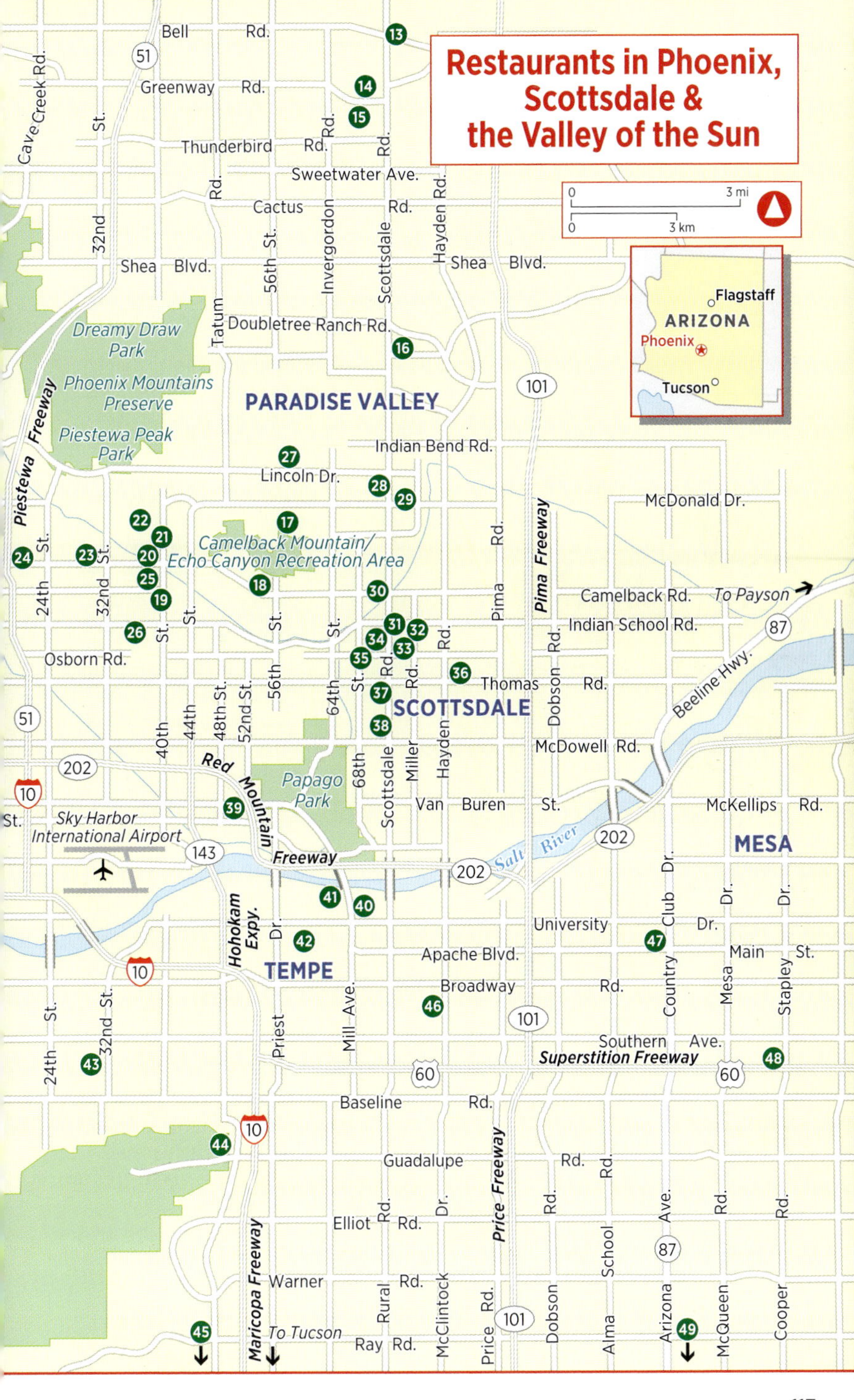
Restaurants in Phoenix, Scottsdale & the Valley of the Sun
0
3 mi
0
3 km
Flagstaff
ARIZONA
Phoenix
Tucson
PARADISE VALLEY
SCOTTSDALE
TEMPE
MESA
Dreamy Draw Park
Phoenix Mountains Preserve
Piestewa Peak Park
Camelback Mountain/ Echo Canyon Recreation Area
Papago Park
Sky Harbor International Airport
Salt River
Bell Rd.
Greenway Rd.
Thunderbird Rd.
Sweetwater Ave.
Cactus Rd.
Shea Blvd.
Doubletree Ranch Rd.
Indian Bend Rd.
Lincoln Dr.
McDonald Dr.
Camelback Rd.
To Payson
Indian School Rd.
Osborn Rd.
Thomas Rd.
McDowell Rd.
Van Buren St.
McKellips Rd.
University Dr.
Apache Blvd.
Main St.
Broadway Rd.
Southern Ave.
Superstition Freeway
Baseline Rd.
Guadalupe Rd.
Elliot Rd.
Warner Rd.
Ray Rd.
To Tucson
Cave Creek Rd.
Piestewa Freeway
32nd St.
Tatum Rd.
56th St.
Invergordon Rd.
Scottsdale Rd.
Hayden Rd.
Pima Rd.
Pima Freeway
24th St.
40th St.
44th St.
48th St.
52nd St.
64th St.
68th St.
Miller Rd.
Dobson Rd.
Beeline Hwy.
Red Mountain Freeway
Hohokam Expy.
Priest Dr.
Mill Ave.
McClintock Dr.
Price Freeway
Price Rd.
Country Club Dr.
Mesa Dr.
Stapley Dr.
Maricopa Freeway
Rural Rd.
School Rd.
Alma
Arizona Ave.
McQueen Rd.
Cooper Rd.
51
202
10
143
101
87
60
13
14
15
16
17
18
19
20
21
22
23
24
25
26
27
28
29
30
31
32
33
34
35
36
37
38
39
40
41
42
43
44
45
46
47
48
49

rattlesnake. It's better than spaghetti and pasta fazul, too. A fun, "cowboy chic" atmosphere and delicious food with a global influence make a meal here unforgettable. You absolutely must start your meal with the Stetson chopped salad; it's both a work of art and an explosion of flavors and textures. Other not-to-be-missed dishes include the exotic mushroom pan-fry and the daily soup. Cowboy Ciao is also notable for its wine list and bar. Located in downtown Scottsdale, the restaurant attracts a diverse crowd.

7133 E. Stetson Dr. (at 6th Ave.). ✆ **480/946-3111.** www.cowboyciao.com. Reservations recommended. Main courses $10–$32 lunch, $13–$32 dinner. AE, DC, DISC, MC, V. Sun–Thurs 11:30am–2:30pm and 5–10pm; Fri–Sat 11:30am–2:30pm and 5–11pm.

deseo ★ NUEVO LATINO Jaded palates and sleepy taste buds will thank you profusely when you introduce them to the vibrant flavors on this restaurant's ceviche menu. Don't bother trying to decide between rainbow ceviche (tuna, *hamachi*, and salmon with white soy sauce, citrus juices, sesame seeds, and pickled jalapeños) and lobster *escabeche* (with avocado, chives, and garlic chips); just order both. If you're more in the mood for a hot appetizer, try the duck empanadas or the Kobe beef tenderloin with truffle aioli. If you're like me, you'll never make it past the appetizers list, but if you do, the grilled beef dishes are well worth trying.

Westin Kierland Resort, 6902 E. Greenway Pkwy. ✆ **480/624-1202.** www.kierlandresort.com. Reservations recommended. Main courses $26–$32. AE, DC, DISC, MC, V. Wed–Sun 6–10pm.

Eddie's House ★★ NEW AMERICAN Eddie Matney has been one of my favorite local chefs for more than 2 decades now, and here at his latest restaurant, he continues to dish up some of the best food the Valley has to offer. While this place has a glitzy facade, it's all warm and homey inside, with photos of Eddie's family all around the dining room. Don't-miss dishes include the MoRockin' shrimp, which come with dough balls (simple and simply delicious) and a spicy chili-beer dipping sauce. After this tasty starter, consider the perennially popular "What's in this?" steak (tenderloin wrapped in Parmesan mashed potatoes), the bacon-infused meatloaf, or the diver scallops. All winners.

7042 E. Indian School Rd. ✆ **480/946-1622.** www.eddieshouseaz.com. Reservations recommended. Main courses $12–$30. AE, DISC, MC, V. Mon–Thurs 11am–2pm and 4–9pm; Fri 11am–2pm and 4–10pm; Sat 4–10pm.

El Chorro Lodge ★ NEW AMERICAN Built in 1934 as a girls school and set on 11 acres of desert near Camelback Mountain, this Arizona landmark has been a restaurant since 1937 and has one of the biggest and prettiest patios in the Valley. Weekend brunches are among the most popular meals here, and the sticky buns are one of the main reasons why. Luckily, those buns are served with any meal, so you don't have to wait until the weekend to enjoy them. Steaks, beef stroganoff, trout almandine, and rack of lamb are perennial favorites here. A major renovation a few years ago added solar hot water, photovoltaic panels, and other sustainable features. The restaurant has a bocce ball court, and there's live music Tuesday through Saturday nights.

5550 E. Lincoln Dr., Paradise Valley. ✆ **480/948-5170.** www.elchorrolodge.com. Reservations recommended. Main courses $12–$21 lunch, $25–$47 dinner. AE, DISC, MC, V. Mon–Fri 11am–2pm and 5–10pm; Sat 11am–3pm and 5–10pm; Sun 9am–3pm and 5–10pm.

FnB ★★ NEW AMERICAN This little hole-in-the-wall serves comfort food so comforting that it was quickly voted the best new restaurant in town when it opened. It's not just that chef Charlene Badman has a way of transforming the familiar into the fabulous, but she also sources ingredients as locally as possible, which is partly why the menu here is always very short. Expect only four entrees when you visit, but expect them all to be perfectly prepared. You might order pasta with Brussels sprouts, chestnut pesto, bacon, and pecorino, or you might have lamb loin with Arizona-grown tepary beans. There are always lots of interesting appetizers and salads as well, and assembling a dinner of small plates (such as fried green tomatoes with green goddess dressing, potatoes roasted in pork fat, or pickled beets with hazelnuts and goat cheese) is encouraged.

7133 E. Stetson Dr. ✆ **480/425-9463.** www.fnbrestaurant.com. Reservations recommended. Main courses $21–$29. AE, DISC, MC, V. Wed–Fri and Sun 5–10pm; Sat 5pm–midnight.

Rancho Pinot ★★ NEW AMERICAN Rancho Pinot, hidden at the back of a nondescript shopping center adjacent to the upscale Borgata shopping plaza, combines a homey cowboy-chic decor with contemporary American cuisine, and has long been a favorite with Scottsdale and Phoenix residents. Look elsewhere if you crave wildly imaginative flavor combinations, but if you like simple, well-prepared food, Rancho Pinot is a great choice. That said, the salads and starters here can be surprisingly creative and surprisingly good. Keep an eye out for the grilled squid-and-shrimp salad with preserved lemons. For an entree, you can always count on the handmade pasta or Nonni's chicken, braised with white wine, mushrooms, and herbs. As much as possible, Rancho Pinot uses organic, local produce, eggs, and dairy products.

In Lincoln Village Shops, 6208 N. Scottsdale Rd. (southwest corner of Scottsdale Rd. and Lincoln Dr.). ✆ **480/367-8030.** www.ranchopinot.com. Reservations recommended. Main courses $11–$16 lunch, $19–$35 dinner. AE, DISC, MC, V. Oct–May Mon–Fri 11:30am–2pm and 5:30–9:30pm, Sat 5:30–9:30pm; June–Sept Tues–Sat 5:30–9pm.

Roaring Fork ★ SOUTHWESTERN This restaurant has been around for years and still serves some of the most creative Southwestern fare in the Valley. While no meal here is complete without a starter of the green-chili pork stew and a side of the green-chili macaroni and cheese, you'll probably also want an entree. Try the delicious duck breast with onion jam and sour-cherry mustard or the braised beef short ribs made with Dr Pepper. If you can't get a table, dine in the saloon or on the saloon patio. Happy hour (Sun–Mon 4–10pm, Tues–Sat 4–7pm) is a good time for an early meal from the saloon menu, actually worth eating from just so you can order the "big ass burger." Wash it all down with a huckleberry margarita.

4800 N. Scottsdale Rd., Ste. 1700 (at the corner of Chaparral Rd.). ✆ **480/947-0795.** www.eddiev.com. Reservations highly recommended. Main courses $13–$39. AE, DC, DISC, MC, V. Daily 4–10pm.

MODERATE

Arcadia Farms ★ NEW AMERICAN Long a favorite of the Scottsdale ladies-who-lunch crowd, this Old Town restaurant features well-prepared contemporary fare. Try the delicious raspberry goat cheese salad with jicama and candied pecans. The warm mushroom, spinach, and goat-cheese tart is another winner. Try to get a seat on the shady patio. This restaurant also operates cafes at the Phoenix Art Museum and the Scottsdale Center for the Performing Arts.

7014 E. 1st Ave. ✆ **480/941-5665.** www.arcadiafarmscafe.com. Reservations recommended. Main courses $12–$15. AE, MC, V. Daily 8am–5pm.

Bandera AMERICAN Once you've gotten a whiff of the wood-roasted chickens turning on the rotisseries in Bandera's back-of-the-building, open-air stone oven, you'll know exactly what to order when you finally get a seat at this popular spot in Old Town. What an aroma! The succulent spit-roasted chicken is the meal to have here. Sure, you could order prime rib or barbecued salmon, but you'd be a fool if you did. Stick with the chicken or maybe the pork ribs, and you won't go wrong.

3821 N. Scottsdale Rd. ✆ **480/994-3524.** www.hillstone.com. Reservations recommended. Main courses $11-$29. AE, MC, V. Sun-Thurs 4:30-10pm; Fri-Sat 4:30-11pm.

Bloom ★ NEW AMERICAN In the upscale SHOPS gainey village, Bloom is part of a regional chain that includes several great Phoenix-area restaurants and one of my favorite Tucson restaurants—Wildflower. An elegant wine bar serves a wide range of flights (tasting selections), and the bistro-style menu has lots of great dishes in a wide range of prices. Be sure to start with one of the tasty salads; there are also enough interesting appetizers to create a very satisfying dinner. The entree menu includes lots of simple comfort foods, as well as a few more exotic flavors. This place is big and always buzzing with energy.

8877 N. Scottsdale Rd. ✆ **480/922-5666.** www.foxrc.com. Reservations recommended. Main courses $9-$18 lunch, $12-$25 dinner. AE, DC, DISC, MC, V. Sun-Thurs 11am-3pm and 5-9pm; Fri-Sat 11am-3pm and 5-9:30pm.

Carlsbad Tavern NEW MEXICAN Carlsbad Tavern blends the fiery tastes of New Mexican cuisine with a hip and humorous bat-theme atmosphere (a reference to Carlsbad Caverns). A lagoon makes this place feel like a beach bar, while the patio fireplace is cozy on a cold night. The menu lists traditional New Mexican dishes such as *carne adovada* (pork simmered in a fiery red-chili sauce), as well as contemporary Southwestern specialties such as crab-stuffed poblano chilies and pasta with an unusual chipotle chicken stroganoff.

3313 N. Hayden Rd. (south of Osborn). ✆ **480/970-8164.** www.carlsbadtavern.com. Reservations accepted for 5 or more. Main courses $9.75-$24. AE, DISC, MC, V. Daily 11am-2am (limited menu daily 10 or 11pm-2am).

5th and Wine NEW AMERICAN "Scottsdale" and "wine"—it's hard to imagine a more pretentious word pairing. So it came as a total shock when I sat down at this casual wine bar/restaurant in downtown Scottsdale and was handed the most reasonably priced wine list I have ever seen in a city known for serving glasses of wine that cost as much as entrees at most restaurants. Pair your $7 glass of Italian sangiovese with some bruschetta, a burger, or perhaps a daily special of beef bourguignon. Between 3 and 6pm on weekdays, great happy hour deals abound.

7051 E. Fifth Ave. ✆ **480/699-8001.** www.5thandwine.com. Reservations recommended. Main courses $11-$23. AE, DISC, MC, V. Mon-Sat 11am-11pm; Sun noon-10pm.

Los Sombreros ★ MEXICAN Although this casual Mexican restaurant is in an attractive old house, it doesn't look all that special from the outside. However, the menu is surprisingly creative and veers from the standard dishes served at most Mexican restaurants. Start with the chunky guacamole, which is some of the best in the city. Be sure to order the chicken *mole poblano* or the *puerco en chipotle,* succulent, slow-roasted pork in tomatillo-chipotle sauce. Finish it all off with the flan, which will spoil you for flan anywhere else. For a real treat, get it with almond-flavored tequila. Unfortunately, service here can be slow.

2534 N. Scottsdale Rd. (at McKellips Rd.). ✆ **480/994-1799.** www.lossombreros.com. Reservations accepted for 5 or more. Main courses $17–$22. AE, DC, DISC, MC, V. Sun–Thurs 4–9pm; Fri–Sat 4–10pm.

Malee's Thai Bistro ★ THAI While there are now upscale Asian restaurants all over the Valley, this was one of the first to move the spicy flavors of Asia out from under fluorescent lights and into a setting that would impress a date. The decor is not as over the top as at the nearby P.F. Chang's (which also got its start here in Scottsdale), but it is certainly elegant for a Thai restaurant, an ideal place for lunch or dinner during a day of gallery hopping. Start with the creamy *tom ka gai* and then be sure to try the spicy crispy fish or the tropical pineapple dish (seafood and chicken curry served in a half pineapple).

7131 E. Main St. ✆ **480/947-6042.** www.maleesthaibistro.com. Reservations recommended. Main courses $13–$21. AE, MC, V. Mon–Thurs 11am–9 or 9:30pm; Fri–Sat 11am–10pm; Sun 4:30–9pm.

The Mission ★ NUEVO LATINO With its Spanish colonial decor and backlit wall of salt blocks, this downtown Scottsdale restaurant melds old-world decor and cuisine with a modern aesthetic. Taking its name from the historic adobe mission church next door, the Mission is a good bet for lunch or dinner. I like to get a few appetizers and a drink and call it a meal. Try the duck *carnitas empanadas,* the pineapple-glazed pork shoulder tacos, or the Peruvian clam stew. The fries here should not be missed. The bar emphasizes its extensive tequila selection and makes a great margarita. If the weather is good, try to get a seat on the small patio out front. Be sure to find out if the Mission will be doing its Sunday afternoon pig roast (yes, they roast a whole pig); you won't want to miss it.

3815 N. Brown Ave. ✆ **480/636-5005.** www.themissionaz.com. Reservations recommended. Main courses $10–$16 lunch, $12–$32 dinner. AE, MC, V. Sun–Thurs 11am–10pm; Fri–Sat 11am–11pm.

Old Town Tortilla Factory MEXICAN Located in an old house surrounded by attractive patios and citrus trees that bloom in winter and spring, this moderately priced Mexican restaurant has a great atmosphere, good food, and a lively bar scene (with more than 120 premium tequilas). As you enter the restaurant grounds, you might even see someone making fresh tortillas, which come in two dozen different flavors. The rich tortilla soup and the tequila-lime salad make good starters. For an entree, try the pork chops crusted with ancho chili powder and raspberry sauce.

6910 E. Main St. ✆ **480/945-4567.** www.oldtowntortillafactory.com. Reservations not accepted. Main courses $15–$33. AE, DC, DISC, MC, V. Sun–Thurs 5–9pm; Fri–Sat 5–10pm.

Petite Maison ★ FRENCH Reasonably priced French food? In Scottsdale? *Mon dieu!* With barely a handful of tables inside (and about the same number outside on the patio), this little house of a restaurant truly lives up to its French moniker. Pine paneling on the walls and ceiling give the dining room the feel of a cozy alpine cabin, the absolute antithesis of Scottsdale hip. The menu is short and sticks to such French bistro classics as steak tartare, duck confit, *escargot en croute,* steak *frites,* and rotisserie chicken. For dessert, the soufflé is a must.

7216 E. Shoeman Lane. ✆ **480/991-6887.** www.petitemaisonaz.com. Reservations recommended. Main courses $9–$15 lunch, $18–$21 dinner. AE, DISC, MC, V. Mon–Wed 11am–2pm and 5–10pm; Thurs–Fri 11am–2pm and 5pm–midnight; Sat 10am–2pm and 5pm–midnight; Sun 10am–2pm and 5–10pm.

Veneto Trattoria Italiana ★ ITALIAN This pleasantly low-key trattoria, specializing in the cuisine of Venice, serves satisfying "peasant food," including traditional pork-and-garlic sausages served with grilled polenta and braised savoy cabbage. *Baccala mantecato* (creamy fish mousse on grilled polenta, made with dried salt cod soaked overnight in milk) may sound unusual, but it's absolutely heavenly. Other good bets include the salad of thinly sliced smoked beef, shaved Parmesan, and arugula. For a finale, try the *semifreddo,* a partially frozen meringue. There's a welcoming bistro ambience and outdoor seating on the patio.

In Hilton Village, 6137 N. Scottsdale Rd. ✆ **480/948-9928.** www.venetotrattoria.com. Reservations recommended. Main courses $11–$21 lunch, $15–$26 dinner. AE, DISC, MC, V. Mon–Sat 11:30am–2:30pm and 5–10pm; Sun 4:30–9:30pm.

Zinc Bistro ★ 🎁 FRENCH It may seem incongruous to find a French bistro in sunny Scottsdale, and in a modern outdoor shopping center at that, but here it is. This place is a perfect reproduction of the sort of bistro you may have loved on your last trip to Paris. Everything is authentic, from the zinc bar to the sidewalk cafe seating to the hooks under the bar for ladies' purses. Try the *moules marinieres* or the crab-and-truffle omelet, both of which come with addictive shoestring potatoes. Steak eaters should be sure to try the melt-in-your-mouth *sous vide* steak, which is cooked for hours in a vacuum bag. For dessert, there is decadent chocolate soufflé.

In Kierland Commons, 15034 N. Scottsdale Rd. ✆ **480/603-0922.** www.zincbistroaz.com. Reservations recommended. Main courses $10–$16 lunch, $18–$36 dinner. AE, MC, V. Tues–Sat 11am–10pm; Sun–Mon 11am–9pm.

INEXPENSIVE

El Molino Mexican Café 🎁 MEXICAN Located a bit out of the Old Town Scottsdale mainstream, this Mexican joint is little more than a fast-food place, but it serves the best chimichangas (a deep-fried burrito) in town. The chimis here have crispy, light shells and are packed with tasty fillings. Try one with *machaca* (shredded and spiced beef) or green-chili beef, and I'm sure you'll become a convert. If fried food just doesn't do it for you, opt for a couple of green corn tamales, an Arizona specialty.

3554 N. Goldwater Blvd. ✆ **480/994-3566.** www.elmolinocafe.com. Reservations not accepted. Main courses $2.25–$14. AE, DISC, MC, V. Mon–Sat 9am–8pm.

Frank & Lupe's MEXICAN On the same street as some of Scottsdale's top contemporary art galleries, this casual Mexican restaurant is a welcome throwback to the days when Scottsdale was still a real cow town. Friends of mine who have been eating here for years insist the only dish to get is the *carne adobada* burrito plate served enchilada style (smothered in a spicy red sauce). I have to agree. If at all possible, eat on the back patio; it feels so much like a restaurant patio in Mexico that you'll be shocked to find you're still in Scottsdale at the end of your meal.

4121 N. Marshall Way. ✆ **480/990-9844.** www.frankandlupes.com. Reservations not accepted. Main courses $8–$20. AE, DISC, MC, V. Daily 11am–10pm.

Grazie Pizzeria Winebar ★ 🎁 PIZZA This little neighborhood pizzeria is in downtown Scottsdale at the west end of Main Street near the Valley Ho resort and is a little gem of a place. It's also very popular on weekends, and the noise level can be deafening. Come on a weeknight or for lunch if you want to carry on a conversation without shouting. The weekend buzz aside, this is a great place to sip Italian wines and share a couple of designer pizzas from the wood-fired oven. Start your meal with the *carpaccio di bresaola,* which is served with arugula, parmigiano-reggiano cheese, and a lemon vinaigrette; or a salad made with arugula, baby greens, parmigiano-reggiano, red onions, red bell peppers, and pine nuts. The pizzas here have paper-thin crusts, so don't worry about filling up before it's time to order the signature ice-cream calzone.

6952 E. Main St. ✆ **480/663-9797.** www.grazie.us. Reservations recommended Fri–Sat nights. Main courses $10–$16. AE, DISC, MC, V. Daily 11am–10pm.

Humble Pie PIZZA I know, I know, pizza is such a guilty pleasure that even on vacation you find yourself craving it. So, if you're staying at one of the resorts along Scottsdale Road and the urge suddenly strikes, head to this classy pizza place. The only thing humble here is the name. The menu lists more than a dozen designer pizzas, including some of my personal favorites such as one made with local sausage, housemade mozzarella, and roasted fennel and another with prosciutto, pears, and Gorgonzola. Humble Pie is a bit more upscale than your average pizza joint, so you might want to dress up a bit. There's a second Humble Pie in north Phoenix in the Desert Ridge Market Place, 21050 N. Tatum Blvd. (✆ **480/502-2121**).

In Hilton Village, 6149 N. Scottsdale Rd. ✆ **480/556-9900.** www.humblepieusa.com. Reservations recommended. Main courses $8–$14. AE, DISC, MC, V. Mon–Sat 11am–10pm; Sun 11am–9pm.

Stax Burger Bistro ★ AMERICAN The retro-style molded white-plastic chairs and the front-and-center bar might have you thinking this is some sort of hipster hangout, but you couldn't be more wrong. Stax is just a burger joint with style. The burgers are served slider style, which means they're small. You'll need to order two or three plus a side of fries to make a full meal, but, when you see all the cool burgers on the menu, you'll be glad you get to order several. There are Kobe beef burgers, turkey burgers, buffalo burgers, and even exotic burgers (maybe ostrich on the night you're there). You can also build your own burgers with toppings that include fresh mozzarella and various aiolis.

4400 N. Scottsdale Rd., no. 12. ✆ **480/946-4222.** www.staxburgerbistro.com. Reservations not accepted. Main courses $5–$7. AE, DISC, MC, V. Sun–Thurs 11am–10pm; Fri–Sat 11am–midnight.

North Scottsdale, Carefree & Cave Creek

VERY EXPENSIVE

Binkley's ★★★ NEW AMERICAN Foodies up on the latest trends in molecular gastronomy (the science of cooking) will want to make sure they have at least one meal at this astonishing little restaurant in Cave Creek. Utterly unpretentious yet sophisticated enough to hold its own with the finest restaurants in the world, Binkley's is the sort of place people dream of finding while on vacation. Every dish here is a work of art, and unexpected flavor combinations and presentations are the rule. Chef Kevin Binkley likes to leave his customers marveling at the meal they've just had. For the most enjoyable experience, opt for a four-, five-, or six-course tasting menu, which might include white-wine braised baby octopus with wasabi root, quail with butter-poached chanterelle mushrooms, a white-truffle risotto, or even root beer–braised short ribs with porcini mushrooms.

6920 E. Cave Creek Rd., Cave Creek. ✆ **480/437-1072.** www.binkleysrestaurant.com. Reservations highly recommended. Main courses $40–$46; tasting menus $65–$89 ($105–$139 with wine). AE, MC, V. Tues–Sat 5–9:30pm.

Bourbon Steak ★★★ STEAK This posh steakhouse from celebrated chef Michael Mina is one of the Valley's best and most expensive restaurants. If you have an appreciation for lobster and foie gras, then you'll be glad this restaurant is here. If you've never had beef tartare, this is the place to try it, and for a delicious twist on an old favorite, try the lobster potpie. Obviously, however, steaks are the thing here. Keep in mind that the steaks are served a la carte, and there are lots of tempting side dishes and accompaniments. How about some truffled macaroni and cheese or roasted marrow bones to accompany your main dish?

At the Fairmont Scottsdale, 7575 E. Princess Dr. (about 12 miles north of downtown Scottsdale). ✆ **480/513-6002.** www.michaelmina.net. Reservations highly recommended. Main courses $29–$78. AE, MC, V. Mon–Sat 5:30–10pm.

EXPENSIVE

Sassi ★★ ITALIAN If you've had to forego this year's vacation in Italy, then don't miss an opportunity to have a meal at this Tuscan villa transplanted to the Arizona desert. Every room in this beautiful, sprawling building is gorgeous and has a distinctive character of its own. The menu is not your standard southern Italian menu, so don't go looking for spaghetti and meatballs (although you might find an excellent four-cheese manicotti in tomato sauce or Roman-style meatballs braised with San Marzano tomatoes). Instead, try some skewered scallops or a dish prepared with the housemade sausage. In fact, the best thing to do here is order a bunch of dishes and then share everything, as any good Italian family would.

10455 E. Pinnacle Peak Pkwy., Scottsdale. ✆ **480/502-9095.** www.sassi.biz. Reservations highly recommended. Main courses $22–$36; 3-course menu $39 ($64 with wine). AE, DC, DISC, MC, V. Tues–Sun 5:30–9 or 10pm.

MODERATE

Café Bink ★★ NEW AMERICAN This casual spinoff from the legendary Binkley's over in Cave Creek is my favorite lunch spot in Carefree. The menu is limited and a bit pricey at lunch, but the food is perfectly and beautifully prepared. Good French onion soup is an option, and the corned beef, available as a sandwich at lunch and with cabbage and apples at dinner, is another good choice. If your tastes are simple, Amy's Bolognese is a good bet. If you've got expensive tastes but can't get a table at Binkley's, go ahead and order the crispy seared foie gras here at Café Bink. As much as possible, ingredients are organic and local.

36889 N. Tom Darlington Dr., Carefree. ✆ **480/488-9796.** www.cafebink.com. Reservations accepted only for 5 or more. Main courses $9–$24 lunch, $16–$28 dinner. AE, DISC, MC, V. Tues–Sun 11am–9pm.

INEXPENSIVE

Bryan's Black Mountain Barbecue BARBECUE Cave Creek loves to play up its cowboy character, and nothing says "cowboy grub" quite like smoked meats. This little barbecue joint gets you in the cowboy mood with Western movie posters and old Hollywood Western movies projected on the wall. There's even a guitar on the wall with a sign that says PLAY ME. Just don't pick up the guitar until you're done with your half rack of pork ribs or ribs and beef brisket combo. Don't despair if there's a vegetarian in your group; Bryan's has a "pulled" squash sandwich on the menu.

Backyard Bounty

If you happen to be in Phoenix in the late winter or early spring, watch for roadside signs advertising fresh citrus fruit. Many homeowners throughout the city have orange and grapefruit trees in their yards and often sell (or even give away) the fruit from the trees. I always stock up on fresh citrus whenever I see one of these signs.

6130 E. Cave Creek Rd., Cave Creek. ✆ **480/575-7155.** www.bryansbarbecue.com. Reservations not accepted. Main courses $7–$19. AE, DISC, MC, V. Tues–Sat 11am–8pm.

Greasewood Flat ★ AMERICAN Burgers and beer are the mainstays at this rustic open-air restaurant in the Pinnacle Peak area of north Scottsdale. Located down a potholed gravel road behind Reata Pass steakhouse, Greasewood Flat is a desert party spot where families, motorcycle clubs, cyclists, and horseback riders all rub shoulders. Place your order at the window and grab a seat at one of the picnic tables. While you wait for your meal, you can check out the old farm equipment. This place is the antithesis of Scottsdale posh, and that's exactly why I love it. Only in Arizona could you find a place like this.

27375 N. Alma School Pkwy., Scottsdale. ✆ **480/585-9430.** www.greasewoodflat.net. Main courses $4–$8.25. AE, DC, DISC, MC, V. Daily 11am–10pm.

Central Phoenix & the Camelback Corridor

EXPENSIVE

Chelsea's Kitchen ★ ☺ NEW AMERICAN Although this restaurant can seem a bit expensive for what you get, the setting, on the banks of a canal just a block off Camelback Road, is gorgeous. The patio, with a wood-burning fireplace, is nearly as large as the dining room and is where you should try to get a table. The sunsets can be absolutely unforgettable. Separating the dining room and patio is a fun indoor-outdoor bar. Under the same ownership as the nearby La Grande Orange Pizzeria and Postino wine bar, Chelsea's Kitchen features a menu of familiar comfort foods with a few more creative dishes thrown into the mix. The seasonal salads are usually a good choice, as are the fish tacos. Be sure to try the fried chicken and the short ribs. Note that kids eat free daily between 3 and 6pm.

5040 N. 40th St. ✆ **602/957-2555.** www.chelseaskitchenaz.com. Reservations accepted. Main courses $12–$27. AE, MC, V. Mon–Sat 11am–10pm; Sun 10am–9pm.

Coup des Tartes ★★ COUNTRY FRENCH Chain restaurants, theme restaurants, restaurants that are all style and little substance: Sometimes in Phoenix it seems impossible to find a homey little hole in the wall that serves good food. Don't despair; Coup des Tartes is just the ticket. With barely a dozen tables and no liquor license (bring your own wine; $9 corkage fee), it's about as removed from the standard Phoenix glitz as you can get without boarding a plane and leaving town. Start your meal with *pâté de campagne* or the scrumptious brie brûlée, which is covered with caramelized apples. The Moroccan lamb shank is a long-time favorite here, and the filet mignon is also good. For dessert, you must have a tart. As often as possible, organic and local produce is used, as is wild-caught fish and naturally raised meat.

4626 N. 16th St. (a couple of blocks south of Camelback Rd.). ✆ **602/212-1082.** www.nicetartes.com. Reservations recommended. Main courses $9–$15 lunch, $19–$31 dinner. AE, DISC, MC, V. Mon 11am–2pm; Tues–Thurs 11am–2pm and 5–10pm; Fri 11am–2pm and 5–11pm; Sat 5–11pm; Sun 10am–2pm.

LON's at the Hermosa ★ NEW AMERICAN In a beautiful old adobe hacienda built by cowboy artist Lon Megargee and surrounded by colorful gardens, this restaurant is one of the most classically Arizonan places in the Phoenix area, and the patio, with its view of Camelback Mountain, is blissfully tranquil. Lunch on the patio is the meal to have here, although the menu at dinner is far more Southwestern than at lunch. Keep an eye out for salads made with prickly-pear vinaigrette and any dish with Arizona-farmed shrimp. The bar here has a cozy and romantic Wild West feel. Dishes often include herbs grown in the restaurant's own garden, and other ingredients are, as much as possible, from ecologically sound sources.

At the Hermosa Inn, 5532 N. Palo Cristi Rd. ✆ **602/955-7878.** www.lons.com. Reservations recommended. Main courses $10–$17 lunch, $26–$36 dinner. AE, DC, DISC, MC, V. Mon–Fri 7–10am, 11am–2pm, and 5–10pm; Sat–Sun 7am–2pm and 5–10pm.

noca ★★ NEW AMERICAN Self-confessed foodie Eliott Wexler hit on something Phoenix was craving when he opened noca—casual fine dining that incorporates the latest trends in molecular gastronomy and upscale comfort foods. The menu here is a foodie's dream come true, and because it is driven by the season, you might start with butternut squash soup with candied hazelnuts and tempura jalapeños or a salad of baby heirloom beets with pumpernickel croutons. Entrees might include haddock with *matsutake* mushrooms, preserved lemon, and cannellini bean ragout or skirt steak with chanterelle mushrooms, braised Tuscan kale, risotto, and butternut-squash puree. If you can resist the trio of doughnuts with mouth-watering dipping sauces, you have far more willpower than I.

3118 E. Camelback Rd. ✆ **602/956-6622.** www.restaurantnoca.com. Reservations highly recommended. Main courses $18–$34; 4-course tasting menu $50 ($70 with wine). AE, DISC, MC, V. Tues–Sat 5:30–10pm; Sun 5:30–9pm (Dec–Mar, also Mon 5:30–10pm).

T. Cook's ★★ MEDITERRANEAN Ready to pop the question? On your honeymoon? Celebrating an anniversary? This is the place for you. There isn't a more romantic restaurant in the Valley. Located within the walls of the Mediterranean-inspired Royal Palms Resort and Spa, it's surrounded by decades-old gardens and even has palm trees growing right through the roof of the dining room. The focal point of the open kitchen is a wood-fired oven that turns out a fabulous spit-roasted chicken as well as an impressive platter of paella. T. Cook's continues to make big impressions right through to the dessert course.

At the Royal Palms Resort and Spa, 5200 E. Camelback Rd. ✆ **602/808-0766.** www.royalpalmshotel.com. Reservations highly recommended. Main courses $11–$16 lunch, $26–$53 dinner. AE, DC, DISC, MC, V. Mon–Sat 6–10am, 11am–2pm, and 5:30–10pm; Sun 6–10am, 10am–2pm (brunch), and 5:30–10pm.

Vincent on Camelback ★★ SOUTHWESTERN Vincent is a Phoenix bastion of Southwestern cuisine and has long enjoyed a devoted local following. The menu blends Southwestern influences with classic European dishes, and while there are plenty of delicious traditional dishes on the menu, if you're from outside the region, you should stick with Southwestern flavors. The menu changes daily, but among the appetizers, the duck tamale is perennially popular (if it's not on the menu, try the lobster chimichanga). For an entree, you might opt for grilled wild boar with celery-root puree and habanero sauce or salmon with chipotle beurre blanc. For dessert, it's hard to beat the tequila soufflé. For a casual breakfast or lunch, try the attached Vincent Market Bistro (see below).

3930 E. Camelback Rd. ✆ **602/224-0225.** www.vincentsoncamelback.com. Reservations highly recommended. Main courses $32–$36 dinner. AE, DISC, MC, V. Mon–Sat 5–10pm.

MODERATE

Beckett's Table ★ NEW AMERICAN On the edge of the trendy Arcadia neighborhood, Beckett's Table is a great place for upscale yet reasonably priced comfort food. You can start with a trio of local sausages and creamy grits (that's polenta to you foodies) or a starter-size grilled cheese sandwich made with pancetta (that's bacon to you nonfoodies). Feeling famished after a long hard day of having fun on your vacation? Opt for the chicken and dumplings, which are made with an herbed, saffron cream sauce. Mac and cheese, skillet chicken, burgers, short ribs—they're all here, as are wood-fired mussels, pork *osso buco* confit, and blood orange–glazed salmon. This place is off the tourist track, so you'll be dining with in-the-know locals.

3717 E. Indian School Rd. ✆ **602/954-1700.** www.beckettstable.com. Reservations recommended. Main courses $13–$19. AE, DC, DISC, MC, V. Tues–Sun 5–10pm.

The Grind AMERICAN I've had burgers that looked like coal, but this is the only place I've ever had a burger that was cooked in a coal-fired oven. It may sound a bit Dickensian to cook with coal, but, trust me, the 1,000° oven here does great things for burgers (and other meats, too). Tucked into an unassuming little shopping center along the south side of Camelback Road, the Grind is basically a bar with a short list of well-prepared burgers and sandwiches. The beef and chicken are hormone-free, and the vegetables are locally grown and organic as much as possible.

3961 E. Camelback Rd. ✆ **602/954-7463.** www.thegrindaz.com. Main courses $8–$17. AE, DISC, V. Sun–Thurs 11am–10pm; Fri–Sat 11am–midnight.

La Grande Orange Pizzeria PIZZA Good pizza and an off-the-beaten-tourist-path neighborhood location make this casual restaurant a good place to feel like a local. Best of all, La Grande Orange is convenient to both downtown Scottsdale and the pricey Camelback corridor. Gourmet pizzas are what this place is all about, but you should be sure to start with the orange-fennel salad or one of the other great salads. While you're here, check out the adjacent La Grande Orange gourmet grocery (great for stocking a picnic).

4410 N. 40th St. (at Campbell Ave.). ✆ **602/840-7777.** www.lagrandeorangepizzeria.com. Reservations not accepted. Main courses $11–$14. AE, MC, V. Mon–Thurs 4–10pm; Fri–Sun 11am–10pm.

The Parlor ★ PIZZA I love this bustling pizza parlor both for its tasty pizzas and for its hip, warehouselike setting. Vegetable and herb gardens line the sidewalk as you approach the front door, and lots of recycled wood has been used in the interior decor. You can assemble your own dream pizza from such ingredients as wild mushrooms, goat cheese, roasted chicken, calamari, and cilantro, or order one of the house pizzas. My favorite is the *salsiccia* (sausage) pizza, which is prepared with a local sausage that's custom-made for the Parlor. There are also a few sandwiches and some great salads, including a steak salad and one made with roasted beets. Unless you sit in one of the barber chairs at the counter, you'd probably never guess that this space once housed a beauty parlor.

1916 E. Camelback Rd. ✆ **602/248-2480.** www.theparlor.us. Reservations not accepted. Main courses $9–$22. AE, MC, V. Mon–Thurs 11am–10pm; Fri–Sat 11am–midnight.

Sierra Bonita Grill ★ SOUTHWESTERN This neighborhood restaurant is the sort of place you dream about finding—flavorful food, big portions, moderate prices. What's not to like? Well, it is a bit off the usual tourist route, but don't let that scare you. Start with the guacamole and the bacon-wrapped shrimp, and then maybe order the same thing again. Then, do not pass up the buttermilk chicken with the heavenly mashed sweet potatoes. The space is dark and a bit rustic, with a ranch feel and cowboy art on the walls.

6933 N. 7th St. ✆ **602/264-0700.** www.sierrabonitagrill.com. Reservations recommended. Main courses $9–$27. AE, MC, V. Mon 11am–9pm; Tues–Sat 11am–10pm; Sun 10am–9pm.

St. Francis ★★ NEW AMERICAN With its brick walls, loft dining room, unusual exposed-beam ceiling, and underlit onyx bar, St. Francis is hip without being pretentious. It's the sort of place you'd expect to find in any major city, but which is surprisingly hard to find in Phoenix. Packed into this compact space just off Central Avenue, you'll find a patio and outdoor bar, a copper counter overlooking the kitchen, and a couple of dining rooms. Nearly everything on the menu is either cooked in the restaurant's wood-fired oven or has ingredients that have been roasted in the big wood oven. That includes the wonderful rustic bread that's stacked on the counter, as well as the green-chili pork stew and the roasted chicken.

111 E. Camelback Rd. ✆ **602/200-8111.** www.stfrancisaz.com. Reservations recommended. Main courses $11–$25. AE, DISC, MC, V. Mon–Thurs 7am–10pm; Fri 7am–11pm; Sat 11am–11pm; Sun 10am–9pm.

Vincent Market Bistro ★★ FRENCH Located in back of the ever-popular Vincent's restaurant, this casual place does a respectable job of conjuring up a casual back-street bistro in Paris. It's quaint without being froufrou. This place stays packed on Saturday mornings when Vincent's farmers' market attracts crowds of shoppers in search of gourmet snacks and fresh produce. Be sure to order the coq au vin. You can also get great dinners to go.

3930 E. Camelback Rd. ✆ **602/224-3727.** www.vincentsoncamelback.com. Main courses $7–$16. AE, DISC, MC, V. Mon–Fri 7am–8pm; Sat 7am–2pm and 5–8pm; Sun 7am–2pm.

INEXPENSIVE

Delux ★ AMERICAN With a sleek and stylish decor, a very limited menu (you'd better like burgers), and one of the best selections of draft beers in the Valley, this is the ultimate ultrahip burger-and-beer joint. The burgers get my vote for best burgers in the city, but it's the cute Barbie-size shopping carts full of crispy french fries that are the real reason to dine here. Talk about your guilty pleasures—it just doesn't get much better than a cart of fries and a pint of Old Rasputin imperial stout. If you're not a fan of burgers, don't despair; there are great salads and a few nonbeef sandwiches.

In the Biltmore Plaza, 3146 E. Camelback Rd. ✆ **602/522-2288.** www.deluxburger.com. Reservations not accepted. Main courses $6–$13. AE, DC, DISC, MC, V. Daily 11am–2am.

Pane Bianco ★ 🎁 LIGHT FARE Chris Bianco, owner of downtown's immensely popular Pizzeria Bianco (see below), has another winner on his hands with this casual counter-service bakery and sandwich shop not far from the Heard Museum. The menu consists of only four sandwiches and a couple of salads, but all the breads are baked on the premises in a wood-fired oven. The housemade mozzarella is exquisitely fresh and is served both as a caprese salad with tomatoes and basil and in a focaccia sandwich with the same ingredients. And that focaccia? The best in Phoenix.

4404 N. Central Ave. ✆ **602/234-2100.** www.pizzeriabianco.com. Reservations not accepted. Sandwiches and salads $8. AE, MC, V. Tues–Sat 11am–3pm. Closed late Aug to mid-Sept.

Downtown, South Phoenix & the Airport Area

EXPENSIVE

Nobuo at Teeter House ★★★ JAPANESE In this little Craftsman bungalow on downtown Phoenix's Heritage Square, James Beard–award-winner Nobuo Fukuda serves his distinctive style of Japanese food. The menu lists barely more than a dozen dishes, so it's almost impossible to go wrong here. Not one of these dishes can really be considered sushi, so don't show up expecting to get a California roll. Instead, consider the *shiromi* (white-fish) carpaccio or house-cured salmon. The lunch menu includes many of the same dishes served at dinner, including the *okonomiyaki* (a sort of savory pancake made with pork and seafood), which is one of my favorite dishes here. While Nobuo has long been known for his wine pairings, here he also features rare Japanese microbrews.

At Heritage Square, 622 E. Adams St. ✆ **602/254-0600.** www.nobuofukuda.com. Reservations not accepted. Small plates $8–$14. AE, DISC, MC, V. Tues–Sun 11am–4pm and 5:30–9 or 10pm.

Quiessence ★★ NEW AMERICAN You won't find your typical Phoenix/Scottsdale dining experience here, and that's exactly why I love it. Quiessence is set at the back of a shady pecan grove not far from South Mountain Park and is surrounded by organic vegetable gardens. These gardens, and the freshness of the ingredients they provide, is what makes the food here so wonderful, and the delightfully rural setting is what makes Quiessence truly special. Fresh, seasonal ingredients are the rule here, so the menu changes often. Be sure to start your meal with the Chef Spread, a platter of cheeses, terrines, and housemade salami.

6106 S. 32nd St. ✆ **602/276-0601.** www.quiessencerestaurant.com. Reservations recommended. Main courses $23–$32 dinner; prix-fixe menu $75–$95 ($120–$140 with wine). AE, MC, V. Tues–Sat 5–9pm. Closed late June to early Aug.

The Stockyards Restaurant & 1889 Saloon ★ STEAK In business for more than 60 years, this steakhouse is on the site of what was once the largest cattle feed lot in the world. Although you'll no longer find steaks on the hoof outside the restaurant's back door, you will still find plenty of steaks on the menu. The menu, which is a blend of classic and more contemporary dishes, also emphasizes game meats. You might find elk medallions, buffalo meatloaf, or wild boar and venison sausages. The saloon is a Wild West classic, with a gorgeous hand-carved mahogany back bar. Don't miss it.

5009 E. Washington St. ✆ **602/273-7378.** www.stockyardssteakhouse.com. Reservations recommended. Main courses $9–$20 lunch, $22–$75 dinner. AE, DISC, MC, V. Mon–Fri 11am–2pm and 5–9pm; Sat 5–9pm; Sun 5–8pm.

MODERATE

Alice Cooper'stown BARBECUE Owned by Alice Cooper himself, this sports-and-rock-themed restaurant/bar is downtown's premier eat-o-tainment center. Sixteen video screens (usually showing sporting events) are the centerpiece, but there's also an abundance of memorabilia, including guitars once used by the likes of Fleetwood Mac and Eric Clapton. The waitstaff even wears Alice Cooper makeup. Barbecue is served in various permutations, including a huge barbecue sandwich. If you're an Alice Cooper fan, or hope to spot some local pro athletes, this place is a must.

101 E. Jackson St. ✆ **602/253-7337.** www.alicecooperstown.com. Reservations accepted only for parties of 7 or more. Sandwiches/barbecue $8–$20. AE, DISC, MC, V. Mon–Thurs 11am–8:30pm; Fri–Sat 11am–9:30pm; Sun (football season only) 9:30am–4pm.

Pizzeria Bianco ★ PIZZA It's not often that a pizza place ranks as one of the most famous restaurants in a city, but this little downtown hole in the wall is exactly that. Chef/owner Chris Bianco has a huge reputation both here in the Valley and across the nation. That's why you're going to have to wait and wait and wait to get a seat here. When you finally get seated, you can judge for yourself whether the rustic, brick-oven pizzas are worth the wait. I'm a fan (my personal favorite is made with red onion, Parmesan, rosemary, and crushed pistachios), but I'm not convinced these pizzas are really as good as the line out the door would suggest. If you do eat here, be sure to order something with the fresh, house-made mozzarella. You can ease the pain of the wait by going next door to Bar Bianco (p. 185).

At Heritage Sq., 623 E. Adams St. ✆ **602/258-8300.** www.pizzeriabianco.com. Reservations accepted for 6–10 people. Pizzas $10–$14. AE, MC, V. Tues–Sat 5–10pm. Closed late Aug to mid-Sept.

Tuck Shop 🎁 AMERICAN Set in the quiet Coronado residential neighborhood a few blocks east of Seventh Street, this little gem of a restaurant is a bit hard to find but well worth searching out. Housed in a 1950s building and decorated in vintage Scandinavian modern style, Tuck Shop feels both hip and casual. You can show up in jeans and just have a drink and some appetizers or get dressed up and make a night of it. The menu leans toward small plates and shareable dishes with lots of comfort foods, including macaroni and cheese with prosciutto and a delicious citrus-brined fried chicken served with cheddar-cheese waffles. The Medjool dates stuffed with local chorizo sausage should not be missed.

2245 N. 12th St. ✆ **602/354-2980.** www.tuckinphx.com. Reservations accepted for parties of 6 or more. Main courses $16–$19. AE, DISC, MC, V. Tues–Sat 5–10pm.

INEXPENSIVE

America's Taco Shop ★ MEXICAN In a little yellow bungalow in central Phoenix, you'll find some of the best carne asada (grilled beef strips) in the city. Here at America's (named for the owner, not the country), you can get carne

Forbidden City in the Desert

So you're driving along the Loop 202 freeway near Sky Harbor Airport and this strange mirage materializes. You think you're seeing a mall-size complex of classical Chinese buildings. You are! It's the **COFCO Chinese Cultural Center,** 668 N. 44th St. (✆ **602/273-7268;** www.phxchinatown.com). This fascinating complex includes several Chinese restaurants, gift shops, and an Asian supermarket. There's also a Chinese garden with numerous traditional viewing pavilions.

asada tacos, carne asada burritos, carne asada *torta* (sandwiches), and carne asada quesadillas. You get the picture? Carne asada is the name of the game here. Wash yours down with a huge glass of *jamaica* (hibiscus tea), *horchata* (rice milk with cinnamon), or *tamarindo* (a tart drink made from the pod of the tamarind tree). Other America's locations include 4447 N. Seventh Ave. (✆ **602/515-0856**) in Phoenix, and 735 E. University Dr. (✆ **480/751-6250**) in Tempe

2041 N. 7th St. ✆ **602/682-5627.** www.americastacoshop.net. Main courses $2.25–$8. AE, MC, V. Mon–Thurs 7:30am–9pm; Fri–Sat 7:30am–10pm; Sun 10am–9pm.

Carolina's 🎁 MEXICAN Located in a somewhat run-down neighborhood south of the US Airways Center and Chase Field, Carolina's is a Phoenix institution. As such you'll find everyone from Hispanic construction workers to downtown corporate types (men in suits, women in high heels and pearls). Everyone enjoys the down-home Mexican cooking here, but Carolina's flour tortillas are what really set this place apart. Order a burrito, perhaps with shredded beef in a spicy green sauce, and you'll be handed what feels like a down-filled pillow, so soft you'll want to lay your head on it. Or get the tortillas to go and use them as the basis for a fun Phoenician picnic.

There's a second Carolina's in north Phoenix at 2126 E. Cactus Rd. (✆ **602/275-8231**).

1202 E. Mohave St. ✆ **602/252-1503.** www.carolinasmex.com. Main dishes $3–$7. AE, DISC, MC, V. Mon–Fri 7am–7:30pm; Sat 7am–6pm.

The Farm at South Mountain/The Farm Kitchen ★ ☺ LIGHT FARE If being in the desert has you dreaming of shady trees and green grass, you'll enjoy the Farm Kitchen, an oasis reminiscent of a deep South pecan orchard. A rustic outbuilding has been converted to a counter-service lunch restaurant where you can order a filling sandwich or a delicious pecan turkey Waldorf salad. The grassy lawn, shaded by pecan trees, is ideal for a picnic. And you can let the kids run all over while you enjoy your salad or sandwich. At the back of the farm, you'll find the **Morning Glory Café** (✆ **602/276-8804**), a cozy little breakfast place.

6106 S. 32nd St. ✆ **602/276-7288.** www.thefarmatsouthmountain.com. Sandwiches and salads $10. AE, MC, V. Early Sept to May Tues–Sun 10am–3pm. (If weather is inclement, call to be sure it's open.) Closed mid-June to early Sept. Take exit 151A off I-10 and go south on 32nd St.

Fry Bread House ★ 🎁 NATIVE AMERICAN Fry bread is just what it sounds like—fried bread—and it's a mainstay on Indian reservations throughout the West. Although you can eat these thick, chewy slabs of fried bread plain, salted, or with honey, they also serve as the wrappers for Indian tacos, which are made with meat, beans, and lettuce. If you've already visited the Four Corners region of Arizona, then you've probably had an Indian taco or two. Forget them—the ones here are the best in the state. Try one with green chili. If you still have room for dessert, do not miss the fry bread with chocolate and butter.

4140 N. 7th Ave. ✆ **602/351-2345.** Reservations not accepted. Main courses $4.25–$7.75. DISC, MC, V. Mon–Thurs 10am–8pm; Fri–Sat 10am–9pm.

MacAlpine's Restaurant and Soda Fountain ★ AMERICAN This is the oldest operating soda fountain in the Southwest, and it hasn't changed much since its opening in 1928. Wooden booths and worn countertops show the patina of age. Big burgers and sandwiches make up the lunch offerings and should be washed down with a root beer float, chocolate malt, or egg cream.

2303 N. 7th St. ✆ **602/262-5545.** www.macalpines1928.com. Reservations not accepted. Sandwiches/specials $4.75–$8. AE, DISC, MC, V. Sun–Thurs 11am–7pm; Fri–Sat 11am–8pm.

Sacred Hogan Navajo Frybread NATIVE AMERICAN I admit it. Frybread tacos are one of my guilty pleasures, and now that there are two places in central Phoenix serving this traditional Native American food, I (and you) have options when a fry-bread craving strikes. This place is totally lacking in atmosphere (Formica booths, fluorescent lights, counter service), but it more than makes up for this with delicious red chili beef and green chili beef fry-bread tacos. If you want to expand your culinary horizons, you can also get mutton stew, a lamb sandwich, or even an egg-and-Spam sandwich on fry bread.

842 E. Indian School Rd. ✆ **602/277-5280.** Main courses $5.25–$20. AE, DISC, MC, V. Mon–Wed 9am–7pm; Thurs–Fri 9am–8pm; Sat 9am–6:30pm.

Tempe & Mesa

MODERATE

House of Tricks ★ NEW AMERICAN Despite the name, you'll find far more treats here than tricks. Housed in a pair of old Craftsman bungalows surrounded by a garden of shady trees, this restaurant seems a world away from the bustle on nearby Mill Avenue. This is a nice spot for a romantic evening and a good place to try some innovative cuisine. The garlicky Caesar salad and the house-smoked salmon with avocado, capers, red onion, and lemon cream are good bets for starters. Entrees change regularly, but the menu usually includes plenty of dishes inspired by the Mediterranean and the Southwest. Try to get a seat on the grape-arbor-covered patio.

114 E. 7th St., Tempe. ✆ **480/968-1114.** www.houseoftricks.com. Reservations recommended. Main courses $8.50–$13 lunch, $20–$32 dinner. AE, DC, DISC, MC, V. Mon–Sat 11am–10pm.

Monti's La Casa Vieja AMERICAN If you're tired of the Scottsdale glitz and are looking for Old Arizona, try this sprawling steakhouse. The adobe building was constructed in 1873 (*casa vieja* means "old house" in Spanish) on the site of the Salt River ferry, which operated in the days when the river flowed year-round. Today, local families know Monti's well and rely on the restaurant for solid meals and low prices. The dark dining rooms are filled with memorabilia of the Old West.

100 S. Mill Ave. (at Rio Salado Pkwy.), Tempe. ✆ **480/967-7594.** www.montis.com. Reservations recommended for dinner. Main courses $7–$12 lunch, $11–$28 dinner. AE, DISC, MC, V. Sun–Thurs 11am–10pm; Fri–Sat 11am–11pm.

The Original Blue Adobe Grille ★ MEXICAN This restaurant looks like the sort of place you should drive right past. Don't! Despite appearances, this New Mexican–style restaurant serves deliciously creative Southwestern fare at very economical prices. To get an idea of what the food here is all about, try the Cruz Kitchen combination plate (a tenderloin relleno and a smoked-pork tamale) or the lobster tamales with mango salsa and raspberry chipotle sauce. Of course, there are great Chicago margaritas, but there's also a surprisingly good wine list. This place is a hangout for Cubs fans and makes a good dinner stop on the way back from driving the Apache Trail.

144 N. Country Club Dr., Mesa. ✆ **480/962-1000.** www.originalblueadobe.com. Reservations recommended. Main courses $8–$20. AE, DISC, MC, V. Mon–Thurs 11am–9pm; Fri–Sat 11am–10pm; Sun noon–8pm.

INEXPENSIVE

Café Lalibela ETHIOPIAN/VEGETARIAN If you've never had Ethiopian food, this casual and inexpensive restaurant near the Arizona State University campus is a good place to give it a try. The various stews, many of which are quite spicy, are eaten with pieces of a traditional Ethiopian crepelike bread called *injera*. For the best introduction to this flavorful cuisine, try the "Lalibela Exclusive" platter, which feeds three and comes with a dozen different dishes. There are lots of meatless dishes on the menu, so this is a good choice for vegetarians.

849 W. University Dr., Tempe. ✆ **480/829-1939.** www.cafelalibela.com. Reservations recommended on weekends. Main courses $4.75–$15. AE, DISC, MC, V. Mon–Thurs 11am–9pm; Fri 11am–10pm; Sat noon–10pm; Sun noon–9pm.

Organ Stop Pizza ★ ☺ PIZZA The pizza here may not be the best in town, but the mighty Wurlitzer theater organ, the largest in the world, sure is memorable. This massive instrument, which contains more than 5,500 pipes, has four turbine blowers to provide the wind to create the sound, and with 40-foot ceilings in the restaurant, the acoustics are great. As you marvel at the skill of the organist, who performs songs ranging from the latest pop tunes to *The Phantom of the Opera,* you can enjoy simple pizzas, pastas, or snacks.

1149 E. Southern Ave. (at Stapley Dr.), Mesa. ✆ **480/813-5700.** www.organstoppizza.com. Reservations for large groups only. Pizzas and pastas $5.50–$19. No credit cards. Thanksgiving to mid-Apr Sun–Thurs 4–9pm, Fri–Sat 4–10pm; mid-Apr to Thanksgiving Sun–Thurs 5–9pm, Fri–Sat 5–10pm.

Ted's Hot Dogs 🎁 AMERICAN Would you stand in line 30 minutes for a hot dog? No? You might want to reconsider and drop by Ted's Hot Dogs in Tempe. At this, the only Arizona outpost of a small chain of hot dog stands based in western New York State, there always seems to be a line, but no one seems to mind the wait. The dogs are all charcoal-broiled, and you get to pick what toppings you want (I always get the special hot sauce). Sure it's going to take you less time to eat your dog than to order it, but these pups are so tasty they're well worth the wait.

1755 E. Broadway, Tempe. ✆ **480/968-6678.** www.tedsonline.com. Main dishes $2.50–$5.25. MC, V. Mon–Thurs 10am–9pm; Fri–Sat 10am–10pm; Sun 10:30am–9pm.

Chandler & Gilbert

EXPENSIVE

Kai ★★★ NEW AMERICAN With ingredients that are frequently sourced from Native American tribes around the country, the food at Kai is as adventurous and alluring as any you'll find in Arizona. Whether you order buffalo tenderloin with saguaro-blossom syrup and cholla-cactus flower buds, or veal rib-eye rubbed with sandalwood and served with mesquite-cooked desert-fruit chutney, you'll savor some of the most exotic flavors in the Southwest. Add service that is second to none in the state and, if you're lucky, a big-sky sunset, and you have an unforgettable meal. There just isn't another restaurant in the state to compare with Kai, which is gorgeous, sophisticated, and subdued, with a pleasant patio overlooking the pool and desert beyond.

At Sheraton Wild Horse Pass Resort & Spa, 5594 W. Wild Horse Pass Blvd., Chandler. ✆ **602/385-5726** or 602/225-0100. www.wildhorsepassresort.com. Reservations highly recommended. Main courses $40–$54; tasting menu $90–$120 ($150–$225 with wine). AE, DC, DISC, MC, V. Wed–Thurs 6–9pm; Fri–Sat 5:30–10pm. Closed early Aug to early Sept.

INEXPENSIVE

Guedo's Cantina Grille ★ MEXICAN Taco stands are a peso a dozen around the greater Phoenix metro area, but few have the cult following of Guedo's in downtown Chandler. This colorful place looks as if it were transported from a Mexican beach town; the patios even have sand floors and palm-thatched shade umbrellas. The food is simple yet fresh and bursting with flavor. Order two or three tacos (I like the fish and shrimp tacos), and then load them with toppings from the salsa bar. Accompany your meal with a cold beer or a margarita, and you just might forget you're still in the States.

71 E. Chandler Blvd., Chandler. ✆ **480/899-7841.** Main dishes $2–$6.50. No credit cards. Tues–Sat 11am–9pm.

Joe's Farm Grill ★ ☺ AMERICAN Before I ate at Joe's, I hardly knew where the town of Gilbert was. However, now that you can get from Scottsdale to this booming southeast Valley suburb entirely on freeways (and in as little as 30 min. if it isn't rush hour), there's no reason not to search out this unique eatery. Designed to resemble a 1950s burger stand and set in the middle of a farm that's part of the Agritopia housing development, Joe's serves creative comfort food and is a huge hit with families. There are big salads with various toppings, barbecued ribs, chicken sandwiches, pizzas, and, best of all, burgers that are among the best in the Valley. As much as possible, produce comes from the surrounding Agritopia farm. After a meal, be sure to walk next door to the **Coffee Shop** (✆ **480/279-3144**) for a pastry.

3000 E. Ray Rd., Gilbert. ✆ **480/563-4745.** www.joesfarmgrill.com. Main dishes $6–$20. AE, DISC, MC, V. Daily 8am–9pm.

Joe's Real BBQ BARBECUE Affiliated with Joe's Farm Grill and located in downtown Gilbert, this place serves huge portions of barbecued ribs, chopped brisket, and pulled pork. The meats are smoked over pecan wood and come with your choice of one or two sides. As you would expect, this place is totally casual, with a John Deere tractor in the middle of the dining room and food served cafeteria-style. There's a sunroom dining area and a shady side yard that's the perfect place to eat on warm days. This east Valley restaurant is a good bet if you're on your way back from driving the Apache Trail.

301 N. Gilbert Rd., Gilbert. ✆ **480/503-3805.** www.joesrealbbq.com. Reservations not accepted. Main courses $7–$19. AE, DISC, MC, V. Daily 11am–9pm.

Dining with a View

elements at Sanctuary Camelback Mountain ★★ NEW AMERICAN Even though it has one of the best views around and some of the best patio dining, elements, the stylish restaurant at the Sanctuary Camelback Mountain resort, doesn't try to slide by on looks alone; it also serves great food. That said, the view is a big part of dinner here, so try to make a reservation so that you can catch sunset. The menu changes regularly and includes influences from around the world. On the appetizer menu, expect the likes of ahi tuna tartare and fiery calamari with Chinese sausage and miso-scallion vinaigrette. Entrees are equally wide-ranging in their culinary influences; the seasonal menu might include duck breast with braised greens, candied turnips, and garlic-cherry glaze or butter-braised scallops with pearl pasta and arugula pesto. If you'll be eating inside, try to get one of the lower-level booths.

At Sanctuary Camelback Mountain Resort and Spa, 5700 E. McDonald Dr., Paradise Valley. ✆ **800/245-2051** or 480/948-2100. www.elementsrestaurant.com. Reservations highly recommended. Main courses $11–$23 lunch, $28–$38 dinner. AE, DC, DISC, MC, V. Mon–Thurs 7–10:30am, 11:30am–2pm, and 5:30–9:30pm; Fri–Sat 7–10:30am, 11:30am–2pm, and 5:30–10pm; Sun 7am–2pm (brunch) and 5:30–9:30pm.

Cowboy Steakhouses

Cowboy steakhouses are family restaurants that generally provide big portions of grilled steaks and barbecued ribs, outdoor and "saloon" dining, live country music, and various other sorts of entertainment.

Rawhide Steakhouse ★ ☺ STEAK Of the many cowboy steakhouses around the Valley, this is by far your best bet for a family dinner. Not only are the steaks some of the best you'll find at a family steakhouse, but there's also an entire Western-town theme park surrounding the restaurant, so there's plenty to keep you and your kids entertained before and after dinner. If you feel adventurous, start your meal with some pan-fried rattlesnake. Cowboy bands keep the crowds entertained during dinner. From February to May and in October and November, there are also weekly sundown cookouts ($48 adults, $15 children) that include a hayride, chuck-wagon dinner, live country music, and lots of other traditional Wild West entertainment.

5700 W. North Loop Rd., Chandler. ✆ **480/502-5600.** www.rawhide.com. Reservations recommended. Main courses $13–$60. AE, DISC, MC, V. Thurs–Fri 5:30–9:30pm; Sat 2–9:30pm; Sun 2–8:30 or 9pm.

Reata Pass ★ STEAK This is by far the most authentic cowboy steakhouse in the Phoenix area. Part of the large restaurant is even housed in an old stagecoach stop, and the building incorporates an adobe building that dates back to 1882. With live music and a huge patio set with picnic tables, this place is a nonstop party. In the warmer months, have your steak out under the stars or the clear blue Sonoran Desert sky. In business since the 1950s, this rustic roadhouse, its bar ceiling plastered with dollar bills, is a local favorite, a place to see what Phoenix was like before it began to sprawl.

27500 N. Alma School Pkwy. ✆ **480/585-7277.** www.reatapass.com. Reservations recommended. Main courses $7–$24. AE, DC, DISC, MC, V. Thurs–Fri 4–10pm; Sat noon–10pm; Sun noon–9pm.

Rustler's Rooste ☺ STEAK This restaurant's location, in the middle of a sprawling golf resort, isn't exactly cowboy country, but back in the day, they say, rustlers used to hide out up here. Today, at the top of the hill, you'll find a fun Western-themed restaurant where you can start your evening by scooting down a big slide from the bar to the main dining room. There's a good view over the city, and cowboy bands play for those who like to kick up their heels. Daring diners always start with the fried snake appetizer and follow up with the enormous "cowboy stuff" platter, which includes steak and seafood kabobs, barbecued pork ribs, fried shrimp, barbecued chicken, and cowboy beans.

At the Arizona Grand Resort, 8383 S. 48th St., Phoenix. ✆ **602/431-6474.** www.rustlersrooste.com. Reservations accepted for 8 or more, but there's a call-ahead waiting list. Main courses $15–$30. AE, DISC, MC, V. Daily 5–10pm.

Espresso Bars, Bakeries & Ice-Cream Parlors

Perhaps it's the heat or the sunshine, but espresso is not the ubiquitous drink in Phoenix that it is in many other parts of the country. However, there are a handful of places to get a good latte or cappuccino. In Scottsdale, try the **Village Coffee Roastery,** 8120 N. Hayden Rd., Ste. E-104 (✆ **480/905-0881;** www.villagecoffee.com), which roasts its own beans and makes what just might be the best lattes in Scottsdale. Alternatively, try **Coffee Bean & Tea Leaf,** which has locations all over the Valley, including in the SHOPS gainey village, 8877 N. Scottsdale Rd. (✆ **480/315-9335;** www.coffeebean.com). If you're wandering around downtown Scottsdale's gallery district or the Scottsdale Waterfront and need an espresso, head to **Sola,** 7124 E. Fifth Ave. (✆ **480/779-7652;** www.solacoffeebar.com).

Up on the north side of the Valley, I always get my espresso at **Firecreek Coffee Company,** 6501 E. Cave Creek Rd., Cave Creek (✆ **480/437-9999;** www.firecreekcoffee.com), which doubles as a wine bar and the Valley's best live-music venue.

Along the Camelback Corridor, there's **Hava Java,** 3166 E. Camelback Rd. (✆ **602/954-9080**), in the Safeway Shopping Center. Not far from the Heard Museum, **Lola Coffee ★**, 4700 N. Central Ave. (✆ **602/265-5652;** www.lolacoffeebar.com), serves the best espresso in Phoenix. It's also the hippest espresso bar in town. Right next door there's a great little bakery run by the owners of Pizzeria Bianco (p. 130).

If ever there were a place where ice cream is a necessity, it is Arizona. In the desert heat, ice cream is a survival food, a means to cool off when temperatures soar. When the heat gets to be too much for you, head to some of these great chill-out spots. Scottsdale's **Sugar Bowl,** 4005 N. Scottsdale Rd. (✆ **480/946-0051;** www.sugarbowlscottsdale.com), in the heart of Old Town, is a longtime locals' favorite that has been immortalized in "Family Circus" cartoons. If you find yourself dying from the heat as you motor through central Phoenix on a toasty afternoon, there's no better antidote than **Mary Coyle,** 5521 N. Seventh Ave. (✆ **602/265-6266;** www.marycoyle.net), which makes its own ice cream and has been in business for more than 50 years. If old-fashioned ice cream just doesn't do it for you, and you absolutely have to have gelato, check out the **Gelato Spot,** 3164 E. Camelback Rd. (✆ **602/957-8040;** www.gelatospot.com), which is right next door to Hava Java in the Safeway shopping plaza. There are other Gelato Spots at 7366 E. Shea Blvd., no. 102, Scottsdale (✆ **480/367-9900**), and 4166 N. Scottsdale Rd., Scottsdale (✆ **480/425-8100**). Alternatively, there is the delightful **Grateful Spoon Gelato,** 4410 N. 40th St. (✆ **602/955-2448**), next door to La Grande Orange Pizzeria (p. 127).

When you're in the neighborhood of the Heard Museum and craving sweets, head down Central Avenue to **Tammie Coe Cakes,** 610 E. Roosevelt St., no. 145 (✆ **602/253-0829;** www.tammiecoecakes.com), a tiny pastry shop in downtown Phoenix. The cases here are filled with irresistibly tempting goodies. There's a second Tammie Coe Cakes at 4410 N. 40th St. (✆ **602/840-3644**). If you're struck with a craving for something sweet while driving Scottsdale Road, head to **Cupcakes,** 6137 N. Scottsdale Rd., Scottsdale (✆ **480/656-3816;** www.gotcupcakes.com), which is in the Hilton Village shopping center and bakes the best cupcakes in town. If you're in Tempe when you're struck with a craving for cookies or a croissant, head to **Essence Bakery,** 825 W. University Dr. (✆ **480/966-2745;** www.essencebakery.com).

Breakfast & Brunch

Although I prefer a pastry and a cappuccino for breakfast when I'm on vacation, I know there are plenty of people who want to tuck into something a bit more filling. If you're in the mood for a big breakfast, try one of the following. In downtown Phoenix, there's **Matt's Big Breakfast,** 801 N. First St. (✆ **602/254-1074;** www.mattsbigbreakfast.com), where ingredients are natural and organic whenever possible. South of downtown, in a bucolic farm setting, there's **Morning Glory Café,** 6106 S. 32nd St. (✆ **602/276-8804;** www.thefarmatsouthmountain.com). In the Arcadia neighborhood south of Camelback Road, try **Over Easy,** 4730 E. Indian School Rd. (✆ **602/468-3447;** www.eatatovereasy.com). In Old Town Scottsdale, you've got several good options, including the **Breakfast Club,** 4400 N. Scottsdale Rd. (✆ **480/222-2582;** www.thebreakfastclub.us); and **Daily Dose,** 4020 N. Scottsdale Rd. (✆ **480/994-3673;** www.dailydosegrill.com).

Most of Phoenix's best Sunday brunches are to be had at restaurants in major hotels and resorts. Among the finest are those served at **LON's** (at the Hermosa Inn, p. 108), **T. Cook's** (at the Royal Palms Resort and Spa, p. 107), **Il Terrazzo** (at the Phoenician, p. 101), and **Top of the Rock** (at the Buttes, a Marriott Resort, p. 112). However, for a unique experience, make a brunch reservation at **Geordie's at the Wrigley Mansion,** 2501 E. Telawa Trail (✆ **602/955-4079;** www.wrigleymansionclub.com). The meal is served in the historic mansion that chewing gum built. Brunch here is served Sunday from 10:30am to 2:30pm and costs $45 per person.

SEEING THE SIGHTS

The Desert & Its Native Cultures

Although the **Sears-Kay Ruins** 15 miles northeast of Cave Creek have never been restored and are, in fact, in ruins, they are close enough to north Scottsdale to be worth searching out. They're also just far enough away to feel like a real discovery. It's an easy 1-mile round-trip hike to this hilltop Hohokam pueblo ruin, and along the way, interpretive plaques explain aspects of Hohokam culture. The pueblo, which dates to between 1050 and 1500, consisted of 40 rooms in four compounds. To find the ruins, head northeast from Carefree on Cave Creek Road, which becomes first Seven Springs Road and then Forest Service Road 24. For more information, contact the Tonto National Forest's Cave Creek Ranger District, 40202 N. Cave Creek Rd., Scottsdale (✆ **480/595-3300;** www.fs.fed.us/r3/tonto/home).

On the south side of the Superstition Mountains, near the Gold Canyon Resort, a relatively short hike will lead you to a small canyon where ancient petroglyphs cover a rock wall beside several pools of water. Known as **Hieroglyphic Canyon,** this rock-art site is reached via a 1.1-mile trail up a gentle slope through dense stands of cactus. To reach the trail head, drive east from Phoenix on U.S. 60 to Gold Canyon. Turn north on King's Ranch Road and follow this road to a right turn onto Baseline Road. Then turn left on Mohican Road, left again on Valley View Drive, and right on Cloudview Avenue, which leads into the trail head parking lot. For more information, contact the Tonto National Forest's Mesa Ranger District, 5140 E. Ingram St. (✆ **480/610-3300;** www.fs.fed.us/r3/tonto/home).

Deer Valley Rock Art Center ★ Located in the Hedgepeth Hills in the northwest corner of the Valley of the Sun, the Deer Valley Rock Art Center

Arizona Biltmore **13**
Arizona Capitol Museum **6**
Arizona Doll & Toy Museum **9**
Arizona Historical Society Museum **23**
Arizona Mining & Mineral Museum **7**
Arizona Museum for Youth **28**
Arizona Museum of Natural History **29**
Arizona Science Center **9**
Arizona State University Art Museum **27**
The Bead Museum **2**
Burton Barr Library **5**
Castles & Coasters **1**
Center for Meteorite Studies **27**
Ceramics Research Center and Gallery **27**
Children's Museum of Phoenix **10**
Cosanti **17**
CrackerJax Family Fun & Sports Park **15**
Desert Botanical Garden **21**
Hall of Flame Firefighting Museum **24**
Heard Museum **3**
Historic Heritage Square **9**
Huhugam Heritage Center **31**
McCormick-Stillman Railroad Park **18**
Mesa Contemporary Arts **30**
Mystery Castle **11**
Penske Racing Museum **14**
Phoenix Art Museum **4**
Phoenix Zoo **22**
Pueblo Grande Museum and Archaeological Park **25**
Scottsdale Center for the Arts **20**
Scottsdale Museum of Contemporary Art **20**
Shemer Art Center and Museum **19**
Taliesin West **16**
Tempe Center for the Arts **26**
Wells Fargo History Museum **8**
Wrigley Mansion **12**

Bell Rd.
Greenway Rd.
Thunderbird Rd.
Sweetwater Ave.
Cactus Rd.
Turf Paradise Racetrack
North Mountain Preserve
PEORIA
Peoria Rd.
Arizona Canal
Black Canyon Freeway
Dunlap Ave.
To Wickenburg
GLENDALE
Northern Ave.
Glendale Ave.
Maryland Ave.
Bethany Home Rd.
Grand Ave.
Missouri Ave.
Camelback Rd.
Indian School Rd.
Grand Canal
Osborn Rd.
Thomas Rd.
DOWNTOWN PHOENIX
McDowell Rd.
Papago Freeway
To Los Angeles
Van Buren St.
Buckeye Rd.
Maricopa Freeway
Broadway Rd.
Salt River
Southern Ave.
Baseline Rd.
Dobbins Rd.
Elliot Rd.
Estrella Dr.
PHOENIX SOUTH MOUNTAIN PARK
59th Ave.
43rd Ave.
35th Ave.
27th Ave.
19th Ave.
7th Ave.
Central Ave.
7th St.
16th St.
0 3 mi
0 3 km

Phoenix, Scottsdale & the Valley of the Sun Attractions
ARIZONA
Flagstaff
Phoenix
Tucson
PARADISE VALLEY
SCOTTSDALE
TEMPE
MESA
Dreamy Draw Park
Phoenix Mountains Preserve
Piestewa Peak Park
Camelback Mountain/ Echo Canyon Recreation Area
Papago Park
Sky Harbor International Airport
Salt River
Bell Rd.
Greenway Rd.
Thunderbird Rd.
Sweetwater Ave.
Cactus Rd.
Shea Blvd.
Doubletree Ranch Rd.
Indian Bend Rd.
Lincoln Dr.
McDonald Dr.
Camelback Rd.
Indian School Rd.
Osborn Rd.
Thomas Rd.
McDowell Rd.
Van Buren St.
Washington St.
McKellips Rd.
University Dr.
Main St.
Apache Blvd.
Broadway Rd.
Southern Ave.
Superstition Freeway
Baseline Rd.
Guadalupe Rd.
Elliot Rd.
Warner Rd.
Ray Rd.
Frank Lloyd Wright Blvd.
Cave Creek Rd.
Piestewa Freeway
Pima Freeway
Price Freeway
Red Mountain Freeway
Hohokam Expy.
Maricopa Freeway
Beeline Hwy.
To Payson
To Tucson
24th St.
32nd St.
40th St.
44th St.
48th St.
52nd St.
56th St.
64th St.
68th St.
Tatum Blvd.
Invergordon Rd.
Scottsdale Rd.
Hayden Rd.
Miller Rd.
Pima Rd.
Dobson Rd.
Alma School Rd.
Country Club Dr.
Mesa Dr.
Stapley Dr.
Priest Dr.
Mill Ave.
Rural Rd.
McClintock Dr.
Arizona Ave.
McQueen Rd.
Cooper Rd.
51
202
10
143
101
87
60
12
13
14
15
16
17
18
19
20
21
22
23
24
25
26
27
28
29
30
31

preserves an amazing concentration of Native American petroglyphs, some of which date back 5,000 years. Although these petroglyphs may not at first seem as impressive as those at more famous sites, the sheer numbers make this a fascinating spot. The drawings, which range from simple spirals to much more complex renderings of herds of deer, are on volcanic boulders along a quarter-mile trail. An interpretive center provides background information on this site and on rock art in general.

3711 W. Deer Valley Rd., Phoenix. ✆ **623/582-8007.** http://dvrac.asu.edu. Admission $7 adults, $4 seniors and students, $3 children 6–12. Oct–Apr Tues–Sat 9am–5pm, Sun noon–5pm; May–Sept Tues–Sun 8am–2pm. Closed major holidays. Take the Loop 101 hwy. west to 27th Ave., go north to Deer Valley Rd., and go west 2½ miles to just past 35th Ave.

Desert Botanical Garden ★★★ In Papago Park adjacent to the Phoenix Zoo, this botanic garden displays more than 20,000 desert plants from around the world, and its Plants and People of the Sonoran Desert Trail is the state's best introduction to Southwestern ethnobotany (human use of plants). Along this trail you can make your own yucca-fiber brush and practice grinding corn as Native Americans once did. On the Desert Wildflower Trail, you'll find colorful wildflowers throughout much of the year. Each spring, there's usually a butterfly pavilion filled with live butterflies. If you come late in the day, you can stay until after dark and see night-blooming flowers and dramatically lit cacti. A cafe on the grounds makes a great lunch spot. During the cooler months, concerts are held in the garden. In December, during Las Noches de las Luminarias, the gardens are lit at night by *luminarias* (candles inside small bags).

In Papago Park, 1201 N. Galvin Pkwy., Phoenix. ✆ **480/941-1225.** www.dbg.org. Admission $15 adults, $14 seniors, $7.50 students 13–18, $5 children 3–12 (free for all on 2nd Tues of each month from 1–8pm). Oct–Apr daily 8am–8pm; May–Sept daily 7am–8pm. Closed July 4th, Thanksgiving, and Christmas. Bus: 1 or 3. METRO light rail: Priest Dr./Washington St.

Heard Museum ★★★ The Heard Museum is one of the nation's finest museums dealing exclusively with Native American cultures and is an ideal introduction to the indigenous peoples of Arizona. From pre-Columbian to contemporary, if it's art created by Native Americans, you'll find it here. If you're interested in the Native cultures of Arizona, this should be your very first stop in the state. The museum is an invaluable introduction to the state's many tribes. The **Home: Native People in the Southwest** exhibit examines the culture of each of the major tribes of the region and is the heart and soul of the museum. Included in this exhibit are more than 500 kachina dolls. In another gallery, you'll find fascinating exhibits of contemporary Native American art. Guided tours are offered daily. The annual **Guild Indian Fair and Market,** held on the first weekend in March, includes traditional dances along with arts and crafts. The museum's cafe is a good place for lunch.

The museum also operates the **Heard Museum North Scottsdale,**

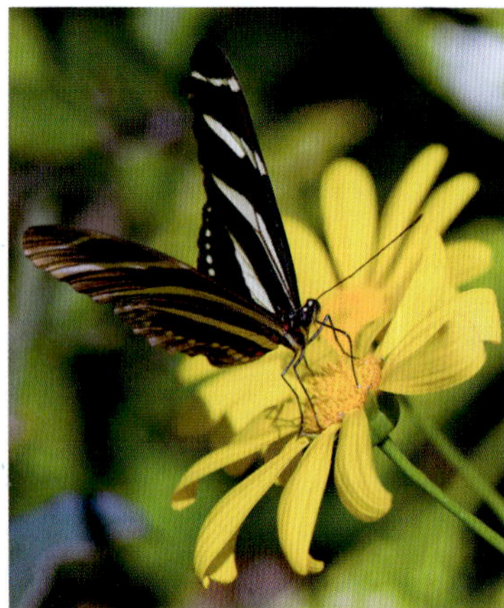

The butterfly pavilion at Desert Botanical Garden.

The Guild Indian Fair and Market at Heard Museum.

32633 N. Scottsdale Rd. (✆ **480/ 344-3380** or 480/488-9817), in Carefree. This gallery features changing exhibits and is open Monday through Saturday from 10am to 5pm, and Sunday from 11am to 5pm. Admission is $5 for adults, $4 for seniors, and $2 for students and children 6 to 12.

2301 N. Central Ave., Phoenix. ✆ **602/252-8848.** www.heard.org. Admission $15 adults, $14 seniors, $7.50 students and children 6–12. Mon–Sat 9:30am–5pm; Sun 11am–5pm. Closed Christmas. Bus: O. METRO light rail: Encanto Blvd./Central Ave.

Huhugam Heritage Center ★ This architectural gem adjacent to the Sheraton Wild Horse Pass Resort is operated by the Pima and Maricopa tribes and offers a glimpse into the cultural heritage of the two tribes. Although the center has only a few small exhibits, it is well worth a visit for its architecture and ethnobotanical garden. The center complex is built within a huge berm that was designed to resemble a giant pot buried in the ground. Exhibits include an outstanding display of Pima and Maricopa baskets dating back to the 1920s.

4759 N. Maricopa Rd., Chandler. ✆ **520/796-3500.** Admission $5 adults, $3 seniors and students, $2 children 6–12; free children 5 and under. Wed–Fri 10am–4pm. Take exit 164 (Queen Creek Rd.) off I-10 and continue 1 mile west.

Pueblo Grande Museum and Archaeological Park Located near Sky Harbor Airport and downtown Phoenix, the Pueblo Grande Museum and Archaeological Park houses the ruins of an ancient Hohokam village that was one of several villages along the Salt River between A.D. 300 and 1400. Sometime around 1450, this and other villages were mysteriously abandoned. Some speculate that drought and a buildup of salts from irrigation water reduced the fertility of the soil and forced the people to seek better growing conditions elsewhere. The small museum here displays many of the artifacts that have been dug up at the site. Although these exhibits are actually more interesting than the ruins themselves, some furnished replicas of Hohokam-style houses give a good idea of how the Hohokam lived. The museum sponsors interesting workshops, demonstrations, and tours (including petroglyph hikes). The **Pueblo Grande Indian Market,** held in

Native Trails in Scottsdale

If you happen to be shopping in Old Town Scottsdale and hear the sound of drumming coming from the Scottsdale Civic Center Mall, be sure to follow the sound to its source. On a stage in front of the Scottsdale Center for the Arts, you'll find members of several Native American tribes performing traditional songs and dances. The show is a cross-cultural journey and is a great way to learn a bit about a few Native cultures. The free programs, called **Native Trails,** are held late January through early April on most Thursdays and Saturdays between noon and 1:30pm. For more information, contact **Scottsdale Convention & Visitors Bureau** (✆ **800/782-1117;** www.scottsdalecvb.com).

mid-December, is one of the largest of its kind in the state and features more than 250 Native American artisans.

4619 E. Washington St. (btw. 44th and 48th sts.), Phoenix. ✆ **877/706-4408** or 602/495-0900. www.pueblogrande.com. Admission $6 adults, $5 seniors, $3 children 6–17. Oct–Apr Mon–Sat 9am–4:45pm, Sun 1–4:45pm; May–Sept Tues–Sat 9am–4:45pm. Closed major holidays. Bus: 1. METRO light rail: 44th St./Washington St.

Art Museums

Arizona State University Art Museum at Nelson Fine Arts Center ★ Although it isn't very large, this museum is memorable for its innovative architecture and excellent temporary exhibitions. With its colorful stucco facade and pyramidal shape, the stark, angular building conjures up images of sunsets on desert mountains. The entrance is down a flight of stairs that leads to a cool underground garden area. Inside are galleries for crafts, prints, contemporary art, and Latin American art, along with outdoor sculpture courts and a gift shop. The collection of American art includes works by Georgia O'Keeffe, Edward Hopper, and John James Audubon. It's definitely a must for both art and architecture fans. Across the street is the affiliated **Ceramics Research Center,** a gallery that showcases the university's extensive collection of fine-art ceramics. You just won't believe the amazing creativity on display.

10th St. and Mill Ave., Tempe. ✆ **480/965-2787.** http://asuartmuseum.asu.edu. Free admission. Tues 11am–8pm; Wed–Sat 11am–5pm. Closed major holidays. Bus: 66. METRO light rail: Mill Ave./Third St.

Mesa Contemporary Arts ★ Although this contemporary arts museum is not very large, it is located in the Mesa Arts Center, which is one of the Valley's architectural gems. You'll find the art museum down in a sunken courtyard beneath the arts center's sail-like canopies. Exhibits change regularly in the five small galleries, and there are occasional sculpture installations in the courtyard.

1 E. Main St., Mesa. ✆ **480/644-6560.** www.mesaartscenter.com. Admission $3.50, free for children 7 and under; free for all on Thurs. Tues–Wed and Fri–Sat 10am–5pm; Thurs 10am–8pm; Sun noon–5pm. Closed major holidays and early Aug to early Sept. Bus: 30.

Phoenix Art Museum ★★ This is one of the largest art museums in the Southwest, and within its labyrinth of halls and galleries is a respectable collection that spans the major artistic movements from the Renaissance to the present. Exhibits cover decorative arts, historical fashions, Spanish colonial furnishings and religious art, and, of course, works by members of the Cowboy Artists of America. The collection of modern and contemporary art is particularly good, with works by Diego Rivera, Frida Kahlo, Pablo Picasso, Alexander Calder, Henry Moore, Georgia O'Keeffe, Henri Rousseau, and Auguste Rodin. The popular Thorne Miniature Collection consists of tiny rooms on a scale of 1

The Mesa Contemporary Arts museum.

inch to 1 foot. Because this museum is so large, it frequently mounts traveling blockbuster exhibits. The cafe here is a good spot for lunch.

1625 N. Central Ave. (at McDowell Rd.), Phoenix. ✆ **602/257-1222.** www.phxart.org. Admission $10 adults, $8 seniors and students, $4 children 6–17, free for children 5 and under; free for all on Wed 3–9pm and first Fri of each month 6–10pm. Wed 10am–9pm; Thurs–Sat 10am–5pm (also 6–10pm on 1st Fri of each month); Sun noon–5pm. Closed major holidays. Bus: O. METRO light rail: McDowell Rd./Central Ave.

Phoenix Art Museum's Thorne Miniature Collection.

Scottsdale Museum of Contemporary Art ★★ Scottsdale may be obsessed with art featuring lonesome cowboys and solemn Indians, but this boldly designed museum makes it clear that patrons of contemporary art are also welcome here. Cutting-edge art, from the abstract to the absurd, fills the galleries, with exhibits rotating every few months. Don't miss James Turrell's "skyspace" *Knight Rise,* which is accessed from a patio off the museum shop and can be visited for free. By the way, the museum shop is full of beautiful items that will fit in your suitcase.

7374 E. 2nd St., Scottsdale. ✆ **480/874-4666.** www.smoca.org. Admission $7 adults, $5 students, free for children 15 and under; free for all on Thurs. Early Sept to late May Tues–Wed and Fri–Sat 10am–5pm, Thurs 10am–8pm, Sun noon–5pm; late May to early Sept Wed and Fri–Sat 10am–5pm, Thurs 10am–8pm, Sun noon–5pm. Closed major holidays. Bus: 41, 50, or 72. Also accessible via Scottsdale Trolley shuttle bus.

Shemer Art Center and Museum ★ This art center may be small, but it mounts some of the more interesting little shows in the Valley. Exhibits change monthly and showcase Arizona artists. You might catch an exhibit of ceramic art, jewelry, or photography. The art center, which is housed in a 1920s Santa Fe mission–style home in the Arcadia neighborhood, also offers a variety of art classes. It's easy to miss as you're speeding along Camelback Road, so keep your eyes peeled.

5005 E. Camelback Rd., Phoenix. ✆ **602/262-4727.** www.phoenix.gov/shemer. Free admission. Mon 9am–3pm; Tues and Thurs 9am–4pm and 6–8:30pm; Wed 9am–4pm; Fri–Sat 9am–1pm (shorter hours in summer). Closed major holidays. Bus: 50.

Tempe Center for the Arts This big, modern art center on the shores of Tempe Town Lake is primarily a performing arts center, but it also has a small gallery that mounts interesting exhibitions throughout the year. Be sure to check the calendar.

700 W. Rio Salado Pkwy., Tempe. ✆ **480/350-2829.** www.tempe.gov/tca. Free admission. Tues–Fri 10am–6pm; Sat 11am–6pm. Closed major holidays. Bus: 48. METRO light rail: Mill Ave./3rd St.

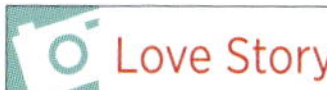

Love Story

Take a walk around the Scottsdale Mall, a refuge of green lawns and shade trees in downtown Scottsdale, and you just might fall in love—make that *on Love.* Robert Indiana's famous pop-art *Love* image, the one with the skewed letter *O*—yes, the one that became a postage stamp—has been installed as a 12-foot-tall sculpture on the lawn outside the Scottsdale Center for the Arts.

History Museums & Historic Landmarks

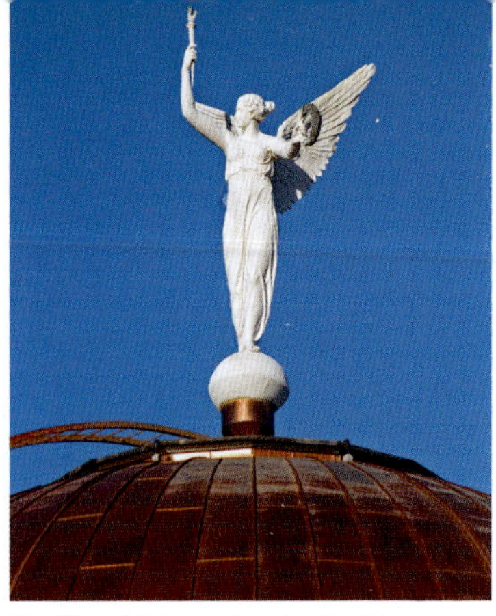
The *Winged Victory* statue atop the Arizona Capitol Museum.

Arizona Capitol Museum ★ In the years before Arizona became a state, the territorial capital moved from Prescott to Tucson, then back to Prescott, before finally settling in Phoenix. In 1898, a stately territorial capitol building was erected (with a copper roof to remind the local citizenry of the importance of that metal in the Arizona economy). Atop this copper roof was placed the statue *Winged Victory,* which still graces the old capitol building today. This building no longer serves as the actual state capitol, but has been restored to the way it appeared in 1912, the year Arizona became a state. Among the rooms on view are the senate and house chambers, as well as the governor's office. Excellent exhibits provide interesting perspectives on early Arizona events and lifestyles.

1700 W. Washington St. ✆ **602/926-3620.** www.lib.az.us/museum. Free admission. Mon–Fri 9am–4pm. Closed state holidays. Bus: 1 or DASH downtown shuttle.

Arizona Historical Society Museum at Papago Park ★ This museum, at the headquarters of the Arizona Historical Society, focuses its well-designed exhibits on the history of central Arizona. Temporary exhibits on the lives and works of the people who helped shape this region are always the highlights of a visit. An interesting permanent exhibit features life-size statues of everyday people from Arizona's past (a Mexican miner, a Chinese laborer, and so on). Quotes relate their individual stories, while props reveal what items they might have traveled with during their days in the desert.

1300 N. College Ave. (just off Curry Rd.), Tempe. ✆ **480/929-9499.** www.arizonahistoricalsociety.org. Admission $5 adults, $4 seniors and students 12–18, free for children 11 and under; free on 1st Sat of each month. Tues–Sat 10am–4pm; Sun noon–4pm.

Historic Heritage Square/Heritage and Science Park The city of Phoenix was founded in 1870, but today few of the city's early homes remain. If you want a glimpse of how Phoenix once looked, stroll around this collection of historic homes on the original town site. Although most of the houses are modest buildings from the early 20th century, there is one impressive Victorian home that dates to 1895. Today, the buildings house museums, restaurants, and gift shops. The Eastlake Victorian **Rosson House** (✆ **602/262-5070;** www.rossonhousemuseum.org), furnished with period antiques, is open for tours. The Stevens House is home to the Arizona Doll & Toy Museum (see later in this chapter). In the Teeter House, you'll find Nobuo at Teeter House (a Japanese restaurant; see "Where to Eat," earlier in this chapter). The old Baird Machine Shop contains Pizzeria Bianco (see "Where to Eat," earlier in this chapter), and the Thomas House is home to Bar Bianco (see "Phoenix & Scottsdale After Dark," later in this chapter).

115 N. 6th St., at Monroe. ✆ **602/262-5029.** www.phoenix.gov/PARKS/heritage.html. Rosson House tours $7.50 adults, $6 seniors and students, $4 children 6–12. Wed and Fri–Sat 10am–4pm; Thurs 1–4pm; Sun noon–4pm. Hours vary for other buildings; call for information. Closed New

Year's Day, Easter, July 4th, mid-Aug to early Sept, Thanksgiving, and Christmas. Bus: Red 0, 1, or DASH downtown shuttle. METRO light rail: Central Station.

Wells Fargo History Museum ★ Yes, this museum is small, and, yes, it's run by the Wells Fargo Bank, but the collection of artifacts here goes a long way toward conjuring up the Wild West so familiar from Hollywood movies. Not only is there an original Wells Fargo stagecoach on display, but there are also gold nuggets to ogle, old photos from the *real* Wild West, and plenty of artifacts and memorabilia from the days of stagecoach travel. There are also original paintings by N. C. Wyeth and bronze sculptures by Frederic Remington and Charles Russell.

145 W. Adams St. ✆ **602/378-1852.** www.wellsfargohistory.com. Free admission. Mon–Fri 9am–5pm. Closed major holidays. Bus: 0 or DASH downtown shuttle. METRO light rail: Central Station.

Science & Industry Museums

Arizona Museum of Natural History ★★ ☺ This is one of the best museums in the Valley, and its wide variety of exhibits appeals to people with a range of interests. For the kids, there are animated dinosaurs on an indoor "cliff" with a roaring waterfall. Of course, there are also plenty of dinosaur skeletons. Also of interest are an exhibit on Mesoamerican cultures, a display on Arizona mammoth kill sites, some old jail cells, and a walk-through mine mock-up with exhibits on the Lost Dutchman Mine. There's also a mock-up of a Hohokam village.

Kids love the dinosaurs at the Arizona Museum of Natural History.

53 N. MacDonald St. (at 1st St.), Mesa. ✆ **480/644-2230.** www.azmnh.org. Admission $10 adults, $9 seniors, $8 students, $6 children 3–12. Tues–Fri 10am–5pm; Sat 11am–5pm; Sun 1–5pm. Closed major holidays. Bus: 30.

Arizona Science Center ★ ☺ So, the kids weren't impressed with the botanical garden or the Native American artifacts at the Heard Museum. Bring 'em here. They can spend the afternoon pushing buttons, turning knobs, and interacting with all kinds of cool science exhibits. In the end, they might even learn something in spite of all the fun they have. The science center also includes a planetarium and an IMAX theater, both of which carry additional charges.

600 E. Washington St. ✆ **602/716-2000.** www.azscience.org. Admission $12 adults, $10 seniors and children 3–17. Planetarium and film combination tickets also available. Daily 10am–5pm. Closed Thanksgiving and Christmas. Bus: 0 or DASH downtown shuttle. METRO light rail: Central Station.

Challenger Space Center ☺ If one of your kids dreams of being a rocket scientist, then a visit to this science center in the northwest Valley is in order. Through space-themed movies, tours, planetarium shows, simulated space missions, and various classes and workshops, visitors can learn about travel in space.

21170 N. 83rd Ave., Peoria. ✆ **623/322-2001.** www.azchallenger.org. Admission $8 adults, $7 seniors, $5 children 4–18, free for children 3 and under. Mon–Fri 9am–4pm; Sat 10am–4pm. Closed major holidays.

Out-of-This-World Rocks

On October 9, 1992, a meteorite slammed into a car in Peekskill, New York. It was a nightmare for the car's owner, but a dream come true for the tabloids. Here was a reminder of just how dangerous out-of-this-world rocks can be. You can see a piece of the Peekskill meteorite and dozens of other otherworldly rocks at Arizona State University's **Center for Meteorite Studies,** Bateman Physical Sciences Center, C wing, Room 139, Palm Walk and University Drive (✆ **480/965-6511;** meteorites.asu.edu), on the ASU campus. The center, which is just a single small room, is open Monday through Friday from 9:30am to 4:30pm, and admission is free.

Museum Miscellany: Planes, Flames, Cars & More

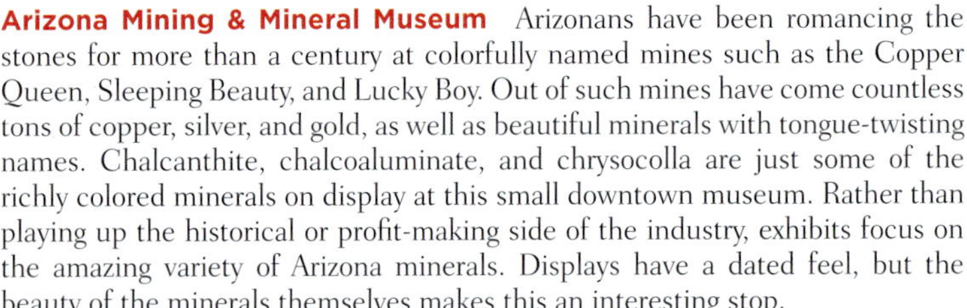

Arizona Mining & Mineral Museum Arizonans have been romancing the stones for more than a century at colorfully named mines such as the Copper Queen, Sleeping Beauty, and Lucky Boy. Out of such mines have come countless tons of copper, silver, and gold, as well as beautiful minerals with tongue-twisting names. Chalcanthite, chalcoaluminate, and chrysocolla are just some of the richly colored minerals on display at this small downtown museum. Rather than playing up the historical or profit-making side of the industry, exhibits focus on the amazing variety of Arizona minerals. Displays have a dated feel, but the beauty of the minerals themselves makes this an interesting stop.

1502 W. Washington St. ✆ **602/771-1600.** www.admmr.state.az.us. Admission $2 adults, free for children 17 and under. Mon–Fri 8am–5pm; Sat 11am–4pm. Closed state holidays. Bus: 1 or DASH downtown shuttle.

Arizona Wing of the Commemorative Air Force Fans of World War II bombers won't want to miss this small air museum in Mesa. The museum is home to *Sentimental Journey,* a B-17G bomber that was built in 1944 and is still flying today. The museum also has a B-25, a couple of Russian MiGs, and an F4 Phantom. Flights in *Sentimental Journey* and a couple of other aircraft can be arranged here, with tour prices ranging from $275 to $425 per person.

Falcon Field, 2017 N. Greenfield Rd., Mesa. ✆ **480/924-1940.** www.arizonawingcaf.com. Oct–May admission $10 adults, $9 seniors, $3 children 5–12, free for children 4 and under; June–Sept admission $7 adults, $3 children 5–12, free for children 4 and under. Oct–May daily 10am–4pm; June–Sept Wed–Sun 9am–3pm. Closed New Year's Day, Thanksgiving, and Christmas. Bus: 136.

Hall of Flame Firefighting Museum ★ ☺ This is the nation's largest firefighting museum and houses a fascinating collection of vintage firetrucks. The displays date from a 1725 English hand pumper to several classic engines from the 20th century. All are beautifully restored and, mostly, fire-engine red. In all, more than 90 vehicles are on display.

At Papago Park, 6101 E. Van Buren St. ✆ **602/275-3473.** www.hallofflame.org. Admission $6 adults, $5 seniors, $4 students 6–17, $1.50 children 3–5, free for children 2 and under. Mon–Sat 9am–5pm; Sun noon–4pm. Closed New Year's Day, Thanksgiving, and Christmas. Bus: 1 or 3. METRO light rail: Priest Dr./Washington St.

The Penske Racing Museum is tucked into a local car dealership.

Musical Instrument Museum ★ I could easily spend the better part of a day at this fascinating museum, and I don't even play an instrument. Vast halls broken down by content showcase an astonishing variety of musical instruments from all over the world. Not only will you see countless unfamiliar instruments, but you'll get to watch videos of them being played in their countries of origin. Think world anthropology as seen through strings and reeds and drums and horns and you'll have an idea of what this museum is all about. Among the many displays are the first Steinway piano ever made (built in 1836 in the Steinweg family's kitchen in Seesen, Germany) and the tools brought to America in 1833 by guitar-maker C. F. Martin. One room that is especially popular with children has instruments you can play yourself. A performance hall stages frequent events, and musicians often give impromptu concerts in the museum itself.

4725 E. Mayo Blvd., Phoenix. ✆ **480/478-6000.** www.themim.org. $15 adults, $13 seniors, $10 youths 6–17, free for children 5 and under. Mon–Wed 9am–5pm; Thurs–Fri 9am–9pm; Sat 9am–5pm; Sun 10am–5pm. Closed Thanksgiving and Christmas. Just south of U.S. 101 at the corner of E. Mayo and N. Tatum boulevards.

Penske Racing Museum ★ 🎁 At first you may think I've sent you to the local Jaguar dealer, but tucked inside the car dealerships here is the coolest little museum in Scottsdale. Inside this museum, you'll find the personal collection of Roger Penske, which includes more than a dozen immaculately maintained race cars, many of them Indianapolis 500 winners. If you follow Indy car racing, you know that the Penske team is the winningest team in the business, and the cars in here are why.

7125 E. Chauncey Lane, Scottsdale. ✆ **480/538-4444.** www.penskeracingmuseum.com. Free admission. Mon–Sat 8am–4pm; Sun noon–5pm.

Architectural Highlights

Arizona Biltmore This resort hotel, although not designed by Frank Lloyd Wright, shows the famed architect's hand in its distinctive cast-cement blocks. It also displays sculptures, furniture, and stained glass designed by Wright. The best way to soak up the ambience of this exclusive resort (if you aren't staying here) is over dinner, a cocktail, or tea. To learn more about the building, however, take a tour, given Tuesday, Thursday, and Saturday at 10am.

2400 E. Missouri Ave. ✆ **602/955-6600.** Tours $10 (free for resort guests).

Burton Barr Library This library is among the most daring pieces of public architecture in the city, and no fan of futuristic art or science fiction should miss it. The five-story cube is partially clad in enough ribbed copper sheeting to produce roughly 17.5 million pennies. The building's design makes use of the desert's plentiful sunshine to provide light for reading, but also incorporates computer-controlled louvers and shade sails to reduce heat and glare.

1221 N. Central Ave. ✆ **602/262-4636.** www.phoenixpubliclibrary.org. Free admission. Mon, Fri, Sat 9am–5pm; Tues–Thurs 11am–7pm; Sun 1–5pm. Bus: 0. METRO light rail: McDowell Rd./Central Ave.

Paolo Soleri's famous bronze bells are cast at Cosanti.

Cosanti This complex of cast-concrete structures served as a prototype and learning project for architect Paolo Soleri's much grander Arcosanti project, currently under construction north of Phoenix (see "En Route to Northern Arizona," later in this chapter). It's here at Cosanti that Soleri's famous bells are cast, and most weekday mornings you can see the foundry in action. Visit between 10am and noon Monday through Friday for the best chance of seeing bronze bells being poured.

6433 E. Doubletree Ranch Rd., Paradise Valley. ✆ **480/948-6145.** www.arcosanti.org. Free admission. Mon–Sat 9am–5pm; Sun 11am–5pm. Closed major holidays. Drive 1 mile west of Scottsdale Rd. on Doubletree Ranch Rd.

Mystery Castle ★ Built for a daughter who longed for a castle more permanent than those built in the sand at the beach, Mystery Castle is a wondrous work of folk-art architecture. Boyce Luther Gulley, who had come to Arizona in hopes of curing his tuberculosis, constructed the castle during the 1930s and early 1940s using stones from the property. The resulting 18-room fantasy has 13 fireplaces, parapets, and many other unusual touches.

800 E. Mineral Rd. ✆ **602/268-1581.** Admission $5 adults, $3 ages 5–12. Thurs–Sun 11am–4pm. Closed June–Sept. Take 7th St. south to Mineral Rd. (2 miles south of Baseline Rd.).

Taliesin West ★★★ Frank Lloyd Wright loved the Arizona desert and, in 1937, built Taliesin West as a winter camp that served as his home, office, and school. Today, the buildings of Taliesin West are the headquarters of the Frank Lloyd Wright Foundation and School of Architecture.

Tours include a general introduction to Wright and his theories of architecture, and also explain the campus buildings. Wright believed in using local materials in his designs, and this is much in evidence at Taliesin West, where local stone

Hunt's Tomb: The Great Pyramid of Phoenix

If you're driving through Papago Park, perhaps on your way to the Desert Botanical Garden, and see a shimmering white pyramid on a hilltop, you might at first imagine that you're having a heat-induced hallucination. Not so. The pyramid is real. However, it was *not* built by wandering Aztecs or ancient Egyptians. It is the tomb of Gov. George W. P. Hunt, who was the first, second, third, sixth, seventh, eighth, and tenth governor of Arizona. No other governor in any state has served as many terms in office as Hunt, who was born in 1859 and died in 1934. The tomb is accessible from a parking area near the zoo.

was used for building foundations. With its glass-walled buildings and patio areas, Taliesin West also showcases Wright's ability to integrate indoor and outdoor spaces.

For a brief introduction to Wright and his theories of architecture, take a basic introductory tour (listed below) or an Insights Tour ($26–$32), which will take you inside Wright's personal living area. There are also behind-the-scenes tours ($60), guided desert walks ($32), apprentice shelter tours ($40), and night hikes ($35). Many of these tours are available only at certain times of year. Call ahead for schedule information.

12621 Frank Lloyd Wright Blvd. (at Cactus/114th St.), Scottsdale. ✆ **480/860-2700,** ext. 494. www.franklloydwright.org. Basic tours $18–$24 adults, $18–$20 seniors and students, $7–$10 children 4–12. Daily 9am–4pm. Closed Easter, Thanksgiving, Christmas, and occasional special events. From Scottsdale Rd., go east on Shea Blvd. to 114th St., then north 1 mile to the entrance road.

TOP: **Frank Lloyd Wright's Taliesin West.** ABOVE, RIGHT: **Wrigley Mansion.**

Wrigley Mansion Situated on a hilltop adjacent to the Arizona Biltmore, this elegant mansion was built by chewing-gum magnate William Wrigley, Jr., between 1929 and 1931 as a present for his wife, Ada. Designed with Italianate styling, the mansion has so many levels and red-tile roofs that it looks like an entire village. The mansion is now a National Historic Landmark, with the interior restored to its original elegance. Tours of the mansion are offered 5 days a week and offer a fascinating glimpse into the lives of the Wrigleys. Tour reservations are required.

2501 E. Telawa Trail. ✆ **602/955-4079.** www.wrigleymansionclub.com. Tours $11. Tues–Sat 10am and 3pm (call for summer hours).

Wild West Theme Towns

Despite a population running to the millions, Phoenix and Scottsdale occasionally like to present themselves as grown-up Wild West cow towns. But since there are more Ford Mustangs than wild mustangs around these parts, you'll have to get out of town way before sundown if you want a taste of the Old West. At the outer edges of the Valley, you'll find a couple of Hollywood-style cow towns that are basically tourist traps, but, hey, if you've got the kids along, you owe it to them to visit at least one of these places.

Cave Creek, founded as a gold-mining camp in the 1870s, is the last of the Valley towns that still has some semblance of Wild West character, but this is rapidly fading as area real-estate prices have skyrocketed and Scottsdale's population center moves ever northward. Still, you'll find several steakhouses and saloons, as well as shops selling Western and Native American crafts and antiques. The main family attraction is a place called **Frontier Town,** 6245 E. Cave Creek Rd. (✆ **480/488-3317;** www.frontiertownaz.com), which is in the center of town. It's a sort of mock cow town with lots of little shops, a restaurant, and a saloon. To learn more about the history of this area, stop in at the **Cave Creek Museum,** at Skyline Drive and Basin Road (✆ **480/488-2764;** www.cavecreekmuseum.org). It's open from October to May on Wednesday, Thursday, Saturday, and Sunday from 1 to 4:30pm and Friday from 10am to 4:30pm. Admission is $5 for adults, $3 for seniors and students 12 and older, and free for children 11 and under.

Goldfield Ghost Town ★ ☺ Over on the east side of the Valley, just 4 miles northeast of Apache Junction, you'll find a reconstructed 1890s gold-mining town. Although it's a bit of a tourist trap—with gift shops, an ice-cream parlor, and the like—it's also home to **Goldfield's Historic Museum** (✆ **480/677-6463**), which has interesting exhibits on the history of the area. Of particular note is the exhibit on the Lost Dutchman gold mine, perhaps the most famous mine in the country, despite the fact that no one knows where it is. Goldfield Mine Tours provides guided tours of the gold mine beneath the town. The Superstition Narrow Gauge Railroad circles the town, and the **Goldfield Livery Stables** (✆ **480/982-0133**) offers horseback riding and carriage rides. If you're here at lunchtime, you can get a meal at the steakhouse/saloon.

4650 N. Mammoth Mine Rd. (4 miles northeast of Apache Junction on Ariz. 88). ✆ **480/983-0333.** www.goldfieldghosttown.com. Museum admission by donation; train rides $6 adults, $5 seniors, $4 children 5–12; mine tours $7 adults, $6 seniors, $4 children 6–12; horseback rides $33 for 1 hr., $55 for 2 hr. Town daily 10am–5pm; museum, tour, and ride hours vary. Closed Christmas.

Rawhide at Wild Horse Pass ☺ Sure, Rawhide is a tourist trap, but this fake cow town, originally located in north Scottsdale, is so much fun and such a quintessentially Phoenician experience that no family should get out of town

Carefree Living

Carefree, a planned community established in the 1950s and popular with retirees, is much more subdued than its neighbor Cave Creek, which effects a sort of Wild West character. Ho Hum Road and Easy Street are just two local street names that reflect the sedate nature of Carefree, which is home to the **Boulders Resort.** This resort boasts a spectacular setting, a 33,000-square-foot spa, and a couple of excellent restaurants. On Easy Street, in what passes for Carefree's downtown, you'll find one of the world's largest sundials. The dial is 90 feet across, and the gnomon (the part that casts the shadow) is 35 feet tall. In the middle of the dial are a pool of water and a fountain. Also downtown is a sort of reproduction Spanish-village shopping area, and just south of town, adjacent to the Boulders resort, is the upscale **el Pedregal** shopping center, with interesting boutiques, galleries, and a few restaurants.

without first moseying down its dusty streets. Those streets are lined with lots of tourist shops and plenty of places for refreshments, including a steakhouse. Attractions and activities include stunt shows, gunfights, trick-roping demonstrations, a mechanical bull, and stagecoach, burro, and train rides. March through May and October and November, there are also Saturday-night sundown cookouts ($48 adults, $15 children) with hayrides, live music, and storytellers.

5700 W. North Loop Rd., Chandler. ✆ **480/502-5600.** www.rawhide.com. Free admission (individual shows and rides $2–$5). Hours vary with the seasons; call for details.

Parks & Zoos

Perhaps the most unusual park in the Phoenix metro area centers on **Tempe Town Lake,** 620 N. Mill Ave., Tempe (✆ **480/350-8625;** www.tempe.gov/lake), which was created in 1999 by damming the Salt River with inflatable dams. With parks and bike paths lining both the north and south shores, this 2-mile-long lake is a good place to stretch your legs. The best lake access is at Tempe Town Beach, at the foot of the Mill Avenue Bridge. Tempe Town Lake is the focus of a large development that also includes the Tempe Center for the Arts.

Among Phoenix's most popular parks are its natural areas and preserves. These include Phoenix South Mountain Park, Papago Park, Phoenix Mountains Preserve (site of Piestewa Peak), North Mountain Preserve, North Mountain Recreation Area, and Camelback Mountain–Echo Canyon Recreation Area. For more information on these parks, see "Bicycling," "Hiking," and "Horseback Riding" under "Outdoor Pursuits," below.

Not far from downtown Phoenix, you can wander around the **Steele Indian School Park,** 300 E. Indian School Rd. (✆ **602/495-0739;** www.phoenix.gov/PARKS/sisp.html). This park, as its name implies, was once an Indian school. Several of the old buildings are still standing, but it's the many new fountains, gardens, and interpretive displays that make this park such a fascinating place. A stop here can easily be combined with a visit to the nearby Heard Museum.

The Phoenix Zoo's African savanna gives visitors the chance to feed giraffes.

Phoenix Zoo ★ ☺ Forget about polar bears and other cold-climate creatures; this zoo focuses its attention primarily on animals that come from climates similar to that of the Phoenix area. Most impressive of the displays are the African savanna, where you can feed a giraffe, and the baboon colony. The Southwestern exhibits are also of interest, as are the Komodo dragons and the exhibit featuring monkeys from Central and South America. All animals are kept in naturalistic enclosures, and what with all the palm trees and tropical vegetation, the zoo sometimes manages to make you forget you're in the desert. Be sure to ride the camel while you're here. *Zoolights,* an after-hours holiday-light display, is held late November to early January.

At Papago Park, 455 N. Galvin Pkwy. ✆ **602/273-1341.** www.phoenixzoo.org. Admission $18 adults, $9 children 3–12, free for children 2 and under. Sept to early Nov and mid-Jan to May daily 9am–5pm; early Nov to mid-Jan daily 9am–4pm; June–Aug Mon–Fri 7am–2pm, Sat–Sun 7am–4pm. Closed Christmas. Bus: 1 or 3. METRO light rail: Priest Dr./Washington St.

Wildlife World Zoo & Aquarium ☺ While the animals at the Phoenix Zoo are interesting enough, the animals here are way cool; just ask your kids. Best of all, you can get really close to some and even feed a few. There are informative animal shows, including parrot feedings, throughout the day. While the desert may seem like an odd place for a public aquarium, the aquarium here is a real kid-pleaser, with sharks, stingrays, piranhas, and an albino alligator. Combine a visit to this zoo with time at the nearby Challenger Space Center or Deer Valley Rock Art Center, and you have a fun, full day for the family.

16501 W. Northern Ave., Litchfield Park. ✆ **623/935-9453.** www.wildlifeworld.com. Zoo and Aquarium admission $28 adults, $14 children 3–12, free for children 2 and under; Aquarium (only available evenings) admission $17 adults, $9 children 3–12, free for children 2 and under. Zoo daily 9am–6pm. Aquarium daily 9am–9pm. Take I-10 west to Ariz. 303 (exit 124) and drive north 6 miles to Northern Ave. eastbound or take Ariz. 101 west to Northern Ave. (exit 101) and continue west for 8 miles.

Especially for Kids

In addition to the following suggestions, kids are likely to enjoy the Arizona Science Center, the Arizona Museum of Natural History, the Hall of Flame Firefighting Museum, and the Phoenix Zoo—all described in detail earlier in this chapter.

Arizona Doll & Toy Museum This small museum is located in the historic Stevens House on Heritage Square in downtown Phoenix. The miniature classroom peopled by doll students is a favorite exhibit. With dolls dating from the 19th century, this is a definite must for doll collectors.

At Heritage Sq., 602 E. Adams St. ✆ **602/253-9337.** Admission $3 adults, $1 children 12 and under. Tues–Sat 10am–4pm; Sun noon–4pm (call for hours in Aug). Bus: 0 or DASH downtown shuttle. METRO light rail: Central Station.

Arizona Museum for Youth Using both traditional displays and participatory activities, this museum allows children to explore the fine arts and their own

Now That's a Fountain

Arizona loves its water features. Reservoirs, canals, pools, fountains—they're everywhere in the desert. You'd never think that water is in short supply around these parts. One of the most unusual water features is the Fountain Hills fountain, less than 20 miles northeast of Scottsdale. This fountain, for which the town is named, is one of the tallest fountains in the world. Using three 500-horsepower pumps, it can shoot water 560 feet into the air. However, the fountain usually operates on only two pumps, with the plume reaching a mere 330 feet on average. Unless there are high winds, the fountain operates daily from 9am to 9pm every hour on the hour for 15 minutes. To find the fountain, take Shea Boulevard east from Scottsdale Road or U.S. 101.

creativity. It's housed in a refurbished grocery store, and the highlight is Artville, an arts-driven kid-size town. Exhibits are geared mainly toward toddlers through 12-year-olds, but all ages can work together to experience the activities.

35 N. Robson St. (btw. Main and 1st sts.), Mesa. ✆ **480/644-2467.** www.arizonamuseumforyouth.com. Admission $7, free for children under 1. Tues–Sat 10am–4pm; Sun noon–4pm. Closed major holidays. Bus: 30.

Castles-n-Coasters Located adjacent to Metrocenter, one of Arizona's largest shopping malls, this small amusement park boasts an impressive double-loop roller coaster, plenty of tamer rides, four 18-hole miniature-golf courses, and a huge pavilion full of video games.

9445 N. Metro Pkwy. E. ✆ **602/997-7575.** www.castlesncoasters.com. Ride and game prices vary; all-day passes $21–$25. Daily (hours change seasonally; call ahead). Bus: 27.

Children's Museum of Phoenix Housed in a large downtown Phoenix building that was once a school, this children's museum makes learning fun for the little ones. Hands-on, interactive exhibits include an art studio, a cool climbing structure, a noodle forest, a giant ballroom full of balls, and a place for toddlers. In one exhibit, kids can learn about the flora and fauna of the Sonoran Desert.

215 N. 7th St. ✆ **602/253-0501.** www.childrensmuseumofphoenix.org. Admission $11 adults, $10 seniors, free for children under 1; free for all 1st Fri of each month. Tues–Sun 9am–4pm. Closed New Year's Day, Thanksgiving, and Christmas. Bus: DASH downtown shuttle. METRO light rail: 3rd St./Washington station.

CrackerJax Family Fun & Sports Park Two miniature-golf courses are the main attractions here, but you'll also find a driving range, a professional putting course for grown-up golfers, batting cages, go-cart tracks, a bumper-boat lagoon, a bungee dome, and a video-game arcade.

16001 N. Scottsdale Rd. (¼ mile south of Bell Rd.), Scottsdale. ✆ **480/998-2800.** www.crackerjax.com. Activity prices vary; multiple-activity pass $15–$25. Sun–Thurs 10am–10pm; Fri–Sat 10am–midnight (driving range opens at 8am). Bus: 72.

McCormick-Stillman Railroad Park.

McCormick-Stillman Railroad Park If you or your kids happen to like trains, you won't want to miss this park. On the grounds are restored railroad cars and engines, two old railway depots, model railroad layouts, and, best of all, a 5⁄12-scale model railroad that takes visitors around the park. A 1929 carousel and a general store round out the attractions.

7301 E. Indian Bend Rd. (at Scottsdale Rd.), Scottsdale. ✆ **480/312-2312.** www.therailroadpark.com. Train $2; carousel rides $1; museum admission $2 adults, free for children 2 and under. Hours vary with the season; call for schedule. Closed Thanksgiving and Christmas (museum closed June–Sept). Bus: 72.

WALKING TOUR: OLD TOWN SCOTTSDALE

START:	**Scottsdale Historical Museum.**
FINISH:	**Scottsdale Waterfront.**
TIME:	**2 hours (not including shopping and visiting the museums).**
BEST TIMES:	**Thursdays, when the Scottsdale Museum of Contemporary Art waives its usual admission charge and art galleries stay open late.**
WORST TIMES:	**Mondays, when galleries and the Scottsdale Museum of Contemporary Art are closed, and summer, when it's just too hot to do any walking.**

From tacky souvenir shops to art galleries dealing in $100,000 paintings, downtown Scottsdale has a lot going on. With half a dozen distinct shopping districts around the area, it's easy to miss many of the highlights. This walking tour leads you past the best downtown Scottsdale has to offer.

After finding a parking space in the large public garage at the corner of Brown Avenue and First Street, walk to the northwest corner of the garage where, at 7333 E. Scottsdale Mall, you will find the:

1 Scottsdale Historical Museum

Housed in a little red schoolhouse that was built in 1909, this museum will help you understand that despite all the modern buildings, Scottsdale really does have a past. Here at the museum, you can pick up a map to the various historic buildings in the neighborhood. On this walking tour, you'll pass most of the buildings on the museum's map.

After acquainting yourself with Scottsdale's history, turn right as you leave the museum and take a stroll around the:

2 Scottsdale Civic Center Mall

Oddly enough, in such a shopping-obsessed city, this mall is a park rather than a shopping center. (Conversely, the nearby Biltmore Fashion Park is a shopping mall, not a park—go figure.) Amid the mall's green lawns and flowering shade trees, you'll find nearly a dozen sculptures. You might also catch some sort of event going on here. In the spring there are Native American dancers and musicians a couple of days a week, and live music on Sunday afternoons.

Near the main entrance to the Scottsdale Center for the Arts, which faces the mall, you'll find the city's most beloved sculpture:

3 Robert Indiana's Love

With its canted letter O, this image, which consists of the word "love" spelled out in large block letters, will likely be quite familiar. The iconic image is nearly as symbolic of the 1960s as the peace sign, and was once used on a postage stamp.

Robert Indiana's *Love.*

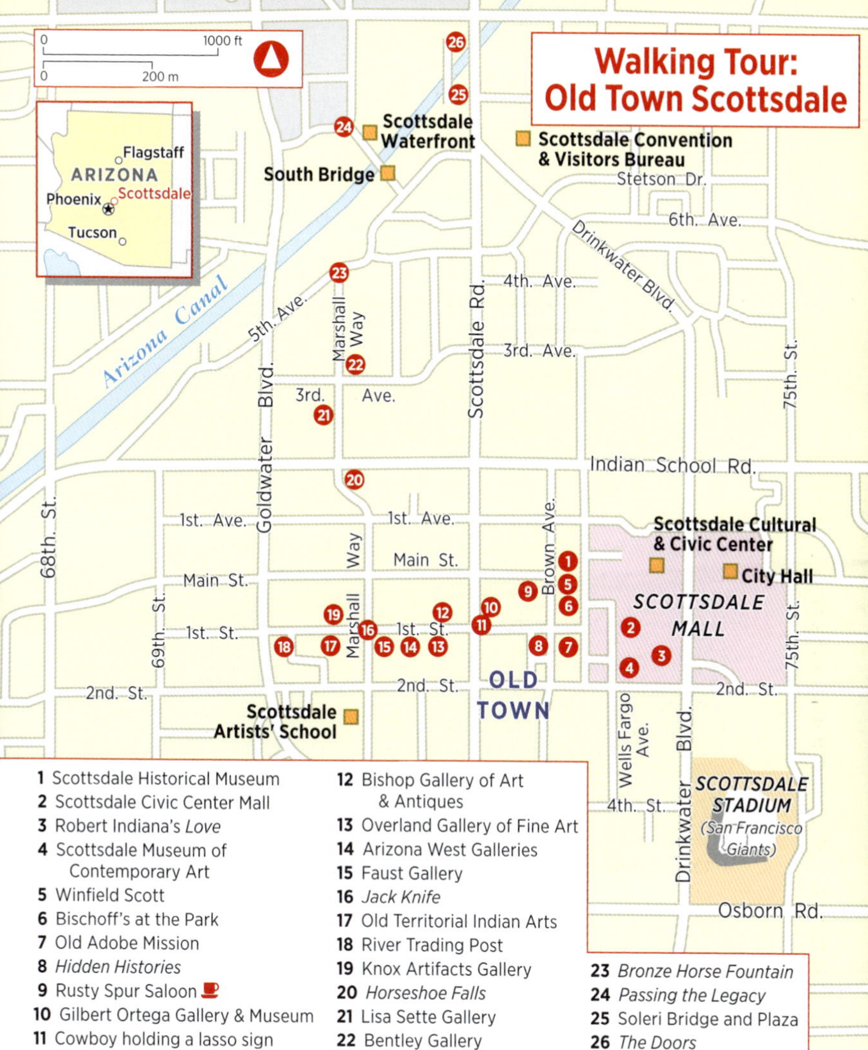

Primed with a bit of pop art, head around the side of the arts center to the:

4 Scottsdale Museum of Contemporary Art

The galleries of this museum are used for a wide variety of often-challenging contemporary art exhibitions. Even if you aren't interested in contemporary art, you might want to check out *Knight Rise,* a room-size art installation off the gift shop. There's never a charge to visit this unusual space that uses light and the sky as canvas.

Head back out of the mall by way of the walkway in front of the little red schoolhouse, and you will see a statue of:

5 Winfield Scott

If you haven't already guessed, Scott was the founder of this city, and it is for him that Scottsdale is named. This statue, which shows Scott with his wife and his mule, Maude, is on the site of Scott's original homestead.

To the left as you exit the mall, at 3925 N. Brown Ave., you'll find:

6 Bischoff's at the Park

Don't confuse this shop full of Native American jewelry and other Southwestern arts and crafts with the affiliated Bischoff's Shades of the West across the street. The latter is a low-end souvenir shop, while the former is full of higher-quality merchandise and is fascinating to explore.

Turn left when you come out of Bischoff's and walk a block and a half south to the:

7 Old Adobe Mission

This small mission church was built in 1933 by Hispanic and Yaqui Indian families and has been undergoing restoration in recent years. Inside, you'll usually find someone ready to answer questions about the building.

Across the street, you'll see the colorful sculptures of Elizabeth Conner's:

8 Hidden Histories

These sculptures are colorful, oversize renditions of familiar objects, including a cowboy hat and an old tire. The sculptures are adjacent to the public parking lot that on Saturday mornings, from November through May, is the site of the Old Town Farmer's Market. If the market is going on, be sure to wander through and try some free samples.

Now walk back north on Brown Avenue to Main Street and turn left. On this block, you'll find lots of souvenir shops and stores selling Native American jewelry. In the middle of the block, you'll find a longtime favorite Scottsdale watering hole.

9 Rusty Spur Saloon

For many years, Scottsdale billed itself as the West's most Western town, and at the **Rusty Spur Saloon,** 7245 E. Main St., the West lives on with country bands playing throughout the day and couples dancing and drinking the night (and day) away. If you're a cowboy or cowgirl at heart, you owe it to yourself to stop in for a beer.

Continue on down Main Street to the intersection with busy Scottsdale Road, and across Main Street, at 3925 N. Scottsdale Rd., you'll see the:

10 Gilbert Ortega Gallery & Museum

This shop has one of the best selections of Native American jewelry in Scottsdale and also has museum-quality displays of Native artifacts around the store.

In front of this store stands a metal cutout of a:

11 Cowboy Holding a Lasso

This unofficial welcome-to-Scottsdale sign has been around for more than 50 years and is another of the city's top photo-op spots.

A large cowboy sign greets visitors to Scottsdale.

From here, cross Scottsdale Road and continue along East Main Street. You will now leave the souvenir shops behind. This end of the street is lined on both sides with art galleries and antiques stores. At 7164 Main St., you'll find one of my favorite antiques shops, the cluttered and cramped:

12 Bishop Gallery of Art & Antiques

This place is divided into two rooms, one full of rare and unusual antiques from around the world and another filled with original works of art. I could spend hours in here.

Across the street, you'll find several more interesting shops and galleries, including, at 7155 E. Main St.:

13 Overland Gallery of Fine Art

At this gallery, you can see the angular Southwestern landscapes of Ed Mell and the more traditional landscapes of contemporary American realist Gary Ernest Smith.

A few doors down, at 7149 Main St., there's:

14 Arizona West Galleries

Antique cowboy gear and the trappings of the American West are the specialty of this antiques shop.

Next watch for, at 7103 E. Main St.:

15 Faust Gallery

Stop in here to look for old Native American baskets and ceramics, as well as Navajo rugs.

At the intersection of East Main Street and Marshall Way, you'll see, in the middle of the roundabout, Ed Mell's sculpture:

16 Jack Knife

This was Mell's first large-scale sculpture, and the horse shows the same sort of angularity that you will have seen in his landscape paintings at the Overland Gallery.

Continue through the intersection, and, at 7077 E. Main St., you'll come to:

17 Old Territorial Indian Arts

This is the oldest Indian arts-and-crafts shop on Main Street, and features a good selection of Hopi kachina dolls, Zuni fetishes, and Navajo silver jewelry.

A few doors away, at 7033 E. Main St., there's also:

18 River Trading Post

Here you'll find ancient Southwestern pottery, Navajo rugs, and a good selection of reasonably priced Native American crafts.

Now walk back to the roundabout and cross the street to 7056 E. Main St. and:

19 Knox Artifacts Gallery

You won't believe your eyes when you step through the doors of this amazing shop. Museum-quality pre-Columbian artifacts, as well as antiquities from ancient Greece, Rome, and Egypt, fill the shelves and cases.

Continue north on Marshall Way, and at the intersection with Indian School Road, you'll find the unusual:

20 Horseshoe Falls

The columns of Michael Maglich's sculpture are actually stacks of horseshoes arranged in the shape of a horseshoe. Mist periodically rises from the ground beneath the statute.

Now cross Indian School Road to the Marshall Way contemporary-arts district where you'll find a dozen galleries scattered along the 2 blocks between Indian School Road and Fifth Avenue. Galleries not to miss include, at 4142 N. Marshall Way, on the west side of the street:

21 Lisa Sette Gallery

It's difficult to categorize the eclectic shows mounted at this gallery, but whatever is on the walls, it will likely be intriguing.

Across the street, at 4161 N. Marshall Way, there is:

22 Bentley Gallery

This is the most cutting-edge major gallery in the Valley. It also has an outpost in a large warehouse south of downtown Phoenix.

In the middle of the roundabout at the intersection of North Marshall Way and East Fifth Avenue, you'll see Bob Parks's:

23 Bronze Horse Fountain

The four life-size bronze horse statues thundering away from this fountain have long been a symbol of the Fifth Avenue shopping district.

Bentley Gallery presents contemporary art in an area dominated by Southwestern galleries.

From the roundabout, walk a block up Stetson Drive to the pedestrian bridge that connects the SouthBridge area with the Scottsdale Waterfront. At the north end of the bridge, you'll come to yet another horse sculpture, Herb Mignery's:

24 Passing the Legacy

This classic Western bronze statue shows two Pony Express riders passing the mail at a full gallop. One sculpture is meant to represent cowboys of the past, while the other represents cowboys of the present.

From this sculpture, head 2 blocks along the landscaped walkway on the north bank of the Arizona Canal. Across the canal, you can see the shops and restaurants of the Mix, while on the north bank, you'll be skirting residential condominiums and the shops of the Scottsdale Waterfront shopping center. Just before the canal reaches Scottsdale Road, you'll find the:

25 Soleri Bridge and Plaza

Arizona-based architect Paolo Soleri, well known in the state for his bronze wind bells and his Arcosanti architectural experiment in the desert north of Phoenix, has been designing bridges for decades, but this stainless-steel pedestrian bridge was the first to ever be constructed. Dedicated in late 2010, the bridge is anchored by a 64-foot pylon that has massive bronze wind bells suspended from it. Each day at solar noon, sunlight shines through the bridge pylon onto a red stripe on the bridge deck. ***Note:*** Solar noon is different from noon on your watch.

Walk back across the bridge and continue a few steps to the corner of Scottsdale and Camelback roads where you'll find Donald Lipski's unusual sculpture:

26 The Doors

From the outside, this sculpture looks like three huge colonial doors leaning against each other, but step inside the doors, and you'll find yourself inside a giant mirrored kaleidoscope.

From here, you can continue shopping your way through the Scottsdale Waterfront, the Mix on the SouthBridge side of the Arizona Canal, or across Camelback Road in the huge Scottsdale Fashion Square shopping mall.

ORGANIZED TOURS & EXCURSIONS

The Valley of the Sun is a sprawling, often congested place, and if you're unfamiliar with the area, you may be surprised at how great the distances between attractions are. If map reading and urban navigation are not your strong points, consider taking a guided tour. If you want a different sort of perspective on the area, consider a jeep tour, hot-air balloon ride, or a flight in a glider.

BUS TOURS If you'd like to get a quick overview of Phoenix and Scottsdale, there are a couple of local tour companies I recommend. **Open Road Tours** (✆ **800/766-7117** or 602/997-6474; www.openroadtours.com) does a half-day tour of the Valley's highlights, with an hour for shopping in Old Town Scottsdale. These tours cost $59 for adults and $39 for children 11 and under. This company also offers day-long tours to Tucson, Sedona, and the Grand Canyon. **Detours** (✆ **866/438-6877;** www.detoursaz.com) also offers half-day tours of the Valley, and these tours, which cost $75 for adults and $40 for children 12 and under, include lunch at a local restaurant.

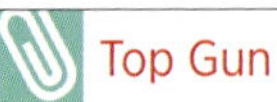

Top Gun

Ever wanted to be a fighter pilot? Well, at **Fighter Combat International** (✆ **866/359-4273;** www.fightercombat.com) you can find out if you've got the right stuff. This company, which operates out of the Phoenix-Mesa Gateway Airport in Mesa, offers a variety of exciting aerobatic flights, including mock dogfights. Best of all, on some flights, you get to learn how to do loops, rolls, spins, and other aerobatic moves. Flights start at $485; for a mock air-combat mission, you'll have to shell out $795.

GLIDER RIDES The thermals that form above the mountains in the Phoenix area make this an ideal place for flying sailplanes (gliders). On the south side of the Valley at the Estrella Sailport, **Arizona Soaring,** 22548 N. Sailport Way, Maricopa (✆ **520/568-2318;** www.azsoaring.com), offers sailplane rides, with a basic 20-minute flight going for $105. An aerobatic flight with loops, rolls, and inverted flying costs $160. To reach the airstrip, take I-10 E to exit 164 (Queen Creek Rd.), go west on Queen Creek Road (which becomes Maricopa Rd. [Ariz. 347]) for 15 miles, turn right on Ariz. 238, and continue 6½ miles. On the north side of the Valley, there's **Turf Soaring School,** 8700 W. Carefree Hwy., Peoria (✆ **602/439-3621;** www.turfsoaring.com), which charges $109 for a basic flight and $159 for a deluxe aerobatic flight. Reservations are a good idea at either place.

HOT-AIR BALLOON RIDES The still morning air of the Valley of the Sun is perfect for hot-air ballooning, and because of the stiff competition, prices are among the lowest in the country. **Over the Rainbow** (✆ **602/225-5666;** www.letsgoballooning.com) charges only $165 for a 1- to 1½-hour flight, while **Adventures Out West** (✆ **800/755-0935** or 480/991-3666; www.adventuresoutwest.com) charges $185 to $205 (or $205–$225 with transportation from your Scottsdale hotel) for a 1-hour flight. Check websites for discounted rates.

JEEP TOURS After spending a few days in Scottsdale, you'll likely start wondering where the desert is. Well, it's out there, and the easiest way to explore it is to book a jeep tour. Most hotels and resorts work with particular companies, so start by asking your concierge. Alternatively, you can contact one of the following companies. Most will pick you up at your hotel, take you off through the desert, and maybe let you pan for gold or shoot a six-gun. Depending on how many people are in your party and where you're staying, expect to pay between $65 to $100 per person for a 3-hour tour. Companies include **Arizona Desert Mountain Jeep Tours** (✆ **800/567-3619;** www.azdesertmountain.com) and **Southwest Desert Adventures** (✆ **877/962-6620** or 480/962-6620; www.arizonabound.com).

If you want to really impress your friends when you get home, you'll need to try something a little different. How about a Hummer tour? Contact **Desert Storm Hummer Tours** (✆ **480/922-0020;** www.dshummer.com), which charges $100 for a 4-hour tour ($75 for children 16 and under). This company also offers night tours ($125 for adults and $100 for children) that let you spot wildlife with night-vision equipment. Alternatively, there's **Stellar Adventures** (✆ **877/878-3552** or 602/402-0584; www.stellaradventures.com), which charges $135 for a basic 4-hour tour ($95 for children 10 and under) and $165 for its advanced tour.

Get a bird's-eye view of the Valley from a hot-air balloon.

If rumbling through the desert on a guided Hummer tour still isn't rugged enough for you, then you might be a candidate for driving yourself through the desert. A couple of companies in the area do tours in Tomcars, which, like the Hummer, were originally developed for military uses. Tomcars are little open-sided buggies that let you get covered with desert dust as you four-wheel past cactus and creosote bushes. If this sounds like your kind of outing, contact **Desert Wolf Tours** (✆ **877/613-9653;** www.desertwolftours.com), which charges $145 for a half-day tour ($87 for children under 12), or **Green Zebra Adventures** (✆ **866/703-2622** or 480/629-6262; www.gogreenzebra.com), which charges $129 for a half-day tour ($59 for children under 12). Full-day, sunset, and night tours are also offered by Desert Wolf Tours.

SCENIC FLIGHTS If you're short on time but want to at least see the Grand Canyon, book an air tour in a small plane. **Westwind Scenic Air Tours,** 732 W. Deer Valley Rd., Phoenix (✆ **888/869-0866** or 480/991-5557; www.westwindairservice.com), charges $349 to $599 (per person) for its Grand Canyon tours, $259 to $350 (per person) for its Sedona tours, and $599 (per person) for its Monument Valley tour. This company flies out of the Deer Valley Airport in the northwest part of the Valley. Flights last 3 to 7 hours for Grand Canyon tours, 1½ to 5 hours for Sedona tours, and 8 hours for Monument Valley tours.

WALKING TOURS Want to get a taste for the Scottsdale dining scene? Take a food tour with **Arizona Food Tours** (✆ **800/979-3370** or 212/209-3370; www.arizonafoodtours.com) and you'll wander the streets of Old Town Scottsdale visiting local restaurants and tasting some of their most popular dishes.

OUTDOOR PURSUITS

BICYCLING Although the Valley of the Sun is a sprawling place, it's mostly flat and has numerous paved bike paths, which makes bicycling a breeze as long as it isn't windy or, in the summer, too hot. In Scottsdale, **Arizona Outback Adventures,** 16447 N. 91st St., Ste. 101 (✆ **866/455-1601** or 480/945-2881; www.azoutbackadventures.com), rents road bikes for $50 to $95 per day, hybrid/comfort bikes for $40 per day, and mountain bikes for $40 to $95 per day. Mountain-biking trail maps are also available. This company also does half-day guided mountain-bike tours ($150 per person with a two-person minimum). Bike rentals and tours are also available from **Cactus Adventures** (✆ **480/688-4743;** www.cactusadventures.com), which charges $25 to $100 for a 24-hour bike rental and $89 to $159 for a half-day bike tour. This company is located near South Mountain Park, which has some of the best mountain-bike riding in the city. Guided rides can also be arranged through **360 Adventures** (✆ **602/795-1877;** www.360-adventures.com).

Papago Park is one of the Valley's best mountain-biking spots.

Among the best mountain-biking spots in the city are Papago Park (at Van Buren St. and Galvin Pkwy.), Phoenix South Mountain Park (use the entrance off Baseline Rd. on 48th St.), and North Mountain Preserve (off 7th St. btw. Dunlap Ave. and Thunderbird Rd.). With its rolling topography and wide dirt trails, Papago Park is the best place for novice mountain bikers to get in some desert riding (and the scenery here is great). For hard-core pedalers, Phoenix South Mountain Park is the place to go. The National Trail is the ultimate death-defying ride here, but there are lots of trails for intermediate riders, including the Desert Classic Trail and the short loop trails just north of the parking area at the 48th Street entrance. North Mountain is another good place for intermediate riders.

If you'd rather confine your cycling to a paved surface, there's no better route than Scottsdale's **Indian Bend Wash greenbelt,** a paved path that extends for more than 10 miles along Hayden Road (from north of Shea Blvd. to Tempe). The Indian Bend Wash pathway can be accessed at many points along Hayden Road. At the south end, the path connects to paved paths on the shores of Tempe Town Lake and provides easy access to Tempe's Mill Avenue shopping district.

GOLF With more than 200 courses in the Valley of the Sun, golf is just about the most popular sport in Phoenix and one of the main reasons people flock here in winter. Sunshine, spectacular views, and the company of coyotes, quails, and doves make playing a round of golf here a truly memorable experience.

However, despite the number of courses, it can be difficult to get a tee time on any of the more popular courses (especially during the months of Feb, Mar, and Apr). If you're staying at a resort with a course, be sure to make your tee-time reservations at the same time you make your room reservations. If you aren't staying at a resort, you might still be able to play a round on a resort course if you can get a last-minute tee time. Try one of the tee-time reservations services below.

The only thing harder than getting a winter or spring tee time in the Valley is facing the bill at the end of your 18 holes. Greens fees at most public and resort courses range from $100 to $190, with the top courses often charging $200 to $250 or more. Some municipal courses, on the other hand, charge less than $60. Of course, you can save money on many courses by opting for twilight play, which usually begins between 1 and 3pm.

You can get more information on Valley of the Sun golf courses from the **Greater Phoenix Convention & Visitors Bureau,** 125 N. Second St. (✆ **877/225-5749** or 602/452-6282; www.visitphoenix.com).

It's a good idea to make reservations well in advance. You can avoid the hassle of booking tee times yourself by contacting **Golf Xpress** (✆ **888/679-8246** or 602/404-4653; www.azgolfxpress.com), which can make reservations further in advance than you could if you called the golf course directly, and can sometimes get you lower greens fees as well. This company also makes hotel reservations, rents golf clubs, and provides other assistance to golfers visiting the Valley. For last-minute reservations, call **Stand-by Golf** (✆ **800/655-5345** or 480/874-3133; www.discountteetimes.com).

The many resort courses are the favored fairways of Valley visitors, and for spectacular scenery, the two Jay Morrish–designed 18-hole courses at the **Boulders ★★★**, 34631 N. Tom Darlington Dr., Carefree (✆ **480/488-9028;** www.bouldersclub.com), just can't be beat. Given the option, play the South Course, and watch out as you approach the tee box on the 7th hole—it's a real heart-stopper. Tee times for nonresort guests are very limited in winter and spring. You'll pay $220 to $250 for a round in winter if you aren't staying at the resort.

Jumping over to Litchfield Park, on the far west side of the Valley, there's the **Wigwam Golf Resort & Spa ★**, 300 Wigwam Blvd. (✆ **800/909-4224** or 623/935-9414; www.wigwamgolfclub.com), which has three championship 18-hole courses. The Gold Course is legendary, but even the Blue and Red courses are worth playing. These are traditional courses for purists who want vast expanses of green rather than cacti and boulders. In high season, the greens fees are $99 to $115 on any of the three courses here. Reservations can be made up to 120 days in advance.

Way over on the east side of the Valley at the foot of the Superstition Mountains is the **Gold Canyon Golf Resort ★★**, 6100 S. Kings Ranch Rd., Gold Canyon (✆ **480/982-9449;** www.gcgr.com), which has been rated the best public course in the state and has three of the state's best holes—the 2nd, 3rd, and 4th on the visually breathtaking, desert-style Dinosaur Mountain course. Greens fees on this course range from $175 to $195 in winter. The Sidewinder course is more traditional and less dramatic, but much more economical. Greens fees are $79 to $89 in winter. You can make tee-time reservations 10 days in advance over the phone or 60 days in advance online. It's well worth the drive.

If you want a traditional course that has been played by presidents and celebrities alike, try to get a tee time at one of the two 18-hole courses at the **Arizona Biltmore Golf Club,** 2400 E. Missouri Ave. (✆ **602/955-9655;** www.azbiltmoregc.com). The courses here are more relaxing than challenging, good to play if you're not yet up to par. Greens fee is $185 in winter and spring ($99 after 2pm). Reservations can be made only 5 days in advance if you aren't staying at the Biltmore and are not an Arizona resident.

Of the two courses at the **Camelback Golf Club,** 7847 N. Mockingbird Lane (✆ **480/596-7050;** www.camelbackinn.com), the tree-shaded Padre Course is more challenging. The Indian Bend Course is a links-style course with great mountain views and lots of water hazards. Padre Course greens fee is $139 in winter ($79 for twilight play); Indian Bend Course fee is $99 ($59 for twilight play) in winter. Reservations can be made up to 60 days in advance.

Set at the base of Camelback Mountain, the **Phoenician Golf Club,** 6000 E. Camelback Rd. (✆ **800/888-8234** or 480/423-2449; www.the phoenician.com), at the Valley's most glamorous resort, has 27 holes that mix traditional and desert styles. Greens fee for those not staying at the resort is $189 in winter and spring ($109 twilight rate for 9 holes), and tee-time reservations can be made up to 60 days in advance.

Of the Valley's many daily-fee courses, it's the two 18-hole courses at **Troon North Golf Club ★★★**, 10320 E. Dynamite Blvd., Scottsdale (✆ **480/585-7700;** www.troonnorthgolf.com), seemingly carved out of raw desert, that garner the most local accolades. This is the finest example of a desert course that you'll find anywhere in the state, and with five tee boxes on each hole, golfers of all levels can enjoy this course. Greens fees in winter and spring are $245 to $295 ($120–$145 for twilight play).

If you want to swing where the pros do, beg, borrow, or steal a tee time on the Tom Weiskopf and Jay Morrish–designed Stadium Course at the **Tournament Players Club (TPC) of Scottsdale ★★**, 17020 N. Hayden Rd. (✆ **888/400-4001** or 480/585-4334; www.tpc.com/scottsdale), which hosts the PGA's Waste Management Phoenix Open. The 18th hole has standing room for 40,000 spectators, but hopefully there won't be that many around the day you double-bogey this hole. The TPC's second 18, the Champions Course, is actually a municipal course, thanks to an agreement with the landowner, the Bureau of Land Management. Stadium Course fees top out at $299 in winter ($194 for twilight play), while Champions Course fees are a somewhat more reasonable $137 in winter ($97 for twilight play).

We-Ko-Pa Golf Club, 18200 E. Toh Vee Circle, Fort McDowell (✆ **866/660-7700** or 480/836-9000; www.wekopa.com), is located off the Beeline Highway (Ariz. 87) on the Fort McDowell Yavapai Nation in the northeast corner of the Valley, and gets rave reviews. The course name is Yavapai for "Four Peaks," which is the mountain range you'll be marveling at as you play. Unlike at other area courses, fairways at the two 18-hole courses here are bounded by desert, not luxury homes, so make sure you keep your ball on the grass. Greens fees are $175 to $195 in winter. Reservations are taken up to 90 days in advance.

The **Kierland Golf Club,** 15636 N. Clubgate Dr., Scottsdale (✆ **480/922-9283;** www.kierlandgolf.com), which was designed by Scott Miller and consists of three 9-hole courses that can be played in combination, is another much-talked-about local daily-fee course. It's affiliated with the Westin Kierland Resort and is conveniently located adjacent to the Kierland Commons shopping center. Greens fees are $199 to $209 in winter ($119 for twilight play).

The Pete Dye–designed **ASU Karsten Golf Course,** 1125 E. Rio Salado Pkwy., Tempe (✆ **480/921-8070;** www.asukarsten.com), part of Arizona State University, is also highly praised and a very challenging training ground for top collegiate golfers. Greens fees are $59 to $99 in winter. Phone reservations are taken up to 14 days in advance; online reservations are taken up to 30 days in advance.

If you're looking for good value in traditional or links-style courses, try the Legacy Golf Resort or Ocotillo Golf Resort. The **Legacy Golf Resort,** 6808 S. 32nd St. (✆ **888/828-3673** or 602/305-5500; www.legacygolfresort.com), is a fairly forgiving course on the south side of the Valley. Greens fees are $149 to $159 in winter ($99 for twilight play). **Ocotillo Golf Resort,** 3751 S. Clubhouse Dr., Chandler (✆ **888/624-8899** or 480/917-6660; www.ocotillogolf.com), in the southeast part of the Valley, has three 9-hole courses centered on 95 acres of man-made lakes, and that means a lot of challenge. Greens fees are $130 to $150 in winter ($65–$80 for twilight play).

If you want to take a crack at a desert-style course or two but don't want to take out a second mortgage for the experience, try Dove Valley Ranch Golf Club or Rancho Mañana Golf Club, both of which are on the north side of the Valley. **Dove Valley Ranch Golf Club,** 33750 N. Dove Lakes Dr., Cave Creek (✆ **480/488-0009;** www.dovevalleyranch.com), designed by Robert Trent Jones, Jr., is something of a merger of desert and traditional styles. Greens fees are $95 to $105 in winter ($85 for twilight play). **Rancho Mañana Golf Club,** 5734 E. Rancho Mañana Blvd., Cave Creek (✆ **480/488-0398;** www.ranchomanana.com), makes a good introduction to desert-style courses, as it's not as challenging as some other options in the area. Greens fee is $139 in winter ($59 for twilight play).

Of the municipal courses in Phoenix, **Papago Golf Course,** 5595 E. Moreland St. (✆ **602/275-8428;** www.papagogolfcourse.net), at the foot of the red sandstone Papago Buttes, offers fine views and a killer 17th hole. Greens fee here is $99 in the winter/spring high season. **Encanto Golf Course,** 2775 N. 15th Ave. (✆ **602/253-3963**), is the third-oldest course in Arizona and, with its wide fairways and lack of hazards, is very forgiving. **Cave Creek Golf Course,** 15202 N. 19th Ave. (✆ **602/866-8076**), in north Phoenix, is another good, economical choice; this course was built atop a former landfill. **Aguila Golf Course,** 8440 S. 35th Ave., Laveen (✆ **602/237-9601**), although a bit inconveniently located in the southwest corner of the Valley, was designed by Gary Panks. In winter, greens fees at Encanto, Cave Creek, and Aguila are $25 to $57 depending on when you play and whether you use a golf cart. For details on these courses, contact **Phoenix Golf** (✆ **866/865-4653** for reservations or 602/237-9601; http://phoenix.gov/recreation/rec/facilities/golf/index.html#a4).

Tempe's **Rolling Hills Golf Course,** 1415 N. Mill Ave., Tempe (✆ **480/350-5275;** www.tempe.gov/golf), on the south side of Papago Park, is another good little municipal course with economical rates. There are two executive 9-hole courses here, and cool-season greens fee is a very reasonable $24 for 18 holes. A golf cart will cost you another $22. Reservations can be made a week in advance.

HIKING Several mountains around Phoenix, including Camelback Mountain and Piestewa Peak, have been set aside as parks and nature preserves, and these natural areas are among the city's most popular hiking spots. The city's largest nature preserve, **South Mountain Park/Preserve ★** (✆ **602/495-0222;** www.phoenix.gov/PARKS), covers 16,000 acres and is one of the largest city parks in the world. This park contains more than 50 miles of hiking, mountain-biking, and horseback-riding trails, and the views of Phoenix (whether from along the National Trail or from the parking lot at the Buena Vista Lookout) are spectacular, especially at sunset. To reach the park's main entrance, drive south on Central Avenue, which leads right into the park. Once inside the park, turn left on Summit Road and follow it to the Buena Vista Lookout, which provides a great view of the city and is the trail head for the National Trail. If you hike east on this trail for 2 miles, you'll come to an unusual little natural tunnel that makes a good turnaround point. The Holbert Trail, a 5-mile round-trip hike that passes numerous petroglyphs, is another of my favorite trails here at South Mountain Park. To access this trail, turn left at the signed activity complex just inside the Central Avenue gate and drive to the last covered picnic area near the restrooms.

Camelback Mountain is the city's most popular hike.

Another place to get in some relatively easy and convenient hiking is **Papago Park,** Galvin Parkway and McDowell Road (✆ **602/261-8318;** www.phoenix.gov/PARKS), home to the Desert Botanical Garden, the Phoenix Zoo, and the fascinating Hole in the Rock (a red-rock butte with a large natural opening in it). There are both paved and dirt trails within the park; the most popular hikes are around the Papago Buttes (park on W. Park Dr.) and up onto the rocks at Hole in the Rock (park past the zoo at the information center). During World War II, there was a German POW camp here.

Perhaps the most popular hike in the city is the trail to the top of **Camelback Mountain ★**, in the **Echo Canyon Recreation Area** (✆ **602/261-8318;** www.phoenix.gov/PARKS), near the boundary between Phoenix and Scottsdale. At 2,704 feet high, this is the highest mountain in Phoenix and boasts the finest mountaintop views in the city. The 1.2-mile Summit Trail that leads to the top of Camelback Mountain is outrageously steep and gains 1,200 feet from trail head to summit. Yet on any given day there will be ironmen and ironwomen nonchalantly jogging up and down to stay fit. At times, it almost feels like a health-club singles scene. To reach the trail head, drive up 44th Street until it becomes McDonald Drive, turn right on East Echo Canyon Parkway, and continue up the hill until the road ends at a parking lot, which is often full. Don't attempt this one in the heat of the day, and bring at least a quart of water. Although people do this hike in sneakers, I would never dream of bagging this peak without good hiking boots on my feet.

At the east end of Camelback Mountain is the Cholla Trail, which, at 1.5 miles in length, isn't as steep as the Summit Trail (at least not until you get close to the summit, where the route gets steep, rocky, and very difficult). The only parking for this trail is along Invergordon Road at Chaparral Road, just north of Camelback Road (along the east boundary of the Phoenician resort). Be sure to park in a legal parking space and watch the hours in which parking is allowed. There's a good turnaround point below the summit, and great views down onto the fairways of the golf course at the Phoenician resort.

The 2,608-foot-tall **Piestewa Peak,** in the **Phoenix Mountains Park and Recreation Area/Dreamy Draw Recreation Area** (✆ **602/262-7901;** www.phoenix.gov/PARKS), offers another aerobic workout of a hike and has views almost as spectacular as those from Camelback Mountain. It is 1.2 miles to the summit, and the trail gains almost 1,200 feet. Piestewa Peak is reached from Squaw Peak Drive off Lincoln Drive between 22nd and 23rd streets. Another section of this park, with much easier trails, can be reached by taking the Northern Avenue exit off Ariz. 51 and then driving east into Dreamy Draw Park.

Of all the popular mountain trails in the Phoenix area, the trail through **Pinnacle Peak Park,** 26802 N. 102nd Way (✆ **480/312-0990;** www.scottsdaleaz.gov/parks/pinnacle), in north Scottsdale, is my favorite. The trail through the park is a 3.5-mile round-trip hike and is immensely popular with the local fitness crowd. Forget about stopping to smell the desert penstemon; if you don't keep up the pace, someone's liable to knock you off the trail into a prickly pear. If you can find a parking space (arrive before 9am on weekends) and can ignore the crowds, you'll be treated to views of rugged desert mountains (and posh desert suburbs). November through April, there are guided hikes Tuesday through Sunday at 10am. There are also astronomy evenings and other events here. To find the park from central Scottsdale, go north on North Pima Road, turn right on East Happy Valley Road, left on North Alma School Parkway, left on East Pinnacle Peak Parkway, and left on North 102nd Way.

For much less vigorous hiking (without the crowds), try **North Mountain Park** (✆ **602/262-6412;** www.phoenix.gov/PARKS), in North Mountain Preserve. This natural area, located on either side of Seventh Street between Dunlap Avenue and Thunderbird Road, has more flat hiking than Camelback Mountain or Piestewa Peak.

Another great place to go for a hike in the desert is north Scottsdale's **McDowell Sonoran Preserve** (✆ **480/998-7971;** www.mcdowellsonoran.org), where you'll find miles of relatively easy and uncrowded trails. The preserve's main access is at the Gateway Trailhead, 18333 N. Thompson Peak Pkwy., where you'll find many miles of trails. To reach this trail head, take E. Bell Road east from U.S. 101 and turn left on N. Thompson Peak Parkway. The best place to access these trails is at the Lost Dog Wash Access Area at 124th Street north of Via Linda. To reach this trail head, drive east on Shea Boulevard, turn north on 124th Street, and watch for the parking lot after you pass Via Linda. The 2.5-mile Ringtail Loop Trail is a good choice for an hour's hike.

North of Scottsdale, in the town of Cave Creek, you'll find a couple of my favorite hikes. The **Black Mountain Trail** is an uncrowded alternative to such popular hikes as Camelback Mountain and Piestewa Peak. This 1-mile trail leads to the summit of Black Mountain, and from the top you can gaze out over all of Cave Creek and Carefree. Keep an eye out for lizards lounging on the rocks at the summit. To find the trail head, take Schoolhouse Road south from Cave Creek Road for ¼ mile and park on the side of the road at the end of the pavement. The hike starts on the road that seems to lead straight up the mountain and then veers off onto the narrow trail. Both longer and less strenuous hikes can be found 3 miles north of Cave Creek at **Spur Cross Ranch Conservation Area,** 44000 N. Spur Cross Rd. (✆ **480/488-6601;** www.maricopa.gov/parks/spur_cross). Here you can wander by the water along Cottonwood Creek or hike up on the slopes of Elephant Mountain. In spring, the wildflowers here can be gorgeous. Best of all, this is the closest desert hiking that really has the feel of being away from the city. To reach the trail head, take Spur Cross Road north from Cave Creek Road. There is a $3 day-use fee. Also in the same general area, you'll find **Cave Creek Regional Park** (✆ **623/465-0431;** www.maricopa.gov/parks/cave_creek), which is even larger than the Spur Cross Ranch park and has 11 miles of hiking trails. For a hike of just under 6 miles, head out on the Go John Trail. You'll find the park west of the town of Cave Creek off Carefree Highway (Ariz. 74) at 32nd Street.

The **Peralta Trail,** way out on the east side of the Valley in the impossibly steep and jagged Superstition Mountains, just might be my favorite hike in the entire state. Unfortunately, a lot of other people feel the same way, and on weekends, the trail is almost always packed with people. However, if you come early on a weekday, you can have this trail almost all to yourself. The route climbs steadily, though not too steeply, past huge old saguaros to a saddle with a view that will take your breath away (or was it the hike up from the trail head that left you gasping?). The view is an in-your-face look at Weaver's Needle, the Superstition Mountains' most famous pinnacle. The hike to the view at Fremont Saddle is 4.6 miles round-trip. To reach the trail head, drive east from Phoenix on U.S. 60 for 8½ miles past Apache Junction to Peralta Road, and then drive 8 miles north, mostly on a gravel road, to the trail head. For information, contact the **Tonto National Forest's Mesa Ranger District,** 5140 E. Ingram St., Mesa (✆ **480/610-3300;** www.fs.fed.us/r3/tonto).

Way out on the west side of the Valley, where suburban sprawl bumps up against the rugged mountains, you'll find **White Tank Mountain Regional Park,** 20304 W. White Tank Mountain Rd., Waddell (✆ **623/935-2505;** www.maricopa.gov/parks/white_tank), and the popular but very rewarding **Waterfall Trail.** This 1.8-mile round-trip hike leads past Indian petroglyphs to, you guessed it, a waterfall. Well, sometimes. Most of the year, the waterfall isn't running, but after a rainstorm, water cascades over the rocks here. Whether the creek is running or not, this is a pretty spot. You can escape the crowds by heading out on some of the park's more remote and rugged trails.

If you'd prefer to have an experienced local guide lead you on a desert hike, contact **Take A Hike Arizona** (✆ **866/615-2748** or 480/634-8488; www.takeahikearizona.com), which offers hikes of varying lengths and difficulty levels. Guided hikes are also available from **360 Adventures** (✆ **602/795-1877;** www.360-adventures.com) and **Cactus Adventures** (✆ **480/688-4743;** www.cactusadventures.com).

HORSEBACK RIDING Even in the urban confines of the Phoenix metro area, people like to play at being cowboys, and there are plenty of places around the Valley to saddle up your palomino. Because any guided ride is going to lead you through interesting desert scenery, your best bet is to pick a stable close to where you're staying. Keep in mind that most stables require or prefer reservations.

The most centrally located place to ride is **Papago Stable,** 400 N. Scottsdale Rd. (✆ **480/966-9793;** www.papagoridingstable.com), which is on the north shore of Tempe Town Lake. You'll pay $30 for a 1-hour ride through Papago Park, and while the park is bordered by a freeway, it still has the feel of the desert, complete with old Indian ruins.

Numerous companies offer horseback riding in the Valley.

On the south side of the city, try **Ponderosa Stables,** 10215 S. Central Ave. (✆ **602/268-1261;** www.arizona-horses.com), which leads rides into South Mountain Park and charges $33 for a 1-hour ride or $55 for a 2-hour ride. These stables also offer dinner rides ($45) to a steakhouse, where you buy your own dinner before riding back under the stars. Because these rides are in one of the city's most popular parks, a ride here is more of an urban experience than a genuine Western horseback adventure. For a more adventurous experience, try one of the following stables.

On the north side of the Valley, **Cave Creek Outfitters,** off Dynamite Boulevard at 31313 N. 144th St., Scottsdale (✆ **888/921-0040** or 480/471-4635; www.cavecreekoutfitters.com), offers 1-hour rides for $50, 2-hour rides for $70, and half-day rides for $125. Between October and May, if you are doing a 2-hour or half-day ride, you can arrange for transportation from your Scottsdale resort for $10 per person. Mid-October through mid-April, you can also ride through Cave Creek Regional Park with **Cave Creek Trail Rides** (✆ **623/742-6700;** www.cavecreektrailrides.com). A 1-hour ride costs $41 for adults and $36 for children 6 to 12. Longer rides are also offered.

On the east side of the Valley, on the southern slopes of the Superstitions, you'll find **Don Donnelly D-Spur Ranch & Riding Stables,** 15371 Ojo Rd. (off Peralta Rd.), Gold Canyon (✆ **602/810-7029;** www.dondonnelly.com), which charges $32 for a 1-hour ride, $60 for a 2-hour ride, and $100 for a half-day ride. November through April, overnight rides are available for $200 per person. **OK Corral Horseback Riding Stables** (✆ **480/982-4040;** www.okcorrals.com), near Apache Junction, also leads riders through the desert near the Superstition Mountains. A 1-hour ride is $33 and a 2-hour ride is $55. There are also steak-dinner rides, all-day rides, and even multiday trips.

TENNIS Most major hotels in the area have tennis courts, and there are several tennis resorts around the Valley. If you're staying someplace without a court, try the **Scottsdale Ranch Park & Tennis Center,** 10400 E. Via Linda, Scottsdale (✆ **480/312-7774;** www.scottsdaleaz.gov/parks/srp.asp). Court fees range from $4 to $12 for 1½ hours; call for hours.

WATER PARKS If you happen to be visiting during the hotter months, consider taking the family to one of the Valley's water parks. At **Mesa Golfland Sunsplash,** 155 W. Hampton Ave., Mesa (✆ **480/834-8319;** www.golfland.com), you can splash in a wave pool and ride a variety of water slides. This park is generally open from Memorial Day weekend to Labor Day weekend (call for hours) and charges $26 for anyone taller than 48 inches, $20 for seniors and anyone under 48 inches, and $3 for children 2 and under. There are also three slides here that open at the start of spring break.

WHITE-WATER RAFTING & TUBING The desert may not seem like the place for white-water rafting, but up in the mountains to the northeast of Phoenix, the **Upper Salt River** still flows wild and free and offers some exciting rafting. Most years from about late February to late May, snowmelt from the White Mountains floods the river and fills it with exciting Class III and IV rapids (sometimes, however, there just isn't enough water). Companies operating full-day, overnight, and multiday rafting trips on the Upper Salt River (conditions permitting) include **Wilderness Aware Rafting** (✆ **800/462-7238;** www.inaraft.com), **Canyon Rio Rafting** (✆ **800/272-3353;** www.canyonrio.com), and **Mild to Wild Rafting** (✆ **800/567-6745;** www.mild2wildrafting.com). Prices range from $119 to $141 for a day trip.

Tamer river trips can be had from **Salt River Tubing and Recreation** (✆ **480/984-3305;** www.saltrivertubing.com), which has its headquarters 20 miles northeast of Phoenix on Power Road at the intersection of Usery Pass Road in Tonto National Forest. For $15, the company will rent you a large inner tube and shuttle you by bus upriver for the float down. Because tubing the Salt River is very popular with partying high-school and college students, I don't recommended these trips for families. Alcohol, drug use, and nudity are common on the river. The inner-tubing season runs from May to September.

SPECTATOR SPORTS

Phoenix is nuts for pro sports and is one of the few cities in the country with teams for all four of the major sports (baseball, basketball, football, and hockey). Add to this baseball's spring training, professional women's basketball, golf and tennis tournaments, the annual Fiesta Bowl college football classic, and ASU football, basketball, and baseball, and you have enough action to keep even the most rabid sports fans happy. The all-around best month to visit is March, when you could feasibly catch baseball's spring training, the Suns, the Coyotes, and ASU basketball and baseball.

Call **Ticketmaster** (✆ **866/448-7849** or 800/745-3000; www.ticketmaster.com) for tickets to most of the events below. For sold-out events, try **Tickets Unlimited** (✆ **800/289-8497** or 602/840-2340; www.ticketsunlimitedinc.com) or **Ticket Exchange** (✆ **800/800-9811;** www.ticketexchangeusa.com).

AUTO RACING At the **Phoenix International Raceway,** 7602 S. Avondale Blvd. at Baseline Road, Avondale (✆ **866/408-7223;** www.phoenixintlraceway.com), there's NASCAR and Indy Car racing on the world's fastest 1-mile oval. Tickets generally range from around $10 to $120.

BASEBALL The **Arizona Diamondbacks** (✆ **888/777-4664** or 602/462-6500; www.diamondbacks.com) have a devoted fan base and regularly pack downtown Phoenix's impressive Chase Field. The ballpark's retractable roof allows for comfortable play during the blistering summers and makes this one of only a few enclosed baseball stadiums with natural grass. Tickets to ballgames are available through the Chase Field ticket office and cost between $8 and $150. The best seats are in sections J and Q. If you'd like to get a behind-the-scenes look at Chase Field, you can take a guided tour. Tours cost $7 for adults, $5 for seniors and children ages 7 to 12, and $3 for children ages 4 to 6.

For decades, baseball's spring-training season has been immensely popular, especially with fans from northern teams, and don't think that the Cactus League's preseason exhibition games are any less popular just because the Diamondbacks play all summer. **Spring-training games** may rank second only to golf in popularity with winter visitors to the Valley. Fifteen major-league baseball teams have spring-training camps around the Valley in the month of March, and exhibition games are scheduled at 10 different stadiums. Most tickets cost between $8 and $28. Get a schedule from a visitor center, check the *Arizona Republic* while you're in town, or check the website of the Cactus League (www.cactusleague.com). Games often sell out, especially on weekends, so be sure to order tickets in advance.

Teams training in the Valley include the **Arizona Diamondbacks,** Salt River Fields at Talking Stick, 7555 N. Pima Rd., Scottsdale (✆ 888/490-0383 or 480/270-5000; www.dbacks.com); the **Chicago Cubs,** HoHoKam

Stadium, 1235 N. Center St., Mesa (✆ 480/964-4467; www.chicagocubs.com); the **Chicago White Sox,** Camelback Ranch, 10710 W. Camelback Rd., Glendale (✆ 623/302-5000; www.chicagowhitesox.com); the **Cincinnati Reds,** Goodyear Ballpark, 1933 S. Ballpark Way, Goodyear (✆ 800/745-3000 or 623/882-3130; www.cincinnatireds.com); the **Cleveland Indians,** Goodyear Ballpark, 1933 S. Ballpark Way, Goodyear (✆ 800/745-3000 or 623/882-3130; www.clevelandindians.com); the **Colorado Rockies,** Salt River Fields, 7555 N. Pima Rd., Scottsdale (✆ 800/388-7625 or 480/270-5000; www.coloradorockies.com); the **Kansas City Royals,** Surprise Stadium, 15850 N. Bullard Ave., Surprise (✆ 800/745-3000 or 623/222-2222; www.kcroyals.com); the **Los Angeles Angels of Anaheim,** Tempe Diablo Stadium, 2200 W. Alameda Dr. (48th St. and Broadway Rd.), Tempe (✆ 480/777-4444 or 480/350-5205; www.angelsbaseball.com); the **Los Angeles Dodgers,** Camelback Ranch, 10710 W. Camelback Rd., Glendale (✆ 623/302-5000; www.losangelesdodgers.com); the **Milwaukee Brewers,** Maryvale Baseball Park, 3600 N. 51st Ave., Phoenix (✆ 800/933-7890 or 623/245-5555; www.milwaukeebrewers.com); the **Oakland Athletics,** Phoenix Municipal Stadium, 5999 E. Van Buren St., Phoenix (✆ 877/493-2255 or 602/392-0074; www.oaklandathletics.com); the **San Diego Padres,** Peoria Sports Complex, 16101 N. 83rd Ave., Peoria (✆ 800/677-1227 or 623/773-8700; www.padres.com); the **San Francisco Giants,** Scottsdale Stadium, 7408 E. Osborn Rd., Scottsdale (✆ 877/473-4849 or 480/312-2580; www.sfgiants.com); the **Seattle Mariners,** Peoria Sports Complex, 16101 N. 83rd Ave., Peoria (✆ 800/677-1227 or 623/773-8700; www.seattlemariners.com); and the **Texas Rangers,** Surprise Stadium, 15930 N. Bullard Ave., Surprise (✆ 800/745-3000 or 623/222-2222; www.texasrangers.com).

BASKETBALL The NBA's **Phoenix Suns** play at the US Airways Center, 201 E. Jefferson St. (✆ **800/462-2849** or 602/379-7867; www.suns.com). Most tickets cost between $10 and $275. Suns tickets are hard to come by; if you haven't planned ahead, try contacting the box office the day before or the day of a game to see if tickets have been returned. Otherwise, you'll have to try the team's ticket exchange website or a ticket agency and pay a premium.

Phoenix also has a WNBA team, the **Phoenix Mercury** (✆ **602/252-9622** or 602/514-8331; www.phoenixmercury.com), which plays at the US Airways Center between May and August. Tickets cost $10 to $195.

FOOTBALL The **Arizona Cardinals** (✆ **800/999-1402** or 602/379-0102; www.azcardinals.com) play at the state-of-the-art University of Phoenix Stadium in the west Valley city of Glendale. This stadium has a retractable roof made of translucent fabric that lets lots of light in when the roof is closed. However, the stadium's most distinctive feature is its movable playing field, which is rolled out into the sun outside the stadium until a game is scheduled. This 2-acre, grass-covered tray is the first of its kind in North America. Ticket prices range from $50 to $445, and single-game tickets for the entire season go on sale in late July. Tickets can be purchased through Ticketmaster (✆ **866/448-7849** or 800/745-3000; www.ticketmaster.com).

GOLF TOURNAMENTS It's not surprising that, with more than 200 golf courses and ideal golfing weather throughout the fall, winter, and spring, the Valley of the Sun hosts some major golf tournaments. Late January's **Waste Management Phoenix Open Golf Tournament** (✆ **602/870-0163;**

The Phoenix Suns' Steve Nash.

Alvadora Spa at Royal Palms.

www.wastemanagementphoenixopen.com) is by far the biggest. Held at the Tournament Players Club (TPC) of Scottsdale, it attracts more spectators than any other golf tournament in the world (usually more than 500,000 each year). The 18th hole has standing room for 40,000. Tickets start at $25.

HOCKEY Ice hockey in the desert? It may not make sense, but even Phoenicians are crazy about ice hockey (maybe it's all those northern transplants). The NHL's **Phoenix Coyotes** (✆ **480/563-7825;** www.phoenixcoyotes.com) plays at the state-of-the-art Jobing.com Arena in Glendale (northwest of downtown Phoenix). Tickets cost $36 to $354.

HORSE RACING **Turf Paradise,** 1501 W. Bell Rd. (✆ **602/942-1101;** www.turfparadise.com), is Phoenix's horse-racing track. The season runs from early October to early May. Admission ranges from free to $5.

RODEOS, POLO & HORSE SHOWS Cowboys, cowgirls, and other horsy types will find plenty of the four-legged critters going through their paces most weeks at **WestWorld of Scottsdale,** 16601 N. Pima Rd., Scottsdale (✆ **480/312-6802;** www.scottsdaleaz.gov/westworld). With its hundreds of stables, numerous equestrian arenas, and a polo field, this complex provides an amazing variety of entertainment and sporting events. There are rodeos, polo matches, and horse shows.

SPAS

Ever since the first "lungers" showed up in the Phoenix area hoping to cure their tuberculosis, the desert has been a magnet for those looking to get healthy. In the first half of the 20th century, health spas were all the rage in Phoenix, and today spas are still immensely popular in the Valley of the Sun. All of the area's top resorts have impressive full-service spas that cater to guests' ever-increasing requests for massages, body wraps, mud masks, and salt glows.

If you can't or don't want to spend the money to stay at a luxury resort and avail yourself of the spa, you may still be able to indulge. Most resorts open their spas to the public, and for the cost of a body treatment or massage, you can spend the day at the spa taking classes, working out in an exercise room, or lounging by the pool. Barring this indulgence, you can slip into one of the Valley's many day spas and take a stress-reduction break the way other people take a coffee break.

Romance and relaxation take center stage at **Alvadora Spa at Royal Palms,** 5200 E. Camelback Rd. (✆ **866/579-3637** or 602/977-6400; www.royalpalmshotel.com), where a Mediterranean ambience prevails. The citrus ritual and orange-blossom body buff are two of the spa's signature treatments. Most 60-minute treatments cost $135, and packages run $232 to $380.

The historic setting and convenient location of the **Arizona Biltmore Spa,** 2400 E. Missouri Ave. (✆ **602/381-7632;** www.arizonabiltmore.com), make this facility an excellent choice if you're spending time along the Camelback Corridor. The spa menu includes dozens of different treatments, including a variety of massages, body scrubs, wraps, and facials. If you have just one 50-minute treatment (priced $135–$185), you can use all of the spa's facilities for the rest of the day. Packages cost $225 to $770.

If you want truly spectacular surroundings as well as bragging rights, head north to the Boulders Resort and the **Golden Door Spa,** 34631 N. Tom Darlington Dr., Carefree (✆ **480/595-3500;** www.goldendoorspas.com). Although this spa has the best name recognition of any spa in the Valley, it is not the most impressive. However, at 33,000 square feet and with 24 treatment spaces, it is certainly large. Also, the list of services is one of the most extensive in the Valley and includes both ayurvedic and Native American–inspired treatments. The turquoise wrap, the spa's signature treatment, is a real desert experience. Most 50-minute treatments cost between $135 and $230. Packages are $450 to $1,900.

The **Centre for Well Being** at the Phoenician, 6000 E. Camelback Rd., Scottsdale (✆ **800/843-2392** or 480/423-2452; www.centreforwellbeing.com), is one of the Valley's most prestigious spas. For $140 to $165, you can get a 50-minute spa treatment (anything from a desert serenity scrub to a shea butter wrap with honey-avocado foot therapy) and then spend the day using the many facilities. Packages range from $290 to $620.

At **Joya Spa,** 4949 E. Lincoln Dr., Paradise Valley (✆ **888/691-5692** or 480/627-3020; www.joyaspa.com), in the luxurious InterContinental Montelucia Resort & Spa, you'll find the most romantic spa in the valley. With its couples suites, it's the perfect place for a day of relaxing with the one you love. The spa's signature treatment is the *hammam* ritual ($45), which involves relaxing in a warming room, then a scrub followed by an herbal steam bath, whirlpool, sauna, and cold deluge; it's best as an add-on to full treatment. Most 50-minute massages run $145 to $165.

Located high on the flanks of Mummy Mountain, the **Spa at Camelback Inn ★**, 5402 E. Lincoln Dr., Scottsdale (✆ **800/922-2635** or 480/596-7040; www.camelbackspa.com), has long been one of the Valley's premier spas and gets my vote for all-around best spa in the Valley. The location is convenient, the views are fabulous, the setting is tranquil, and there's a long menu of relaxing spa services. For the cost of a single 1-hour treatment—between $130 and $175—you can use all the facilities, which include a fitness center and pool. Among the treatments available are the Para-Joba Body Moisturizer, which will leave your skin feeling like silk, and the Sonoran Rose facial, perfect for making sure you come back from vacation looking like you were actually on one. Packages run from $190 to $360.

Spa Avania, Hyatt Regency Scottsdale Resort and Spa at Gainey Ranch, 7500 E. Doubletree Ranch Rd., Scottsdale (✆ **480/444-1234;** www.spaavania.com), takes its name from the Greek work for "tranquil" and offers spa treatments designed to stimulate all the senses and also take into consideration the time of day and the body's natural rhythms. One-hour treatments run $165 to $180, while packages cost anywhere from $297 to $555.

Willow Stream–The Spa at the Fairmont Scottsdale Princess ★, 7575 E. Princess Dr. (✆ **800/908-9540** or 480/585-2732; www.fairmont.com/scottsdale), is my favorite Valley spa. Designed to conjure up images of the journey to Havasu Canyon, it includes a rooftop swimming pool and a large hot tub in a grotto below the pool. Because this is one of the largest spas in the Valley, you stand a better chance of getting last-minute reservations. Most 60-minute treatments cost $169 to $189. There are also several options for couples.

4 SHOPPING

For the most part, shopping in the Phoenix area means malls. They're everywhere, and they're air-conditioned, which, I'm sure you'll agree, makes shopping in the desert far more enjoyable when it's 110°F (43°C) outside.

Scottsdale and Phoenix's Biltmore District (along Camelback Rd.) are the Valley's main upscale shopping areas, with several high-end shopping centers and malls. The various distinct shopping districts of downtown Scottsdale are among the few upscale outdoor shopping areas in the Valley and are home to hundreds of boutiques, galleries, jewelry stores, Native American crafts stores, and souvenir shops. The Western atmosphere of Old Town Scottsdale is partly real and partly a figment of the local merchants' imaginations, but nevertheless it's the most popular tourist shopping area in the Valley. With dozens of galleries in the Main Street Arts and Antiques District and the nearby Marshall Way Contemporary Arts District, it also happens to be the heart of the Valley's art market.

For locals, Scottsdale's shopping scene has been moving steadily northward over the past decade. Kierland Commons and the SHOPS gainey village are both north of Old Town Scottsdale on North Scottsdale Road and are packed with women's fashion boutiques.

Antiques & Collectibles

With more than 100 antiques shops and specialty stores, downtown Glendale (northwest of downtown Phoenix) is the Valley's main antiques district. You'll find the greatest concentration of antiques stores just off Grand Avenue between 56th and 59th avenues. A half-dozen times each year, the **Arizona Antique Shows** (✆ **602/717-7337;** www.azantiqueshow.com), Arizona's largest collectors' shows, are held at America's Home & Garden Center, 13802 N. Scottsdale Rd., Ste. 142 (at the corner of Thunderbird Rd.).

Antique Trove If you love browsing through packed antiques malls searching for your favorite collectibles, then this should be your first stop in the Valley. With more than 100 dealers, it's one of the biggest antiques malls in the area. 2020 N. Scottsdale Rd., Scottsdale. ✆ **480/947-6074.** www.antiquetrove.com.

Arizona West Galleries ★★ Nowhere else in Scottsdale will you find such an amazing collection of cowboy collectibles and Western antiques. There are antique saddles and chaps, old rifles and six-shooters, sheriffs' badges, spurs, and the like. 7149 E. Main St., Scottsdale. ✆ **480/994-3752.**

Bishop Gallery for Art & Antiques ★ This cramped shop is wonderfully eclectic, featuring everything from Asian antiques to unusual original art. It's definitely worth a browse. 7164 E. Main St., Scottsdale. ✆ **480/949-9062.** www.bishop gallery.net.

Femme Fatales & Fantasies The name is a bit odd, but what this shop in Scottsdale is all about is old movie posters. Not only are there lots of gorgeous old posters for sale, but there are also lots of rare posters from the owner's collection on display. Well worth a visit. 7013 E. Main St. ✆ **480/429-6800.** www.fffmovieposters.com.

Knox Artifacts Gallery ★★ Ancient ceramics pieces from around the Southwest are among the specialties at this amazing antiques store. There are lots of other pre-Columbian artifacts as well as Roman, Greek, and Egyptian pieces. These are museum-quality artifacts with prices to prove it. 7056 E. Main St., Ste. B, Scottsdale. ✆ **480/874-1007.** www.fortknoxartifacts.com.

Art

In the Southwest, only Santa Fe is a more important art market than Scottsdale, and along the streets of Scottsdale's Main Street Arts and Antiques District and the Marshall Way Contemporary Arts District, you'll see dozens of galleries selling everything from monumental bronzes to contemporary art created from found objects. On Main Street, you'll find primarily cowboy art, both traditional and contemporary, while on North Marshall Way, you'll discover much more daring contemporary art.

In addition to the galleries listed here, you'll usually find a huge tent full of art along Scottsdale Road in north Scottsdale. The annual **Celebration of Fine Art** (✆ **480/443-7695;** www.celebrateart.com) takes place each year between mid-January and late March. Not only will you get to see the work of 100 artists, but on any given day, you'll also find dozens of the artists at work on the premises. Admission is $8 for adults and $7 for seniors. Call or check the website for location and hours of operation.

Art One This gallery specializes in works by art students and other area cutting-edge artists. The works here can be surprisingly good, and prices are very reasonable. 4130 N. Marshall Way, Scottsdale. ✆ **480/946-5076.** www.artonegalleryinc.com.

Bentley Projects Housed in a huge old warehouse south of Chase Field in downtown Phoenix, this massive gallery is one of the city's most cutting-edge contemporary-art spaces. You may not be in the market for any Dale Chihuly glass art, but if you'd like to see some, stop by this gallery. There's a second gallery in Scottsdale at 4161 N. Marshall Way (✆ **480/946-6060**). 215 E. Grant St., Phoenix. ✆ **602/340-9200.** www.bentleygallery.com.

Gebert Contemporary With other galleries in Santa Fe, this is one of the Southwest's premier contemporary-art galleries. Abstract art tends to dominate the exhibit schedule here. 7160 Main St., Scottsdale. ✆ **480/429-0711.** www.gebertartaz.com.

Lisa Sette Gallery If you aren't a fan of cowboy or Native American art, don't despair. Instead, drop by this gallery, which always mounts eclectic and fascinating shows. You might even catch a show by William Wegman, America's favorite dog photographer. 4142 N. Marshall Way, Scottsdale. ✆ **480/990-7342.** www.lisasettegallery.com.

Overland Gallery of Fine Art ★★ Traditional Western and Russian Impressionist paintings form the backbone of this gallery's offerings. The works on display here are museum-quality and prices sometimes approach $100,000. Definitely worth a look. The gallery also shows the angular Southwest landscapes of Ed Mell, one of my favorite Southwest artists. 7155 Main St., Scottsdale. ✆ **800/920-0220** or 480/947-1934. www.overlandgallery.com.

Riva Yares Gallery This is one of Scottsdale's largest and most respected contemporary-art galleries, and has a second location in Santa Fe. You may not have room in your car for the monumental sculptures sold here, but I'm sure they'll deliver for you. If you're lucky, you might stumble on a show by the likes of Milton Avery or Frank Stella. 3625 Bishop Lane, Scottsdale. ✆ **480/947-3251.** www.rivayaresgallery.com.

Wilde Meyer Gallery Brightly colored and playful are the norm at this gallery, which represents Linda Carter Holman, a Southwestern favorite who does cowgirl-inspired paintings. The associated Colores by Wilde Meyer is at 7100 E. Main St., Scottsdale (✆ **480/947-1489**). 4142 N. Marshall Way, Scottsdale. ✆ **480/945-2323.** www.wildemeyer.com.

Xanadu Gallery Featuring glass art, colorful and graphic two-dimensional works, and the fun Wild West collages and paintings of Dave Newman, this gallery always seems to show art that's distinctly different from that at most of the other galleries on Main Street. 7039 E. Main St., Ste. 101, Scottsdale. ✆ **866/483-1306** or 480/368-9929. www.xanadugallery.com.

Books

Major chain bookstores in the area include four **Barnes & Noble** locations: 10235 N. Metro Pkwy. E., Phoenix (✆ **602/678-0088**); in Kierland Commons, North Scottsdale Road and East Greenway Parkway, Scottsdale (✆ **480/948-8551**); 10500 N. 90th St., Scottsdale (✆ **480/391-0048**); and Tempe Marketplace, 2000 E. Rio Salado Pkwy. (✆ **480/894-6954**).

Charles Parkhurst Rare Books and Autographs If you're looking for an 1890 first edition of Henry Stanley's *In Darkest Africa* or a 1755 translation of Miguel de Cervantes's *The History and Adventures of the Renowned Don Quixote,* you just might find it here. This store, which also deals in ephemera signed by various signers of the Declaration of Independence, is an absolute treasure-trove and a must for bibliophiles. 7079 E. 5th Ave. ✆ **480/947-3558.** www.parkhurstrarebooks.com.

Guidon Books Whether you're already a student of Western and Civil War history or have only recently developed an interest in the past, this cramped little bookshop in Old Town Scottsdale should not be missed. Rare and out-of-print books are a specialty, but there are plenty of new books as well. Western Americana and the Civil War are the main focus here. 7117 Main St., Scottsdale. ✆ **480/945-8811.** www.guidon.com.

The Poisoned Pen The store name should give you a clue as to what sort of bookstore this is: It specializes in mysteries. In addition to shelves packed with whodunits, there are lots of collectible first editions and books signed by the authors. 4014 N. Goldwater Blvd., Ste. 101, Scottsdale. ✆ **888/560-9919** or 480/947-2974. www.poisonedpen.com.

Chocolate

Cerreta Candy Company Want to feel like a kid in Willy Wonka's candy factory? Head west to Glendale and the Cerreta Candy Company factory, which is open for tours Monday through Friday at 10am and 1pm (shopping hours are longer). The store here is packed with all kinds of sweet treats. 5345 W. Glendale Ave., Glendale. ✆ **623/930-1000.** www.cerreta.com.

Fashion

In addition to the options mentioned below, there are lots of great shops in malls all over the city. Favorite destinations for upscale fashions include Scottsdale Fashion Square, Biltmore Fashion Park, the SHOPS gainey village, the Borgata of Scottsdale, and el Pedregal Shops & Dining at the Boulders. See "Malls & Shopping Centers," below, for details.

For cowboy and cowgirl attire, see "Western Wear," below.

Conrad Leather Boutique It may be hot when you visit Arizona, but remember, you have to go home where it's probably a whole lot cooler. If you need a new leather jacket or belt, there's no better place in the Valley to look than this north Scottsdale boutique. Beautiful leather jackets for both men and women fill the shop. In el Pedregal, 34505 N. Scottsdale Rd., Ste. E-7, Scottsdale. ✆ **480/488-2190.**

Scottsdale Jean Company If you're searching for the latest high-fashion jeans, don't leave town without dropping by this shop in north Scottsdale. It has the biggest and best selection of jeans in the city. In Northsight Crossing Center, 14747 N. Northsight Blvd., Ste. 106 (at Raintree Dr., on the northeast corner), Scottsdale. ✆ **480/905-9300.** www.scottsdalejc.com.

Stefan Mann Purses, purses, purses. Gorgeous leather purses, wallets, and luggage are to be had at Stefan Mann, which has been in business for more than 25 years. If you're constantly on the prowl for a standout handbag, you'll certainly find something here. In el Pedregal, 34505 N. Scottsdale Rd., Ste. J-6, Scottsdale. ✆ **480/488-3371.** www.stefanmann.com.

Gifts & Souvenirs

Bischoff's Shades of the West This is a one-stop shop for all things Southwestern. From T-shirts to regional foodstuffs, this sprawling store has it all, with good selections of candles, Mexican crafts, and wrought-iron cabinet hardware that can give your kitchen a Western look. 7247 Main St., Scottsdale. ✆ **480/945-3289.** www.shadesofthewest.com.

Sphinx Date Ranch Dates—love 'em or hate 'em, there's no denying the connection these supersweet little palm fruits have to the desert. At this old-fashioned shop just south of Old Town Scottsdale, you can buy all kinds of dates and date products. 3039 N. Scottsdale Rd., Scottsdale. ✆ **800/482-3283** or 480/941-2261. www.sphinxdateranch.com.

The Store @ Scottsdale Center for the Performing Arts ★ This gift shop on the downtown Scottsdale mall has a wonderful selection of fun, contemporary, and artistic gifts, including lots of jewelry. There's another gift shop next door at the Scottsdale Museum of Contemporary Art. 7380 E. 2nd St., Scottsdale. ✆ **480/874-4644.** www.scottsdaleperformingarts.com.

Two Plates Full I love wandering through this shop just to marvel at all the bright colors and fun designs. Featuring functional art and crafts, home accessories, and jewelry, this is a great place to shop for unique gifts. In the Borgata, 6166 N. Scottsdale Rd., Ste. 402, Scottsdale. ✆ **480/443-3241.** www.twoplatesfull.com.

Jewelry

Cornelis Hollander Although this shop is much smaller and not nearly as dramatic as the nearby Jewelry by Gauthier store (see below), the designs are just as cutting edge. Whether you're looking for classic chic or trendy modern designs, you'll find plenty to interest you here. 4151 N. Marshall Way, Scottsdale. ✆ **800/677-6821** or 480/423-5000. www.cornelishollander.com.

The Jewelry Boutique at Molina If you can spend as much on a necklace as you can on a Mercedes, then this is *the* place to shop for your baubles. Although you don't need an appointment, it's highly recommended. You'll then get personalized service as you peruse the classically styled jewelry. 3134 E. Camelback Rd. ✆ **602/508-1653.** www.finejewelers.com.

Jewelry by Gauthier This elegant store sells the designs of the phenomenally talented Scott Gauthier. The stylishly modern pieces use precious stones and are miniature works of art. There's a second, much smaller shop in Kierland Commons, 15034 N. Scottsdale Rd., Ste. 120 (✆ **480/443-4030**). 4211 N. Marshall Way, Scottsdale. ✆ **888/411-3232** or 480/941-1707. www.jewelrybygauthier.com.

Sami This little jewelry store, northeast of Scottsdale in the city of Fountain Hills, specializes in amethyst from a mine in the nearby Four Peaks Mountains. The mine has been producing gemstones since Spanish colonial times, and the very best of the stones wind up at this shop. You'll also find Arizona peridot and "anthill" garnet jewelry here. 16704 Ave. of the Fountains, Ste. 100, Fountain Hills. ✆ **877/376-6323** or 480/837-8168. www.samifinejewelry.com.

Malls & Shopping Centers

While locals don't want to call it a shopping center, the **Scottsdale Waterfront,** an ambitious mixed-use development along a canal at the corner of Camelback and Scottsdale roads, is essentially just that. There are shops, most of which are either national chains or satellites of popular local boutiques, restaurants (once again national and local chains), and high-rise residential towers. The only real difference between the Scottsdale Waterfront and the attached Scottsdale Fashion Square is that at the waterfront you actually have to (get to?) walk around outside. On the south side of the canal, you'll find the fun little boutiques of the **Mix Shops** (www.shopthemix.com), which is part of the **SouthBridge** development. This bank of the canal also has several good restaurants.

Now, when I say this development is along a canal, don't start thinking Venice-style canals. Scottsdale's canal, a cement-lined trough, is not exactly a romantic watercourse, although it is lined with attractive pathways, gardens, fountains, and sculptures that together make this the prettiest shopping and dining destination in town.

Biltmore Fashion Park ★ This open-air shopping plaza with garden courtyards is one of the most pleasant places to shop in Phoenix. Saks Fifth Avenue and Macy's are the two anchors, while smaller storefronts bear familiar names including Tommy Bahama, Brooks Bothers, and Ralph Lauren. There are also lots of restaurants here. 2502 E. Camelback Rd. (at 24th St.). ✆ **602/955-8400.** www.shopbiltmore.com.

The Borgata of Scottsdale ★ Designed to resemble the medieval Italian village of San Gimignano, complete with turrets, stone walls, and ramparts, the Borgata is far and away the most architecturally interesting mall in the Valley.

Outdoor shopping at Kierland Commons.

Within its walls, you'll find about a dozen upscale boutiques, galleries, and restaurants. 6166 N. Scottsdale Rd. ✆ **602/953-6538.** www.borgata.com.

el Pedregal Shops & Dining at the Boulders ★ Adjacent to the Boulders resort 30 minutes north of Old Scottsdale, el Pedregal is the most self-consciously Southwestern shopping center in the Valley, and it's worth the long drive out just to see the neo–Santa Fe/Moroccan architecture. The shops offer high-end merchandise, fashions, and art. 34505 N. Scottsdale Rd., Carefree. ✆ **480/488-1072.** www.elpedregal.com.

Kierland Commons ★★ The urban-village concept of a shopping center—narrow streets, sidewalks, and residences mixed in with retail space—has taken off all over the country, and here in Scottsdale, the concept has taken on Texas-size proportions. However, despite the grand scale of this shopping center, it has a great feel. You'll find Tommy Bahama, Ann Taylor Loft, Crate & Barrel, and even a few local boutiques, including 42 Saint, which stocks fashions not found elsewhere. 15205 N. Scottsdale Rd. ✆ **480/348-1577.** www.kierlandcommons.com.

Scottsdale Fashion Square Scottsdale has long been the Valley's shopping mecca, and for years this huge mall has been the reason why. It now houses five major department stores—Nordstrom, Dillard's, Neiman Marcus, Macy's, and Barney's New York—and smaller stores such as Coach, Eddie Bauer, J. Crew, and Louis Vuitton. 7014–590 E. Camelback Rd. (at Scottsdale Rd.), Scottsdale. ✆ **480/941-2140.** www.fashionsquare.com.

the SHOPS gainey village This upscale shopping center is much smaller than Kierland Commons farther up Scottsdale Road, but is no less impressive, especially after dark when lights illuminate the tall palm trees. There may not be a more impressive concentration of women's clothing stores anywhere in Scottsdale. 8777–8989 N. Scottsdale Rd. (at Doubletree Ranch Rd.). ✆ **602/953-6150.** www.theshopsgaineyvillage.com.

Native American Arts, Crafts & Jewelry

Bischoff's at the Park ★★ This museumlike store and gallery is affiliated with another Bischoff's right across the street (see "Gifts & Souvenirs," above). However, this outpost carries higher-end jewelry; Western-style home furnishings; and clothing, ceramics, sculptures, contemporary paintings, and books and music with a regional theme. 3925 N. Brown Ave., Scottsdale. ✆ **480/946-6155.**

Faust Gallery ★ Old Native American baskets and pottery, as well as old and new Navajo rugs, are the specialties at this interesting shop. It also sells Native American and Southwestern art, including ceramics, paintings, bronzes, and unusual sculptures. 7100 E. Main St., Ste. 3, Scottsdale. ✆ **480/200-4290.** www.faustgallery.com.

Gilbert Ortega Gallery & Museum You'll find Gilbert Ortega shops all over the Valley, but this is the biggest and best. As the name implies, there are museum displays throughout the store. Jewelry is the main attraction, but there are also baskets, sculptures, pottery, rugs, paintings, and kachina dolls. 3925 N. Scottsdale Rd. ✆ **480/990-1808.**

Heard Museum Gift Shop The Heard Museum (see "Seeing the Sights," earlier in this chapter) has an astonishing collection of well-crafted Native American jewelry, art, and crafts of all kinds. This is the best place in the Valley to shop for Native American arts and crafts; you can be absolutely assured of the quality. Because the store doesn't have to charge sales tax, you'll also save a bit of money. Also be sure to check out the affiliated Berlin Gallery, which features contemporary Native American art. At the Heard Museum, 2301 N. Central Ave. ✆ **602/252-8344.** www.heard.org.

John C. Hill Antique Indian Art ★★ While shops selling Native American art and artifacts abound in Scottsdale, few offer the high quality available in this tiny shop. Not only does the store have one of the finest selections of Navajo rugs in the Valley, including quite a few older rugs, but there also are kachina dolls, superb pieces of Navajo and Zuni silver-and-turquoise jewelry, baskets, and pottery. 6962 E. 1st Ave., Ste. 104, Scottsdale. ✆ **480/946-2910.** www.johnhillgallery.com.

Old Territorial Shop ★★ Owned and operated by Alston and Deborah Neal, this is the oldest Indian arts-and-crafts store on Main Street, and it offers good values on jewelry, concho belts, kachina dolls, fetishes, pottery, and Navajo rugs. 7077 E. Main St., Ste. 7, Scottsdale. ✆ **480/945-5432.** www.oldterritorialshop.com.

River Trading Post If you are interested in getting into collecting Native American art or artifacts, this is a good place to get in on the ground floor. Quality is high and prices are relatively low. Not only are there high-quality Navajo rugs, but there are also museum-quality pieces of ancient Southwestern pottery. 7033 E. Main St., Scottsdale. ✆ **866/426-6901** or 480/444-0001. www.rivertradingpost.com.

Outlet Malls & Discount Shopping

Arizona Mills This huge mall in Tempe is a temple of budget consumerism that attracts primarily young, cash-strapped shoppers. You'll find lots of name-brand outlets, a multiplex theater, and an IMAX theater. 5000 S. Arizona Mills Circle, Tempe. ✆ **480/491-7300.** www.arizonamills.com. From I-10, take the Baseline Rd. east exit. From U.S. 60, exit Priest Dr. south.

My Sister's Closet This is where the crème de la crème of Scottsdale's used clothing comes to be resold. You'll find reasonable prices on such labels as Armani, Donna Karan, and Calvin Klein. Locations are also at Town & Country shopping plaza, 2033 E. Camelback Rd., Phoenix (✆ **602/954-6080**), and Desert Village, 23233 N. Pima Rd., Ste. 105 (✆ **480/419-6242**). At Lincoln Village, 6204 N. Scottsdale Rd., Scottsdale. ✆ **480/443-4575.** www.mysisterscloset.com.

Western Wear

Az-Tex Hat Company If you're looking to bring home a cowboy hat, this is the best place in Scottsdale to do your shopping. The small shop in Old Scottsdale offers custom shaping and fitting of both felt and woven hats. 3903 N. Scottsdale Rd., Scottsdale. ✆ **800/972-2116** or 480/481-9900. www.aztexhats.com.

Out West ★ If the revival of 1950s cowboy fashions and interiors has hit your nostalgia button, then you'll want to high-tail it up to this eclectic shop. All things Western are available, and the fashions are both beautiful and fun (although fancy and pricey). 7003 E. Cave Creek Rd., Cave Creek. ✆ **480/488-0180.** www.outwestmercantile.com.

Saba's Western Stores Since 1927, this store has been outfitting Scottsdale's cowboys and cowgirls, visiting dude ranchers, and anyone else who wants to adopt the look of the Wild West. There's another Saba's around the corner at

3965 N. Brown Ave. (✆ **480/947-7664**). Call or check the website for other locations around Phoenix. 7254 Main St., Scottsdale. ✆ **877/342-1835** or 480/949-7404. www.sabaswesternwear.com.

Sheplers Western Wear This is the largest Western-wear store in the Valley, a veritable department store of cowboy duds. If you can't find it here, it just ain't available in these parts. 829 N. Dobson Rd., Mesa. ✆ **480/668-1211.** www.sheplers.com.

PHOENIX & SCOTTSDALE AFTER DARK

If you're looking for nightlife in the Valley of the Sun, you won't have to look hard, but you may have to drive quite a way. Although much of the nightlife scene is centered on downtown Scottsdale, Tempe's Mill Avenue, and downtown Phoenix, you'll find things going on all over.

The weekly *Phoenix New Times* tends to have the most comprehensive listings for clubs and concert halls. The Thursday edition of the *Arizona Republic* also lists upcoming events and performances. Another publication to check for abbreviated listings is *Where Phoenix/Scottsdale,* which is free and can usually be found at hotels and resorts.

Tickets to many concerts, theater performances, and sporting events are available through **Ticketmaster** (✆ **866/448-7849** or 800/745-3000; www.ticketmaster.com), which has outlets at Fry's Marketplace grocery stores.

The Club & Music Scene

Even if it were not in the middle of the desert, the Scottsdale club scene would be red-hot. Packed into a few dozen blocks surrounding Old Town Scottsdale, near the corner of Camelback and Scottsdale roads, are dozens of trendy dance clubs and chic bars. This is where visiting celebrities, wealthy fashionistas, and wannabes all come to party. The crowd is young, affluent, and attractive, and with all the beautiful people cruising around in Porsches and limousines, it's easy to think you're in L.A. Cruise along **Stetson Drive,** which is divided into two sections (east and west of Scottsdale Rd.), to find the latest hot spots.

While Scottsdale is the nexus of nightclubbing for the fashion-conscious, the Valley has plenty of clubs and bars for those who don't wear Prada. Other nightlife districts include Tempe's Mill Avenue and downtown Phoenix. This latter area comes into its own after basketball and baseball games and concerts at US Airways Center.

Mill Avenue in Tempe is a good place to wander around in search of your favorite type of music. The bars and clubs here are mostly within walking distance of one another. Because Tempe is a college town, the crowd tends to be young and rowdy.

Downtown Phoenix is home to Symphony Hall, the Herberger Theater Center, and several sports bars. However, much of the action revolves around sports events and concerts at US Airways Center and Chase Field.

As most denizens of any urban nightlife scene know, clubs come and go. To find out what's hot, get a copy of the *Phoenix New Times.* Many dance clubs in the Phoenix area are open only on weekends, so be sure to check what nights the doors will be open.

Myst nightclub.

COUNTRY

Buffalo Chip Saloon & Steakhouse So you think you're a studly urban cowboy? Well, maybe you've never met a mechanical bull you couldn't ride, but at this barnlike Cave Creek roadhouse they've got genuine rip snortin' live bull riding. You man enough? There's live country music Thursday through Saturday nights, all-you-can-eat fish fries featuring walleye, and s'mores on the dessert menu. This place is also popular with Green Bay Packers fans, a lot of whom transplanted themselves to the Phoenix area after deciding to leave cold winters behind. 6811 E. Cave Creek Rd., Cave Creek. ✆ **480/488-9118.** www.buffalochipsaloon.com. No cover.

Handlebar-J This Scottsdale landmark is about as genuine a cowboy bar as you'll find in Phoenix, and cowpokes often stop by when they come in from the ranch. You'll hear live git-down two-steppin' music nightly; free dance lessons are given Wednesday, Thursday, and Sunday at 7pm. 7116 Becker Lane (1 block north of the northwest corner of Scottsdale Rd. and Shea Blvd.), Scottsdale. ✆ **480/948-0110.** www.handlebarj.com. No cover to $5.

Rusty Spur Saloon A small, rowdy, drinkin'-and-dancin' place frequented by tourists, this bar is the oldest saloon in Old Town Scottsdale and is loads of fun, with peanut shells all over the floor, dollar bills stapled to the walls, and live country-music afternoons and evenings. If you're a cowboy or cowgirl at heart, this is the place to party when you're in Scottsdale. 7245 E. Main St., Scottsdale. ✆ **480/425-7787.** www.rustyspursaloon.com. No cover.

DANCE CLUBS & DISCOS

Axis/Radius If you're looking to do a bit of celebrity-spotting, Axis is one of the best places in town to keep your eyes peeled. For many years now, this has been one of Scottsdale's hottest dance clubs and liveliest singles scenes. The two-story glass box is a bold contemporary space with an awesome sound system. These twin clubs are open Thursday through Saturday. 7340 E. Indian Plaza (2 blocks east of Scottsdale Rd. and 1 block south of Camelback Rd.), Scottsdale. ✆ **480/970-1112.** www.axis-radius.com. Cover $10.

Myst Always packed to the walls with the Valley's beautiful people, Myst is one of the top spots in Scottsdale to see and be seen. The atmosphere is lavishly ostentatious, with various themed rooms. The club is usually open Friday and Saturday. 7340 E. Shoeman Lane, Scottsdale. ✆ **480/970-5000.** www.mystaz.com. Cover $10.

Pepin Friday and Saturday starting at 10pm and Sunday beginning at 9pm, a DJ plays Latin dance music at this small Spanish restaurant located on the Scottsdale Mall. Friday and Saturday evenings, there are also live flamenco performances. 7363 Scottsdale Mall, Scottsdale. ✆ **480/990-9026.** www.pepinrestaurant.com. Cover $10.

ROCK, BLUES & JAZZ

Char's Has the Blues You wouldn't think to look at this little cottage, but it really does have those mean-and-dirty, low-down blues. All of the best blues brothers and sisters from around the city and around the country make the scene here. 4631 N. 7th Ave., 4 blocks south of Camelback Rd. ✆ **602/230-0205.** www.charshastheblues.com. No cover to $6.

Geordie's at the Wrigley Mansion Open only on Friday and Saturday nights, this lounge is inside the historic Wrigley Mansion, which was built between 1929 and 1931 by chewing-gum magnate William Wrigley, Jr. The sprawling mansion is located on a hilltop adjacent to the Arizona Biltmore resort. Come for the sparkling city lights after dark. 2501 E. Telawa Trail. ✆ **602/955-4079.** www.wrigleymansionclub.com. No cover.

The Rhythm Room This blues club, long the Valley's most popular, books quite a few national acts as well as the best of the local scene, and has a dance floor if you want to move to the beat. 1019 E. Indian School Rd. ✆ **602/265-4842.** www.rhythmroom.com. Cover $7–$35.

The Bar & Pub Scene

SCOTTSDALE, CAREFREE & CAVE CREEK

AZ88 Located across the park from the Scottsdale Center for the Arts, this sophisticated bar/restaurant has a hip, contemporary ambience that's just right for a martini or a basket of waffle fries before or after a performance. There's also a great patio area. Wednesday through Saturday, DJs spin everything from acid jazz to vintage rock and pop. Weekend nights, the crowd is primarily gay. 7353 Scottsdale Mall, Scottsdale. ✆ **480/994-5576.** www.az88.com.

Cave Creek Coffee Co. & Wine Bar Located way up north in the cow town of Cave Creek, this hip coffeehouse doubles as a lively wine bar that also happens to book some great music. Past performers have included Kelly Joe Phelps, Michelle Shocked, Richie Havens, and Rickie Lee

Axis/Radius.

AZ88 is known for its martinis.

Jones. 6033 E. Cave Creek Rd., Cave Creek. ✆ **480/488-0603.** www.cavecreekcoffee.com. No cover to $40.

Coach House No, this place is definitely not a trendy boutique selling overpriced black handbags. It's an open-air, all-day drinking establishment where you have to check your Scottsdale pretentions at the door, make that the patio gate. In business for more than 50 years, the Coach House captures the feel of old Scottsdale without going too heavy on the cowboy kitsch. 7011 E. Indian School Rd. ✆ **480/990-3433.** www.coachhousescottsdale.com.

Don & Charlie's Although this is primarily a steakhouse, it also has the best sports bar in Scottsdale. What makes Don & Charlie's such a great sports bar is not the size or number of its TVs, but rather all the sports memorabilia on the walls. 7501 E. Camelback Rd., Scottsdale. ✆ **480/990-0900.** www.donandcharlies.com.

Dos Gringos For young partyers who don't feel like getting dressed up to go out on the town, this is a great choice. With its open-air bar, Dos Gringos is patterned after Mexican beach bars and can be loads of fun on a Saturday night. 4209 N. Craftsman Court, Scottsdale. ✆ **480/423-3800.** www.dosgringosaz.com.

Hyatt Regency Scottsdale Lobby Bar ★★ The open-air lounge just below the main lobby of this posh Scottsdale resort sets a romantic stage for nightly live music (often flamenco or Caribbean steel drum music). Wood fires burn in patio fire pits, and the terraced gardens offer plenty of dark spots for a bit of romance. 7500 E. Doubletree Ranch Rd., Scottsdale. ✆ **480/444-1234.** www.scottsdale.hyatt.com.

Kazimierz World Wine Bar ★ Sort of a spacious speak-easy crossed with a wine cellar, this place, which is associated with the nearby Cowboy Ciao restaurant (p. 115), offers the same wide selection of wines available at the restaurant. There are dozens of wines by the glass and live music ($5 cover after 8pm) several nights each week. The entrance is hard to find, but it's worth seeking out (look around back for the big wooden door with a sign that says THE TRUTH IS INSIDE). 7137 E. Stetson Dr., Scottsdale. ✆ **480/946-3004.** www.kazbar.net.

Olive & Ivy ★ With a huge patio right on the canal in the Scottsdale Waterfront, the bar at this restaurant has become *the* place to see and be seen in Scottsdale. There are more than 45 wines available by the glass, and the bartenders mix decent drinks, too. Be sure to dress the part. 7135 E. Camelback Rd., Ste. 195, Scottsdale. ✆ **480/751-2200.** www.foxrestaurantconcepts.com.

Papago Brewing Brewing some of the best beers in the valley and serving lots of great beers from other breweries, this pub south of Old Town Scottsdale is a beer geek's nirvana. This is a great place to escape the glitz of Scottsdale's swanky nightclubs. See you there. 7107 E. McDowell Rd., Scottsdale. ✆ **480/425-7439.** www.papagobrewing.com.

Salty Señorita As you might guess from the name, this open-air bar on the southern edge of Old Town Scottsdale serves delicious margaritas. In fact, they repeatedly have been voted best in the Valley. Best of all, on Monday nights, they're half-price. This is a great place to kick back on a hot afternoon. 3636 N. Scottsdale Rd., Scottsdale. ✆ **480/946-7258.** www.saltysenorita.com.

Uncorked: The Unpretentious Wine Bar ★ This unpretentious little north Scottsdale wine bar is a challenge to locate, but that's what makes it such an enjoyable spot. You'll find Uncorked in the courtyard of the Promenade Corporate Center at the intersection of Scottsdale Road and Frank Lloyd Wright Boulevard in the same shopping center that houses the big blue Frank Lloyd Wright spire. 16427 N. Scottsdale Rd., Ste. 130, Scottsdale. ✆ **480/699-9230.** www.uncorkedwinebar.com.

IN PHOENIX

Alice Cooper'stown Sports and rock mix it up at this downtown restaurant/bar run by, you guessed it, Alice Cooper. Chase Field, where the Arizona Diamondbacks play ball, is only a block away. See p. 129 for more information. 101 E. Jackson St. ✆ **602/253-7337.** www.alicecooperstown.com.

Bar Bianco ★ Located downtown on Heritage Square, this little wine bar is in a restored historic home and is affiliated with Pizzeria Bianco (p. 130), the tiny and ever-popular designer-pizza place next door. This is a very romantic spot for a drink. 609 E. Adams St. ✆ **602/528-3699.** www.pizzeriabianco.com.

Bomberos Café & Wine Bar Housed in a former fire station, this off-the-beaten-path wine bar is a great place to feel like a local. You won't find too many tourists here, but you will find plenty of wines from all over South America. There are regular wine tastings, live South American music on Saturday nights, and a beautiful little patio. 8801 N. Central Ave. ✆ **602/687-8466.** www.bomberoswinebar.com.

Durant's In business for decades, Durant's has long been downtown Phoenix's favorite after-work watering hole. Although especially popular with the old guard, this classic bar has caught on with the young martini-drinking crowd as well. 2611 N. Central Ave. ✆ **602/264-5967.** www.durantsfinefoods.com.

Fez If you happen to be in downtown Phoenix and are looking for a stylish place for a cocktail, drop by this hip bar/restaurant on Central Avenue. Although the name sounds like this might be some exotic Moroccan place, nothing is further from the truth. About the only thing remotely North African here is the pomegranate juice used in the cocktails. 3815 N. Central Ave. ✆ **602/287-8700.** www.fezoncentral.com.

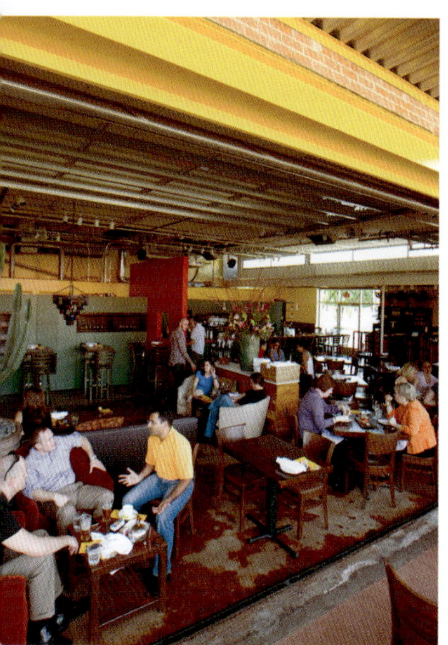
Postino is housed in a former post office.

Majerle's Sports Grill If you're a Phoenix Suns fan, you won't want to miss this sports bar located only a couple of blocks from US Airways Center, where the Suns play. Suns memorabilia covers the walls, and who knows, you just might bump into a team member or two while you're here. 24 N. 2nd St. ✆ **602/253-0118.** www.majerles.com.

MercBar With bars in Phoenix and New York, this dark and seductive bar in the heart of the Camelback corridor is the place in the neighborhood for martinis and eye candy. You won't find a better place to escape the tourists and conventioneers at your resort. 2525 E. Camelback Rd. ✆ **602/508-9449.** www.mercbar.com.

Postino ★★ This immensely popular wine bar is in the heart of the Arcadia neighborhood, south of Camelback Road, and is housed in a former post office. Casual yet stylish, the bar has garage-style doors that roll up to open the restaurant to the outdoors. Choose from a great selection of wines by the glass and a limited menu of European-inspired appetizers. There's a second Postino at 5144 N. Central Ave. (✆ **602/274-5144**). 3939 E. Campbell Ave. ✆ **602/852-3939.** www.postinowinecafe.com.

The Rose and Crown Pub In a historic Craftsman bungalow on downtown's Heritage Square, this place does a very respectable job of replicating an English pub. The only real difference is that when you sit out on the front porch with your pint of beer, the air is balmy not damp. I'll drink to that. 628 E. Adams St. ✆ **602/256-0223.** www.theroseandcrownaz.com.

Sun Up Brewing This excellent little brewpub is a bit hard to spot as you drive down busy Camelback Road in central Phoenix, but keep an eye out on the north side of the road and you'll find it. There are usually more than a half-dozen brews on tap, and the seasonal can be quite distinctive. 322 E. Camelback Rd. ✆ **602/279-8909.** www.sunupbrewing.com.

T. Cook's Lounge ★★ If you aren't planning on having dinner at this opulent Mediterranean restaurant, at least stop by for a cocktail in the bar. With its mix of Spanish colonial and 1950s tropical furnishings, this is as romantic a lounge as you'll find anywhere in the Valley. You can also snuggle with your sweetie out on the patio by the fireplace. At the Royal Palms Resort and Spa, 5200 E. Camelback Rd. ✆ **602/840-3610.** www.royalpalmshotel.com.

The Vig This midcentury modern tavern in the Arcadia neighborhood is a great place to escape the resort scene and maybe meet some locals over cocktails. Best of all, you can even play some bocce ball on the bar's little artificial lawn. There's also a second Vig (Vig Uptown) at 6015 N. 16th St. (✆ **602/633-1187**), that is just as midcentury modern and cool as the original. 4041 N. 40th St. ✆ **602/553-7227.** www.thevig.us.

IN TEMPE & CHANDLER

Dave's Electric Beer This little brewpub started out years ago in Bisbee, where it was the state's very first microbrewery. Today, Dave's pub is across the street from Sun Devil Stadium and is surrounded by the ASU campus. 502 S. College Ave., Tempe. ✆ **480/967-5353.** www.daveselectricbrewpub.com.

Four Peaks Brewing Company Consistently voted the best brewpub in Phoenix, this Tempe establishment, housed in a former creamery, brews good beers and serves decent pub grub. Four Peaks is a favorite of ASU students, and you'll find the pub south of East University Drive between South Rural Road and South McClintock Drive. There's a second Four Peaks in north Scottsdale at 15730 N. Pima Rd., Ste. D5-7 (✆ **480/991-1795**). 1340 E. 8th St., Tempe. ✆ **480/303-9967.** www.fourpeaks.com.

Rula Bula ★ The middle of the desert may seem like an odd place for an Irish pub, but Rula Bula has such an authentic feel that it's easy to imagine that it's damp and dreary outside. There's live Irish music 2 or 3 nights a week. The pub stays packed primarily with college students. 401 S. Mill Ave., Tempe. ✆ **480/929-9500.** www.rulabula.com.

San Tan Brewing Company This brewpub is another of the reasons I like to hang out in downtown Chandler. With good beer, live music, and walls that roll back to let the warm Arizona air inside, San Tan Brewing is a fun place to cool off on a hot day. 8 S. San Marcos Plaza, Chandler. ✆ **480/917-8700.** www.santanbrewing.com.

The Sanctuary on Camelback's jade bar offers a stunning view of the Valley.

COCKTAILS WITH A VIEW

The Valley of the Sun has more than its fair share of spectacular views. Unfortunately, most of them are from expensive restaurants. All these restaurants have lounges, though, where, for the price of a drink (and perhaps valet parking), you can sit back and ogle a crimson sunset and the purple mountains' majesty. Among the best choices are the **Terrace Room at Different Pointe of View,** at the Pointe Hilton Tapatio Cliffs Resort; **Rustler's Rooste,** at the Arizona Grand Resort; and both the cozy outdoors **edge** and the swanky **jade bar,** at the Sanctuary on Camelback Mountain.

Thirsty Camel Whether you've already made your millions or are still working your way up the corporate ladder, you owe it to yourself to spend a little time in the lap of luxury. You may never drink in more ostentatious surroundings than here at Arizona's most luxurious resort. The view is one of the best in the city. At the Phoenician, 6000 E. Camelback Rd. ✆ **480/941-8200.** www.thephoenician.com.

The Wright Bar & Squaw Peak Terrace Can't afford the lifestyles of the rich and famous? For the cost of a couple of drinks, you can sink into a seat here at the Biltmore's main lounge and watch the sunset test its color palette on Piestewa Peak. Alternatively, you can slide into a seat near the piano and let the waves of mellow jazz wash over you. At the Arizona Biltmore, 2400 E. Missouri Ave. ✆ **602/381-7632.** www.arizonabiltmore.com.

GAY & LESBIAN BARS & CLUBS

Amsterdam Bar This downtown Phoenix nightclub complex may not look like much from the outside, but through the doors, you'll find a classy spot that's known across the Valley for its great martinis. There's usually a female impersonator 1 night of the week, and other nights, live music or DJ dance music plays. 718 N. Central Ave. ✆ **602/258-6122.**

BS West In business since 1988, this bar is open daily from 2pm to 2am. Currently Sundays are karaoke night, and on Friday nights, female impersonators strut their stuff. There are also nightly specials. 7125 E. 5th Ave., Scottsdale. ✆ **480/945-9028.** www.bswest.com. No cover to $3.

Charlie's If you're a cowpoke and want to do some boot scootin' while you're in town, head on over to Charlie's. This club is the home of the Arizona Gay Rodeo Association, and there's country music, clogging and line dance lessons, and an after-hours scene on the weekends. 727 W. Camelback Rd. ✆ **602/265-0224.** www.charliesphoenix.com. No cover to $3.

Forbidden Night Club Forbidden, on the western edge of Old Town Scottsdale, is pretty much the only gay nightclub in a town packed with nightclubs for straights. So, if you're gay and you're staying in Scottsdale it's either this or a long drive into Phoenix (and back). 6820 E. 5th Ave., Scottsdale. ✆ **480/994-5176.** No cover to $5.

The Performing Arts

Although downtown Phoenix claims the Valley's greatest concentration of performance halls, including Symphony Hall, the Orpheum Theatre, and the Herberger Theater Center, there are major performing arts venues scattered across the Valley. No matter where you happen to be staying, you're likely to find performances being held somewhere nearby.

Calling these many Valley venues home are such major companies as the Phoenix Symphony, Arizona Opera Company, Ballet Arizona, Center Dance Ensemble, Actors Theatre of Phoenix, and Arizona Theatre Company. Adding to the performances held by these companies are the wide variety of touring companies that make stops here throughout the year.

While you'll find box-office phone numbers listed below, you can also purchase most performing arts tickets through **Ticketmaster** (✆ **866/448-7849** or 800/745-3000; www.ticketmaster.com). For sold-out shows, check with your hotel concierge, or try **Tickets Unlimited** (✆ **800/289-8497** or 602/840-2340; www.ticketsunlimitedinc.com).

MAJOR PERFORMING ARTS CENTERS

Symphony Hall, 75 N. Second St. (✆ **602/262-7272;** www.phoenix.gov/extranet/pccd/symphonyhall.html), is Phoenix's premier performance venue and

Symphony Hall is home to the Phoenix Symphony.

Grady Gammage Auditorium hosts touring Broadway shows.

is home to the Phoenix Symphony, Ballet Arizona, and the Arizona Opera Company. It also hosts touring Broadway shows and various other concerts and theatrical productions. The hall's Grand Drape is the world's largest piece of machine-made embroidery.

The **Orpheum Theatre,** 203 W. Adams St. (✆ **602/262-7272;** www.phoenix.gov/extranet/pccd/orpheum.html), is the most elegant hall in the Valley. The historic Spanish colonial baroque-revival theater was built in 1929 and at the time was considered the most luxurious theater west of the Mississippi. Today, its ornately carved sandstone facade stands in striking contrast to the adjacent glass-and-steel City Hall building, with which the theater shares a common wall.

Although not the largest performance venue in town, the **Celebrity Theatre,** 440 N. 32nd St. (✆ **602/267-1600;** www.celebritytheatre.com), often books good shows. With its revolving stage and no seat farther than 75 feet from the performers, this is a great place to catch the likes of Manhattan Transfer or Kenny G.

The **Comerica Theatre,** 400 W. Washington St. (✆ **602/379-2800** or 602/379-2888; www.livenation.com), is another of Phoenix's major downtown performance halls and seats from 2,000 to 5,000 people. It books many top names in entertainment, as well as the occasional Broadway show or international touring company.

The Frank Lloyd Wright–designed **Grady Gammage Auditorium,** 1200 S. Forest Ave. (at Mill Ave. and Apache Blvd.), Tempe (✆ **480/965-3434;** www.asugammage.com), on the Arizona State University campus, is at once massive and graceful. This 3,000-seat hall is where touring Broadway shows perform when they come to the Valley.

The **Scottsdale Center for the Arts,** 7380 E. Second St., Scottsdale (✆ **480/994-2787;** www.scottsdaleperformingarts.org), hosts a variety of performances and series, ranging from classical music to alternative dance. This center seems to get the best of the touring performers who come through the Valley.

In Scottsdale, the ASU **Kerr Cultural Center,** 6110 N. Scottsdale Rd. (✆ **480/596-2660;** www.asukerr.com), a tiny venue in a historic home near the

Borgata shopping center, offers up an eclectic season that includes music from around the world. The Kerr Cultural Center sponsors a couple of different free concert series.

With its sail-like shade canopies, sunken sculpture courtyard, numerous water features, and colorful architecture, the **Mesa Arts Center,** 1 E. Main St. (✆ **480/644-6500;** www.mesaartscenter.com), is the prettiest performing arts center in the Valley. Check out the performance schedule when planning your visit.

The **Tempe Center for the Arts,** 700 W. Rio Salado Pkwy., Tempe (✆ **480/350-2822;** www.tempe.gov/TCA), is centrally located and is on the shore of Tempe Town Lake. There are water views out its big wall of glass, and in the two performance halls, there are frequent jazz concerts, as well as performances by the Tempe Symphony, Tempe Little Theatre, and Childsplay, a local children's theater company.

OUTDOOR VENUES & SERIES

Given the weather, it should come as no surprise that Phoenicians like to attend performances under the sun and stars.

Cricket Wireless Pavilion, 2121 N. 83rd Ave., Phoenix (✆ **602/254-7200;** www.cricket-pavilion.com), west of downtown and ½ mile north of I-10 between 75th and 83rd avenues, is the city's top outdoor venue. This 20,000-seat amphitheater is open year-round and hosts everything from Broadway musicals to rock concerts.

Mesa Amphitheater, 201 N. Center St. (at University Dr.), Mesa (✆ **480/644-2560;** www.mesaamp.com), is a much smaller amphitheater that holds a wide variety of concerts in spring and summer, and occasionally other times of year as well.

Throughout the year, the **Scottsdale Center for the Performing Arts,** 7380 E. Second St., Scottsdale (✆ **480/994-2787;** www.scottsdaleperformingarts.org), stages outdoor performances in the adjacent Scottsdale Amphitheater on the Scottsdale Civic Center Mall. The Sunday A'fair series runs from January to April, with free concerts from noon to 4pm on selected Sundays of each month. Performances range from acoustic blues to zydeco.

Two perennial favorites of Valley residents take place in particularly attractive surroundings. The Music in the Garden concerts at the **Desert Botanical Garden,** 1201 N. Galvin Pkwy. in Papago Park (✆ **480/941-1225** or 480/481-8188; www.dbg.org), are held on Sundays in January and February. The season always includes an eclectic array of musical styles. Tickets are $21 for adults and $8 for children 3 to 12; garden admission is included. In the spring and fall, there are also Friday-night jazz concerts. Up on the north side of the Valley, just outside Carefree, **el Pedregal at the Boulders,** 34505 N. Scottsdale Rd., Scottsdale

Lunch & a Show

At downtown Phoenix's Herberger Theater Center, 222 E. Monroe St. (✆ 602/254-7399; www.herbergertheater.org), lunch break means the actors hit the stage while the audience grabs sandwiches for Lunch Time Theater. Throughout much of the year, 30- to 45-minute plays are staged at noon Tuesday through Thursday. Tickets are only $6, and inexpensive boxed salads, sandwiches, and pasta salads can be ordered in advance.

(✆ **480/488-1072;** www.elpedregal.com), often has free live music on weekends (usually Sun afternoon).

Outdoor concerts are also held at various parks and plazas around the Valley during the warmer months. Check local papers for listings.

CLASSICAL MUSIC, OPERA & DANCE

The **Phoenix Symphony** (✆ **800/776-9080** or 602/495-1999; www.phoenixsymphony.org), the Southwest's leading symphony orchestra, performs at Symphony Hall (tickets mostly run $18–$88).

Opera buffs will want to see what the **Arizona Opera** (✆ **602/266-7464;** www.azopera.org) has scheduled. Each season, this company stages up to five operas, both familiar and more obscure, and splits its time between Phoenix and Tucson. Tickets cost $25 to $144. Performances are held at Symphony Hall.

Ballet Arizona (✆ **602/381-1096;** www.balletaz.org) performs at both the Orpheum Theatre and Symphony Hall and stages both classical and contemporary ballets; tickets run $17 to $121. The **Center Dance Ensemble** (✆ **602/252-8497;** www.centerdance.com), the city's contemporary dance company, stages several productions a year at the Herberger Theater Center. Tickets cost $22.

THEATER

With nearly a dozen professional companies and at least as many major nonprofessional companies taking to the boards throughout the year, a play is always being staged somewhere in the Valley. So, for much of the year, theater fans will have plenty to choose from on a visit to Phoenix.

The **Herberger Theater Center,** 222 E. Monroe St. (✆ **602/254-7399;** www.herbergertheater.org), which is located downtown and vaguely resembles a Spanish colonial church, is the city's main venue for live theater. Its two Broadway-style theaters together host hundreds of performances each year, including productions by the Actors Theatre and the Arizona Theatre Company (ATC). **Actors Theatre** (✆ **602/253-6701** or 602/252-8497 for tickets; www.atphx.org) tends to stage smaller, lesser-known off-Broadway–type works, with musicals, dramas, and comedies equally represented; tickets go for $28 to $70. The annual production of *A Christmas Carol* is always a big hit. **ATC** (✆ **602/256-6995;** www.aztheatreco.org) is the state theater company and splits its performances between Phoenix and Tucson. Founded in 1967, it's the major force on the Arizona thespian scene. Productions range from world premieres to recent Tony Award winners to classics. Tickets run $30 to $69.

Phoenix Theatre, 100 E. McDowell Rd. (✆ **602/254-2151;** www.phoenixtheatre.net), has its performance venue in the Phoenix Art Museum building and has been around for more than 90 years. Musicals are the mainstays here; tickets to most shows are $30 to $62. If your interest lies in Broadway plays, see what **Broadway Across America–Arizona** (✆ **480/965-3434;** www.broadwayacrossamerica.com/tempe) has scheduled. The series, focusing mostly on comedies and musicals, is held at the Gammage Auditorium in Tempe; tickets usually cost between $20 and $64, with the occasional higher-price tickets for a real blockbuster show. The **Theater League** (✆ **800/776-7469** or 602/262-7272; www.theaterleague.com) is another series that brings in Broadway musicals. Performances are held in the Orpheum Theatre, and tickets range from $50 to $60.

If you're staying in Scottsdale and are looking for something to do with the whole family, the **Scottsdale Desert Stages Theatre,** 4720 N. Scottsdale Rd.

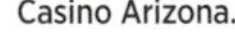
Casino Arizona.

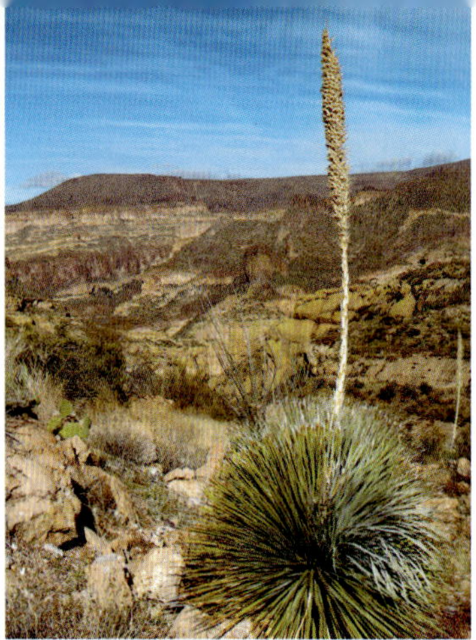
One of the most scenic desert drives can be found along the Apache Trail.

(✆ **480/483-1664;** www.desertstages.com), stages primarily musicals and children's theater productions. Tickets range from $12 to $25.

Casinos

Casino Arizona at Talking Stick Resort Operated by the Salt River Pima–Maricopa Indian Community, this is the most conveniently located casino in the area. Just off U.S. 101 on the east side of Scottsdale, it offers plenty of slot machines, cards, and other games of chance. There's also a second casino, Casino Arizona at Salt River, at U.S. 101 and McKellips Road. U.S. 101 and Indian Bend Rd. ✆ **480/850-7777.** www.casinoaz.com.

Fort McDowell Casino Located about 45 minutes northeast of downtown Scottsdale, this Indian casino is the oldest in the state, offering slot machines, poker, keno, bingo, and free shuttles from hotels around the Valley. There's also a very attractive resort hotel here. 10424 N. Fort McDowell Rd., Fort McDowell (off Ariz. 87, 2 miles northeast of Shea Blvd. and Fountain Hills). ✆ **800/843-3678.** www.fortmcdowellcasino.com.

A SIDE TRIP FROM PHOENIX: THE APACHE TRAIL ★★

There isn't a whole lot of desert or history left in Phoenix, but only an hour's drive to the east you'll find quite a bit of both. The **Apache Trail,** a narrow, winding, partially gravel road that snakes its way around the north side of the Superstition Mountains, offers some of the most scenic desert driving in central Arizona. Along the way are ghost towns and ancient ruins, saguaros and century plants, reservoirs and hiking trails. You could easily spend a couple of days traveling this route, though most people make it a day trip. Pick and choose the stops that appeal to you, and be sure to get an early start. The gravel section of the road is well graded and is passable for regular passenger cars.

If you'd rather leave the driving to someone else, **Apache Trail Tours** (✆ **480/982-7661;** www.apachetrailtours.com) offers a variety of guided tours along the Apache Trail. This company also offers off-road adventures in the Superstition Mountains and Four Peaks area. Tours range in price from $45 to $165.

To start this drive, head east on U.S. 60 to the town of Apache Junction, and then go north on Ariz. 88. About 4 miles out of town is **Goldfield Ghost Town,** a reconstructed gold-mining town (see "Wild West Theme Towns" under "Seeing the Sights," earlier in this chapter). Allow plenty of time if you plan to stop here.

Not far from Goldfield is **Lost Dutchman State Park,** 6109 N. Apache Trail (✆ **480/982-4485;** www.azstateparks.com), where you can hike into the rugged Superstition Mountains and see what the region's gold seekers were up against. Springtime wildflower displays here can be absolutely gorgeous. Park admission is $7 per vehicle; the campground here charges $15 to $17 per site.

Continuing northeast, you'll reach **Canyon Lake,** set in a deep canyon flanked by colorful cliffs and rugged rock formations. This is the first of three reservoirs you'll pass on this drive, and together the three lakes provide much of Phoenix's drinking water, without which the city would never have been able to grow as large as it is today. At Canyon Lake, you can swim at the Acacia Picnic Area or the nearby Boulder Creek Picnic Area, which is in a pretty side cove. You can also take a cruise on the ***Dolly* steamboat** (✆ **480/827-9144;** www.dollysteamboat.com). A 90-minute jaunt on this reproduction paddle-wheeler costs $20 for adults, $18 for seniors, and $12 for children 5 to 12. Lunch ($47) and dinner ($68 for adults and $47 for children) cruises are also available, and once a month, there is even a twilight astronomy cruise. There's also a lakeside restaurant at the boat landing. But if you're at all hungry, hold out for nearby **Tortilla Flat** (✆ **480/984-1776;** www.tortillaflataz.com), an old stagecoach stop with a restaurant, saloon, and general store. The ceiling and interior walls of this funky old place are plastered with thousands of dollar bills that have been left by previous customers. If it's hot out, be sure to stop in at the general store for some prickly-pear ice cream (guaranteed spineless). From December through April, there are staged gunfights here on the second and fourth Saturdays of the month.

A few miles past Tortilla Flat, the pavement ends and the truly spectacular desert scenery begins. Among the rocky ridges, arroyos, and canyons of this stretch of road, you'll see saguaro cacti and century plants (a type of agave that dies after sending up its flower stalk, which can be as much as 15 ft. tall). Next you'll come to **Apache Lake,** which is not nearly as spectacular as Canyon Lake, though it does have the **Apache Lake Marina and Resort** (✆ **928/467-2511;** www.apachelake.com), with a motel, restaurant, and general store. If you're inclined to turn this drive into an overnight trip, this would be a good place to spend the night. Room rates are $80 to $105; boat rentals are available.

Shortly before reaching pavement again, you'll see **Theodore Roosevelt Dam.** This dam, built in 1911, forms Roosevelt Lake and, despite its concrete face, is the largest masonry dam in the world.

Continuing on Ariz. 88, you'll next come to **Tonto National Monument** ★ (✆ **928/467-2241;** www.nps.gov/tont), which preserves some of the southernmost cliff dwellings in Arizona. These pueblos were occupied between about 1300 and 1450 by the Salado people and are some of the few remaining traces of this tribe, which once cultivated lands now flooded by Roosevelt Lake. The lower ruins, open daily year round, are a half-mile up a steep trail from the visitor center. The upper ruins are reached by a 3-mile round-trip hike, and can only be visited on a guided hike. The upper ruins are open November through April with tours offered three or four times each week at 10am. In May and October, there are tours on Saturday mornings at 8am. Tour reservations are required (reserve at least 2 weeks in advance). The park is open daily (except Christmas) from 8am to 5pm (you must begin the lower ruin trail by 4pm); admission is $3.

Thousands of dollar bills plaster the walls at Tortilla Flat.

Boyce Thompson Arboretum.

Keep going on Ariz. 88 to the copper-mining town of **Globe.** Although you can't see the mines themselves, the tailings (remains of rock removed from the copper ore) can be seen piled high all around the town. Be sure to visit **Besh-Ba-Gowah Archaeological Park ★** (✆ **928/425-0320;** www.globeaz.gov/visitors/besh-ba-gowah), on the eastern outskirts of town. This Salado Indian pueblo site has been partially reconstructed, and several rooms are set up to reflect the way they might have looked when they were first occupied about 700 years ago. For this reason, they're among the most fascinating ruins in the state. Besh-Ba-Gowah is open daily from 9am to 5pm (closed New Year's Day, Thanksgiving, and Christmas); admission is $4 for adults, $3 for seniors, and free for children 11 and under. To get here, head out of Globe on South Broad Street to Jesse Hayes Road.

From Globe, head west on U.S. 60. Three miles west of Superior, you'll come to **Boyce Thompson Arboretum ★★**, 37615 U.S. 60 (✆ **520/689-2811;** http://arboretum.ag.arizona.edu), dedicated to researching and propagating desert plants. This was the nation's first botanical garden established in the desert and is set in two small, rugged canyons. From the impressive cactus gardens, you can gaze up at sunbaked cliffs before ducking into a forest of eucalyptus trees that grow along a stream. As you hike the nature trails of this 320-acre arboretum, watch for the two bizarre boojum trees. September through April, the arboretum is open daily from 8am to 5pm, and May through August, it's open 6am to 3pm. Admission is $7.50 for adults and $3 for children 5 to 12. There are regularly scheduled guided tours of the garden; call for the schedule.

If after a long day on the road you're looking for a place to eat, stop in at **Gold Canyon Golf Resort,** 6100 S. Kings Ranch Rd., Gold Canyon (✆ **800/827-5281** or 480/982-9090; www.gcgr.com), which has a good formal dining room and a more casual bar and grill.

EN ROUTE TO TUCSON

Driving southeast from Phoenix for about 60 miles will bring you to the Casa Grande and Coolidge area, where you can learn about the Hohokam people who once inhabited this region. If you're continuing south toward Tucson and you're not in a big hurry, I suggest taking the scenic **Pinal Pioneer Parkway** (Ariz. 79), which was the old highway between Phoenix and Tucson before the interstate was built.

Attractions Along the Way

Attention discount shoppers! In the town of Casa Grande you can shop 'til you drop at the **Outlets at Casa Grande,** 2300 E. Tanger Dr. (✆ **800/405-5016** or 520/836-9663; www.outletsatcasagrande.com). You'll find this collection of discount outlet stores at exit 198 off I-10.

Casa Grande Ruins National Monument ★★ Located outside the town of Coolidge, this national monument preserves one of the most unusual Indian ruins in the state. In Spanish, *casa grande* means "big house," and that's exactly what you'll find here. In this instance, the big house is the ruin of an earth-walled structure built 650 years ago by the Hohokam people. It is speculated that the building was once some sort of astronomical observatory, but this is not known for certain. Whatever the original purpose of the building was, today it provides a glimpse of a style of ancient architecture rarely seen. Instead of using adobe bricks or stones, the people who built this structure used layers of hard-packed soil, which have survived the ravages of the weather and still stand in silent testament to the Hohokam's long-ago architectural endeavors. The Hohokam began farming the valleys of the Gila and Salt rivers about 1,500 years ago, and eventually built an extensive network of irrigation canals for watering their fields. By the middle of the 15th century, the Hohokam had abandoned both their canals and their villages and disappeared without a trace.

1100 W. Ruins Dr., Coolidge (Ariz. 87, 1 mile north of Coolidge). ✆ **520/723-3172.** www.nps.gov/cagr. Admission $5. Daily 9am–5pm. Closed Thanksgiving and Christmas.

Picacho Peak State Park ★★ If you're heading to Tucson by way of I-10, consider a stop at this state park, 35 miles northwest of Tucson at exit 219. Picacho Peak, a wizard's cap of rock rising 1,500 feet above the desert, is a visual landmark for miles around. Hiking trails lead around the lower slopes of the peak and up to the summit; these trails are especially popular in spring, when the wildflowers bloom (the park is known as one of the best places in Arizona to see spring wildflowers). In addition to its natural beauty, Picacho Peak was the site of the only Civil War battle to take place in the state. Each March, Civil War reenactments are staged here. Campsites in the park cost $25.

Exit 219 off I-10. ✆ **520/466-3183.** www.azstateparks.com. Admission $7 per car. Daily 8am–5pm.

Picacho Peak State Park is one of the best places to see spring wildflowers.

Rooster Cogburn Ostrich Ranch ☺ While you may need true grit to ride an ostrich, even a child can feed one of these giant birds (that is, as long as the ostrich is on the other side of a fence). This sprawling roadside ranch has not only a huge flock of ostriches that you can feed, but also an aviary full of lorikeets. On weekends and holidays, tours of the ranch in a monster truck are also offered.

27480 S. Marez Dr., Picacho. ✆ **520/466-3658.** www.roostercogburn.com. Admission $6, free for children 5 and under; monster truck tours $10 for children 6 and older, $5 for children 5 and under. Nov–Apr daily 9am–5pm; May–Oct Fri–Mon 9am–5:30pm.

Arcosanti is Italian architect Paolo Soleri's version of a future city.

EN ROUTE TO NORTHERN ARIZONA

If you enjoy searching out deals at factory-outlet stores, then you'll be in heaven at the **Outlets at Anthem,** 4250 W. Anthem Way (✆ **623/465-9500;** www.outletsanthem.com). Among the offerings are Ann Taylor, Polo Ralph Lauren, and Levi's. Take exit 229 (Anthem Way) off I-17.

Some 13 miles farther north is the town of Rock Springs, which is barely a wide spot in the road and is easily missed by drivers roaring up and down I-17. However, if you're a fan of pies, then do *not* miss exit 242. Here you'll find the **Rock Springs Café,** 35769 S. Old Black Canyon Hwy., Rock Springs (✆ **623/374-5794;** www.rockspringscafe.com), in business since 1918. Although this aging, nondescript building looks like the sort of place that would best be avoided, the packed parking lot says different. Why so popular? It's not the barbecue or steaks or even the "mountain oysters." No, this place stays packed because of its legendary pies, which many people claim are the best in the state. So popular are the pies here that every year, the Rock Springs Café sells upwards of 50,000 of them. If one slice isn't enough, order a whole pie to go.

If you appreciate innovative architecture, don't miss the Cordes Junction exit (exit 262) off I-17 (see the "Central Arizona" map on p. 201). Here you'll find **Arcosanti** (✆ **928/632-7135;** www.arcosanti.org), Italian architect Paolo Soleri's vision of the future—a "city" that merges architecture and ecology. Soleri, who came to Arizona to study with Frank Lloyd Wright at Taliesin West, envisions a compact, energy-efficient city that disturbs the natural landscape as little as possible—and that's just what's rising out of the desert here at Arcosanti. The organic design built of cast concrete will fascinate both students of architecture and those with only a passing interest in the discipline. Arcosanti has been built primarily with the help of students and volunteers who live here for various lengths of time. To help finance the construction, Soleri designs and sells wind bells cast in bronze or made of ceramic. These distinctive bells are available at the gift shop. Arcosanti is open daily from 9am to 5pm, and tours are held hourly (except at noon) between 10am and 4pm ($10 suggested donation). If you'd like to stay overnight, basic accommodations ($40–$100 double) are available by reservation. There's also a cafe that serves buffet meals to overnight guests.

East of I-17 between Black Canyon City and Cordes Junction lies **Agua Fria National Monument,** which is administered by the Bureau of Land Management, Hassayampa Field Office, 21605 N. Seventh Ave., Phoenix (✆ **623/ 580-5500;** www.blm.gov/az/st/en/prog/blm_special_areas/natmon/afria.html). The monument protects the region's numerous prehistoric Native American ruin sites, which date from between 1250 and 1450 (at least 450 prehistoric sites are known to exist in this area). There is very limited access to the monument, and there are no facilities for visitors. If you have a high-clearance vehicle, preferably four-wheel-drive, you can enter the monument from I-17 at the Badger Springs exit (exit 256) or the Bloody Basin Road exit (exit 259).

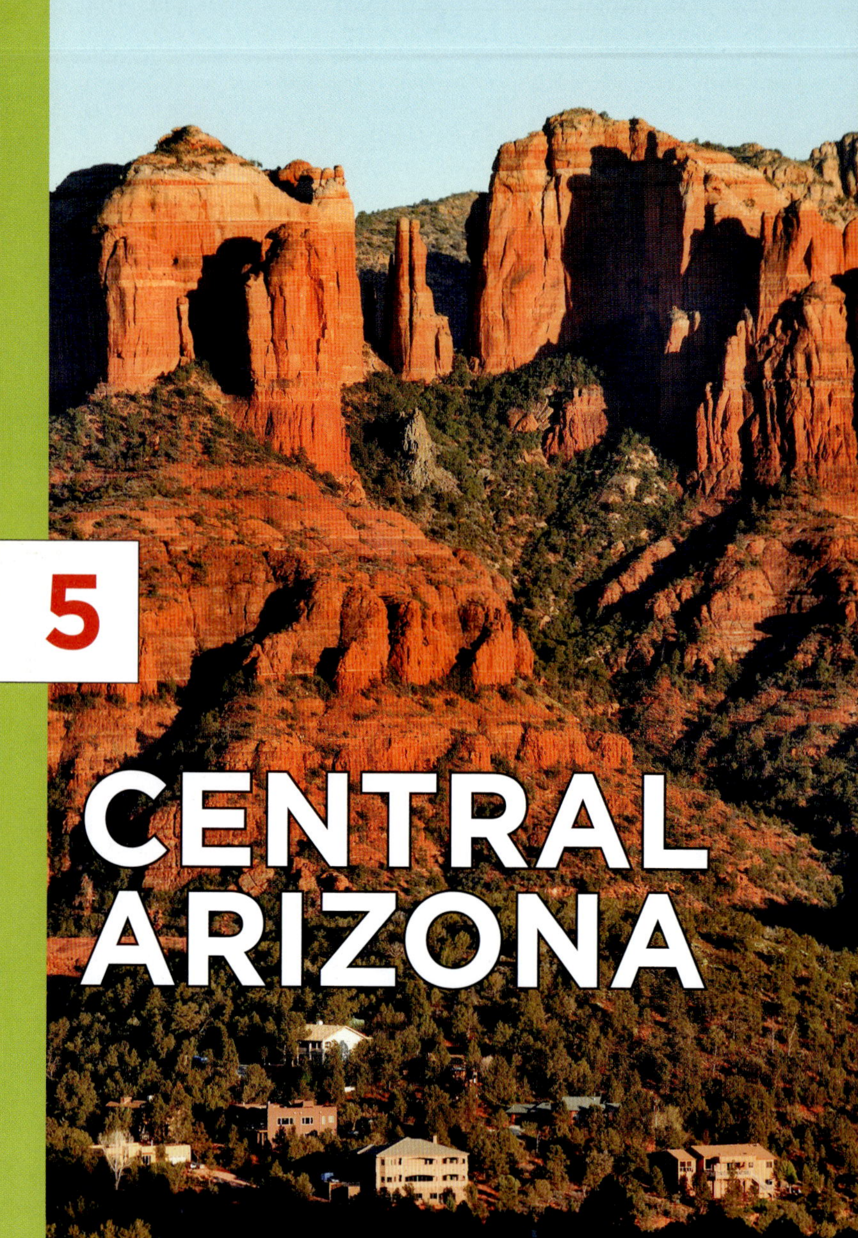

5

CENTRAL ARIZONA

Let's say you're planning a trip to Arizona. You're going to fly in to Phoenix, rent a car, and head north to the Grand Canyon. Glancing at a map of the state, you might easily imagine that there's nothing to see or do between Phoenix and the Grand Canyon. This is the desert, right? Miles of desolate wasteland, that sort of thing. Wrong!

Between Phoenix and the Grand Canyon lies one of the most beautiful landscapes on earth, the red-rock country of Sedona. But don't get the idea just because a neighbor went last year and loved it that Sedona is some sort of pristine wilderness waiting to be discovered. Decades ago, Hollywood came to Sedona to shoot Westerns; then came the artists and the retirees and the New Agers. Now Hollywood (and just about everyone with money from both coasts) is back, but this time the stars aren't shooting Westerns; they're building huge homes on the range.

While the Sedona area is absolutely drop-dead gorgeous, Central Arizona is more than just red rock and retirees. It also has the former territorial capital of Prescott, historic sites, ancient Indian ruins, an old mining town turned artists' community, and even a few good old-fashioned dude ranches out Wickenburg way. There are, of course, thousands of acres of cactus-studded desert, but there are also high mountains, cool pine forests, and a fertile river valley, appropriately named the Verde (Green) Valley. And north of Sedona's red rocks is Oak Creek Canyon, a tree-shaded cleft in the rocks with one of the state's most scenic stretches of highway running through it.

If you should fall in love with this country, don't be too surprised. People have been drawn to the region for hundreds of years. The Hohokam people farmed the fertile Verde Valley as long ago as A.D. 600, followed later by the Sinagua. Although these early tribes had disappeared by the time the first white settlers arrived in the 1860s, Apache and Yavapai tribes did inhabit the area. It was to protect settlers from these hostile tribes that the U.S. Army established Fort Verde here in 1871.

When Arizona became a U.S. territory in 1863, Prescott, due to its central location, was chosen as the territorial capital. Although the town would eventually lose that title to Tucson and then to Phoenix, it was the most important city in Arizona for part of the late 19th century. Wealthy merchants and legislators rapidly transformed this pioneer outpost into a beautiful town filled with stately Victorian homes surrounding an imposing county courthouse.

Settlers were lured to this region not only by fertile land, but also by the mineral wealth that lay hidden in the ground. Miners founded a number of communities in central Arizona, among them Jerome. When the mines finally shut down, Jerome was almost completely abandoned, but now artists and craftspeople have moved in to reclaim and revitalize the old mining town.

In the middle of the 20th century, it was sunshine and a chance to ride the range that lured people to central Arizona, and many of those visitors headed to Wickenburg. This former cow town still clings to its Western roots and has

PREVIOUS PAGE: **Sedona's Cathedral Rock at sunset.**

restored part of its downtown to its 1880s appearance. It is here you'll find the region's few remaining dude ranches, which now call themselves "guest ranches."

WICKENBURG

53 miles NW of Phoenix; 61 miles S of Prescott; 128 miles SE of Kingman

Known a half-century ago as the dude-ranch capital of the world, Wickenburg once attracted celebrities and families from all over the country. Those were the days when the West had only just stopped being wild, and spending the winter in Arizona was an adventure, not just a chance to escape snow and ice. Today, although the area has only a handful of dude (or guest) ranches still in business, Wickenburg still clings to its Wild West image. The guest ranches that remain range from rustic to luxurious, but a chance to ride the range is still the area's main attraction.

When dude ranches first flourished back in the 1920s and 1930s, Wickenburg realized that visitors wanted a taste of the Wild West, so the town gave the tenderfoots what they wanted: trail rides, hayrides, cookouts—the works. The town is still providing those same activities and has now preserved one of its downtown streets much as it may have looked in the early 1900s when this was a booming mining town.

Wickenburg was founded in 1863 by Henry Wickenburg, a Prussian prospector who came to the desert in search of riches. He hit pay dirt just south of the town that now bears his name, and his Vulture Mine eventually became the most profitable gold and silver mine in Arizona. Although the mine closed in 1942, it is now operated as a tourist attraction. If you've come to Arizona searching for the West the way it used to be, Wickenburg, with its ranches and old gold mine, is a good place to look. Just don't expect shootouts staged in the streets every day—this ain't Tombstone.

Wickenburg is filled with historic buildings.

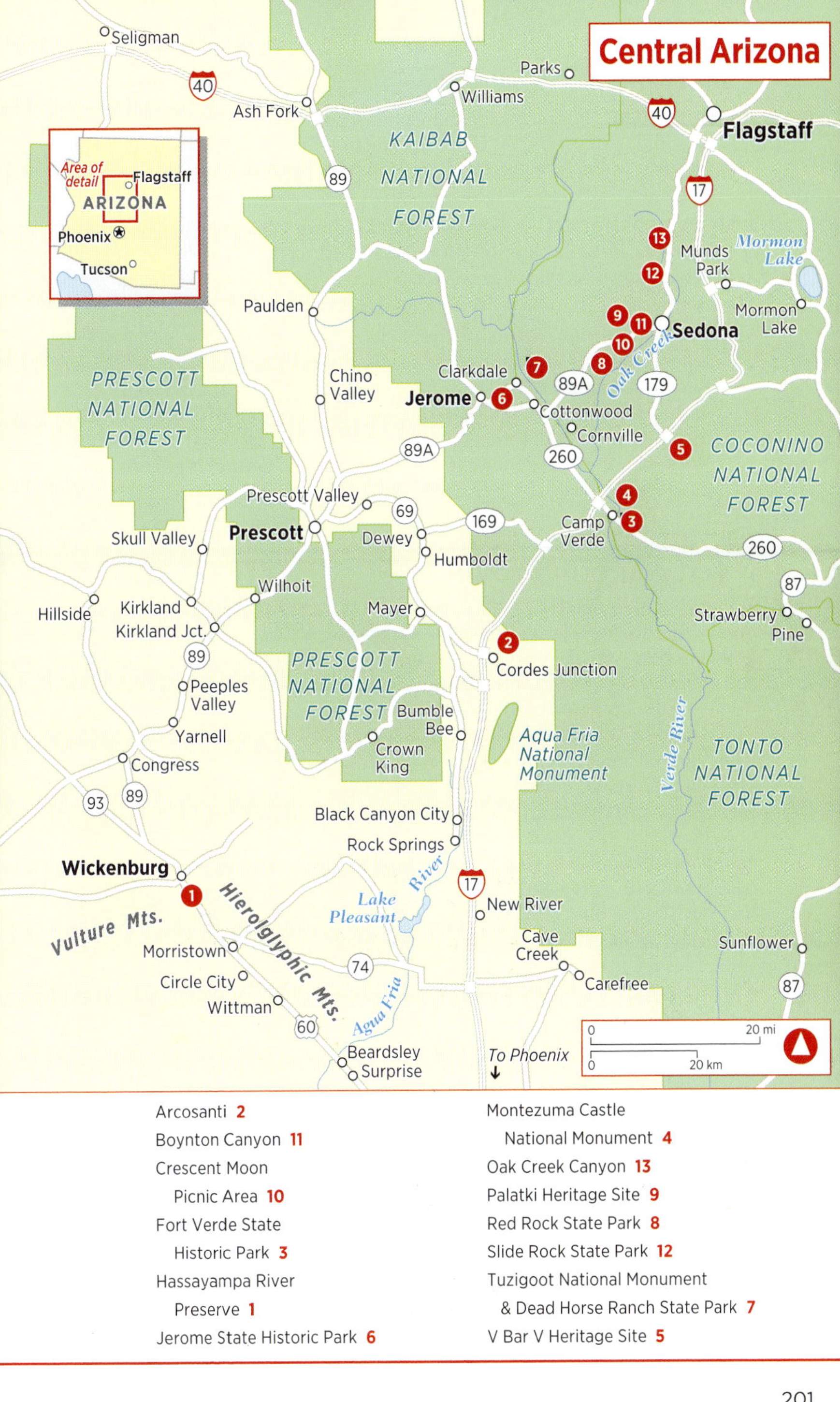
Central Arizona
Area of detail
Flagstaff
ARIZONA
Phoenix
Tucson
Seligman
Ash Fork
Williams
Parks
Flagstaff
KAIBAB NATIONAL FOREST
Mormon Lake
Munds Park
Mormon Lake
Sedona
Oak Creek
Paulden
Chino Valley
Clarkdale
Jerome
Cottonwood
Cornville
PRESCOTT NATIONAL FOREST
COCONINO NATIONAL FOREST
Prescott Valley
Prescott
Skull Valley
Dewey
Humboldt
Camp Verde
Wilhoit
Hillside
Kirkland
Kirkland Jct.
Mayer
Strawberry
Pine
Cordes Junction
Peeples Valley
Yarnell
Congress
PRESCOTT NATIONAL FOREST
Bumble Bee
Crown King
Aqua Fria National Monument
Verde River
TONTO NATIONAL FOREST
Black Canyon City
Rock Springs
Wickenburg
Vulture Mts.
Hieroglyphic Mts.
Lake Pleasant
River
New River
Morristown
Circle City
Wittman
Cave Creek
Carefree
Sunflower
Agua Fria
Beardsley
Surprise
To Phoenix
0
20 mi
0
20 km
Arcosanti 2
Boynton Canyon 11
Crescent Moon Picnic Area 10
Fort Verde State Historic Park 3
Hassayampa River Preserve 1
Jerome State Historic Park 6
Montezuma Castle National Monument 4
Oak Creek Canyon 13
Palatki Heritage Site 9
Red Rock State Park 8
Slide Rock State Park 12
Tuzigoot National Monument & Dead Horse Ranch State Park 7
V Bar V Heritage Site 5

Essentials

GETTING THERE From Phoenix, drive north on I-17, then west on Ariz. 74, continuing west on U.S. 60. From Prescott, take Ariz. 89. If you're coming from the west, take U.S. 60 from I-10. U.S. 93 comes down from I-40 in northwestern Arizona.

VISITOR INFORMATION Contact the **Wickenburg Chamber of Commerce,** 216 N. Frontier St. (✆ **800/942-5242** or 928/684-5479; www.outwickenburgway.com). The visitor center is open Monday through Friday from 9am to 5pm, Saturday and Sunday from 10am to 2pm.

SPECIAL EVENTS **Gold Rush Days,** held on the second full weekend in February, is the biggest festival of the year in Wickenburg and has been for more than 60 years. Events include gold panning, a rodeo, and shootouts in the streets. On the second full weekend in November, the **Bluegrass Festival** features fiddle and banjo contests. On the first weekend in December, Wickenburg holds its annual **Cowboy Poetry Gathering,** with lots of poetry and music.

Exploring the Area

A WALK AROUND TOWN

While Wickenburg's main attractions remain the guest ranches outside of town, a walk around downtown also provides a glimpse of the Old West. Most of the buildings here were built between 1890 and the 1920s (although a few are older), and although not all of them look their age, there is just enough Western character to make a stroll worthwhile (if it's not too hot).

The old **Santa Fe train station,** on Frontier Street, is now the Wickenburg Chamber of Commerce, where you can pick up a map that tells a bit about the history of the town's buildings. The brick **post office,** almost across the street from the train station, once had a ride-up window providing service to people on horseback. Frontier Street is preserved as it looked in the early 1900s. The covered sidewalks and false fronts are characteristic of frontier architecture; the false fronts often disguised older adobe buildings that were considered "uncivilized" by settlers from back east. At the **Garcia Little Red Schoolhouse,** 245 N. Tegner St. (✆ **928/684-7473;** www.wco.org), which has a gift shop and is open Tuesday through Saturday from 10am to 2pm, you can even go back to school. You'll find the old schoolhouse next door to the Basha's supermarket.

Two of the town's most unusual attractions aren't buildings at all. The **Jail Tree,** behind the convenience store at the corner of Wickenburg Way and Tegner Street, is an old mesquite tree that served as the local hoosegow. Outlaws were simply chained to the tree. Their families would often come to visit and have a picnic in the shade of the tree. The second, equally curious, town attraction is the **Wishing Well,** which stands beside the bridge over the Hassayampa. Legend has it that anyone who

Wickenburg After Dark

These days, stargazing and telling stories around the campfire aren't the only things to do after dark. The **Del E. Webb Center for the Performing Arts,** 1090 S. Vulture Mine Rd. (✆ **928/684-6624;** www.delewebbcenter.org), brings a wide range of cultural performances to a town that once knew only horse operas.

Desert Caballeros Western Museum.

drinks from the Hassayampa River will never tell the truth again. How the well adjacent to the river became a wishing well is unclear.

MUSEUMS & MINES

Desert Caballeros Western Museum ★★ Wickenburg thrives on its Western heritage, and inside this museum you'll find an outstanding collection of Western art depicting life on the range, including works by Albert Bierstadt, Thomas Moran, Charles Russell, Frederic Remington, Maynard Dixon, and other members of the Cowboy Artists of America. The Hays "Spirit of the Cowboy" collection is an impressive display of historical cowboy gear that alone makes this museum worth a stop.

21 N. Frontier St. ✆ **928/684-2272.** www.westernmuseum.org. Admission $7.50 adults, $6 seniors, free for children 16 and under. Mon–Sat 10am–5pm; Sun noon–4pm. Closed Mon June–Aug, and major holidays.

The Vulture Mine ☺ Lying at the base of Vulture Peak (the most visible landmark in the Wickenburg area), the Vulture Mine was first staked by Henry Wickenburg in 1863, fueling the small gold rush that helped populate this section of the Arizona desert. Today, the Vulture Mine has the feel of a ghost town, and though you can't go down into the old mine itself, you can wander around the aboveground shacks and mine structures on a self-guided tour. It's all mildly interesting for those who appreciate old mines, and fun for kids.

Vulture Mine Rd. ✆ **602/859-2743.** Admission $10, free for children 11 and under. Sept to early June daily 9am–3pm; early June to Sept daily 8am–2pm. Closed Thanksgiving and Christmas. Take U.S. 60 W. out of town, turn left on Vulture Mine Rd., and drive 12 miles south.

A BIRDER'S PARADISE

Hassayampa River Preserve ★ At one time, the Arizona desert was laced with rivers that flowed for most, if not all, of the year. In the past century, however, these rivers, and the riparian forests they once supported, have disappeared at an alarming rate because of the damming of rivers and the lowering of water tables by wells. Riparian areas support trees and plants that require more water than is usually available in the desert, and this lush growth provides food and

Hassayampa River Preserve.

shelter for hundreds of species of birds, mammals, and reptiles. Today, the riparian cottonwood-willow forests of the desert Southwest are considered the country's most endangered forest type.

The Nature Conservancy, a nonprofit organization dedicated to purchasing and preserving threatened habitats, owns and manages the Hassayampa River Preserve, which is now one of the state's most important bird-watching sites (280 species of birds have been spotted here). Nature trails lead along the river beneath cottonwoods and willows, and past the spring-fed Palm Lake. On-site are a visitor center and bookshop. October through April, free naturalist-guided walks are offered on the last Saturday of the month at 8:30am (reservations recommended).

49614 N. U.S. 60 (milepost 114, 3 miles southeast of Wickenburg). ✆ **928/684-2772.** www.nature.org. Suggested donation $5 ($3 for Nature Conservancy members). Mid-Sept to mid-May Wed–Sun 8am–5pm; mid-May to mid-Sept Fri–Sun 7–11am. Closed Thanksgiving, day after Thanksgiving, Christmas Eve, Christmas Day, New Year's Eve, and New Year's Day.

OUTDOOR PURSUITS

If you're in the area for more than a day or just can't spend another minute in the saddle, you can go out on a jeep tour and explore the desert backcountry, visit Vulture Peak, see some petroglyphs, or check out old mines. Call B.C. **Jeep Tours** (✆ **928/684-7901** or 928/231-1010; www.bcjeeptours.com), which charges $60 to $100 per person with a two-person minimum. However, if you've got time for only one jeep tour on your Arizona vacation, make it in Sedona.

Los Caballeros Golf Club ★, 1551 S. Vulture Mine Rd. (✆ **928/684-2704;** www.loscaballerosgolf.com), has been rated one of the best courses in the state. Greens fee is $90 in the cooler months.

Hikers should head southwest of town to the end of Vulture Mine Road (off U.S. 60) to climb **Vulture Peak,** which is a steep but rewarding climb best done in the cooler months. The views from up top (or even just the saddle near the top) are well worth the effort. There are sometimes spectacular wildflower displays here in the spring.

Where to Stay

Flying E Ranch ☺ This is a working cattle ranch with 20,000 high, wide, and handsome acres for you and the cattle to roam. In business since 1946, the Flying E attracts plenty of repeat business, with families finding it a particularly appealing and down-home kind of place. Accommodations vary in size, but all have Western-style furnishings and either twin or king-size beds. Three family-style meals are served in the wood-paneled dining room; but there's no bar, so you'll need to bring your own liquor. However, the main lodge does have a spacious lounge where guests like to gather by the fireplace. There are also breakfast cookouts, lunch rides, hayrides, and evening chuck-wagon dinners. Horseback riding costs an additional $40 to $60 per person per day.

2801 W. Wickenburg Way, Wickenburg, AZ 85390. www.flyingeranch.com. ✆ **888/684-2650** or 928/684-2690. Fax 928/684-5304. 17 units. $308–$392 double. Rates include all meals. 2- to 4-night minimum stay. MC, V. Closed May–Oct. Drive 4 miles west of town on U.S. 60. **Amenities:** Dining room; exercise room; Jacuzzi; outdoor pool; sauna; tennis court. *In room:* A/C, TV, fridge, free Wi-Fi.

Kay El Bar Guest Ranch ★ This is the smallest and oldest of the Wickenburg guest ranches, and its adobe buildings, built between 1914 and 1925, are listed on the National Register of Historic Places. The well-maintained ranch is quintessentially Wild West in style, and the setting, on the shady banks of the Hassayampa River (usually dry), lends the ranch a surprisingly lush feel compared with the arid surrounding landscape. While the Homestead House and the Casa Grande are the most spacious, the smaller rooms in the adobe main lodge have original Monterey-style furnishings and other classic 1950s dude-ranch decor. I like this place because it's so small you feel like you're on a friend's ranch. Guests can go out horseback riding twice a day, except on Sunday when there's a long morning ride followed by lunch on a hilltop.

Rincon Rd., off U.S. 93 (P.O. Box 2480), Wickenburg, AZ 85358. www.kayelbar.com. ✆ **800/684-7583** or 928/684-7593. Fax 928/684-4497. 11 units. $375–$420 double; $795–$895 cottage for 4. Rates do not include 15% service charge. Rates include all meals and horseback riding. 2- to 4-night minimum stay. Children 3 and under stay free in parent's room. MC, V. Closed May to mid-Oct. **Amenities:** Dining room; lounge; access to nearby health club; Jacuzzi; small outdoor pool. *In room:* Hair dryer, no phone.

Rancho de los Caballeros ★★ Located on 20,000 acres 2 miles west of Wickenburg, Rancho de los Caballeros is part of an exclusive country-club community and, as such, feels more like a resort than a guest ranch. However, the main lodge itself, with its flagstone floor, copper fireplace, and colorfully painted furniture, has a very Southwestern feel. Peace and quiet are the keynotes of a visit here, and most guests focus on golf (the golf course is one of the best in the state) and horseback riding (not included in room rates). In addition, the ranch has a spa and offers trap and skeet shooting and guided nature walks. Guest rooms are filled with handcrafted furnishings, exposed-beam ceilings, Indian rugs, and, in some, tile floors and fireplaces. While breakfast and lunch are quite casual, dinner is more formal, with proper attire required.

Horseback riding at Kay El Bar Guest Ranch.

1551 S. Vulture Mine Rd. (off U.S. 60 west of town), Wickenburg, AZ 85390. www.sunc.com. ✆ **800/684-5030** or 928/684-5484. 79 units. Mid-Oct to Jan and late Apr to early May $405–$520 double; Feb to mid-Apr $465–$625 double. Rates do not include 15% gratuity charge. Rates include all meals. Children 4 and under stay free in parent's room. MC, V. Closed early May to mid-Oct. **Amenities:** Dining room; lounge; babysitting; children's programs; concierge; 18-hole golf course; exercise room and access to nearby health club; small outdoor pool; full-service spa; 4 tennis courts. *In room:* A/C, TV, fridge, hair dryer, free Wi-Fi.

Where to Eat

If you'll be staying at a guest ranch, all your meals will be provided. In town, you can get a quick salad, sandwich, or coffee at the friendly **Pony Espresso Café,** 233 W. Wickenburg Way (✆ **928/684-0208;** www.theponyespressocafe.com), or next door at the **Horseshoe Café,** 207 E. Wickenburg Way (✆ **928/684-7377**).

En Route to Prescott

Between Wickenburg and Prescott, Ariz. 89 climbs out of the desert at the town of **Yarnell,** which lies at the top of a steep stretch of road. The landscape around Yarnell is a jumble of weather-worn granite boulders that give the town a unique appearance. Several little crafts and antiques shops here are worth a stop. However, the town's main claim to fame is the **Shrine of St. Joseph of the Mountains** (✆ **928/778-5229;** www.stjoseph-shrine.org), which is known for its carved stone Stations of the Cross. Watch for the sign to the shrine as you drive through town.

PRESCOTT

100 miles N of Phoenix; 66 miles SW of Sedona; 87 miles SW of Flagstaff

Prescott, the former territorial capital, is an Arizona anomaly; it doesn't seem like the Southwest at all. With its stately courthouse on a tree-shaded square, its well-preserved historic downtown business district, and its old Victorian homes, Prescott wears the air of the quintessential small Midwestern town, the sort of place where the Broadway show *The Music Man* might have been staged. Prescott has just about everything a small town should have: an 1890s saloon (the Palace), an old cattlemen's hotel (the Hassayampa Inn), a burger shop (Kendall's), and a brewpub (the Prescott Brewing Company). Add to this several small museums, a couple of other historic hotels, the strange and beautiful landscape of the Granite Dells, and the nearby Prescott National Forest, and you have a town that appeals to visitors with a diverse range of interests.

The town's pioneer history dates from 1863, when the Walker party discovered gold in the mountains of central Arizona. Soon miners were flocking to the area to seek their own fortunes. A year later, Arizona became a U.S. territory, and the new town of Prescott, located right in the center of Arizona, was made the territorial capital. Prescott lost its statewide influence when the capital moved to Phoenix, but because of the importance of ranching and mining in central Arizona, Prescott continued to be a major regional town. Today Prescott has become an upscale retirement community, heralded as much for its historical heritage as for its mild year-round climate. In summer, Prescott is also a popular weekend getaway for Phoenicians; it is usually 20° cooler here than it is in Phoenix (and most winters even see some snow).

Essentials

GETTING THERE Prescott is at the junction of Ariz. 89, Ariz. 89A, and Ariz. 69. If you're coming from Phoenix, take the Cordes Junction exit (exit 262) from I-17. From Flagstaff, the most direct route is I-17 to Ariz. 169 to Ariz. 69. From Sedona, just take Ariz. 89A all the way.

Shuttle "U" (✆ **800/304-6114** or 928/442-1000; www.shuttleu.com) provides service to Prescott from Sky Harbor Airport for $34 one-way, $56 round-trip.

VISITOR INFORMATION The **Prescott Chamber of Commerce** is at 117 W. Goodwin St. (✆ **800/266-7534** or 928/445-2000; www.visit-prescott.com). The visitor center is open Monday through Friday from 9am to 5pm, and Saturday and Sunday from 10am to 2pm.

ORIENTATION Ariz. 89 comes into Prescott on the northeast side of town, where it joins with Ariz. 69 coming in from the east. Five miles north of town, Ariz. 89A from Sedona also merges with Ariz. 89. The main street into town is **Gurley Street,** which forms the north side of Courthouse Plaza. **Montezuma Street,** also known as Whiskey Row, forms the west side of the plaza. If you continue south on Montezuma Street, you'll be on Ariz. 89 heading toward Wickenburg.

SPECIAL EVENTS The **World's Oldest Rodeo** (✆ **800/358-1888** or 928/445-3103; www.worldsoldestrodeo.com) is Prescott's biggest annual event and is held in early July. In early June, there's **Territorial Days,** which includes special art exhibits, performances, tournaments, races, and lots of food and free entertainment. In mid-July, the Sharlot Hall Museum hosts the **Prescott Indian Art Market.** In December, the city is decked out with lights, and there are numerous holiday events.

Exploring the Town

A walk around **Courthouse Plaza** should be your first introduction to Prescott. The stately old courthouse in the middle of the tree-shaded plaza sets the tone for the whole town. The building, far too large for a small regional town such as this, dates from the days when Prescott was the capital of the Arizona territory. Under the big shade trees, you'll find several bronze statues of cowboys and soldiers.

Surrounding the courthouse and extending north for a block is Prescott's **historic business district.** Stroll around admiring the brick buildings, and you'll realize that Prescott was once a very important place. Duck into an old saloon or the lobby of one of the historic hotels, and you'll understand that the town was also part of the Wild West.

Fort Whipple Museum Located north of town off Ariz. 89 on the grounds of what is now a Veterans Affairs hospital, this museum focuses on the history of this fort, which was active from 1863 to 1922 and has many stately officers' homes. Don't miss the display about Fiorello LaGuardia's time at the fort.

Veterans Affairs campus, Bldg. 11, 500 N. Ariz. 89. ✆ **928/445-3122.** Free admission. Thurs–Sat 10am–4pm. Closed New Year's Day, Thanksgiving, and Christmas.

Phippen Museum ★ If you're a fan of classic Western art, you won't want to miss this small museum. Located on a hill a few miles north of town, the Phippen is named after the first president of the prestigious Cowboy Artists of America organization and exhibits works by both established Western artists and

Prescott's Courthouse Plaza.

Frémont House at the Sharlot Hall Museum.

newcomers. Also on display are artifacts and photos that help place the artwork in the context of the region's history. The **Phippen Museum Western Art Show & Sale** is held each year on Memorial Day weekend. This museum underwent a major expansion in 2011.

4701 Ariz. 89 N. **928/778-1385.** www.phippenartmuseum.org. Admission $5 adults, $4 seniors and students, free for children 11 and under. Tues–Sat 10am–4pm; Sun 1–4pm.

Sharlot Hall Museum ★ Opened in 1928 in a log home that once served as the governor's mansion of the Arizona territory, this museum was founded by Sharlot Hall, who served as the territorial historian from 1909 to 1911. In addition to the governor's "mansion," which is furnished much as it might have been when it was built, several other interesting buildings can be toured. With its traditional wood-frame construction, the Frémont House, which was built in 1875 for the fifth territorial governor, shows how quickly Prescott grew from a remote logging and mining camp into a civilized little town. The 1877 Bashford House reflects the Victorian architecture that was popular throughout the country around the end of the 19th century. The Sharlot Hall Building houses exhibits on Native American cultures and territorial Arizona. Every year in early summer, artisans, craftspeople, and costumed exhibitors participate in the **Folk Arts Fair.**

A Big Little Collection

Prescott is home to Embry-Riddle Aeronautical University, and in the university library, you can marvel at the world's largest collection of miniature airplanes. The **Kalusa Miniature Airplane Collection,** which includes more than 5,500 hand-carved and hand-painted miniature airplanes, was created by John W. Kalusa over a period of more than 50 years. The planes are built to a scale of ⅛th inch to 1 foot. Many of the planes are barely an inch across, while others, such as Howard Hughes's famed "Spruce Goose," are much larger. You'll find the airplane collection in cases on the first and second floors of the Christine and Steven F. Udvar-Hazy Library and Learning Center, Embry-Riddle Aeronautical University, 3700 Willow Creek Rd. (**928/777-3811;** http://library.pr.erau.edu/collections/kalusa.php). Contact the library for current hours.

415 W. Gurley St. ✆ **928/445-3122.** www.sharlot.org. Admission $5 adults, free for children 17 and under. May–Sept Mon–Sat 10am–5pm, Sun noon–4pm; Oct–Apr Mon–Sat 10am–4pm, Sun noon–4pm. Closed New Year's Day, Thanksgiving, and Christmas.

The Smoki Museum This interesting little museum, which houses a collection of Native American artifacts in a historic stone building, is named for the fictitious Smoki tribe. The tribe was dreamed up in 1921 by a group of non-Indians who wanted to inject some new life into Prescott's July 4th celebrations. Despite its phony origins, the museum contains genuine artifacts and basketry from many different tribes, mainly Southwestern. The museum also sponsors interesting lectures on Native American topics.

147 N. Arizona St. ✆ **928/445-1230.** www.smokimuseum.org. Admission $5 adults, $4 seniors, $3 students, free for children 12 and under. Mon–Sat 10am–4pm; Sun 1–4pm. Closed Thanksgiving and Christmas.

Outdoor Pursuits

Prescott is situated on the edge of a wide expanse of high plains with the pine forests of **Prescott National Forest** at its back. Within the national forest are lakes, campgrounds, and many miles of hiking and mountain biking trails. My favorite hiking and biking areas in the national forest are Thumb Butte (west of town) and the Granite Mountain Wilderness (northwest of town).

Thumb Butte, a rocky outcropping that towers over the forest just west of town, is Prescott's most easily recognizable natural landmark. A 1.2-mile trail leads nearly to the top of this butte, and from the saddle near the summit, there's a panoramic vista of the entire region. The trail is very steep but paved much of the way. The summit of the butte is a popular rock-climbing spot. An alternative return trail makes a loop hike possible. To reach the trail head, drive west out of town on Gurley Street, which becomes Thumb Butte Road. Follow the road until you see the National Forest signs, after which there's a parking lot, picnic area, and trail head. The parking fee is $5.

The Granite Basin Recreation Area provides access to the **Granite Mountain Wilderness.** Trails lead beneath the cliffs of Granite Mountain, where you might spot peregrine falcons. For the best views, hike 1.5 miles to Blair Pass and then on up the Granite Mountain trail as far as you feel like going. To reach this area, take Gurley Street west from downtown, turn right on Grove Avenue, and follow it around to Iron Springs Road, which will take you northwest out of town to the signed road for the Granite Basin Recreation Area (less than 8 miles from downtown). There is a $5 parking fee here.

Both of the above areas also offer mountain biking trails. Although the scenery isn't as spectacular as in the Sedona area, the trails are great. You can rent a bike and get maps and specific trail recommendations at **Ironclad Bicycles,** 710 White Spar Rd.

Prescott's landmark Thumb Butte.

Granite Dells is a maze of boulders.

(✆ **928/776-1755;** www.ironcladbicycles.com), which charges $24 to $48 per day for mountain bikes.

For maps and information on these and other hikes and bike rides in the area, stop by the **Bradshaw Ranger Station,** 344 S. Cortez St. (✆ **928/443-8000;** www.fs.fed.us/r3/prescott).

North of town 5 miles on Ariz. 89 is an unusual and scenic area known as the **Granite Dells ★★**. Jumbled hills of rounded granite suddenly jut from the landscape, creating a maze of huge boulders and smooth rock. In the middle of this dramatic landscape lies **Watson Lake,** the waters of which push their way in among the boulders to create one of the prettiest lakes in the state. On the highway side of the lake, you'll find **Watson Lake Park,** 3101 Watson Lake Rd. (✆ **928/777-1122;** www.cityofprescott.net/services/parks), which has picnic tables and great views. Spring through fall (weather permitting), you can rent **canoes and kayaks** ($15–$20 for the first hour and $10–$15 per hour after that) at the lake Friday through Sunday from 8am to 4pm. Reservations aren't accepted, but you can call **Prescott Outdoors** (✆ **928/925-1410;** www.prescottoutdoors.com) to make sure they'll be at the lake with their boats. There's a $2 parking fee in the park.

For hiking in the Watson Lake area, I recommend heading to the scenic **Peavine Trail ★★**, which is one of the most gratifying easy hikes in the state. To find the trail head, turn east onto Prescott Lake Parkway, which is between Prescott and the Granite Dells, and then turn left onto Sun Dog Ranch Road. This rails-to-trails path extends for several miles through the middle of the Granite Dells and is the best way to fully appreciate the Dells (you'll be away from both people and the highway). Although this is a fascinating, easy hike, it also makes a great, equally easy, mountain bike ride that can be extended 7.5 miles on the Iron King Trail. Also accessible from this same trail head is the **Watson Woods Riparian Preserve,** which has some short trails through the wetlands and riparian zone along Granite Creek. There's a $2 parking fee at the trail head.

A couple of miles west of Watson Lake you can hike in **Willow Lake Park,** 1497 Heritage Park Rd. (✆ **928/777-1122;** www.cityofprescott.net/services/parks). Parking areas on Willow Creek Road provide access to several miles of trails that lead through grasslands and groves of huge cottonwood trees adjacent to Willow Lake. The trails eventually lead to the edge of the Granite Dells. There's great bird-watching in the trees in this park, and there are even great blue heron and cormorant rookeries. The trail head on Heritage Park Road provides access to the Willow Dells Trails network. These trails meander through the jumbled boulders of the Granite Dells and are some of the most fascinating trails in the state. There's a $2 parking fee at park trail heads.

If you want to explore the area on horseback, try **Granite Mountain Stables,** 2400 Shane Dr. (✆ **928/771-9551;** www.granitemountainstables.com), which offers guided trail rides in the Prescott National Forest. A 1-hour ride is $35.

Reasonably priced golf is available at the 36-hole **Antelope Hills Golf Course,** 1 Perkins Dr. (✆ **800/972-6818** or 928/777-1888; www.antelopehillsgolf.com). Greens fees range from $30 to $45.

Prescott's North Cortez Street is filled with antiques stores.

Shopping

Downtown Prescott is filled with antiques stores, especially along North Cortez Street, and is the best place in Arizona to do some antiques shopping. For Native American crafts and Old West memorabilia, be sure to stop in at **Ogg's Hogan,** 111 N. Cortez St. (✆ **928/443-9856**). In the Hotel St. Michael's shopping arcade, check out **Hotel Trading,** 110 S. Montezuma St. (✆ **928/778-7276**), which carries some genuine Native American artifacts at reasonable prices. Owner Ernie Lister also makes silver jewelry in the 19th-century Navajo style. In this same arcade, you'll find the **Old Sage Bookshop,** 110 S. Montezuma St. (✆ **928/776-1136**), a wonderful little used-book store selling primarily hardback editions. On the same block are both the **Arts Prescott Gallery,** 134 S. Montezuma St. (✆ **928/776-7717;** www.artsprescott.com), a cooperative of local artists, and **Van Gogh's Ear,** 156B S. Montezuma St. (✆ **928/776-1080;** www.vgegallery.com), which was founded by a splinter group from the co-op. Also on this block you'll find the **Newman Gallery,** 106-A S. Montezuma St. (✆ **928/442-9167;** www.newmangallery.net), which features the colorful Western-inspired pop-culture imagery of artist Dave Newman.

Want to sample some local wine while you're in the area? Head north of Prescott to **Granite Creek Vineyards,** 2515 Rd. 1 E., Chino Valley (✆ **928/636-2003;** www.granitecreekvineyards.com), which produces organic, sulfite-free wines that are surprisingly good. The winery is open Friday through Sunday from 1 to 5pm. Call for directions.

Where to Stay

MODERATE

Hassayampa Inn ★ Built as a luxury hotel in 1927, the Hassayampa Inn, which is listed on the National Register of Historic Places, evokes the time when Prescott was the bustling territorial capital. In the lobby, exposed ceiling beams, wrought-iron chandeliers, and arched doorways all reflect the place's Southwestern heritage. Unfortunately, guest rooms are not as impressive as the lobby. Rooms tend to be very small but do have original furnishings or antiques. Some suites are very oddly configured; you might find the shower in one converted closet and the commode in another. One room is said to be haunted; any hotel employee will be happy to tell you the story of the ill-fated honeymooners whose ghosts supposedly reside here.

122 E. Gurley St., Prescott, AZ 86301. www.hassayampainn.com. ✆ **800/322-1927** or 928/778-9434. Fax 928/717-0143. 67 units. $79–$199 double; $129–$219 suite. Rates include full breakfast. Children 12 and under stay free in parent's room. AE, DC, DISC, MC, V. Pets accepted ($10 per night). **Amenities:** Restaurant; lounge; exercise room and access to nearby health club; room service. *In room:* A/C, TV, hair dryer, free Wi-Fi.

The Pleasant Street Inn Downtown Prescott is full of beautiful old Victorian homes, but this is one of the only ones that's a bed-and-breakfast inn. In this old house, innkeeper Jeanne Watkins eschews the sort of over-the-top decor characteristic of most Victorian B&Bs. What you'll find is simply furnished but very comfortable guest rooms and common areas. Although the large upstairs Pine View Suite, which has a fireplace, is my favorite, the downstairs Terrace Suite, with its little deck, is also a good choice. This pleasant inn is only 3 blocks from Courthouse Plaza.

142 S. Pleasant St., Prescott, AZ 86303. www.pleasantbandb.com. ✆ **877/226-7128** or 928/445-4774. 4 units. $130 double; $160–$185 suite. DISC, MC, V. Children 12 and older welcome. **Amenities:** Concierge; access to nearby health club. *In room:* A/C, no phone, free Wi-Fi.

Rocamadour Bed & Breakfast for (Rock) Lovers ★★ The Granite Dells, just north of Prescott, is the area's most unforgettable feature. Should you wish to stay amid these jumbled boulders, there's no better choice than Rocamadour. Mike and Twila Coffey honed their innkeeping skills as owners of a 40-room château in France, and antique furnishings from that château can now be found throughout this inn. The most elegant pieces are in the Chambre Trucy, which also boasts an amazing underlit whirlpool tub. A cottage built on top of the boulders has a large deck. The unique setting, engaging innkeepers, and thoughtful details everywhere you turn make this one of the state's must-stay inns.

3386 N. Ariz. 89, Prescott, AZ 86301. ✆ **928/771-1933.** 3 units. $149–$169 double; $219 suite. Rates include full breakfast. AE, MC, V. *In room:* A/C, TV/VCR, free Wi-Fi.

INEXPENSIVE

Hotel St. Michael Located right on Whiskey Row, this hotel, complete with resident ghost and the oldest elevator in Prescott, offers a historic setting at budget prices (don't expect the most stylish furnishings). All rooms are different; some have bathtubs but no showers. Its restaurant, the casual Caffe St. Michael, overlooks Courthouse Plaza.

205 W. Gurley St., Prescott, AZ 86301. www.stmichaelhotel.com. ✆ **800/678-3757** or 928/776-1999. Fax 928/776-7318. 72 units. $59–$99 double; $89–$119 suite. Rates include full breakfast. AE, DC, DISC, MC, V. **Amenities:** Restaurant; access to nearby health club. *In room:* A/C, TV, free Wi-Fi.

Haunted Hotels

Jerome may be the region's top ghost town, but in Prescott, three hotels claim to be haunted. The Hassayampa Inn, Hotel St. Michael, and Hotel Vendome are all said to have resident ghosts.

Hotel Vendome ☺ Not quite as luxurious as the Hassayampa, yet not as basic as the St. Michael, the Vendome is a good middle-price choice for those who want to stay in a historic hotel. Built in 1917 as a lodging house, the restored brick building is only 2 blocks from the action of Whiskey Row, but far enough away that you can get a good night's sleep. Guest rooms are outfitted with modern furnishings, but some of the bathrooms still contain original claw-foot tubs.

The two-bedroom units, with an interconnected bathroom, are ideal for families. I just hope your kids will be able to sleep in this haunted hotel. (Like a couple of other hotels in town, the Vendome has its own resident ghost.)

230 S. Cortez St., Prescott, AZ 86303. www.vendomehotel.com. ✆ **888/468-3583** or 928/776-0900. 20 units. $59–$149 double; $99–$199 2-bedroom unit. Rates include continental breakfast. AE, DC, DISC, MC, V. **Amenities:** Lounge; concierge. *In room:* A/C, TV, free Wi-Fi.

The Motor Lodge Originally opened in 1910 as a collection of summer cabins, this vintage getaway has been revived as a midcentury modern motor court. Rooms are decorated with retro furnishings that are more Scottsdale hip than Prescott country, but if you want to stay someplace with a hip aesthetic, this is about your only choice in town. Keep in mind that this is budget hip and rooms vary in size and amenities.

503 S. Montezuma St., Prescott, AZ 86303. www.themotorlodge.com. ✆ **928/717-0157.** 12 units. $89–$139 double. 2-night minimum on certain holidays. AE, DISC, MC, V. **Amenities:** Bikes. *In room:* TV, hair dryer, free Wi-Fi.

Where to Eat

Grab picnic fare at **New Frontiers Natural Foods,** 1112 W. Iron Springs Rd. (✆ **928/445-7370**). For delicious baked goods, including savory turnovers, stop in at the **Pangaea Bakery,** 220 W. Goodwin St., Ste. 1 (✆ **928/778-2953;** www.pangaeabakery.com), which is half a block off Whiskey Row. For a quick, juicy burger or some ice cream, stop in at **Kendall's Famous Burgers & Ice Cream,** 113 S. Cortez St. (✆ **928/778-3658**). For coffee, I like the **Wild Iris Coffeehouse,** 124 S. Granite St. (✆ **928/778-5155;** www.wildiriscoffee.com), which is on the street behind Whiskey Row and overlooks Granite Creek.

MODERATE

El Gato Azul ★ MEDITERRANEAN Whether you're ravenous from a long day of hiking in the Granite Mountain Wilderness or still full from a big lunch, this casual creekside restaurant in downtown Prescott is a great choice. You can have as few or as many *tapas* (small plates) as it takes to fill you up. I like to order as many little appetizers as possible so I can pack in lots of different flavors. Try the blackened scallops, the bacon-wrapped shrimp, or the chicken *satay.* If you want something substantial, you can also order a nice big entree such as snapper with romesco sauce or shrimp in a creamy cilantro pesto.

316 W. Goodwin St. ✆ **928/445-1070.** www.elgatoazulprescott.com. Reservations recommended. Main courses $8–$11 lunch, $14–$23 dinner; *tapas* $4–$9. DISC, MC, V. Daily 11am–9pm.

Murphy's AMERICAN Murphy's, housed in an 1890 mercantile building that's on the National Register of Historic Places, has long been one of Prescott's favorite special-occasion restaurants. Sparkling leaded-glass doors usher diners into a high-ceilinged room with fans revolving slowly overhead. Many of the shop's original shelves can still be seen in the lounge area, and the restaurant does a good job of creating a historical ambience. The best bets on the menu are the mesquite-grilled meats, but the fish specials can also be good. You can save a bit of money by dining early (btw. 4 and 5:30pm) and ordering one of the sunset dinners.

201 N. Cortez St. ✆ **928/445-4044.** Reservations recommended. Main courses $9.25–$36. AE, DISC, MC, V. Sun–Thurs 11am–10pm; Fri–Sat 11am–11pm.

129½ ★ NEW AMERICAN Prescott, a classic small-town-America sort of place, may seem an odd location for a classic New York–style jazz club, but this restaurant has it down. It may not be in a basement and it isn't smoky, but everything else has just the right feel. Best of all, the restaurant has great food. Steaks are the specialty and can be had with an assortment of delicious sauces, such as rosemary cream, mushroom ragout, and pinot noir and green peppercorn (my personal favorite). There's live jazz Thursday through Sunday nights.

129½ N. Cortez St. ✆ **928/443-9292.** www.129andahalf.com. Reservations recommended. Main courses $14–$29. DISC, MC, V. Sun–Thurs 5–9pm; Fri–Sat 5–10pm.

The Rose Restaurant ★ CONTINENTAL This little restaurant, housed in a building that was constructed in 1900 and moved to this spot around 1910, has long satisfied Prescott locals and visitors alike. While much of the menu has a distinctly continental flavor, there are also plenty of dishes drawing on Asian and Latin American influences. You can start your meal with escargot, foie gras, or seared-duck potstickers, and then move on to lamb chops with fennel pollen and minted demi-glace, hunter-style veal with forest mushrooms, or shrimp-and-scallop risotto with truffles and cremini mushrooms. The wine list includes plenty of reasonably priced options. Although prices here are high, the Rose is one of Prescott's best restaurants and is your best bet for an elegant fine-dining experience while in town.

234 S. Cortez St. ✆ **928/777-8308.** www.theroserestaurant.com. Reservations recommended. Main courses $17–$36. AE, DISC, MC, V. Wed–Sun 5–9pm.

INEXPENSIVE

Dinner Bell Café ☺ 🎁 AMERICAN This casual little breakfast-and-lunch place is a big hit with local students and other people in the know who come to order either the waffles (served with a variety of toppings) or the thick, juicy burgers. The waffles are available at lunch, but I don't think you can get the burger at breakfast. The Dinner Bell has a split personality. Up front there's a classic old diner that's been in business since 1939, while in back there's a colorful modern space with walls that roll up. The setting, a block off Whiskey Row, makes this a great little hideaway for a quick, casual meal, and kids will want to wander along the adjacent creekside path.

321 W. Gurley St. ✆ **928/445-9888.** Main courses $4.75–$9.50. No credit cards. Mon–Fri 6:30am–2pm; Sat–Sun 7am–2pm.

Prescott After Dark

Back in the days when Prescott was the territorial capital and a booming mining town, it supported dozens of rowdy saloons, most of which were concentrated along Montezuma Street on the west side of Courthouse Plaza. This section of town was known as **Whiskey Row,** and legend has it there was a tunnel from the courthouse to one of the saloons so lawmakers wouldn't have to be seen ducking into the saloons during regular business hours. On July 14, 1900, a fire consumed most of Whiskey Row. However, concerned cowboys and miners managed to drag the tremendously heavy bar of the Palace saloon across the street before it was damaged.

Today, Whiskey Row is no longer the sort of place where respectable women shouldn't be seen, although it does still have a few noisy saloons with genuine Wild West flavor. Most of them feature live country music on weekends and are the dark, dank sorts of places that provide solace to a cowboy (or a construction worker) after a long day's work. However, within a few blocks of Whiskey Row, you can hear country, folk, jazz, and rock at a surprisingly diverse assortment of bars, restaurants, and clubs. In fact, Prescott has one of the densest concentrations of live-music clubs in the state.

To see what this street's saloons looked like back in the old days, drop by the **Palace,** 120 S. Montezuma St. (✆ **928/541-1996;** www.historicpalace.com), which still has a classic bar up front. These days, the Palace is more of a restaurant than a saloon, but there's live music on the weekends. A couple of times a month, there are also dinner-theater performances. Call to find out if anything is happening while you're in town.

If you want to drink where the ranchers drink and not where the hired hands carouse, head upstairs to the **Jersey Lilly Saloon,** 116 S. Montezuma St. (✆ **928/541-7854;** www.jerseylillyprescott.com), which attracts a more well-heeled clientele than the street-level saloons. On weekends, there is live music in a wide range of styles. Just around the corner from the Palace and the Jersey Lilly is the **Prescott Brewing Company,** 130 W. Gurley St. (✆ **928/771-2795;** www.prescottbrewingcompany.com), which is today's answer to the saloons of yore, brewing and serving its own tasty microbrews. A block away you'll find the **Raven Café,** 142 N. Cortez St. (✆ **928/717-0009;** www.ravencafe.com), which is the most artsy and eclectic nightlife venue in town. Not only does the Raven have the best beer list in Prescott (with an emphasis on Belgian beers and American microbrews), but the entertainment lineup ranges from Monday-night movies to live jazz and bluegrass.

The **Prescott Fine Arts Association,** 208 N. Marina St. (✆ **928/445-3286;** www.pfaa.net), sponsors plays, music performances, children's theater, and art exhibits. The association's main building, a former church built in 1899, is on the National Register of Historic Places. A block away, you'll find the **Elks Opera House,** 117 E. Gurley St. (✆ **928/777-1367;** www.elksoperahouse.com), a renovated theater that was built in 1905. **Yavapai College Performance**

The Palace is a good example of the saloons of Prescott's past.

Hall (✆ **877/928-4253** or 928/776-2000; www.yc.edu/content/community events) also stages a wide range of shows. And check the schedule at the Sharlot Hall Museum's **Blue Rose Theater** (✆ **928/445-3122;** www.sharlot.org). Also, each year in early December, Prescott stages the **Acker Musical Showcase** (www.ackershowcase.com), a citywide showcase of local talent. As many as 80 Prescott businesses host musical groups on the night of the event.

JEROME

35 miles NE of Prescott; 28 miles W of Sedona; 130 miles N of Phoenix

Few towns anywhere in Arizona make more of an impression on visitors than Jerome, a historic mining town that clings to the slopes of Cleopatra Hill high on Mingus Mountain. The town is divided into two sections that are separated by an elevation change of 1,500 vertical feet, with the upper part of town 2,000 feet above the Verde Valley. On a clear day, the view from Jerome is stupendous—it's possible to see for more than 50 miles, with the red rocks of Sedona, the Mogollon Rim, and the San Francisco Peaks all visible in the distance. Add to the unforgettable views the abundance of interesting shops and galleries and the winding narrow streets, and you have a town that should not be missed.

Once known as the billion-dollar copper camp, Jerome was founded in 1883 and by the 1920s was the fourth largest city in Arizona. In the early years, Jerome's ore was mined using an 88-mile-long network of underground railroads. However, in 1918 a fire broke out in the mine tunnels, and mining companies were forced to abandon the tunnels in favor of open-pit mining.

Jail Brakes?

One unforeseen hazard of open-pit mining next to a town built on a 30-degree slope was the effect dynamiting would have on Jerome. Mine explosions would regularly rock Jerome's world, and eventually buildings in town began sliding downhill. Even the town jail broke loose. With no jail brakes to stop it, the jail slid 225 feet downhill. (Now that's a jailbreak.)

Between 1883 and 1953, Jerome experienced an economic roller-coaster ride as the price of copper rose and fell. In the early 1950s, when it was no longer profitable to mine the copper ore of Cleopatra Hill, the last mining company shut down its operations, and almost everyone left town. By the early 1960s, Jerome looked as though it were on its way to becoming just another ghost town—but then artists who had discovered the phenomenal views and dirt-cheap rents began moving in, and slowly the would-be ghost town developed a reputation as an artists' community. Soon tourists began visiting to see and buy the artwork that was being created in Jerome, and old storefronts turned into galleries.

Jerome is now far from a ghost town, and on summer weekends the streets are packed with visitors browsing the galleries and crafts shops. The same remote and rugged setting that once made it difficult and expensive to mine copper has now become one of the town's main attractions. Because Jerome is built on a steep slope, streets through town switch back from one level of houses to the next, with narrow alleys and stairways connecting the different levels of town. All these winding streets, alleys, and stairways are lined with old brick and wood-frame buildings that cling precariously to the side of the mountain. The entire town has been designated a National Historic Landmark, and today, residences,

Jerome sits on the slopes of Cleopatra Hill on Mingus Mountain.

studios, shops, and galleries stand side by side looking (externally, anyway) much as they did when Jerome was an active mining town.

Essentials

GETTING THERE Jerome is on Ariz. 89A roughly halfway between Sedona and Prescott. Coming from Phoenix, take Ariz. 260 from Camp Verde.

VISITOR INFORMATION Contact the **Jerome Chamber of Commerce** (✆ **928/634-2900;** www.jeromechamber.com) for information.

Exploring the Town

Wandering the streets, soaking up the atmosphere, and shopping are the main pastimes in Jerome. But before you launch yourself on a shopping tour, you can learn about the town's past at the **Jerome State Historic Park,** off Ariz. 89A on Douglas Road in the lower section of town (✆ **928/634-5381;** www.azstateparks.com). Located in a mansion built in 1916 as a home for mine owner "Rawhide Jimmy" Douglas and as a hotel for visiting mining executives, the Jerome State Historic Park contains exhibits on mining as well as a few of the mansion's original furnishings. From its perch on a hill above Douglas's Little Daisy Mine, the mansion overlooks Jerome and, dizzyingly far below, the Verde Valley. The mansion was constructed of adobe bricks made on the site and once contained a wine cellar, billiards room, marble shower, steam heat, and central vacuum system. The park is open Thursday through Monday from 8:30am to 5pm, and admission is $5 for adults and $2 for children 7 to 13.

To learn more about Jerome's history, stop in at the **Jerome Historical Society's Mine Museum,** 200 Main St. (✆ **928/634-5477;** www.jeromehistoricalsociety.org), which has some small and old-fashioned displays on mining. It's open daily from 9am to 5pm; admission is $2 for adults, $1 for seniors, and free for children 12 and under. The second floor of the gift shop **Liberty Theatre & Gifts,** 110 Jerome Ave. (✆ **928/649-9016;** www.jerome libertytheater.com), was a theater back in the town's heyday. The theater is now being slowly restored and is open to the public. Although small, the theater museum here is fun to wander through, and a film about the history of Jerome is usually playing in the old theater. For that classic mining-town tourist-trap experience, follow the signs up the hill from downtown Jerome to the **Gold King Mine** (✆ **928/634-0053;** www.goldkingmineghosttown.com), where you can see lots of old, rusting mining equipment and maybe even catch a demonstration. The mine is open 10am to 5pm daily, and admission is $5 for adults, $4 for seniors, and $3 for children ages 6 to 12.

Most visitors come to Jerome for the shops, which offer an eclectic blend of contemporary art, chic jewelry, one-of-a-kind handmade fashions, and unusual imports. Of course, the inevitable ice-cream parlors and shops full of tacky souvenirs are present, too. To see what local artists are creating, stop in at the **Jerome Artists Cooperative Gallery,** 502 Main St. (✆ **928/639-4276;** www.jeromeartistscoop.com), on the west side of the street where Hull Avenue and Main Street fork as you come up the hill into town. For leather goods, stop in at **Altai Leather Designs,** 415 Main St. (✆ **928/639-2221;** www.altaileather.com), which is across the street from the co-op gallery. Don't miss the eclectic offerings—everything from surplus Russian army and navy uniforms to feather boas—of the **House of Joy,** 416 N. Hull Ave. (✆ **928/634-5339;** www.jeromesfinest.com), which is just up the street from the co-op gallery. A little farther up the road, the **Raku Gallery,** 250 Hull Ave. (✆ **928/639-0239;** www.rakugallery.com), has gallery space on two floors and walls of glass across the back, with views of the red rocks of Sedona in the distance. Don't miss **Nellie Bly,** 136 Main St. (✆ **928/634-0255;** www.nellieblyscopes.com), a shop full of handmade kaleidoscopes. Head down Main Street to find **Aurum Jewelry,** 369 Main St. (✆ **928/634-3330;** www.aurumjewelry.com), which has a beautiful and eclectic collection of jewelry. A couple of doors away, you'll find **Pura Vida Gallery,** 501 School St. (✆ **928/634-0937;** www.puravidagalleryjerome.com), which has a fascinating and eclectic selection of fine art, jewelry, and unusual Southwest-inspired furniture and fashions.

Jerome now has three winery tasting rooms, two of which are affiliated. My favorite of the town's wineries is **Caduceus Cellars,** 158 Main St. (✆ **928/639-9463;** www.caduceus.org), which charges $5.50 to $13 to taste four wines. This tasting room is open Sunday through Thursday from 11am to 6pm and Friday and Saturday from 11am to 8pm. The town's other two wineries are not as reliable as Caduceus Cellars, but some good wines can be found at both the **Jerome Winery,** 403 Clark St. (✆ **928/639-9067;** www.jeromewinery.com), and **Bitter Creek**

Jerome's side streets are filled with shops and galleries.

Works at the Jerome Artists Cooperative Gallery.

Winery, 240 Hull St. (✆ **928/634-7033;** www.bittercreekwinery.com). Both of these tasting rooms charge $6 for four tastes. These two tasting rooms are open Sunday through Friday from 11am to 4 or 5pm and Saturday from 10am to 5pm.

If you're in the market for local art, be sure to drop by the **Old Jerome High School,** which is on Ariz. 89A downhill from the main part of town and is full of artists' studios. On the first Saturday of each month, all of the studios here are open from 5 to 9pm for the Jerome Art Walk. Across the street from the old high school, you'll find **Copper Mountain Antiques** (✆ **928/634-3273**), which is filled with fascinating antiques, many made of copper and many from France.

Where to Stay

Connor Hotel of Jerome Housed in a renovated historic hotel, this lodging has spacious rooms with large windows; views of the valley, however, are limited. Although a few of the rooms are located directly above the hotel's popular bar, which can be quite noisy on weekends, most rooms are quiet enough to provide a good night's rest. Better yet, come on a weekday when the Harley-Davidson poseur crowd from the Scottsdale area isn't thundering through the streets on their hogs.

164 Main St. (P.O. Box 1177), Jerome, AZ 86331. www.connorhotel.com. ✆ **800/523-3554** or 928/634-5006. Fax 928/649-0981. 12 units. $90–$165 double. Children 11 and under stay free in parent's room. AE, DISC, MC, V. Pets accepted. **Amenities:** Bar. *In room:* TV, fridge, hair dryer, free Wi-Fi.

Ghost City Inn With its long verandas on both floors, this restored old house is hard to miss as you drive into town from Clarkdale. It manages to capture the spirit of Jerome, with a mix of Victorian and Southwestern decor. Most bedrooms have great views across the Verde Valley (and these are definitely worth requesting). Two units feature antique brass beds. The rooms are on the small side, so if space is a priority, opt for the suite.

541 Main St., Jerome, AZ 86331. www.ghostcityinn.com. ✆ **888/634-4678.** 6 units. $95–$145 double; $145 suite. Rates include full breakfast. 2-night minimum on some weekends and holidays. DISC, MC, V. Pets accepted ($25 fee). No children 13 or under. *In room:* A/C, TV, hair dryer, no phone, free Wi-Fi.

Mile High Inn In classic European tradition, this inn is upstairs from a restaurant (the Mile High Grill) and is reached by a flight of stairs. Therein lies this inn's greatest charm. Although half the rooms have shared bathrooms, all the rooms are attractively decorated, some with antiques and some with more modern furnishings. Although the rooms are not very large, a couple do have king-size beds, and there is an apartment for rent as well.

309 Main St. (P.O. Box 1311), Jerome, AZ 86331. www.jeromemilehighinn.com. ✆ **414/634-5094.** 7 units, 4 with private bathroom. $85–$105 double with shared bathroom; $120–$130 double with private bathroom. Rates include full breakfast (except Mon–Wed in winter). 2-night minimum on holidays. AE, DISC, MC, V. **Amenities:** Restaurant; lounge. *In room:* A/C, no phone.

Where to Eat

The Asylum ★ SOUTHWESTERN As the name would imply, this restaurant (inside a former hospital building high above downtown Jerome) is a bit out of the ordinary. The bedpan full of candy at the front desk and the odd little notes in the menu will also make it absolutely clear that this place doesn't take much, other than good food, seriously. I like the distinctly Southwestern dishes, including the prickly-pear barbecued pork tenderloin with tomatillo salsa, and an unusual butternut-squash soup made with a cinnamon-lime cream sauce. Cocktails all get wacky loony-bin names, and there's also a superb, award-winning wine list.

200 Hill St. ✆ **928/639-3197.** www.theasylum.biz. Reservations recommended. Main courses $10–$16 lunch, $20–$32 dinner. AE, DISC, MC, V. Daily 11am–3pm and 5–9pm.

Flatiron Café LIGHT FARE The tiny Flatiron Café is a simple breakfast-and-lunch spot in, you guessed it, Jerome's version of a flatiron building. The limited menu includes the likes of lox and bagels, a breakfast burrito, black-bean hummus, smoked-salmon quesadillas, fresh juices, and espresso drinks. It looks as though you could hardly squeeze in here, but there's more seating across the street. It's definitely not your usual ghost-town lunch counter.

416 Main St. (at Hull Ave.). ✆ **928/634-2733.** www.flatironcafejerome.com. Reservations not accepted. Most items $8.50–$13. MC, V. Wed–Mon 7am–3pm.

Haunted Hamburger AMERICAN Perched precariously high above Jerome's main shopping street, this restaurant seems poised to come crashing down into the Verde Valley far below. Although you can get steaks, fajitas, barbecued ribs, and other dishes here, it would be a mistake not to order the namesake haunted hamburger, which is made with mushrooms, bacon, cheese, green chilies, grilled onion, and guacamole. While this burger is memorable, it's the view from the restaurant that will truly haunt you.

410 Clark St. ✆ **928/634-0554.** Reservations not accepted. Main courses $5–$21. MC, V. Daily 11am–9pm.

THE VERDE VALLEY

Camp Verde: 20 miles E of Jerome; 30 miles S of Sedona; 95 miles N of Phoenix

Named by early Spanish explorers who were impressed by the sight of such a verdant valley in an otherwise brown desert landscape, the Verde Valley has long been a magnet for both wildlife and people. Today, the valley is one of Arizona's richest agricultural and ranching regions. The valley is also popular with retirees, and housing subdivisions now sprawl across much of the landscape. Cottonwood and Clarkdale, the valley's two largest towns, are old copper-smelting towns, while Camp Verde was an army post back in the days of the Indian Wars. All three towns have some interesting historic buildings, but it is the valley's two national monuments—Tuzigoot and Montezuma Castle—that are the main attractions.

These two national monuments preserve the ruins of Sinagua villages that date from long before the first European explorers entered the Verde Valley. By the time the first pioneers began settling in this region, the Sinaguas had long since moved on, and Apaches had claimed the valley as part of their territory. When settlers came into conflict with the Apaches, Fort Verde, now a state park, was established. Between this state park and the two national monuments, hundreds of years of Verde Valley history and prehistory can be explored. This valley is also the site of the most scenic railroad excursion in the state.

Essentials

GETTING THERE Camp Verde is just off I-17 at the junction with Ariz. 260. The latter highway leads northwest through the Verde Valley for 12 miles to Cottonwood.

VISITOR INFORMATION Contact the **Cottonwood Chamber of Commerce,** 1010 S. Main St., Cottonwood (✆ **928/634-7593;** www.cottonwoodchamberaz.org).

FESTIVALS Avid birders may want to plan their visit to coincide with the annual **Verde Valley Birding & Nature Festival** (✆ **928/282-2202;** www.birdyverde.org), which is held the last weekend in April.

A Railway Excursion

Verde Canyon Railroad ★★ When the town of Jerome was busily mining copper, a railway was built to link the booming town with the territorial capital at nearby Prescott. Because of the rugged mountains between Jerome and Prescott, the railroad was forced to take a longer but less difficult route north along the Verde River before turning south toward Prescott. Today, you can ride these same tracks aboard the Verde Canyon Railroad. The route through the canyon traverses both the remains of a copper smelter and unspoiled desert that is inaccessible by car and is part of Prescott National Forest. The views of the rocky canyon walls and green waters of the Verde River are quite dramatic, and if you look closely along the way, you'll see ancient Sinagua cliff dwellings. In late winter and early spring, nesting bald eagles can also be spotted. Although the Grand Canyon Railway travels to a more impressive destination, this is a more scenic excursion.

Verde Canyon Railroad.

300 N. Broadway, Clarkdale. ✆ **800/582-7245.** www.verdecanyonrr.com. Tickets $55 adults, $50 seniors, $35 children 2–12; 1st-class tickets $80. Call or visit the website for schedule and reservations.

National Monuments & State Parks

Dead Horse Ranch State Park You'll find this state park on the outskirts of Cottonwood, not far from Tuzigoot National Monument. Set on the banks of the Verde River, the park offers picnicking, fishing, swimming, hiking, mountain biking, and camping. Trails wind through the riparian forests along the banks of the river and visit marshes that offer good bird-watching; they also lead into the adjacent national forest, so you can get in many miles of scenic hiking and mountain biking. The ranch was named in the 1940s, when the children of a family looking to buy a ranch told their parents they wanted to buy the place with the dead horse by the side of the road.

For a guided horseback ride in the park, contact **Trail Horse Adventures** (✆ **866/958-7245** or 928/634-5276; www.trailhorseadventures.com). A 1-hour ride will cost you $64 and a 3-hour lunch ride costs $125.

675 Dead Horse Ranch Rd., Cottonwood. ✆ **928/634-5283.** www.azstateparks.com. Admission $7 per car. Visitor center daily 8am–5pm. Closed Christmas. From Main St. on the east side of Cottonwood, drive north on N. 10th St.

Fort Verde State Historic Park Just south of Montezuma Castle and Montezuma Well, in the town of Camp Verde, you'll find Fort Verde State Historic Park. Established in 1871, Fort Verde was the third military post in the Verde Valley and was occupied until 1891, by which time tensions with the Indian population had subsided and made the fort unnecessary. The military had first come to the Verde Valley in 1865 at the request of settlers who wanted protection from the local Tonto Apache and Yavapai. The tribes, traditionally hunters and gatherers, had been forced to raid farms for food after their normal economy was disrupted by the sudden influx of settlers into the area. Between 1873 and 1875, most of the Indians in the area were rounded up and forced to live on various reservations. An uprising in 1882 led to the last clash between local tribes and Fort Verde's soldiers.

The state park, which covers 10 acres, preserves three officers' quarters, an administration building, and some ruins. The buildings that have been fully restored house exhibits on the history of the fort and what life was like here in the 19th century. With their gables, white picket fences, and shake-shingle roofs, the buildings of Fort Verde suggest that life at this remote post was not so bad, at least for officers. Costumed military reenactments are held here throughout much of the year; call for details.

125 E. Hollaman St., Camp Verde. ✆ **928/567-3275.** www.azstateparks.com. Admission $4 adults, $2 children 7–13, free for children 6 and under. Thurs–Mon 9am–5pm. Closed Christmas.

Montezuma Castle National Monument ★★ Despite the name, the ruins within this monument are neither castle nor Aztec dwelling (as the reference to Aztec ruler Montezuma implies). This Sinagua ruin is, however, one of the best-preserved cliff dwellings in Arizona. The site consists of two impressive stone pueblos that were, for some unknown reason, abandoned by the Sinagua people in the early 14th century.

The more intriguing of the two ruins is set in a shallow cave 100 feet up a cliff overlooking Beaver Creek. Construction on this five-story, 20-room village began sometime in the early 12th century. Because Montezuma Castle has been protected from the elements by the overhanging roof of the cave in which it was built, the original adobe mud that was used to plaster over the stone walls of the dwelling is still intact. Another structure, containing 45 rooms on a total of six levels, stands at the base of the cliff. This latter dwelling, which has been subjected to rains and floods over the years, is not nearly as well-preserved as the cliff dwelling. In the visitor center, you'll see artifacts that have been unearthed from the two ruins.

Montezuma Well, located 11 miles north of Montezuma Castle (although still part of the national monument), is a spring-fed sinkhole that was, for the Native peoples of this desert, a genuine oasis. This sunken pond was formed when a cavern in the area's porous limestone bedrock collapsed. Underground springs quickly filled the sinkhole, which today contains a pond measuring more than 360 feet across and 65 feet deep. Over the centuries, the presence of year-round water attracted first the Hohokam and later the Sinagua peoples, who built irrigation canals to use the water for growing crops. Some of these channels can still be seen. Sinagua structures and an excavated Hohokam pit house built around 1100 are clustered in and near the sinkhole. To reach Montezuma Well, take exit 293 off I-17.

Exit 289 off I-17. ✆ **928/567-3322.** www.nps.gov/moca. Admission $5 adults ($8 with Tuzigoot National Monument admission), free for children 15 and under; no charge to visit Montezuma Well. June–Aug daily 8am–6pm; Sept–May daily 8am–5pm. Closed Christmas.

Montezuma Castle National Monument.

Out of Africa Wildlife Park ★ ☺ Lions and tigers and bears, oh my. And zebras and giraffes and wildebeests, oh yes. That's what you'll encounter at this sprawling wildlife park between Camp Verde and Cottonwood. The park includes both a "wildlife preserve" of large fenced predator enclosures and an "African Bush Safari" area. In this latter area, you ride on a rugged safari vehicle through a vast enclosure populated by giraffes, zebras, ostriches, wildebeests, and other African animals. You may even get to feed a giraffe or zebra. The other half of the park is home to numerous lions, tigers, wolves, panthers, hyenas, and other large predators. All these carnivores are fed on Sunday, Wednesday, and Friday at 3pm, and following the feeders is one of the highlights of a visit to the park. One of the park's most popular attractions, especially with kids, is the Tiger Splash, in which big cats and their caretakers demonstrate predator-prey interactions in a large pool.

3505 W. Ariz. 260 (at Verde Valley Justice Rd.), Camp Verde. ✆ **928/567-2840** or 928/567-2842. www.outofafricapark.com. Admission $36 adults, $34 seniors, $20 children ages 3–12, free for children 2 and under. Daily 9:30am–5pm. Closed Thanksgiving and Christmas.

Tuzigoot National Monument Perched atop a hill overlooking the Verde River, this small, stone-walled pueblo was built by the Sinagua people and was inhabited between 1125 and 1400. The Sinagua, whose name is Spanish for "without water," were traditionally dry-land farmers relying entirely on rainfall to water their crops. When the Hohokam, who had been living in the Verde Valley since A.D. 600, moved on to more fertile land around 1100, the Sinagua moved into this valley. Their buildings progressed from individual homes called pit houses to the type of communal pueblo seen here at Tuzigoot.

An interpretive trail leads through the Tuzigoot ruins, explaining different aspects of Sinaguan life, and inside the visitor center is a small museum displaying many of the artifacts unearthed here. Desert plants, many of which were used by the Sinagua, are identified along the trail.

Just outside Clarkdale off Ariz. 89A. ✆ **928/634-5564.** www.nps.gov/tuzi. Admission $5 adults ($8 with Montezuma Castle National Monument admission), free for children 15 and under. Memorial Day weekend to Labor Day weekend daily 8am–6pm; rest of year daily 8am–5pm. Closed Christmas.

Other Verde Valley Attractions & Activities

IN & AROUND CAMP VERDE

Out on the edge of town, you'll find Camp Verde's top attraction—**Cliff Castle Casino,** 555 Middle Verde Rd. (✆ **800/381-7568** or 928/567-7900; www.cliffcastlecasino.net), at exit 289 off I-17.

About halfway between Camp Verde and Cottonwood, you'll find **Alcantara Vineyards,** 3445 S. Grapevine Way, Verde Valley (✆ **888/569-0756** or 928/649-8463; www.alcantaravineyard.com), which, although away from the area's other wineries (which are in the community of Page Springs), is far and away the most beautiful winery in Arizona. The terraced vineyards overlook limestone cliffs and a bend of the Verde River. The wines, primarily big reds, can be quite good. The tasting room is open daily from 11am to 5pm, and there is an $10 per person tasting fee.

IN & AROUND COTTONWOOD & CLARKDALE

Cottonwood, 6 miles from Jerome, isn't nearly as atmospheric as the old copper-mining town up on the hill, but in the Old Town district, where one side of Main Street has an old-fashioned covered sidewalk, you'll find quite a few interesting shops, galleries, and cafes. As in Jerome, there are a couple of winery tasting rooms here where you sample local wines. At the **Pillsbury Wine Company,** 1012 N. Main St. (✆ **928/639-0646;** www.pillsburywine.com), you can choose from among more than a dozen wines. Wines here are produced by several area wineries, which makes this one of the best places in the region to get an idea of the breadth of wines being produced in Arizona. For $12 to $16, you can taste five wines (additional tastes are $2 each). The tasting room is open Monday through Thursday from 11am to 6pm, Friday and Saturday from 11am to 9pm, and Sunday from noon to 6pm. Across the street, you'll find **Arizona Stronghold Winery,** 1023 Main St. (✆ **928/639-2789;** www.azstronghold.com), a joint operation of Page Spring Cellars' Eric Glomski and Caduceus Cellars' Maynard Keenan. The tasting room is open Monday, Thursday, and Sunday from noon to 7pm, Tuesday and Wednesday from noon to 5pm, and Friday and Saturday from noon to 9pm. The tasting fee is $9.

If it's a hot day, you may want to head up to **Sycamore Creek** to cool off in one of the creek's swimming holes. It's only a ¼-mile hike to the first swimming hole, but there are more farther up the creek. To reach the trail head for this hike, follow signs to Tuzigoot National Monument, and after crossing the bridge over the Verde River, turn left onto Forest Road (F.R.) 131 (signed for the Sycamore Canyon Wilderness). The road quickly turns to gravel and then dirt and is very rough in places. Don't try driving this road without a high-clearance vehicle and preferably one with four-wheel-drive. The trail head is 11 miles up this road.

Alcantara Vineyards uses its own grapes to produce excellent wines.

Where to Eat

If you need some espresso to get you through the rest of the day, the best place in the area to get it is at **Crema Coffee & Creamery,** 917 N. Main St., Cottonwood (✆ **928/649-5785;** www.cremacoffeeandcreamery.com). Crema also sells sandwiches, soup, pastries, and gelato and is open Monday through Friday from 7am to 4pm and Saturday and Sunday from 8am to 4pm. If you're planning a picnic and need some artisan bread for your sandwiches, stop by the **Orion Bread Co.,** 1028 N. Main St. (✆ **928/649-1557;** www.orionbread.com). This bakery is open Monday and Tuesday from 9am to 5pm, Sunday and Wednesday through Friday from 7am to 5pm, and Saturday from 7am to 3pm.

Bing's Burger Station AMERICAN In what was once a gas station on the edge of old town Cottonwood, you can get some of the best burgers in the region. This burger joint, with its wall of license plates from around the country, is a throwback to the burger stands of the 1950s. The menu is short and simple and is on a pad of paper. Mark down what you want on your burger and what sides and drink you want, and hand it over to the waiter. Be sure to try one of the fountain sodas (peach, lime, root beer, and mulberry), that are made with syrups produced exclusively for Bing's.

794 N. Main St., Cottonwood. ✆ **928/649-1718.** www.bingsburgers.com. Reservations not accepted. Main courses $4–$6. DISC, MC, V. Tues–Sat 11am–7pm.

Blazin' M Ranch Wild West Adventure ☺ AMERICAN Located adjacent to Dead Horse Ranch State Park, the Blazin' M Ranch is classic Arizona-style family entertainment—barbecue and beans accompanied by cowboy music and comedy. Although this place is geared primarily toward the young 'uns, if you're young at heart, you might also enjoy the Blazin' M. However, it's definitely more fun if you bring the whole family. Highlights include a reproduction of a Yavapai Apache camp, a mining camp, mechanical horse roping, and a gallery of animated woodcarvings, which features humorous Western scenes.

1875 Maberry Ranch Rd. (off 10th St., signed for Dead Horse Ranch State Park), Cottonwood. ✆ **800/937-8643.** www.blazinm.com. Reservations recommended. Dinner $35 adults, $33 seniors, $25 children ages 3–12. AE, DISC, MC, V. Wed–Sat gates open at 4pm, dinner at 6:30pm, show at 7:30pm. Closed Thurs–Fri in Dec.

Old Town Café 🎁 LIGHT FARE Good pastries, salads, and sandwiches, such as a grilled panini of smoked turkey, spinach, tomatoes, and mozzarella, make Old Town my favorite lunch spot in the Verde Valley. It's a bright, cheery little cafe with a handful of tables.

1025-A N. Main St., Cottonwood. ✆ **928/634-5980.** www.oldtownroaster.com/cafe.html. Reservations not accepted. Salads and sandwiches $6–$9.50. AE, DISC, MC, V. Tues–Sat 8am–3pm.

SEDONA & OAK CREEK CANYON ★★★

66 miles NE of Prescott; 116 miles N of Phoenix; 106 miles S of the Grand Canyon

Nowhere in Arizona, or the entire country for that matter, will you find a town or city in a more beautiful setting. On the outskirts of Sedona, red-rock buttes, eroded canyon walls, and mesas rise into cerulean skies. Off in the distance, the Mogollon Rim looms, its forests of juniper and ponderosa pine dark against the

Sedona's red rocks create a unique landscape.

rocks. With a wide band of rosy sandstone predominating in this area, Sedona has come to be known as red-rock country, and each evening at sunset, the rocks put on an unforgettable light show that is reason enough for a visit.

All this may sound perfectly idyllic, but if you lower your eyes from the red rocks, you'll see the flip side of Sedona—a sprawl of housing developments, highways lined with unattractive strip malls, and bumper-to-bumper traffic. However, not even this can mar the beauty of the backdrop.

With national forest surrounding the city (and even fingers of forest extending into what would otherwise be the city limits), Sedona also has some of the best outdoor access of any city in the Southwest. All around town, alongside highways and down side streets in suburban neighborhoods, there are trail heads. Trek down any one of these trails, and you leave the city behind and enter the world of the red rocks. Just don't be surprised if you come around a bend in the trail and find yourself in the middle of a wedding ceremony or a group of 30 people doing tai chi.

Located at the mouth of Oak Creek Canyon, Sedona was first settled by pioneers in 1877 and was named for the first postmaster's wife. Word of Sedona's beauty (the town's not the wife's) did not begin to spread until Hollywood filmmakers began using the region's red rock as backdrop to their Western films. Next came artists, lured by the colorful landscapes and desert light (it was here that the Cowboy Artists of America organization was formed). Although still touted as an artists' community, Sedona's art scene these days is geared more toward tourists than toward collectors of fine art.

More recently, the spectacular views and mild climate were discovered by retirees. Until the crash of the real estate market, Sedona's hills were alive with the sound of construction as ostentatious retirement mansions and celebrity trophy homes sprouted from the dust like desert toads after an August rainstorm. Although the souring of the economy has slowed the building boom considerably, Sedona is still the sort of town that believes, if you come, they will build it.

Sedona is also a magnet for New Age believers, who come to experience unseen cosmic energy fields known as vortexes. The vortexes are such a powerful attraction that many New Age types have stayed in the area and have turned Sedona into a hotbed of alternative therapies. You can hardly throw a smudge stick around these parts without hitting a psychic (shouldn't they have seen it coming?). Mountain bikers have also discovered the red rock, and word has spread that the biking here is almost as good as up north in Moab, Utah.

The waters of Oak Creek were what first attracted settlers and Native peoples to this area, and today this stream still lures visitors to Sedona—especially in summer when the cool shade and even cooler creek waters are a glorious respite from the heat of the desert. Two of Arizona's finest swimming holes are located on Oak Creek only a few miles from Sedona, and one of these, Slide Rock, has been made into a state park.

With its knock-your-hiking-boots-off scenery, dozens of motels, hotels, and inns, and smattering of good restaurants, Sedona makes an excellent base for exploring central Arizona. Several ancient Indian ruins (including an impressive cliff dwelling), the "ghost town" of Jerome, and the scenic Verde Canyon Railroad are all within easy driving distance, and even the Grand Canyon is but a long day trip away.

Essentials

GETTING THERE Sedona is on Ariz. 179 at the mouth of Oak Creek Canyon. From Phoenix, take I-17 to Ariz. 179 N. From Flagstaff, head south on I-17 until you see the turnoff for Ariz. 89A and Sedona. Ariz. 89A also connects Sedona with Prescott.

Sedona Phoenix Shuttle (✆ **800/448-7988** in Arizona, or 928/282-2066; www.sedona-phoenix-shuttle.com) operates several trips daily between Phoenix's Sky Harbor Airport and Sedona. The fare is $50 one-way, $90 round-trip.

VISITOR INFORMATION The **Sedona Chamber of Commerce Visitor Center/Uptown Gateway Visitor Center,** 331 Forest Rd. (✆ **800/288-7336** or 928/282-7722; www.visitsedona.com), is at the corner of Ariz. 89A and Forest Road in uptown Sedona. The visitor center is open Monday through Saturday from 8:30am to 5pm, and Sunday and holidays from 9am to 3pm.

You can also get information, as well as a Red Rock Pass for parking at area trail heads, at the **Visitor Contact Center,** 8375 Ariz. 179, Village of Oak Creek (✆ **928/203-2900**), which is open daily from 8am to 5pm, or the **North Gateway Visitor Center,** Oak Creek Vista Overlook, Ariz. 89A (✆ **928/203-2900**), which is open March 1 through November 1, weather permitting, daily from 9am to 4:30pm, and sometimes on weekends in other months.

GETTING AROUND Whether traveling by car or on foot, you'll need to cultivate patience when trying to cross major roads in Sedona. Traffic here, especially on weekends, can be some of the worst in the state. Also be prepared for slow traffic on roads that have good views; drivers are often distracted by the red rocks. You may hear or see references to the **"Y,"** which refers to the intersection of Ariz. 179 and Ariz. 89A between the Tlaquepaque shopping plaza and uptown Sedona.

Rental cars are available through **Enterprise** (✆ **800/261-7331** or 928/282-2052). You can also rent a jeep from **Barlow Jeep Rentals,** 3009 W. Ariz. 89A (✆ **888/928-5337** or 928/282-8700; www.barlowjeeprentals.com), which charges $150 for 4 hours and $250 for 24 hours. Or you can get around Sedona on the **Sedona Roadrunner** (✆ **928/282-0938;** www.roadrunner.az.gov), a free shuttle bus that operates daily from 11am to 6pm with shuttles every 10 minutes between uptown, Tlaquepaque, and the Hillside Sedona shopping plaza.

SPECIAL EVENTS The **Sedona International Film Festival** (✆ **928/282-1177;** www.sedonafilmfestival.com), held between late February and early March, always books plenty of interesting films. In mid-December at the

Tlaquepaque shopping plaza, Sedona celebrates the **Festival of Lights** (✆ **928/282-4838;** www.tlaq.com) by lighting thousands of *luminarias* (paper bags partially filled with sand and containing a single candle). From mid-November to early January, more than a million lights illuminate Los Abrigados Resort (✆ **800/521-3131** or 928/282-1777; www.redrockfantasy.com) in a **Red-Rock Fantasy.**

Exploring Red-Rock Country

The Grand Canyon may be Arizona's biggest attraction, but there's actually far more to do in Sedona. If you aren't an active type, there's the obvious option of just sitting down and gazing in awe at the rugged cliffs, needle-like pinnacles, and isolated buttes that rise from the green forest floor at the mouth of Oak Creek Canyon. Want to see more but don't want to break a sweat? Head out into the red rocks on a jeep tour or soar over them in a biplane. Want to go *mano a mano* with

vortex POWER

For many years now, Sedona has been one of the world's centers for the New Age movement, and large numbers of people make the pilgrimage here to experience the "power vortexes" of the surrounding red-rock country. Around town you'll see bulletin boards and publications advertising such diverse services as past-life regressions, crystal healing, tarot readings, reiki, axiatonal therapy, electromagnetic field balancing, soul recovery, channeling, aromatherapy, myofascial release, and aura photos and videos.

According to believers, a vortex is a site where the earth's unseen lines of power intersect to form a particularly powerful energy field. Psychic Page Bryant determined through channeling that there were four vortexes around Sedona. Scientists may scoff, but Sedona's vortexes have become so well known that the visitor centers have several handouts to explain them and a map to guide you to them. (Many of the most spectacular geological features of the Sedona landscape also happen to be vortexes.)

The four main vortexes are Bell Rock, Cathedral Rock, Airport Mesa, and Boynton Canyon. **Bell Rock** and **Airport Mesa** are both said to contain masculine or electric energy that boosts emotional, spiritual, and physical energy. **Cathedral Rock** is said to contain feminine or magnetic energy, good for facilitating relaxation. The **Boynton Canyon** vortex is considered an electromagnetic energy site, which means it has a balance of both masculine and feminine energy.

If you're not familiar with vortexes and want to learn more about the ones in Sedona, consider a vortex tour. These are offered by several companies, including **Earth Wisdom Jeep Tours** (✆ **928/282-4714;** www.earthwisdomtours.com), **Spirit Steps** (✆ **866/508-0094** or 928/282-4562; www.spiritsteps.org), and **Sedona Vortex Tours** (✆ **800/943-3266** or 928/282-2733; www.sedonaretreats.com). All three offer tours that combine aspects of Native American and New Age beliefs. Tours last 2½ to 3 hours and cost around $68 to $114 per person.

You can also stock up on books, crystals, and other spiritual supplies at stores such as **Crystal Magic,** 2978 W. Ariz. 89A (✆ **928/282-1622**), or **Center for the New Age,** 341 Ariz. 179 (✆ **888/881-6651** or 928/282-2085; www.sedonanewagecenter.com).

Cliff dwellings in Boynton Canyon.

this wild landscape? Go for a hike, rent a mountain bike, or go horseback riding. (See "Organized Tours" and "Outdoor Pursuits," later in this section, for details.)

Although **Schnebly Hill Road,** which climbs into the red rocks east of Sedona, is a rough dirt road, it's a must for superb views. This road is best driven in a high-clearance vehicle. To reach this scenic road, head south out of Sedona on Ariz. 179, turn left after you cross the bridge over Oak Creek (at the Tlaquepaque shopping center), and head up the road, which starts out paved but soon turns to dirt. As this road climbs to the top of the Mogollon Rim, each switchback and cliff-edged curve yields a new and more astonishing view. At the top, the Schnebly Hill overlook offers a view that just begs to be savored over a long picnic. If you don't feel comfortable doing this drive in your own vehicle, you can book a jeep tour that heads up this way.

The Name Game

If you're having a hard time remembering which rock is which here in Sedona, you aren't alone. Cathedral Rock was originally named Courthouse Rock, but many years ago it was incorrectly marked on a map and the change stuck.

Just south of Sedona, on the east side of Ariz. 179, you'll see the aptly named **Bell Rock.** There's a parking area at the foot of this formation, and trails lead up to the top. Adjacent to Bell Rock is **Courthouse Butte,** and to the west stands **Cathedral Rock.** From the Chapel of the Holy Cross (see "Attractions & Activities Around Town," below) on Chapel Road, you can see **Eagle Head Rock** (from the front door of the chapel, look three-quarters of the way up the mountain to see the eagle's head), the **Twin Nuns** (two pinnacles standing side by side), and **Mother and Child Rock** (to the left of the Twin Nuns).

If you head west out of Sedona on Ariz. 89A and turn left onto Airport Road, you'll drive up onto **Airport Mesa,** which commands an unobstructed panorama of Sedona and the red rocks. About halfway up the mesa is a small parking area from which easy trails radiate, and at the top of the mesa is a huge parking area and viewpoint park that attracts large crowds of sunset gazers. The views from here are among the best in the region.

Boynton Canyon, located 8 miles west of the "Y," is a narrow red-rock box canyon and is one of the most beautiful spots in the Sedona area. This canyon is also the site of the deluxe Enchantment Resort, but hundreds of years before there were luxury suites here, there were Sinagua cliff dwellings. Several of these cliff dwellings can still be spotted high on the canyon walls. **Boynton Canyon Trail** leads 3 miles up into this canyon from a trail head parking area just outside the gates of Enchantment. To get to the trail head, drive west out of Sedona on Ariz. 89A, turn right on Dry Creek Road, take a left at the first T intersection, and a right at the second T.

On the way to Boynton Canyon, look north from Ariz. 89A, and you'll see **Coffee Pot Rock,** also known as Rooster Rock, rising 1,800 feet above Sedona. Three pinnacles, known as the **Three Golden Chiefs** by the Yavapai tribe, stand beside Coffee Pot Rock. As you drive up Dry Creek Road, on your right you'll see **Capitol Butte,** which resembles the U.S. Capitol.

To the west of Boynton Canyon, you can visit the well-preserved Sinagua cliff dwellings at **Palatki Heritage Site** (✆ **928/282-3854;** www.redrockcountry.org). These small ruins, tucked under the red cliffs, are the best place in the area to get a feel for the ancient Native American cultures that once lived in this region. Among the ruins, you'll see numerous pictographs (paintings) created by the past residents of Palatki. Before heading out to these ruins, be sure you make a reservation by calling the number above. To reach the ruins, follow the directions to Boynton Canyon, but instead of turning right at the second T intersection, turn left onto Boynton Pass Road (F.R. 152C), which is one of the most scenic roads in the area. This road is paved for the first couple of miles but then becomes a sometimes rough dirt road. Follow this road to another T intersection and go right onto F.R. 525, then veer right onto F.R. 795, which dead-ends at the ruins. You can also get here by driving west from Sedona on Ariz. 89A to F.R. 525, a gravel road leading north to F.R. 795. To visit Palatki, you'll need a Red Rock Pass (see "The High Cost of Red-Rock Views," below); the ruins are usually open daily from 9:30am to 3pm and reservations are recommended due to limited parking spaces. The dirt roads around here become impassable to regular cars when they're wet, so don't try coming out here if the roads are at all muddy.

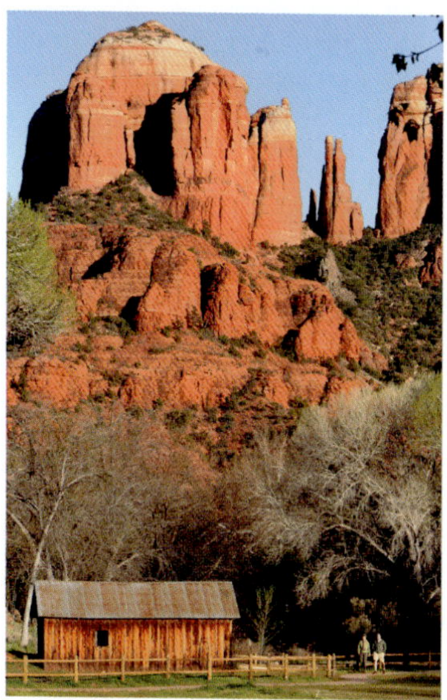

Crescent Moon Picnic Area.

South of Ariz. 89A and a bit west of the turnoff for Boynton Canyon is Upper Red Rock Loop Road, which leads to **Crescent Moon Picnic Area ★★**, a national forest recreation area that has become a must-see for visitors to Sedona. Its popularity stems from a beautiful photograph of Oak Creek with **Cathedral Rock** in the background—an image that has been reproduced countless times in Sedona promotional literature and on postcards. Hiking trails lead up to Cathedral Rock. Admission is $9 per vehicle. For more information, contact the Coconino National Forest's **Red Rock District,** 8375 Ariz. 179, Village of Oak Creek (✆ **928/203-2900;** www.fs.fed.us/r3/coconino).

If you continue on Red Rock Loop Road, you will come to **Red Rock State Park,** 4050 Red Rock

Loop Rd. (✆ **928/282-6907;** www.azstateparks.com), which flanks Oak Creek. The views here take in many of the rocks listed above, and you have the bonus of being right on the creek (though swimming and wading are prohibited). Park admission is $10 per car. The park offers lots of guided walks and interpretive programs.

South of Sedona, near the junction of I-17 and Ariz. 179, you can visit one of the premier petroglyph sites in Arizona. The rock art at the **V Bar V Heritage Site** (✆ **928/282-3854;** www.redrockcountry.org) covers a small cliff face and includes images of herons and turtles. To get here, take the dirt road that leads east for 2⅔ miles from the junction of I-17 and Ariz. 179 to the Beaver Creek Campground. The entrance to the petroglyph site is just past the campground. From the parking area, it's about a half-mile walk to the petroglyphs, which are open Friday through Monday from 9:30am to 3pm. To visit this site, you'll need a Red Rock Pass or another valid pass.

Oak Creek Canyon

The **Mogollon Rim** (pronounced *Mug*-ee-un by the locals) is a 2,000-foot escarpment cutting diagonally across central Arizona and on into New Mexico. At the top of the Mogollon Rim are the ponderosa pine forests of the high mountains, while at the bottom the lowland deserts begin. Of the many canyons cutting down from the rim, Oak Creek Canyon is the most beautiful (and one of the few that has a paved road down through it). Ariz. 89A runs through the canyon from just outside Flagstaff to Sedona, winding its way down from the rim and paralleling Oak Creek. Along the way are overlooks, parks, picnic areas, campgrounds, and a variety of lodges and inns.

Approaching Oak Creek Canyon from the north, your first stop after traveling south from Flagstaff will be the **Oak Creek Canyon Vista,** which provides a view far down the valley to Sedona and beyond. The overlook is at the edge of the Mogollon Rim, and the road suddenly drops in tight switchbacks just south of here. You may notice that one rim of the canyon is lower than the other. This is because Oak Creek Canyon is on a geologic fault line; one side of the canyon is moving in a different direction from the other.

Although the top of the Mogollon Rim is a ponderosa pine forest and the bottom a desert, Oak Creek Canyon supports a forest of sycamores and other

Swimmers cool off at Slide Rock State Park.

Chapel of the Holy Cross.

THE high cost OF RED-ROCK VIEWS

A quick perusal of any Sedona real-estate magazine will convince you that property values around these parts are as high as the Mogollon Rim. However, red-rock real estate is also expensive for those who want only a glimpse of the rocks. With the land around Sedona split up into several types of National Forest Service day-use sites, state parks, and national monuments, visitors find themselves pulling out their wallets just about every time they turn around to look at another rock. Here's the lowdown on what it's going to cost you to do the red rocks right.

A **Red Rock Pass** will allow you to visit Palatki Ruins and the V Bar V petroglyph site and park at any national forest trail head parking areas. The cost is $5 for a 1-day pass, $15 for a 7-day pass, and $20 for a 12-month pass (this annual pass is not a good value, and I don't recommend it). Passes are good for everyone in your vehicle. However, be aware that these passes are not valid at Grasshopper Point (a swimming hole), Call of the Canyon (the West Fork Oak Creek trail head), or Crescent Moon (Sedona's top photo-op site), all of which charge $8 to $9 admission per vehicle.

Two state parks are in the area—Slide Rock ($10–$20 per car) and Red Rock ($10 per car). Admission to the Montezuma Castle or Tuzigoot national monuments will cost you $5 per adult or $8 if you buy a combination pass that lets you visit both national monuments.

If two or more of you are traveling together and you plan on visiting the Grand Canyon and three or four other national parks or monuments, you might want to consider getting an **America the Beautiful Pass** ($80). This pass is good for a year and will get you into any national park or national monument in the country. If you're 62 or older, definitely get an **America the Beautiful Senior Pass** ($10), which is good for the rest of your life. Persons with disabilities can get a free lifetime **America the Beautiful Access Pass.** Any of these three passes can be used in lieu of a Red Rock Pass.

For more information on the Red Rock passes, visit www.redrockcountry.org.

deciduous trees. There is no better time to drive scenic Ariz. 89A than between late September and mid-October, when the canyon is ablaze with red and yellow leaves.

In the desert, swimming holes are powerful magnets during the hot summer months, and consequently, **Slide Rock State Park,** 6871 N. Ariz. 89A (© **928/282-3034;** www.azstateparks.com), 7 miles north of Sedona on the site of an old homestead, is the most popular spot in Oak Creek Canyon during the summer. What pulls in the crowds of families and teenagers is the park's natural water slide and great little swimming hole. On hot days, the park is jammed with people splashing in the water and sliding over the algae-covered sandstone bottom of Oak Creek. Open daily, year-round; admission is $10 per vehicle ($20 during the summer). There's another popular swimming area at **Grasshopper Point,** several miles closer to Sedona. Admission is $8 per vehicle.

Within Oak Creek Canyon, several hikes of different lengths are possible. By far the most spectacular and popular is the 6-mile round-trip up the **West Fork of Oak Creek ★**. This is a classic canyon-country hike with steep canyon walls rising from the creek. At some points, the canyon is no more than 20 feet wide, with walls rising up more than 200 feet. You can also extend the hike many more miles up the canyon for an overnight backpacking trip. The trail head for the West

Fork of Oak Creek hike is 9½ miles up Oak Creek Canyon from Sedona at the Call of the Canyon Recreation Area, which charges a $9 day-use fee per vehicle.

Stop by the Sedona Chamber of Commerce Visitor Center for a free map of area hikes. The **Coconino National Forest's Red Rock District,** 8375 Ariz. 179 (✆ **928/203-2900;** www.redrockcountry.org), just south of the Village of Oak Creek, is an even better source of hiking information. It's open daily from 8am to 5pm.

If you get thirsty while driving through the canyon, hold out for **Garlands Indian Gardens Market,** 3951 N. Ariz. 89A (✆ **928/282-7702**), about 4 miles north of Sedona. Here, in the fall, you can usually buy delicious organic apple juice made from apples grown in the canyon. For one last view down the canyon, stop at **Midgely Bridge** (watch for the parked cars and small parking area at the north end of the bridge).

Attractions & Activities Around Town

Sedona's most notable architectural landmark is the **Chapel of the Holy Cross ★**, 780 Chapel Rd. (✆ **928/282-4069;** www.chapeloftheholycross.com), a small church built right into the red rock on the south side of town. If you're driving up from Phoenix, you can't miss it—the chapel sits high above the road just off Ariz. 179. With its contemporary styling, it is one of the most architecturally important modern churches in the country. Marguerite Brunswig Staude, a devout Catholic painter, sculptor, and designer, had the inspiration for the chapel in 1932, but it wasn't until 1957 that her dream was finally realized. The chapel's design is dominated by a simple cross forming the wall that faces the street. The cross and the starkly beautiful chapel seem to grow directly from the rock, allowing the natural beauty of the red rock to speak for itself. It's open Monday through Saturday from 9am to 5pm and Sunday from 10am to 5pm; admission is free.

The **Sedona Arts Center,** 15 Art Barn Rd. (✆ **888/954-4442** or 928/282-3809; www.sedonaartscenter.com), near the north end of uptown Sedona on Ariz. 89A, has a gallery that specializes in works by local and regional artists.

To learn a bit about the local history, stop by the **Sedona Heritage Museum,** 735 Jordan Rd. (✆ **928/282-7038;** www.sedonamuseum.org), in Jordan Historical Park. The museum, which is housed in a historic home, is furnished with antiques and contains exhibits on the many movies that have been filmed in the area. The farm was once an apple orchard, and there's still apple-processing equipment in the barn. Hours are daily from 11am to 3pm; admission is $3.

Sunset at the Amitabha Stupa

There's just something about Sedona that brings out people's spirituality, and one of the latest spiritual attractions to find a home among the red rocks is the **Amitabha Stupa Park** (✆ **928/282-5195;** www.stupas.org), a Tibetan Buddhist shrine erected in a residential neighborhood in west Sedona. The 36-foot-tall stupa is up a short path that winds through juniper trees festooned with prayer flags. The stupa is often visited by devout Buddhists, who leave offerings at the base of the stupa, but the public is welcome anytime from dawn to dusk. To find the stupa, drive north from Ariz. 89A on Andante Drive and turn left on Pueblo Drive. Park outside the gate on the right.

While Sedona isn't yet a resort spa destination on par with Phoenix or Tucson, it does have an ever-growing number of spas that can add just the right bit of pampering to your vacation. **Therapy on the Rocks,** 676 N. Ariz. 89A (✆ **928/282-3002;** www.myofascialrelease.com), with its creekside setting, is a longtime local favorite that offers massage, myofascial release, and great views of the red rocks. A half-day of therapy here will run you $350. For personal attention, try the little **Red Rock Healing Arts Center,** Creekside Plaza, 251 Ariz. 179 (✆ **888/316-9033;** www.redrockhealing.com), which is just up the hill from the Tlaquepaque shopping plaza and offers a variety of massages, wraps, scrubs, and facials. A 60-minute massage or other body treatment is only $80 to $90. In west Sedona, try **Sedona's New Day Spa,** 1449 W. Ariz. 89A (✆ **928/282-7502;** www.sedonanewdayspa.com), a beautiful day spa with a resortlike feeling. A 1-hour treatment will run you between $105 and $155. In the Village of Oak Creek, there's the **Hilton Sedona Spa,** at the Hilton Sedona Resort & Spa, 90 Ridge Trail Dr. (✆ **928/284-6900;** www.hiltonsedonaspa.com), offering a variety of treatments. There are also exercise and yoga classes, a pool, and tennis courts. Most 50-minute treatments cost $125.

It may be a bit premature to start calling Sedona the next Napa Valley, but there are a few wineries in the area. Three of them, located in the community of Page Springs about 20 minutes west of Sedona, are open to the public for tastings. To reach these wineries, drive west from Sedona on Ariz. 89A, and turn south on Page Springs Road. You'll first come to **Javelina Leap Vineyard & Winery,** 1565 N. Page Springs Rd. (✆ **928/649-2681;** www.javelinaleapwinery.com), where winemaker and owner Rod Snapp focuses on premium red wines. The winery produces wines made from both estate-grown grapes and grapes from other Arizona vineyards. The tasting room is open daily from 11am to 5pm. The tasting fee is $8. Right next door is **Oak Creek Vineyards and Winery,** 1555 N. Page Springs Rd. (✆ **928/649-0290;** www.oakcreekvineyards.net), which is across the street from the Page Springs Fish Hatchery. The tasting room here is open daily from 10am to 6pm, and the tasting fee is $5. **Page Springs Cellars,** 1500 N. Page Springs Rd. (✆ **928/639-3004;** www.pagespringscellars.com), is the most impressive and reliable of the three wineries. Rhone varietals are the specialty of Page Springs winemaker/owner Eric Glomski, who is one of the state's top winemakers. The tasting room is open Sunday through Thursday from 11am to 6pm and Friday and Saturday from 11am to 9pm. There is a $10 tasting fee.

If you'd prefer to do your wine tasting with a guide, contact **Sedona Wine Country Tours** (✆ **928/554-4072;** www.sedonawinecountrytours.com), which offers a variety of tours in the area and charges $98 to $150 per person.

Organized Tours

For an overview of Sedona, take a tour on the **Sedona Trolley,** 276 N. Ariz. 89A (✆ **928/282-4211;** www.sedonatrolley.com), which leaves several times daily on two separate tours. One tour visits the Tlaquepaque shopping plaza, the Chapel of the Holy Cross, and several art galleries, while the other goes out through west Sedona to Boynton Canyon and Enchantment Resort. Tours are $12 for adults ($22 for both tours) and $6 for children 12 and under ($11 for both tours).

The red-rock country surrounding Sedona is the city's greatest natural attraction, and there's no better way to explore it than by four-wheel-drive vehicle. Although you may end up feeling like every other tourist in town, you quite simply should not leave Sedona without going on a jeep tour. These tours will get you out onto rugged roads and 4×4 trails with spectacular views. The unchallenged leader in Sedona jeep tours is **Pink Jeep Tours,** 204 N. Ariz. 89A (✆ **800/873-3662** or 928/282-5000; www.pinkjeep.com), which has been heading deep into the Coconino National Forest since 1958. It offers tours ranging in length from 1½ to 11 hours; however, the 2-hour Broken Arrow tour ($75 adults, $56 children 12 and under) is the most adventurous and is the tour I recommend. Pink Jeep Tours also offers tours to Grand Canyon National Park.

If a jeep just isn't manly enough for you, how about a Hummer? Better yet, how about a Hummer that runs on enviro-friendly bio-diesel (have your quiche and eat it, too)? **Sedona Offroad Adventures,** 273 N. Ariz. 89A, Ste. C (✆ **928/282-6656;** www.sedonaoffroadadventures.com), will take you out in the red rocks in the ultimate off-road vehicle. One-hour tours run $39 to $49 ($29–$39 for children), and while there are 1½- and 2-hour tours, the 2½-hour Jeep Eater Tour for $94 ($74 for children) is the most fun.

How about a chance to play cowboy? **A Day in the West,** 252 N. Ariz. 89A (✆ **800/973-3662** or 928/282-4320; www.adayinthewest.com), has its own private ranch for some of its jeep tours and horseback rides. There are cowboy cookouts, too. Prices range from $45 to $169.

If you'd like to have a very knowledgeable local tour guide show you around places you're interested in seeing at your own pace, I recommend getting in touch with Steven "Benny" Benedict at **Earth Tours** (✆ **928/203-9132;** www.earthtours.com). Benny likes to take clients to spots that even many locals don't know about. Half-day excursions run $150 per person, and full-day outings are $295 per person. These tours have a three-person minimum.

Just because it's too dark to see the red rocks doesn't mean there's nothing to see and do in Sedona at night. How about a tour of the heavens? **Evening Sky Tours** (✆ **928/203-0006;** www.eveningskytours.com) takes advantage of the dark night skies over Sedona to lead people on astronomy tours of the stars and planets. Tours cost $60 for adults and $20 for children.

As spectacular as Sedona is from the ground, it is even more so from the air. **Red Rock Helicopter Tours** offers short flights to different parts of this colorful region. A 15-minute tour costs $70 per person. This same company also operates **Sky Safari Air Tours,** which does a variety of flights in small planes. A 20-minute air tour will run you $69 per person (two-person minimum), while a 45-minute tour will cost $109 per person (two-person minimum). Flights as far afield as the Grand Canyon and Canyon de Chelly can also be arranged. However, my favorite Sedona air tours are those offered by the affiliated **Red Rock Biplane Tours,** which operates modern Waco open-cockpit biplanes. With the wind in your hair, you'll feel as though you've entered the world of Snoopy and the Red Baron. Tours lasting 20 to 60 minutes are offered; a 20-minute tour costs $119 per person with a two-person minimum. All three of these companies can be reached at **Sedona Air Tours** (✆ **888/866-7433** or 928/204-5939; www.sedonaairtours.com).

If something a bit slower is more your speed, how about drifting over the sculpted red buttes of Sedona in a hot-air balloon? **Northern Light Balloon Expeditions** (✆ **800/230-6222** or 928/282-2274; www.northernlightballoon.com) charges $195 per person. **Red Rock Balloon Adventures** (✆ **800/258-3754;** www.redrockballoons.com) also charges $195 per person, while the affiliated **Sky High Balloon Adventures** (✆ **800/551-7597;** www.skyhighballoons.com), which floats over the Verde Valley, charges $180 per person.

Outdoor Pursuits

Hiking is the most popular outdoor activity in the Sedona area, with dozens of trails leading off into the red rocks. The only problem is that nearly everyone who comes to Sedona wants to go hiking, so finding a little solitude along the trail can be difficult. Not surprisingly, the most convenient trail heads also have the most crowded trails. If you want to ditch the crowds, pick a trail head that is *not* on Ariz. 179 or Ariz. 89A. That means that if you stop at any of the trail heads in Oak Creek Canyon or between the Village of Oak Creek and Sedona, you'll likely encounter lots of other people along the trail. You'll enjoy your Sedona hikes more if you start from a trail that begins down a side road. Among my personal favorites are the trails that originate at the end of Jordan Road in uptown Sedona; the Cathedral Rock Trail, which starts in a housing development between Sedona and the Village of Oak Creek; and the trails off Boynton Pass Road. ***Note:*** Don't forget to get your Red Rock Pass before heading out for a hike. See the box, "The High Cost of Red-Rock Views" on p. 233 for details on how to obtain your pass.

This said, the most convenient place to get some red dust on your boots is along the **Bell Rock Pathway ★**, which begins alongside Ariz. 179 just north of the Village of Oak Creek. This trail winds around the base of Bell Rock and accesses many other trails that lead up onto the sloping sides of Bell Rock. Although this is one of the most popular hiking trails in the area and is always crowded, it is the single best introduction to hiking in Sedona's beautiful red-rock country. It's about 4 miles to go all the way around Bell Rock and the adjacent Courthouse Butte.

You'll see fewer tourists if you head to the .75-mile **Cathedral Rock Trail,** which is also located between the Village of Oak Creek and uptown Sedona. The trail follows cairns (piles of rocks) up the slickrock slopes on the north side of Cathedral Rock. To reach this trail, turn off Ariz. 179 at the sign for the Back o' Beyond housing development and watch for the trail head at the end of the paved road. Be aware, however, that calling this route a trail is being very generous. In places it is almost a hand-over-hand crawl across the rocks. However, even if you stop when the going gets steep, you'll get great views. For convenience and solitude, you can't beat the **Mystic Trail,** which begins at an unmarked roadside pull-off on Chapel Road halfway between Ariz. 179 and the Chapel of the Holy Cross. This is an easy out-and-back trail that runs between a couple of housing developments, but once you're on the trail, you'll feel all alone.

Hikers take a break on the red rocks outside of Sedona.

Among the most popular trails in the Sedona area are those that lead into **Boynton Canyon** (site of Enchantment Resort). Here you'll glimpse ancient Native American ruins built into the red-rock cliffs. Although the scenery is indeed stupendous, the great numbers of other hikers on the trail detract considerably from the experience, and the parking lot usually fills up early in the day. The 1.5-mile **Vultee Arch Trail,** which leads to an impressive sandstone arch, is another great hike. The turnoff for this hike's trail head is 2 miles up Dry Creek Road and then another 3½ miles on a very rough dirt road. The **Devil's Bridge Trail,** which starts on the same dirt road, is a little easier to get to and leads to the largest natural sandstone arch in the area. This one is a 1.8-mile round-trip hike.

For the hands-down best views in Sedona, hike all or part of the **Airport Mesa Trail,** a 3.5-mile loop that circles Airport Mesa. With virtually no elevation gain, this is an easy hike. You'll find the trail head about halfway to the top of Airport Mesa on Airport Road. Try this one as early in the day as possible; by midday, the parking lot is usually full and it stays that way right through sunset.

For more information on hiking in Oak Creek Canyon (site of the famous West Fork Oak Creek Trail), see "Oak Creek Canyon," earlier in this section. For more information on all these hikes, contact the **Coconino National Forest's Red Rock District,** 8375 Ariz. 179, Village of Oak Creek (✆ **928/203-2900;** www.fs.fed.us/r3/coconino).

Sedona is rapidly becoming one of the Southwest's meccas for mountain biking. The red rock here is every bit as challenging and scenic as the famed slickrock country of Moab, Utah, and much less crowded. Using Sedona as a base, mountain bikers can ride year-round by heading up to Flagstaff in the heat of summer. One of my favorite rides is around the base of Bell Rock. Starting at the trail head parking area just north of the Village of Oak Creek, you'll find not only the easy Bell Rock Path, but also numerous more-challenging trails.

Another great ride starts above uptown Sedona, where you can take the Jim Thompson Trail to Midgely Bridge or the network of trails that head toward Soldier Pass. The riding here is only moderately difficult and the views are superb. To reach these trails, take Jordan Road to a left onto Park Ridge Road, and follow this road to where it ends at a trail head parking area. You can rent bikes from **Mountain Bike Heaven,** 1695 W. Ariz. 89A (✆ **928/282-1312;** www.mountainbikeheaven.com). Bikes rent for $45 to $65 per day. **Sedona Bike & Bean,** 6020 Ariz. 179, Village of Oak Creek (✆ **928/284-0210;** www.bike-bean.com), across the street from the popular Bell Rock Pathway and its adjacent mountain-bike trails, also rents bikes (and serves coffee). Bikes go for $40 to $55 for a full day. Any of these stores can sell you a good local trail map or Cosmic Ray's *Fat Tire Tales and Trails* guidebook to the best rides in Arizona. If you'd prefer to have a guide take you out on a road-bike tour, contact **Road Bike Sedona,** 6101 Ariz. 179 (✆ **928/202-1194;** www.sedonamtbadventures.com).

If you'd rather saddle up a palomino than pedal a bicycle, you can book a horseback ride through **A Day in the West,** 252 N. Ariz. 89A (✆ **800/973-3662** or 928/282-4320; www.adayinthewest.com), which charges $79 for a 1½-hour ride along the Verde River.

Surprisingly, Sedona has not yet been ringed with golf courses. However, what few courses there are offer superb views to distract you from your game. The **Oakcreek Country Club,** 690 Bell Rock Blvd. (✆ **888/284-1660** or 928/284-1660; www.oakcreekcountryclub.com), south of town off Ariz. 179, has stunning views from the course. Greens fee is $99 ($79 after 1pm). The **Sedona Golf Resort ★★**, 35 Ridge Trail Dr. (✆ **877/733-6630;** www.sedonagolfresort.com), south of town on Ariz. 179, offers equally breathtaking views of the red rocks. Greens fee is $95 ($70 after 1pm).

Shopping

Ever since the Cowboy Artists of America organization was founded in Sedona back in 1965 (at what is now the Cowboy Club restaurant), this town has had a reputation as an artists' community. Today, with dozens of galleries around town, it's obvious that art is one of the driving forces behind the local economy. Most of Sedona's galleries specialize in traditional Western, contemporary Southwestern, and Native American art, and in some galleries, you'll see works by members of the Cowboy Artists of America. You'll find the greatest concentration of galleries and shops in the uptown area of Sedona (along Ariz. 89A just north of the "Y") and at Tlaquepaque.

With more than 40 stores and restaurants, **Tlaquepaque Arts & Crafts Village,** 336 Ariz. 179 (✆ **928/282-4838;** www.tlaq.com), at the bridge over Oak Creek on the south side of Sedona, is designed to resemble a Mexican village. (It was named after a famous arts-and-crafts neighborhood in the suburbs of Guadalajara.) The maze of narrow alleys and courtyards, with its fountains, chapel, and bell tower, is worth a visit even if you aren't in a buying mood. Most of the shops here sell high-end art, jewelry, women's fashions, and unique gifts. I wish all shopping centers were such fascinating places.

Unfortunately, many of Sedona's shops now specialize in cheap Southwestern gifts that have little to do with art, and weeding through the tackiness to find the real galleries can be difficult. One place to start is at **Hozho,** which is right on Ariz. 179 just before you cross the Oak Creek bridge in Sedona and has a couple of Sedona's better galleries.

Clear Creek Trading If you're in the market for a bear-skin rug, a cow skull, or some buffalo horns, then do not miss this shop in an old house at the north end of the uptown shopping district. This shop has rooms full of oddities as well as rooms full of kitschy tourist souvenirs. 435 N. Ariz. 89A ✆ **928/204-5805.** www.clearcreektrading.com.

Cowboy Corral If you want to dress like Wyatt Earp or Annie Oakley, this shop can outfit you. Definitely not your standard urban cowboy shop, Cowboy Corral goes for the vintage look. 219 N. Ariz. 89A. ✆ **800/457-2279** or 928/282-2040. www.cowboycorral.com.

El Prado Located in the Hillside Sedona shopping center, this gallery features the unusual stone furniture of artist R. C. Albin and the fascinating copper wind sculptures of Lyman Whittaker. These aren't the sorts of things you can pack in your suitcase for the flight home, but if you've got a new retirement home here in Arizona, these pieces sure would look good in the garden. At Hillside Sedona, 671 Ariz. 179. ✆ **928/282-7390.** www.elpradogalleries.com.

Exposures International Gallery If you've got a big house and need some big art, this is the place to shop for it. Exposures is the largest gallery in the state and usually has lots of monument-size sculptures out front. My favorite artist here is Texas sculptor Bill Worrell. 561 Ariz. 179. ✆ **877/269-0129** or 928/282-1125. www.exposuresfineart.com.

Garland's Indian Jewelry ★★★ A great location in the shade of scenic Oak Creek Canyon and a phenomenal collection of concho belts, squash-blossom necklaces, and bracelets make this the best place in Arizona to shop for Indian jewelry. There are also lots of kachinas for sale. At Indian Gardens, 3953 N. Ariz. 89A (4 miles north of Sedona). ✆ **928/282-6632.** www.garlandsjewelry.com.

Tlaquepaque is modeled after a Mexican village.

Garland's Navajo Rugs ★★★ Garland's isn't just the premier Navajo rug shop in Sedona; it has one of the largest selections of contemporary and antique Navajo rugs in the country. It also carries Native American baskets and pottery, Hopi kachina dolls, and Navajo sand paintings. 411 Ariz. 179. ✆ **928/282-4070.** www.garlandsrugs.com.

Geoffrey Roth Ltd. If you're in the market for some unique jewelry or a gorgeous handmade wristwatch, check out this shop in the Tlaquepaque shopping center. At Tlaquepaque, 336 Ariz. 179, Ste. A102. ✆ **800/447-7684** or 928/282-7756. www.geoffreyrothltd.com.

George Kelly Fine Jewelers This is another great place to shop for beautiful jewelry. The designs are highly creative and incorporate a wide range of stones, even the occasional meteorite. At Hyatt Shops at Piñon Pointe, 101 N. Ariz. 89A., Suite 23. ✆ **928/282-8884.**

Gifted Hands Gallery Although primarily a gallery of fine crafts, it is worth stopping by this gallery to see the playful tabletop bronzes of Deanne McKeown, one of this gallery's original owners. Also be sure to check out Deanne's husband Byron's unusual canes and her daughter Lesley's distinctive jewelry. Mesquite-wood cutting boards, baskets, and ceramics round out the offerings here. At Tlaquepaque, 336 Ariz. 179, Ste. A117. ✆ **928/282-4822.** www.giftedhandssedona.com.

The Hike House If you've come to Sedona for the great hiking in the area, be sure to stop by the Hike House. This shop across Oak Creek from the Tlaquepaque shopping center not only sells hiking gear and clothes, but also has a cafe. An interactive computer trail finder can help you plan your day's hike. 431 Ariz. 179. ✆ **928/282-5820.** www.thehikehouse.com.

Hillside Sedona This shopping center just south of Tlaquepaque is dedicated to art galleries and upscale retail shops, and also has a couple of good restaurants. The hillside location means there are some good views to be had while you shop. 671 Ariz. 179. ✆ **928/282-4500.** www.hillsidesedona.net.

Hoel's Indian Shop ★★ Located 10 miles north of Sedona in a private residence in Oak Creek Canyon, this Native American arts-and-crafts gallery is one of the finest in the region and sells pieces of the highest quality. It's a good idea to call before coming out to make sure the store will be open. 9589 N. Ariz. 89A. ✆ **928/282-3925.** www.hoelsindianshop.com.

Hummingbird House ★ Looking for an unusual gift to take home to someone? Tired of the crowds of tourists at Tlaquepaque and in uptown? Check out this hidden gift shop in an attractively restored historic general store set behind a picket fence. You'll find the shop on a back street behind the Burger King that's at the junction of Ariz. 89A and Ariz. 179. 100 Brewer Rd. ✆ **928/282-0705.**

Isadora Handweaving Gallery ★★ This tiny shop in the Tlaquepaque shopping plaza has been around for more than 20 years and is one of the top fiber-arts galleries in the country. Gorgeous handmade women's fashions fill the racks, and there are also plenty of beautiful accessories to go with the handwoven silk jackets, felted scarves, and colorful shawls. At Tlaquepaque, 336 Ariz. 179, Ste. A120. ✆ **928/282-6232.** www.isadoragallery.com.

Lanning Gallery In business for more than 20 years, this gallery in the Hozho Center across Oak Creek from Tlaquepaque carries both classic and contemporary art, with an emphasis on colorful two-dimensional works. At Hozho Center, 431 Ariz. 179. ✆ **928/282-6865.** www.lanninggallery.com.

Sedona Arts Center Members Gallery Located at the north end of uptown Sedona, this shop is the best place in town to see the work of area artists—everything from jewelry and fiber arts to photography and ceramics. Because it's a nonprofit shop, you won't pay any tax here. 15 Art Barn Rd. ✆ **928/282-3865.** www.sedonaartscenter.com.

Son Silver West/Robson Design For those who love everything Southwestern, this shop is a treasure-trove of all kinds of interesting stuff, including Native American and Hispanic art and crafts, antique *santo* (saint) carvings, antique rifles, imported pots, dried-chili *ristras* (garlands), and garden art. 1476 Ariz. 179 (on the south side of town). ✆ **928/282-3580.** www.sonsilverwest.com.

Victorian Cowgirl ★★ This is not your usual urban cowgirl attire. No, this is the sort of place you shop when you need an $800 Victorian lace-and-velvet dress for an upcoming soiree. Shop owner Candace Walters has designed dresses for Crystal Gayle, Diana Ross, Morgan Fairchild, and Jaclyn Smith, among others. Oh, and there are less expensive outfits as well. 181 Ariz. 179. ✆ **877/232-3455** or 928/282-0778. www.victoriancowgirl.com.

Where to Stay

Sedona is one of the most popular destinations in the Southwest, with dozens of hotels and motels around town. However, accommodations here tend to be overpriced for what you get. (Blame it on the incomparable views.) My advice is to save money elsewhere on your trip and make Sedona the place where you splurge on a room with a view.

SEDONA & OAK CREEK CANYON

Very Expensive

Enchantment Resort ★★★ ☺ Located at the mouth of Boynton Canyon, this resort more than lives up to its name. The setting is breathtaking, and the pueblo-style architecture blends in with the landscape. The individual casitas can be booked as two-bedroom suites, one-bedroom suites, or single rooms, but it's worth reserving a suite just so you can enjoy the casita living rooms, which feature high-beamed ceilings and beehive fireplaces. All the rooms, however, have patios with dramatic views. Both the Yavapai Restaurant (p. 250) and a less formal bar and grill offer tables outdoors; lunch on the terrace should not be missed. Guests have access to the facilities at Mii amo spa (see separate review, below). With its great setting amid the red rocks, suites, croquet court, swimming pool, and children's programs, Enchantment is a great choice for families. 525 Boynton Canyon Rd., Sedona, AZ 86336. www.enchantmentresort.com. ✆ **800/826-4180** or 928/282-2900. Fax 928/282-9249. 218 units. $350–$450 double; $450–$550 junior suite; $750–$950 1-bedroom suite; $1,125–$1,425 2-bedroom suite. Rates do not include $22 resort fee. Children 12 and under stay free in parent's room. AE, DC, DISC, MC, V. **Amenities:** 3 restaurants, including Yavapai Restaurant (review, p. 250); 2 lounges; babysitting; bikes; children's programs; concierge; executive-level rooms; putting green and 6-hole par-3 golf course; health club; 6 Jacuzzis; 7 pools; room service; full-service spa; 7 tennis courts. *In room:* A/C, TV/VCR/DVD, CD player, fridge (in some), hair dryer, Internet (included in resort fee), kitchen (in some), minibar.

L'Auberge de Sedona ★ Set on the banks of Oak Creek and shaded by towering sycamore trees, this luxurious boutique resort is a sort of French country retreat in the middle of the desert. L'Auberge's cottages, which are surrounded by lushly landscaped grounds and look like rustic log cabins from the outside, have a classic styling worthy of a luxury French country inn (leather couches, gorgeous beds, plush towels, wood-burning fireplaces). The hillside cottages are among the largest and most luxurious accommodations in Sedona. Fabulous views and outdoor showers are just two features of these cottages. The restaurant, which serves American cuisines with Mediterranean influences, has a glass-walled dining room and a creekside terrace.

5

301 L'Auberge Lane, Sedona, AZ 86336. www.lauberge.com. ✆ **800/272-6777** or 928/282-1661. Fax 928/282-2885. 88 units. $250–$375 double; $350–$1,025 cottage. Rates do not include 10% resort fee. Rates include continental breakfast and evening wine reception. Children 12 and under stay free in parent's room. AE, DISC, MC, V. Pets accepted ($35 per night). **Amenities:** Restaurant; lounge; babysitting; concierge; executive-level rooms; access to nearby health club; room service; small full-service spa. *In room:* A/C, TV, fridge, hair dryer, MP3 docking station, Wi-Fi (included in resort fee).

Mii amo, a destination spa at Enchantment ★★★ This full-service destination spa inside the gates of the Enchantment Resort easily claims the state's best spa location. Designed to resemble a modern Native American–style pueblo, the spa backs up to the red-rock cliffs of Boynton Canyon and is shaded by cottonwood trees. Mii amo is well designed, with indoor and outdoor pools and outdoor massage cabanas at the foot of the cliffs. Guest rooms, which open onto a courtyard, have a bold, contemporary styling (mixed with Native American art and artifacts) that makes them some of the finest accommodations in the state. All units have private patios and gas fireplaces. Mii amo is a world unto itself in this hidden canyon, and no other spa in Arizona has a more Southwestern feel. 525 Boynton Canyon Rd., Sedona, AZ 86336. www.miiamo.com. ✆ **888/749-2137** or 928/203-8500. Fax 928/203-8599. 16 units. 3-night packages: Apr–May and Sept–Oct $4,470–$6,390 double; Nov–Jan $3,810–$5,730 double; Feb–Mar and June–Aug $4,140–$6,060 double. Rates include 3 meals per day, 2 daily spa treatments, and a variety of activities. AE, DC, DISC, MC, V. **Amenities:** Restaurant; lounge; bikes; concierge; exercise room; 3 Jacuzzis; 2 pools (indoor and outdoor); room service; full-service spa w/25 treatment areas and wide variety of body treatments. *In room:* A/C, TV/VCR/DVD, CD player, hair dryer, Internet (included in resort fee), minibar, MP3 docking station.

Expensive

Amara Hotel, Restaurant & Spa ★★ It's hip, it's convenient, and it's got drop-dead-gorgeous views. What's not to love about this hidden gem of a boutique hotel hidden behind the shops of uptown Sedona? Oh, did I mention the creekside setting shaded by grand old sycamores? There's even a swimming hole. How cool is that? This stylish hotel definitely offers the best of both worlds here in Sedona. The resort is hip and sophisticated, yet close to nature, and the minimalist decor and Zen-inspired style make Amara one of Sedona's most tranquil accommodations. From the outside, the hotel fits right in with the red-rock surroundings, while inside, bold splashes of color contrast with black-and-white photos. Guest rooms all have balconies or patios, wonderful pillow-top beds, and furnishings in black and red. The resort also has a small full-service spa.

100 Amara Lane, Sedona, AZ 86336. www.amararesort.com. ✆ **800/815-6152** or 928/282-4828. Fax 928/282-4825. 100 units. $175–$315 double; from $255–$365 suite. Rates include full breakfast. Rates do not include $20 resort fee. Children 18 and under stay free in parent's room. AE, DISC, MC, V. Pets accepted ($75 fee). **Amenities:** Restaurant; lounge; concierge; exercise room; Jacuzzi; outdoor saltwater pool; room service; sauna; full-service spa. *In room:* A/C, TV/DVD, fridge, hair dryer, free Wi-Fi.

Briar Patch Inn ★★ If you're searching for tranquillity or a romantic retreat amid the cool shade of Oak Creek Canyon, this is the place. Located 3 miles north of Sedona on the banks of Oak Creek, this inn's cottages are surrounded by beautiful grounds where bird songs and the babbling creek set the mood. There's even a swimming hole right here. The cottages date from the 1940s but have been attractively updated. A Western/rustic-Mexican style predominates. Most units have fireplaces and kitchenettes. In summer, breakfast is served on a creekside terrace. Despite a lack of red-rock views, the Briar Patch offers a delightful combination of solitude and sophistication.

3190 N. Ariz. 89A, Sedona, AZ 86336. www.briarpatchinn.com. ✆ **888/809-3030** or 928/282-2342. Fax 928/282-2399. 19 units. $219–$395 double. Rates include full breakfast. Children 3 and under stay free in parent's room. AE, DISC, MC, V. **Amenities:** Concierge; access to nearby health club; spa services; free Wi-Fi. *In room:* A/C, CD player, fridge, hair dryer, kitchen or kitchenette (in most).

El Portal Sedona ★★★ You just can't help but fall in love with this amazing inn. Owners Steve and Connie Segner have done everything right, and the overall experience here makes this one of the very best lodgings in the state. Located adjacent to the Tlaquepaque shopping center and built of hand-formed adobe blocks, El Portal is designed to resemble a 200-year-old hacienda and is a monument to fine craftsmanship. The inn is filled with Arts and Crafts–period antiques, and in the dining room the ceiling beams were salvaged from a railroad bridge. Each of the large guest rooms has its own distinctive character, from Arts and Crafts to cowboy chic. Most rooms have whirlpool tubs, and many rooms have private balconies with red-rock views. Exquisite breakfasts are served at an additional cost. Guided hikes and jeep tours can be arranged.

95 Portal Lane, Sedona, AZ 86336. www.elportalsedona.com. ✆ **800/313-0017** or 928/203-9405. Fax 928/203-9401. 12 units. Feb–June and Sept–Nov and late Dec to early Jan $259–$399 double; early to late Jan, July–Aug, and early Dec $200–$359 double. Rates include afternoon hors d'oeuvres. 2-night minimum on weekends and holidays. AE, DC, DISC, MC, V. Pets accepted. **Amenities:** Concierge; access to nearby health club and adjacent resort pools; room service. *In room:* A/C, TV/DVD, CD player, fridge, hair dryer, free Wi-Fi.

Garland's Oak Creek Lodge ★ Located 8 miles north of Sedona in the heart of Oak Creek Canyon, this may be the hardest place in the area to book a room. People have been coming here for so many years and like it so much that

A Taxing Situation

You can save a little bit on your hotel bill by staying in the Village of Oak Creek rather than in Sedona proper. Not only are there several budget hotels here, but also the room tax is only 7.35% vs. 13.737% in Sedona.

they reserve a year in advance (however, cancellations do occur). What makes the lodge so special? Maybe it's that you have to drive *through* Oak Creek to get to your log cabin. Maybe it's the beautiful gardens or the relaxing atmosphere of an old-time summer getaway. The well-maintained cabins, most of which have air-conditioning, are rustic but comfortable; the larger ones have fireplaces. Meals include organic fruits and vegetables grown on the property, and there's a yoga pavilion overlooking the creek.

P.O. Box 152, Sedona, AZ 86339. www.garlandslodge.com. ✆ **928/282-3343.** 16 units. $245–$295 double. Rates do not include 15% service charge. Rates include breakfast, afternoon tea, and dinner. 2-night minimum. Children 2 and under stay free in parent's room. MC, V. Closed mid-Nov to late Mar and Sun year-round. **Amenities:** Dining room; tennis court; free Wi-Fi. *In room:* No phone.

The Lodge at Sedona ★ Set amid pine trees a block off Ariz. 89A in west Sedona, this large inn is decorated in the Arts and Crafts/mission style, which makes it one of the more distinctive inns in Sedona. The best rooms are those on the ground floor. These tend to be large, and several are suites. Suites are only slightly more expensive than deluxe rooms, which makes the suites the best choices here. Second-floor rooms are more economical and tend to be fairly small. If you want views, book one of the small upstairs rooms or the Desert Trail, Copper Canyon, or Whispering Winds suite. Breakfasts are five-course affairs that can tide you over until dinner.

125 Kallof Place, Sedona, AZ 86336. www.lodgeatsedona.com. ✆ **800/619-4467** or 928/204-1942. Fax 928/204-2128. 14 units. $189–$229 double; $269–$349 suite. Rates include full breakfast. AE, DISC, MC, V. Pets accepted ($35 per night). Children 11 and over welcome. **Amenities:** Concierge; access to nearby health club. *In room:* A/C, TV, CD player, hair dryer, free Wi-Fi.

Sedona Rouge Hotel & Spa ★ This stylish boutique hotel is one of the most distinctive luxury hotels in Sedona, and although it is located right on busy Ariz. 89A in west Sedona, I highly recommend it. Merging contemporary styling with North African details, the hotel manages to create an ambience that is very international in feel. Antique wrought-iron window grates from Tunisia decorate hallways, and guest rooms have Moroccan-inspired tables. Bathrooms, with dual-head rain-type showers, are a real highlight. If you can, try to get a room on the third floor; these have vaulted ceilings that make the rooms seem larger. The tiny lobby is just off an enclosed courtyard with a splashing fountain. A rooftop patio has the best view at the hotel. This is a good pick for couples in a romantic mood.

2250 W. Ariz. 89A, Sedona, AZ 86336. www.sedonarouge.com. ✆ **866/312-4111** or 928/203-4111. Fax 928/203-9094. 77 units. Jan–Feb $199–$299 double; Mar–May $209–$319 double; June–Aug $159–$299 double; Sept–Oct $189–$289 double; Nov–Dec $159–$289 double. Children 12 and under stay free in parent's room. AE, DC, DISC, MC, V. Pets accepted ($100 deposit, $50 fee). **Amenities:** Restaurant; lounge; concierge; exercise room and access to nearby health club; 2 Jacuzzis; outdoor pool; room service; full-service spa. *In room:* A/C, TV, CD player, fridge, hair dryer, free Wi-Fi.

Moderate

Cedars Resort on Oak Creek Located right at the "Y" and set atop a 100-foot cliff, this motel has fabulous views across Oak Creek to the towering red rocks.

Guest rooms are large and comfortable, and creekside rooms have private balconies. However, for the best views, ask for a "canyon" room. Alternatively, you can save some money by opting for a room without and then hang out at the pool and hot tub, both of which have great views of the red rocks. A long stairway leads down to the creek, and the shops of uptown Sedona are just a short walk away.

20 W. Ariz. 89A (P.O. Box 292), Sedona, AZ 86339. www.sedonacedarsresort.com. ✆ **800/874-2072** or 928/282-7010. Fax 928/282-5372. 38 units. $99–$159 double. Rates include continental breakfast. Children 12 and under stay free in parent's room. AE, DC, DISC, MC, V. **Amenities:** Concierge; exercise room and access to nearby health club; Jacuzzi; small outdoor pool. *In room:* A/C, TV, CD player, fridge, hair dryer, free Wi-Fi.

Forest Houses ★ 🎁 Set at the upper end of Oak Creek Canyon and built right on the banks of the creek, these rustic houses and apartments date back to the 1940s. Built by a stone sculptor, they feature artistic touches that set them apart from other cabins in the canyon. About half of the houses are built right on the creek, and some seem to grow straight from the rocks in the streambed. Terraces let you fully enjoy the setting. One of my favorite units is the two-bedroom Cloud House, with stone floors, peeled-log woodwork, and a loft. This property is certainly not for everyone (no phones, no TVs, and you have to drive through the creek to get here), but those who discover the Forest Houses often come back year after year.

9275 N. Ariz. 89A, Sedona, AZ 86336. www.foresthousesresort.com. ✆ **928/282-2999.** Fax 928/282-0663. 16 units. $110–$145 double. 2- to 4-night minimum stay. Children 8 and under stay free in parent's room. AE, MC, V. Pets accepted ($20 deposit). Closed Jan to mid-Mar. *In room:* Kitchen, no phone.

Matterhorn Inn Located in the heart of the uptown shopping district, this hotel is convenient to restaurants and shops, and all of the attractively furnished guest rooms have excellent views of the red-rock canyon walls. Although the Matterhorn is set above a row of shops fronting busy Ariz. 89A, if you lie in bed and keep your eyes on the rocks, you'd never know there was so much going on below you. This place is a great value for Sedona.

230 Apple Ave., Sedona, AZ 86336. www.matterhorninn.com. ✆ **800/372-8207** or 928/282-7176. 23 units. Mar–Nov $89–$169 double; Dec–Feb $79–$159 double. Children 4 and under stay free in parent's room. AE, MC, V. Pets accepted ($10 per night). **Amenities:** Concierge; Jacuzzi; small outdoor pool. *In room:* A/C, TV, CD player, fridge, hair dryer, MP3 docking station, free Wi-Fi.

Orchards Inn of Sedona For picture-perfect, in-your-face views of the red rocks, few Sedona hotels can compete with the Orchards. The red-rock views from the hotel's hillside setting above Oak Creek are simply spectacular. Best of all, every room here has a view and glass patio doors to let you see plenty of the scenery. Don't be discouraged when you drive up to the front door; although the Orchards, which is more hotel than inn, is located amid the uptown tourist crowds, it seems miles away once you check into your room and gaze out at the red rocks. Rooms were completely remodeled in 2009, giving the hotel a fresh, contemporary look.

254 N. Ariz. 89A, Sedona, AZ 86336. www.orchardsinn.com. ✆ **800/341-6075** or 928/282-2405. Fax 928/282-5710. 69 units. $129–$249 double. Rates include full breakfast. Children 17 and under stay free in parent's room. AE, DC, DISC, MC, V. Pets accepted ($10 per night). **Amenities:** Restaurant; lounge; Jacuzzi; small outdoor pool. *In room:* A/C, TV/DVD, fridge, hair dryer, free Wi-Fi.

Inexpensive

Rose Tree Inn 🎁 This little inn, only a block from Sedona's uptown shopping district, is tucked amid pretty gardens (yes, there are lots of roses) on a quiet street. The property consists of an eclectic cluster of renovated older buildings. Each unit is furnished differently—one Victorian, one Southwestern, two with gas fireplaces. Four guest rooms have kitchenettes, making these rooms good choices for families or for longer stays.

376 Cedar St., Sedona, AZ 86336. www.rosetreeinn.com. ✆ **888/282-2065** or 928/282-2065. 5 units. $95–$149 double. Children 15 and under stay free in parent's room. AE, MC, V. **Amenities:** Concierge; access to nearby health club. *In room:* A/C, TV/VCR, CD player, fridge, hair dryer, kitchen (in some), free Wi-Fi.

Sky Ranch Lodge ★ ☺ This motel is located atop Airport Mesa and has the most stupendous vista in town. From here you can see the entire red-rock country, with Sedona filling the valley below. Although the rooms are fairly standard motel issue and are badly in need of updating, some have gas fireplaces and some have balconies. Only the nonview units fall into the inexpensive category, but those great views are just steps away. With a pool and plenty of space for running around, this place will keep the kids happy. You can even walk up the road to watch planes and helicopters at the airport.

1105 Airport Rd., Sedona, AZ 86336. www.skyranchlodge.com. ✆ **888/708-6400** or 928/282-6400. 94 units. $70–$194 double. Children 12 and under stay free in parent's room. AE, DISC, MC, V. Pets accepted ($10 per night). **Amenities:** Jacuzzi; small outdoor pool. *In room:* A/C, TV, kitchenettes (in some).

VILLAGE OF OAK CREEK

Expensive

Adobe Village Graham Inn ★ A garden full of bronze statues of children greets you when you pull up to this luxurious inn in the Village of Oak Creek, 6 miles south of uptown Sedona. The inn lies almost at the foot of Bell Rock and features a variety of themed accommodations. The villas, the Sundance room, and the Sedona suite are the most impressive rooms here. My favorite is the Purple Lizard villa, which opts for a colorful Taos-style interior and an amazing rustic canopy bed. The Wilderness villa resembles a luxurious log cabin. The Lonesome Dove villa is a sort of upscale cowboy cabin with a fireplace, potbellied stove, and round hot tub in a "barrel." Can you say *romantic?* This inn also operates the Adobe Grand Villas in West Sedona.

150 Canyon Circle Dr., Sedona, AZ 86351. www.adobevillagegrahaminn.com. ✆ **800/228-1425** or 928/284-1425. 11 units. $199–$329 double; $349–$419 suite; $349–$479 villa. Rates include full breakfast and afternoon hors d'oeuvres. 2-night minimum weekends and holidays. AE, DISC, MC, V. **Amenities:** Concierge; Jacuzzi; outdoor pool. *In room:* A/C, TV/VCR/DVD, hair dryer, kitchenette (in some), Wi-Fi (in some).

Canyon Villa ★★ In the Village of Oak Creek, 6 miles south of Sedona, this bed-and-breakfast offers luxurious accommodations and spectacular views of the red rocks. All rooms but one have views, as do the pool area, living room, and dining room. Guest rooms are varied in style—Victorian, Santa Fe, country, rustic—but no matter what the decor, the furnishings are impeccable. All rooms have balconies or patios, and several have fireplaces. Breakfast is a lavish affair meant to be lingered over, and in the afternoon there's an elaborate spread of appetizers.

40 Canyon Circle Dr., Sedona, AZ 86351. www.canyonvilla.com. ✆ **800/453-1166** or 928/284-1226. Fax 928/284-2114. 11 units. $239–$349 double (lower rates in off season). Rates include full breakfast. AE, DC, DISC, MC, V. No children 10 or under. **Amenities:** Concierge; access to nearby health club; outdoor pool. *In room:* A/C, TV/DVD, CD player, hair dryer, free Wi-Fi.

Hilton Sedona Resort & Spa ★★ This resort boasts not only one of the most breathtaking golf courses in the state, but also the best pool area north of Phoenix. While golf is the driving force behind most stays here, anyone looking for an active vacation will find plenty to keep them busy. Guest rooms are suites of varying sizes, with fireplaces and balconies or patios. The resort's restaurant plays up its views of the golf course and red rocks. The only drawback here is that, because it's south of the Village of Oak Creek, the resort is a bit of a drive (about 8 miles) to Sedona's shops and restaurants.

90 Ridge Trail Dr., Sedona, AZ 86351. www.hiltonsedonaresort.com. ✆ **877/273-3762** or 928/284-4040. Fax 928/284-6940. 219 units. $179–$459 double. Children 18 and under stay free in parent's room. AE, DC, DISC, MC, V. Pets accepted ($50 fee). **Amenities:** 2 restaurants; 2 lounges; concierge; 18-hole golf course; exercise room and access to nearby health club; 5 Jacuzzis; 3 pools; room service; sauna; full-service spa; 3 tennis courts. *In room:* A/C, TV, hair dryer, minibar, MP3 docking station, Wi-Fi ($12–$15 per day).

Las Posadas of Sedona ★ Located across the highway from the Hilton resort in the Village of Oak Creek, Las Posadas is a cross between an all-suites boutique hotel and a bed-and-breakfast inn. All of the large suites have separate entrances and kitchenettes, which makes staying here a bit like having your own Sedona apartment. The difference is that here you're served a gourmet breakfast each morning. All the suites have gas fireplaces and a balcony or patio, and some suites have outdoor whirlpool spas. Be sure to ask for a room with a view.

26 Av. de Piedras, Sedona, AZ 86351. www.lasposadasofsedona.com. ✆ **888/284-5288** or 928/284-5288. Fax 928/284-4178. 23 units. $199–$479 double. Rates include full breakfast. AE, DC, DISC, MC, V. Pets accepted ($15 per night). No children 11 or under. **Amenities:** Concierge; access to nearby health club; outdoor pool. *In room:* A/C, TV/DVD, CD player, hair dryer, kitchenette, free Wi-Fi.

Moderate

Red Agave With a gorgeous view of Bell Rock and hiking trails that start at the edge of the property, this is Sedona's premier budget getaway for an active vacation. Affiliated with the nearby Bike and Bean bike shop, Red Agave offers discounts on bike rentals and easy access to miles of great mountain-biking trails. Accommodations are in attractive studios with tile floors, kitchens, and comfortable beds. If you're coming with your family, there are also A-frame cabins with loft sleeping areas. The small pool, two hot tubs, fire pit, and big yard provide lots of options for relaxing.

120 Canyon Circle Dr., Sedona, AZ 86351. www.redagaveresort.com. ✆ **877/284-9237** or 928/284-9327. Fax 928/284-0832. 14 units. $109–$129 double; $209–$229 suite. AE, DISC, MC, V. Pets accepted ($40). **Amenities:** 2 Jacuzzis; small outdoor pool. *In room:* A/C, TV, kitchen, free Wi-Fi.

Inexpensive

Sedona Village Lodge This little hotel in the Village of Oak Creek may be set at the back of a big parking lot shared with a shopping plaza, but it is such a great deal, that I just have to tell you about it. If all you're looking for is an economical place to spend the night and don't need a pool or hot tub, this place is an almost unbelievable value. Now, don't get me wrong, the Sedona Village Lodge is nothing fancy, just clean and comfortable. That said, the suites have kitchenettes, gas fireplaces, and red-rock views.

105 Bell Rock Plaza, Sedona, AZ 86351. www.sedonalodge.com. ✆ **800/890-0521** or 928/284-3626. Fax 928/284-3629. 15 units. $49–$59 double; $79–$89 suite. 2-night minimum holiday

weekends and all weekends Mar–May and Sept–Oct. MC, V. Pets accepted. *In room:* A/C, TV, fridge, hair dryer, kitchenette (some rooms), free Wi-Fi.

Wildflower Inn With the best Bell Rock views of any of the budget hotels in the Village of Oak Creek, this casual place is a good bet for a budget Sedona vacation. Not only do many of the rooms have views, but some have fireplaces and others have double whirlpool tubs. There's even a rooftop deck where you can have your breakfast, or a picnic dinner, if you're so inclined. Rustic log furniture in the guest rooms gives this place a bit more character than you'd expect from a budget motel. The Bell Rock trail head is just across the street.

6086 Ariz. 179, Sedona, AZ 86351. www.sedonawildflowerinn.com. ✆ **888/494-5335** or 928/284-3937. Fax 928/284-3314. 28 units. $89–$149 double. Rates include continental breakfast. Children 12 and under stay free in parent's room. AE, DC, DISC, MC, V. **Amenities:** Concierge; exercise room; sauna. *In room:* A/C, TV, fridge, hair dryer, free Wi-Fi.

CAMPGROUNDS

Within Oak Creek Canyon along Ariz. 89A, there are five national forest campgrounds. **Manzanita,** 6 miles north of town, is both the largest and the most pleasant (and the only one open in winter; $20 per night). Other Oak Creek Canyon campgrounds include **Cave Springs,** 13 miles north of town ($20 per night), and **Pine Flat,** 12 miles north of town ($20 per night). The **Beaver Creek Campground,** 3 miles east of I-17 on F.R. 618, which is an extension of Ariz. 179 (take exit 298 off I-17), is a pleasant spot near the V Bar V Heritage Site ($16 per night). For more information on area campgrounds, contact the **Coconino National Forest's Red Rock Ranger District,** 8375 Ariz. 179 (✆ **928/203-7500;** www.fs.fed.us/r3/coconino), which is located south of the Village of Oak Creek. Reservations can be made for Manzanita, Pine Flat, and Cave Springs campgrounds by contacting the **National Recreation Reservation Service** (✆ **877/444-6777** or 518/885-3639; www.recreation.gov).

Where to Eat

SEDONA

Expensive

Fournos ★★ NEW AMERICAN Although this restaurant has been around for years, it is now overseen by chef Ivan Flowers, who used to cook at Sedona's Amara Resort. Here, in a tiny hole-in-the-wall restaurant no bigger than most home dining rooms in Sedona, the kitchen turns out the best food in Sedona. The lobster bisque is absolutely heavenly and should not be missed, nor should the mushrooms in cognac sauce. If you see anything on the short menu with oven-roasted tomatoes, get it; these tomatoes are intensely flavorful. Among the standout dishes on the menu are the pork *osso buco* (a huge portion of braised pork shank) and the rack of lamb encrusted in basil and oregano. If there happen to be any steak specials the night you dine here, say yes. A T-bone steak I tasted here was one of the best steaks I've ever had.

3000 W. Ariz. 89A. ✆ **928/282-3331.** www.fournossedona.com. Reservations highly recommended. Main courses $22–$29. No credit cards. Mon and Thurs–Sat 5–8:30pm.

The Heartline Café ★★ SOUTHWESTERN/INTERNATIONAL The heart line, from Zuni mythology, is a symbol of health and longevity; it is also a symbol for the healthful, creative food served here. To start, don't miss the

Cocktails & More with a View

Because the main reason you're in Sedona is to enjoy the views of those amazing red rocks, it would be a shame not to take every possible opportunity to sit back and ogle the scenery. So why not sip a drink while you stare? In the morning, I like to get coffee at the Pink Jeep tour company's **Pink Java Cafe,** 206 Ariz. 89A (✆ **928/282-0249**), which has a little patio with an astonishing view. Alternatively, you can get coffee and a pastry at **Wildflower Bread Company,** in the Shops at Piñon Point, 101 N. Ariz. 89A (✆ **928/204-2223;** www.wildflowerbread.com), which is in the shopping complex between uptown Sedona and the "Y." Although there's a bit of traffic noise here, the view of Snoopy Rock is hard to beat.

When it's time to watch the sunset light show, I like to head to the bar at uptown's **Open Range Grill & Tavern,** 320 N. Ariz. 89A (✆ **928/282-0002;** www.openrangesedona.com), which is located in Sinagua Plaza. This place does decent margaritas. Because only a handful of tables have views, try to arrive early. The view tables are tucked around behind the bar. If these tables are already taken, try the nearby **Canyon Breeze,** Sedona Center, 300 N. Ariz. 89A (✆ **928/282-2112;** www.canyon-breeze.com), where you can sit at the bar and gaze out at the red rocks. There's a big terrace, too.

tea-smoked chicken dumplings with spicy peanut sauce or warm red-cabbage salad. The must-have entree here is the heavenly pecan-crusted local trout with Dijon cream sauce. Those searching out variety in vegetarian choices will find it here. The beautiful courtyard and traditionally elegant interior are both good places to savor a meal. Lunch and gourmet takeout are available at the adjacent Heartline Gourmet Take-Out & Market, which is a good place to pick up a picnic lunch before heading out into the red rocks.

1600 and 1610 W. Ariz. 89A. ✆ **928/282-0785** (cafe) or 928/282-3365 (Gourmet Take-Out). www.heartlinecafe.com. Reservations recommended. Cafe main courses $17–$27; Gourmet Express $6–$15. AE, DC, DISC, MC, V. Cafe Wed–Mon 5:30–9:30pm. Gourmet Take-Out daily 8am–4pm.

René at Tlaquepaque ★ CONTINENTAL/AMERICAN Although a formal dining experience and traditional French fare may seem out of place in a town that celebrates its cowboy heritage, René's makes fine dining seem as natural as mesquite-grilled steak and cowboy beans. Located in Tlaquepaque, the city's upscale south-of-the-border-themed shopping center, this restaurant is the best place in Sedona for a special meal. The house specialty is rack of lamb. More adventurous diners may want to try the excellent tenderloin of venison with whiskey–juniper berry sauce. Finish with a flambéed dessert. To save money, I recommend eating here at lunch.

At Tlaquepaque, 336 Ariz. 179, Ste. 118. ✆ **928/282-9225.** www.rene-sedona.com. Reservations recommended. Main courses $10–$17 lunch, $19–$45 dinner. AE, MC, V. Mon–Thurs 11:30am–2pm and 5:30–8:30pm; Fri–Sat 11:30am–2:30pm and 5:30–9pm; Sun 11:30am–2:30pm and 5:30–8:30pm.

Shugrue's Hillside Grill ★ NEW AMERICAN/CONTINENTAL Located at the back of the Hillside Sedona shopping plaza, this is the most upscale outpost in a small chain of popular Arizona restaurants. Although the prices are high at dinner, if you come before the sun sets, you'll be treated to unforgettable views through the walls of glass. The extensive menu includes influences from around the world. For a starter, try the blackened shrimp *saganaki*. There are plenty of good steak and fish entrees, too.

671 Ariz. 179. ✆ **928/282-5300.** www.shugrues.com. Reservations highly recommended. Main courses $11–$19 lunch, $14–$36 dinner. AE, MC, V. Daily 11:30am–3pm and 5–9pm.

Yavapai Restaurant ★ SOUTHWESTERN The Yavapai Restaurant, at the exclusive Enchantment Resort, has the best views and most memorable setting of any restaurant in Sedona. It is also one of the town's most formal restaurants, which doesn't quite fit with the rugged setting but is in keeping with Enchantment's exclusive character. The menu changes regularly to take advantage of seasonal ingredients, but keep an eye out for venison with the sauce of the moment. Because the scenery is every bit as important as the food here, make sure you make dinner reservations to take in the sunset on the red rocks. You can also soak up the views at breakfast and lunch and save quite a bit of money.

At Enchantment Resort, 525 Boynton Canyon Rd. ✆ **928/204-6000.** www.enchantmentresort.com. Reservations required. Main courses $16–$24 lunch, $32–$45 dinner; Sun brunch $49 adults ($25 for children 11 and under). AE, DISC, MC, V. Mon–Sat 6:30am–2:15pm and 5:30–9:30pm; Sun 10:30am–2:30pm and 5:30–9:30pm.

Moderate

Barking Frog Grille ★ ☺ SOUTHWESTERN This sprawling Southwestern restaurant is under the same management as the Cowboy Club (below) and is a good bet for a casual family dinner. There's plenty on the menu to keep everyone happy, but be sure to start with the delicious guacamole (prepared tableside). Other standout dishes include caramelized sea scallops with citrus butter and rotisserie game hen. Of course, for the kids, there are great burgers. Because this restaurant is away from the touristy parts of town, it is often easy to get a table on short notice during the busy spring season.

2620 W. Ariz. 89A. ✆ **928/204-2000.** www.barkingfroggrille.com. Reservations recommended. Main courses $8–$30 lunch; $11–$30 dinner. AE, DISC, MC, V. Daily 11am–10pm.

Café Elote ★ MEXICAN *Elote* is a Mexican preparation of corn on the cob that is made with freshly roasted corn that is slathered with spicy mayonnaise and sprinkled with white *cotija* cheese. Squirt on a little lime, and you have the ultimate south-of-the-border street food. Here at this treat's namesake restaurant, the *elote* is sliced from the cob and served as a sort of dip. This dish alone, maybe with a side of guacamole and a margarita, is reason enough to eat at this highly creative Mexican restaurant. For an entree, try the braised lamb in sweet-and-spicy ancho-chili sauce. This is a casual and colorful spot, and feels a bit like a Mexican beach bar.

At King's Ransom Sedona Hotel, 771 Ariz. 179. ✆ **928/203-0105.** www.elotecafe.com. Reservations not accepted. Main courses $17–$22. AE, DISC, MC, V. Tues–Sat 5–9pm.

Cowboy Club Grille & Spirits ☺ SOUTHWESTERN With its big booths, huge steer horns over the bar, and cowboy gear adorning the walls, this restaurant is Sedona's quintessential New West steakhouse. Start out with fried cactus strips with a prickly-pear sauce or perhaps some snake skewers. The buffalo tenderloin, served with brandied peppercorn cream sauce, may be the most expensive item on the menu, but it's worth the splurge. Frugal travelers can opt for the buffalo cheeseburger. Service is friendly but can be slow during the peak tourist season. The adjacent Silver Saddle Room is a more upscale spin on the same concept, with similar menu prices. The kids should get a kick out of the cowboy decor and, who knows, you may even get them to taste your snake or cactus appetizer. It was in this building in 1965 that the Cowboy Artists of America organization was formed.

241 N. Ariz. 89A. ✆ **928/282-4200.** www.cowboyclub.com. Reservations not accepted for Cowboy Club; recommended for Silver Saddle Room. Main courses $11–$37. AE, DISC, MC, V. Daily 11am–10pm.

Dahl & DiLuca ★ ITALIAN A faux-Tuscan villa interior, complete with a bar in a grotto, makes this the most romantic restaurant in Sedona, and the excellent Italian food makes it that much more unforgettable. Be sure to start with calamari, which is some of the best I've ever had. Pasta predominates here, and portions are big. I like the gnocchi with mushrooms and truffle cream sauce. However, the veal dishes here are also excellent, and there are plenty of good seafood, chicken, and vegetarian dishes. The eggplant Parmesan and portobello *alla griglia* are real standouts. Keep in mind that during the high season (spring), this place stays packed with tourists and service can, at times, be brusque.

2321 W. Ariz. 89A (in west Sedona diagonally across from the Safeway Plaza). ✆ **928/282-5219.** www.dahl-diluca.com. Reservations recommended. Main courses $13–$32. AE, DISC, MC, V. Daily 5–10pm.

Oak Creek Bar & Grill AMERICAN If you find yourself lost in the maze of shops at the Tlaquepaque shopping plaza, don't despair of finding sustenance before you find your way back to your car; just consult one of the shopping center maps and head to this casual second-floor brewpub. The menu features such pub standards as pizzas, barbecued ribs, and fish and chips, plus a few slightly more creative dishes—all of which go well with the pub's beers. If you feel like having some fun, order the "Seven Dwarfs," a sampler of all the beers they brew here.

In Tlaquepaque Arts Village, 336 Ariz. 179 downhill from the "Y." ✆ **928/282-3300.** www.oakcreekpub.com. Reservations not accepted. Main courses $10–$19 lunch, $12–$28 dinner. AE, DISC, MC, V. Daily 11:30am–8:30 or 9pm.

Open Range Grill & Tavern SOUTHWESTERN In a town boasting some of the most astonishing scenery in the country, it seems foolish *not* to dine with a view. While restaurants with great views rarely offer food to match the scenery, Open Range is an exception. Sure the prices are a bit high, but the view out the wall of glass at the back of this restaurant is more than worth the premium charged for meals here. The menu offerings are fairly simple, but well prepared and with the occasional unusual ingredient or two. At lunch, there's a tasty grilled-chicken Caesar club sandwich made with sun-dried tomatoes, arugula, and bacon, and at lunch or dinner you can get this same dish as a salad. Steaks, pork chops, crab cakes, and salmon dishes all get a Southwestern spin. Be sure to try the green-chili macaroni and cheese.

In Sedona Center, 320 N. Ariz. 89A. ✆ **928/282-0002.** www.openrangesedona.com. Reservations accepted for parties of 6 or more. Main courses $12–$15 lunch, $15–$28 dinner. AE, MC, V. Sun–Thurs 11:30am–10pm; Fri–Sat 11:30am–11pm.

Inexpensive

Dining in Sedona tends to be expensive, so your best bets for economical meals are sandwich shops or ethnic restaurants. For breakfast, locals swear by the **Coffee Pot Restaurant,** 2050 W. Ariz. 89A (✆ **928/282-6626;** www.coffeepotsedona.com), although I personally am not a fan. You can decide for yourself. For filling sandwiches, try **Sedona Memories,** 321 Jordan Rd. (✆ **928/282-0032**), 1 block off Ariz. 89A in the uptown shopping area. Having a picnic? You can stock up on exotic imported meats, cheeses, and other fun foods or get a gourmet sandwich to go at west Sedona's **Euro-Deli,** 3190 W. Ariz. 89A (✆ **928/282-4798;** www.eurodelisedona.com). For picnic supplies, head to **New Frontiers Natural Foods,** 1420 W. Ariz. 89A (✆ **928/282-6311**). You can also get organic and vegan fare at **Chocolatree Organic Eatery,** 1595 W. Ariz. 89A (✆ **928/282-2997;** www.chocolatreecafe.com), which specializes in live foods, including raw chocolate treats.

When you need good espresso, perhaps for that long drive to the Grand Canyon, you've got a few good options around town. I like to start my days in Sedona at **Pink Java Café,** 206 N. Ariz. 89A (✆ **928/282-0249**), which serves organic coffee and has a patio where you can sit and gaze at the red rocks while you sip your latte. In west Sedona, stop by **Heart of Sedona Coffee,** at the Old Marketplace shopping center, 1370 W. Ariz. 89A, Ste. 12 (✆ **928/282-5777**). In the Village of Oak Creek, try **Posse Grounds Coffeehouse,** 7000 Ariz. 179, Ste. B110 (✆ **928/284-4620;** www.possegrounds.com).

Casa Bonita MEXICAN Located in the same shopping center as the Basha's supermarket, this casual and colorful Mexican restaurant is a local favorite. Both the food and the service are usually very reliable. I like the fried fish tacos, which are made with tartar sauce. Don't miss the apple chimichanga dessert. Also, be sure to have a designated driver; the margaritas here are the best in town.

164 Coffee Pot Dr., Ste. H. ✆ **928/282-2728.** www.casabonitaaz.com. Main courses $4.25–$16. AE, DC, DISC, MC, V. Mon–Fri 11am–9pm; Sat–Sun noon–9pm.

The Hideaway Restaurant ☺ ITALIAN Hidden at the back of a shopping plaza near the "Y," this casual family restaurant is as popular with locals as it is with visitors. Basic pizzas, subs, sandwiches, salads, and pastas are the choices here. However, most people come for the knockout views. From the shady porch, you can see the creek below and the red rocks rising across the canyon. Lunch or an early sunset dinner is your best bet. The antipasto salad is an absolute must. Keep an eye out for hummingbirds and great blue herons.

Country Sq., 251 Ariz. 179. ✆ **928/282-4204.** Reservations accepted only for parties of 10 or more. Main courses $5.50–$12 lunch, $12–$15 dinner. AE, DISC, MC, V. Daily 11am–9pm.

Javelina Cantina MEXICAN Although Javelina Cantina is part of a chain of Arizona restaurants, the formula works, and few diners leave disappointed. Sure, the restaurant is touristy, but what it has going for it is good Mexican food, a lively atmosphere, decent views, and a convenient location in the Hillside shops. The grilled fish tacos are tasty, as is the pork adobo sandwich. The salmon tostadas are also worth trying. There are also plenty of different margaritas and tequilas to accompany your meal. Expect a wait.

At Hillside Sedona shopping plaza, 671 Ariz. 179. ✆ **928/203-9514.** www.javelinacantina.com. Reservations recommended. Main courses $9–$18. AE, DISC, MC, V. Daily 11:30am–8:30 or 9pm.

Picazzo's Organic Italian Kitchen ★ PIZZA For down-home pizza in an upscale setting, nothing in Sedona can compare with this artistic pizza place. Throw in an attractive walled patio dining area and a view of Coffee Pot Rock, and you have one of the best values in town. You get a great setting, a great view, and great pizza, and best of all, by eating here you can avoid the crowds in uptown

Sedona. There are also good by-the-slice lunch specials and half-price appetizers during happy hour. Try the pesto and goat cheese pizza, or a spinach and wild mushroom pizza with Alfredo sauce. Gluten-free pizzas are available, and, as much as possible, ingredients are organic and hormone and preservative free.

1855 W. Ariz. 89A. ✆ **928/282-4140.** www.picazzos.com. Reservations not accepted. Pizzas $12–$25. AE, MC, V. Sun–Thurs 11am–9pm; Fri–Sat 11am–10pm.

VILLAGE OF OAK CREEK

Moderate

Cucina Rústica ★ MEDITERRANEAN/SOUTHWESTERN With its various distinct dining rooms and numerous antique doors, this sister restaurant to west Sedona's wonderful Dahl & DiLuca (see above) feels like a luxurious villa. My favorite room in which to dine here is one with a central dome that is lit by what appear to be thousands of stars, but for a genuine starlit dinner, you can ask for a seat on the patio. You can get some of the same delicious dishes served at Dahl & DiLuca, but they also serve some of the best prawns I've ever had. They're wrapped in radicchio and prosciutto and then grilled.

7000 Ariz. 179, Village of Oak Creek. ✆ **928/284-3010.** www.cucinarustica.com. Reservations recommended. Main courses $13–$34. AE, MC, V. Sun–Thurs 5–9pm; Fri–Sat 5–9:30 or 10pm.

Inexpensive

Tara Thai Cuisine THAI Friends who have a house in Sedona love this restaurant, and if you like Thai food, I'm sure you will, too. Not only is the food packed with all those great, exotic Thai flavors, but also, in this overpriced tourist town, the reasonable prices are a welcome relief. I like the pad Thai, and, if it's on the menu, be sure to try the mango and sticky rice for dessert. You'll find Tara Thai tucked into a shopping center near the north end of the Village of Oak Creek.

34 Bell Rock Plaza, Village of Oak Creek. ✆ **928/284-9167.** Reservations recommended. Main courses $9–$18. AE, DISC, MC, V. Tues–Fri 11am–3pm and 5–9pm; Sat 11am–9pm; Sun noon–9pm.

Sedona After Dark

If you'd like to catch some live classical music while you're in town, check the schedule of **Chamber Music Sedona** (✆ **877/768-2415** or 928/204-2415; www.chambermusicsedona.org).

If you're searching for good microbrewed beer, head to the **Oak Creek Brewing Co.,** 2050 Yavapai Dr. (✆ **928/204-1300;** www.oakcreekbrew.com), north of Ariz. 89A off Coffee Pot Drive. There's also the affiliated **Oak Creek Brewery and Grill,** 336 Ariz. 179 (✆ **928/282-3300;** www.oakcreekpub.com) in the Tlaquepaque shopping complex. If you're looking for some live music, check out **Olde Sedona Bar & Grille,** 1405 W. Ariz. 89A (✆ **928/282-5670;** www.oldesedona.com). Down in the Village of Oak Creek, you can do a little dancing at the **Full Moon Saloon,** 7000 N. Ariz. 179 (✆ **928/284-1872;** www.thefullmoonsaloon.com), which is located in the Tequa Plaza shopping center and has live music and karaoke several nights a week.

6

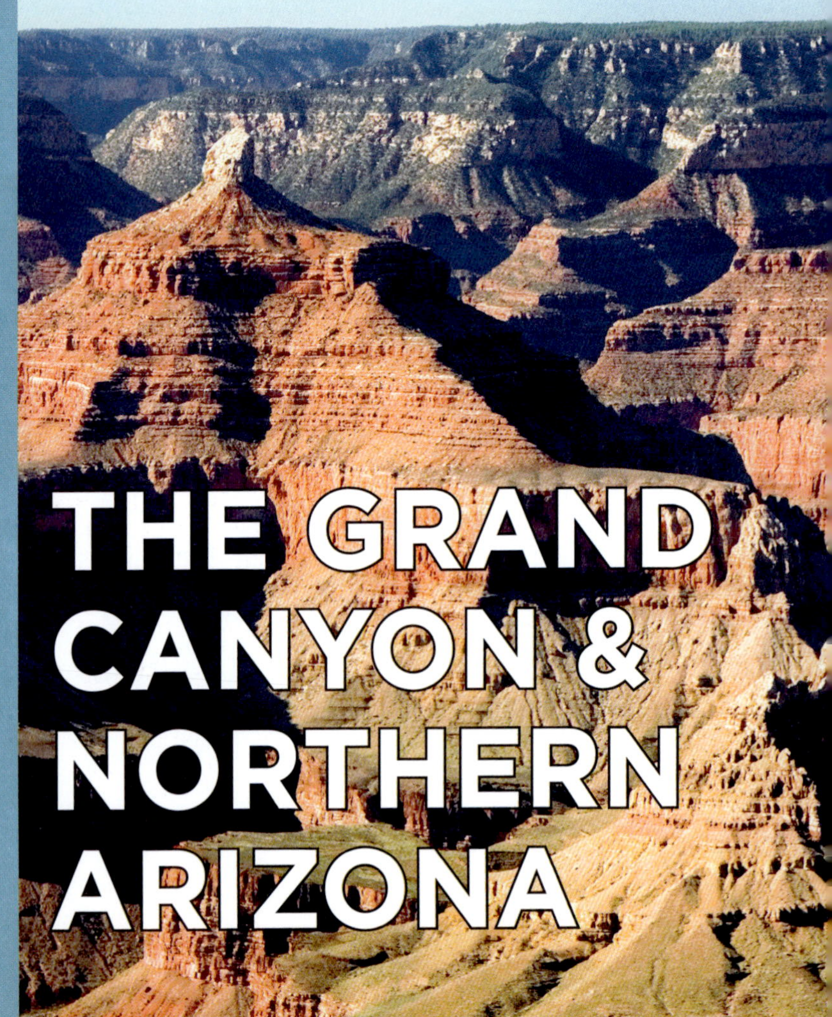

THE GRAND CANYON & NORTHERN ARIZONA

The Grand Canyon—the name is at once both apt and inadequate. How can words sum up the grandeur of 2 billion years of the earth's history sliced open by the power of a single river? Once an impassable and forbidding barrier to explorers and settlers, the Grand Canyon today is a magnet that each year attracts millions of visitors from all over the world. The pastel layers of rock weaving through the canyon's rugged ramparts, the interplay of shadows and light, the wind in the pines, California condors soaring overhead, the croaking of ravens on the rim—these are the sights and sounds that never fail to transfix the hordes of visitors who gaze awestruck into the canyon's seemingly infinite depths.

While the Grand Canyon is undeniably the most awe-inspiring natural attraction anywhere in the state, northern Arizona contains other natural attractions that are also worthwhile, and certainly less crowded. Only 60 miles south of the great yawning chasm stand the San Francisco Peaks, the tallest of which, Humphreys Peak, rises to 12,643 feet. These peaks, sacred to the Hopi and Navajo, are ancient volcanoes that today are popular with skiers, hikers, and mountain bikers.

Volcanic eruptions 900 to 1,000 years ago helped turn the land east of the San Francisco Peaks into fertile farmland that allowed the Sinagua people to thrive in this otherwise inhospitable environment. Within a few hundred years, however, the Sinagua disappeared. Today the ruins of their ancient villages, scattered across lonely, windswept plains, are all that remain of their culture.

Just as the region once attracted Native Americans, it also attracted pioneers, who settled on the south side of the San Francisco Peaks. Amid expansive ponderosa pine forests now stands the city of Flagstaff, which at 7,000 feet in elevation is one of the highest cities in the U.S. Flagstaff is home to Northern Arizona University, whose students ensure that this is a lively, liberal town. Born of the railroads and named for a flagpole, Flagstaff is now the main jumping-off point for trips to the Grand Canyon. Because the city has preserved much of its Western heritage in its restored downtown historic district, it's well worth a visit.

While it's the Grand Canyon that brings many people to northern Arizona, most visitors spend only a day or so in Grand Canyon National Park, so you may want to take a look at what else there is to do in this part of the state. If, on the other hand, you only want to visit the canyon, there are many different ways to accomplish this goal. You can do so on your own or in a group; on foot or on a mule; or from a raft, a train, or a helicopter. Regardless of what you decide, you'll find that the Grand Canyon more than lives up to its name.

FACING PAGE: **Each year the Grand Canyon attracts millions of visitors from around the world.**

THE GRAND CANYON SOUTH RIM ★★★

60 miles N of Williams; 80 miles NE of Flagstaff; 230 miles N of Phoenix; 340 miles N of Tucson

Whether you merely stand on the rim gazing in awe, spend several days hiking deep in the canyon, or ride the roller-coaster rapids of the Colorado River, a trip to the Grand Canyon is an unforgettable experience. A mile deep, 277 miles long, and up to 18 miles wide, the canyon is so large that it is absolutely overwhelming in its grandeur, truly one of the great natural wonders of the world. Clarence Dutton, a 19th-century geologist who published one of the earliest studies of Grand Canyon geology and who named many of the canyon's prominent landscape features, held the canyon in such reverence that he named land formations for Solomon, Apollo, Venus, Thor, Zoroaster, Horus, Buddha, Vishnu, Krishna, Shiva, and Confucius.

Something of this reverence infects nearly every first-time visitor. Nothing in the slowly changing topography of the approach to the Grand Canyon prepares you for what awaits. You hardly notice the elevation gain or the gradual change from windswept sagebrush scrubland to juniper woodlands to ponderosa pine forest. Suddenly, it's there. No preliminaries, no warnings. Stark, quiet, a maze of cathedrals and castles sculpted by nature.

Layers of sandstone, limestone, shale, and schist give the canyon its colors, and from dawn to dusk, the interplay of shadows and light creates an ever-changing palette of hues and textures. In this landscape layer cake of stone can be read 2 billion years of geologic history, though geologists believe it has taken only 17 million years for the erosive action of the Colorado River to carve the canyon. That the canyon has a complex geologic history is written all over the landscape, which is now an open book exposing the secrets of this region's geology.

The story of the Grand Canyon begins millions of years ago, when vast seas covered this region. Sediments carried by seawater were deposited and, over millions of more years, those sediments were turned into limestone and sandstone. According to the most widely accepted theory, the Colorado River began its work of

The Grand Canyon's bright colors come from layers of sandstone, limestone, shale, and schist.

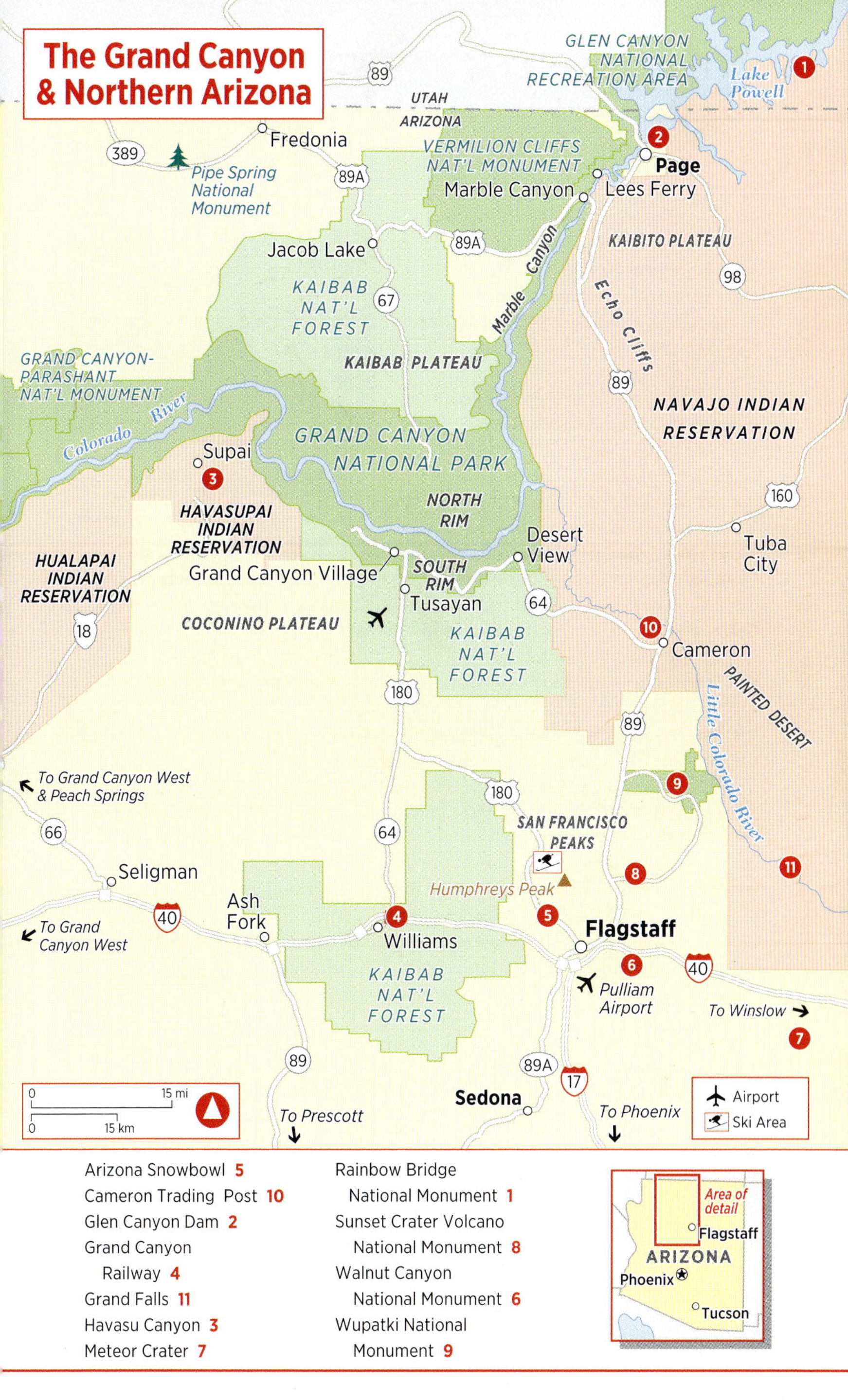
The Grand Canyon & Northern Arizona
Glen Canyon National Recreation Area
Lake Powell
Utah
Arizona
Fredonia
Pipe Spring National Monument
Vermilion Cliffs Nat'l Monument
Page
Marble Canyon
Lees Ferry
Kaibito Plateau
Jacob Lake
Kaibab Nat'l Forest
Marble Canyon
Echo Cliffs
Kaibab Plateau
Grand Canyon-Parashant Nat'l Monument
Colorado River
Navajo Indian Reservation
Grand Canyon National Park
Supai
Havasupai Indian Reservation
North Rim
Desert View
Tuba City
Hualapai Indian Reservation
Grand Canyon Village
South Rim
Tusayan
Coconino Plateau
Kaibab Nat'l Forest
Cameron
Painted Desert
Little Colorado River
To Grand Canyon West & Peach Springs
San Francisco Peaks
Seligman
Humphreys Peak
Ash Fork
Williams
Flagstaff
To Grand Canyon West
Kaibab Nat'l Forest
Pulliam Airport
To Winslow
Sedona
To Prescott
To Phoenix
Airport
Ski Area
15 mi
15 km
Arizona Snowbowl 5
Cameron Trading Post 10
Glen Canyon Dam 2
Grand Canyon Railway 4
Grand Falls 11
Havasu Canyon 3
Meteor Crater 7
Rainbow Bridge National Monument 1
Sunset Crater Volcano National Monument 8
Walnut Canyon National Monument 6
Wupatki National Monument 9
Area of detail
Flagstaff
Arizona
Phoenix
Tucson

cutting through the plateau when the ancient seabed was thrust upward to form the Kaibab Plateau. Today, 21 sedimentary layers, the oldest of which is more than a billion years old, can be seen in the canyon. Beneath all these layers, at the very bottom, is a stratum of rock so old that it has metamorphosed, under great pressure and heat, from soft shale to a much harder stone. Called Vishnu Schist, this layer is the oldest rock in the Grand Canyon, dating from 2 billion years ago.

The one-armed John Wesley Powell navigated the Colorado River in a wooden boat.

In the more recent past, the Grand Canyon has been home to several Native American cultures, including the Ancestral Puebloans (Anasazi), who are best known for their cliff dwellings in the Four Corners region. About 150 years after the Ancestral Puebloans and Coconino peoples abandoned the canyon in the 13th century, another tribe, the Cerbat, moved into the area. Today, the Hualapai and Havasupai tribes, descendants of the Cerbat people, still live in and near the Grand Canyon on the south side of the Colorado River.

In 1540, Spanish explorer Garcia Lopez de Cárdenas became the first European to set eyes on the Grand Canyon, but it would be another 329 years before the first expedition traveled through the entire canyon. John Wesley Powell, a one-armed Civil War veteran, was deemed crazy when he set off to navigate the Colorado River in wooden boats. His small band of men spent 98 days traveling 1,000 miles down the Green and Colorado rivers. So difficult was the endeavor that when some of the expedition's boats were wrecked by powerful rapids, part of the group abandoned the journey and set out on foot, never to be seen again.

How wrong the early explorers were about this supposedly Godforsaken landscape. Instead of being abandoned as a worthless wasteland, the Grand Canyon has become one of the most-visited natural wonders on the planet, a magnet for people from all over the world. By raft, by mule, on foot, and in helicopters and small planes—approximately four million people each year come to gaze into this great chasm.

However, there have been those in the recent past who regarded the canyon as mere wasted space, suitable only for filling with water. Upstream of the Grand Canyon stands Glen Canyon Dam, which forms Lake Powell, while downstream lies Lake Mead, created by Hoover Dam. The Grand Canyon might have suffered the same fate, but luckily the forces for preservation prevailed. Today, the Grand Canyon is the last major undammed stretch of the Colorado River.

Named by early Spanish explorers for the pinkish color of its muddy waters, the Colorado River once carried immense loads of silt. Because much of the Colorado's silt load now gets deposited on the bottom of Lake Powell (behind Glen Canyon Dam), the water in the Grand Canyon is much clearer (and colder) than it once was. Today, only when rainstorms and snowmelt feed the side canyons of the Grand Canyon does the river still flow murky and pink from heavy loads of eroding sandstone.

The Colorado River once carried large amounts of silt, giving it a pinkish color.

While the waters of the Colorado are now usually clearer than before, the same cannot be said for the air in the canyon. Yes, you'll find smog here, smog that has been blamed on both Las Vegas and Los Angeles to the west and a coal-fired power plant to the east, near Page. Scrubbers have been installed on the power plant's smokestacks, but there isn't much to be done about smog drifting from the west.

Far more visible and frustrating is the traffic congestion at the South Rim during the busy months from spring to fall. With more than four million people visiting the park each year, traffic during the summer months has become almost as bad at the South Rim as it is during rush hour in any major city, and finding a parking space can be the biggest challenge of a visit to Grand Canyon National Park. But don't let these inconveniences dissuade you from visiting. Despite the crowds, the Grand Canyon more than lives up to its name and is one of the most memorable sights on earth.

Essentials

GETTING THERE

During the summer, if at all possible, travel to the park by some means other than car. Alternatives include taking the Grand Canyon Railway from Williams, flying into Grand Canyon Airport and then taking a taxi, taking the Arizona Shuttle from Flagstaff, or coming to the park on a guided tour. There are plenty of scenic overlooks, hiking trails, restaurants, and lodges in the Grand Canyon Village area, and free shuttle buses operate along both Hermit Road and Desert View Drive.

BY CAR The South Rim of the Grand Canyon is 60 miles north of Williams and I-40 on Ariz. 64 and U.S. 180. Flagstaff, the nearest city of any size, is 80 miles away. From Flagstaff, it's possible to take U.S. 180 directly to the South Rim or U.S. 89 to Ariz. 64 and the east entrance to the park. This latter route is my preferred way of getting to the canyon since it sees slightly less traffic. Be sure you have plenty of gasoline in your car before setting out for the canyon; there are few service stations in this remote part of the state, and what gas stations there are charge exorbitant prices.

Long waits at the entrance gates, parking problems, and traffic congestion have long been the norm at the canyon during the popular summer months, and even during the spring and fall there can be backups at the entrance gates and visitors can have a hard time finding a parking space. However, extra ticketing lanes and additional parking lots built in recent years have somewhat alleviated the congestion at the south entrance to the park.

BY PLANE The Grand Canyon Airport is in Tusayan, 6 miles south of Grand Canyon Village. However, there are no regularly scheduled commercial flights into this airport other than day-tours from Las Vegas on **Scenic Airlines** (✆ **800/634-6801;** www.scenic.com), **Grand Canyon Airlines** (✆ **866/235-9422** or 928/638-2359; www.grandcanyonairlines.com), and **Maverick Airlines** (✆ **800/962-3869** or 702/405-4300; www.maverickairlines.com). These tours last from 6½ to 8 hours and cost between $219 and $319. The closest airport with commercial service is in Flagstaff. From there, you'll need to arrange another mode of transportation the rest of the way to the national park (see "Flagstaff," later in this chapter, for details).

BY TRAIN The **Grand Canyon Railway** operates excursion trains between Williams and the South Rim of the Grand Canyon. See "Williams," later in this chapter, for details.

For long-distance connections, **Amtrak** (✆ **800/872-7245;** www.amtrak.com) provides service to Flagstaff and Williams. From Flagstaff, it's then possible to take a bus directly to Grand Canyon Village. From Williams, you can take the Grand Canyon Railway excursion train to Grand Canyon Village. ***Note:*** The Amtrak stop in Williams is undeveloped and is on the outskirts of town. If you plan to take an Amtrak train to Williams, a shuttle from the Grand Canyon Railway Hotel will pick you up where the Amtrak train drops you off.

BY BUS Shuttle bus service between Phoenix, Flagstaff, Williams, and Grand Canyon Village is provided by **Arizona Shuttle** (✆ **877/226-8060** or 928/226-8060; www.arizonashuttle.com). Between Phoenix and Flagstaff, adult fares are $39 one-way and $78 round-trip ($35 and $70 for Internet bookings); between Flagstaff and the Grand Canyon, fares are $28 one-way and $56 round-trip ($24 and $48 for Internet bookings). Shuttles also connect Williams with Flagstaff and Grand Canyon Village, and there are shuttles between Flagstaff and Sedona as well.

The Grand Canyon Railway.

VISITOR INFORMATION

You can get advance information on the Grand Canyon by contacting **Grand Canyon National Park,** P.O. Box 129, Grand Canyon, AZ 86023 (✆ **928/638-7888;** www.nps.gov/grca).

When you arrive at the park, stop by the **Grand Canyon Visitor Center,** 4½ miles from the south entrance. Here you'll find an information desk, exhibits, a theater, and a shop selling maps, books, and videos. The center is open daily 8am to 5pm (9am–5pm in winter). Three large parking lots are adjacent to the information plaza, and these are the best places to leave your car once you reach the park. From these lots, you can easily access the park's system of free shuttle buses. Wherever you park in Grand Canyon Village, you can catch the Village Route bus to the visitor center and other parts of the village. If you park at Yaki Point, you can take the Kaibab Trail Route bus. *The Guide,* a small newspaper full of useful information about the park, is available at both South Rim park entrances. Although smaller, the **Verkamp's Visitor Center,** near El Tovar Hotel, is a much more convenient place to get park information. This latter visitor center is open daily from 8am to 7pm in summer (until 6pm other months). Displays here focus on the history of development in Grand Canyon Village.

ORIENTATION

Grand Canyon Village is built on the South Rim of the canyon and divided roughly into two sections. At the east end of the village are the Grand Canyon Visitor Center, Yavapai Lodge, Trailer Village, and Mather Campground. At the west end are El Tovar Hotel and Bright Angel, Kachina, Thunderbird, and Maswik lodges, as well as several restaurants, the train depot, and the trail head for the Bright Angel Trail.

GETTING AROUND

As I mentioned earlier, the Grand Canyon Village area can be extremely congested, especially in summer. If possible, you may want to use one of the transportation options below to avoid the park's traffic jams and parking problems. To give you an idea, in summer you can expect at least a 20- to 30-minute wait at the South Rim entrance gate just to get into the park. You can cut the waiting time here by acquiring an America the Beautiful–National Parks and Federal Recreational Lands Pass before arriving. The standard pass costs $80 and is good for 1 year. This pass is not an especially good value unless you plan to visit several other major national parks or lots of smaller parks and monuments. The senior pass and access pass are, on the other hand, exceptional bargains. With any of the three America the Beautiful passes in hand, you can use the express lane. See p. 54 for info.

BY BUS Free shuttle buses operate on three routes within the park. The **Village Route** bus circles through Grand Canyon Village throughout the day with frequent stops at the Grand Canyon Visitor Center, hotels, campgrounds, restaurants, Market Plaza (site of a general store, bank, laundry, and showers), and other facilities. The **Hermit's Rest Route** bus takes visitors to eight canyon overlooks west of Bright Angel Lodge (this bus does not operate Dec–Feb). The **Kaibab Trail Route** bus stops at the Grand Canyon Visitor Center, Mather Point, Yavapai Geology Museum, Pipe Creek Vista, the South Kaibab Trailhead, and Yaki Point. There's also a morning Hikers' Express bus to the South Kaibab Trailhead. This bus stops at Bright Angel Lodge, the Back Country Information Office, and the Grand Canyon Visitor Center. Hikers needing transportation to or from Yaki Point when the bus is not running can use a taxi (✆ **928/638-2631,** ext. 6563). Between mid-May and mid-September, the **Tusayan Route** operates between the town of Tusayan, outside the park, and Grand Canyon Village, inside the park. To use this shuttle, you must have a valid park entrance pass.

Between mid-May and mid-October, **Trans Canyon** (✆ **928/638-2820;** www.trans-canyonshuttle.com) offers shuttle-bus service between the South Rim and the North Rim. The vans leave the South Rim at 1:30pm and arrive at the North Rim at 6pm. The return trip leaves the North Rim at 7am, arriving at the South Rim at 11:30am. The fare is $80 one-way and $150 round-trip; reservations are required.

BY CAR Service stations are outside the south entrance to the park in Tusayan, at Desert View near the east entrance (no cash sales in winter), and east of the park at Cameron. Because of the long distances within the park and to towns outside the park, fill up before setting out on a drive. Gas at the canyon is very expensive.

BY TAXI Taxi service is available to and from the airport, trail heads, and other destinations (✆ **928/638-2631,** ext. 6563). The fare from the airport to Grand Canyon Village is $10 for up to two adults ($5 for each additional person).

[Fast FACTS] THE GRAND CANYON

Accessibility Check *The Guide* for park programs, services, and facilities that are partially or fully accessible. You can also get the Grand Canyon National Park *Accessibility Guide* at Grand Canyon Visitor Center, Yavapai Geology Museum, Kolb Studio, Verkamp's Visitor Center, Tusayan Museum, and Desert View Visitor Center, as well as on the park's website. Temporary accessibility parking permits are available at the park entrances and the Grand Canyon Visitor Center, Verkamp's Visitor Center, Kolb Studio, El Tovar concierge desk, and the Bright Angel, Yavapai, and Maswik transportation desks. The national park has wheelchairs available at no charge for temporary use inside the park. You can usually find one of these wheelchairs at the Grand Canyon Visitor Center. All park shuttle buses are wheelchair-accessible. Accessible tours can also be arranged by contacting any lodge transportation desk or by calling **Grand Canyon National Park Lodges** (✆ **928/638-2631**).

Banks & ATMs There's an ATM at the **Chase** bank (✆ **928/638-2437**) at Market Plaza, which is near Yavapai Lodge. The bank is open Monday through Thursday from 9am to 5pm and Friday from 9am to 6pm.

Climate The climate at the Grand Canyon is dramatically different from that of Phoenix, and between the rim and the canyon floor there's also a pronounced difference. The South Rim is at 7,000 feet and consequently gets very cold in winter. You can expect snow anytime between November and May, and winter temperatures can be below 0°F (–18°C) at night, with daytime highs in the 20s or 30s (minus single digits to single digits Celsius). Summer temperatures at the rim range from highs in the 80s (20s Celsius) to lows in the 50s (teens Celsius). The North Rim of the canyon, which is slightly higher than the South Rim and stays a bit cooler throughout the year, is open to visitors only from May through October because the access road is not kept cleared of snow in winter.

On the canyon floor, temperatures are considerably higher. In summer, the mercury can reach 120°F (49°C) with lows in the 70s (20s Celsius), while in winter, temperatures are quite pleasant with highs in the 50s (teens Celsius) and lows in the 30s (single digits Celsius). July, August, and September are the wettest months because of frequent afternoon thunderstorms. April, May, and June are the driest months, but it still might rain or even snow. Down on the canyon floor, there is much less rain year-round.

Fees The entry fee for Grand Canyon National Park is $25 per car (or $12 per person if coming in on foot or by bicycle). Your admission ticket is good for 7 days. Don't lose it, or you'll have to pay again to reenter the park.

Festivals The **Grand Canyon Music Festival** (✆ **800/997-8285** or 928/638-9215; www.grandcanyonmusicfest.org), which primarily features chamber music, takes place in late August and early September. Performances are $15 for adults and $8 for children, and are held indoors at the Shrine of the Ages in the South Rim's Grand Canyon Village.

Hospitals & Clinics The **North Country Grand Canyon Clinic** (✆ **928/638-2551**) is on Clinic Drive, off Center Road (the road that runs past the National Park Service ranger office). The clinic is open daily from 8am to 6pm (shorter hours Oct–May). It provides 24-hour emergency service as well.

Laundry A coin-operated laundry is located near Mather Campground in the Camper Services building.

Lost & Found Report lost items or turn in found items at the Grand Canyon Visitor Center; call ✆ **928/638-7798.** For items lost or found at a hotel, restaurant, or lounge, call ✆ **928/638-2631.**

Parking If you want to avoid parking headaches, use one of the three large lots by the Grand Canyon Visitor Center or the lot at Market Plaza (the general store), which is up a side road near Yavapai Lodge. From these parking areas, a paved walking trail leads to the historic section of the village in less than 1.5 miles, and most of the route is along the rim. Another option is to park at the Maswik Transportation Center parking lot, which is served by the Village Route shuttle bus.

Police In an emergency, dial ✆ **911.** Ticketing speeders is one of the main occupations of the park's police force, so obey the posted speed limits.

Post Office The post office (✆ **928/638-2512**) is at Market Plaza near Yavapai Lodge. It's open Monday through Friday from 9am to 4:30pm and Saturday from 11am to 1pm.

Road Conditions Information on road conditions in the Grand Canyon area is available by calling ✆ **888/411-7623** or 511.

Safety The most important safety tip to remember is to be careful near the edge of the canyon. Footing can be unstable and may give way. Also, be sure to keep your distance from wild animals, no matter how friendly they may appear. Avoid hiking alone if at all possible, and keep in mind that the canyon rim is more than a mile above sea level (it's harder to breathe up here). Do not leave valuables in your car or tent.

Desert View Drive

While the vast majority of visitors to the Grand Canyon enter through the south entrance, head straight for Grand Canyon Village, and proceed to get caught up in traffic jams and parking problems, you can avoid much of this congestion and have a much more enjoyable experience if you enter the park through the east entrance. To reach this entrance from Flagstaff, take U.S. 89 north to Ariz. 64, and then head west. Following this route, you'll get great views of the canyon sooner after you enter the park and have fewer parking problems. Even before

The best views of the Colorado from the South Rim are at Lipan Point.

you reach the park, you can stop and take in views of the canyon of the Little Colorado River. These viewpoints are on the Navajo Reservation, and at every stop you'll have opportunities to shop for Native American crafts and souvenirs at the numerous vendors' stalls.

Desert View Drive, the park's only scenic road open to cars year-round, extends for 25 miles between Desert View, which is just inside the park's east entrance, and Grand Canyon Village, the site of all the park's hotels and most of its other commercial establishments. Along Desert View Drive, you'll find not only good viewpoints, but also several picnic areas. Much of this drive is through forests, and canyon views are limited; but where there are viewpoints, they are among the best in the park.

Pack a Lunch

Lunch options are very limited inside Grand Canyon National Park, so if you are driving up from Flagstaff, I suggest packing a picnic lunch. Try stopping at a grocery store in Flagstaff for supplies. Otherwise, you're going to be stuck eating burgers in a cafeteria when you could be sitting on the edge of the canyon gazing out at one of the most awe-inspiring vistas on earth.

Desert View is the first stop on this scenic drive, and with its historic watchtower, general store, snack bar, service station, information center, bookstore, and big parking lot, it is better designed for handling large numbers of tourists than Grand Canyon Village. I find it a much more memorable and enjoyable experience to start a park visit here at Desert View rather than at the south entrance to the park (at Tusayan) and Grand Canyon Village.

From anywhere at Desert View, the scenery is breathtaking, but the very best perspective here is from atop the **Desert View Watchtower.** Although the watchtower looks as though it was built centuries ago, it actually dates from 1932. Architect Mary Elizabeth Jane Colter, who is responsible for much of the park's historic architecture, designed it to resemble the prehistoric towers that dot the Southwestern landscape. Built as an observation tower and rest stop for tourists, the watchtower incorporates Native American designs and art. The curio shop on the ground floor is a replica of a kiva (sacred ceremonial chamber) and has lots of interesting souvenirs, regional crafts, and books. The tower's second floor features work by Hopi artist Fred Kabotie. Covering the walls are pictographs incorporating traditional designs. On the walls and ceiling of the upper two floors are more

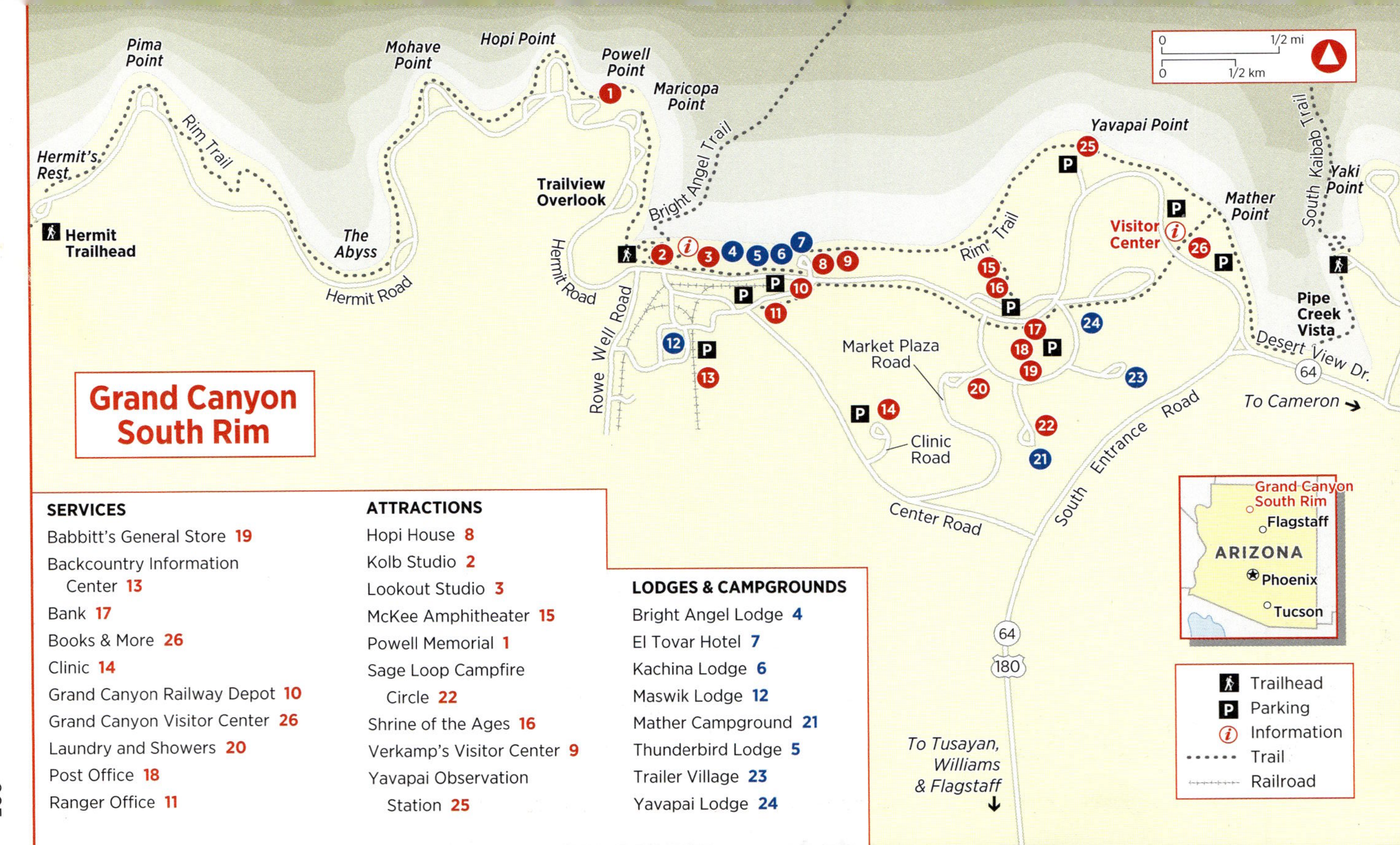
Grand Canyon South Rim
Pima Point
Mohave Point
Hopi Point
Powell Point
Maricopa Point
Hermit's Rest
Hermit Trailhead
Rim Trail
The Abyss
Hermit Road
Trailview Overlook
Bright Angel Trail
Rowe Well Road
Market Plaza Road
Clinic Road
Center Road
Rim Trail
Yavapai Point
Visitor Center
Mather Point
South Kaibab Trail
Yaki Point
Pipe Creek Vista
Desert View Dr.
64
To Cameron
South Entrance Road
64
180
To Tusayan, Williams & Flagstaff
0
1/2 mi
0
1/2 km
Grand Canyon South Rim
Flagstaff
ARIZONA
Phoenix
Tucson
Trailhead
Parking
Information
Trail
Railroad
SERVICES
Babbitt's General Store 19
Backcountry Information Center 13
Bank 17
Books & More 26
Clinic 14
Grand Canyon Railway Depot 10
Grand Canyon Visitor Center 26
Laundry and Showers 20
Post Office 18
Ranger Office 11
ATTRACTIONS
Hopi House 8
Kolb Studio 2
Lookout Studio 3
McKee Amphitheater 15
Powell Memorial 1
Sage Loop Campfire Circle 22
Shrine of the Ages 16
Verkamp's Visitor Center 9
Yavapai Observation Station 25
LODGES & CAMPGROUNDS
Bright Angel Lodge 4
El Tovar Hotel 7
Kachina Lodge 6
Maswik Lodge 12
Mather Campground 21
Thunderbird Lodge 5
Trailer Village 23
Yavapai Lodge 24

traditional images by artist Fred Geary, this time reproductions of petroglyphs from throughout the Southwest. From the roof, which at 7,522 feet above sea level is the highest point on the South Rim, it's possible to see the Colorado River, the Painted Desert to the northeast, the San Francisco Peaks to the south, and Marble Canyon to the north. Several black-mirror "reflectoscopes" provide interesting darkened views of some of the most spectacular sections of the canyon.

At **Navajo Point,** the next stop along the rim, the Colorado River and Escalante Butte are both visible, and there's a good view of the Desert View Watchtower. However, I suggest heading straight to **Lipan Point ★★**, where you get the South Rim's best views of the Colorado River. You can actually see several stretches of the river, including a couple of major rapids. From here you can also view the Grand Canyon supergroup: several strata of rock tilted at an angle to the other layers of rock in the canyon. The supergroup's angle indicates there was a period of mountain building before the layers of sandstone, limestone, and shale were deposited in this region. The red, white, and black rocks of the supergroup are composed of sedimentary rock and layers of lava. One of the park's best-kept secrets, a little-known though very rugged trail, begins here at Lipan Point (see "Hiking the Canyon," below, for details).

The **Tusayan Museum** (daily 9am–5pm) is the next stop along Desert View Drive. This small museum is dedicated to the Hopi tribe and the Ancestral Puebloan people who inhabited the region 800 years ago. Outside the museum, there are the ruins of an Ancestral Puebloan village, and inside the museum, there are artfully displayed exhibits on various aspects of life in the village. A short self-guided trail leads through the ruins. Free guided tours are available.

Next along the drive is **Moran Point,** from which you can see a layer of red shale in the canyon walls. This point is named for 19th-century landscape painter Thomas Moran, who is known for his paintings of the Grand Canyon.

The next stop, **Grandview Point,** affords a view of Horseshoe Mesa, another interesting feature of the canyon landscape. The mesa was the site of the Last Chance Copper Mine in the early 1890s. Later that same decade, the Grandview Hotel was built and served canyon visitors until its close in 1908. The steep, unmaintained Grandview Trail leads down to Horseshoe Mesa from here. This trail makes a good less-traveled alternative to the South Kaibab Trail, although it is somewhat steeper.

The last stop along Desert View Drive is **Yaki Point,** which is no longer open to private vehicles. The park service would prefer it if you parked your car in Grand Canyon Village and took the Kaibab Trail Route shuttle bus from the Grand Canyon Visitor Center to Yaki Point. The reality is that people passing by in cars want to see what this viewpoint is all about and now park their cars alongside the main road and

Wotan's Throne is one of the canyon's most recognizable points.

Return of the Condor

With wingspans approaching 10 feet and weighing as much as 25 pounds, California condors are the largest flying land birds in North America (both mute and trumpeter swans are heavier). In the 1980s, there were only 22 California condors left in the wild, and these were captured so that a captive-breeding program could be instituted in hopes of bringing these birds back from the brink of extinction.

Between 1924 and 1996, if you had seen a California condor in Arizona, you would likely have been in a zoo. There were none of these giant birds living free in a state where once they had been plentiful. That all changed in 1996 when six captive-raised condors were released atop the Vermilion Cliffs (north of Grand Canyon National Park). Since then between 6 and 10 birds have been released annually, and there are now more than 50 condors flying free over northern Arizona. In 2003, for the first time in more than a century, a pair of condors hatched and raised a chick, and since then, several more condor pairs have successfully raised offspring.

Condors are curious birds, and they are often attracted to human activity. Consequently, they are often seen in or near Grand Canyon Village on the South Rim of the canyon. Captive-raised condors are easily recognized by the large numbers affixed to their wings. If you see a condor without a wing number, it is one of the handful of birds that have hatched in the wild in recent years. One of the best places to spot condors is on the way to the North Rim on House Rock Valley Road, north of U.S. 98A between Lees Ferry and Jacob Lake. A few miles up this road, you will find interpretive plaques and a viewpoint from which you can see the condor release site high atop the cliffs to the east. For more information on the condor-release program, visit the **Peregrine Fund** website (www.peregrinefund.org), which is the organization that administers the program.

walk up the Yaki Point access road. The spectacular view from here encompasses a wide section of the central canyon. The large, flat-topped butte to the northeast is Wotan's Throne, one of the canyon's most readily recognizable features. Yaki Point is the site of the trail head for the South Kaibab Trail and consequently is frequented by hikers headed down to Phantom Ranch at the bottom of the canyon. The South Kaibab Trail is the preferred downhill hiking route to Phantom Ranch and is a more scenic route than the Bright Angel Trail. If you're planning a day hike into the canyon, this should be your number-one choice. Be sure to bring plenty of water.

Grand Canyon Village & Vicinity

Grand Canyon Village is the first stop for the vast majority of the nearly four million people who visit the Grand Canyon every year (though I recommend coming in from the east entrance and avoiding the crowds). Consequently, it is the most crowded area in the park, but it also has the most overlooks and visitor services. Its many historic buildings add to the popularity of the village, which, if it weren't so crowded all the time, would have a pleasant atmosphere. For visitors who have entered the park through the south entrance, that unforgettable initial gasp-inducing glimpse of the canyon is usually at **Mather Point,** which is down a short paved path from the Grand Canyon Visitor Center. The visitor center, with its large parking lots, is also a good place to park your car. From here you can get around the South Rim by shuttle bus.

Continuing west toward the village proper, you next come to **Yavapai Point,** which has the best view from anywhere in the vicinity of Grand Canyon Village. If you can bring yourself to drive past Mather Point and delay your initial glimpse of the canyon for a few minutes longer, Yavapai Point actually makes a better first view of the canyon (although parking spaces here are limited). From here you can see the Bright Angel Trail, Indian Gardens, Phantom Ranch, the Colorado River, and even the suspension bridge that hikers and mule riders use to cross the river to Phantom Ranch. Between Hoover Dam (downstream) and the Navajo Bridge upstream near Lees Ferry, a distance of 340 miles, this is the only bridge across the Colorado. Here you'll also find the historic **Yavapai Geology Museum,** which houses a small geology museum and has big walls of glass to take in the extraordinary vistas. The geology displays here are the park's best introduction to the forces that created the Grand Canyon and should not be missed. The museum is open daily from 8am to 8pm in summer (shorter hours other months). Yavapai Point is a particularly good spot from which to take sunrise and sunset photos. If you want to do some walking, the paved Grand Canyon Greenway extends 3.5 miles east to the South Kaibab Trailhead and 3 miles west, passing through Grand Canyon Village along the way.

FROM TOP: **Yavapai Observation Station; Kolb Studio, a one-time photo studio, is now a bookstore and houses exhibits.**

Continuing west from Yavapai Point, you'll come to a parking lot at park headquarters and a side road that leads to parking at the Market Plaza. Grand Canyon Village proper is west of these parking areas, and a paved pathway that leads along the rim here provides lots of good (though crowded) spots for taking pictures. The village is the site of such historic buildings as **El Tovar Hotel** and **Bright Angel Lodge,** both of which are worth brief visits to take in the lodge ambience of their lobbies. Inside Bright Angel Lodge you'll find the **Bright Angel History Room,** which has displays on Mary Elizabeth Jane Colter and the Harvey Girls. Be sure to check out this room's fireplace, which is designed with all the same geologic layers that appear in the canyon. Adjacent to El Tovar is the **Hopi House Gift Store and Art Gallery,** a historic souvenir-and-curio shop. Built in 1905 to resemble a Hopi pueblo and to serve as a place for Hopi artisans to work and sell their crafts, this was the first shop inside the park. Today, it's full of Hopi and Navajo arts and crafts, including expensive kachina dolls, rugs, jewelry, and pottery. This shop is open daily; hours vary seasonally.

To the west of Bright Angel Lodge, two buildings cling precariously to the rim of the canyon. These are the Kolb and Lookout studios, both of which are listed on the National Register of Historic Places. **Kolb Studio** is named for Ellsworth and Emory Kolb, two brothers who set up a photographic studio on the rim of the Grand Canyon in 1904. The construction of this studio generated one of the Grand Canyon's first controversies—over whether buildings should be allowed on the canyon rim. Because the Kolbs had friends in high places, their sprawling studio and movie theater remained. Emory Kolb lived here until his death in 1976, by which time the studio had been listed as a historic building. It now serves as a bookstore, while the auditorium houses special exhibits. **Lookout Studio,** built in 1914 from a design by Mary Elizabeth Jane Colter, was the Fred Harvey Company's answer to the Kolb brothers' studio and incorporates architectural styles of the Hopi and the Ancestral Puebloans. The use of native limestone and an uneven roofline allow the studio to blend in with the canyon walls and give it the look of an old ruin. It now houses a souvenir store and two lookout points. Both the Kolb and Lookout studios are open daily; hours vary seasonally.

Hermit Road

Hermit Road leads 8 miles west from Grand Canyon Village to Hermit's Rest, and mile for mile, it has the greatest concentration of breathtaking viewpoints in the park. Because it is closed to private vehicles March through November, it is also one of the most pleasant places to do a little canyon viewing or easy hiking during the busiest times of year: no traffic jams, no parking problems, and plenty of free shuttle buses operating along the route. Westbound buses stop at eight overlooks (Trailview, Maricopa Point, Powell Point, Hopi Point, Mohave Point, the Abyss, Pima Point, and Hermit's Rest); eastbound buses stop at only Pima, Mohave, and Powell points. December through February, you can drive your own vehicle along this road, but keep in mind that winters usually mean a lot of snow, and the road can sometimes be closed due to hazardous driving conditions.

Because you probably won't want to stop at every viewpoint along this route, here are some tips to help you get the most out of an excursion along Hermit Road. First of all, keep in mind that the earlier you catch a shuttle bus, the more likely you are to avoid the crowds (buses start 1 hr. before sunrise, so photographers can get good shots of the canyon in dawn light). Second, remember that the closer you are to Grand Canyon Village, the larger the crowds will be. So, I recommend heading out early and getting a couple of miles between you and the village before getting off the shuttle bus.

The first two stops are **Trailview Overlook** and **Maricopa Point,** both on the paved section of the Rim Trail and within 1½ miles of the village, and thus usually pretty crowded. If you just want to do a short, easy walk on pavement, get out at Maricopa Point and walk back to the village. From either overlook, you have a view of the Bright Angel Trail winding down into the canyon from Grand Canyon Village. The trail, which leads to the bottom of the canyon, crosses the Tonto Plateau about 3,000 feet below the rim. This plateau is the site of Indian

The Abyss is named for its 3,000-foot drop.

Garden, where there's a campground in a grove of cottonwood trees. Because the views from these two overlooks are not significantly different from those in the village, I suggest skipping these stops if you've already spent time gazing into the canyon from the village.

Powell Point, the third stop, is the site of a memorial to John Wesley Powell, who, in 1869 with a party of nine men, became the first person to navigate the Colorado River through the Grand Canyon. Visible at Powell Point are the remains of the Orphan Mine, a copper mine that began operation in 1893. The mine went out of business because transporting the copper to a city where it could be sold was too expensive. Uranium was discovered here in 1951, but in 1969 the mine was shut down, and in 1987 the land became part of Grand Canyon National Park. Again, I recommend continuing on to the more spectacular vistas that lie ahead.

The next stop is **Hopi Point,** which is one of the three best stops along this route. From here you can see a long section of the Colorado River far below you. Because of the great distance, the river seems to be a tiny, quiet stream, but in reality the section you see is more than 100 yards wide and races through Granite Rapids. Because Hopi Point juts into the canyon, it is one of the best spots in the park for taking sunrise and sunset photos (remember, shuttle buses operate from 1 hr. before sunrise to 1 hr. after sunset).

The view is even more spectacular at the next stop, **Mohave Point.** Here you can see the river in two directions. Three rapids are visible from this overlook, and on a quiet day, you can sometimes even hear Hermit Rapids. As with almost all rapids in the canyon, Hermit Rapids are at the mouth of a side canyon where boulders loosened by storms and carried by flooded streams are deposited in the Colorado River. Don't miss this stop; it's got the best view on Hermit Road.

Next you come to the **Abyss,** the appropriately named 3,000-foot drop created by the Great Mojave Wall. This vertiginous view is one of the most

Leave the Driving to Them

Now, I'm not a big fan of guided tours, but sometimes they just make a lot of sense. The Grand Canyon is one of those places, especially if you are usually the designated driver. Why should you have to keep your eyes on the road when there's all that gorgeous scenery right outside the window? Why not let someone else do the driving?

If you plan on making your visit to the Grand Canyon a day trip from Flagstaff rather than an overnight stay at the park, consider taking a tour with **American Dream Tours** (✆ **888/203-1212** or 928/527-3369; www.americandreamtours.com). Not only will you get to enjoy the scenery more, but knowledgeable guides will also fill you with fascinating information about the canyon. Tours are $98 for adults and $69 for children 10 and under (lower rates may be available on their website).

The view from Hermit's Rest, which is on the National Register of Historic Places.

awe-inspiring in the park. The walls of the Abyss are red sandstone that's more resistant to erosion than the softer shale in the layer below. Other layers of erosion-resistant sandstone have formed the free-standing pillars that are visible from here. The largest of these pillars is called the Monument. If you're looking for a good hike along this road, get out here and walk westward to either Pima Point (3 miles away) or Hermit's Rest (4 miles away).

The **Pima Point** overlook, because it is set back from the road, is another good place to get off the bus. From here, the Greenway Trail leads through the forest near the canyon rim, providing good views undisturbed by traffic on Hermit Road. From this overlook, it's also possible to see the remains of Hermit Camp on the Tonto Plateau. Built by the Santa Fe Railroad, Hermit Camp was a popular tourist destination between 1911 and 1930 and provided cabins and tents.

The final stop on Hermit Road is at **Hermit's Rest,** which was named for Louis Boucher, a prospector who came to the canyon in the 1890s and was known as the Hermit. The log-and-stone Hermit's Rest building, designed by Mary Elizabeth Jane Colter and built in 1914, is on the National Register of Historic Places and is one of the most fascinating structures in the park. With its snack bar, it makes a great place to linger while you soak up a bit of park history. The steep Hermit Trail, which leads down into the canyon, begins just past Hermit's Rest.

Hiking the Canyon

No visit to the canyon is complete without journeying below the rim on one of the park's hiking trails. While the views don't necessarily get any better than they are from the top, they do change considerably. Gazing up at all those thousands of feet of vertical rock walls provides a very different perspective from that atop the rim. Should you venture far below the rim, you also stand a chance of seeing fossils, old mines, petroglyphs, wildflowers, and wildlife. However, with around four million people visiting the Grand Canyon annually, you can forget about finding any solitude on the park's main hiking trails.

That said, there is no better way to see the canyon than on foot (my apologies to the mules), and a hike down into the canyon will likely be the highlight of your visit. You can get away from *most* of the crowds simply by heading down the Bright Angel or South Kaibab trail for 2 to 3 miles. Keep in mind, though, that these are the two busiest trails below the canyon rim and can see hundreds of hikers per day. If you want to see fewer other hikers and are in good shape, consider heading down the Grandview Trail or the Hermit Trail instead. If you're just looking for an easy walk that doesn't involve hiking back up out of the canyon, the Rim Trail is for you.

The Grand Canyon offers some of the most rugged and strenuous hiking anywhere in the United States, and for this reason anyone attempting even a short walk should be well prepared. Each year, injuries and fatalities are suffered by day hikers who set out without sturdy footgear or without food and adequate amounts of water. Even a 30-minute hike in summer can dehydrate you, and a long hike in the heat can necessitate drinking more than a gallon of water. So, carry and drink at least 2 quarts of water if you go for a day hike during the summer. Don't attempt to hike from the rim to the Colorado River and back in a day. Although there are very fit individuals who have managed the grueling hike to the bottom and back in a day, there are also plenty who have tried and died. Finally, remember that mules have the right of way.

DAY HIKES

Hikers tend to gravitate to loop trails, but here on the South Rim, you'll find no such trails. Thus, day hikers must reconcile themselves to out-and-back hikes. Still, the vastly different scenery in every direction makes out-and-back hikes here as interesting as any loop trail could be. The only problem is that the majority of the out-and-back trails are the reverse of what you'll find at most other places. Instead of starting out by slogging up a steep mountain, you let gravity assist you in hiking down into the canyon. With little negative reinforcement and few natural turnaround destinations, it is easy to hike so far that the return trip back up the trail becomes an arduous death march. Know your limits and turn around before you become tired. On the canyon rim, the only hiking trail is the Rim Trail/Greenway Trail, while the Bright Angel, South Kaibab, Grandview, and Hermit trails all head down into the canyon.

For an easy, flat hike, your main option is the **Rim Trail,** which stretches for 13 miles from the South Kaibab Trailhead east of Grand Canyon Village to Hermit's Rest, 8 miles west of the village. Around 8½ miles of this trail are paved, and the portion that passes through Grand Canyon Village is always the most crowded stretch of trail in the park. To the west of the village, after the pavement ends, the Rim Trail leads another 5.8 miles out to Hermit's Rest. For most of this distance, the trail follows Hermit Road, which means you'll have to deal with traffic noise (although only from shuttle buses for most of the year). The last 2.8 miles of the Rim Trail is now part of the paved Greenway Trail. To avoid the crowds and get the most enjoyment out of a hike along the Rim Trail, I like to head out as early in the morning as possible and get off at the Abyss shuttle stop. From here it's a 4-mile hike to Hermit's Rest; for more than half of this distance, the

Avoid the crowds with a hike of Shoshone Point.

trail isn't as close to the road as it is at the Grand Canyon Village e[illegible] Plus, Hermit's Rest makes a great place to rest, and from here you [illegible] shuttle bus back to the village. Alternatively, you could start hiking [illegible] Canyon Village (it's right around 8 miles from the west end of the vill[illegible] mit's Rest) or any of the seven shuttle-bus stops en route, or take the [illegible] the way to Hermit's Rest and then hike back.

"Now this is more like I pictured it," said a woman who walked up to [illegible] edge of the canyon just as I was leaving **Shoshone Point** on my first visit to this little known canyon overlook. At the time, she and her companion and I were the only people there despite huge crowds elsewhere in the park. If you, too, have dreamed of a Grand Canyon without the crowds of gawkers at all the scenic viewpoints, then you're a candidate for a hike to this hidden viewpoint. The route to this secluded overlook (actually a reservable group picnic area) is along a flat dirt access road that makes this a good bet for a family walk (just keep a tight rein on the kids once you get to the canyon rim since there are no fences here). There are no signs for Shoshone Point, so you'll just have to watch for the small dirt parking area and gate on the north side of the road at milepost 246. You can't drive in without a permit (permits are only for groups and cost $225), and if the gate is open, it usually means that a group is using the site. If this is the case, you'll probably want to skip this hike. You'll find the parking area 19 miles west of the Desert View entrance to the park and 2⅓ miles east of the Grand Canyon Village end of Desert View Drive.

The **Bright Angel Trail,** which starts just west of Bright Angel Lodge in Grand Canyon Village, is the most popular trail into the canyon because it starts right where the greatest number of park visitors tend to congregate (near the ice-cream parlor and the hotels). It is also the route traditionally used by mule riders headed down into the canyon. Bear in mind that this trail follows a narrow side canyon for several miles and thus has somewhat limited views. For these reasons, this trail is worth avoiding. On the other hand, it's the only maintained trail into the canyon that has potable water, and there are four destinations along the trail that make good turnaround points. Both 1½ Mile Resthouse (1,131 ft. below the rim) and 3 Mile Resthouse (2,112 ft. below the rim) have water (except in winter, when the water is turned off). Keep in mind that these rest houses take their names from their distance from the rim; if you hike to 3 Mile Resthouse, you still have a 3-mile hike back up. Destinations for longer day hikes include Indian Garden (9 miles round-trip) and Plateau Point (12 miles round-trip), which are both slightly more than 3,000 feet below the rim. There is year-round water at Indian Garden.

The **South Kaibab Trail ★★★** begins near Yaki Point east of Grand Canyon Village and is the preferred route down to Phantom Ranch. This trail also offers the best views of any of the trails into the canyon, so should you have time for only 1 day hike, make it the South Kaibab Trail. From the trail head, it's 3 miles round-trip to Cedar Ridge and 6 miles round-trip to Skeleton Point. The hike is very strenuous, and no water is available along the trail.

If you're looking to escape the crowds and are an experienced mountain or desert hiker with good, sturdy boots, consider the unmaintained **Hermit Trail,** which begins at Hermit's Rest, 8 miles west of Grand Canyon Village at the end of Hermit Road. It's a 5-mile round-trip hike to Santa Maria Spring on a trail that loses almost all of its elevation (1,600–1,700 ft.) in the first 1.5 miles. Beyond Santa Maria Spring, the Hermit Trail descends to the Colorado River, but it is a 17-mile hike, one-way, from the trail head. Alternatively, you can do a 7-mile round-trip hike

to Dripping Springs. Water from these two springs must be treated with a water filter, iodine, or purification tablets, or by boiling for at least 10 minutes, so you're better off just carrying sufficient water for your hike. March through November, Hermit Road is closed to private vehicles, so during these months, you'll need to take the free shuttle bus out to the trail head. If you take the first bus of the day, you'll likely have the trail almost all to yourself.

FROM TOP: The South Kaibab Trail offers the best views of any of the trails into the canyon; the Tanner Trail is so secret that it's not listed on the National Park Service map.

The **Grandview Trail,** which begins at Grandview Point 12 miles east of Grand Canyon Village, is another steep and unmaintained trail that's a good choice for physically fit hikers. A strenuous 6-mile round-trip hike leads down to Horseshoe Mesa, 2,600 feet below the trail head. No water is available, so carry at least 2 quarts. Just to give you an idea of how steep this trail is, you'll lose more than 2,000 feet of elevation in the first .8 mile down to Coconino Saddle.

There's one other trail I have to tell you about, but you have to promise not to tell anyone else. This trail is so secret that the National Park Service doesn't mark it on the maps it hands out to park visitors. It's called the **Tanner Trail ★**, and it starts just downhill from the beginning of the parking lot at Lipan Point near the east end of Desert View Drive. The Tanner Trail started out as a trail used by horse thieves to move stolen horses between Utah and Arizona. This is one of the shortest, steepest, and most challenging trails down into the canyon, and it is probably for good reason that the park service doesn't want you to know about it. They don't want to have to rescue you when you collapse from dehydration hiking back up.

Now that you are suitably warned, let me tell you about the single best day-hiking experience I've ever had in the Grand Canyon. The Tanner Trail is so unknown that I hiked the upper section of it twice in 2 days and saw only one other hiker. He was sitting at the top of the trail dripping with sweat after having hiked all the way to the Colorado River and back (this is an activity that the park service works hard to discourage people from attempting). Therein lies the beauty of this trail—you can have it all to yourself even when the park is packed with tourists! Of course, there is a cost. This trail is not for everyone. You must be in excellent shape, with good knees and strong quadriceps. Don't even think of setting foot on this trail unless you are wearing very sturdy boots with excellent ankle support. Take lots of water and drink it. Finally, remember that it will take you considerably longer to hike back up than it took you to hike down. So how far can you hike on this trail? Well, that's up to you. It's 3 miles and a 1,700-foot elevation drop to Escalante Butte, from which you get a good view of Marble Canyon, Hance Rapids, and the bottom of the canyon.

BACKPACKING

Backpacking the Grand Canyon is an unforgettable experience. Although most people are content to simply hike down to Phantom Ranch and back, there are many miles of trails deep in the canyon. Keep in mind, however, that to backpack the canyon, you'll need to do a lot of planning. A **Backcountry Use Permit** is required of all hikers planning to overnight in the canyon, unless you'll be staying at Phantom Ranch in one of the cabins or a dormitory.

Because a limited number of hikers are allowed into the canyon on any given day, it's important to make permit requests as soon as it is possible to do so. Permit requests are taken in person, by mail, by fax (but not by phone), and online. Contact the **Backcountry Information Center,** Grand Canyon National Park, P.O. Box 129, Grand Canyon, AZ 86023 (✆ **928/638-7875** Mon–Fri 1–5pm for information; fax 928/638-2125; www.nps.gov/grca). The office begins accepting written permit requests on the first of every month for the following 5 months. In-person, verbal permit requests can be made only for the following 4 months. Holiday periods are the most popular—if you want to hike over the Labor Day weekend, be sure you make your reservation on May 1. If you show up without a hiking permit, go to the Backcountry Information Center (daily 8am–noon and 1–5pm), adjacent to Maswik Lodge, and put your name on the waiting list. When applying for a permit, you must specify your exact itinerary, and once in the canyon, you must stick to this itinerary. Backpacking fees include a nonrefundable $10 backcountry permit fee and a $5 per-person per-night backcountry camping fee. Keep in mind that you'll still have to pay the park entry fee when you arrive at the Grand Canyon.

There are **campgrounds** at Indian Garden, Bright Angel Campground (near Phantom Ranch), and Cottonwood, but hikers are limited to 2 nights per trip at each of these campgrounds (except Nov 15–Feb 28, when 4 nights are allowed at each campground). Other nights can be spent camping at undesignated sites in certain regions of the park.

The *Grand Canyon Trip Planner* contains information to help you plan your itinerary. It's available through the Backcountry Information Center (see contact information, above). Maps are available through the **Grand Canyon Association,** P.O. Box 399, Grand Canyon, AZ 86023 (✆ **800/858-2808** or 928/638-2481; www.grandcanyon.org), and at bookstores and gift shops within the national park, including Grand Canyon Visitor Center, Verkamp's Visitor Center, Kolb Studio, Desert View Information Center, Yavapai Observation Station, Tusayan Museum, and, on the North Rim, Grand Canyon Lodge.

The best times of year to backpack are spring and fall. In summer, temperatures at the bottom of the canyon are frequently above 100°F (38°C), while in winter, ice and snow at higher elevations make footing on trails precarious (crampons are recommended). Plan to carry at least 2 quarts, and preferably 1 gallon, of water whenever backpacking in the canyon.

The Grand Canyon is an unforgiving landscape and, as such, many people might want a professional guide while backpacking through this rugged corner of the Southwest. To arrange a guided backpacking trip into the canyon, contact **Discovery Treks,** 28248 N. Tatum Blvd., Ste. B1-414, Cave Creek, AZ 85331 (✆ **888/256-8731** or 480/247-9266; www.discoverytreks.com), which offers 2- to 5-day all-inclusive hikes into the canyon with rates starting at $695 per person.

Other Ways of Seeing the Canyon

BUS TOURS

If you'd rather leave the driving to someone else and enjoy more of the scenery, opt for a bus or van tour of one or more sections of the park. **Xanterra South Rim** (✆ **888/297-2757,** 303/297-2757, or, for same-day reservations, 928/638-2631; www.grandcanyonlodges.com) offers several tours within the park. These can be booked by calling or stopping at one of the transportation desks, which are at Bright Angel, Maswik, and Yavapai lodges (see "Where to Stay," below). Prices range from around $20 for a 1½-hour sunrise or sunset tour to around $57 for a combination of Desert View tour with any of the company's other three tours—Hermit's Rest, sunrise, and sunset.

TRAIL RIDES BY MULE & HORSE ★

Mule rides into the canyon have been popular since the beginning of the 20th century, when the Bright Angel Trail was a toll road. After having a look at the steep drop-offs and narrow path of the Bright Angel Trail, you might decide this isn't exactly the place to trust your life to a mule. Never fear: Wranglers will be quick to reassure you they haven't lost a rider yet. There are mule rides along the rim and down to Phantom Ranch at the bottom of the canyon. The 3-hour rides meander through the forest and eventually arrive at the Abyss, a spectacular viewpoint along Hermit Road. Those who want to spend a night down in the canyon can choose an overnight trip to Phantom Ranch, where cabins and dormitories are available at the only lodge actually in the canyon. From November to March, a 2-night trip to Phantom Ranch is offered; other times of year, you'll ride down one day and back up the next. Mule trips range in price from $119 for the 3-hour ride to $482 for an overnight ride to $674 for the 2-night ride. Couples get discounts on overnight rides.

Mules to the bottom of the canyon book at least 6 months in advance.

Riders must weigh less than 200 pounds fully dressed; stand at least 4 feet, 7 inches tall; and speak and understand English fluently. Pregnant women are not allowed on mule trips.

Because these trail rides are very popular (especially in summer), they often book up 6 months or more in advance (reservations are taken up to 13 months in advance). For more information or to make a reservation, contact **Xanterra Parks & Resorts** (✆ **888/297-2757** or 303/297-2757; www.grandcanyonlodges.com). If, at the last minute (5 days or fewer from the day you want to ride), you decide you want to go on a mule trip, contact **Xanterra South Rim** at its Arizona phone number (✆ **928/638-2631**) for the remote possibility that there may be space available. If you arrive at the canyon without a reservation and decide that you'd like to go on a mule ride, stop by the Bright Angel Transportation Desk to get your name put on the next day's waiting list.

If you'd rather spend less time in the saddle and don't mind not seeing the canyon from the back of your horse or mule, head out of the park to **Apache Stables** (✆ **928/638-2891;** www.apachestables.com), which is located a mile north of Tusayan on Moqui Drive. A 1-hour ride costs $49 and a 2-hour ride is $89. There are also wagon rides ($26) and campfire rides ($59; be sure to bring something to cook over the fire). The stables are closed in winter.

THE GRAND CANYON RAILWAY ★★

In the early 20th century, most visitors to the Grand Canyon arrived by train, and it's still possible to travel to the canyon along the steel rails. The **Grand Canyon Railway** (✆ **800/843-8724** or 303/843-8724; www.thetrain.com), which runs from Williams to Grand Canyon Village, uses both diesel engines and, occasionally, early-20th-century steam engines that now run on waste vegetable oil. Trains depart from the Williams Depot, which is housed in the historic 1908 Fray Marcos Hotel and also contains a railroad museum, gift shop, and cafe. (Grand Canyon Railway also operates the adjacent Grand Canyon Railway Hotel.) At Grand Canyon Village, the trains use the 1910 log railway terminal in front of El Tovar Hotel.

Passengers have the choice of four classes of service: coach, first class, observation dome (upstairs in the dome car), and luxury parlor class. Actors posing as cowboys provide entertainment, including musical performances, aboard the train. The round-trip takes 8 hours, including a 3¼- to 3¾-hour layover at the canyon. Fares range from $70 to $190 for adults, and $40 to $110 for children 2 to 12 (these rates do not include taxes or the park entry fee).

Not only is this a fun trip that provides great scenery and a trip back in time, but taking the train also allows you to avoid the traffic congestion and parking problems in Grand Canyon Village. When booking your train trip, you can also book a bus tour in the park, which will help you see more than you would on foot. The railway offers room/train packages as well.

In November, December, and January, the railway's Polar Express provides service to the North Pole and a visit from Santa.

A BIRD'S-EYE VIEW

Despite controversies over noise and safety (there have been a few crashes over the years), airplane and helicopter flights over the Grand Canyon remain one of the most popular ways to see this natural wonder. Personally, I would rather enjoy the canyon on foot or from a saddle. However, the volume of flights over the canyon each day would indicate that quite a few people don't share my opinion. If you want to join the crowds buzzing above the canyon, you'll find several companies operating out of Grand Canyon Airport in Tusayan. Air tours last anywhere from 30 minutes to about 2 hours.

Helicopter rides are one of the most popular ways to see the Grand Canyon.

Companies offering tours by small plane include **Air Grand Canyon** (✆ **800/247-4726** or 928/638-2686; www.airgrandcanyon.com) and **Grand Canyon Airlines** (✆ **866/235-9422** or 928/638-2359; www.grandcanyonairlines.com). This latter company has been offering air tours since 1927 and is the oldest scenic airline at the canyon. Fifty-minute flights cost $114 to $126 for adults and $94 to $106 for children.

Helicopter tours are available from **Maverick Helicopters** (✆ **888/261-4414** or 928/638-2622; www.airstar.com), **Grand Canyon Helicopters** (✆ **800/541-4537** or 928/638-2764; www.grandcanyonhelicoptersaz.com), and **Papillon Grand Canyon Helicopters** (✆ **888/635-7272** or 928/638-2419; www.papillon.com). Rates range from $139 to $185 for a 25- to 30-minute flight and from $189 to $235 for a 45- to 55-minute flight. Children sometimes receive a discount (usually around $20).

INTERPRETIVE PROGRAMS

Numerous interpretive programs are scheduled throughout the year at various South Rim locations. Walks led by rangers explore different aspects of the canyon; rangers give geology talks, offer lectures on the cultural and natural resources of the canyon, lead nature hikes, organize trips to fossil beds, and hold stargazing gatherings. At Tusayan Ruin, guided tours are offered. Many programs are held at Mather Point Amphitheater and the Shrine of the Ages. Consult your copy of *The Guide* for information on times and meeting points.

THE GRAND CANYON FIELD INSTITUTE

If you're the active type or would like to turn your visit to the Grand Canyon into more of an educational experience, you may want to consider doing a trip with the **Grand Canyon Field Institute** (✆ **866/471-4435** or 928/638-2485; www.grandcanyon.org/fieldinstitute). Cosponsored by Grand Canyon National Park and the Grand Canyon Association, the Field Institute schedules a wide variety of guided educational trips, such as challenging backpacking trips through the canyon (some for women only) and programs lasting anywhere from 1 day to more than a week. Subjects covered include wilderness studies, geology, natural history, human history, photography, and art.

JEEP TOURS

If you'd like to explore parts of Grand Canyon National Park that most visitors never see, contact **Grand Canyon Jeep Tours & Safaris** (✆ **800/320-5337** or 928/638-5337; www.grandcanyonjeeptours.com), which offers three different tours that visit the park as well as the adjacent Kaibab National Forest. One tour stops at a lookout tower that affords an elevated view of the canyon, while another visits an Indian ruin and site of petroglyphs and cave paintings. Prices range from $45 to $104 for adults and $35 to $84 for children 11 and under.

Rafting trips can last from a half-day to 2 weeks.

RAFTING THE COLORADO RIVER ★★★

Ever since John Wesley Powell ignored everyone who knew better and proved that it was possible to travel by boat down the tumultuous Colorado, running the big river has become a passion and an obsession with adventurers. Today, rafting down the Colorado River as it roars and tumbles through the mile-deep gorge of the Grand Canyon is the adventure of a lifetime, and anyone from grade-schoolers to grandmothers can join the elite group of people who have made the run. However, be prepared for some of the most furious white water in the world.

Numerous companies offer trips through various sections of the canyon. You can spend as little as half a day on the Colorado (downstream from Glen Canyon Dam; see "Lake Powell & Page," in chapter 7) or more than 2 weeks. You can go down the river in a huge motorized rubber raft (the quickest and noisiest way to see the entire canyon), a paddle- or oar-powered raft (more thrills and, if you have to help paddle, more energy expended on your part), or a wooden dory (the biggest thrill of all). In a motorized raft, you can travel the entire canyon from Lees Ferry to Lake Mead in only 8 days; however, you'll have to listen to the outboard motor whenever you aren't in the middle of a rapid. Should you opt for a dory or an oar- or paddle-powered raft, expect to spend 5 to 6 days getting from Lees Ferry to Phantom Ranch, or 7 to 9 days getting from Phantom Ranch to Diamond Creek, just above Lake Mead. Aside from the half-day trips near Glen Canyon Dam, any Grand Canyon rafting trip will involve lots of monster rapids. Variables to consider include hiking in or out of Phantom Ranch for a combination rafting-and-hiking adventure.

Most trips start from Lees Ferry near Page and Lake Powell. It's also possible to start a trip at Phantom Ranch, hiking in from either the North or South Rim. The main rafting season is April through October, but some companies operate year-round. Rafting trips tend to book up more than a year in advance, and some companies begin taking reservations as early as January for the following year's trips. Although it is possible to book a rafting trip for around $250 per day, the majority of trips fall in the $300 to $350 per day range, with rates depending on the length of the trip and the type of boat used.

The following are companies I recommend checking out when you start planning your Grand Canyon rafting adventure:

- **Arizona Raft Adventures,** 4050 E. Huntington Rd., Flagstaff, AZ 86004 (✆ **800/786-7238;** www.azraft.com); 6- to 16-day motor, oar, and paddle trips. Although this is not one of the larger companies operating on the river, it offers lots of different trips, including those that focus on natural history and others that double as yoga workshops. They also do trips in paddle rafts that allow you to help navigate and provide the power while shooting the canyon's many rapids.

- **Canyoneers,** P.O. Box 2997, Flagstaff, AZ 86003 (✆ **800/525-0924** or 928/526-0924; www.canyoneers.com); 3- to 10-day motorized-raft trips and 6- to 14-day oar-powered trips. Way back in 1938, this was the first company to take paying customers down the Colorado, and Canyoneers is still one of the top companies on the river.
- **Grand Canyon Whitewater,** 916 Vista St. (P.O. Box 1300), Page, AZ 86040 (✆ **800/343-3121** or 928/645-8866; www.grandcanyonwhitewater.com); 4- to 8-day motorized-raft trips and 5- to 13-day oar trips.
- **Grand Canyon Expeditions Company,** P.O. Box O, Kanab, UT 84741 (✆ **800/544-2691** or 435/644-2691; www.gcex.com); 8-day motorized trips and 14- and 16-day dory trips. If you've got the time, I highly recommend these dory trips—they're among the most thrilling adventures in the world.
- **Hatch River Expeditions,** HC 67 Box 35, Marble Canyon, AZ 86036 (✆ **800/856-8966** or 928/355-2241; www.hatchriverexpeditions.com); 4- to 8-day motorized trips and 6-, 7-, and 12-day oar trips. All of this company's trips, except their upper-canyon expedition, end with a helicopter flight out of the canyon. This company has been in business since 1929 and claims to be the oldest commercial rafting company in the U.S. With so much experience, you can count on Hatch to provide you with a great trip.
- **Outdoors Unlimited,** 6900 Townsend Winona Rd., Flagstaff, AZ 86004 (✆ **800/637-7238** or 928/526-4511; www.outdoorsunlimited.com); 5- to 15-day oar and paddle trips. This company has been taking people through the canyon for more than 40 years and usually sends them home very happy.
- **Wilderness River Adventures,** P.O. Box 717, Page, AZ 86040 (✆ **800/992-8022;** www.riveradventures.com); 4- to 8-day motorized-raft trips and 6-, 7-, 10-, 12-, 14-, and 16-day oar trips. The 4-day trips (actually 3½ days) involve hiking out from Phantom Ranch. This is one of the bigger companies operating on the canyon, and it offers a wide variety of trips, which makes it a good one to check with if you're not sure which type of trip you want to do.

For information on 1-day rafting trips at the west end of the Grand Canyon, see "Havasu Canyon & Grand Canyon West," later in this chapter. For information on half-day trips near Page, see "Lake Powell & Page," in chapter 7.

Activities Outside the Canyon

If you aren't completely beat at the end of the day, check the entertainment schedule at Tusayan's **Grand Hotel** (✆ **928/638-3333**). Cowboy singers, country bands, and Native American dancers all perform here regularly.

For a virtual Grand Canyon experience, you can see an IMAX movie at the **National Geographic Visitor Center,** 450 Ariz. 64 (✆ **928/638-2468;** www.grandcanyonimaxtheater.com), in Tusayan outside the south entrance to the park. A short IMAX film covering the history and geology of the canyon is shown throughout the day on the theater's six-story screen. Admission is $13 for adults and $9.50 for children 5 to 10. March to October, there are shows daily between 8:30am and 8:30pm; November to February, shows are daily between 10:30am and 6:30pm.

Outside the east entrance to the park, the **Cameron Trading Post** (✆ **800/338-7385** or 928/679-2231; www.camerontradingpost.com), at the crossroads of Cameron where Ariz. 64 branches off U.S. 89, is the best trading post in the state. The original stone trading post, a historic building, now houses a gallery of Indian artifacts, clothing, and jewelry. This gallery sells museum-quality pieces, but even if you don't have $10,000 to drop on a rug or basket, you can still look around. The main trading post is a more modern building and is the largest trading post in northern Arizona. Don't miss the beautiful terraced gardens in back of the original trading post.

Where to Stay

Keep in mind that the Grand Canyon is one of the most popular national parks in the country, and hotel rooms both within and just outside the park are in high demand. Make reservations as far in advance as possible. Don't expect to find a room if you head up here in summer without a reservation. You'll likely wind up driving back to Williams or Flagstaff to find a vacancy. There, is, however, one long-shot option. See "Inside the Park," below, for details. Who knows? You might get lucky.

INSIDE THE PARK

All hotels inside the park are operated by **Xanterra South Rim/Xanterra Parks & Resorts.** Reservations are taken up to 13 months in advance, beginning on the first of the month. If you want to stay in one of the historic rim cabins at Bright Angel Lodge, reserve at least a year in advance. However, rooms with shared bathrooms at Bright Angel Lodge are often the last in the park to book up, and although they're small and very basic, they're your best bet if you're trying to get a last-minute reservation.

To make reservations at any of the in-park hotels listed below, contact **Xanterra South Rim/Xanterra Parks & Resorts,** 6312 S. Fiddlers Green Circle, Ste. 600N, Greenwood Village, CO 80111 (✆ **888/297-2757** or 303/297-2757; www.grandcanyonlodges.com). It is sometimes possible, due to cancellations and no-shows, to get a same-day reservation; it's a long shot, but it happens. Same-day reservations can be made by calling ✆ **928/638-2631.** Xanterra accepts American Express, Diners Club, Discover, MasterCard, and Visa. Children 16 and under stay free in their parent's room.

Expensive

El Tovar Hotel ★★ El Tovar Hotel, which first opened its doors in 1905, is the park's premier lodge. Built of local rock and Oregon pine by Hopi craftsmen, it's a rustic yet luxurious mountain lodge that perches on the edge of the canyon (although with views from only a few rooms). The lobby, entered from a veranda set with rustic furniture, has a small fireplace, cathedral ceiling, and log walls on which moose, deer, and antelope heads are displayed. Although guest rooms are comfortable and attractively decorated, the standard units are rather small, as are the bathrooms. For more legroom, book a deluxe unit. Suites, with private terraces and stunning views, are extremely spacious. El Tovar Dining Room (see "Where to Eat," below) serves a mix of Continental and Southwestern cuisine and is the best restaurant in the village. Just off the lobby is a cocktail lounge with a view.

78 units. $178–$273 double; $335–$426 suite. **Amenities:** Restaurant, El Tovar Dining Room (review, p. 286); lounge; concierge; room service. *In room:* A/C, TV, fridge, hair dryer.

Moderate

Thunderbird & Kachina Lodges If you want great views, these hotels are your best bets—but only if you get a room with a view. These two side-by-side hotels date from the 1960s and, with their dated exteriors, are a far cry from what you might imagine a national park hotel would look like. They do, however, have the biggest windows of any of the hotels on the canyon rim, and they also have the most modern rooms. If you get a second-story room on the canyon side of either hotel, you'll get some of the best views in the park (these rooms at the Kachina Lodge get the nod for having *the* best views). Book early—these two lodges are some of the park's most popular accommodations. Just remember, if it's not a view room, you'll be staring at the parking lot, and the lodge will not guarantee canyon-view rooms.

104 units. $173–$184 double. *In room:* TV, fridge, hair dryer.

Yavapai Lodge Located in several buildings at the east end of Grand Canyon Village (a 1-mile hike from the main section of the village, but convenient to the Grand Canyon Visitor Center), the Yavapai is the largest lodge in the park and thus is where you'll likely wind up if you wait too long to make a reservation. Unfortunately, it's also the least-appealing hotel in the park. There are no canyon views, which is why Yavapai is less expensive than the Thunderbird and Kachina lodges. If you must stay here, try for a room in the nicer Yavapai East wing, which is set under shady pines. Rooms in this wing have air-conditioning. However, I recommend that you plan ahead and try to stay at one of the lodges right on the rim.

358 units. $114–$163 double (winter discounts available). **Amenities:** Restaurant. *In room:* TV.

Inexpensive

Bright Angel Lodge & Cabins ★ Bright Angel Lodge, which began operation in 1896 as a collection of tents and cabins on the edge of the canyon, is the most affordable lodge in the park, and, with its flagstone-floor lobby and huge fireplace, it has a genuine, if crowded, mountain-lodge atmosphere. It also happens to offer the greatest variety of accommodations in the park. The best and most popular units are the rim cabins, which should be booked a year in advance. In fact, any rooms here should be booked as far in advance as possible. Most of the rooms and cabins feature rustic furnishings. The Buckey Suite, the oldest structure on the canyon rim, is arguably the best room in the park, with a canyon view, gas fireplace, and king-size bed. The tour desk, big fireplace, museum, and restrooms account for the constant crowds in the lobby.

86 units (20 with shared bathrooms). $70 double with shared bathroom; $92 double with private bathroom; $113–$178 cabin; $141–$340 suite. **Amenities:** 2 restaurants, Arizona Room and Bright Angel Restaurant (reviews, p. 286); snack bar; lounge. *In room:* No phone.

Maswik Lodge Set back ¼ mile or so from the rim, the Maswik Lodge offers spacious rooms and cabins that have been comfortably modernized without losing their appealing rustic character. If you don't mind roughing it a bit, the 28 old cabins, which are available only in summer, have lots of character. These cabins have high ceilings and ceiling fans, and are my top choice away from the rim. If you crave modern appointments, lots of space, and predictably comfortable air-conditioned accommodations, opt for one of the large Maswik North rooms, which also have refrigerators and coffeemakers. Second-floor rooms have high ceilings and balconies, which makes them your most comfortable choice away from the rim.

278 units. $92–$173 double (winter discounts available); $92 cabin. **Amenities:** Restaurant; lounge. *In room:* TV, fridge.

Phantom Ranch ★ Built in 1922, Phantom Ranch is the only lodge at the bottom of the Grand Canyon and has a classic ranch atmosphere. Accommodations are in rustic stone-walled cabins or 10-bed gender-segregated dormitories. Evaporative coolers keep both the cabins and the dorms cool in summer. Make reservations as early as possible, and don't forget to reconfirm. (It's sometimes possible to get a room on the day of departure if there are any last-minute cancellations, though. To attempt this, you must put your name on the waiting list at the Bright Angel Lodge transportation desk the day before you want to stay at Phantom Ranch.)

Family-style meals must be reserved in advance. The menu consists of beef-and-vegetable stew ($26) and steak ($42). Breakfasts ($20) are hearty, and sack lunches ($13) are available as well. Between meals, the dining hall becomes a canteen selling snacks, drinks, gifts, and necessities. After dinner, it serves as a beer hall. There's a public phone here, and mule-back duffel transfer ($64) between Grand Canyon Village and Phantom Ranch can be arranged.

11 cabins, 40 dorm beds. $105 double in cabin; $41 dormitory bed. Mule-trip overnights (with all meals and mule ride included) $477 for 1 person, $843 for 2 people. 2-night trips available Nov–Mar. **Amenities:** Restaurant; lounge. *In room:* No phone.

IN TUSAYAN (OUTSIDE THE SOUTH ENTRANCE)

If you can't get a reservation for a room in the park, this is the next closest place to stay. Unfortunately, this area can be very noisy because of the many helicopters and airplanes taking off from the airport. Also, hotels outside the park are very popular with tour groups, which during the busy summer months keep many hotels full. All of the hotels listed here are lined up along U.S. 180/Ariz. 64.

Best Western Grand Canyon Squire Inn ☺ If you're worried that the kids might get restless after they've spent 30 seconds looking at the Grand Canyon, you might want to consider staying here. With a pool in the summer and a video-game room and bowling alley year-round, this hotel offers plenty to distract the kids. Parents will likely appreciate the large guest rooms with comfortable easy chairs and big windows. In the lobby, which is more Las Vegas glitz than mountain rustic, cases are filled with old cowboy paraphernalia. Down in the basement are an impressive Western sculpture, a waterfall wall, and the hotel's bowling alley and game room.

100 Ariz. 64 (P.O. Box 130), Grand Canyon, AZ 86023. www.grandcanyonsquire.com. ✆ **800/622-6966** or 928/638-2681. Fax 928/638-2782. 250 units. $80–$206 double. Children 12 and under stay free in parent's room. AE, DC, DISC, MC, V. **Amenities:** 2 restaurants, including Coronado Room (review, p. 287); 2 lounges; exercise room; Jacuzzi; seasonal outdoor pool; sauna. *In room:* A/C, TV, hair dryer, free Wi-Fi.

Canyon Plaza Resort The setting behind the IMAX theater and surrounded by parking lots is none too pretty, but guest rooms, most of which have a bit of contemporary styling, are large and comfortable, and have balconies or patios. The hotel is built around two enclosed skylit courtyards, one of which houses a restaurant and the other a bar and whirlpool. Families will want to opt for one of the suites, which contain separate small living rooms. Unfortunately, the hotel is very popular with tour groups and can often feel crowded.

406 Canyon Plaza Lane (P.O. Box 520), Grand Canyon, AZ 86023-0520. www.grandcanyonplaza.com. ✆ **800/995-2521** or 928/638-2673. Fax 928/638-9537. 232 units. Mid-Mar to mid-Oct $198–$218 double, $228–$248 suite; mid-Oct to mid-Mar $67–$148 double, $107–$178 suite.

Rates include continental breakfast. Children 16 and under stay free in parent's room. AE, DC, DISC, MC, V. Pets accepted ($50 fee). **Amenities:** Restaurant; lounge; 2 Jacuzzis; seasonal outdoor pool. *In room:* A/C, TV, fridge, hair dryer, free Wi-Fi.

Grand Hotel ★ With its mountain lodge–style lobby, this modern hotel lives up to its name and is your best bet outside the park. There's a flagstone fireplace, log-beam ceiling, and fake ponderosa-pine tree trunks holding up the roof. Just off the lobby are a dining room (with evening entertainment ranging from Native American dancers to country-music bands), a small bar that even has a few saddles for bar stools, and an espresso stand. Guest rooms are spacious, with a few Western touches, and some have small balconies.

Ariz. 64 (P.O. Box 3319), Grand Canyon, AZ 86023. www.grandcanyongrandhotel.com. ✆ **888/634-7263** or 928/638-3333. Fax 928/638-3131. 121 units. Mid-Mar to mid-Oct $159–$289 double, $289–$409 suite; mid-Oct to mid-Mar $99–$139 double, $209–$269 suite. Children 12 and under stay free in parent's room. AE, DC, DISC, MC, V. **Amenities:** Restaurant, Canyon Star Restaurant and Saloon (review, p. 286); lounge; exercise room; Jacuzzi; indoor pool; free Wi-Fi. *In room:* A/C, TV, hair dryer.

Holiday Inn Express Hotel & Suites-Grand Canyon ☺ This hotel has modern, well-designed, and predictably clean and comfortable guest rooms. The hotel also includes a separate building that houses 32 large suites that are ideal for families. These suites are among the nicest accommodations inside or outside the park. ***Parents take note:*** In the main building, there are also "Kids' Suites" that have bunk beds, three TVs, and a video-game machine.

226 N. Ariz. 64, Grand Canyon, AZ 86023. www.gcanyon.com. ✆ **888/473-2269** or 928/638-3000. Fax 928/638-0123. 194 units. $74–$199 double; $84–$250 suite. Rates include full breakfast. Children 19 and under stay free in parent's room. AE, DC, DISC, MC, V. **Amenities:** 2 Jacuzzis; indoor pool. *In room:* A/C, TV, hair dryer, free Wi-Fi.

Red Feather Lodge With more than 200 units, this motel is often slow to fill up, so it's a good choice for last-minute bookings. Try to get one of the newer rooms, which are a bit more comfortable than the older ones. In summer, the pool here makes this place a good bet for families.

300 Ariz. 64 (P.O. Box 1460), Grand Canyon, AZ 86023. www.redfeatherlodge.com. ✆ **866/561-2425** or 928/638-2414. Fax 928/638-2707. 216 units. Mid-Mar to mid-Oct $120–$170 double; mid-Oct to mid-Mar $70–$120 double. Children 17 and under stay free in parent's room. AE, DC, DISC, MC, V. Pets accepted ($50 deposit plus $25 per night). **Amenities:** Restaurant; Jacuzzi; seasonal outdoor pool. *In room:* A/C, TV, fridge (in some), free Wi-Fi.

ANOTHER AREA ACCOMMODATION

Cameron Trading Post Motel ★ 🎁 Located 54 miles north of Flagstaff on U.S. 89 at the junction with the road to the east entrance of the national park, this motel offers some of the most attractive rooms in the vicinity of the Grand Canyon and is part of one of the best trading posts in the state. The motel, adjacent to the historic Cameron Trading Post, is built around the shady oasis of the old trading post's terraced gardens. Guest rooms feature Southwestern-style furniture and attractive decor. Most have balconies, and some have views of the Little Colorado River (which, however, rarely has much water in it). Don't miss the Navajo tacos in the dining room; the small ones are plenty big enough for a meal.

466 U.S. 89 (P.O. Box 339), Cameron, AZ 86020. www.camerontradingpost.com. ✆ **800/338-7385** or 928/679-2231. Fax 928/679-2501. 62 units. Jan–Feb $59–$69 double, $99–$129 suite;

Mar–Apr $79–$89 double, $129–$159 suite; May–Oct $99–$109 double, $149–$179 suite; Nov–Dec $69–$79 double, $129–$159 suite. AE, DISC, MC, V. Pets accepted ($15 fee). **Amenities:** Restaurant. *In room:* A/C, TV, hair dryer, free Wi-Fi.

CAMPGROUNDS

Inside the Park

On the South Rim, there are two campgrounds and an RV park. **Mather Campground,** in Grand Canyon Village, has 327 campsites. Reservations can be made up to 6 months in advance and are highly recommended for stays between March and late November (reservations not accepted for other months). Contact the National Recreation Reservation Service (✆ **877/444-6777** or 518/885-3639; www.recreation.gov). Between late spring and early fall, don't even think of coming up here without a reservation; you'll just set yourself up for disappointment. If you don't have a reservation, your next-best bet is to arrive in the morning, when sites are being vacated. Campsites are $18 per night ($15 per night mid-Nov to Feb; reservations not accepted).

Desert View Campground, with 50 sites, is 25 miles east of Grand Canyon Village and open from May to mid-October only. No reservations are accepted. Campsites are $12 per night.

The **Trailer Village RV park,** with 75 RV sites, is in Grand Canyon Village and charges $36 per night (for two adults) for full hookup. Reservations can be made up to 13 months in advance by contacting **Xanterra South Rim/Xanterra Parks & Resorts,** 6312 S. Fiddlers Green Circle, Ste. 600N, Greenwood Village, CO 80111 (✆ **888/297-2757** or 303/297-2757; www.xanterra.com or www.grandcanyonlodges.com). For same-day reservations, call ✆ **928/638-2631.**

Outside the Park

Two miles south of Tusayan is the U.S. Forest Service's **Ten-X Campground.** This campground has 70 campsites, is open May through September, and charges $10. It's usually your best bet for finding a site late in the day.

You can also camp just about anywhere within the **Kaibab National Forest,** which borders Grand Canyon National Park. Several dirt roads lead into the forest from the highway, and although you won't find designated campsites or toilets along these roads, you will find spots where others have obviously camped before. This so-called dispersed camping is usually used by campers who have been unable to find sites in campgrounds. One of the most popular roads for this sort of camping is on the west side of the highway between Tusayan and the park's south entrance. For more information, contact the **Tusayan Ranger District,** Kaibab National Forest, 176 Lincoln Log Loop (P.O. Box 3088), Grand Canyon, AZ 86023 (✆ **928/638-2443;** www.fs.fed.us/r3/kai).

Where to Eat

INSIDE THE PARK

If you're looking for a quick, inexpensive meal, there are plenty of options. In Grand Canyon Village, choices include **cafeterias** at the Yavapai and Maswik lodges and a **delicatessen** at Canyon Village Marketplace on Market Plaza. The **Bright Angel Fountain,** at the back of the Bright Angel Lodge, serves hot dogs, sandwiches, and ice cream and is always crowded on hot days. My favorite place in the park to grab a quick bite is the **Hermit's Rest Snack Bar** at the west end of Hermit Road. The stone building that houses this snack bar was designed by

Mary Elizabeth Jane Colter, who also designed several other buildings on the South Rim. At Desert View (near the east entrance to the park), there's the **Desert View Trading Post Cafeteria.** All of these places are open daily, and all serve meals for $10 and under.

The Arizona Room SOUTHWESTERN Because this restaurant has the best view of the three dining establishments right on the South Rim, it is immensely popular and is my favorite restaurant in the park. Add to this the fact that the Arizona Room has a Southwestern menu almost as creative as that of El Tovar Dining Room, and you'll understand why there is often a long wait for a table here. To avoid the wait and take in the views, arrive early, which should assure you of getting a good table without too much of a wait. Once you finally sit down to eat, I recommend both the pan-seared salmon with melon salsa and the baby back ribs with either the prickly-pear or chipotle glaze. Because this restaurant is open for lunch part of the year, you've got another great option for dining with a billion-dollar view.

At the Bright Angel Lodge. ✆ **928/638-2631.** Reservations not accepted. Main courses $7.50–$13 lunch, $12–$26 dinner. AE, DC, DISC, MC, V. Daily 4:30–10pm (Mar–Oct also lunch daily 11:30am–3pm). Closed Jan–Feb.

Bright Angel Restaurant ☺ AMERICAN As the least expensive of the three restaurants right on the rim of the canyon, this casual Southwestern-themed coffeehouse in the historic Bright Angel Lodge stays packed with families throughout the day. Meals are simple and none too memorable, but if you can get one of the few tables near the windows, at least you get something of a view. The menu includes everything from burgers to fajitas to spaghetti (foods calculated to comfort tired and hungry hikers), but my favorite offerings are the bread bowls full of chili and stew that are served at lunch. Wines are available, and service is generally friendly and efficient.

At the Bright Angel Lodge. ✆ **928/638-2631.** Reservations not accepted. Main courses $7.50–$10 lunch, $8.50–$26 dinner. AE, DC, DISC, MC, V. Daily 6:30am–10pm.

El Tovar Dining Room ★★ CONTINENTAL/SOUTHWESTERN If you're staying at El Tovar, you'll want to have dinner in the hotel's rustic yet elegant dining room. But before making reservations at the most expensive restaurant in the park, be aware that few tables have views of the canyon. However, despite the limited views, the meals served here are the best on the South Rim. The menu includes a bit of Southwestern flavor, but for the most part, it sticks to familiar Continental dishes. The New York steak is a good bet, as is the wild salmon tostada. Start your meal with the interesting little roulades (flavorful bite-size tortilla roll-ups). Service is generally quite good. Have a drink in the bar before dinner (you might even be able to snag a table with a view).

At El Tovar Hotel. ✆ **928/638-2631,** ext. 6432. Reservations highly recommended for dinner. Main courses $10–$15 lunch, $18–$34 dinner. AE, DC, DISC, MC, V. Daily 6:30–11am, 11:30am–2pm, and 5–10pm.

IN TUSAYAN (OUTSIDE THE SOUTH ENTRANCE)

In addition to the restaurants listed below, you'll find a steakhouse and a pizza place, as well as familiar chains such as McDonald's, Pizza Hut, and Wendy's.

Canyon Star Restaurant and Saloon ★ AMERICAN/MEXICAN This place aims to compete with El Tovar Dining Room and the Arizona Room, and serves the most creative Southwestern fare this side of the park boundary, plus you'll have live entertainment while you eat. Try the barbecued buffalo brisket. Evening shows include cowboy music and performances of Native American songs and dances. This place is big, so there usually isn't too long a wait for a table; and even if there is, you can relax in the saloon where you can saddle up a bar stool (some of the stools have saddles instead of seats).

At the Grand Hotel, Ariz. 64. ✆ **928/638-3333.** Reservations recommended in summer. Main courses $10–$20 lunch, $11–$27 dinner. AE, DISC, MC, V. Spring–fall daily 7–10am, 11am–2pm, and 5–9pm; winter daily 7–10am and 5–9pm.

Coronado Room CONTINENTAL/SOUTHWESTERN If you should suddenly be struck by an overpowering desire to have escargot for dinner, don't despair—head for the Best Western Grand Canyon Squire Inn (p. 283). Now, I'm well aware that Best Western and escargot go together about as well as the Eiffel Tower and rattlesnake fritters, but this place really does serve classic Continental fare way out here in the Arizona high country. You'll probably want to stick to the steaks, though (or the wild game such as elk tournedos). You might also want to try a few of the Southwestern appetizers on the menu. Be prepared for slow service.

At the Best Western Grand Canyon Squire Inn, 100 Ariz. 64. ✆ **928/638-2681.** Reservations recommended. Main courses $19–$30. AE, DC, DISC, MC, V. Daily 5–10pm.

THE GRAND CANYON NORTH RIM ★★★

42 miles S of Jacob Lake; 216 miles N of Grand Canyon Village (South Rim); 354 miles N of Phoenix; 125 miles W of Page/Lake Powell

Although the North Rim of the Grand Canyon is only 10 miles from the South Rim as the raven flies, it's more than 200 miles by road, and because it is such a long drive from population centers such as Phoenix and Las Vegas, the North Rim is much less crowded than the South Rim. Additionally, due to heavy snowfall, the North Rim is open only from mid-May to late October or early November. There are also far fewer activities or establishments on the North Rim than there are on the South Rim (no helicopter or plane rides, no IMAX theater, no McDonald's). For these reasons, most of the millions of people who annually visit the Grand Canyon never make it to this side—and that is exactly why, in my opinion, the North Rim is a far superior place to visit. If Grand Canyon Village turns out to be more human zoo than the wilderness experience you expected, the North Rim will probably be much more to your liking, although crowds, traffic congestion, and parking problems are not unheard of here, either.

Fall means colorful leaves along the North Rim of the Grand Canyon.

An Important Note

Visitor facilities at the North Rim are open only from mid-May to mid-October. From mid-October to November (or until snow closes the road to the North Rim), the park is open for day use only. The campground may be open after mid-October, weather permitting.

The North Rim is on the Kaibab Plateau, which is more than 8,000 feet high on average and takes its name from the Paiute word for "mountain lying down." The higher elevation of the North Rim means that instead of the mix of junipers interspersed with ponderosa pines of the South Rim, you'll see dense forests of ponderosa pines, Douglas firs, and aspens interspersed with large meadows. Consequently, the North Rim has a much more alpine feel than the South Rim. The elevation—1,000 feet higher than the South Rim—also means that the North Rim gets considerably more snow in winter than the South Rim. The highway south from Jacob Lake is not plowed in winter, when Grand Canyon Lodge closes down.

Essentials

GETTING THERE The North Rim is at the end of Ariz. 67 (the North Rim Pkwy.), reached from U.S. 89A. **Trans Canyon** (✆ **928/638-2820;** www.trans-canyonshuttle.com) operates a shuttle between the North Rim and the South Rim of the Grand Canyon during the months the North Rim is open. The trip takes 5 hours; the fare is $80 one-way and $150 round-trip (reservations are required).

FEES The park entry fee is $25 per car and is good for 1 week. Remember not to lose the little paper receipt that serves as your admission pass.

VISITOR INFORMATION For information before leaving home, contact **Grand Canyon National Park,** P.O. Box 129, Grand Canyon, AZ 86023 (✆ **928/638-7888;** www.nps.gov/grca). At the entrance gate, you'll be given a copy of *The Guide,* a small newspaper with information on park activities. When you arrive at the park, stop by the **North Rim Visitor Center,** which is adjacent to the Grand Canyon Lodge and is open mid-May to mid-October daily 8am to 6pm.

Exploring the Park

While it's hard to beat the view from a chair on the terrace of the Grand Canyon Lodge, the best spots for seeing the canyon are Bright Angel Point, Point Imperial, and Cape Royal. **Bright Angel Point** is at the end of a half-mile trail near the Grand Canyon Lodge, and from here you can see and hear Roaring Springs, which is 3,600 feet below the rim and are the North Rim's only water source. You can also see Grand Canyon Village on the South Rim.

At 8,803 feet, **Point Imperial** is the highest point on the North Rim. A short section of the Colorado River can be seen far below, and off to the east the Painted Desert is visible. The Point Imperial/Nankoweap Trail leads north from here along the rim of the canyon. However, this area was burned in a forest fire in 2000.

Cape Royal is the most spectacular setting on the North Rim, and along the 23-mile road to this viewpoint you'll find several other scenic overlooks. Across the road from the **Walhalla Overlook** are the ruins of an Ancestral

FROM TOP: **Angel's Window Overlook; the Navajo Bridge is 470 feet above the Colorado River and affords a great view of Marble Canyon.**

Puebloan structure, and just before reaching Cape Royal, you'll come to the **Angel's Window Overlook,** which gives you a breathtaking view of the natural bridge that forms Angel's Window. Once at Cape Royal, you can follow a trail across this natural bridge to a towering promontory overlooking the canyon.

Once you've had your fill of simply taking in the views, you may want to get out and stretch your legs on a trail or two. Quite a few day hikes of varying lengths and difficulty are possible. The shortest is the .5-mile paved trail to Bright Angel Point, along which you'll have plenty of company but also plenty of breathtaking views. If you have time for only one hike while you're here, make it down the **North Kaibab Trail.** This trail is 14 miles long and leads down to Phantom Ranch and the Colorado River. To hike the entire trail, you'll need to have a camping permit and be in very good physical condition (it's almost 6,000 ft. to the canyon floor). For a day hike, most people make Roaring Springs their goal. This hike is 9.5 miles round-trip, involves a descent and ascent of 3,000 feet, and takes 7 to 8 hours. You can shorten this hike considerably by turning around at the Supai Tunnel, which is fewer than 1,500 feet below the rim at the 2-mile point. For a relatively easy hike away from the crowds, try the Widforss Point Trail.

If you want to see the canyon from a saddle, contact **Grand Canyon Trail Rides** (✆ **435/679-8665;** www.canyonrides.com), which offers mule rides varying in length from 1 hour ($40) to a half-day ($75). One half-day ride goes down into the canyon to the Supai Tunnel.

En Route to or from the North Rim

Between Page and the North Rim of the Grand Canyon, U.S. 89A crosses the Colorado River at **Lees Ferry** in Marble Canyon. The original **Navajo Bridge** over the river here was replaced in 1995, and the old bridge is now open to pedestrians. From the bridge, which is 470 feet above the Colorado River, there's a beautiful view of Marble Canyon. At the west end of the bridge, you'll find the Navajo Bridge Interpretive Center, which is operated by the National Park Service and is partly housed in a stone building built during the Depression by the Civilian Conservation Corps (CCC). At the east end of the bridge, which is on the Navajo Reservation, interpretive signs tell the story of Lees Ferry from the Native American perspective.

Lees Ferry is the starting point for raft trips through the Grand Canyon, and for many years it was the only place to cross the Colorado River for hundreds of miles in either direction. This stretch of the river is now legendary among anglers for its trophy trout fishing. Lees Ferry has a 54-site campground charging $12 per night. Reservations are not accepted.

Lees Ferry Anglers (✆ **800/962-9755** or 928/355-2261; www.leesferry.com), 11 miles west of the bridge at Lees Ferry, is fishing headquarters for the region. Not only does it sell all manner of fly-fishing tackle and offer advice about good spots to try your luck, it also operates a guide service and rents waders and boats. A guide and boat cost $350 per day for one person, and $425 per day for two people.

Continuing west, the highway passes under the **Vermilion Cliffs,** so named for their deep-red coloring and now the namesake of the **Vermilion Cliffs National Monument** (✆ **435/688-3200;** www.blm.gov/az/st/en/prog/blm_special_areas/natmon/vermilion.html). At the base of these cliffs are huge boulders balanced on narrow columns of eroded soil. The balanced rocks give the area an otherworldly appearance. Access to the national monument is very limited, and for the most part, a four-wheel-drive vehicle is required. Along this unpopulated stretch of road are three rustic lodges.

Along this same stretch of road, you'll find the gravel road that leads north to the **Coyote Buttes ★★★**, which are among the most unusual rock formations in Arizona. Basically, these striated conical sandstone hills are petrified sand dunes, which should give you a good idea of why one area of the Coyote Buttes is called the Wave. The buttes are a favorite of photographers. You must have a permit ($7

Coyote Buttes is also called the Wave for its unusual rock formations.

per person) to visit this area, and only 20 people are allowed to visit each day (with a maximum group size of six people). Permits are issued by lottery, and applications must be submitted 4 months in advance. There's no actual trail to the buttes, so you have to navigate by way of the photos and map that you'll be sent when you receive your permit. For more information, contact the Bureau of Land Management's **Arizona Strip Field Office,** 345 E. Riverside Dr., St. George, UT 84790 (✆ **435/688-3200;** www.blm.gov/az/st/en/arolrsmain/paria/coyote_buttes.html).

One last detour to consider before or after visiting the national park is an area known as the **East Rim.** This area lies just outside the park in Kaibab National Forest and can be reached by turning east on gravel Forest Road (F.R.) 611 about ¾ mile south of DeMotte Campground, which is a few miles north of the park entrance. Follow F.R. 611 for 4½ miles to the East Rim Viewpoint (crossing F.R. 610 at about 1½ miles). Another good view can be had from the Marble viewpoint at the end of F.R. 219, a 4-mile-long dead-end spur road off F.R. 610 about 6 miles from the junction with F.R. 611. For more information, contact the **North Kaibab Ranger Station,** 430 S. Main St. (P.O. Box 248), Fredonia, AZ 86022 (✆ **928/643-7395;** www.fs.fed.us/r3/kai), or in summer, the **Kaibab Plateau Visitors Center** (✆ **928/643-7298**), in Jacob Lake at the junction of Ariz. 67 and U.S. 89A.

North of the Park

To learn more about the pioneer history of this remote and sparsely populated region of the state (known as the Arizona Strip), continue west from Jacob Lake 45 miles on Ariz. 389 to **Pipe Spring National Monument,** 406 N. Pipe Spring Rd., Fredonia (✆ **928/643-7105;** www.nps.gov/pisp), which preserves an early Mormon ranch house that was built in the style of a fort for protection from Indians. This "fort" was also known as Winsor Castle and occasionally housed the wives of polygamists hiding out from the law. A small museum contains exhibits on both Mormon settlers and the Paiute Indians who have long inhabited this region. Throughout the day, there are tours of Winsor Castle. In summer, there are living-history demonstrations. The monument is open daily from 7am to 5pm June through August, and from 8am to 5pm September through May (closed New Year's Day, Thanksgiving, and Christmas). Admission is $5 per adult.

Southwest of Pipe Spring, in an area accessible only via long gravel roads, lies the **Grand Canyon–Parashant National Monument.** This monument preserves a vast and rugged landscape north of the east end of Grand Canyon National Park. The monument has no facilities and no paved roads. For more information, contact the Bureau of Land Management's **Interagency Information Center,** 345 E. Riverside Dr., St. George, UT 84790 (✆ **435/688-3200;** www.nps.gov/para).

If you have an interest in Native American rock art and are searching for a memorable and uncrowded adventure, make time to visit the remote **Snake Gulch,** west of Jacob Lake. The red-and-yellow pictographs in this remote canyon date from the Basketmaker period (300 B.C.–A.D. 800) and are among the most impressive and extensive in the state. The first pictographs are in a shallow cave about 2 miles from the trail head. Continue down the canyon for 2 or 3 miles to find many more shallow caves with pictographs. To reach the Snake Gulch trail head, drive ¼ mile south of Jacob Lake Visitor Center on Ariz. 67, turn west on F.R. 461, and follow this road and F.R. 462 for about 9 miles. Turn south on F.R. 422 and continue 2 miles, and then go west on F.R. 423 for 1¼ miles to F.R. 642. Drive north 2 miles on F.R. 642 to the trail head at the end of the road. This route involves about 15 miles of driving on gravel roads that are passable to regular passenger vehicles unless there has been recent rain or snow. Alternatively, you can drive south from Fredonia on a good paved road (F.R. 422), which turns to gravel a short distance before the F.R. 642 junction. Carry plenty of water, especially in summer, when it can be extremely hot here. Spring and fall are the best times to visit. For more information, contact the North Kaibab Ranger District, 430 S. Main St. (P.O. Box 248), Fredonia, AZ 86022 (✆ **928/643-7395;** www.fs.fed.us/r3/kai).

Where to Stay

INSIDE THE PARK

Grand Canyon Lodge ★★ Perched right on the canyon rim, this classic mountain lodge is listed on the National Register of Historic Places and is as impressive a lodge as any you'll find in a national park. The stone-and-log main building has a soaring ceiling and a viewing room set up with chairs facing a wall of glass, and on either side of this room are flagstone terraces furnished with rustic chairs. Accommodations vary from standard motel units to rustic mountain cabins to comfortable modern cabins. My favorites are the frontier cabins, which, although cramped and paneled with dark wood, were renovated in 2009 and capture the feeling of a mountain retreat better than the other options. The two-bedroom pioneer cabins, good for families, were also remodeled in 2009. Only a few units have views of the canyon. The dining hall has two walls of glass to take in the awesome canyon views.

Forever Resorts, 7501 E. McCormick Pkwy., Scottsdale, AZ 85258. www.grandcanyonlodgenorth.com. ✆ **877/386-4383** or 480/337-1320. 220 units. $113–$182 double. Children 15 and under stay free in parent's room. AE, DC, DISC, MC, V. Closed mid-Oct to mid-May. **Amenities:** 3 restaurants; lounge; bikes; free Wi-Fi. *In room:* Hair dryer.

OUTSIDE THE PARK

North of the national park, the next-closest lodgings are the Kaibab Lodge and the Jacob Lake Inn. You'll also find lots of budget accommodations in Kanab, Utah, 37 miles west of Jacob Lake.

Jacob Lake Inn This is one of only two lodges outside the entrance to the North Rim of Grand Canyon National Park, and, because it is at the crossroads of Jacob Lake, it is always a busy spot in summer. While most of the units here are old cabins that tend to be cramped and old-fashioned, there are also two dozen modern motel-style rooms in a contemporary mountain-rustic lodge. It is these latter rooms, which are the inn's only rooms with TVs, telephones, and high-speed Internet access, that I recommend. Sure, they're more expensive than the cabins, but they are the nicest rooms in the area. Be sure to stock up on cookies at the inn's bakery.

Ariz. 67/U.S. 89A, Jacob Lake, AZ 86022. www.jacoblake.com. ✆ **928/643-7232.** 62 units. $86–$134 cabin double; $112–$135 motel/lodge double (lower rates in winter). AE, DISC, MC, V. Pets accepted ($10 per night). **Amenities:** Restaurant. *In room:* TV (in some), Internet (in some), no phone (in some).

EN ROUTE TO THE PARK

If you don't have a reservation at the North Rim's Grand Canyon Lodge, you should call the places recommended below to see if you can get a reservation. If so, you can continue on to the North Rim the next morning. Lodges anywhere near the canyon fill up early in the day if they aren't already fully booked with reservations made months in advance.

Cliff Dwellers Lodge Affiliated with Lees Ferry Anglers, this motel is the area's de facto fly anglers' headquarters and tends to stay filled up with people who have come here to fish for the Colorado's huge rainbow trout. The newer, more expensive rooms here are standard motel units with combination tub/showers, and are the best and most predictable rooms in the Vermilion Cliffs area. Older rooms, in an interesting stone-walled building, have knotty pine walls and showers only. The lodge is close to some spectacular balanced rocks, and it's about 11 miles east to Lees Ferry. The views are unforgettable.

U.S. 89A milepost 547 (H.C. 67, Box 30), Marble Canyon, AZ 86036. www.cliffdwellerslodge.com. ✆ **800/962-9755** or 928/355-2261. Fax 928/355-2271. 20 units. $80–$90 double (lower rates in winter). AE, DISC, MC, V. **Amenities:** Restaurant. *In room:* A/C, TV, no phone.

Lees Ferry Lodge at Vermilion Cliffs Located at the foot of the Vermilion Cliffs, 4 miles west of the Colorado River, Lees Ferry Lodge, built in 1929 of native stone and rough-hewn timber beams, is a small place with simple, rustic accommodations. However, the lodge's restaurant serves as a sort of de facto community center for area residents, and owner Maggie Sacher is usually on hand to answer questions and share stories. Also, the patio seating area in front of the lodge has fabulous views. The restaurant here has a great, old-fashioned atmosphere. With its rustic character and friendly feel, this is my favorite place to stay in the area. Don't miss it.

U.S. 89A (H.C. 67, Box 1), Marble Canyon, AZ 86036. www.vermilioncliffs.com. ✆ **928/355-2231.** 10 units. $70–$90 double. Children 4 and under stay free in parent's room. AE, MC, V. Pets accepted. **Amenities:** Restaurant. *In room:* A/C, no phone.

Marble Canyon Lodge The Marble Canyon Lodge, built in the 1920s just 4 miles from Lees Ferry, is the closest lodge to the put-in spot for people rafting the Grand Canyon, and consequently this lodge is popular primarily with rafters. Accommodations are mostly in aging motel-style rooms that lack the modernity of the rooms at Cliff Dwellers Lodge or the character of the rooms at the Lees Ferry Lodge at Vermilion Cliffs. In addition to the restaurant, there's a general store that specializes in rafting supplies.

U.S. 89A, Marble Canyon, AZ 86036. www.marblecanyoncompany.com. ✆ **800/726-1789** or 928/355-2225. Fax 928/355-2227. 56 units. $70–$80 double ($48 in winter). Children 11 and under stay free in parent's room. AE, DISC, MC, V. Pets accepted. **Amenities:** Restaurant; lounge; free Wi-Fi. *In room:* A/C, TV, kitchenette (in some), no phone.

CAMPGROUNDS

Just north of Grand Canyon Lodge, the **North Rim Campground** (✆ **928/638-7888** or 928/638-7814), with 90 sites and no hookups for RVs, is the only campground at the North Rim. It's open mid-May to mid-October. Reservations can be made up to 6 months in advance by calling the National Recreation Reservation Service (www.recreation.gov; ✆ **877/444-6777** or 518/885-3639). Campsites cost $18 to $25 per night.

There are two nearby campgrounds outside the park in the Kaibab National Forest. The **DeMotte Campground** (May 15–Nov 1) is the closest to the park entrance, has 38 sites, and charges $17. **Jacob Lake Campground** (May 15–Oct 1) is 30 miles north of the park entrance, has 51 sites, and also charges $17 per night. Neither campground takes reservations. You can also camp anywhere in the Kaibab National Forest as long as you're more than 200 feet from a main roadway or a quarter-mile from a water source. So if you can't find a site in a campground, simply pull off the highway in the national forest and park your RV or pitch your tent. Contact the North Kaibab Ranger District, 430 S. Main St., Fredonia (✆ **928/643-7395;** www.fs.fed.us/r3/kai), for information.

The **Kaibab Camper Village** (✆ **800/525-0924,** 928/643-7804 May 14–Oct 15, or 928/526-0924 other months; www.kaibabcampervillage.com) is a privately owned campground in the crossroads of Jacob Lake, 30 miles north of the park entrance. It's open from mid-May to mid-October and has around 100 sites. Rates are $17 for tent sites, $35 for RV sites with full hookups. Make reservations well in advance.

Where to Eat

INSIDE THE PARK

Grand Canyon Lodge (see above) has a dining room with a splendid view. More casual choices at the lodge include a cafeteria and a saloon that serves light meals.

OUTSIDE THE PARK

Your only choices for a meal outside the park are the **Kaibab Lodge** (✆ **928/638-2389;** www.kaibablodge.com), just north of the entrance, and the **Jacob Lake Inn** (✆ **928/643-7232;** www.jacoblake.com), 45 miles north at the junction with U.S. 89A.

FLAGSTAFF ★★

150 miles N of Phoenix; 32 miles E of Williams; 80 miles S of Grand Canyon Village

With its wide variety of accommodations and restaurants, the great outdoors at the edge of town, three national monuments nearby, one of the state's finest museums, and a university that supports a lively cultural community, Flagstaff makes an ideal base for exploring much of northern Arizona.

The San Francisco Peaks, just north of the city, are the site of the Arizona Snowbowl ski area, one of the state's main winter playgrounds. In summer, miles of trails through these same mountains attract hikers and mountain bikers, and it's even possible to ride the chairlift for a panoramic vista that stretches 70 miles north to the Grand Canyon. Of the area's national monuments, two preserve ancient Indian ruins and the third is an otherworldly landscape of volcanic cinder cones.

It was as a railroad town that Flagstaff made its fortunes, and the historic downtown offers a glimpse of the days when the city's fortunes rode the rails. The railroad still runs right through the middle of Flagstaff, but the loud train horns that once plagued visitors hoping for a good night's sleep are now a thing of the past. In early 2010, the city finally negotiated an arrangement with the railroad to eliminate the noisy horns. So, today, Flagstaff really is a good place to spend a night or two.

Essentials

GETTING THERE Flagstaff is on I-40, one of the main east-west interstates in the United States. I-17 starts here and heads south to Phoenix. Ariz. 89A connects Flagstaff to Sedona by way of Oak Creek Canyon. U.S. 180 connects Flagstaff with the South Rim of the Grand Canyon, and U.S. 89 connects the city with Page.

Flagstaff Pulliam Airport, 3 miles south of Flagstaff off I-17, is served by **US Airways** (✆ **800/428-4322;** www.usairways.com) from Phoenix.

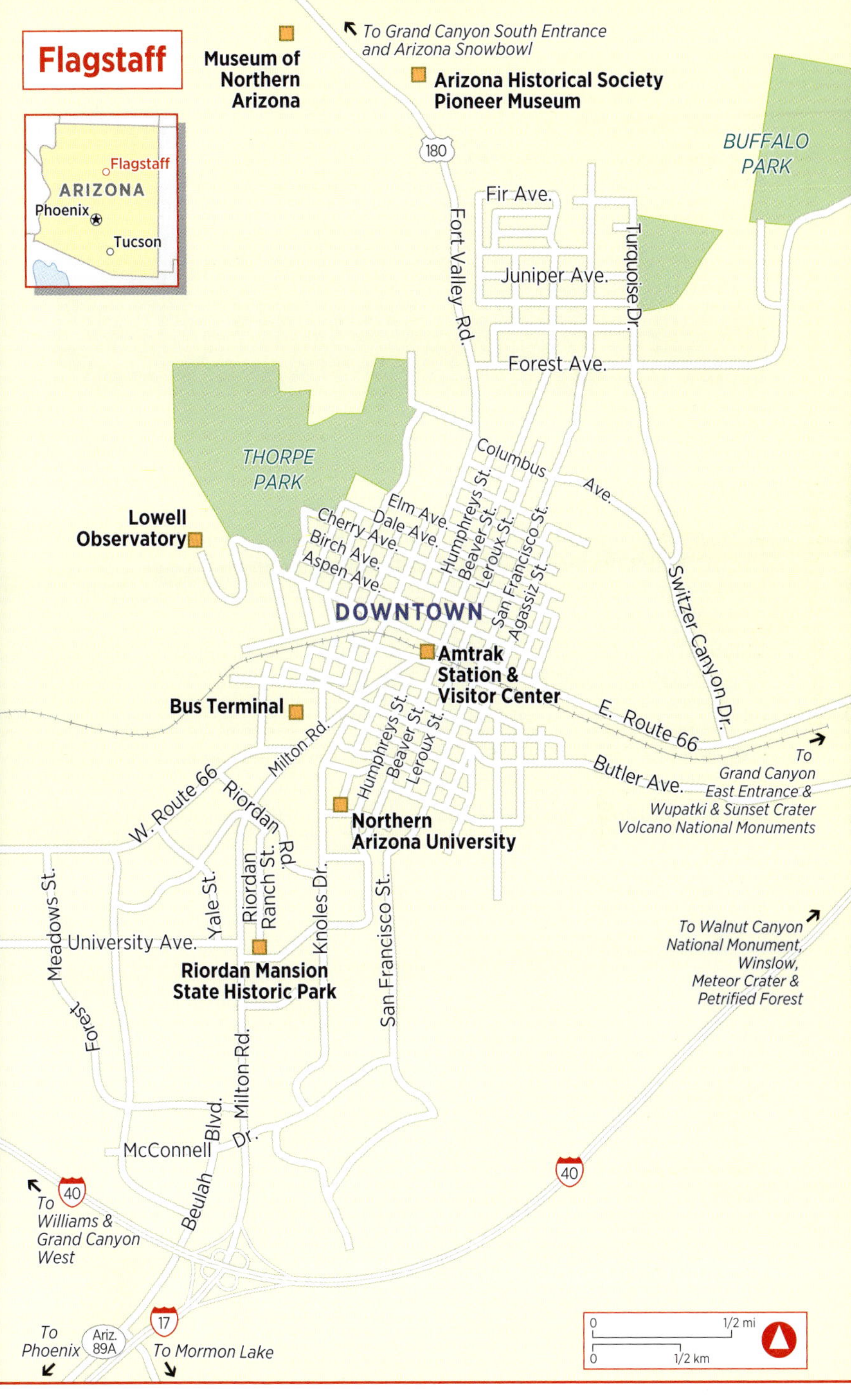
Flagstaff
Flagstaff
ARIZONA
Phoenix
Tucson
Museum of Northern Arizona
To Grand Canyon South Entrance and Arizona Snowbowl
Arizona Historical Society Pioneer Museum
180
BUFFALO PARK
Fir Ave.
Fort Valley Rd.
Juniper Ave.
Turquoise Dr.
Forest Ave.
THORPE PARK
Columbus Ave.
Lowell Observatory
Elm Ave.
Dale Ave.
Cherry Ave.
Birch Ave.
Aspen Ave.
Humphreys St.
Beaver St.
Leroux St.
San Francisco St.
Agassiz St.
Switzer Canyon Dr.
DOWNTOWN
Amtrak Station & Visitor Center
Bus Terminal
E. Route 66
Milton Rd.
Butler Ave.
To Grand Canyon East Entrance & Wupatki & Sunset Crater Volcano National Monuments
W. Route 66
Riordan Rd.
Northern Arizona University
Meadows St.
Yale St.
Riordan Ranch St.
Knoles Dr.
San Francisco St.
University Ave.
Riordan Mansion State Historic Park
To Walnut Canyon National Monument, Winslow, Meteor Crater & Petrified Forest
Forest
Milton Rd.
McConnell Dr.
Beulah Blvd.
40
To Williams & Grand Canyon West
40
To Phoenix
Ariz. 89A
17
To Mormon Lake
0
1/2 mi
0
1/2 km

The Historic Hotel Monte Vista in Flagstaff.

Amtrak (✆ **800/872-7245**) offers service to Flagstaff from Chicago and Los Angeles. The train station is at 1 E. Rte. 66.

VISITOR INFORMATION Contact the **Flagstaff Visitor Center,** 1 E. Rte. 66 (✆ **800/379-0065** or 928/774-9541; www.flagstaffarizona.org). The visitor center is open Monday to Saturday from 8am to 5pm and Sunday from 9am to 4pm.

ORIENTATION Downtown Flagstaff is just north of I-40. Milton Road, which at its southern end becomes I-17 to Phoenix, leads past Northern Arizona University on its way into downtown and becomes Route 66, which runs parallel to the railroad tracks. San Francisco Street is downtown's main street. Humphreys Street leads north out of town toward the San Francisco Peaks and the South Rim of the Grand Canyon.

GETTING AROUND Car rentals are available from **Avis** (✆ **800/331-1212,** 928/774-8421 at the airport, or 928/714-0713 downtown), **Budget** (✆ **800/527-0700,** 928/779-5235 at the airport, or 928/213-0156 downtown), **Enterprise** (✆ **800/261-7331** or 928/526-1377), **Hertz** (✆ **800/654-3131,** 928/774-4452 at the airport, or 928/226-0120 downtown), and **National** (✆ **877/222-9058** or 928/774-3321).

Call **A Friendly Cab** (✆ **800/853-4445** or 928/774-4444; www.afriendlycab.com) if you need a taxi. **Mountain Line Transit** (✆ **928/779-6624;** www.mountainline.az.gov) provides public bus transit around the city; the fare is $1.

Outdoor Pursuits

Flagstaff is northern Arizona's center for outdoor activities. Chief among them is skiing at **Arizona Snowbowl** (✆ **928/779-1951;** www.arizonasnowbowl.com), on the slopes of Mount Agassiz, from which you can see all the way to the North Rim of the Grand Canyon. There are four chairlifts, 32 runs, 2,300 vertical feet of slopes, ski rentals, and a children's ski program. With an excellent mix of beginner, intermediate, and advanced slopes, and as the ski area that's most easily accessed from Phoenix, Snowbowl sees a lot of weekend traffic from the snow-starved denizens of the desert. Conditions are, however, very unreliable, and the ski area can be shut down for weeks on end due to lack of snow. All-day lift tickets are $49 to $57 for adults, $26 for seniors and children 8 to 12, and free for children 7 and under and seniors 70 and over. In summer, you can ride a chairlift almost to the summit of Mount Agassiz and enjoy the expansive views across seemingly all of northern Arizona. The round-trip lift-ticket price is $12 for adults, $8 for seniors and children 8 to 12. To get here, take U.S. 180 N. from Flagstaff for 7 miles and turn right onto Snow Bowl Road.

When no snow is on the ground, there are plenty of trails for hiking amid the San Francisco Peaks, and many national forest trails are open to mountain bikes. Late September, when the aspens have turned a brilliant golden yellow, is one of the best times of year for a hike in Flagstaff's mountains. If you've got the stamina, do the **Humphreys Trail,** which climbs more than 3,300 feet in 4.5 miles. Needless to say, the views from the 12,633-foot summit are stupendous. After all, this is the highest point in Arizona. To reach the trail head, take U.S. 180 N. out of Flagstaff for 7 miles, turn right on Snow Bowl Road, and continue to the parking area by the ski lodge. This is my favorite Flagstaff area hike and is nearly as awe-inspiring in its own way as hiking down into the Grand Canyon.

If you'd like a short hike with a big payoff, hike to **Red Mountain.** This hike is only about 2.5 miles round-trip, but leads to a fascinating red-walled cinder cone that long ago collapsed to reveal its strange interior walls. To find the trail head, drive north from Flagstaff toward the Grand Canyon on U.S. 180. At milepost 247, watch for a forest road leading west for about a quarter-mile to the trail head parking area.

For information on other hikes in the Coconino National Forest, contact the **Flagstaff Ranger Districts,** 5075 N. U.S. 89, Flagstaff 86004 (✆ **928/526-0866;** www.fs.fed.us/r3/coconino).

Seeing the Sights

Downtown Flagstaff—along Route 66, San Francisco Street, Aspen Avenue, and Birch Avenue—is the city's **historic district.** These old brick buildings are now filled with shops selling Native American crafts, works by local artists and artisans, Route 66 souvenirs, and various other Arizona mementos such as rocks, minerals, and crystals. Don't miss **Jonathan Day's Indian Arts,** 21 N. San

Skiers and snowboarders spend winters at Arizona Snowbowl.

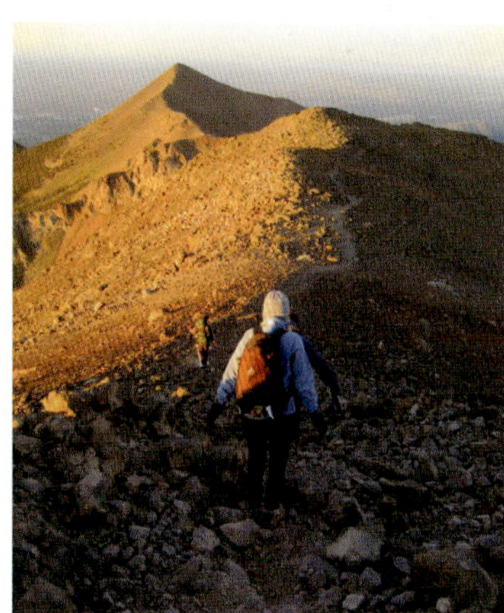

Humphreys Trail climbs more than 3,300 feet in 4.5 miles.

Francisco St. (✆ **928/779-6099;** www.traditionalhopikachinas.com), a small shop with what just might be the best selection of traditional Hopi kachinas in the state. **Puchteca Indian Art,** 20 N. San Francisco St. (✆ **928/774-2414**), is also worth a visit for its interesting Native American jewelry and pottery. Fans of old books should be sure to check out **Starrlight Books,** 15 N. Leroux St. (✆ **928/774-6813**), which is full of first editions and other hard-bound books. There's a good selection of Southwest titles. The **Artists Gallery,** 17 N. San Francisco St. (✆ **928/773-0958;** www.flagstaffartistsgallery.com), which is full of art by local artists, is also worth a visit. The historic district is worth a walk-through even if you aren't shopping. If you need any outdoors gear, head to **Babbitt's Backcountry Outfitters,** 12 E. Aspen Ave. (✆ **928/774-4775;** www.babbittsbackcountry.com).

MUSEUMS, PARKS & CULTURAL ACTIVITIES

The Arboretum at Flagstaff Covering 200 acres, this arboretum, the highest-elevation research garden in the U.S., focuses on plants of the high desert, coniferous forests, and alpine tundra, all of which are environments found in the vicinity of Flagstaff. On the grounds are a butterfly garden, an herb garden, a shade garden, and a passive solar greenhouse. There are guided tours daily at 11am, 1, and 3pm. The arboretum also has regularly scheduled birds-of-prey presentations.

4001 S. Woody Mountain Rd. ✆ **928/774-1442.** www.thearb.org. Admission $7 adults, $6 seniors, $3 children 3–17, free for children 2 and under. Apr–Oct daily 9am–5pm. Closed Nov–Mar.

Arizona Historical Society Pioneer Museum This small historical museum is housed in a stone building that was constructed in 1908 as a hospital for the indigent (in other words, a poor farm). Today, the old hospital contains a historical collection from northern Arizona's pioneer days. Barbed wire, livestock brands, saddles, and trapping and timber displays round out the collection.

2340 N. Fort Valley Rd. ✆ **928/774-6272.** www.arizonahistoricalsociety.org. Admission $5 adults, $4 seniors and students 12–18, free for children 11 and under. Mon–Sat 9am–5pm. Closed New Year's Day, Thanksgiving, and Christmas.

The 24-inch telescope at Lowell Observatory.

Lowell Observatory ★ This historic observatory is located atop aptly named Mars Hill and is one of the oldest astronomical observatories in the Southwest. Founded in 1894 by Percival Lowell, the observatory has played important roles in contemporary astronomy. Among the work carried out here was Lowell's study of the planet Mars and the calculations that led him to predict the existence of Pluto. It wasn't until 13 years after Lowell's death that Pluto was finally discovered almost exactly where he had predicted it would be.

The facility consists of outdoor displays, several observatories, and a visitor center with numerous fun and educational exhibits. During the day, there are

Grand Falls: The Chocolate Niagara

Calm down all you chocoholics. Grand Falls, 33 miles east of Flagstaff, only looks like liquid chocolate; it isn't a real chocolate waterfall. This said, it's still worth the drive out to see it. At 185 feet tall, these falls on the Little Colorado River are higher than Niagara Falls, although the falls do not carry nearly the volume of water that Niagara does. In fact, for most of the year, there's no water at all in Grand Falls. These falls run only during the spring snowmelt season (in years when there has been any snow) and after summer monsoons. Consequently, to see these falls, you need to have good timing. You also need a high-clearance vehicle, because the last 10 miles of the route are on a washboard gravel road that can be impassable if it has rained recently.

To find Grand Falls, drive north from Flagstaff on U.S. 89A, and turn east on Townsend-Winona Road. Drive 8 miles to Leupp Road, and turn left. Follow this road 14 miles to Indian Route 70, which is immediately after the sign marking the boundary of the Navajo Reservation (you may see a sign for GRAND FALLS BIBLE CHURCH). Turn north (left) onto this gravel road and drive 10 miles north to the Little Colorado River. Now turn around and go back ¼ mile to the unmarked rough dirt track on your right. The falls are a few hundred yards down this dirt road.

guided tours every hour between 1 and 4pm, and between 12:15 and 12:50pm, you can look at the sun through a small telescope. However, the main attraction is the chance to observe the stars and planets through the observatory's 24-inch telescope. Keep in mind that the telescope domes are not heated, so if you come up to stargaze, be sure to dress appropriately. There are no programs on cloudy nights.
1400 W. Mars Hill Rd. ✆ **928/774-3358.** www.lowell.edu. Admission $8 adults, $7 seniors and students, $4 children 5–17. Mar–Oct daily 9am–5pm; Nov–Feb daily noon–5pm. Telescope viewings: June–Aug Mon–Sat 5:30–10pm; Sept–May Mon, Wed, and Fri–Sat 5–9:30pm. Closed New Year's Day, Easter, Thanksgiving, and Dec 24–25.

Museum of Northern Arizona ★★ This small but surprisingly thorough museum is the ideal first stop on an exploration of northern Arizona. You'll learn, through state-of-the-art exhibits, about the archaeology, ethnology, geology, biology, and fine arts of the region. The cornerstone of the museum is an exhibit that explores life on the Colorado Plateau from 15,000 B.C. to the present. Among the other displays are a life-size kiva (ceremonial room) and a small but interesting collection of kachinas. The large gift shop is full of contemporary Native American arts and crafts, and during the summer special exhibits and sales focus on Hopi and Navajo arts and crafts.

The museum building itself is made of native stone and incorporates a courtyard featuring vegetation from the six life zones of northern Arizona. Outside is a short self-guided nature trail that leads through a narrow canyon.
3101 N. Fort Valley Rd. (3 miles north of downtown Flagstaff on U.S. 180). ✆ **928/774-5213.** www.musnaz.org. Admission $7 adults, $6 seniors, $5 students, $4 children 7–17. Daily 9am–5pm. Closed New Year's Day, Thanksgiving, and Christmas.

Riordan Mansion State Historic Park ★ Built in 1904 for local timber barons Michael and Timothy Riordan, this 13,000-square-foot mansion—Arizona's finest example of an Arts and Crafts–era building—is actually two houses connected by a large central hall. Each brother and his family occupied half of the house (they had the rooflines constructed differently so that visitors could tell the two sides apart). Although the mansion appears to be built of logs, it's actually just faced with log slabs. Inside, mission-style furnishings and touches of Art Nouveau styling make it clear that this family was keeping up with the times. The west wing of the mansion holds displays on, among other things, Stickley furniture. Guided tours provide a glimpse into the lives of two of Flagstaff's most influential pioneers.

409 W. Riordan Rd. (off Milton Rd./Ariz. 89A, just north of the junction of I-40 and I-17). ✆ **928/779-4395.** www.azstateparks.com. Admission $7 adults, $3 children 7–13. Thurs–Mon 9:30am–5pm. Guided tours on the hour. Closed Christmas.

Sunset Crater Volcano National Monument ★ Dotting the landscape northeast of Flagstaff are more than 400 volcanic craters, of which Sunset Crater Volcano is the youngest. Taking its name from the colors of the cinders near its summit, Sunset Crater Volcano stands 1,000 feet tall and began forming around 1040. Over a period of more than 150 years, the volcano erupted repeatedly (creating the red-and-yellow cinder cone seen today) and eventually covered an area of 800 square miles with ash, lava, and cinders. A 1-mile interpretive trail passes through a desolate landscape of lava flows, cinders, and ash as it skirts the base of this volcano. If you want to climb to the top of a cinder cone, take the 1-mile Lenox Crater Trail. In the visitor center (at the west entrance to the national monument), you can learn more about the formation of Sunset Crater and about volcanoes in general. Near the visitor center is the 44-site Bonito Campground, which is open from early May to mid-October and charges $18 for a campsite.

14 miles north of Flagstaff off U.S. 89. ✆ **928/526-0502.** www.nps.gov/sucr. Admission $5 adults, free for children 15 and under (admission also valid for Wupatki National Monument). Daily sunrise–sunset; visitor center daily May–Oct 8am–5pm, Nov–Apr 9am–5pm. Visitor center closed Christmas.

Walnut Canyon National Monument ★ The remains of 300 small 13th-century Sinagua cliff dwellings can be seen in the undercut layers of limestone in this 400-foot-deep wooded canyon east of Flagstaff. These cliff dwellings,

Riordan Mansion.

Sunset Crater Volcano is the youngest of Flagstaff's 400 volcanic craters.

though not nearly as impressive as the ruins at Montezuma Castle National Monument (50 miles to the south) or Wupatki National Monument (20 miles to the north), are worth a visit for the chance to poke around inside the well-preserved rooms, which were well protected from the elements (and from enemies). The Sinagua were the same people who built and then abandoned the stone pueblos in Wupatki National Monument, and it is theorized that when the land to the north lost its fertility, the Sinagua began migrating southward, settling for 150 years in Walnut Canyon.

A self-guided trail leads from the visitor center on the canyon rim down 185 feet to a section of the canyon wall where 25 cliff dwellings can be viewed up close (some can even be entered). Bring binoculars so that you can scan the canyon walls for other cliff dwellings. From Memorial Day to Labor Day twice a month, on the first and last Saturday, there are guided hikes into the monument's backcountry (reservations required). There's also a picnic area near the visitor center.

7½ miles east of Flagstaff on Walnut Canyon Rd. (take exit 204 off I-40). ✆ **928/526-3367.** www.nps.gov/waca. Admission $5 adults, free for children 15 and under. May–Oct daily 8am–5pm; Nov–Apr daily 9am–5pm. Visitor center closed Christmas.

Wupatki National Monument ★★ The landscape northeast of Flagstaff is desolate and windswept, a sparsely populated region carpeted with volcanic ash deposited in the 11th century. It may come as a surprise, then, to learn that this area contains hundreds of archaeological sites. The most impressive are pueblo ruins left by the Sinagua (the name means "without water" in Spanish), who inhabited this area from around 1100 until around 1250. According to contemporary Hopis and Zunis, the people who lived in this area were their ancestors, and it is easy to see the similarity between the stone-walled pueblos here and the traditional homes on the nearby Hopi Reservation. Today the ruins of several ancient villages can be seen in this national monument.

The largest of the pueblos is Wupatki Ruin, in the southeastern part of the monument. Here the Sinagua built a sprawling three-story pueblo containing nearly 100 rooms. They also constructed what is believed to be a ball court, which, although quite different in design from the courts of the Aztec and Maya, suggests that a similar game may have been played in this region. Another circular stone structure just below the main ruins may have been an amphitheater or a dance plaza.

The most unusual feature of Wupatki, however, is a natural phenomenon: a blowhole, which may have been the reason this pueblo was constructed here. A network of small underground tunnels and chambers acts as a giant barometer, blowing air through the blowhole when the underground air is under greater pressure than the outside air. On hot days, cool air rushes out of the blowhole with amazing force.

Join an Archaeological Dig

Elden Pueblo, on the north side of Flagstaff on U.S. 89, is a small archaeological site that is open to the public free of charge. Although these Sinagua ruins are not much to look at, you can help out with the excavation of the site if you're interested. Each summer, the Arizona Archaeological Society (www.azarchsoc.org) operates the **Elden Pueblo Field School** (✆ **928/527-3452**). Field schools cost $100 to $150 per week (plus AAS membership dues).

Several other ruins within the national monument are easily accessible by car. They include Nalakihu, Citadel, and Lomaki, which are the closest to U.S. 89, and Wukoki, near Wupatki. Wukoki Ruin, built atop a huge sandstone boulder, is particularly picturesque. The visitor center is adjacent to the Wupatki ruins and contains interesting exhibits on the Sinagua and Ancestral Puebloan people who once inhabited the region. November through March, there are reservation-only guided hikes on Saturdays.

33 miles north of Flagstaff off U.S. 89. ✆ **928/679-2365.** www.nps.gov/wupa. Admission $5 adults, free for children 15 and under (admission also valid for Sunset Crater Volcano National Monument). Daily sunrise–sunset; visitor center daily 9am–5pm (closed Christmas).

Where to Stay

EXPENSIVE

Shooting Star Inn ★ Although this rustic inn has only three simply furnished rooms and is a bit out of the way (about midway btw. Flagstaff and the Grand Canyon), it is so unusual I think you should know about it. It's definitely not for everyone, but a stay here just might be the most memorable part of a visit to northern Arizona. The modern log inn is an off-the-grid home, which means that electricity here is produced by an array of photovoltaic panels. The Shooting Star is operated by professional photographer Tom Taylor, whose real passion is astronomy; as part of your stay, you'll get to study the stars and planets through some of Taylor's many telescopes. Because the inn is so far from town, you may want to arrange to have Taylor cook dinners for you.

27948 N. Shooting Star Lane, Flagstaff, AZ 86001. www.shootingstarinn.com. ✆ **928/606-8070.** 3 units. $195 double. Rates include full breakfast and astronomy program. AE, DISC, MC, V. *In room:* No phone, free Wi-Fi.

MODERATE

England House Bed & Breakfast ★★ This B&B, just 3 blocks from Flagstaff's historic downtown, is a beautiful two-story Victorian red-sandstone house built in 1902. This old house was lovingly restored by owners Richard and Laurel Dunn, who are devoted to details. Consequently, the England House has a delightful period authenticity. The three large guest rooms are on the second floor and are furnished with 1870s French antiques. There's also a small guest room, called the Pantry (though it isn't really *that* small), on the ground floor. One room has a Tempur-Pedic mattress, while another has a feather bed. Breakfasts are served in a bright sunroom just off the kitchen.

614 W. Santa Fe Ave., Flagstaff, AZ 86001. www.englandhousebandb.com. ✆ **877/214-7350** or 928/214-7350. 4 units. $129–$199 double. Rates include full breakfast. DISC, MC, V. No children 11 or under. **Amenities:** Concierge. *In room:* A/C, hair dryer, no phone, free Wi-Fi.

The Inn at 410 ★★ Situated only 2 blocks from historic downtown Flagstaff, this restored 1894 Craftsman home is one of the best B&Bs in Arizona, providing convenience, pleasant surroundings, comfortable rooms, and delicious breakfasts. Guests can lounge and enjoy afternoon tea on the front porch, in the comfortable dining room, or in the garden. Each guest room features a distinctive theme; my favorites are Canyon Memories and the Southwest Suite, which conjure up the inn's Western heritage. All rooms have fireplaces, and three have two-person whirlpool tubs. Some of the guest rooms are in an adjacent building that overlooks the gardens. Brix, one of Flagstaff's best restaurants, is right next door.

410 N. Leroux St., Flagstaff, AZ 86001. www.inn410.com. ✆ **800/774-2008** or 928/774-0088. Fax 928/774-6354. 9 units. Mar–Oct $160–$210 double; Nov–Feb $150–$200 double. 2-night minimum on weekends Apr–Oct. Rates include full breakfast and afternoon refreshments. MC, V. No children 4 or under. **Amenities:** Concierge; exercise room and access to nearby health club. *In room:* A/C, TV/DVD/VCR, fridge, hair dryer, no phone, free Wi-Fi.

Little America Hotel ★ Set on 500 acres of pine forest and with a trail that winds for 2 miles through the property, this hotel on the east side of Flagstaff might seem at first to be little more than a giant truck stop. However, on closer inspection, you'll find that behind the truck stop stands a surprisingly luxurious and economical hotel set beneath shady pines. The decor is dated but fun, with a sort of French Provincial style predominating. Rooms vary in size, but all have small private balconies.

2515 E. Butler Ave., Flagstaff, AZ 86004. www.littleamerica.com/flagstaff. ✆ **800/865-1401** or 928/779-2741. Fax 928/779-7983. 247 units. $99–$229 double; $249–$349 suite. Children 17 and under stay free in parent's room. AE, DC, DISC, MC, V. Take exit 198 off I-40. **Amenities:** Restaurant; lounge; free airport transfers; concierge; exercise room; Jacuzzi; outdoor pool; room service. *In room:* A/C, TV, fridge, hair dryer, free Wi-Fi.

Radisson Woodlands Hotel Flagstaff ★ With its elegant marble-floored lobby, the Woodlands Hotel is easily the most upscale lodging in Flagstaff. A white baby grand, a crystal chandelier, traditional European furnishings, and contemporary sculpture all add to the unexpected luxury in the public spaces, as do intricately carved pieces of furniture and architectural details from different Asian countries. Guest rooms are quite comfortable and have Sleep Number® beds.

1175 W. Rte. 66, Flagstaff, AZ 86001. www.radisson.com/flagstaffaz. ✆ **800/395-7046** or 928/773-8888. Fax 928/773-0597. 183 units. $99–$139 double; $144–$184 suite. AE, DC, DISC, MC, V. **Amenities:** 2 restaurants; lounge; free airport transfers; exercise room; indoor and outdoor Jacuzzis; seasonal outdoor pool; room service; sauna. *In room:* A/C, TV, hair dryer, free Wi-Fi.

INEXPENSIVE

Historic Hotel Monte Vista This hotel is definitely not for everyone. Although it is historic, it is also a bit run-down and appeals primarily to young travelers who appreciate the low rates and the nightclub just off the lobby. So why stay here? In its day, the Monte Vista hosted the likes of Clark Gable, John Wayne, Carole Lombard, and Gary Cooper, and today, the hotel is supposedly haunted (ask at the front desk for the list of resident ghosts). Opened in 1927, the Monte Vista now has creatively decorated rooms that vary in size and decor. Although the hotel has plenty of old-fashioned flair, don't expect perfection. Check out a room first to see if this is your kind of place.

100 N. San Francisco St., Flagstaff, AZ 86001. www.hotelmontevista.com. ✆ **800/545-3068** or 928/779-6971. Fax 928/779-2904. 50 units, 5 with shared bathrooms. May to early Nov $65

double with shared bathroom, $80–$130 double with private bathroom, $120–$175 suite; early Nov to Apr $50–$55 double with shared bathroom, $70–$110 double with private bathroom, $100–$140 suite. Children 17 and under stay free in parent's room. AE, DISC, MC, V. Pets accepted ($25 fee). **Amenities:** Restaurant; lounge; free Wi-Fi. *In room:* TV, hair dryer.

Hotel Weatherford This historic hotel in downtown Flagstaff is a casual sort of place popular with young travelers, but it has loads of character. The distinctive stone-walled 1897 building has a wraparound veranda on its third floor, where you'll also find the beautifully restored Zane Grey Ballroom (now an elegant bar). Downstairs are a casual restaurant and the ever-popular Charly's Pub & Grill, which has been booking live rock, blues, and jazz acts for more than 3 decades. The hotel is the site of the annual New Year's Eve giant pine-cone drop.

23 N. Leroux St., Flagstaff, AZ 86001. www.weatherfordhotel.com. ✆ **928/779-1919.** 11 units, 3 with shared bathrooms. $49–$79 double with shared bathroom; $89 double with private bathroom; $130 suite. Children 12 and under stay free in parent's room. AE, DC, DISC, MC, V. **Amenities:** Restaurant; 3 lounges. *In room:* A/C (in 3 rooms), TV (in 3 rooms), MP3 docking station, no phone, free Wi-Fi.

Where to Eat

If you're headed north to the Grand Canyon and need a good espresso to get you there, stop at **Late for the Train Espresso,** 1800 N. Fort Valley Rd. (✆ **928/773-0308;** www.lateforthetrain.com), on U.S. 180 as you drive north out of town. Just watch for the old gas station. There's another location downtown at 107 N. San Francisco St. (✆ **928/779-5975**). On cold mornings, though, only one Flagstaff coffee drink will do, and that's the "Hot Monte" at the Hotel Monte Vista's **Rendezvous Coffee House/Martini Bar,** 100 N. San Francisco St. (✆ **928/779-6971;** www.hotelmontevista.com). It's made with espresso, chocolate, milk, cinnamon, and cayenne. If you need to stock up on picnic supplies, try **New Frontiers Natural Marketplace,** 320 S. Cambridge Lane at Butler Avenue (✆ **928/774-5747**). For good old-fashioned pies, head east of downtown Flagstaff to **Miz Zip's,** 2924 E. Rte. 66 (✆ **928/526-0104**).

EXPENSIVE

Brix Restaurant and Wine Bar ★★ NEW AMERICAN Although it's a bit hard to find (tucked into a corner of an old brick carriage house), Brix, Flagstaff's most contemporary restaurant, is well worth searching out. The menu relies on fresh, seasonal ingredients, so it changes regularly. However, any time of year, you'll find a great selection of artisanal cheeses, which make a good starter to a meal here. The chef's creativity shines through in such dishes as pancetta-wrapped scallops with pumpkin risotto and sage brown butter; lamb shanks with lentil-and-eggplant ragout; and porcini gnocchi with leeks, oyster mushrooms, and greens. There's an excellent wine list to accompany the food.

413 N. San Francisco St. ✆ **928/213-1021.** www.brixflagstaff.com. Reservations recommended. Main courses $23–$34. AE, DISC, MC, V. Sun–Thurs 5–9pm; Fri–Sat 5–10pm.

Cottage Place Restaurant ★ CONTINENTAL/NEW AMERICAN On the south side of the railroad tracks in a neighborhood mostly frequented by college students, Cottage Place is just what its name implies—an unpretentious little cottage. But despite the casual appearance, dining here is a formal affair. The menu, which tends toward the rich side, is primarily Continental, with a few Southwestern influences as well. The house specialties are chateaubriand and rack of lamb (both served for two), and there are always a couple of choices for vegetarians as well. The appetizer sampler, with herb-stuffed mushrooms, grilled shrimp, and crab cake, is a winner. There's a long, award-winning wine list, and between 5 and 6pm, there are twilight dinners for $16 to $20.

126 W. Cottage Ave. ✆ **928/774-8431.** www.cottageplace.com. Reservations recommended. Main courses $20–$42; tasting menu $55. AE, DISC, MC, V. Wed–Sun 5–9:30pm.

Josephine's Modern American Bistro ★ REGIONAL AMERICAN Housed in a restored Craftsman bungalow with a beautiful stone fireplace and a wide front porch for summer dining, this restaurant combines a historical setting with excellent food that draws on a wide range of influences. For these reasons, this is my favorite Flagstaff restaurant. The pork *osso buco* with green-chili risotto is a real winner. At lunch, try the crab-cake po' boy sandwich. There's a good selection of reasonably priced wines also.

503 N. Humphreys St. ✆ **928/779-3400.** www.josephinesrestaurant.com. Reservations recommended. Main courses $9.75–$13 lunch, $19–$30 dinner. AE, DISC, MC, V. Mon–Fri 11am–2:30pm and 5–9pm; Sat–Sun 5–9pm.

MODERATE

Criollo ★ LATIN AMERICAN Utilizing locally grown and sustainably produced ingredients as much as possible, this casually hip restaurant in downtown Flagstaff serves flavorful food from a range of Latin American countries. The chicken *mole* burrito and the fish tacos are excellent, and for a starter, I like the *hallaca,* which is basically a tamale made with a banana-leaf wrapper instead of a corn husk. There are lots of small plates, in case you just want a light meal, and the bar whips up some very interesting cocktails. Best of all, this place is open late (for Flagstaff), which means you won't have to go without dinner if you spent longer than you planned at the Grand Canyon.

16 N. San Francisco St. ✆ **928/774-0541.** www.criollolatinkitchen.com. Reservations recommended. Main courses $10–$16 lunch, $12–$18 dinner. AE, DISC, MC, V. Mon–Thurs 11am–10pm; Fri 11am–midnight; Sat 9am–midnight; Sun 9am–10pm.

Pasto ★ ITALIAN Located in downtown Flagstaff, Pasto has a lively urban feel and serves some of the best food in town. It is always reliable, but be aware that it can get boisterous on the weekends. Casual yet sophisticated, Pasto is less formal than Brix, Cottage Place, or Josephine's, so if you don't feel like getting dressed up after a day at the canyon, come here. As the restaurant's name implies, the menu includes a good assortment of pastas; however, entrees here are so creative that I always start with a small order of pasta so I'll have room for the likes of seared scallops with mushroom risotto or grilled salmon with fired gnocchi and Gorgonzola-grilled pear.

19 E. Aspen St. ✆ **928/779-1937.** www.pastorestaurant.com. Reservations recommended. Main courses $8–$10 lunch, $15–$30 dinner. AE, DISC, MC, V. Mon–Sat 11am–2pm and 5–9pm.

INEXPENSIVE

Beaver Street Brewery AMERICAN/PIZZA This big microbrewery, cafe, and billiards parlor on the south side of the railroad tracks serves up several good brews, and it also does great pizzas and salads. The Beaver Street pizza, made with roasted-garlic pesto, sun-dried tomatoes, fresh basil, and goat cheese, is particularly tasty. Among the large, filling salads, my favorite is the Mongolian beef, which is served on a bed of greens with sesame-ginger dressing. This place stays packed with college students, but a good pint of ale helps any wait pass quickly, especially if you can grab a seat by the woodstove. The brewery also operates the adjacent **Beaver Street Brews & Cues,** 3 S. Beaver St., which has pool tables and a vintage bar.

11 S. Beaver St. ✆ **928/779-0079.** www.beaverstreetbrewery.com. Reservations not accepted. Main courses $9.25–$15. AE, DISC, MC, V. Sun–Thurs 11am–11pm; Fri–Sat 11am–midnight.

Diablo Burger 🎁 AMERICAN If ever there were the quintessential hole in the wall, this is it. With little more than a small sign on the door of what looks to be an old silo but is actually a parking-garage support column, Diablo Burger may be hard to find, but it is definitely worth the search. Burgers are made from locally raised natural beef and, as often as possible, produce is local. The burgers are served on English muffins and come with some of the best fries in Arizona. I'm a fan of the Blake burger, which is made with a roasted green chili, but the Vitamin B, with bacon, blue cheese, and beets, is also pretty good. To find Diablo Burger, look to the left of the Pesto Brothers restaurant on the plaza in downtown Flagstaff.

120 N. Leroux St. ✆ **928/774-3274.** www.diabloburger.com. Reservations not accepted. Main courses $7.75–$9.75. No credit cards. Mon–Wed 11am–9pm; Thurs–Sat 11am–11pm.

Himalayan Grill INDIAN/TIBETAN The food of India and Tibet are featured at this restaurant in a little strip mall south of downtown Flagstaff. While the Indian dishes here are quite good, I like to order the less familiar Tibetan dishes. The *momos* are similar to Japanese *gyoza* or Chinese potstickers. Here you can get them stuffed with either meat or vegetables. Follow your *momos* with a bowl of *thupka* (a hearty noodle soup) or *chau chau* (pan-fried noodles). Both of these latter dishes can be ordered with chicken or lamb. At lunch, there's a $9 buffet, and on Sundays, brunch is served.

801 S. Milton Ave. ✆ **928/213-5444.** www.himalayangrill.com. Main courses $10–$21. AE, DISC, MC, V. Daily 11am–2:30pm and 5–10:30pm.

Karma Sushi Bar Tapas ★ JAPANESE Located on historic Route 66 directly across from the Flagstaff Visitor Center, this stylish sushi place has a fun Asian rustic feel. The clientele tends to be college students, not tourists, which is why I like to eat here. Of course, since this place specializes in sushi and small plates, it's also a great place for a light meal, especially after one too many cowboy-size steaks. I'm a sucker for fancy sushi rolls, and here I like to get the caterpillar (freshwater eel, cucumber, artificial crab, and avocado slices) and the black cat roll (tempura asparagus, spicy lobster, mango, and avocado with black sesame seeds).

6 E. Rte. 66. ✆ **928/774-6100.** www.karmaflagstaff.com. Reservations not accepted. Sushi $3.50–$13; main courses $8–$17. AE, DISC, MC, V. Mon–Sat 11am–10pm; Sun 4:30–10pm.

Macy's European Coffee House & Bakery COFFEEHOUSE/BAKERY Good espresso and baked goodies draw people in here the first time, but there are also decent vegetarian pasta dishes, soups, salads, and other college-town standbys. This is Flagstaff's counterculture hangout, attracting both students and professors. For the true Macy's experience, order one of the huge lattes and a scone or other pastry.

14 S. Beaver St. ✆ **928/774-2243.** www.macyscoffee.net. Meals $3.25–$7.75. MC, V. Daily 6am–8pm.

Flagstaff After Dark

For events taking place during your visit, check *Flagstaff Live* (www.flaglive.com), a free weekly newspaper available at shops and restaurants downtown. The university has many musical and theatrical groups that perform throughout most of the year, and several clubs around town book a variety of live acts.

The **Orpheum Theater,** 15 W. Aspen St. (✆ **928/556-1580;** www.orpheumpresents.com), in downtown Flagstaff, gets the best of touring rock, folk, and country acts, so be sure to check the schedule while you're in town. In summer, also check out what's showing at **Movies on the Square** (✆ **928/853-4292;** www.heritagesquaretrust.org), a free outdoor movie series shown at downtown Flagstaff's Heritage Square on Friday nights. There's live entertainment before the movies, as well as on Thursday nights and Saturday and Sunday afternoons. In addition, during the warmer months, regular outdoor concerts are performed at the **Pine Mountain Amphitheater,** Fort Tuthill County Park (✆ **928/774-0899;** www.pinemountainamphitheater.com), which is located at exit 337 off I-17 south of Flagstaff.

Flagstaff has four good brewpubs. My favorite is the **Beaver Street Brewery,** 11 S. Beaver St. (✆ **928/779-0079;** www.beaverstreetbrewery.com), described under "Where to Eat," above. This brewery also operates the **Lumberyard Brewing Company Taproom and Grille,** 5 S. San Francisco St. (✆ **928/779-2739;** www.lumberyardbrewingcompany.com). Also try **Flagstaff Brewing Co.,** 16 E. Rte. 66 (✆ **928/773-1442;** www.flagbrew.com). Climb the stairs to the **Wine Loft ★**, 17 N. San Francisco St. (✆ **928/773-9463**), a wine bar located above the Artists Gallery in downtown Flagstaff; if you're like me, you'll wish you had a place like this in your town. Local musicians play live several nights per week. I wouldn't think of leaving Flagstaff without hanging out here at least one evening. Also check out **Cuveé 928,** 6 E. Aspen Ave., Ste. 110 (✆ **928/214-9463;** www.cuvee928winebar.com), a wine bar/bar right on Heritage Square in downtown Flagstaff.

For a livelier scene, check out the **Museum Club,** 3404 E. Rte. 66 (✆ **928/526-9434**), a Flagstaff institution and one of America's classic roadhouses. Built in the early 1900s and often called the Zoo, this cavernous log saloon is filled with deer antlers, stuffed animals, and trophy heads. There's live music (mostly country) on weekends.

Other places around town with live music include **Charly's Pub,** 23 N. Leroux St. (✆ **928/779-1919;** www.weatherfordhotel.com), inside the historic Weatherford Hotel. This place has long been a popular student hangout featuring live blues and rock. For a mellower scene, see what's on the schedule at the **Campus Coffee Bean,** 1800 S. Milton Rd. (✆ **928/556-0660;** www.flagcampuscoffeebean.com).

WILLIAMS

32 miles W of Flagstaff; 58 miles S of the Grand Canyon; 220 miles E of Las Vegas, NV

Although it's almost 60 miles south of the Grand Canyon, Williams is still the closest real town to the national park. Consequently, it has dozens of motels catering to those unable to get a room in or just outside the park. Founded in 1880 as a railroading and logging town, Williams also has a bit of Western history to boast about, which makes it an interesting place to explore for a morning or

Williams is home to the Grand Canyon Railway depot.

afternoon. Old brick commercial buildings dating from the late 19th century line the main street, while modest Victorian homes sit on the tree-shaded streets that spread south from the railroad tracks. In recent years, however, mid-20th-century history has taken center stage: Williams was the last town on historic Route 66 to be bypassed by I-40, and the town now plays up its Route 66 heritage.

Most important for many visitors, however, is that Williams is where you'll find the Grand Canyon Railway depot. The excursion train that departs from here not only provides a fun ride on the rails, but also serves as an alternative to dealing with traffic congestion in Grand Canyon National Park. Of course, there are also the obligatory on-your-way-to-the-Grand-Canyon tourist traps nearby, and these family-oriented attractions make Williams a good choice for families.

Named for famed mountain man Bill Williams, the town sits at the edge of a ponderosa pine forest atop the Mogollon Rim. Surrounding Williams is the Kaibab National Forest, and within the forest not far from town are good fishing lakes, hiking and mountain-biking trails, and even a small downhill ski area.

Essentials

GETTING THERE Williams is on I-40 just west of the junction with Ariz. 64, which leads north to the South Rim of the Grand Canyon.

Amtrak (✆ **800/872-7245**) has service to Williams on its *Southwest Chief* line. There's no station, though—the train stops on the outskirts of town. However, a shuttle van from the Grand Canyon Railway Hotel will pick you up and drive you into town, and since most people coming to Williams by train are continuing on to the Grand Canyon on the Grand Canyon Railway, this arrangement works well.

For information on the **Grand Canyon Railway** excursion trains to Grand Canyon Village, see "Exploring the Area: Route 66 & Beyond," below.

VISITOR INFORMATION For information on the Williams area, including details on hiking, mountain biking, and fishing, contact the **Williams/Forest Service Visitors Center,** 200 W. Railroad Ave. (✆ **800/863-0546** or 928/635-4061; www.williamschamber.com). The visitor center, which includes some interesting historical displays, is open daily from 8am to 5pm. The shop carries books on the Grand Canyon and trail maps for the adjacent national forest.

Exploring the Area: Route 66 & Beyond

These days, most people coming to Williams are here to board the **Grand Canyon Railway** ★★, Williams Depot, 233 N. Grand Canyon Blvd. (✆ **800/843-8724** or 303/843-8724; www.thetrain.com), which operates vintage steam and diesel locomotives between Williams and Grand Canyon Village. Round-trip fares (not including tax or the national park entrance fee) range from $70 to $190 for adults, $40 to $110 for children 2 to 12. Although this is primarily a day-excursion train, it's possible to ride up one day and return on a different day—just let the reservations clerk know that's what you want to do. The same company that operates the train also manages the hotels in Grand Canyon Village. If you can't get a reservation at one of the hotels inside the park, you'll end up having to take a shuttle bus or taxi out of the park to your hotel, which can be inconvenient and add a bit to your daily costs.

Route 66 fans will want to drive Williams's main street, which, not surprisingly, is named Route 66. Along this stretch of the old highway, you can check out the town's vintage buildings, many of which house shops selling Route 66 souvenirs. A few antiques stores sell collectibles from the heyday of the famous highway.

The Williams stretch of Route 66.

Both east and west of town you can drive more sections of the "Mother Road." However, with the exception of the section that begins at exit 139, these stretches are not very remarkable and are recommended only for die-hard fans of Route 66. East of town, take exit 167 off I-40 and follow the graveled **Old Trails Highway** (the predecessor to Route 66). A paved section of Route 66 begins at exit 171 on the north side of the interstate and extends for 7 miles to the site of the Parks General Store. From Parks, you can continue to Brannigan Park on a graveled section of Route 66.

West of Williams, take exit 157 and go south. If you turn east at the T intersection, you'll be on a gravel section of the old highway; if you turn west, you'll be on a paved section. Another stretch can be accessed at exit 106. If you continue another 12 miles west and take exit 139, you'll be on the longest uninterrupted stretch of Route 66 left in the country. It extends from here all the way to Kingman, and along the way, passes through the town of **Seligman,** which has several interesting buildings.

Family Attractions

Bearizona ☺ If your kids start whining that they didn't see any mountain lions, wolves, or bears at the Grand Canyon, oh my, bring them to this drive-through wildlife park on the eastern outskirts of Williams. Not only are there the black bears for which the park is named, but also wolves, bighorn sheep, and bison. As of 2011, the park was quite new, so there were still many more animal enclosures planned.

1500 E. Rte. 66, Williams. ✆ **928/635-2289.** www.bearizona.com. $16 adults, $15 seniors, $8 children 4–12, free for children 3 and under. Daily 8am–5pm (later in summer). Closed Thanksgiving, Christmas, and Jan–Feb.

Grand Canyon Deer Farm ☺ If you have the kids with you, be sure to stop at this private petting zoo, where you'll find both axis deer and reindeer, as well as miniature horses, donkeys, and cattle. Best of all, you get to pet and feed the deer and some of the other animals. You'll also see bison, llamas, a camel, a coatimundi, and even wallabies and marmosets. Between April and August, you're likely to see newborns.

6769 E. Deer Farm Rd. ✆ **800/926-3337** or 928/635-4073. www.deerfarm.com. Admission $8.50 adults, $7.50 seniors, $5 ages 3–13, free for children 2 and under. Oct 16–Mar 15 daily 10am–5pm; Mar 16–Oct 15 daily 9am–6pm. Closed Thanksgiving and Christmas. Take exit 171 (Deer Farm Rd.) off I-40, 8 miles east of Williams.

Planes of Fame Air Museum Fans of old fighter planes may want to spend a little time wandering around the hangar at this air museum. Among the planes on display are American, Japanese, and Russian fighters. You can also see an old Ford Trimotor (the sort of plane that once flew tourists over the Grand Canyon).

Valle Airport, 755 Mustang Way, Valle. ✆ **928/635-1000.** www.planesoffame.org. Admission $5.95 adults, $1.95 ages 5–11, free for children 4 and under. Daily 9am–5pm. Closed Thanksgiving and Christmas. 30 miles north of Williams on Ariz. 64.

Where to Stay

MODERATE

Grand Canyon Railway Hotel ★ This hotel is operated by the Grand Canyon Railway and combines modern comforts with the style of a classic Western railroad hotel. The high-ceilinged lobby features a large flagstone fireplace and paintings of the Grand Canyon. The very comfortable guest rooms feature Southwestern styling; ask for a unit in the wing with the fitness room, pool, and hot tub. The hotel's elegant lounge, which features a 100-year-old English bar, serves simple meals, and there's a buffet-style restaurant adjacent. Although this hotel does not accept pets, they do have a pet "resort."

233 N. Grand Canyon Blvd., Williams, AZ 86046. www.thetrain.com. ✆ **800/843-8724** or 928/635-4010. Fax 928/773-1610. 298 units. Mid-Mar to mid-Oct and holidays $169–$189 double, $219–$350 suite; mid-Oct to mid-Mar $109–$119 double, $350 suite. Railroad/hotel packages available (mid-Mar to mid-Oct and holidays $225 per person; mid-Oct to mid-Mar $158 per person). Children 15 and under stay free in parent's room. AE, DC, DISC, MC, V. **Amenities:** 2 restaurants; lounge; exercise room; indoor pool. *In room:* A/C, TV, hair dryer, Wi-Fi ($10 per day).

The Red Garter Inn ★ 🎁 The Wild West lives again at this restored 1897 bordello, but these days the only tarts that come with the rooms are in the bakery downstairs. Located across the street from the Grand Canyon Railway terminal at the top of a steep flight of stairs, this B&B sports high ceilings, attractive wood trim, and reproduction period furnishings. Walls in a couple of rooms have graffiti written by bordello visitors in the early 20th century. The great historical atmosphere makes this my favorite place to stay in Williams.

137 W. Railroad Ave., Williams, AZ 86046. www.redgarter.com. ✆ **800/328-1484** or 928/635-1484. 4 units. $120–$145 double. Rates include continental breakfast. DISC, MC, V. No children 7 or under. **Amenities:** Restaurant. *In room:* TV, no phone, free Wi-Fi.

INEXPENSIVE

In addition to the following choice, there are numerous budget chain motels in Williams.

The Canyon Motel & RV Park ★ You'll find this updated 1940s Route 66 motor lodge on the eastern outskirts of Williams, tucked against the trees. While the setting and the rooms in 1940s flagstone cottages are nice enough, the real attractions are the railroad cars parked in the front yard. You can stay in a caboose or a Pullman car, which makes this a fun place to overnight if you plan to take the excursion train to the Grand Canyon. I prefer the caboose rooms, which have a more authentic feel. An indoor pool, a horseshoe pit, a swing set, and nature trails provide plenty of entertainment for the whole family. There's also a deluxe RV park here.

1900 E. Rodeo Rd., Williams, AZ 86046. www.thecanyonmotel.com. ✆ **800/482-3955** or 928/635-9371. Fax 928/635-4138. 23 units. $40–$79 double; $159 caboose; $105 Pullman double. DISC, MC, V. **Amenities:** Small indoor pool. *In room:* TV, fridge, hair dryer, no phone, free Wi-Fi.

CAMPGROUNDS

There are several campgrounds near Williams in the Kaibab National Forest. They include **Cataract Lake,** 1 mile northwest of Williams on Cataract Lake Road, with 18 sites ($14 per night); **Dogtown Lake,** 6½ miles southeast of Williams off Fourth Street/Perkinsville Road/F.R. 173, with 52 sites ($18 per night); **Kaibab Lake,** 4 miles northeast of Williams off Ariz. 64, with 63 sites ($18 per night); and **Whitehorse Lake,** 19 miles southeast of Williams off Fourth Street/Perkinsville Road/F.R. 173, with 94 sites ($18 per night).

Where to Eat

Red Raven Restaurant ★ NEW AMERICAN A cheeseburger and a milkshake may be the meal of choice for most visitors to this Route 66 town, but here at the Red Raven, culinary horizons are a bit broader. Start your meal with Southwestern egg rolls that are served with a smoky chipotle dipping sauce. Then try the pork loin with cilantro pesto or the basil butter salmon with cranberry–pine nut couscous. There are also plenty of steaks. Although it is a fairly casual place, this is by far the most sophisticated restaurant in town.

135 W. Rte. 66. ✆ **928/635-4980.** www.redravenrestaurant.com. Reservations recommended. Main courses $5–$10 lunch, $12–$27 dinner. AE, DISC, MC, V. Tues–Sun 11am–2pm and 5–9pm.

Rod's Steak House AMERICAN For a good dinner in Williams, just look for the red neon steer at the east end of town. The menu here may be short, but the food is reliable. Prime rib au jus, the house specialty, comes in three different weights to fit your hunger. If you're not in the mood for steak, opt for barbecued ribs, trout, or fried chicken.

301 E. Rte. 66. ✆ **928/635-2671.** www.rods-steakhouse.com. Reservations recommended. Main courses $6.50–$13 lunch, $13–$42 dinner. AE, DISC, MC, V. Mar–Oct Mon–Sat 11am–9:30pm; Nov–Feb Mon–Sat noon–9pm.

HAVASU CANYON ★★ & GRAND CANYON WEST

Havasu Canyon: 200 miles W of Grand Canyon Village; 70 miles N of Ariz. 66; 155 miles NW of Flagstaff; 115 miles NE of Kingman

Grand Canyon West: 240 miles W of Grand Canyon Village; 70 miles N of Kingman; 115 miles E of Las Vegas, NV

With roughly four million people each year visiting the South Rim of the Grand Canyon, and traffic congestion and parking problems becoming the most memorable aspects of many people's trips, you may want to consider an alternative to the South Rim. For most travelers, this means driving around to the North Rim; however, the North Rim is open only from mid-May to late October and, unfortunately, is not immune to parking problems and traffic congestion.

There are a couple of lesser-known alternatives. A visit to Havasu Canyon, on the Havasupai Indian Reservation, entails a 20-mile round-trip hike or horseback ride similar to that from Grand Canyon Village to Phantom Ranch, although with a decidedly different setting at the bottom of the canyon. Grand Canyon West, home to the much-hyped Skywalk, is on the Hualapai Indian Reservation and is primarily a tour-bus destination for vacationers from Las Vegas. With bus tours, cafeteria-style restaurants, contrived attractions, and as much buzzing helicopter and small-plane traffic as any busy airport, Grand Canyon West is definitely someplace that can be appreciated only by those who have very little time to spare but who desperately want to see something that looks like the Grand Canyon. This is also the only place where you can fly down into the canyon, which accounts for all the air traffic.

Essentials

GETTING THERE It isn't possible to drive all the way to **Havasu Canyon**'s Supai village. The nearest road ends 8 miles from Supai at Hualapai Hilltop. This is the trail head for the trail into the canyon and is at the end of Indian Rte. 18, which runs north from Ariz. 66. The turnoff is 7 miles east of Peach Springs and 31 miles west of Seligman.

The easiest and fastest way to reach Havasu Canyon is by helicopter from Hualapai Hilltop. Flights are operated by **Airwest Helicopters** (✆ **623/516-2790;** www.airwesthelicopters.com). The one-way fare is $85.

If you're headed to **Grand Canyon West,** you've got a couple of options. The best route is to head northwest out of Kingman on U.S. 93. After 27 miles, turn right onto the Pearce Ferry Road (signed for Dolan Springs and Meadview). After 28 miles on this road, turn right onto Diamond Bar Road, which is signed for Grand Canyon West. Another 14 miles down this road brings you to the Hualapai Indian Reservation. A little farther along, you'll come to the Grand Canyon West Terminal (there's actually an airstrip here), where visitor permits and bus-tour tickets are sold. You can also drive to Grand Canyon West from Peach Springs via Buck and Doe Road, which adds almost 50 miles of gravel road to your trip and is not passable if it has rained any time recently.

VISITOR INFORMATION For information on Havasu Canyon, contact the **Havasupai Tourism,** P.O. Box 160, Supai, AZ 86435 (✆ **928/448-2121** or 928/448-2141; www.havasupaitribe.com), which handles all campground reservations.

The water at Havasu Canyon is crystal clear.

For information on Grand Canyon West, contact **Hualapai Tourism** (✆ **888/868-9378** or 928/769-2636; www.grandcanyonwest.com).

Havasu Canyon ★★★

Imagine hiking for hours through a dusty brown landscape of rocks and cacti. The sun overhead is blistering and bright. The air is hot and dry. Rock walls rise higher and higher as you continue your descent through a mazelike canyon. Eventually, the narrow canyon opens into a wide plain shaded by cottonwood trees, a sure sign of water, and within a few minutes you hear the sound of a babbling stream. The water, when you finally reach it, is cool and crystal clear, a pleasant surprise. Following the stream, you pass through a dusty Indian village of small homes. Not surprisingly, in a village 8 miles beyond the last road, every yard seems to be a corral for horses. Passing through the village, you continue along the stream.

As the trail descends again, you spot the first waterfall. At the foot of the falls, the creek's waters, previously crystal-clear, are a brilliant turquoise blue. The sandstone walls rising above look redder than before. No, you aren't having a heat-induced hallucination—the water really is turquoise, and it fills terraces of travertine that form deep pools of cool water at the base of the canyon's waterfalls. Welcome to Havasu Canyon, home of the Havasupai tribe, whose name means "people of the blue-green waters." For centuries, the Havasupai have called this idyllic desert oasis home.

Together this canyon's waterfalls form what many claim is the most beautiful spot in the entire state. I'm not going to argue with them. The waterfalls and the pools that form below them are the canyon's main attraction, and most people are content to go for swims in the cool waters, sun themselves on the sand, and gaze for hours at the turquoise waters.

In August 2008, a massive flood roared through the canyon, gouging out a new creek channel that created two new waterfalls but bypassed one of the former falls. Then, in 2010, there were two flash floods that stranded campers in the canyon and prompted a closure of the canyon. There is speculation that the flood of 2008 has made the campground more prone to flooding, and while floods have occurred here regularly over the years, the canyon has always been quick to hide the scars caused by flooding. That said, be sure to check current conditions when planning a trip to Havasupai, and if possible, plan your visit in the spring when flash flooding is less likely. Also, keep in mind that the water, when not in flood, is still that amazing turquoise color.

The Havasupai entry fee is $40 per person to visit Havasu Canyon, and everyone entering the canyon is required to register at the tourist office in the village of Supai. Because it's a long walk to the campground, be sure you have a confirmed reservation before setting out from Hualapai Hilltop. It's good to make reservations as far in advance as possible, especially for holiday weekends.

If you plan to hike down into the canyon, start early to avoid the heat of the day. The hike is beautiful, but it's 10 miles to the campground. The steepest part of the trail is the first mile or so from Hualapai Hilltop. After this section, it's relatively flat.

Through **Havasupai Tourism** (✆ **928/448-2121** or 928/448-2141; www.havasupaitribe.com), you can hire a horse to carry you or your gear down into the canyon from Hualapai Hilltop. Horses cost $70 to $94 each way. Many people who hike in decide that it's worth the money to ride out, or at least have their backpacks carried out. Be sure to confirm your horse reservation a day before driving to Hualapai Hilltop. Sometimes no horses are available, and it's a long drive back to the nearest town. There are also pack mules that will carry your gear into and out of the canyon.

If you'd like to hike into Havasu Canyon with a guide, **Arizona Outback Adventures,** 16447 N. 91st St., Ste. 101, Scottsdale, AZ 85260 (✆ **866/455-1601** or 480/945-2881; www.aoa-adventures.com), leads 3- to 5-day hikes into Havasu Canyon and charges $848 to $1,698 per person. **Discovery Treks,** 28248 N. Tatum Blvd., Ste. B1, no. 414, Cave Creek, AZ 85331 (✆ **888/256-8731** or 480/247-9266; www.discoverytreks.com), offers similar 3-day trips for $895 to $1,169 per person.

The Skywalk juts over the edge of the canyon.

Grand Canyon West

Located on the Hualapai Indian Reservation on the south side of the Colorado River, **Grand Canyon West** (✆ **888/868-9378;** www.grandcanyonwest.com) overlooks the little-visited west end of Grand Canyon National Park. Although the view is not as spectacular as at either the South Rim or the North Rim, Grand Canyon West is noteworthy for one thing: It is one of the only places where you can legally take a helicopter ride down into the canyon. This is possible because the helicopters operate on land that is part of the Hualapai Indian Reservation. At this point, the south side of the Colorado lies within the reservation, while the north side of the river is within Grand Canyon National Park. The tours are operated by **Papillon Helicopters** (✆ **888/635-7272** or 702/736-7243; www.papillon.com), which charges $159 per person for a quick trip to the bottom of the canyon and a boat ride on the Colorado River.

Grand Canyon West is a self-styled major destination, with plans for a full-fledged resort and airport. The first phase of this development is called the **Skywalk,** and contrary to what you may have read about this Vegas-style attraction, the Skywalk is not over the Colorado River and is not in Grand Canyon National Park. The horseshoe-shaped glass observation platform juts over a side canyon of the Grand Canyon, and from the deck you can glimpse the Colorado River a short distance away and 4,000 feet below. However, you'll have to cough up $71 for the privilege of walking out on the Skywalk for a view that is only marginally better than the view from solid ground. For your $71, you'll also get to ride a **shuttle bus** along the rim of the canyon. The shuttle stops at Eagle Point, which is the site of the Skywalk and a collection of traditional Native American dwellings; at Guano Point, where bat guano was once mined commercially; and at Hualapai Ranch, a faux cow town where there are wagon and horseback rides, cowboy cookouts, and gunfight shows. Tours operate daily throughout the year and start at $41 per person (without the Skywalk; $71 to $86 with the Skywalk). A horseback ride can be added for $10 to $75. A helicopter ride down into the canyon and a brief boat trip on the Colorado River can be added for $159. Reservations are recommended.

Because this is about the closest spot to Las Vegas that actually provides a glimpse of the Colorado River and Grand Canyon National Park, the bus tours and helicopter rides are very popular with tour groups from Las Vegas. Busloads of visitors come and go throughout the day, and the air is always filled with the noise of helicopters ferrying people down into the canyon.

While Grand Canyon West and the Skywalk are pretty much the biggest tourist rip-off in the state and can be recommended only as a side trip from Las Vegas for travelers who absolutely must fly down into the canyon, the drive out here is one of the most scenic routes in Arizona. Along Diamond Bar Road, you'll be driving below the Grand Wash Cliffs, and for much of the way, the route traverses a dense forest of Joshua trees. If you're coming from Kingman, allow at least 2 hours to get here.

Other Area Activities

If you long to raft the Grand Canyon but have only a couple of free days in your schedule to realize your dream, then you have just one option. Here at the west end of the canyon, it's possible to do a 1-day rafting trip that begins on the Hualapai Indian Reservation. These trips are operated by **Hualapai River Runners** (✆ **888/868-9378;** www.grandcanyonwest.com), a tribal rafting company, and are offered between March and October. Expect a mix of white water and flat water. Although it's not as exciting as longer trips in the main section of the canyon, you'll still plow through some pretty big waves. Be ready to get wet. These trips stop at a couple of side canyons where you can get out and do some exploring. The one-day trips cost $328 per person.

If you aren't interested in (or can't afford) one of these rafting trips, you still might want to consider driving down to the bottom of the Grand Canyon. That's right, the Diamond Creek Road leads to the bottom of the canyon. This gravel road is on the Hualapai Indian Reservation and is the only place in the Grand Canyon where it is possible to drive to the Colorado River. Bear in mind that this is a rough road and you'll need a high-clearance vehicle and a permit ($15 per person). Get your permit at the Hualapai Lodge. You can also take a jeep tour to the bottom of the canyon with **Grand Canyon Old West Jeep Tours** (✆ **800/716-9389;** www.grandcanyonjeeps.com), which has its office in Williams and charges $249 per person for a full-day tour that also includes a visit to Grand Canyon Caverns.

Also in this area, you can visit **Grand Canyon Caverns** (✆ **928/422-3223** or 928/422-4565; www.grandcanyoncaverns.com), just outside Peach Springs. The caverns, which are accessed via a 210-foot elevator ride, are open from Memorial Day to October 15 daily from 9am to 5pm, and other months daily from 10am to 4pm. Admission is $15 for adults, $9.95 for children 4 to 12. Explorers' Tours ($45 adults and kids) head off into parts of the caverns that aren't seen on the regular tour. These caverns are unusual in that they are dry caverns that were formed when lava flows encountered limestone. Also, at one time the caverns were a designated fallout shelter and supplies are still stored in one large chamber.

Where to Stay & Eat

The Caverns Inn Ever dreamed of spending the night 220 feet underground? The underground cavern suite at this old Route 66 motel is surprisingly popular for an accommodation that costs $700 a night. Most of the rooms here are far more traditional and far more economical. Built on the site of the Grand Canyon Caverns, which are open to the public, the Caverns Inn makes a good choice if you are heading down to the bottom of nearby Havasu Canyon. Although this motel is not as modern as the nearby Hualapai Lodge, rooms are comfortable and service is good. Horseback rides and guided jeep tours to the bottom of the Grand Canyon can be arranged, and there's a general store with camping supplies and food.

Mile Marker 115, Route 66, Peach Springs, AZ 86434. www.grandcanyoncaverns.com. ✆ **928/422-3223** or 928/422-4565. Fax 928/422-4471. 49 units. $75–$90 double; $700 cavern suite. Children 12 and under stay free in parent's room. DISC, MC, V. Pets accepted ($25 deposit plus $5 per night). **Amenities:** Restaurant; lounge; seasonal outdoor pool; free Wi-Fi. *In room:* A/C, TV, fridge, hair dryer.

Hualapai Lodge 🎁 Located in the Hualapai community of Peach Springs, this lodge, although fairly basic, offers the most luxurious accommodations anywhere in the region. Guest rooms are spacious and modern, with a few bits of regional decor for character. Most people staying here are in the area to visit Grand Canyon West, to go rafting with Hualapai River Runners, or to hike into Havasu Canyon. The dining room is just about the only place in town to get a meal and serves some Native American dishes. Light sleepers should be aware that there is a railroad track behind the hotel.

900 Rte. 66 (P.O. Box 538), Peach Springs, AZ 86434. www.grandcanyonwest.com. ✆ **888/868-9378** or 928/769-2636. Fax 928/769-2372. 56 units. $100–$110 double. Rates include continental breakfast. Children 16 and under stay free in parent's room. AE, DISC, MC, V. Pets accepted ($25 per day). **Amenities:** Restaurant; exercise room; Jacuzzi; outdoor pool; room service. *In room:* A/C, TV, hair dryer, free Wi-Fi.

IN HAVASU CANYON

Havasu Campground, 2 miles beyond Supai village between Havasu Falls and Mooney Falls, is the only campground in the canyon. Campsites ($17 per night) are mostly in the shade of cottonwood trees on either side of Havasu Creek, and picnic tables are provided. No firewood is available, so be sure to bring a camp stove. Spring water is available, but it needs to be purified before you drink it. To make a campsite reservation, contact **Havasupai Tourism,** P.O. Box 160, Supai, AZ 86435 (✆ **928/448-2141** or 928/448-2121; www.havasupaitribe.com).

Havasupai Lodge Located in Supai village, this lodge offers, aside from the campground, the only accommodations in the canyon. The two-story building features standard motel-style rooms that lack only TVs and telephones, neither of which is much in demand at this isolated retreat. The only real drawback of this comfortable though basic lodge is that it's 2 miles from Havasu Falls and 3 miles from Mooney Falls. A cafe, across from the general store, serves breakfast, lunch, and dinner. It's a very casual place, and prices are high for what you get because all ingredients must be packed in by horse.

P.O. Box 159, Supai, AZ 86435. www.havasupaitribe.com. ✆ **928/448-2111** or 928/448-2201. 24 units. $145 double. MC, V. *In room:* A/C, no phone.

KINGMAN

180 miles SW of Grand Canyon Village; 150 miles W of Flagstaff; 30 miles E of Laughlin, NV; 90 miles SE of Las Vegas, NV

Although Kingman is the only town of any size between the Grand Canyon and Las Vegas, it is primarily a place to gas up before heading out across the desert. However, if you have a couple of hours to spare, the city does have interesting little museums and downtown historic buildings. The town's other claim to fame is that it is on the longest extant stretch of historic Route 66.

That Kingman today is more way station than destination is not surprising, considering its history. In 1857, Lieut. Edward Fitzgerald Beale passed through this region leading a special corps of camel-mounted soldiers on a road-surveying expedition. Some 60 years later, the road Beale surveyed would become the National Old Trails Highway, the precursor to Route 66. Gold and silver were discovered in the nearby hills in the 1870s, and in the early 1880s, the railroad laid its tracks through what would become the town of Kingman. Kingman flourished briefly around the start of the 20th century as a railroad town, and today, buildings constructed during this railroading heyday give downtown a bit of historical character.

In the nearby hills, such mining towns as Oatman and Chloride sprang up and boomed until the 1920s, when the mines became unprofitable and were abandoned. Then, during the 1930s, tens of thousands of the impoverished and unemployed following Route 66 from the Midwest to Los

Kingman is typically a place to fuel cars and stomachs.

Angeles passed through Kingman, which became an important stop on the road to the promised land of California. Route 66 has long since been replaced by I-40, but the longest remaining stretch of the old highway runs east from Kingman to Ash Fork. Over the years, Route 66 has taken on legendary status, and today people come from all over the world searching for pieces of this highway's historic past.

Remember Andy Devine? No? Well, Kingman is more than happy to tell you all about its squeaky-voiced native-son actor. Devine starred in hundreds of short films and features beginning in the silent-screen era, but he's perhaps best known as cowboy sidekick Jingles on the 1950s TV western *Wild Bill Hickok.* In the 1950s and 1960s, he hosted *Andy's Gang,* a popular children's TV show, and in the 1960s, he played Captain Hap on *Flipper.* Devine died in 1977, but here in Kingman his memory lives on—in a room in the local museum and every September when the town celebrates Andy Devine Days.

Essentials

GETTING THERE Kingman is on I-40 at the junction with U.S. 93 from Las Vegas. One of the last sections of old Route 66 (Ariz. 66) connects Kingman with Ash Fork.

Amtrak (✆ **800/872-7245**) offers rail service to Kingman from Chicago and Los Angeles. The station is at Fourth Street and Andy Devine Avenue.

VISITOR INFORMATION The **Powerhouse Tourist Information & Visitor Center,** 120 W. Rte. 66 (✆ **866/427-7866** or 928/753-6106; www.kingmantourism.org), is in a restored 1907 powerhouse that also houses the Historic Route 66 Museum, a Route 66 gift shop, and a model railroad. The visitor center is open daily from 8am to 5pm.

Exploring the Area

There isn't much to do right in Kingman, but while you're in town, you can learn more about local history at the **Mohave Museum of History and Arts,** 400 W. Beale St. (✆ **928/753-3195;** www.mohavemuseum.org). Plenty of Andy Devine memorabilia is on display. The museum is open Monday through Friday from 9am to 5pm, Saturday from 1 to 5pm. Admission is $4 for adults, $3 for seniors, free for children 12 and under. Afterward, take a drive or a stroll around downtown Kingman to view the town's many historic buildings. (You can pick up a map at the museum.)

If you're interested in historic homes, you can tour the **Bonelli House,** 430 E. Spring St. (✆ **928/753-1413**), a two-story stone home built in 1915 and furnished much as it may have been at that time. It's open Monday through Friday from 11am to 3pm (last tour starts at 2:30pm), but before heading over, check at the Mohave Museum of History and Arts to see if there will be a guide on hand to show you around. Admission is by donation.

The **Historic Route 66 Museum,** 120 W. Rte. 66 (✆ **928/753-9889;** www.kingmantourism.org), has exhibits on the history of not just Route 66, but also the roads, railroads, and trails that preceded it. A great collection of old photos taken during the Depression, and even an "Okie" truck are on display. You'll also see a Studebaker Champion and mock-ups of a gas station, diner, hotel lobby, and barbershop. Hours are daily from 9am to 5pm; admission is $4 for adults, $3 for seniors, and free for children 12 and under.

When you're tired of the heat and want to cool off, head southeast of Kingman to **Hualapai Mountain Park,** 6250 Hualapai Mountain Rd. (✆ **928/681-5700;** www.mcparks.com), which covers 2,300 acres and is at elevations between 4,984 and 8,417 feet. The park offers picnicking, hiking, mountain biking, camping, and rustic rental cabins built in the 1930s by the Civilian Conservation Corps. Daily admission to the park is $5.

OATMAN

Located 30 miles southwest of Kingman on old Route 66, the busy little mining camp of **Oatman** is a classic Wild West ghost town full of tourist shops selling tacky souvenirs. Founded in 1906 when gold was discovered here, Oatman quickly grew into a lively town of 12,000 people and was an important stop on Route 66. In 1942, when the U.S. government closed down many of Arizona's gold-mining operations, Oatman's population plummeted. Today the once-abandoned old buildings have been preserved as a ghost town. The historic look of Oatman has attracted numerous filmmakers over the years; *How the West Was Won* is just one of the movies that was shot here.

One of Oatman's biggest attractions is its population of feral burros. These animals, which roam the streets of town begging for handouts, are descendants of burros used by gold miners. Be careful—they bite!

And, of course, the Wild West isn't the Wild West if you don't spend some time in the saddle. **Oatman Stables** (✆ **928/768-3257;** www.oatmanstables.com), which operates between October and May, offers 1-hour horseback rides for $35 per person and 2-hour rides for $60.

Annual events staged here are among the strangest in the state, including January bed races, a Fourth of July high-noon sidewalk egg fry, and a Christmas season bush-decorating competition. Saloons and restaurants provide options for

Oatman is a classic Wild West ghost town.

GET YOUR KICKS ON route 66

It was the Mother Road, the Main Street of America, and for thousands of Midwesterners devastated by the Dust Bowl days of the 1930s, the road to a better life. On the last leg of its journey from Chicago to California, Route 66 meandered across the vast empty landscape of northern Arizona, and today, much of this road is still visible.

Officially dedicated in 1926, Route 66 was the first highway in America to be uniformly signed from one state to the next. Less than half of the highway's 2,200-mile route was paved, and in those days, the stretch between Winslow and Ash Fork was so muddy in winter that drivers had their cars shipped by railroad between the two points. By the 1930s, however, the entire length of Route 66 had been paved, and the westward migration was underway.

The years following World War II saw Americans take to Route 66 in unprecedented numbers for a different reason. A new prosperity and reliable cars made travel a pleasure, and Americans set out to discover the West. Motor courts, cafes, and tourist traps sprang up along the highway's length, and these businesses increasingly turned to eye-catching signs and billboards to lure passing motorists. Neon lit up the once-lonely stretches of highway.

By the 1950s, Route 66 just couldn't handle the traffic. After President Eisenhower initiated the National Interstate Highway System, Route 66 was slowly replaced by a four-lane divided highway. Many of the towns along the old highway were bypassed, and motorists stopped frequenting such roadside establishments as Pope's General Store and the Oatman Hotel. Many closed, while others were replaced by their more modern equivalents. Some, however, managed to survive, and they appear along the road like strange time capsules from another era, vestiges of Route 66's legendary past.

The **Wigwam Motel** (p. 344) in Holbrook is one of the most distinctive Route 66 landmarks. The wigwams (actually tepees) were built out of concrete around 1940 and still contain many of their original furnishings. Also in Holbrook are several rock shops with giant signs—and life-size concrete dinosaurs—that date from Route 66 days.

Flagstaff, the largest town along the Arizona stretch of Route 66, became a major layover spot. Motor courts flourished on the road leading into town from the east. Today, this road has been officially renamed Route 66 by the city of Flagstaff, and a few of the old motor courts remain. Although you probably wouldn't want to stay in most of these old motels, their neon signs were once beacons in the night for tired drivers. Downtown Flagstaff has quite a few shops where you can pick up Route 66 memorabilia.

About 65 miles west of Flagstaff begins the longest remaining stretch of old Route 66. Extending for 160 miles from Ash Fork to Topock, this lonely blacktop passes through some of the most remote country in Arizona (and goes right through the town of Kingman). In Seligman, at the east end of this stretch of the highway, you'll find **Delgadillo's Snow Cap,** 301 E. Rte. 66 (✆ **928/422-3291**), which serves up fast food amid outrageous decor (closed in winter). Next door at **Angel &**

Vilma Delgadillo's Route 66 Gift Shop & Visitor's Center, 217 E. Rte. 66 (✆ **928/422-3352;** www.route66giftshop.com), you'll be entertained by the owner, Angel, one of Route 66's most famous residents and an avid fan of the old highway. The walls of Angel's old one-chair barbershop are covered with photos and business cards of happy customers. Today, Angel's place is a Route 66 information center and souvenir shop.

After leaving Seligman, the highway passes through such waysides as Peach Springs, Truxton, Valentine, and Hackberry. Before reaching Peach Springs, you'll come to **Grand Canyon Caverns,** once a near-mandatory stop for families traveling Route 66. In Hackberry, be sure to stop at the **Hackberry General Store & Visitor's Center,** 11255 E. Ariz. 66 (✆ **928/769-2605;** www.hackberrygeneralstore.com), which is filled with Route 66 memorabilia as well as old stuff from the 1950s and 1960s. At Valle Vista, near Kingman, the highway goes into a 7-mile-long curve. Some claim it's the longest continuous curve on a U.S. highway.

After the drive through the wilderness west of Seligman, Kingman feels like a veritable metropolis; its bold neon signs once brought a sigh of relief to the tired and the hungry. Today, it boasts dozens of modern motels and is still primarily a resting spot for the road-weary. **Mr. D'z Route 66 Diner** (p. 322), a modern rendition of a 1950s diner (housed in an old gas station/cafe), serves burgers and blue-plate specials. Across the street at 120 W. Rte. 66. is a restored powerhouse that dates from 1907 and is home to the **Historic Route 66 Association of Arizona** (✆ **928/753-5001;** www.azrt66.com), the **Historic Route 66 Museum** (see above), and the **Powerhouse Visitor Center.** Each year over the first weekend in May, Kingman hosts the **Historic Route 66 Fun Run,** a drive along 150 miles of old Route 66 between Topock and Seligman.

The last stretch of Route 66 in Arizona heads southwest out of Kingman through the rugged Sacramento Mountains. It passes through **Oatman,** which almost became a ghost town after the local gold-mining industry shut down and the new interstate highway pulled money out of town. Today, mock gunfights and nosy wild burros entice motorists to stop, and shops playing up Route 66's heritage line the wooden sidewalks.

After dropping down out of the mountains, the road once crossed the Colorado River on a narrow metal bridge. Although the bridge is still there, it now carries a pipeline instead of traffic; cars must now return to the bland I-40 to continue their journey into the promised land of California.

a meal and a chance to soak up the Oatman atmosphere for a while. For more information, contact the **Oatman Chamber of Commerce,** P.O. Box 423, Oatman, AZ 86433 (✆ **928/768-6222;** www.oatmangoldroad.org).

Where to Stay & Eat

Most of the budget motel chains have branches in Kingman, and rates are among the lowest in the state. None of these motels is particularly recommendable, but if it's late in the day and you need a place to stay, you're more likely to find a cheap place here than in Las Vegas to the west or Williams to the east.

DamBar & Steak House STEAK This steakhouse has long been Kingman's favorite place for dinner out. It's hard to miss—just look for the steer on the roof of a rustic wooden building. Inside, the atmosphere is very casual, with wooden booths and sawdust on the floor. Mesquite-broiled steaks are the name of the game here, but there are plenty of other hearty dishes as well. On Friday and Saturday nights, there's live country music.

1960 E. Andy Devine Ave. ✆ **928/753-3523.** Reservations recommended on weekends and in summer. Main courses $7.50–$28. AE, DISC, MC, V. Daily 11am–10pm.

Mr. D'z Route 66 Diner AMERICAN This modern version of a vintage roadside diner is painted an eye-catching turquoise and pink, a retro color scheme that continues inside, where you can snuggle into a booth or grab a stool at the counter. Mr. D'z is a big hit with car buffs and people doing Route 66. Punch in a few 1950s tunes on the jukebox, and order up a Route 66 bacon cheeseburger and a root beer float. Unfortunately, service here can be very unpredictable.

105 E. Andy Devine Ave. ✆ **928/718-0066.** www.mrdzrt66diner.com. Main courses $5.50–$17. AE, DISC, MC, V. Daily 7am–9pm.

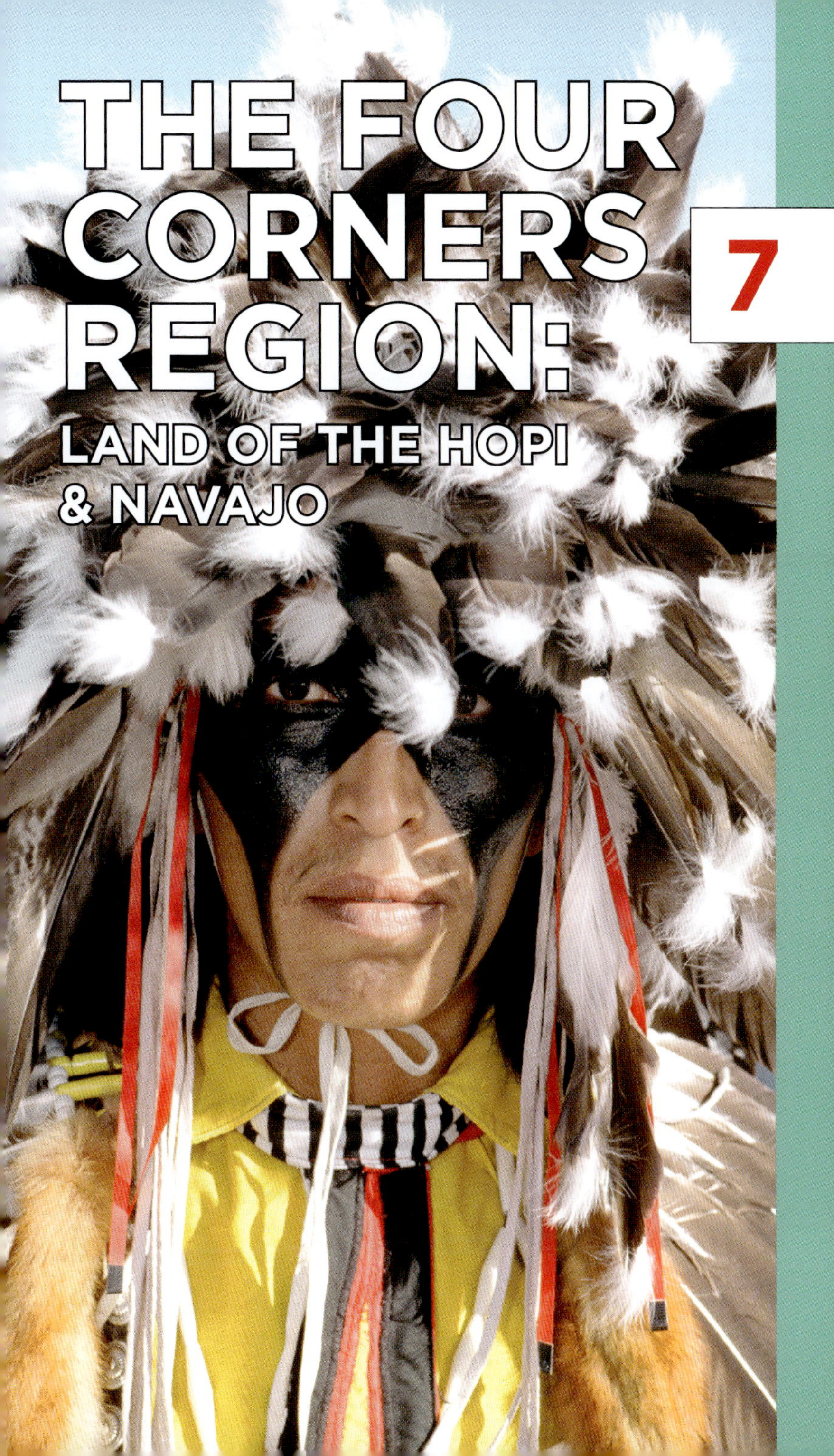

7

THE FOUR CORNERS REGION: LAND OF THE HOPI & NAVAJO

Ready for a little trivia quiz? Where in the U.S. can you stand in four states at the same time? Give up? The answer is way up in the northeastern corner of Arizona, where this state meets New Mexico, Colorado, and Utah. This novelty of the United State's westward expansion has long captured the imagination of vacationing families looking for some way of entertaining the kids in the middle of the desert. "Hey, kids, wanna have your picture taken in four states at the same time?"

Known as Four Corners, this spot is the site of a Navajo Tribal Park. Pay your admission, and you, too, can experience the Four Corners state of mind. However, Four Corners is much more than a surveyor's gimmick. The term also refers to this entire region, most of which is Navajo and Hopi reservation land. The Four Corners region happens to have some of the most spectacular landscapes in the state, with majestic mesas, rainbow-hued deserts, towering buttes, multicolored cliffs, deep canyons, a huge cliff-rimmed reservoir, and even a meteorite crater. Among the most dramatic landscape features are the 1,000-foot buttes of Monument Valley, which for years have symbolized the Wild West of John Wayne movies and car commercials.

The Four Corners region is also home to Arizona's most scenic reservoir, Lake Powell, a flooded version of the Grand Canyon. With its miles of blue water mirroring red-rock canyon walls hundreds of feet high, Lake Powell is one of

PREVIOUS PAGE: **A Navajo man prepares to perform at a powwow.** ABOVE: **Utah, Colorado, New Mexico, and Arizona meet in the Four Corners.**

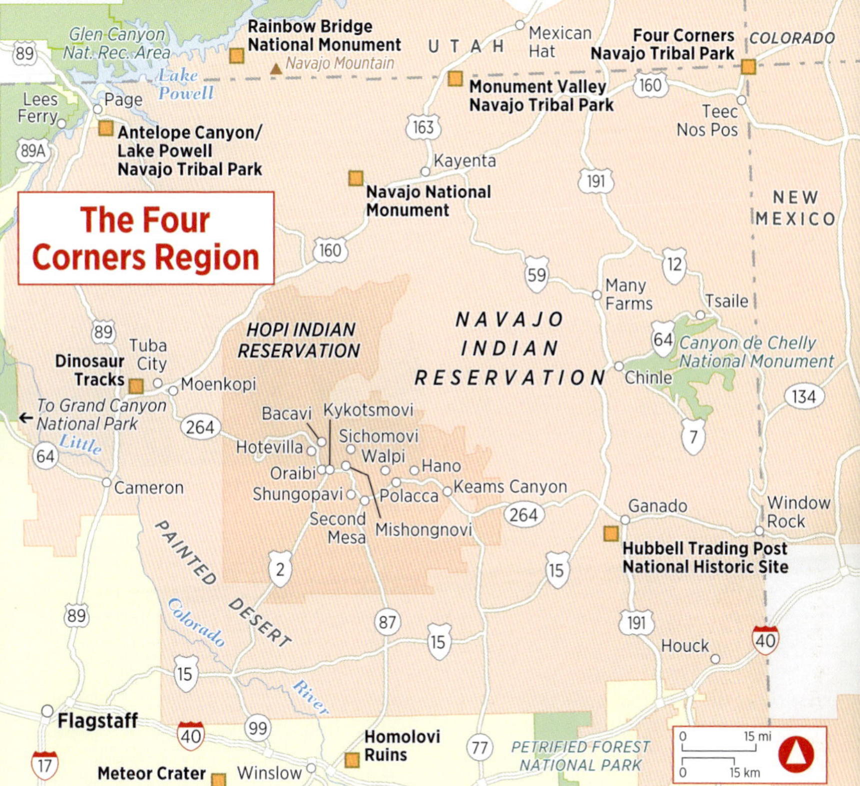

northern Arizona's curious contrasts—a vast artificial reservoir in the middle of barren desert canyons. Although a half-century ago there was a bitter fight over damming Glen Canyon to form Lake Powell, today the lake is among the most popular attractions in the Southwest.

Be forewarned, however: The Four Corners region also claims some of the most desolate, wind-swept, and monotonous landscapes in the state, so be sure to fill up on both gas and coffee before heading out on the highway for another 100-mile drive to the next destination.

While this region certainly offers plenty of scenery, it also provides one of the nation's most fascinating cultural experiences. This is American Indian country, the homeland of both the Navajo and the Hopi, tribes that have lived on these lands for hundreds of years and have adapted different means of surviving in this arid region. The Navajo, with their traditional log homes (called hogans) scattered across the countryside, were herders of sheep, goats, and cattle. The Hopi, on the other hand, congregated in villages atop mesas and built houses of stone. Today, the Hopi still grow corn and other crops at the foot of their mesas in much the same way the indigenous peoples of the Southwest have done for centuries.

These two tribes are only the most recent Native Americans to inhabit what to the casual observer seems to be a desolate, barren wilderness. The Ancestral Puebloans (formerly called Anasazis) left their mark in countless canyons throughout the Four Corners region. Their cliff dwellings date back 700 years or more, and here in Arizona, the most spectacular ruins are in Canyon de Chelly and Navajo national monuments. No one is sure why the Ancestral Puebloans moved up into the cliff walls, but there is speculation that unfavorable growing conditions brought on by drought may have forced them to use every possible inch of arable land. Likewise, no one is certain why the Ancestral Puebloans abandoned their cliff dwellings in the 13th century. With no written record, their disappearance may forever remain a mystery.

A Navajo woman whose tribe, along with the Hopi, inhabits the region.

The Hopi, who claim the Ancestral Puebloans as their ancestors, have for centuries lived atop mesas in northeastern Arizona, and Oraibi, on Third Mesa, may be the oldest continuously inhabited community in the U.S. Most of the villages are built on three mesas, known simply as First Mesa, Second Mesa, and Third Mesa, which are numbered from east to west and are completely surrounded by the Navajo Nation. These villages have always maintained a great deal of autonomy, which over the years has sometimes led to disputes between villages. The activities of missionaries and the policies of the Bureau of Indian Affairs have also created conflicts among and within villages.

The Navajo Nation, the largest reservation in the U.S., is home to nearly 200,000 Navajos and covers an area of 26,000 square miles in northeastern Arizona and parts of New Mexico and Utah. Although the reservation today has modern towns with supermarkets, shopping centers, and hotels, many Navajos still follow a pastoral lifestyle as herders. As you travel the roads of the reservation, you'll frequently encounter flocks of goats and sheep, and herds of cattle and horses. These animals have free range of the reservation and often graze beside the highway.

Compared to such pueblo tribes as the Hopi and Zuni, the Navajo are relative newcomers to the Southwest. Their Athabaskan language is most closely related to the languages spoken by Native Americans in the Pacific Northwest, Canada, and Alaska. It's believed that the Navajo migrated southward from northern Canada beginning around 1000, arriving in the Southwest sometime after 1400. At this time, they were still hunters and gatherers, but contact with the pueblo tribes, which had long before adopted an agricultural lifestyle, began to change the Navajo into farmers. When the Spanish arrived in the Southwest in the early 17th century, the Navajo began raiding Spanish settlements for horses, sheep, and goats and adopted a pastoral way of life, grazing their herds on the high plains and the canyon bottoms.

The continued raids, made even more successful with the acquisition of horses, put the Navajo in conflict with the Spanish settlers who were beginning to encroach on Navajo land. In 1805, the Spanish sent a military expedition into the Navajo's chief stronghold, Canyon de Chelly, and killed 115 people, who, by some accounts, may have been all women, children, and old men. This massacre, however, did not stop the conflicts between the Navajo and Spanish settlers.

In 1846, when this region became part of the United States, American settlers encountered the same problems that the Spanish had. Military outposts were established to protect the new settlers, and numerous unsuccessful attempts were made to establish peace. In 1863, after continued attacks, a military expedition led by Col. Kit Carson burned crops and homes late in the summer, effectively obliterating the Navajo's winter food supplies. Thus defeated, the Navajo were rounded up and herded 400 miles to an inhospitable region of New Mexico near Fort Sumner. This trek became known as the Long Walk. Living conditions at Fort Sumner were deplorable, and the land was unsuitable for farming. Because they were unable to survive at Fort Sumner, the Navajo were allowed to return to their homeland in 1868.

Upon returning home, and after continued clashes with white settlers, the Navajo settled into a lifestyle of herding. Today, however, the Navajo have had to turn to many different livelihoods. Although weaving and silver work have become lucrative businesses for some craftspeople, the amount of money these trades garner for the tribe as a whole is not significant. Many Navajos now take jobs as migrant workers. Gas and oil leases and coal mining on the reservation provide additional income.

Although the reservation covers an immense area, much of it is of little value other than as scenery. Fortunately, the Navajo have recognized the income potential of their spectacular land. Monument Valley is operated as a tribal park, as is the Four Corners monument. Numerous Navajo-owned tour companies also operate on the reservation.

As you travel the reservation, you may notice small hexagonal buildings with rounded roofs. These are hogans, the traditional homes of the Navajo, and are usually made of wood and earth with the doorway facing east to greet the new day. At the Canyon de Chelly and Navajo national monument visitor centers, you can look inside hogans that are part of the parks' exhibits. If you take a tour at Canyon de Chelly or Monument Valley, you may have an opportunity to visit a privately owned hogan. Although most Navajos now live in modest houses or manufactured homes, a family usually has a hogan for religious ceremonies.

The Navajo and Hopi reservations cover a vast area and are laced with a network of well-paved roads, as well as many unpaved roads that are not always passable to cars without four-wheel-drive. Because distances are great, keep your gas tank filled, and keep an eye out for livestock on the road, especially at night.

WINSLOW

55 miles E of Flagstaff; 70 miles S of Second Mesa; 33 miles W of Holbrook

It's hard to imagine that a town could build its tourist fortunes on a mention in a pop song, but that is exactly what Winslow did for decades after the band the Eagles sang about "standin' on a corner in Winslow, Arizona," in their hit song "Take It Easy." On the corner of Second Street and Kinsley Avenue, the town even has an official Standin' on the Corner Park (complete with a mural of a girl in a flatbed Ford).

Popular songs aside, Winslow can claim a couple of more significant attractions. Right in town is the beautifully restored La Posada, one of the Southwest's historic railroad hotels. Twenty miles west of town is mile-wide Meteor Crater. And northeast of town is Homolovi Ruins State Park, which preserves numerous archaeological sites. If you happen to be a rock climber, you'll find great climbing routes in the Moenkopi section of Jacks Canyon south of town.

Meteor Crater.

Essentials

GETTING THERE Winslow is on I-40 at the junction with Ariz. 87, which leads north to the Hopi mesas and south to Payson. **Amtrak** (✆ **800/872-7245**) trains stop in Winslow at La Posada hotel, 501 E. Second St.

VISITOR INFORMATION Contact the **Winslow Chamber of Commerce,** 523 W. Second St. (✆ **928/289-2434;** www.winslowarizona.org), which is housed in the town's restored Hubbell Trading Post. The historic building now houses a visitor center and museum exhibits on Winslow's history.

One Big Hole in the Ground

Meteor Crater ★ Northern Arizona has more than its fair share of natural attractions, and while most of the region's big holes in the ground were created

Communing with the Spirits of the Past

A few years ago, I took a friend on a tour of northern Arizona. At the end of our road trip, I asked which was the most memorable of all the places we had visited. Surprisingly, the answer was not Sedona, Monument Valley, or even the Grand Canyon. It was **Rock Art Ranch ★★** (✆ **928/386-5047** or 928/288-3260), a privately owned historic site southeast of Winslow. Located on part of the old Hashknife Outfit, which was the largest ranch in the country during the late 19th century, Rock Art Ranch is the finest rock-art site in the state. The setting, the narrow little Chevelon Canyon, which is almost invisible until you are right beside it, is absolutely enchanting. Pecked into the canyon's walls are hundreds of Ancestral Puebloan petroglyphs, and because these petroglyphs span more than 8,000 years, this is considered one of the world's most important collections of petroglyphs. Tours (reservations required) are available Monday through Saturday (call to get rate information and directions to the ranch). Also on the ranch are a museum of Ancestral Puebloan artifacts and a bunkhouse that dates from the Hashknife days. If you're interested in petroglyphs, Rock Art Ranch should not be missed.

by the slow process of erosion, there is one hole that has far more dramatic origins. At 550 feet deep and 2½ miles in circumference, the Barringer Meteorite Crater is the best-preserved meteorite impact crater on earth. The meteorite, which estimates put at roughly 150 feet in diameter, was traveling at 40,000 mph when it slammed into the earth 50,000 years ago. Within seconds, more than 175 million tons of rock had been displaced, leaving a gaping crater and a devastated landscape. Today, you can stand on the rim of the crater (there are observation decks and a short trail) and marvel at the power, equivalent to 20 million tons of TNT, which created this otherworldly setting. In fact, so closely does this crater resemble craters on the surface of the moon that in the 1960s, NASA came here to train Apollo astronauts.

On the rim of the crater, there's a small museum that features exhibits on astrogeology and space exploration, as well as a film on meteorites. On display are a 1,400-pound meteorite and an Apollo space capsule. Throughout the day, there are 1-hour hiking tours along the rim of the crater.

20 miles west of Winslow at exit 233 off I-40. ✆ **800/289-5898** or 928/289-5898. www.meteorcrater.com. Admission $15 adults, $14 seniors, $8 children 6–17. Memorial Day to mid-Sept daily 7am–7pm; mid-Sept to Memorial Day daily 8am–5pm. Closed Christmas.

Other Area Attractions

In downtown Winslow, near that famous corner, you'll find the little **Old Trails Museum,** 212 Kinsley Ave., at Second Street (✆ **928/289-5861;** www.oldtrailsmuseum.org), which is something of a community attic and has exhibits on Route 66 and the Harvey Girls (who once worked in the nearby La Posada hotel; see the box "Fred Harvey & His Girls," later in this chapter). The museum is open Tuesday through Saturday from 10am to 4pm. Admission is free.

Even if you aren't planning on staying the night at the restored **La Posada,** 303 E. Second St. (✆ **928/289-4366**), be sure to stop by just to see this historic railway hotel. Self-guided tours are available for a $3 donation.

The Little Painted Desert.

On the windswept plains northeast of Winslow, 1¼ miles north of I-40 at exit 257, is **Homolovi Ruins State Park** (✆ **928/289-4106;** www.azstateparks.com), which preserves more than 300 Ancestral Puebloan archaeological sites, several of which have been partially excavated. Although these ruins are not nearly as impressive as those at Wupatki or Walnut Canyon, a visit here will give you a better understanding of the interrelationship of the many ancient pueblos of this region.

Continuing north from the state park, you'll find the little-known and little-visited **Little Painted Desert ★**, a 660-acre county park. To reach the park and its viewpoint overlooking the painted hills of this stark yet colorful landscape, continue north on Ariz. 87 from Homolovi Ruins State Park for another 12 miles.

While you're in Winslow, be sure to check out the **SNOWDRIFT Art Space,** 120 W. Second St. (✆ **928/289-8201;** www.snowdriftart.com), an art gallery/studio owned by artist Daniel Lutzick, who was one of the people who helped get the historic La Posada hotel up and running again.

Where to Stay

In addition to the following historic hotel, you'll find lots of budget chain motels in Winslow.

La Posada ★★ What an unexpected beauty this place is! Designed by Mary Elizabeth Jane Colter, architect of many of the buildings on the South Rim of the Grand Canyon, this railroad hotel first opened in 1930. Colter gave La Posada the feel of an old Spanish hacienda and even created a fictitious history for the building. In the lobby are numerous pieces of original furniture as well as reproductions of pieces once found in the hotel. The nicest rooms are the large units named for famous guests—Albert Einstein, Howard Hughes, Harry Truman, and Charles Lindbergh. The hotel's Turquoise Room (see "Where to Eat," below) is by far the best restaurant in the entire Four Corners region. La Posada is in the process of being slowly but completely restored and is reason enough to overnight in Winslow.

303 E. 2nd St. (Rte. 66), Winslow, AZ 86047. www.laposada.org. ✆ **928/289-4366.** Fax 928/289-3873. 45 units. $109–$169 double. DISC, MC, V. Pets accepted ($10 fee). **Amenities:** Restaurant; lounge; access to nearby health club; room service. *In room:* A/C, TV, hair dryer, no phone, free Wi-Fi.

Where to Eat

The Turquoise Room ★★ NEW AMERICAN/SOUTHWESTERN When Fred Harvey began his railroad hospitality career, his objective was to provide decent meals to the traveling public. (See "Fred Harvey & His Girls," on p. 351.) Here, in La Posada's reincarnated dining room, chef/owner John Sharpe prepares not just decent meals, but superb meals the likes of which you won't find anywhere else in northern Arizona. In summer, herbs and vegetables often come from the hotel's own gardens, and wild game is a specialty. Be sure to start your meal with the sweet-corn and black-bean soup, which is actually two soups served side by side in the same bowl to create a sort of yin-yang symbol. On top of all this, you can watch the trains rolling by just outside the window while you dine.

At La Posada, 303 E. 2nd St. ✆ **928/289-2888.** www.theturquoiseroom.net. Reservations recommended. Main courses $9–$13 lunch, $17–$34 dinner. AE, DISC, MC, V. Daily 7am–4:15pm and 5–9pm.

THE HOPI RESERVATION

67 miles N of Winslow; 250 miles NE of Phoenix; 100 miles SW of Canyon de Chelly; 140 miles SE of Page/Lake Powell

The Hopi Reservation, often referred to as Hopiland or just Hopi, is completely encircled by the Navajo Nation and has at its center a grouping of mesas upon which the Hopi have lived for nearly 1,000 years. This remote region, with its flat-topped mesas and barren landscape, is the center of the universe for the Hopi people. Here the Hopi follow their ancient customs, and many aspects of pueblo culture remain intact. However, much of the culture is hidden from the view of visitors, and although the Hopi perform elaborate religious and social dances throughout the year, many of these dances are not open to outsiders.

The mesas are home to two of the oldest continuously inhabited villages in North America—Walpi and Old Oraibi. Although these two communities show their age and serve as a direct tie to the pueblos of the Ancestral Puebloan culture, most of the villages on the reservation are scattered collections of modern homes. These villages are not destinations unto themselves, but along Ariz. 264 numerous crafts shops and studios sell kachinas, baskets, pottery, and silver jewelry. The chance to buy crafts directly from the Hopi is the main reason for a visit to this area, although you can also take a guided tour of Walpi village.

Important note: When visiting the Hopi pueblos, remember that you are a guest and your privileges can be revoked at any time. Respect all posted signs at village entrances, and remember that *photographing, sketching, and recording are prohibited in the villages and at ceremonies.* Also, kivas (ceremonial rooms) and ruins are off-limits.

Essentials

GETTING THERE This is one of the state's most remote regions. Distances are great, but highways are generally in good condition. Ariz. 87 leads from Winslow to Second Mesa, and Ariz. 264 runs from Tuba City in the west to the New Mexico state line in the east.

VISITOR INFORMATION For advance information, contact the **Hopi Cultural Preservation Office,** P.O. Box 123, Kykotsmovi, AZ 86039 (© **928/734-3612;** www.nau.edu/~hcpo-p). The Moenkopi Legacy Inn's website (**www.experiencehopi.com**) is another good place to find information on visiting the Hopi reservation.

The Villages

With the exception of Upper and Lower Moenkopi, which are near the Navajo town of Tuba City, and the recently settled Yuh Weh Loo Pah Ki community east of Keams Canyon, the Hopi villages are scattered along roughly 20 miles of Ariz. 264. Although Old Oraibi is the oldest, there are no official tours of this village, and visitors are not likely to feel very welcome here. Consequently, Walpi, one of only two villages with organized tours, is the best place for visitors to learn more about life in the Hopi villages. I mention all of the Hopi villages below to provide a bit of history and perspective on this area, but for the most part, these villages (with the exception of Walpi and Old Oraibi) are not at all picturesque. However, most do have quite a few crafts galleries and stores selling silver jewelry.

FIRST MESA At the top of First Mesa is the village of **Walpi,** parts of which today still look much like the ruins of Ancestral Puebloan villages in such locations as Canyon de Chelly, Navajo National Monument, and Wupatki National Monument. Small stone houses seem to grow directly from the rock of the mesa top, and ladders jut from the roofs of kivas. The view from the village stretches for hundreds of miles, and it is easy to see why the Hopi settled on this spot. Walpi was originally located lower on the slopes of First Mesa, but after the Pueblo Revolt of 1680 brought on fear of reprisal from the Spanish, villagers moved to the top of the mesa so that they could better defend themselves in the event of a Spanish attack.

The Hopi have lived in the area for almost 1,000 years.

Immediately adjacent to Walpi are the two villages of **Sichomovi,** which was founded in 1750 as a colony of Walpi, and **Hano,** which was founded by Tewa peoples who were most likely seeking refuge from the Spanish after the Pueblo Revolt. Neither of these villages has the ancient character of Walpi. At the foot of First Mesa is **Polacca,** a settlement founded in the late 1800s by Walpi villagers who wanted to be closer to the trading post and school.

SECOND MESA Second Mesa is today the center of tourism in Hopiland and is where you'll find the Hopi Cultural Center. Villages on Second Mesa include **Shungopavi,** which was moved to its present site after Old Shungopavi was abandoned in 1680 following the Pueblo Revolt (it no longer exists). Old Shungopavi is said to have been the first Hopi village and was founded by the Bear Clan. Shungopavi is notable for its silver jewelry and its coiled plaques (flat baskets).

Mishongnovi, which means "place of the black man," is named for the leader of a clan that came here from the San Francisco Peaks around 1200. The original Mishongnovi village, located at the base of the mesa, was abandoned in the 1690s, and the village was reestablished at the current site atop the mesa. The Snake Dance is held here during odd-numbered years. It is doubtful that these dances will be open to non-Hopis, although you could check with the Hopi Cultural Preservation Office (see "Visitor Information," above).

Sipaulovi, which is located on the eastern edge of the mesa, was founded after the Pueblo Revolt of 1680.

THIRD MESA **Oraibi,** which the Hopi claim is the oldest continuously occupied town in the United States, is located on Third Mesa. The village dates from 1150 and, according to legend, was founded by people from Old Shungopavi. A Spanish mission was established in Oraibi in 1629, and the ruins are still visible north of the village. Today, Oraibi is a mix of old stone houses and modern ones, mostly constructed of cinder blocks. Wander around Oraibi, and you'll likely be approached by village women and children offering to sell you various local crafts and the traditional blue-corn *piki* bread. You may also be invited into someone's home to see the crafts they have to offer. For this reason, Old Oraibi is the most interesting village in which to shop for local crafts.

For centuries, Oraibi was the largest of the Hopi villages, but in 1906, a schism arose due to Bureau of Indian Affairs policies, and many of the villagers left to form **Hotevilla.** This is considered the most conservative of the Hopi villages and has had frequent confrontations with the federal government. **Kykotsmovi,** also known as Lower Oraibi or New Oraibi, was founded in 1890 by villagers from Oraibi who wanted to be closer to the school and trading post. This village is the seat of the Hopi Tribal Government. **Bacavi** was founded in 1907 by villagers who had helped found Hotevilla but who later decided that they wanted to return to Oraibi. The people of Oraibi would not let them return, and rather than go back to Hotevilla, they founded a new village.

MOENKOPI This village is 40 miles to the west of the Hopi mesas. Founded in 1870 by people from Oraibi, Moenkopi sits in the center of a wide green valley where plentiful water makes farming more reliable. Moenkopi is only a few miles from Tuba City off U.S. 160 and is divided into the villages of Upper Moenkopi and Lower Moenkopi.

Exploring the World of the Hopi

Start your visit to the Hopi pueblos at the **Hopi Cultural Center Museum,** on Ariz. 264 in Second Mesa (✆ **928/734-6650**). This combination museum, motel, and restaurant is the tourism headquarters for the area. The museum is open Monday through Friday from 8am to 5pm and Saturday and Sunday from 9am to 3pm (closed weekends in the winter). Admission is $3 for adults and $1 for children 13 and under.

From here, it's just a few miles to the Second Mesa village of Sipaulovi and the **Sipaulovi Visitor Center** (✆ **928/737-5426;** www.sipaulovihopi informationcenter.org). At the visitor center, you can watch a 20-minute video about the Hopi culture and arrange for a 1-hour walking tour of Sipaulovi. Tours are offered Monday through Friday from 8am to 4pm and cost $15 for adults, $12 for seniors, and $10 for children ages 10 to 17.

The most rewarding Hopi village to visit is **Walpi ★**, on First Mesa. Guided tours of this tiny village are usually offered daily between 9am and 3pm (8am to 4pm in summer). Admission is $13 for adults, $10 for youths age 14 to 17, and $5 for children 5 to 13. To sign up for a tour, drive to the top of First Mesa (in Polacca, take the road that says FIRST MESA VILLAGE) and continue through the village to **Ponsi Hall Visitor Center** (✆ **928/737-2670**), where you'll see signs for the tours. The tours, which last 1 hour, are led by Hopis who will tell you the history of the village and explain a bit about the local culture.

About 1½ miles north of the community of Keams Canyon, in the pretty little canyon for which this historic community is named, you'll find, carved into the stone walls of the canyon, an inscription left by Colonel "Kit" Carson. It was Carson who led the war on the Navajo during the summer of 1863 and who, to defeat the tribe, burned their crops, effectively leaving the Navajo with no winter supplies. The inscription reads simply, "1st Regt. N.M. Vols. Aug 13th 1863 Col. C. Carson Com." To find the inscription, turn off Ariz. 264 in Keams Canyon and drive north on the main road through the community. You'll also find some picnic tables along this road.

Cultural Tours

To get the most out of a visit to the Hopi mesas, it is best to take a guided tour. With a guide, you will learn much more about this rather insular culture than you ever could on your own. Tour companies frequently use local guides and stop at the homes of working artisans. This all adds up to a more in-depth and educational visit to one of the oldest cultures on the continent.

Bertram Tsavadawa at **Ancient Pathways Tours** (✆ **928/797-8145;** www.experiencehopi.com/tourcompanies.html) specializes in tours to Hopi petroglyph sites. These are sites that are not open to the public unless you are with a Hopi guide. Three-hour tours cost $75 for adults and $35 for children under 18; 6-hour tours cost $165 for adults and $85 for children. One-hour tours of Old Oraibi ($15) can also be arranged. Micah Loma'omvaya of **Hopi Tours** (✆ **800/774-0830** or 928/206-7433; www.hopitours.com) offers 1-hour tours of Oraibi for $25 per person, 2-hour petroglyph tours for $35 per person, 3-hour driving tours for $50 per person, and 4-hour rock art tours for $65 per person. Half-day and full-day tours are also available. Half-day and full-day tours are also offered by Gary Tso of the **Left-Handed Hunter Tour Company** (✆ **928/734-2567;** lhhunter68@hopitelecom.net). Half-day tours cost $120 for two people, and full-day tours cost $265 for two people.

Dances & Ceremonies

The Hopi have developed the most complex religious ceremonies of any of the Southwest tribes. The masked kachina dances for which they are most famous are held from January to July. However, most kachina dances are closed to the non-Hopi public. Social dances (usually open to the public) are held August through February. If you're on the reservation during these months, ask if any dances are taking place. Who knows? You might get lucky. Snake Dances (usually closed to the non-Hopi public) are held August through December.

Kachinas, whether in the form of dolls or masked dancers, are representative of the spirits of everything from plants and animals to ancestors and sacred places. More than 300 kachinas appear on a regular basis in Hopi ceremonies, and another 200 appear occasionally. The kachina spirits are said to live in the San Francisco Peaks to the southwest and at Spring of the Shadows in the east. According to legend, the kachinas lived with the Hopi long ago, but the Hopi people made the kachinas angry, causing them to leave. Before departing, though, the kachinas taught the Hopi how to perform their ceremonies.

Today, the kachina ceremonies, performed by men wearing elaborate costumes and masks, serve several purposes. Most important, they bring clouds and rain to water the all-important corn crop, but they also ensure health, happiness, long life, and harmony in the universe. As part of the kachina ceremonies, dancers often bring carved wooden kachina dolls to village children to introduce them to the various spirits.

The kachina season lasts from the winter solstice until shortly after the summer solstice. The actual dates for dances are usually announced only shortly before the ceremonies are to be held. Preparations for the dances take place inside kivas that are entered from the roof by means of a ladder; the dances themselves are usually held in a village square or street.

With ludicrous and sometimes lewd mimicry, clowns known as *koyemsi, koshares,* and *tsukus* entertain spectators between the dances, bringing a lighthearted counterpoint to the very serious nature of the kachina dances. Non-Hopis attending dances have often become the focus of attention for these clowns.

Despite the importance of the kachina dances, it is the **Snake Dance** that has captured the attention of many non-Hopis. The Snake Dance involves the handling of both poisonous and nonpoisonous snakes. The ceremony takes place over 16 days, with the first 4 days dedicated to collecting snakes from the four cardinal directions. Later, footraces are held from the bottom of the mesa to the top. On the last day of the ceremony, the actual Snake Dance is performed. Men of the Snake Society form pairs of dancers—one to carry the snake in his mouth and the other to distract the snake with an eagle feather. When all the snakes have been danced around the plaza, they are rushed down to their homes at the bottom of the mesa to carry the Hopi prayers for rain to the spirits of the underworld.

Due to the disrespectful attitude of some past visitors, many ceremonies and dances are now closed to non-Hopis. However, a couple of Hopi villages do allow visitors to attend some of their dances. The best way to find out about attending dances is to contact the **Hopi Cultural Preservation office** (see "Visitor Information," above).

FROM TOP: **More than 300 kachina spirits appear in Hopi ceremonies; the Snake Dance takes place over 16 days and is closed to non-Hopis.**

Eat Local, Shop Local

The Hopi and Navajo reservations both offer some interesting opportunities to eat locally and shop locally, and in so doing patronize small businesses and individuals, which is one of the key aspects of eco-travel. On the Hopi reservation, residents of the village of Walpi lead tours of this ancient cliff-top village (p. 331). On these walking tours, you're likely to be approached by village residents selling handicrafts and sometimes traditional *piki* bread. The latter, a paper-thin bread made from blue corn, has long been a staple food of the Hopi. If you wander around the village of Old Oraibi, you're also likely to be approached by village residents selling handicrafts, particularly small, wooden dolls. Throughout the Hopi Reservation, you'll see signs in front of people's homes advertising traditional crafts for sale. On the Navajo Nation, you can sample traditional foods at the Ch'ihootso Indian Marketplace in Window Rock (p. 347). The steam corn soup served at several of the little food vendors' stalls here is a particular favorite of local families. Also, anywhere on the Navajo Nation where there is a scenic view, you'll find jewelry vendors set up by the side of the road. Although I have never found much worth buying at these stalls, my wife has gotten some very pretty turquoise earrings.

Shopping

Most visitors come to the reservation to shop for Hopi crafts. Across the reservation, dozens of small shops sell crafts and jewelry of different quality, and some homes, especially at the foot of First Mesa, have signs indicating that they sell crafts. Shops often sell the work of only a few individuals, so you should stop at several to get an idea of the variety of work available. Also, if you tour Walpi or wander around in Oraibi, you will likely be approached by villagers selling various crafts, including kachina dolls. The quality will not be as high as that in shops, but then, the prices won't be as high either.

At Keams Canyon, 30 miles east of Second Mesa on Ariz. 264, you'll find **McGee's Indian Art Gallery** (✆ **928/738-2295;** www.hopiart.com), which is the best place on the reservation to shop for high-quality contemporary kachina dolls. The first trading post to open on this site was built in 1879, and the McGee family has owned the business since 1937. The gallery is adjacent to a grocery store that is the current incarnation of the old trading post.

If you're in the market for Hopi silver jewelry, stop in at **Hopi Fine Arts** (✆ **928/737-2222**), which is at the foot of Second Mesa at the junction of Ariz. 264 and Ariz. 87. This shop also has a good selection of kachina dolls and some beautiful coil and wicker plaque baskets. Hours are limited in the winter.

One of the best places to get a quick education in Hopi art and crafts is **Tsakurshovi** ★ (✆ **928/734-2478**), a tiny shop 1½ miles east of the Hopi Cultural Center on Second Mesa. This shop has a huge selection of traditional kachina dolls and also has lots of jewelry. Janice and Joseph Day, the owners, are very friendly and are always happy to share their expertise with visitors. This is also where you can buy a "Don't Worry Be Hopi" T-shirt.

If you're interested in kachina dolls, be sure to visit Oraibi's **Monongya Gallery** (✆ **928/734-2344**), a big building right on Ariz. 264 outside of Oraibi. It usually has one of the largest selections of kachina dolls in the area.

Where to Stay & Eat

If you've brought your food along, you'll find picnic tables just east of Oraibi on top of the mesa. These tables have an amazing view!

Hopi Cultural Center Restaurant & Inn Although it isn't much, this simple motel is one of only two accommodations on the Hopi reservation. While the Moenkopi Legacy Inn in Moenkopi/Tuba City is newer and more comfortable, the Hopi Cultural Center is more centrally located if you are planning to spend a couple of days shopping for crafts in the area. Guest rooms are comfortable enough, though the grounds are quite desolate. The restaurant menu includes some traditional dishes, including Hopi stew, which is made with hominy, lamb, and green chili. There's also a small museum on the grounds. Because it is the only lodging for miles around, be sure you have a reservation before heading up for an overnight visit. P.O. Box 67, Second Mesa, AZ 86043. www.hopiculturalcenter.com. ✆ **928/734-2401.** Fax 928/734-6651. 30 units. Mar 15–Oct 15 $95–$105 double; Oct 16–Mar 14 $75–$85 double. Children 12 and under stay free in parent's room. AE, DC, DISC, MC, V. Pets accepted ($50 deposit). **Amenities:** Restaurant. *In room:* A/C, TV, free Wi-Fi.

En Route to or from the Hopi Mesas

On the west side of the reservation, in Tuba City, is the **Tuba City Trading Post,** Main Street and Moenave Avenue (✆ **928/283-5441**). This octagonal trading post was built in 1906 of local stone and is designed to resemble a Navajo hogan or traditional home (there's also a real hogan on the grounds). The trading post sells Native American crafts, with an emphasis on books, music, and jewelry. Across the parking lot from the trading post, you'll find **Hogan Espresso,** Main Street and Moenave Avenue (✆ **800/644-8383** or 928/283-4545), one of the few places on the reservation where you can get espresso. It's open Monday to Friday from 7am to 9pm and Saturday and Sunday from 9am to 7pm. Behind the trading post, you'll find the **Explore Navajo Interactive Museum,** 10 N. Main St. (✆ **928/640-0684**), a small museum in a tentlike structure that was used at the 2002 Salt Lake City Olympics. Although small, the museum provides a good introduction to Navajo culture. There is also a good Navajo code talkers exhibit here. In summer, the museum is open Monday through Saturday 8am to 6pm and Sunday noon to 6pm; call for hours in other months. Admission is $9 for adults, $7 for seniors, and $6 for children ages 7 to 12.

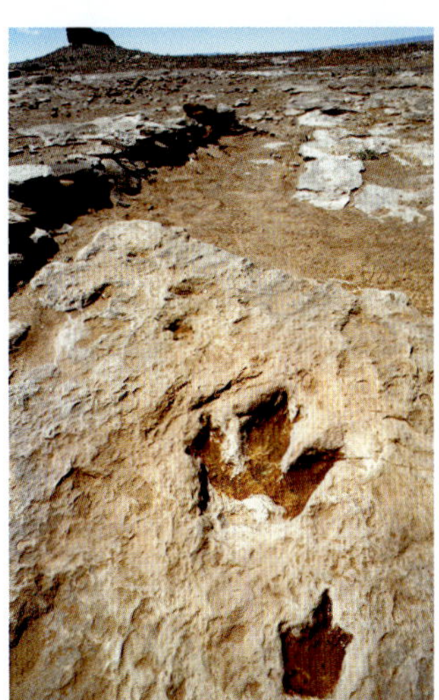

Dinosaur footprints can be seen west of Tuba City.

On the western outskirts of Tuba City, on U.S. 160, you'll find **Van's Trading Co.** (✆ **928/283-5343;** vanstradingcompany.com), in the corner of a large grocery store. Van's has a dead-pawn auction on the 15th of each month at 3pm (any pawned item not reclaimed by the owner by a specified date is considered "dead pawn"). The auction provides opportunities to buy older pieces of Navajo silver-and-turquoise jewelry.

A NATIVE AMERICAN crafts PRIMER

The Four Corners region is taken up almost entirely by the Navajo and Hopi reservations, so Native American crafts are ubiquitous. You'll see jewelry for sale by the side of desolate roads, Navajo rugs in tiny trading posts, and Hopi kachinas being sold out of village homes. The information below will help you make an informed purchase.

Hopi Kachina Dolls These elaborately decorated wooden dolls are representations of the spirits of plants, animals, ancestors, and sacred places. Traditionally, they were given to children to initiate them into the pantheon of kachina spirits, which play important roles in ensuring rain and harmony in the universe. Kachinas have long been popular with collectors, and Hopi carvers have changed their style over the years to cater to the collectors' market. Older kachinas were carved from a single piece of cottonwood, sometimes with arms simply painted on. This older style is much simpler and stiffer than the contemporary style that emphasizes action poses and realistic proportions. A great deal of carving and painting goes into each kachina, and prices today are in the hundreds of dollars for even the simplest. The *tsuku,* or clown kachinas, which are usually painted with bold horizontal black-and-white stripes and are often depicted in humorous situations or carrying slices of watermelon, are popular with tourists and collectors. In the past few years, young carvers have been returning to the traditional style of kachina, so it's now easier to find these simpler images for sale.

Hopi Overlay Silver Work Most Hopi silver work is done in the overlay style, which was introduced to tribal artisans after World War II, when the GI Bill provided funds for former soldiers to study silversmithing at a school founded by Hopi artist Fred Kabotie. The overlay process basically uses two sheets of silver, one with a design cut from it. Heat fuses the two sheets, forming a raised image. Designs often borrow from other Hopi crafts such as basketry and pottery, and from ancient Ancestral Puebloan pottery. Belt buckles, earrings, bolo ties, and bracelets are all popular.

Hopi Baskets On Third Mesa, wicker plaques and baskets are made from rabbit brush and sumac, and colored with bright aniline dyes. On Second Mesa, coiled plaques and baskets are created from dyed yucca fibers. Throughout the reservation, yucca-fiber sifters are made by plaiting over a willow ring.

Hopi Pottery Contemporary Hopi pottery tends toward geometric designs and comes in a variety of styles, including a yellow-orange ware decorated with black-and-white designs and white pottery with red-and-black designs. Nampeyo, who died in 1942, is the most

West of Tuba City and just off U.S. 160, you can see **dinosaur footprints ★** preserved in the stone surface of the desert. There are usually a few people waiting at the site to guide visitors to the best footprints (these guides will expect a tip of a few dollars). The scenery out your car window is some of the strangest in the region—you'll see lots of red-rock sandstone formations that resemble petrified sand dunes.

The **Cameron Trading Post ★** (✆ **800/338-7385** or 928/679-2231; www.camerontradingpost.com), 16 miles south of the junction of U.S. 160 and U.S. 89, is well worth a visit. The main trading post is filled with souvenirs but famous Hopi potter and is credited with bringing Hopi pottery to the attention of collectors. Today, members of the Nampeyo family are still active as potters. Most pottery is produced on First Mesa.

Navajo Silver Work Whereas the Hopi create overlay silver work from sheets of silver and the Zuni use silver work simply as a base for their skilled lapidary or stone-cutting work, Navajo silversmiths highlight the silver itself. Silversmithing caught on with Navajo men in the 1880s, when Lorenzo Hubbell, who had established a trading post in the area, hired Mexican silversmiths as teachers. The earliest pieces of Navajo jewelry were replicas of Spanish ornaments, but as the Navajo silversmiths became more proficient, they began to develop their own designs. The squash-blossom necklace, with its horseshoe-shape pendant, is one of the most distinctive Navajo designs.

Navajo Rugs After the Navajo acquired sheep and goats from the Spanish, they learned weaving from the pueblo tribes, and by the early 1800s, their weavings were widely recognized as being the finest in the Southwest. Women were the weavers among the Navajo, and they primarily wove blankets. However, by the end of the 19th century, the craft was beginning to die out as it became more economical to purchase ready-made blankets. When Lorenzo Hubbell set up his trading post, he recognized a potential market in the East for the woven blankets—if they could be made heavy enough to be used as rugs. Although today the cost of Navajo rugs, which take hundreds of hours to make, has become almost prohibitively expensive, there are still enough women practicing the craft to keep it alive.

The best rugs are those made with homespun yarn and natural vegetal dyes. However, commercially manufactured yarns and dyes are increasingly used to keep costs down. Some weavers are now using wool from Churro sheep, which are descended from sheep that may have been brought to this region by Spanish settlers more than 300 years ago. There are more than 15 regional styles of rugs and there is quite a bit of overlapping and borrowing. Bigger and bolder patterns are likely to cost quite a bit less than very complex and highly detailed patterns.

has large selections of rugs and jewelry as well. In the adjacent stone-walled gallery are museum-quality Native American artifacts (with prices to match). The trading post includes a motel (p. 340), convenience store, and gas station.

WHERE TO STAY

Moenkopi Legacy Inn & Suites ★ With a facade designed to resemble a Hopi village, the Moenkopi Legacy Inn, which opened in 2010, is by far the best hotel in the area. The lobby, with its peeled-log columns, stone chimney, and soaring ceiling, is reminiscent of the interiors of traditional Hopi homes, and incorporates numerous traditional Hopi symbols. Guest rooms are large, comfortable, and modern, and feature old photos of Hopi villages. In the courtyard, there's a small artificial stream beside the swimming pool. There's a small gift shop off the lobby, and display cases feature works by local artists and artisans.

7

P.O. Box 2260, Tuba City, AZ 86045. www.experiencehopi.com. ✆ **928/283-4500.** Fax 928/283-4499. 100 units. $89–$129 double; $105–$179 suite. Rates include continental breakfast. Children 17 and under stay free in parent's room. AE, MC, V. **Amenities:** Lounge (no alcohol served); exercise room; Jacuzzi; outdoor saltwater pool. *In room:* A/C, TV, hair dryer, free Wi-Fi.

Quality Inn Navajo Nation Located in the bustling Navajo community of Tuba City (where you'll find gas stations, fast-food restaurants, and grocery stores), this modern hotel is adjacent to the historic Tuba City Trading Post. The hotel offers comfortable rooms of average size, but the green lawns, shade trees, and old trading post (complete with hogan) are what really set this place apart. This hotel is also adjacent to the Explore Navajo Interactive Museum (see above). The nearby Moenkopi Legacy Inn may be newer, but the trading post and museum here make this a more interesting choice in the area.

10 N. Main St. (P.O. Box 247), Tuba City, AZ 86045. www.explorenavajo.com. ✆ **800/644-8383** or 928/283-4545. Fax 928/283-4144. 80 units. Apr–Oct $108–$153 double; Nov–Mar $88–$123 double. Rates include full breakfast. Children 17 and under stay free in parent's room. AE, DC, DISC, MC, V. Pets accepted ($10 per night). **Amenities:** Restaurant; exercise room. *In room:* A/C, TV, fridge, hair dryer, free Wi-Fi.

THE PETRIFIED FOREST & PAINTED DESERT ★

25 miles E of Holbrook; 90 miles E of Flagstaff; 118 miles S of Canyon de Chelly; 180 miles N of Phoenix

Petrified wood has long fascinated people, and although it can be found in almost every state, the "forest" of downed logs in northeastern Arizona is by far the most extensive. But don't head out this way expecting to see standing trees of stone with leaves and branches intact. Although there is enough petrified timber scattered across this landscape to fill a forest, it is, in fact, in the form of broken logs and not standing trees. Many a visitor has shown up expecting to find some sort of national forest of stone trees. The reality is much less impressive than the petrified forest of the imagination.

However, this area is still unique. When, in the 1850s, this vast treasure-trove of petrified wood was discovered, scattered like stone kindling across the landscape, enterprising people began exporting it wholesale to the East. Within 50 years, so much had been removed that in 1906 several areas were set aside as the Petrified Forest National Monument, which, in 1962, became a national park. A 27-mile scenic drive winds through the petrified forest (and a small corner of the Painted Desert), providing a fascinating high-desert experience.

It may be hard to believe as you drive across this arid landscape, but at one time this area was a vast steamy swamp. That was 225 million years ago, when dinosaurs and huge amphibians ruled the earth and giant now-extinct trees grew on the high ground around the swamp. Fallen trees were washed downstream, gathered in piles in quiet backwaters, and eventually were covered over with silt, mud, and volcanic ash. As water seeped through this soil, it dissolved the silica in

The forest of petrified wood in northeastern Arizona is the most extensive.

the volcanic ash and redeposited it inside the cells of the logs. Eventually, the silica recrystallized into stone to form petrified wood, with minerals such as iron, manganese, and carbon contributing the distinctive colors.

This region was later inundated with water, and thick deposits of sediment buried the logs ever deeper. Eventually, the land was transformed yet again as a geologic upheaval thrust the lake bottom up above sea level. This upthrust of the land cracked the logs into the segments we see today. Wind and water gradually eroded the landscape to create the Painted Desert, and the petrified logs were once again exposed on the surface of the land.

Essentials

GETTING THERE The north entrance to Petrified Forest National Park is 25 miles east of Holbrook on I-40. The south entrance is 20 miles east of Holbrook on U.S. 180.

FEES & HOURS The entry fee is $10 per car. Between early May and early September, the park is open from 7am to 7pm; late February to early May and early September to late October, it's open daily from 7am to 6pm; and late October to late February, it's open daily from 8am to 5pm.

VISITOR INFORMATION For further information on the Petrified Forest or the Painted Desert, contact **Petrified Forest National Park,** P.O. Box 2217, Petrified Forest, AZ 86028 (✆ **928/524-6228;** www.nps.gov/pefo). For information on Holbrook and the surrounding region, contact the **Holbrook Chamber of Commerce Visitor Center & Museum,** 100 E. Arizona St. (✆ **800/524-2459** or 928/524-6558; www.holbrookchamberofcommerce.com).

Exploring a Unique Landscape

Petrified Forest National Park has both a north and a south entrance. If you are coming from the west, it's better to start at the southern entrance and work your way north along the park's 27-mile scenic road, which has more than 20 overlooks. This way, you'll see the most impressive displays of petrified logs early in

The Giant Logs trail.

your visit and save the Painted Desert vistas for last. If you're coming from the east, start at the northern entrance and work your way south.

The **Rainbow Forest Museum** (✆ **928/524-6228**), just inside the south entrance to the park, is the best place to begin your tour. Here you can learn all about petrified wood, watch an introductory film, and otherwise get oriented. Exhibits chronicle the area's geologic and human history. There are also displays on the reptiles and dinosaurs that once inhabited this region. The museum sells maps and books and also issues free backpacking permits. Early May to early September, it's open from 7am to 7pm (daily); early September to late October and late February to early May, it's open daily from 7am to 6pm; late October to late February, it's open from 8am to 5pm (daily). Adjacent to the museum is a snack bar.

The **Giant Logs self-guided trail** starts behind the museum. The trail winds across a hillside strewn with logs that are 4 to 5 feet in diameter. Almost directly across the parking lot from the museum is the entrance to the **Long Logs** and **Agate House** areas. On the 1.6-mile Long Logs trail, you can see more big trees, while at Agate House, a 2-mile round-trip hike will lead you to the ruins of a pueblo built from colorful petrified wood. These two trails can be combined into a 2.5-mile hike.

Heading north, you'll pass by the unusual formations known as the **Flattops.** These structures were caused by the erosion of softer mineral deposits from beneath a harder and more erosion-resistant layer of sandstone. This is one of the park's wilderness areas. The **Crystal Forest** is the next stop to the north, named for the beautiful amethyst and quartz crystals once found in the cracks of petrified logs. Concern over the removal of these crystals was what led to the protection of the petrified forest. A .75-mile loop trail winds past the logs that once held the crystals.

At the **Jasper Forest Overlook,** you can see logs that include petrified roots, and a little bit farther north, at the **Agate Bridge** stop, you can see a petrified log that forms a natural agate bridge. Continuing north, you'll reach **Blue Mesa,** where pieces of petrified wood form capstones over easily eroded clay soils. As wind and water wear away at the clay beneath a piece of stone, the balance of the stone becomes more and more precarious until it eventually comes toppling down. A 1-mile loop trail here leads into the park's badlands.

Erosion has played a major role in the formation of the Painted Desert, and to the north of Blue Mesa you'll see some of the most interesting erosional features of the area. It's quite evident why these hills of sandstone and clay are known as the **Teepees.** The layers of different color are due to manganese, iron, and other minerals in the soil.

By this point, you've probably seen as much petrified wood as you'd ever care to see, so be sure to stop at **Newspaper Rock,** where instead of staring at more ancient logs, you can see a dense concentration of petroglyphs left by generations of Native Americans. Unfortunately you can no longer get close to these petroglyphs, so you'll have to be content to observe them from a distance. At nearby **Puerco Pueblo,** the park's largest archaeological site, you can view the remains of homes built by the people who created the park's petroglyphs. This pueblo was probably occupied around A.D. 1400. Don't miss the petroglyphs on its back side.

North of Puerco Pueblo, the road crosses I-40. From here to the Painted Desert Visitor Center, there are eight overlooks onto the southernmost edge of the **Painted Desert.** Named for the vivid colors of the soil and stone that cover the land here, the Painted Desert is a dreamscape of pastels washed across a barren expanse of eroded hills. The colors are created by minerals dissolved in sandstone and clay soils that were deposited during different geologic periods. There's a picnic area at Chinde Point overlook. At Kachina Point, you'll find the **Painted Desert Inn,** a renovated historic building that is operated as a bookstore and museum. From here, there's access to the park's other wilderness area. The inn, which was built in 1924 and expanded by the Civilian Conservation Corps, is noteworthy for both its architecture and the Fred Kabotie murals on the interior walls. Hours are 9am to 5pm daily. Between Kachina Point and Tawa Point, you can do an easy 1-mile round-trip hike along the rim of the Painted Desert. An even more interesting route leads down into the Painted Desert from behind the Painted Desert Inn.

No Smoke Signals Necessary

If you're driving into Arizona from New Mexico, you can get information on the state at the Painted Cliffs Welcome Center, Grants Road, Lupton (✆ 928/688-2448; www.arizonaguide.com), which is at exit 359 off I-40. The visitor center is open daily from 8am to 5pm.

Just inside the northern entrance to the park is the **Painted Desert Visitor Center** (✆ **928/524-6228**), which is open the same hours as the Rainbow Forest Museum (see above). Here you can watch a short film that explains the process by which wood becomes fossilized (it's the same film that's shown at the Rainbow Forest Museum). Adjacent to the visitor center are a cafeteria, a bookshop, and a gas station.

Other Reasons to Linger in Holbrook

Although the Petrified Forest National Park is the main reason for visiting this area, you might want to stop by downtown Holbrook's **Old West Museum,** 100 E. Arizona St. (✆ **928/524-6558**), which also houses the Holbrook Chamber of Commerce visitor center. This old and dusty museum has exhibits on local history but is most interesting for its old jail cells. It's open Monday through Friday from 8am to 5pm, Saturday and Sunday from 8am to 4pm; admission is free. On weekday evenings in June and July, there are Native American dance performances in front of the visitor center.

Although it is against the law to collect petrified wood inside Petrified Forest National Park, there are several rock shops in Holbrook where you can buy legally collected pieces of petrified wood in all shapes and sizes. You'll find them lined up along the main street through town and out on U.S. 180, the highway leading to the south entrance of Petrified Forest National Park. The biggest and best of these rock shops is **Jim Gray's Petrified Wood Co.,** 147 U.S. 180 (✆ **928/524-1842;** www.petrifiedwoodco.com), which has everything from raw rocks to petrified-wood coffee tables that sell for thousands of dollars. This store also has a fascinating display of minerals and fossils. It's open daily from 7am to 7 or 8pm in the summer (8am–6pm in other months) and is well worth a stop.

Where to Stay

Holbrook, the town nearest to Petrified Forest National Park, offers lots of budget chain motels charging very reasonable rates.

Wigwam Motel If you're willing to sleep on a saggy mattress for the sake of reliving a bit of Route 66 history, don't miss this collection of concrete wigwams. This unique motel was built in the 1940s, when unusual architecture was springing up all along famous Route 66. The motel has been owned by the same family since it was built and still has the original rustic furniture. Old cars are kept in the parking lot for an added dose of Route 66 character.

811 W. Hopi Dr., Holbrook, AZ 86025. www.galerie-kokopelli.com/wigwam. ✆ **928/524-3048.** Fax 928/524-3668. 15 units. $52–$58 double. MC, V. Pets accepted ($5 per night). *In room:* A/C, TV.

Where to Eat

While there are plenty of inexpensive restaurants in Holbrook, none is particularly memorable or recommendable. Your best bet is to drive over to Winslow to the Turquoise Room at La Posada hotel.

THE WINDOW ROCK & GANADO AREAS

74 miles NE of Petrified Forest National Park; 91 miles E of Second Mesa; 190 miles E of Flagstaff; 68 miles SE of Canyon de Chelly National Monument

Window Rock, the capital of the Navajo Nation, is less than a mile from the New Mexico state line and is named for a huge natural opening in a sandstone cliff just outside town. Today, that landmark is preserved as the **Window Rock Tribal Park,** located 2 miles north of Ariz. 264. As the Navajo Nation's capital, Window Rock is the site of government offices, a museum and cultural center, and a zoo. A few miles to the west is the St. Michaels Historical Museum, in the community of St. Michaels. About a half-hour's drive west of St. Michaels is the Hubbell Trading Post, in the community of Ganado.

Essentials

GETTING THERE To reach Window Rock from Flagstaff, take I-40 east to Lupton and go north on Indian Rte. 12.

VISITOR INFORMATION For advance information, contact **Navajo Tourism,** P.O. Box 663, Window Rock, AZ 86515 (✆ **928/810-8501;** www.discovernavajo.com).

SPECIAL EVENTS Unlike the village ceremonies of the pueblo-dwelling Hopi, Navajo religious ceremonies tend to be held in the privacy of family hogans. However, the public is welcome to attend the numerous fairs, powwows, and rodeos held throughout the year. The biggest of these is the **Navajo Nation Fair** (✆ **928/871-6478;** www.navajonationfair.com), held in Window Rock in early September. It features traditional dances, a rodeo, a powwow, a Miss Navajo Pageant, and arts-and-crafts exhibits and sales.

Exploring the Area

Hubbell Trading Post National Historic Site ★ Located just outside the town of Ganado, 26 miles west of Window Rock, the Hubbell Trading Post was established in 1876 by Lorenzo Hubbell and is the oldest continuously operating trading post on the Navajo Nation. Hubbell did more to popularize the arts and crafts of the Navajo people than any other person and was in large part responsible for the revival of Navajo weaving in the late 19th century.

Much more than just a place to trade crafts for imported goods, trading posts were for many years the main gathering spot for meeting people from other parts of the reservation and served as a sort of gossip fence and newsroom. Hubbell Trading Post is still in use today, and in the trading post's general store, you'll see basic foodstuffs (not much variety here) and bolts of the cloth Navajo women use for sewing their traditional skirts and blouses. However, today the trading post is more a living museum. Visitors can explore the grounds on their own or take a guided tour ($2), and can often watch Navajo weavers in the slow process of creating a rug.

Window Rock Tribal Park.

Watch Navajo weavers at work at Hubbell Trading Post.

What Time Is It?

The Navajo Nation observes daylight saving time, contrary to the rest of the state, so if you're coming from elsewhere in Arizona, the time here will be 1 hour later in months when daylight saving is in effect. The Hopi Reservation, however, does not observe daylight saving time, even though it is completely surrounded by the Navajo Nation.

The rug room is filled with a variety of traditional and contemporary Navajo pieces. And although it's possible to buy a small 12×18-inch rug for around $100, most cost thousands of dollars. In another room are baskets, kachinas, and jewelry by Navajo, Hopi, and Zuni artisans. Twice a year, usually in May and October, there are auctions of Native American crafts here at the trading post.

Ariz. 264, Ganado. ✆ **928/755-3475.** www.nps.gov/hutr. Free admission. Apr 30–Sept 8 daily 8am–6pm; Sept 9–Apr 29 daily 8am–5pm. Closed New Year's Day, Thanksgiving, and Christmas.

Navajo Museum, Library & Visitor's Center This museum and cultural center is housed in a large building patterned after a traditional hogan. Inside you'll see temporary exhibits of contemporary crafts and art, as well as exhibits on contemporary Navajo culture. There's also a gift shop.

Ariz. 264 at Loop Rd. (across from the Navajo Nation Inn), Window Rock. ✆ **928/871-7941.** www.navajonationmuseum.org. Free admission. Mon 8am–5pm; Tues–Sat 8am–6pm (until 7pm in summer).

Navajo Nation Zoo & Botanical Park ☺ Located in back of the Navajo Nation Inn, this zoo and botanical park features animals and plants that are significant in Navajo history and culture. Bears, cougars, and wolves are among the creatures you'll see. The setting, which includes several sandstone "haystack" rocks, is very dramatic, and some of the animal enclosures are quite large and incorporate natural rock outcroppings.

Ariz. 264, Window Rock. ✆ **928/871-6574.** www.navajozoo.org. Free admission. Mon–Sat 10am–5pm. Closed New Year's Day, Thanksgiving, and Christmas.

St. Michaels Historical Museum In the community of St. Michaels, 4 miles west of Window Rock, this museum chronicles the lives and influence of Franciscan friars who started a mission in this area in the 1670s. The museum is in a small building adjacent to the impressive stone mission church. Back in the early years of the 20th century, a friar here photographed the Navajos of the area, and the chance to see some of these historical photos is one of the best reasons to visit this museum.

St. Michaels, just south of Ariz. 264. ✆ **928/871-4171.** Free admission. Memorial Day to Labor Day daily 9am–5pm; other months, call for hours.

Shopping

The **Hubbell Trading Post,** although a National Historic Site, is still an active trading post and has an outstanding selection of rugs, as well as lots of jewelry (see "Exploring the Area," above). In Window Rock, be sure to visit the **Navajo Arts and Crafts Enterprise** (✆ **800/871-1829** or 928/871-4090; www.gonavajo.com), which is next to the Quality Inn Navajo Nation Capital and has been operating since 1941. Here you'll find silver-and-turquoise jewelry, Navajo rugs, baskets, pottery, and Native American clothing. The store is open Monday through Saturday from 9am to 8pm and Sunday from noon to 6pm.

Where to Stay

Navajoland Inn & Suites This hotel is 2 miles west of Window Rock near the historic St. Michaels Mission and is centrally located for exploring west to the Hopi mesas, north to Canyon de Chelly, and south to Petrified Forest National Park. With its indoor pool and exercise room, this is your best bet in the area, especially if you're traveling with the family.

392 W. Ariz. 264, St. Michaels, AZ 86511. www.navajoland-innsuites.com. ✆ **928/871-5690.** Fax 928/871-5699. 73 units. $70–$80 double; $90 suite. Children 12 and under stay free in parent's room. AE, DC, DISC, MC, V. Pets accepted ($20 per day). **Amenities:** Exercise room; Jacuzzi; indoor pool; sauna. *In room:* A/C, TV, free Wi-Fi.

Quality Inn Navajo Nation Capital This hotel is in Window Rock, the administrative center of the Navajo Nation. The rooms feature rustic Southwestern-style furnishings and are the best you'll find on this side of the reservation. The restaurant serves American and traditional Navajo dishes, including mutton stew and fry bread.

48 W. Ariz. 264 (P.O. Box 2340), Window Rock, AZ 86515. www.explorenavajo.com. ✆ **800/662-6189** or 928/871-4108. Fax 928/871-5466. 56 units. Apr–Oct $73–$103 double; Nov–Mar $68–$98 double. Rates include full breakfast. Children 17 and under stay free in parent's room. AE, DC, DISC, MC, V. Pets accepted ($10 per night). **Amenities:** Restaurant; exercise room. *In room:* A/C, TV, hair dryer, free Wi-Fi.

Where to Eat

In Window Rock, your best bet is the **Quality Inn Navajo Nation Capital** (see "Where to Stay," above), which serves moderately priced American, Mexican, and Navajo food. Try the Navajo tacos or mutton stew. The restaurant is open daily from 6am to 9pm.

At the **Ch'ihootso Indian Marketplace** (✆ **928/871-5443**), at the junction of Ariz. 264 and Navajo Rte. 12, you'll find several tiny restaurants that specialize in traditional Navajo dishes such as mutton stew and fry bread. On weekends a crafts/flea market is in the parking lot here. Hours vary.

CANYON DE CHELLY NATIONAL MONUMENT ★★★

68 miles NW of Window Rock; 222 miles NE of Flagstaff; 110 miles SE of Navajo National Monument; 110 miles SE of Monument Valley Navajo Tribal Park

It's hard to imagine narrow canyons less than 1,000 feet deep being as impressive as the Grand Canyon, but in some ways Canyon de Chelly National Monument is just that. Gaze down from the rim at an ancient cliff dwelling as the whinnying of horses and clanging of goats' bells drifts up from far below, and you'll be struck by the continuity of human existence. For more than 2,000 years, people have called these canyons home, and today the canyon is the site of not only prehistoric dwelling sites, but also the summer homes of Navajo farmers and shepherds.

Canyon de Chelly National Monument consists primarily of two major canyons—Canyon de Chelly (which is pronounced "Canyon duh Shay" and is derived from the Navajo word *tsegi,* meaning "rock canyon") and Canyon del Muerto (Spanish for "Canyon of the Dead"). The canyons extend for more than

Canyon de Chelly National Monument.

100 miles through the rugged slickrock landscape of northeastern Arizona, draining the seasonal snowmelt runoff from the Chuska Mountains.

In summer, Canyon de Chelly's smooth sandstone walls of red and yellow contrast sharply with the greens of corn, pastures, and cottonwoods on the canyon floor. Vast stone amphitheaters form the caves in which the Ancestral Puebloans built their homes, and as you watch shadows and light paint an ever-changing canyon panorama, it's easy to see why the Navajo consider this sacred ground. The many mysteriously abandoned cliff dwellings and the breathtaking natural beauty make Canyon de Chelly as worthy of a visit as the Grand Canyon.

Essentials

GETTING THERE From Flagstaff, the easiest route to Canyon de Chelly is I-40 to U.S. 191 to Ganado. At Ganado, drive west on Ariz. 264 and pick up U.S. 191 N. to Chinle. If you're coming down from Monument Valley or Navajo National Monument, Indian Rte. 59, which connects U.S. 160 and U.S. 191, is an excellent road with plenty of beautiful scenery.

FEES Admission to the monument is free.

VISITOR INFORMATION Before leaving home, you can contact **Canyon de Chelly National Monument,** P.O. Box 588, Chinle, AZ 86503 (✆ **928/674-5500;** www.nps.gov/cach), for information. The monument itself is open daily from sunrise to sunset. The visitor center is open daily 8am to 5pm (closed Christmas day). Remember that the Navajo Nation observes daylight saving time.

SPECIAL EVENTS The annual **Central Navajo Fair** is held in Chinle in August. It includes, among other activities, a rodeo, a powwow (Native American drumming and dancing), and Navajo food stalls.

Taking Photos on the Reservations

Before taking a photograph of a Navajo, always ask permission. If it's granted, a tip of $1 or more is expected. Photography is not allowed at all in Hopi villages.

Exploring the Canyon

Your first stop should be the **visitor center** (see above), in front of which is an example of a traditional crib-style hogan, a hexagonal structure of logs and earth that Navajos use as both a home and a ceremonial center. Inside the visitor center, a small museum explores the history of Canyon de Chelly, and there's often a silversmith demonstrating Navajo jewelry-making techniques. Interpretive programs are offered at the monument from Memorial Day to Labor Day. Check at the visitor center for daily activities, such as campfire programs and natural-history programs.

From the visitor center, most people tour the canyon by car. Very different views of the monument's system of canyons are provided by the 15-mile North Rim and 16-mile South Rim drives. The North Rim Drive overlooks Canyon del Muerto, while the South Rim Drive overlooks Canyon de Chelly. With stops, the drive along either rim road can easily take 2 to 3 hours. If you have time for only one, make it the South Rim Drive, which provides both a dramatic view of Spider Rock and the chance to hike down into the canyon on the only trail you can explore without hiring a guide. If, on the other hand, you're more interested in the history and prehistory of this area, opt for the North Rim Drive, which overlooks several historically significant sites within the canyon.

THE NORTH RIM DRIVE

The first stop on the North Rim is the **Ledge Ruin Overlook.** On the opposite wall, about 100 feet up from the canyon floor, you can see the Ledge Ruin. This site was occupied by the Ancestral Puebloans between 1050 and 1275. Nearby, at the unmarked Dekaa Kiva Viewpoint, you can see a lone kiva (circular ceremonial building). This structure was reached by means of toeholds cut into the soft sandstone cliff wall.

A view from the Antelope House Overlook.

The second stop is the **Antelope House Overlook,** which is the all-around most interesting overlook in the monument. Not only do you get to hike a quarter-mile over the rugged rimrock landscape, but you also get to view ruins, rock art, and impressive cliff walls. The Antelope House ruin takes its name from the antelope paintings, believed to date back to the 1830s, on a nearby cliff wall. Beneath the ruins of Antelope House, archaeologists have found the remains of an earlier pit house dating from A.D. 693. Although most of the Ancestral Puebloan cliff dwellings were abandoned sometime after a drought began in 1276, Antelope House had already been abandoned by 1260, possibly because of damage caused by flooding. Across the wash from Antelope House, an ancient tomb, known as the Tomb of the Weaver, was discovered by archaeologists in the 1920s. The tomb contained the well-preserved body of an old man wrapped in a blanket of golden eagle feathers and accompanied by cornmeal, shelled and husked corn, pine nuts, beans, salt, and thick skeins of cotton. Also visible from this overlook is Navajo Fortress, a red-sandstone butte that the Navajo once used as a refuge from attackers. A steep trail and system of log ladders led to the top of the butte, and by hauling the ladders up behind them, the Navajo could escape from any pursuers.

The third stop is **Mummy Cave Overlook,** named for two mummies found in burial urns below the ruins. Archaeological evidence indicates that this giant amphitheater consisting of two caves was occupied for 1,000 years, from A.D. 300 to 1300. In the two caves and on the shelf between are 80 rooms, including three kivas. The central structure between the two caves includes an interesting three-story building characteristic of the architecture in Mesa Verde National Park in Colorado. Archaeologists speculate that a group of Ancestral Puebloans migrated here from New Mexico. Much of the original plasterwork is still intact and indicates that the buildings were colorfully decorated.

The fourth and last stop on the North Rim is the **Massacre Cave Overlook,** which got its name after an 1805 Spanish military expedition killed more than 115 Navajos at this site. The Navajo at the time had been raiding Spanish settlements that were encroaching on their territory. Accounts of the battle at Massacre Cave differ. One version claims there were only women, children, and old men taking shelter in the cave, but the official Spanish records claim 90 warriors and 25 women and children were killed. Also visible from this overlook is Yucca Cave, which was occupied about 1,000 years ago.

THE SOUTH RIM DRIVE

The South Rim Drive climbs slowly but steadily, and at each stop you're a little bit higher above the canyon floor. Near the mouth of the canyon is the **Tunnel Overlook,** where a short narrow canyon feeds into Chinle Wash, a wash formed

The 80-room White House Ruin can be reached via the White House Ruins Trail.

Spider Rock rises 800 feet from the canyon floor.

FRED HARVEY & HIS girls

Unless you grew up in the Southwest and can remember back to pre–World War II days, you may have never heard of Fred Harvey and the Harvey Girls. But if you spend much time in northern Arizona, you're likely to run into quite a few references to the Harvey Girls and their boss.

Fred Harvey was the Southwest's most famous mogul of railroad hospitality and was an early promoter of tourism in the Grand Canyon State. Harvey, who was working for a railroad in the years shortly after the Civil War, developed a distaste for the food served at railroad stations. He decided he could do a better job, and in 1876 he opened his first Harvey House railway-station restaurant for the Santa Fe Railroad. By the time of his death in 1901, Harvey operated 47 restaurants, 30 diners, and 15 hotels across the West.

The women who worked as waitresses in the Harvey House restaurants came to be called Harvey Girls. Known for their distinctive black dresses, white aprons, and black bow ties, Harvey Girls had to adhere to very strict behavior codes. In fact, in the late 19th century, they were considered the only real "ladies" in the West, aside from schoolteachers. So celebrated were they in their day that in the 1940s, Judy Garland starred in a Technicolor MGM musical called *The Harvey Girls.* Garland played a Harvey Girl who battles the evil town dance-hall queen (played by Angela Lansbury) for the soul of the local saloonkeeper.

by the streams that cut through the canyons of the national monument. *Tsegi* is a Navajo word meaning "rock canyon," and at the nearby **Tsegi Overlook,** that's just what you'll see when you gaze down from the viewpoint.

The next stop is the **Junction Overlook,** so named because it overlooks the junction of Canyon del Muerto and Canyon de Chelly. Here you can see the Junction Ruin, which has 10 rooms and a kiva. Ancestral Puebloans occupied this ruin during the Great Pueblo Period, which lasted from around 1100 until shortly before 1300. First Ruin, which is perched precariously on a long narrow ledge, is also visible. There are 22 rooms and two kivas in this ruin. Good luck picking out the two canyons in this maze of curving cliff walls.

The third stop is **White House Overlook,** from which you can see the 80-room White House Ruin, which is among the largest ruin sites in the canyon. These buildings were inhabited between 1040 and 1275. From this overlook, you have your only opportunity to descend into Canyon de Chelly without a guide or ranger. The **White House Ruins Trail ★★** descends 600 feet to the canyon floor and crosses Chinle Wash before reaching the White House Ruin. The buildings of this ruin were constructed both on the canyon floor and 50 feet up the cliff wall in a small cave. Although you cannot enter the ruins, you can get close enough to get a good look. Do not wander off this trail, and please respect the privacy of the Navajo living here. The 2.5-mile round-trip hike takes about 2 hours. Be sure to carry water.

Notice the black streaks on the sandstone walls above the White House Ruins. These streaks, known as desert varnish, are formed by seeping water, which reacts with iron in the sandstone (iron is what gives the walls their reddish hue). To create the canyon's many petroglyphs, Ancestral Puebloan artists would chip away at the desert varnish. Later, the Navajo used paints to create pictographs of animals and historical events, such as the Spanish military expedition that killed 115 Navajos at Massacre Cave. Many of these petroglyphs and pictographs can be seen if you take a guided tour into the canyon.

The fifth stop is **Sliding House Overlook.** These ruins were built on a narrow shelf and appear to be sliding down into the canyon. Inhabited from about 900 until 1200, Sliding House contained between 30 and 50 rooms. This overlook is already more than 700 feet above the canyon floor, with sheer walls giving the narrow canyon a very foreboding appearance.

On the last access road to the canyon rim, you'll come to the **Face Rock Overlook,** which provides yet another dizzying glimpse of the ever-deepening canyon. Here you gaze 1,000 feet down to the bottom. However, it is the next stop—**Spider Rock Overlook ★★**—that offers the monument's most spectacular view. This viewpoint overlooks the junction of Canyon de Chelly and Monument Canyon. The monolithic pinnacle known as Spider Rock rises 800 feet from the canyon floor, its two free-standing towers forming a natural monument. Across the canyon from Spider Rock is the similarly striking **Speaking Rock,** which is connected to the far canyon wall.

OTHER WAYS TO SEE THE CANYON

Access to the floor of Canyon de Chelly is restricted. Unless you're on the White House Trail (see "The South Rim Drive," above), you must be on an organized tour or accompanied by an authorized guide in order to enter the canyon. If you want to see a lot of the canyon and don't happen to be driving your own four-wheel-drive vehicle, the best way to see Canyon de Chelly and Canyon del Muerto is on a jeep tour or what locals call **shake-and-bake tours ★**. These latter tours are in rugged military-type trucks that have had seats installed in the truck beds. In summer, these excursions really live up to the name. (In winter, the trucks are enclosed to keep out the elements.) Tours, which leave from two area hotels, make frequent stops for photographs and to visit ruins, Navajo farms, and rock art.

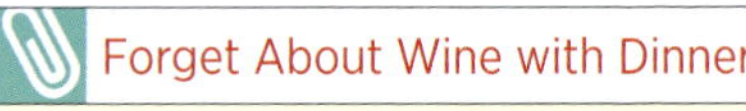

Forget About Wine with Dinner

Alcohol is prohibited on both the Navajo and Hopi reservations. Unfortunately, however, despite this prohibition, drunk drivers are a problem on the reservation, so stay alert.

Thunderbird Lodge (✆ **800/679-2473;** www.tbirdlodge.com), which uses unusual six-wheel-drive trucks for its tours, operates half-day tours costing $49 for adults and $38 for children 12 and under, and full-day trips costing $79 per person. The half-day tours operate year-round with departures at 9am and 1 or 2pm (depending on the season); full-day tours operate spring through fall, departing at 9am and returning at 5pm. Similar tours are offered by **Canyon de Chelly Tours** (✆ **928/674-5433** or 928/349-1600; www.canyondechellytours.com), which departs from the Holiday Inn and will take you into the canyon in a Unimog truck (a powerful four-wheel-drive off-road vehicle). These tours, which operate from March to October, cost $60 to $66 for adults and $40 to $44 for children 12 and under. Reservations are recommended.

For a more personalized experience, I recommend going out in a jeep in a small group. **De Chelly Tours** (✆ **877/343-3243** or 928/674-3772; www.acanyondechellytour.com)charges $150 for a 3-hour guided jeep tour for up to three people. Canyon de Chelly Tours (see above) offers similar jeep tours and charges $175 to $193 for 3-hour tours for up to three people.

Access remote parts of the canyon via horseback.

If you'd rather use a more traditional means of transportation, you can go on a guided horseback ride. To leave the crowds behind, drive east along South Rim Drive to **Totsonii Ranch ★** (✆ **928/755-2037** or 928/220-5524; www.totsoniiranch.com), which is 1¼ miles past the end of the paved stretch of this road. Rides from here visit a remote part of the canyon (including the Spider Rock area) and cost $15 per group per hour for the guide and $15 per person per hour. Totsonii Ranch also offers overnight rides for $335 per person and 2-night rides for $515 per person.

If you're physically fit and enjoy hiking, consider hiring a **Navajo guide** to lead you into the canyon. Hikes can start at the White House Ruin trail, near the Spider Rock overlook, or from near the Antelope House overlook. These latter two starting points are trails that are not open to the public without a guide and should be your top choices. The hike from Antelope House gets my vote for best option for a hike. The monument visitor center maintains a list of guides, and guides can often be hired at the visitor center. The guide fee is usually $15 per hour with a 3-hour minimum.

Shopping

The **Thunderbird Lodge Gift Shop,** in Chinle (✆ **800/679-2473**), is well worth a stop while you're in the area. It has a large collection of rugs, as well as a good selection of pottery and plenty of souvenirs. Anywhere visitors gather in the canyon (such as at ruins and petroglyph sites), you're likely to encounter craftspeople selling jewelry and other types of handwork. These craftspeople accept cash, personal checks, traveler's checks, and sometimes credit cards.

Where to Stay

Holiday Inn–Canyon de Chelly ★ Between the town of Chinle and the national monument entrance, this modern hotel is on the site of the old Garcia Trading Post, which has been incorporated into the restaurant and gift-shop building (although the building no longer has any historical character). All guest rooms have patios or balconies, and most face the cottonwood-shaded pool courtyard. Because Canyon de Chelly truck tours leave from the parking lot here and because the restaurant serves the best food in town, this should be your top choice for a room in Chinle.

Indian Rte. 7, Garcia Trading Post, Chinle, AZ 86503. www.holiday-inn.com/chinle-garcia. ✆ **888/465-4329** or 928/674-5000. Fax 928/674-8264. 108 units. $89–$109 double. Children 19 and under stay free in parent's room; children 12 and under eat free. AE, DC, DISC, MC, V. **Amenities:** Restaurant; concierge; exercise room; outdoor pool; room service. *In room:* A/C, TV, fridge, hair dryer, free Wi-Fi.

Thunderbird Lodge Built on the site of an early trading post at the mouth of Canyon de Chelly, Thunderbird Lodge is the closest hotel to the national monument. The red-adobe construction of the lodge itself is reminiscent of ancient pueblos, and the presence on the property of an old stone-walled trading post gives this place lots of character. However, the rooms here are not quite as modern or as comfortable as those at the nearby Holiday Inn. The old trading post now serves as a cafeteria that serves a few Navajo dishes. There's also a shop that sells Navajo rugs.

P.O. Box 548, Chinle, AZ 86503. www.tbirdlodge.com. ✆ **800/679-2473** or 928/674-5841. Fax 928/674-5844. 73 units. Mar–Oct $110–$120 double, $163 suite; Nov–Feb $66 double, $95 suite. Children 12 and under stay free in parent's room. AE, DC, DISC, MC, V. Pets accepted ($25 fee). **Amenities:** Restaurant. *In room:* A/C, TV, free Wi-Fi.

CAMPGROUNDS

Adjacent to the Thunderbird Lodge is the free **Cottonwood Campground,** which has around 100 sites but does not take reservations. On South Rim Drive 10 miles east of the Canyon de Chelly visitor center, you'll find the private **Spider Rock Campground** (www.spiderrockcampground.com; ✆ **928/674-8261**), which has more than 30 spaces and charges $10 to $15 per night. This campground also has a couple of hogans for rent for $29 to $39 per night.

Where to Eat

Other than a handful of fast-food restaurants in Chinle, the only places to eat in town are hotel dining rooms. While the cafeteria at the Thunderbird Lodge has a memorable setting in a historic trading post, the food is forgettable. The food at the Holiday Inn's dining room is a bit better, though the service isn't. If you need an espresso, stop by **Changing Woman Cafe** (✆ **928/674-5260;** www.changingwomancafe.com), which is in a hogan under the trees across from the national monument's Cottonwood Campground. The coffee is organic, and the cafe owner, Victoria Begay, also offers a variety of four-wheel-drive, hiking, and camping tours.

NAVAJO NATIONAL MONUMENT ★

110 miles NW of Canyon de Chelly; 140 miles NE of Flagstaff; 60 miles SW of Monument Valley; 90 miles E of Page

Navajo National Monument, 30 miles west of Kayenta and 60 miles northeast of Tuba City, encompasses three of the largest and best-preserved Ancestral Puebloan cliff dwellings in the region—Betatakin, Keet Seel, and Inscription House. It's possible to visit both Betatakin and Keet Seel, but, due to its fragility, Inscription House is closed to the public. The name Navajo National Monument is a bit misleading. Although the Navajo do inhabit the area now, the cliff dwellings were built by Kayenta Ancestral Puebloans, the ancestors of today's Hopi and Pueblo peoples. The Navajo did not arrive in this area until centuries after the cliff dwellings had been abandoned.

For reasons unknown, the well-constructed cliff dwellings here were abandoned around the middle of the 13th century. Tree rings suggest that a drought in the latter part of the 13th century prevented the Ancestral Puebloans from growing sufficient crops. In Tsegi Canyon, however, there's another theory for the abandonment. The canyon was usually flooded each year by spring and summer snowmelt, which made farming quite productive, but in the mid-1200s, weather patterns changed and streams began cutting deep into the soil, forming narrow little canyons called arroyos, which lowered the water table and made farming much more difficult.

Essentials

GETTING THERE Navajo National Monument can be reached by taking U.S. 89 N. to U.S. 160 to Ariz. 564 N.

FEES Monument admission is free.

VISITOR INFORMATION For information, contact **Navajo National Monument,** HC 71 Box 3, Tonalea, AZ 86044 (✆ **928/672-2700;** www.nps.gov/nava). Late May through mid-September, the visitor center is open daily from 8am to 6pm; in winter the visitor center is open daily from 9am to 5pm. The monument is open daily from sunrise to sunset.

Exploring the Monument

A visit to Navajo National Monument is definitely not a point-and-shoot experience. You're going to have to expend some energy if you want to see what this monument is all about. The shortest distance you'll have to walk is 1 mile, which is the round-trip from the visitor center to the Betatakin overlook. However, if

Our Daily Bread

The sandwich board beside the pickup was a bit cryptic. KNEEL DOWN BREAD was all it said. I had spotted the sign out of the corner of my eye as I made a turn on a remote section of the Navajo Nation at the foot of Black Mesa. Slamming on the brakes, I pulled a U-turn and went back to find out more.

My travel companion, a baker by trade, leaned out of the car window and asked the Navajo woman sitting in the pickup truck, "What's kneel down bread?"

"It's corn that we roast and then take off the cob," the woman explained. "Then we grind it, put it back in the husk and roast it." She reached into a cooler and pulled out what looked like a long tamale.

"We'll take two," said my friend enthusiastically, handing the Navajo woman $4. And, for the rest of the morning, as we drove across the desert, we nibbled on the sweetest rustic corn bread imaginable.

Keep your eyes open as you travel the Navajo and Hopi reservations and you, too, may stumble upon some unexpected traditional treats.

you want to actually get close to these ruins, you're looking at strenuous day or overnight hikes.

Your first stop should be the **visitor center,** which has informative displays on the Ancestral Puebloan and Navajo cultures, including numerous artifacts from Tsegi Canyon. You can also watch a couple of short films or a slide show.

The only one of the monument's three ruins that can be seen easily is **Betatakin ★**, which means "ledge house" in Navajo. Built in a huge amphitheater-like alcove in the canyon wall, Betatakin was occupied only from 1250 to 1300 and may have housed 125 people. A 1-mile round-trip paved trail from the visitor center leads to overlooks of Betatakin. The strenuous 5-mile round-trip hike to Betatakin itself is led by a ranger, takes 3 to 5 hours, and involves descending more than 700 feet to the floor of Tsegi Canyon and later returning to the rim. Between late May and early September, these guided hikes are offered daily at 8:15 and 10am. Remember, daylight saving time *is* observed here on the Navajo Nation. Other months, tours leave only on weekends at 10am, but call to make sure the tour will be going out. These hikes are offered on a first-come, first-served basis. All participants should carry 1 to 2 quarts of water. While this is a fascinating hike, you will be hiking with a large group.

Keet Seel ★, which means "broken pieces of pottery" in Navajo, has a much longer history than Betatakin, with occupation beginning as early as A.D. 950 and continuing until 1300. At one point, Keet Seel may have housed 150 people. The 17-mile round-trip hike is quite strenuous. During the summer, hikers usually stay overnight at a primitive campground near the ruins, but in the winter, if the hike is offered at all, it is done as a day hike. You must carry enough water for your trip—up to 2 gallons in summer—because none is available along the trail. These hikes are offered between late May and mid-September and reservations can be made up to 5 months in advance. Hikes are sometimes offered in other months.

Where to Stay

There is no lodge at the national monument, but there are two free campgrounds that have a total of 47 campsites. Sunset View Campground is open all year, while Canyon View Campground is open only between April and September. Both campgrounds are free, and neither takes reservations. The nearest reliable motels are 30 miles away in Kayenta. See the section on Monument Valley, below, for details.

MONUMENT VALLEY NAVAJO TRIBAL PARK ★★★

60 miles NE of Navajo National Monument; 110 miles NW of Canyon de Chelly; 200 miles NE of Flagstaff; 150 miles E of Page

In its role as sculptor, nature has, in the north central part of the Navajo Nation, created a garden of monoliths and spires unequaled anywhere on earth. Whether you've been here or not, you've almost certainly seen images of Monument Valley before. This otherworldly landscape has been an object of fascination for years, and since Hollywood director John Ford first came here in the 1930s, it has served as backdrop for countless movies, TV shows, and commercials.

Monument Valley Navajo Tribal Park.

Located 30 miles north of Kayenta and straddling the Arizona-Utah state line (you actually go into Utah to get to the park entrance), Monument Valley is a vast flat plain punctuated by natural sandstone cathedrals. These huge monoliths rise up from the sagebrush with sheer walls that capture the light of the rising and setting sun and transform it into fiery hues. Evocative names including the Mittens, Three Sisters, Camel Butte, Elephant Butte, the Thumb, and Totem Pole reflect the shapes the sandstone has taken under the erosive forces of nature.

While it may at first seem as if this strange landscape is a barren wasteland, it is actually still home to a few hardy Navajo families. The Navajo have been living in the valley for generations, herding their sheep through the sagebrush scrublands, and some families continue to reside here today. In fact, human habitation in Monument Valley dates back hundreds of years. Within the park are more than 100 Ancestral Puebloan archaeological sites, ruins, and petroglyphs dating from before 1300.

Essentials

GETTING THERE Monument Valley Navajo Tribal Park is 200 miles northeast of Flagstaff. Take U.S. 89 north to U.S. 160 to Kayenta, which is 23 miles south of Monument Valley and 29 miles east of Navajo National Monument. Then drive north on U.S. 163.

FEES Admission to the park is $5 per person (free for children 9 and under). ***Note:*** Because this is a tribal park and not a federal park, America the Beautiful passes are not valid here.

VISITOR INFORMATION For information, contact **Monument Valley Navajo Tribal Park** (✆ **435/727-5874** or 435/727-5879; www.navajonationparks.org). May through September, the park is open daily from 6am to 8:30pm; between October and April, it's open daily from 8am to 4:30pm. The park is closed on Christmas.

Exploring the Park

This is big country and, like the Grand Canyon, is primarily a point-and-shoot experience for most visitors. Because this is reservation land and people still live in Monument Valley, most backcountry and off-road travel is prohibited unless you're with a licensed guide. So basically, with one exception, your options for seeing the park on your own are limited. You can take a few pictures from the overlook beside the visitor center and the View Hotel, drive the park's Valley Drive (a scenic but very rough 17-mile dirt road), take a jeep or van tour, or go on a guided hike or horseback ride. At the visitor center, you'll find a small museum and a large gift shop, and, at the View Hotel, you'll find a restaurant with a knockout view. A quarter-mile away from the visitor center there's a picnic area.

Although Valley Drive is best driven in a high-clearance vehicle, plenty of people drive the loop in rental cars and other standard passenger vehicles. Take it slow, and you should do fine. However, if the first stretch of rocky, rutted road convinces you to change your mind about the drive, just return to the visitor center and book a jeep or van tour and let someone else pay the repair bills. Along the loop drive, you'll pass 11 very scenic viewpoints that provide ample opportunities for photographing the valley's many natural monuments. At many of these viewpoints, you'll also encounter Navajos selling jewelry and other crafts. At John Ford's Point, so named because it was a favorite shooting location for film director John Ford, you may even get the chance to photograph a Navajo on horseback posed in front of all that spectacular scenery. He'll expect a tip.

If you're trying to decide whether to take a tour, here's some little-publicized information that might help you with your decision. Most tours don't just drive the 17-mile loop; they go off into a part of the valley that is closed to anyone who is not on a tour. This part of the valley is, in my opinion, the most beautiful. You'll get close-up looks at several natural arches and stop at some beautiful petroglyphs. Before booking a tour, make sure that the tour will go to this "closed" section of the valley. There are always plenty of jeep tour companies waiting for business in the park's main parking lot. If you're staying at Goulding's Lodge, then your best bet is to go out with **Goulding's Tours** (✆ **435/727-3231;** www.gouldings.com), which has its office right at the lodge (see "Where to Stay & Eat," below), just a few miles from the park entrance. Goulding's offers 2½-hour tours ($40 for adults, $27 for children 7 and under), 3½-hour tours ($50 for adults, $30 for children), 5½-hour tours ($70 for adults, $55 for children), and all-day tours ($90 for adults, $70 for children). This company also offers full-moon tours (Sept and Oct are the best months for these). **Monument Valley Simpson's Trailhandler Tours** (✆ **877/686-2848** or 435/727-3362; www.trailhandlertours.com), another reliable company to try, charges $69 to $72 for a 2½-hour tour ($35–$36 for children 6–12). **Sacred Monument Tours** (✆ **435/727-3218** or 928/380-4527; www.monumentvalley.net) charges $73 for a 2½-hour jeep tour ($58 for children 11 and under). A variety of other tours are also available.

The traditional way to explore this quintessentially Wild West landscape, however, is from the back of a horse, a la John Wayne. I recommend going out with **Sacred Monument Tours** (✆ **435/727-3218** or 928/380-4527; www.monumentvalley.net), which charges from $68 for a 1-hour horseback ride up to $286 for an all-day ride.

Monumental Sunsets

Be sure to save some storage space on the memory card of your digital camera (or keep plenty of film in your camera) for sunset at Monument Valley. Sure, these rocks are impressive at noon, but as the sun sets and the shadows lengthen, they are positively enchanting—definitely one of the most spectacular sites in America.

Because the jeep and van tours are such a big business here, there's a steady stream of the vehicles on Valley Drive throughout the day. One way to get away from the rumble of engines is to go out on a guided hike. These are offered by **Sacred Monument Tours** (✆ **435/727-3218** or 928/380-4527; www.monumentvalley.net), which charges between $73 and $166 per person for hikes of different lengths. **Kéyah Hózhóní Tours** (✆ **928/309-7440;** www.monumentvalley.com) also offers hiking tours ($100 per person) and overnight camping trips ($550 for one or two people). Keep in mind that summers can be very hot here.

There are two exceptions to the no-traveling-off-road rule. The 3.3-mile **Wildcat Trail ★★** is a loop trail that circles West Mitten Butte and provides the only opportunity to get close to this picturesque butte. As you circle the butte, you'll get all kinds of different perspectives, even one that completely eliminates the "thumb." Because this is the park's only option for unguided hiking, it's a not-to-be-missed excursion and one of the most memorable hikes in the state. In summer, be sure to carry plenty of water. The other trail open without a guide is the Mesa Rim Trail, a .5-mile trail along the mesa above the View Hotel.

Activities Outside the Park

Before leaving the area, you might want to visit **Goulding's Museum & Trading Post,** at Goulding's Lodge (see "Where to Stay & Eat," below). This old trading post was the home of the Gouldings for many years and is set up as they had it back in the 1920s and 1930s. There are also displays about the many movies that have been shot here. The trading post hours vary with the seasons; admission is by donation.

Inside Kayenta's Burger King, which is next door to the Hampton Inn, there's an interesting exhibit on the Navajo code talkers of World War II. The code talkers were Navajo soldiers who used their own language to transmit military messages, primarily in the South Pacific.

Where to Stay & Eat

In addition to the lodgings listed here, you'll find several budget motels north of Monument Valley in the Utah towns of Mexican Hat and Bluff. There are restaurants at both the View Hotel and Goulding's Lodge, but, aside from the great views, neither is recommendable.

Goulding's Lodge ★ For decades this was the only lodge actually located in Monument Valley, and although you can now stay inside the park at the Navajo-owned View Hotel, Goulding's is still a good bet. Because this is one of the most popular hotels in the area, be sure to make your reservation well in advance. Goulding's offers great views (especially at sunrise) from the private balconies of its large guest rooms. The restaurant serves Navajo and American dishes, and also boasts views that are enough to make any meal an event. Unfortunately, although the setting is memorable, the service in the restaurant can be somewhat lacking. The lodge also has a museum.

P.O. Box 360001, Monument Valley, UT 84536. www.gouldings.com. ✆ **435/727-3231.** Fax 435/727-3344. 62 units. Mar 15–Nov 15 $130–$185 double; Nov 16–Mar 14 $78 double. Children 9 and under stay free in parent's room. AE, DC, DISC, MC, V. Pets accepted ($20 fee). **Amenities:** Restaurant; exercise room; indoor pool. *In room:* A/C, TV/DVD, fridge, hair dryer, free Wi-Fi.

More Big Rocks

Monument Valley isn't the only place in this region with impressive rocks. Just north of Kayenta, on the road to Monument Valley, you'll pass by El Capitan (also called Agathla), a huge plug of volcanic rock that rises from the desert floor. Of course, when you pull over to take a picture, you can also shop for cheap jewelry at Navajo vendors' stalls. East of Kayenta on U.S. 160, watch for the red sandstone cliffs known as Baby Rocks. East of Tuba City, also on U.S. 160, watch for the two sandstone towers known as Elephant Feet.

Hampton Inn–Navajo Nation This is the most modern lodging right in the town of Kayenta and, as such, should be your first choice if you can't get a room in Monument Valley itself. The Hampton Inn is built in a contemporary Santa Fe style and has spacious, comfortable guest rooms. In the hotel's dining room, you can get a few Navajo dishes. Adjacent to the hotel, you'll find the Navajo Cultural Center and a Burger King that has an interesting display on the Navajo code talkers of World War II.

U.S. 160 (P.O. Box 1219), Kayenta, AZ 86033. www.hamptoninn.com. ✆ **800/426-7866** or 928/697-3170. Fax 928/697-3189. 73 units. $89–$169 double. Rates include full breakfast. Children 18 and under stay free in parent's room. AE, DC, DISC, MC, V. Pets accepted ($20 fee plus $20 per night). **Amenities:** Restaurant; small outdoor pool; room service. *In room:* A/C, TV, hair dryer, free Wi-Fi.

Kayenta Monument Valley Inn ☺ This hotel, right in the center of Kayenta, is very popular with tour groups and is almost always crowded. Although the grounds are dusty and a bit run-down, the rooms are spacious and clean and have all been extensively renovated in the past few years. I like the poolside units best. Part of the hotel's dining room is designed to look like an Ancestral Puebloan ruin, and the menu offers both American and Navajo cuisine.

U.S. 160 and U.S. 163 (P.O. Box 307), Kayenta, AZ 86033. www.kayentamonumentvalleyinn.com. ✆ **866/306-5458** or 928/697-3221. Fax 928/697-3349. 164 units. Early Sept to June $139–$189 double; July early Sept $229–$249 double. Children 18 and under stay free in parent's room. AE, DC, DISC, MC, V. **Amenities:** Restaurant; exercise room; small outdoor pool; room service. *In room:* A/C, TV, hair dryer, free Wi-Fi.

The View Hotel ★★ This Navajo-owned hotel inside Monument Valley Navajo Tribal Park is the only hotel inside the park. As such, it should be your first choice for accommodations in the area. With the park's most famous and picturesque buttes right outside the windows, you need do nothing more than sit back and watch the play of light on red-rock pinnacles. The rooms themselves are comfortable enough, though little better than standard freeway off-ramp motel rooms. What you're paying for here is the view, not the room itself. Both the service and the food in the hotel's restaurant are subpar, but the only other option in the area is the dining room at Goulding's, which isn't much better.

P.O. Box 360457, Monument Valley, UT 84536. www.monumentvalleyview.com. ✆ **435/727-5555.** Fax 435/727-4545. 96 units. Mid-Mar to mid-Nov $149–$229 double, $185–$319 suite; mid-Nov to mid-Mar $99–$129 double, $175–$199 suite. AE, DISC, MC, V. **Amenities:** Restaurant; exercise room; free Wi-Fi. *In room:* A/C, TV, fridge.

Wetherill Inn Located in Kayenta a mile north of the junction of U.S. 160 and U.S. 163, and 20 miles south of Monument Valley, the Wetherill Inn doesn't look like much from the outside, but guest rooms are the most modern rooms in Kayenta. While the hotel offers neither the convenience of the View Hotel or Goulding's Lodge nor the amenities of the nearby Holiday Inn or Hampton Inn, if you just want a nice room for the night, this is a good bet. A cafe next door serves Navajo and American food.

1000 Main St., Kayenta, AZ 86033. www.wetherill-inn.com. ✆ **928/697-3231.** Fax 928/697-3233. 54 units. May 1–Oct 15 $131 double; Oct 16–Nov 15 and Apr $90 double; Nov 16–Mar 31 $75 double. Children 12 and under stay free in parent's room. Rates include continental breakfast. AE, DC, DISC, MC, V. **Amenities:** Indoor pool. *In room:* A/C, TV, hair dryer, free Wi-Fi.

CAMPGROUNDS

If you're headed to Monument Valley Navajo Tribal Park, you can camp at **Goulding's Campground** (www.gouldings.com; ✆ **435/727-3231**), which charges $20 to $44 per night. There are also small cabins that go for $79 per night. This campground is open year-round (limited services Nov to mid-Mar) and has an indoor pool, hot showers, a playground, a coin-op laundry, and Wi-Fi.

Driving on to Colorado or New Mexico: The Four Corners Meet

It seems like a supremely silly reason to drive miles out of your way, but lots of people feel they just have to visit the **Four Corners Monument** (✆ **928/871-6647;** www.navajonationparks.org/htm/fourcorners.htm). Why? So they can stand in four states—Arizona, Colorado, Utah, and New Mexico—at once and get their photo taken. Located north of Teec Nos Pos in the very northeast corner of the state, this park is the only place in the United States where the corners of four states come together. The scenery is not exactly the most dramatic in the region, and the exact point is just a cement pad surrounded by flags and vendor stalls. The park also has a few picnic tables and a snack bar serving, among other things, Navajo fry bread. The park is open daily from 8am to 7pm, and admission is $3.

LAKE POWELL ★★ & PAGE

272 miles N of Phoenix; 130 miles E of Grand Canyon North Rim; 130 miles NE of Grand Canyon South Rim

Had the early Spanish explorers of Arizona suddenly come upon Lake Powell after traipsing for months across desolate desert, they would have either taken it for a mirage or fallen to their knees and rejoiced. Imagine the Grand Canyon filled with water, and you have a pretty good picture of Lake Powell. Surrounded by hundreds of miles of parched desert, this reservoir, created by the damming of the Colorado River at Glen Canyon, seems unreal when first glimpsed. Yet real it is, and it draws people from around the region with its promise of relief from the heat.

Construction of the Glen Canyon Dam came about despite the angry outcry of many who felt that this canyon was even more beautiful than the Grand Canyon and should be preserved in its natural state. Preservationists lost the battle, and construction of the dam began in 1960, with completion in 1963. It took another 17 years for Lake Powell to fill to capacity. Today, the lake is a watery powerboat playground, and houseboats and water-skiers cruise where once only bird songs and the splashing of waterfalls filled the canyon air. These days most people seem to agree, though, that Lake Powell is as amazing a sight as the Grand Canyon, and it draws almost as many visitors each year as its downriver neighbor.

Visitors dock houseboats along Lake Powell.

While Lake Powell is something of a man-made wonder of the world, one of the natural wonders of the world—Rainbow Bridge—can also be found on its shores. Called *nonnozhoshi* by the Navajo, or "the rainbow turned to stone," this is the largest natural bridge on earth and stretches 275 feet across a side canyon off Lake Powell.

The town of Page, originally a camp constructed to house the workers who built the dam, has many motels and inexpensive restaurants, and is the main base for most visitors to the area.

Essentials

GETTING THERE Page is connected to Flagstaff by U.S. 89. Ariz. 98 leads southeast onto the Navajo Indian Reservation and connects with U.S. 160 to Kayenta and Four Corners. The Page Airport is served by **Great Lakes Airlines** (✆ **800/554-5111** or 307/433-2899; www.greatlakesav.com), which flies from Phoenix. Round-trip airfares start at around $198.

FEES Admission to Glen Canyon National Recreation Area is $15 per car (good for 1 week). There is also a $16-per-week boat fee if you bring your own boat.

VISITOR INFORMATION For further information on the Lake Powell area, contact the **Glen Canyon National Recreation Area** (✆ **928/608-6404;** www.nps.gov/glca); the **Page–Lake Powell Chamber of Commerce,** 34 S. Lake Powell Blvd., Page (✆ **888/261-7243** or 928/645-2741; www.pagechamber.com); or the **John Wesley Powell Memorial Museum,** 6 N. Lake Powell Blvd., Page (✆ **888/597-6873** or 928/645-9496; www.powellmuseum.org).

GETTING AROUND Rental cars are available at the Page Airport from **Avis** (✆ **800/331-1212** or 928/645-2024).

Glen Canyon National Recreation Area

Until the flooding of Glen Canyon formed Lake Powell, this area was one of the most remote regions in the contiguous 48 states. However, since the construction of Glen Canyon Dam at a spot where the canyon of the Colorado River was less than a third of a mile wide, this remote and rugged landscape has become one of the country's most popular national recreation areas. Today, the lake and much of the surrounding land is designated the Glen Canyon National Recreation Area and attracts around two million visitors each year. The otherworldly setting amid the slickrock canyons of northern Arizona and southern Utah is a tapestry of colors, the blues and greens of the lake contrasting with the reds and oranges of the surrounding sandstone cliffs. This interplay of colors and vast desert landscapes easily makes Lake Powell the most beautiful of Arizona's many reservoirs.

Built to provide water for the desert communities of the Southwest and West, **Glen Canyon Dam** stands 710 feet above the bedrock and contains almost 5 million cubic yards of concrete. The dam also provides hydroelectric power, and deep within its massive wall of concrete are huge power turbines. Although most Lake Powell visitors are more interested in water-skiing and powerboating than they are in drinking water and power production, there would be no lake without the dam, so any visit to this area ought to start at the **Carl Hayden Visitor Center** (✆ **928/608-6404**), which is located beside the dam on U.S. 89 just north of Page. Here you can tour the dam and learn about its construction. Between mid-May and mid-September, the visitor center is open daily from 8am to 6pm; November to February, it's open daily 8:30am to 4:30pm; other months, it's open daily 8am to 5pm (it's closed New Year's Day, Thanksgiving, and Christmas).

More than 500 feet deep in some places, and bounded by nearly 2,000 miles of shoreline, **Lake Powell** is a maze of convoluted canyons where rock walls often rise hundreds of feet straight out of the water. In places, the long, winding canyons are so narrow there isn't even room to turn a motorboat around. The only way to truly appreciate this lake is from a boat, whether a houseboat, a runabout, or a sea kayak. Water-skiing, riding personal watercrafts, and fishing have long been the most popular on-water activities, and consequently, you'll be hard-pressed to find a quiet corner of the lake if you happen to be a solitude-seeking sea kayaker. However, with so many miles of shoreline, you're bound to find someplace to get away from it all. Your best bet for solitude is to head up-lake

Glen Canyon Dam.

Rainbow Bridge.

from Wahweap Marina. This will get you away from the crowds and into some of the narrower reaches of the lake.

In addition to the Carl Hayden Visitor Center mentioned above, there's the **Bullfrog Visitor Center,** in Bullfrog, Utah (✆ **435/684-7423**). It's open intermittently from May to early October; call for hours.

BOAT & AIR TOURS

There are few roads penetrating the Glen Canyon National Recreation Area, so the best way to appreciate this rugged region is by boat. If you don't have your own boat, you can at least see a small part of the lake on a boat tour. A variety of tours depart from **Wahweap Marina** (✆ **888/896-3829** or 928/645-2433; www.lakepowell.com). Your best bet is either the 1½-hour **Antelope Canyon Cruise** ($40 for adults, $26 for children) or the 2½-hour **Canyons Adventure Cruise** ($63 for adults, $39 for children). To see more of the lake, opt for the full-day tour to Rainbow Bridge (see below for details). Dinner cruises are also offered.

The Glen Canyon National Recreation Area covers an immense area, much of it only partially accessible by boat. If you'd like to see more of the area than is visible from car or boat, consider taking an air tour with **Westwind Scenic Air Tours** (✆ **800/245-8668** or 928/645-2494; www.westwindairservice.com), which offers several tours of northern Arizona and southern Utah, including flights over Rainbow Bridge and Monument Valley. Sample rates are $125 for a 30-minute flight over Rainbow Bridge (minimum two passengers) and $259 for a 90-minute flight over Monument Valley (minimum three passengers). Children 12 and under get a 10% discount.

Rainbow Bridge National Monument

Rainbow Bridge ★★★, the world's largest natural bridge and one of the most spectacular sights in the Southwest, rises from the bedrock of a narrow canyon roughly 40 miles up the lake from Wahweap Marina and Glen Canyon Dam.

This massive natural arch of sandstone stands 290 feet high and spans 275 feet and has been preserved in Rainbow Bridge National Monument. Carved by wind and water over the ages, Rainbow Bridge is an awesome reminder of the powers of erosion that have sculpted this entire region into the spectacle it is today.

Rainbow Bridge is accessible only by boat or by way of a 14-mile-long hiking trail, so, going by boat is by far the more popular way to visit this natural attraction. **Lake Powell Resorts and Marinas** (✆ **888/896-3829** or 928/645-2433; www.lakepowell.com) offers 6-hour tours ($113 for adults, $84 for children) that not only get you to Rainbow Bridge in comfort, but also cruise through some of the most spectacular scenery on earth. Tours include a box lunch and a bit more exploring after visiting Rainbow Bridge. Currently, because the lake's water level is so low from years of drought, the boat must stop more than a half-mile from Rainbow Bridge, so if you aren't able to walk this distance, you won't even be able to see the sandstone arch.

Rainbow Bridge National Monument (✆ **928/608-6200;** www.nps.gov/rabr) is administered by Glen Canyon National Recreation Area. For information on hiking to Rainbow Bridge, contact the **Navajo Parks and Recreation Department,** P.O. Box 2520, Window Rock, AZ 86515 (✆ **928/871-6647;** www.navajonationparks.org). The hike to Rainbow Bridge is about 25 miles round-trip and should be done as an overnight backpacking trip. It requires a Navajo Nation hiking permit ($5 per day) and a camping permit ($5 per night), which are available through the Navajo Parks and Recreation Department, at the **Cameron Visitor Center** (✆ **928/679-2303**), in the community of Cameron near the turnoff for the Grand Canyon, and at the **Antelope Canyon Tribal Park Office** (✆ **928/698-2808**), 3 miles south of Page on Navajo Rte. 20 (beside the LeChee Chapter House).

Antelope Canyon

If you've spent any time in Arizona, chances are you've noticed photos of a narrow sandstone canyon only a few feet wide. The pinkish-orange walls of the canyon seem to glow with an inner light, and beams of sunlight slice the darkness of the deep slot canyon. Sound familiar? If you've seen this, you were probably looking at a photo of Antelope Canyon (sometimes called Corkscrew Canyon). Located 2½ miles southeast of Page off Ariz. 98 (at milepost 299), this photogenic canyon comprises the **Antelope Canyon/Lake Powell Navajo Tribal Park** ★★★ (✆ **928/698-2808;** www.navajonationparks.org/htm/antelopecanyon.htm), which is on the Navajo Nation and is divided into upper and lower canyons. The entry fee is $6, and children 7 and under enter free. March through October, Antelope Canyon is open daily from 8am to 5pm; November through February, hours vary and closures are common.

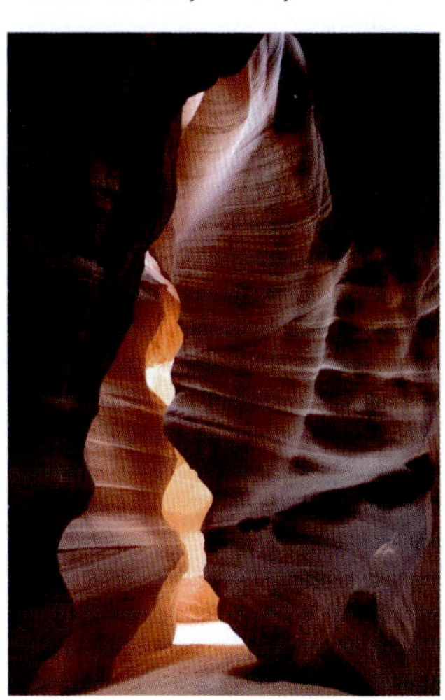

The narrow, sandstone Antelope Canyon.

There are currently two options for visiting Antelope Canyon. You can join a tour

So, What's with the Bathtub Ring?

You'll notice that the red-rock cliff walls above the waters of Lake Powell are no longer red but are instead coated with what looks like a layer of white soap scum. Those are calcium carbonate deposits left on the rock after more than a decade of drought that, at its worst, left the lake level more than 130 feet below what is called "full pool" (when the reservoir is full). Currently, the lake level is down around 66 feet.

that leaves from Page, or you can drive out to the slot canyon yourself. Either way, you'll have to pay a guide. The most convenient and reliable way is to take one of the 1½-hour tours that leave from Page. Try **Antelope Canyon Tours,** 22 S. Lake Powell Blvd. (✆ **866/645-9102** or 928/645-9102; www.antelopecanyon.com), which operates tours to Upper Antelope Canyon and charges $32 for adults, $20 for children 8 to 12, and $14 for children 6 to 7. Photographic tours cost $50, $35 for children 8 to 12, and $29 for children 3 to 7. If you don't want to deal with crowds of tourists ogling the rocks and snapping pictures with their point-and-shoots, I recommend heading out with **Overland Canyon Tours,** 48 S. Lake Powell Blvd. (✆ **928/608-4072;** www.overlandcanyontours.com), to nearby Canyon X, which is much less visited than Antelope Canyon and is a good choice for serious photographers who want to avoid the crowds. One other option for avoiding the crowds is to book a tour with **Slot Canyon Hummer Adventures,** 12 N. Lake Powell Blvd. (✆ **928/645-2266;** www.slotcanyonhummeradventures.com), which leads tours to several other little-visited area slot canyons. A 2½-hour tour is $99 and a 5-hour tour is $159.

Alternatively, at both the upper and lower canyons, you'll find Navajo guides collecting park entry fees and fees for guide services. At Lower Antelope Canyon, these guides charge $20 ($12 for children ages 6–12). At Upper Antelope Canyon, guides charge $25 ($10 for children ages 5–11). Upper Antelope Canyon is a short drive up a sandy streambed from the highway, while Lower Antelope Canyon is a short walk from the parking area just off the highway. You'll get more out of your experience if you go on one of the guided tours mentioned above, but you'll save a little money by visiting the canyon on your own. For more information on visiting Upper Antelope Canyon, contact **Antelope Canyon Navajo Tours** (✆ **928/698-3384;** www.navajotours.com); for information on Lower Antelope Canyon, contact **Ken's Tours** (✆ **928/606-2168;** www.lowerantelope.com).

Just remember that if there's even the slightest chance of rain in the region, you should not venture into this canyon, which is subject to flash floods. In the past, people who have ignored bad weather predictions have been killed by such floods.

Watersports

While simply exploring the lake's maze of canyons on a narrated tour is satisfying enough for many visitors, the most popular activities are still houseboating, waterskiing, riding personal watercrafts, and fishing. Five marinas (only Wahweap is in Arizona) help boaters explore the lake. At the **Wahweap Marina** (✆ **888/896-3829** or 928/645-2433; www.lakepowell.com), you can rent various types of boats, along with personal watercrafts and water skis. Rates range from $400 to

In a kayak, you can explore canyons too narrow for powerboats.

$584 per day, depending on the type of boat. Personal watercrafts go for $335 per day, and sea kayaks rent for $46 per day. For information on renting houseboats, see "Where to Stay," below. A variety of boats, including ski boats and kayaks, can also be rented at **Antelope Point Marina,** 537 Marina Pkwy., Navajo Rte. 22B (✆ **928/645-5900;** www.antelopepointlakepowell.com). Expect to pay $375 to $425 per day for a ski boat and $30 to $45 per day for a kayak.

If roaring engines aren't your speed, you might want to consider exploring Lake Powell by sea kayak. While afternoon winds can sometimes make paddling difficult, the air is often quite still in the morning. With a sea kayak, you can even explore canyons too narrow for powerboats. Rentals are available at **Twin Finn Diving,** 816 Copper Mine Rd. (✆ **928/645-3114;** www.twinfinn.com). Sea kayaks rent for $45 to $55 per day, and sit-on-top kayaks for $35 to $45. Multiday kayak tours are operated by **Hidden Canyon Kayak** (✆ **800/343-3121** or 928/645-8866; www.diamondriver.com/kayak), which charges $760 to $1,000 for 4- to 6-day trips. Guided kayak trips are also offered by **Kayak Powell** (✆ **888/854-7862;** www.kayaklakepowell.com), which charges $95 for a half-day tour; multiday tours range from $495 for a 2-day tour to $895 for a 5-day tour.

While most of Glen Canyon National Recreation Area consists of the impounded waters of Lake Powell, the recreation area also contains a short stretch of the Colorado River that still flows swift and free. If you'd like to see this stretch of river, try a float trip from Glen Canyon Dam to Lees Ferry. These trips are operated by **Colorado River Discovery** (✆ **888/522-6644** or 928/645-9175; www.raftthecanyon.com) between March and November. Half-day trips in motorized rafts cost $84 for adults and $74 for children ages 4 to 11. Try to reserve at least 2 weeks in advance. Spring and fall, this company also offers full-day oar-powered raft trips ($161 for adults and $151 for children). **Kayak Powell** (see above) offers all-day ($49) and overnight ($99) self-guided kayak trips on this stretch of the Colorado River.

If you have a boat (your own or a rental), avail yourself of some excellent year-round fishing. Smallmouth, largemouth, and striped bass, as well as walleye, catfish, crappie, and carp, are all plentiful. Because the lake lies within both Arizona and Utah, you'll need to know which state's waters you're fishing in whenever you cast your line out, and you'll need the appropriate license. (Be sure to pick up a copy of the Arizona and Utah state fishing regulations, or ask about applicable regulations at any of the marinas.) In Wahweap, you can arrange licenses to fish the entire lake at **Lake Powell Resorts and Marinas** (✆ **928/645-2433**), which also sells bait and tackle and can provide you with advice on fishing this massive reservoir. Other marinas on the lake also sell licenses, bait, and tackle. The best season is March through November, but walleye are most often caught during the cooler months. If you'd rather try your hand at catching enormous rainbow trout, try downstream of the Glen Canyon Dam, where cold waters provide ideal conditions for trophy trout. Unfortunately, there isn't much access to this stretch of river. You'll need a trout stamp to fish for the rainbows. If you want a guide to take you where the fish are biting, contact Bill McBurney at **Ambassador Guide Service** (✆ **800/256-7596;** www.ambassadorguides.com).

If you're just looking for a good place for a swim near Lake Powell Resort, take the Coves Loop just west of the marina. Of the three coves, the third one, which has a sandy beach, is the best. The Chains area, another good place to jump off the rocks and otherwise lounge by the lake, is outside Page down a rough dirt road just before you reach Glen Canyon Dam. Although the desert may not immediately jump to mind when considering a scuba-diving vacation, the view underwater at Lake Powell is as scenic as the view above it. To explore the underwater regions of the canyon, contact **Twin Finn Diving,** 816 Copper Mine Rd. (✆ **928/645-3114;** www.twinfinn.com), which charges $45 a day for scuba gear and also rents snorkeling equipment.

Other Outdoor Pursuits

If you're looking for a quick, easy hike with great views, head north on North Navajo Drive from downtown Page. At the end of this street is the main trail head for Page's **Rimview Trail.** This trail runs along the edge of Manson Mesa, upon which Page is built, and has views of Lake Powell and miles of red-rock country. The entire loop trail is 8 miles long, but if you want to do a shorter hike, I recommend the stretch of trail heading east (clockwise) from the trail head. If you happen to have your mountain bike with you, the trail is a great ride.

At Lees Ferry, a 39-mile drive from Page at the southern tip of the national recreation area, you'll find three short trails (Cathedral Wash, River, and Spencer). The 2-mile **Cathedral Wash Trail** is the most interesting of the three day hikes and follows a dry wash through a narrow canyon with unusual rock formations. The trail head is at the second turnout after turning off U.S. 89A. Be aware that this wash is subject to flash floods. The **River Trail** is a 2-mile round-trip hike along the river and starts at the boat ramp. The 4-mile round-trip **Spencer Trail,** which begins along the River Trail, leads up to the top of a 1,700-foot cliff for spectacular views of Marble Canyon. Lees Ferry is also the southern trail head for famed **Paria Canyon ★**, a favorite of canyoneering backpackers. This trail is between 38 and 47 miles long (depending on where you start) and follows the meandering route of a narrow slot canyon for much of its length. Most hikers start from the northern trail head, which is in Utah on U.S. 89. For more

Acrophobes, Beware!

If you have a fear of heights, there are a couple of places in the Page area that you should never visit. On the other hand, if you want some great views, then don't miss the following two scenic vistas.

As you drive down the hill from Page on Lake Powell Boulevard (the road toward Glen Canyon Dam from Page), go straight through the intersection instead of turning right toward the dam. Here you'll find a parking area and a short path to a viewing platform perched on the edge of sheer cliff walls. Far below lie the clear green waters of the Colorado River, while upstream looms Glen Canyon Dam.

If you're up for a short hike, grab the camera and head to the **Horseshoe Bend ★** viewpoint. Horseshoe Bend is a huge loop of the Colorado River, and the viewpoint is hundreds of feet above the water on the edge of a cliff. It's about a half-mile to the viewpoint from the trail head, which is 5 miles south of the Carl Hayden Visitor Center on U.S. 89 just south of milepost 545.

information on hiking in Paria Canyon, contact the **Arizona Strip Interpretive Association/Interagency Visitor Center,** 345 E. Riverside Dr., St. George, UT 84790 (✆ **435/688-3200;** www.blm.gov/az/st/en/fo/arizona_strip_field.html).

The 18-hole **Lake Powell National Golf Course ★**, 400 Clubhouse Dr. (✆ **928/645-2023;** www.golflakepowell.com), is one of the most spectacular in the state. The fairways wrap around the base of the red-sandstone bluff atop which sits the town of Page. The views stretch on forever, and in places, eroded sandstone walls come right down to the greens and fairways. Greens fees run $36 to $69 for 18 holes.

Other Area Attractions

Between April and October, you can learn about Navajo culture at **Navajo Village Heritage Center** (✆ **928/660-0304;** www.navajovillage.com), a living-history center on the northeast corner of Ariz. 98 and Coppermine Road (on the south side of Page). Evening performances here center around programs of Native American dancing, but there are also demonstrations by weavers, silversmiths, and other artisans. Tours, which last 2½ hours, cost $50 ($30 for children) and include dinner and traditional dances. Reservations are required. Although this is definitely a tourist attraction, you will come away with a better sense of Navajo culture.

If you're in the market for Native American crafts, stop by **Blair's Dinnebito Trading Post,** 626 N. Navajo Dr. (✆ **800/644-3008** or 928/645-3008; www.blairstradingpost.com), which has been in business for more than 60 years. The trading post has a good selection of Navajo rugs, Hopi kachinas, silver jewelry, pottery, and baskets.

John Wesley Powell Memorial Museum In 1869, one-armed Civil War veteran John Wesley Powell and a small band of men spent more than 3 months fighting the rapids of the Green and Colorado rivers to become the first people to travel the length of the Grand Canyon. It is for this intrepid—some said crazy—adventurer that Lake Powell is named and to whom this small museum is dedicated. Besides documenting the Powell expedition with photographs, etchings, artifacts, and dioramas, the museum displays Native American artifacts ranging from Ancestral Puebloan pottery to contemporary Navajo and Hopi crafts. The museum also acts as an information center for Page, Lake Powell, and the surrounding region.

6 N. Lake Powell Blvd. ✆ **888/597-6873** or 928/645-9496. www.powellmuseum.org. Admission $5 adults, $3 seniors, $1 children 5–12, free for children 4 and under. Mon–Sat 9am–5pm (closed Sat Nov–Feb).

Where to Stay

HOUSEBOATS

Although there are plenty of hotels and motels in and near Page, the most popular accommodations here are not waterfront hotel rooms, but houseboats, which function as floating vacation homes. With a houseboat, which is as easy to operate as a car, you can explore Lake Powell's beautiful red-rock country, far from any roads. No special license or prior experience is necessary, and plenty of hands-on instruction is given before you leave the marina. Because Lake Powell houseboating is extremely popular with visitors from all over the world, it's important to make reservations as far in advance as possible, especially if you plan to visit in summer.

Antelope Point Resort & Marina ★★ ☺ At this marina, built atop the world's largest floating platform of its kind, you can rent some of the newest and most luxurious houseboats on the lake (the larger ones even have outdoor hot tubs). There are 59-foot, 70-foot, and 75-foot boats available, ranging in quality from deluxe to luxury. Speedboats ($375–$425 per day), personal watercraft ($375 per day), and sea kayaks ($30–$45 per day) can also be rented and are a great way to explore smaller waterways that your houseboat can't navigate. To reach the marina, which has a floating restaurant, a market, and a cafe for ice cream and coffee, head east out of Page on Ariz. 98 and drive 5 miles to the signed Antelope Point Marina turnoff.

537 Marina Pkwy. (P.O. Box 880), Page, AZ 86040. www.lakepowellhouseboating.com. ✆ **800/255-5561** or 928/645-5900. Fax 480/998-7399. $6,790–$14,798 per week. AE, DISC, MC, V. Pets accepted ($100 fee). **Amenities:** Watersports equipment/rentals. *In room:* A/C, TV/DVD, CD player, kitchen.

Lake Powell Resorts & Marinas ★ ☺ This is the original houseboat-rental operation on Lake Powell, and houseboats here range in size from 46 to 75 feet, sleep anywhere from 8 to 12 people, and come complete with showers and a fully equipped kitchen. For deluxe on-the-water accommodations, opt for one of the 62-foot "Journey" houseboats. If you're coming in the summer, splurge on a boat with some sort of cooling system.

100 Lakeshore Dr., Page, AZ 86040. www.lakepowell.com. ✆ **888/896-3829** or 928/645-2433. Fax 928/645-1031. Mid-June to late Sept $3,395–$12,400 per week; lower rates other months. 3-, 4-, 5-, and 6-night rates also available on most houseboats. AE, DC, DISC, MC, V. Pets accepted ($10 per day). *In room:* Kitchen, no phone.

HOTELS & MOTELS

Best Western Arizonainn Perched right at the edge of the mesa on which Page is built, this modern motel has a fine view across miles of desert. While the guest rooms are unremarkable and are basically just standard motel rooms, about half have lake views. Be sure to ask for one of these. If you can't get a room with a view, you can at least hang out by the pool; it's got that same 100-mile view.

716 Rimview Dr., Page, AZ 86040. www.bestwestern.com. ✆ **800/826-2718** or 928/645-2466. Fax 928/645-2053. 102 units. May–Sept $100–$110 double; Oct–Apr $60–$70 double. Rates include continental breakfast. Children 17 and under stay free in parent's room. AE, DC, DISC, MC, V. Pets accepted ($10 per night). **Amenities:** Free airport transfers; exercise room; Jacuzzi, small outdoor pool. *In room:* A/C, TV, hair dryer, free Wi-Fi.

Courtyard by Marriott ★ Located at the foot of the mesa on which Page is built and adjacent to the Lake Powell National Golf Course, this is the top in-town choice. It's also the closest you'll come to a golf resort in this part of the state. Although you'll pay a premium for views of the golf course or lake, it's a worthwhile investment. Guest rooms are larger than those at most area lodgings. Moderately priced meals are served in a casual restaurant that has a terrace overlooking the distant lake. The 18-hole golf course has great views of the surrounding landscape.

600 Clubhouse Dr. (P.O. Box 4150), Page, AZ 86040. www.marriott.com/pgacy. ✆ **877/905-4495** or 928/645-5000. Fax 928/645-5004. 153 units. $89–$199 double. Children 17 and under stay free in parent's room. AE, DC, DISC, MC, V. **Amenities:** Restaurant; lounge; 18-hole golf course; exercise room; Jacuzzi; seasonal outdoor pool. *In room:* A/C, TV, fridge, hair dryer, free Wi-Fi.

Lake Powell Resort ★ This hotel at the sprawling Wahweap Marina 5 miles north of Page should be your first lodging choice in the area. The Lake Powell Resort features lots of resort amenities and activities, but it is often overwhelmed by busloads of tour groups. Consequently, don't expect very good service. Guest rooms are arranged in several long two-story wings, and every unit has either a balcony or a patio. Half of the rooms have lake views; those in the west wing have the better vantage point, as the east wing overlooks a coal-fired power plant. The Rainbow Room (see "Where to Eat," below) offers fine dining.

100 Lakeshore Dr., Page, AZ 86040. www.lakepowell.com. ✆ **888/896-3829** or 928/645-2433. Fax 928/645-1031. 348 units. Apr–Dec $156–$221 double, $236–$266 suite; Jan–Mar $69–$136 double, $216–$266 suite. Children 17 and under stay free in parent's room. AE, DC, DISC, MC, V. Pets accepted ($20 fee). **Amenities:** 2 restaurants; snack bar; lounge; free airport transfers; concierge; exercise room; Jacuzzi; 2 outdoor pools; room service; sauna; watersports equipment/rentals, free Wi-Fi. *In room:* A/C, TV, fridge, hair dryer.

CAMPGROUNDS

There are campgrounds at **Wahweap** and **Lees Ferry** in Arizona, and at Bullfrog, Hite, and Halls Crossing in Utah. Some scrubby trees provide a bit of shade at the Wahweap site, but the wind and sun make this a rather bleak spot in summer. Nevertheless, because of the lake's popularity, these campgrounds stay packed for much of the year. Wahweap (✆ **888/896-3829**) charges $23 to $38 per night (reservations are accepted), and Lees Ferry charges $12 (reservations not accepted).

Where to Eat

Blue Buddha Sushi Lounge JAPANESE Maybe it's the sight of all that Lake Powell water and maybe it's the hip, urban vibe, but whatever the reason, this sushi restaurant is a big hit in Page. This stylish lounge/restaurant attracts a young crowd who come for creative sushi rolls. Blue lights and Buddha statues everywhere set the mood. You'll find this place down an alley next to Blair's Trading Post.

644 N. Navajo Dr. ✆ **928/645-0007.** www.bluebuddhasushi.com. Reservations recommended. Main courses $14–$25; sushi $8–$12. AE, DISC, MC, V. Summer Mon–Sat 5–10pm, Sun 5–9pm; other months Tues–Sat 5–9pm.

The Dam Bar & Grille ☺ AMERICAN This theme restaurant is a warehouse-size space designed to conjure images of the interior of Glen Canyon Dam. Inside, cement walls, hard hats, and a big transformer that sends out bolts of neon "electricity" will put you in a "dam" good mood. Sandwiches, pastas, and steaks dominate the menu, but the slow-roasted chicken is my favorite dish. The lounge area is a popular local hangout, and next door is the affiliated Gunsmoke Saloon nightclub. Kids will love the cool dam decor and old boats around the inside of the restaurant.

644 N. Navajo Dr. ✆ **928/645-2161.** www.damplaza.com. Reservations recommended in summer. Main courses $7–$25. AE, DISC, MC, V. Daily 11am–9pm (until 10pm in summer).

Ja' di' Tooh ★ AMERICAN Even if this wasn't the only floating restaurant on Lake Powell, I'd tell you to be sure to have a meal here while you're in the area. With big walls of glass (some of which roll up like garage doors) and a large patio off the bar, this place is the perfect spot for lingering over a meal and drinks, especially on a hot summer day. The water lapping at the floats and the sandstone rising all around make this the quintessential Lake Powell dining experience. Okay, so the menu isn't creative (a few pizzas, sandwiches, and wraps at lunch and primarily steaks at dinner), but the setting can't be beat.

Antelope Point Marina, 537 Marina Pkwy., Navajo Rte. 22B. ✆ **928/645-5900.** www.antelopepointlakepowell.com. Main courses $8.75–$26. AE, DISC, MC, V. Daily 11am–9pm (closed Mon–Wed in winter).

Rainbow Room AMERICAN/SOUTHWESTERN With sweeping vistas of Lake Powell through the walls of glass, the Rainbow Room is both Page's top restaurant and its most touristy. The menu is short and includes a few dishes with Southwestern flavor, and many of the ingredients are organic. I like the Southwestern buffalo *osso buco*. Be prepared for a wait; this place regularly feeds busloads of tourists. The adjacent bar has a knockout view through a long wall of glass.

At Lake Powell Resort, 100 Lakeshore Dr. ✆ **888/896-3829.** Reservations recommended. Main courses $9–$12 lunch, $10–$36 dinner. AE, DISC, MC, V. Daily 6am–2pm and 5–9pm. Closed Nov–Feb.

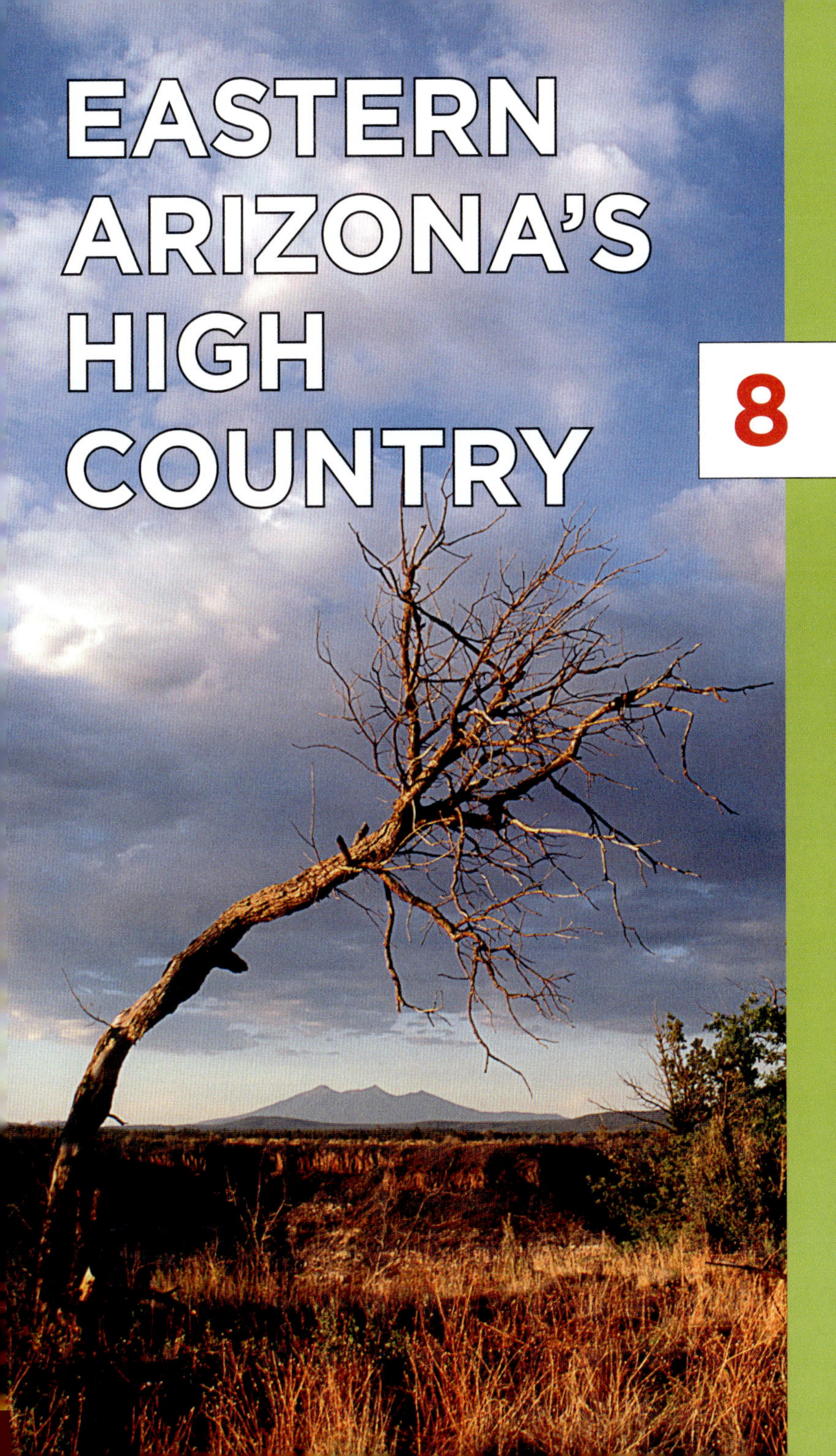
EASTERN ARIZONA'S HIGH COUNTRY
8

Cactus and desert landscapes are what come to mind when most people think of Arizona. But that's only part of the picture. Arizona actually has more mountainous country than Switzerland and more forest than Minnesota, and most of these mountains and forests are here in the highlands of eastern Arizona.

Folks from Phoenix and its surrounding cities discovered long ago how close the White Mountains' cool forests are and have for many decades built cabins and weekend homes in this area. In only a few hours, you can drive up from the cacti and creosote bushes to the meadows and pine forests. In this sparsely populated region, towns with such apt names as Alpine, Lakeside, and Pinetop have now become summer retreats for the residents of the state's low-lying, sunbaked deserts.

Dividing the arid lowlands from the cool pine forests of the highlands is the Mogollon Rim (pronounced *Mug*-ee-un by the locals), a 2,000-foot escarpment that stretches for 200 miles from central Arizona into New Mexico. Along this impressive wall, the climatic and vegetative change is dramatic, with sunshine at the base and snow squalls at the top. This area was made famous by Western author Zane Grey, who lived in a cabin near Payson and set many of his novels in this scenic yet oft-overlooked part of Arizona. Fans of Grey's novels can follow in the author's footsteps and visit a small museum with an exhibit dedicated to Grey.

Trout fishing, hiking, horseback riding, and hunting are the main warm-weather pastimes of eastern Arizona, and when winter weather reports from up north have Phoenicians dreaming about snow, many head to the White Mountains for a bit of skiing. Sunrise Park Resort, operated by the White Mountain

PREVIOUS PAGE: **The Mogollon Rim.** ABOVE: **Author Zane Grey.**

Apache Tribe, is the state's biggest and busiest downhill ski area. There are also plenty of cross-country ski trails in the area.

Much of eastern Arizona is Apache reservation land. Recreational activities abound here, but remember that the Apache tribe requires visitors to have reservation fishing permits and outdoor recreation permits. Fishing is particularly popular on the reservation, which isn't surprising, considering there are 400 miles of trout streams and 25 lakes stocked with rainbow and brown trout.

PAYSON & THE MOGOLLON RIM COUNTRY

94 miles NE of Phoenix; 90 miles SE of Flagstaff; 90 miles SW of Winslow; 100 miles W of Pinetop-Lakeside

Payson, 94 miles from Phoenix and 5,000 feet above sea level, is one of the closest places for Phoenicians to find relief from the summer heat, and though it is not quite high enough to be considered the mountains, it certainly isn't the desert (summer temperatures are 20° cooler than in the Valley of the Sun). The 2,000-foot-high, 200-mile-long Mogollon Rim, the region's main attraction, is only 22 miles north of town, and the surrounding Tonto National Forest provides opportunities for hiking, swimming, fishing, and hunting. The nearly perfect climate of Payson has also made the town a popular retirement spot. Summer highs are usually in the 80s or 90s (30s Celsius), while winter highs are usually in the 50s and 60s (teens Celsius).

Essentials

GETTING THERE Ariz. 87, the Beeline Highway, connects Payson to Phoenix and Winslow. Ariz. 260 runs east from Payson, climbing the Mogollon Rim and continuing into the White Mountains.

VISITOR INFORMATION Contact the **Rim Country Regional Chamber of Commerce,** 100 W. Main St., Payson (✆ **800/672-9766** or 928/474-4515; www.rimcountrychamber.com).

SPECIAL EVENTS Held every year since 1884 (when it started as a friendly gathering of local ranchers and cowboys), the August Doins Rodeo claims to be the world's oldest continuous rodeo. The rodeo is held the third weekend in August.

Outdoor Pursuits

The area's most popular attraction is **Tonto Natural Bridge State Park,** 10 miles northwest of Payson on Ariz. 87 (✆ **928/476-4202;** www.azstateparks.com), which preserves the largest natural travertine bridge in the world. In 1877, gold prospector David Gowan, while being chased by Apaches, became the first white man to see this natural bridge, which stands 183 feet high and 150 feet across at its widest point. Although it sounds very impressive, this natural bridge is more of a tunnel and looks nothing like the picturesque sandstone arches in southern Utah. Admission to the park is $5 for adults and $2 for children 7 to 13. The park is open Thursday through Monday from 9am to 5pm.

If you'd like to go horseback riding, try **Kohl's Ranch Stables,** on Hwy. 260, 17 miles north of Payson (✆ **928/478-0030**). Rates start at $30 for a 1-hour ride.

The **Highline Trail** is a 50-mile hike along the lower slope of the Mogollon Rim. You can find out more about this and other area trails, and learn which ones are open to mountain bikes, at the **Payson Ranger Station,** 1009 E. Ariz. 260 (✆ **928/474-7900;** www.fs.fed.us/r3/tonto), at the east end of town.

You can also hike this area in the company of llamas that will carry your gear for you. John and Joyce Bittner of the **Ranch at Fossil Creek,** 10379 W. Fossil Creek Rd., Strawberry (✆ **928/476-5178;** www.ranchatfossilcreek.com), offer half-day llama hikes ($65 for adults, $40 for children 11 and under). Overnight stays in a yurt can be arranged for $85. This ranch also raises goats and produces both goat cheese and goats-milk fudge. Guided and self-guided tours of the ranch's facilities can be arranged, and cheese, fudge, and soap are all available for sale. You'll find Fossil Creek Creamery's cheeses on the menus of some of the state's best restaurants.

Other Area Attractions

About 5 miles north of town, off Ariz. 87 on Houston Mesa Road, you can visit the ruins of **Shoofly Village,** in the Tonto National Forest. This village was first occupied nearly 1,000 years ago by peoples related to the Hohokam and Salado. It once contained 79 rooms, though today only rock foundations remain. An interpretive trail helps bring the site to life.

To learn more about the history of the area, stop by the **Rim Country Museum,** 700 Green Valley Pkwy. (✆ **928/474-3483;** www.rimcountrymuseums.com), which has displays on the region as well as a special Zane Grey exhibit and a reconstruction of the cabin Grey lived in during his time in the Payson area. The museum, located in Green Valley Park, is housed in the oldest forest ranger station and residence still standing in the Southwest. The museum is open Wednesday through Monday from 10am to 4pm. Admission is $5 for adults, $4 for seniors, and $3 for children 12 to 18.

If you're feeling lucky, spend some time and money at the **Mazatzal Casino** (✆ **800/777-7529** or 928/474-6044; www.777play.com), half a mile south on Ariz. 87. The casino is run by the Tonto Apaches.

Scenic Drives

Scenic drives through this region are popular with visitors. One of the most popular drives is along the top of the Mogollon Rim on 45-mile-long **Forest Road (F.R.) 300.** The road clings to the edge of the rim and has numerous views of the forest far below and plenty of places to stop, including lakes, picnic areas, trail heads, and campgrounds. This is a good gravel road and can be negotiated in summer in a standard passenger car. In winter, however, the road is not maintained. To access the rim road from Payson, head east on Ariz. 260 or north on Ariz. 87 for 30 miles and watch for signs.

Tonto National Bridge State Park.

About 15 miles north of Payson on Ariz. 87 is the village of **Pine,** and another 3 miles beyond this, the village of **Strawberry.** Here, in a quiet setting in the forest, you'll find a few shops selling antiques and crafts and, in Pine, the **Pine-Strawberry Museum,** Ariz. 87, Pine (✆ **928/476-3547;** www.pinestrawhs.org), a small museum that chronicles the history of this area. May 15 to October 15, the museum is open Monday through Thursday from 10am to 2pm and Friday through Sunday from 10am to 4pm; other months the museum is open Monday through Saturday from 10am to 2pm. Admission is free. If you leave Ariz. 87 in Strawberry and drive west 1¾ miles on Fossil Creek Road, you'll come to the old **Strawberry Schoolhouse** (www.pinestrawhs.org/schoolhouse.html), a restored log building dating from 1885. The schoolhouse is open mid-May to mid-October Saturday from 10am to 4pm and Sunday from noon to 4pm; mid-June through early August, the schoolhouse is also open Friday and Monday from 10am to 4pm.

Another interesting drive starts west of the Strawberry Schoolhouse. If you continue west on this road, you'll be on the gravel **Fossil Creek Road ★★**, which leads 10 miles down into a deep and spectacular canyon. It's a bit hair-raising, but if you like views, it's well worth the white knuckles and dust. At the bottom, **Fossil Creek** offers some of the most idyllic little swimming holes you could ever hope to find. If you make it down here on a weekday, you just might have a swimming hole all to yourself.

Fossil Creek offers idyllic swimming holes.

Where to Stay

Majestic Mountain Inn Although located in town, this hotel was built in an attractive, modern mountain-lodge style that makes it the most appealing place to stay right in Payson. There's a large stone chimney and fireplace in the lobby, and all of the deluxe and luxury rooms have fireplaces. The luxury units also have tile floors and a double whirlpool tub facing the fireplace. The standard rooms aren't as spacious or luxurious, but are still quite comfortable.

602 E. Ariz. 260, Payson, AZ 85541. www.majesticmountaininn.com. ✆ **800/408-2442** or 928/474-0185. Fax 928/472-6097. 50 units. $60–$150 double. Rates include continental breakfast. Children 17 and under stay free in parent's room. AE, DC, DISC, MC, V. Pets accepted ($25 fee). **Amenities:** Access to nearby health club; outdoor pool. *In room:* A/C, TV/VCR, fridge, hair dryer, free Wi-Fi.

CAMPGROUNDS

East of Payson on Ariz. 260 are several national forest campgrounds. These include **Upper Tonto Creek** and **Christopher Creek** campgrounds. Neither of these campgrounds takes reservations. Information is available from the **Payson Ranger Station,** 1009 E. Ariz. 260 (✆ **928/474-7900;** www.fs.fed.us/r3/tonto), at the east end of town.

Where to Eat

Fargo's Steakhouse STEAK This modern steakhouse next door to the Majestic Mountain Inn is the classiest restaurant in town and has a contemporary mountain-lodge atmosphere. The menu doesn't break any new ground, but you can get reliable steaks. Start with tenderloin skewers with Cajun dipping sauce or the bacon-wrapped scallops. Steak eaters on a diet will want to consider the black and blue Caesar salad.

620 E. Ariz. 260. ✆ **928/474-7455.** www.fargossteakhouse.com. Reservations recommended. Main courses $7.50–$14 lunch, $14–$31 dinner. AE, DISC, MC, V. Sun–Thurs 11am–9pm; Fri–Sat 11am–10pm.

Gerardo's Italian Bistro ★ ITALIAN Although it's nothing fancy, this casual southern Italian restaurant on the north side of Payson is a local favorite. The classics, including lasagna, spaghetti and meatballs, shrimp scampi, and cioppino are here, and there are also plenty of pizzas and a good selection of vegetarian pasta dishes. The Florentine ravioli in creamy red sauce is another good bet.

A Pleasant Valley Detour

For a bit of back-road adventure, head south from the Mogollon Rim to the remote community of Young, which sits in the middle of the aptly named Pleasant Valley. The town can be reached only via well-graded gravel roads—24 miles of gravel if you come from the north, 32 miles from the south—which is why a trip to Young is an adventure.

Why visit Young? Most people come just to see the land that spawned the worst range war and family feud in the West. Known as the Pleasant Valley War or Graham-Tewksbury Feud, it likely erupted over conflicts about sheep grazing in the valley, and eventually the feud took dozens of lives. Zane Grey memorialized the 1880s range war in his novel *To the Last Man.*

You'll find Young on Ariz. 288, which heads south from Ariz. 260 about midway between Payson and Heber, and connects to Ariz. 88 north of Globe (near Theodore Roosevelt Lake).

512 N. Beeline Hwy. ✆ **928/468-6500.** www.gerardosbistro.com. Reservations recommended. Main courses $7–$16 lunch, $11–$24 dinner. AE, DISC, MC, V. Mon–Thurs 11am–8:30pm; Fri–Sat 11am–9pm.

PINETOP-LAKESIDE

90 miles NE of Payson; 185 miles NE of Phoenix; 50 miles S of Holbrook; 140 miles SE of Flagstaff

Pinetop-Lakeside, two towns that grew together over the years, is the busiest community in the White Mountains, and strung along Ariz. 260 as it passes through this area are dozens of motels and cabin resorts. At first glance, it's easy to dismiss the town as one long commercial strip, what with all the shopping centers and budget motels, but Pinetop-Lakeside has spent many years entertaining families during the summer months, and it has plenty of diversions to keep visitors busy. You just have to look a little harder than you might in nearby Greer.

With Apache and Sitgreaves National Forests on one side and the unspoiled lands of the White Mountain Apaches' Fort Apache Indian Reservation on the other, Pinetop-Lakeside is well situated for anyone who enjoys the outdoors. Nearby are several lakes with good fishing; nearly 200 miles of hiking, mountain-biking, and cross-country ski trails; horseback riding; and downhill skiing. Although summer is the busy season, Pinetop-Lakeside becomes something of a ski resort in winter. Sunrise Park ski area is only 30 miles away, and on weekends the town is packed with skiers.

Pinetop-Lakeside is definitely the family destination of the White Mountains, so if you're looking for a romantic weekend or solitude, continue farther into the White Mountains to Greer.

Essentials

GETTING THERE Pinetop-Lakeside is located on Ariz. 260, and is 90 miles east of Payson.

VISITOR INFORMATION For information on this area, contact the **Pinetop-Lakeside Chamber of Commerce,** 102-C W. White Mountain Blvd., Lakeside, AZ 85929 (✆ **800/573-4031** or 928/367-4290; www.pinetoplakesidechamber.com).

Outdoor Pursuits

Old forts and casinos aside, it's the outdoors (and the cool weather) that really draws people here. Fishing, hiking, mountain biking, and horseback riding are among the most popular activities. Between mid-May and the end of October, you can saddle up at **Porter Mountain Stables,** 4048 Porter Mountain Rd. (✆ **928/368-5306**), which charges $30 for adults ($27 for children) for a 1-hour ride, $48 for adults ($45 for children) for a 2-hour ride. Half-day, all-day, and sunset rides are also offered.

Meandering through the forests surrounding Pinetop-Lakeside are the 180 miles of trails of the **White Mountains Trail System.** Many of these trails are easily accessible (in fact, some are right in town) and are open to both hikers and mountain bikers. The trails at Pinetop's **Woodland Lake Park** are among my favorites. The park is just off Ariz. 260 near the east end of Pinetop and has 6 miles of trails, including a paved path around the lake. For a panoramic vista of the Mogollon Rim, hike the short, flat **Mogollon Rim Interpretive Trail** off Ariz. 260 on the west side of Lakeside. For another short but pleasant stroll, check out the **Big Springs Environmental Study Area,** on Woodland Road in Lakeside. This quiet little preserve encompasses a small meadow through which flows a spring-fed stream. There is often good bird-watching here. You can spot more birds at Woodland Lake Park, mentioned above, and at **Jacques Marsh,** 2 miles north of Ariz. 260 on Porter Mountain Road in Lakeside. For more information on area trails, contact the **Lakeside Ranger District,** 2022 W. White Mountain Blvd., Lakeside (✆ **928/368-2100;** www.fs.fed.us/r3/asnf), on Ariz. 260 in Lakeside, or the **Pinetop-Lakeside Chamber of Commerce** (see "Visitor Information," above).

If you're up here to catch the big one, you can try for native Apache trout, as well as stocked rainbows, browns, and brookies. This is also the southernmost spot in the United States where you can fish for arctic graylings. Right in the Pinetop-Lakeside area, try **Woodland Lake,** in Woodland Lake Park, toward the east end of Pinetop and just south of Ariz. 260, or **Show Low Lake,** east of Lakeside and north of Ariz. 260. On the nearby Fort Apache Indian Reservation, there's good fishing in **Hawley Lake,** which is east of Pinetop-Lakeside and south of Ariz. 260. If you plan to fish at this latter lake, be sure to get a reservation fishing license ($7 per day). Licenses are available at the **Hon-Dah Service Station,** at Ariz. 260 and Ariz. 73 (✆ **928/369-4311**), and at **Hon-Dah Ski & Outdoor Sport,** also at Ariz. 260 and Ariz. 73 (✆ **928/369-7669**).

Several area golf courses are open to the public, including **Pinetop Lakes Golf & Country Club,** 4643 Buck Springs Rd., Pinetop (✆ **928/369-4531;** www.pinetoplakesgolf.com), considered one of the best executive courses in the state (play this one if you have time for only one round while you're in the area); **Silver Creek Golf Club,** 2051 Silver Lake Blvd., Show Low (✆ **928/537-2744;** www.silvercreekgolfclub.com); and the **Bison Golf & Country Club,** 860 N. 36th Dr., Show Low (✆ **928/537-4564;** www.bisongolf.net).

About 50 miles south of Show Low, U.S. 60 crosses a bridge over the narrow and scenic canyon of the Salt River. This stretch of the river is a favorite of white-water rafters, and several companies offer rafting trips of varying lengths. Try **Wilderness Aware Rafting** (✆ **800/462-7238;** www.inaraft.com), **Canyon Rio Rafting** (✆ **800/272-3353;** www.canyonrio.com), or **Mild to Wild Rafting** (✆ **800/567-6745;** www.mild2wildrafting.com). Prices are between $119 and $151 for a day trip.

Other Area Attractions

If you want to learn more about the Apaches, drive south from Pinetop-Lakeside to the **Apache Cultural Center & Museum** (✆ **928/338-4625;** http://wmat.us/wmaculture.shtml), in the town of Fort Apache, which was established in 1870 by the U.S. government. The cultural center, approximately 22 miles south of Pinetop on Ariz. 73, includes a museum with small but informative exhibits on Apache culture. Outside the cultural center and down a short trail is a re-creation of a traditional Apache village. The cultural center is open Monday through Friday (plus Sat in summer) from 8am to 5pm. Admission is $5 for adults, $3 for seniors and students, and free for children 6 and under. The cultural center is on the grounds of a former Indian school that is now called the Fort Apache Historic Park and includes more than 20 historic buildings, but don't expect to see a Hollywood-style fort. The park is more of a collection of aging historic buildings.

Also in this area are the **Kinishba Ruins.** This 200-room pueblo ruin is more than 1,000 years old and was visited by Coronado when he passed through in search of the Seven Cities of Cíbola. Get directions to the ruins at the Cultural Center.

For more information on visiting the Fort Apache Indian Reservation, contact the **White Mountain Apache Tribe Office of Tourism** (✆ **877/338-9628;** http://wmat.us/tourism.shtml), which is located in General Crook's cabin in Fort Apache Historic Park.

If you're looking for something to do after dark, head out to the **Hon-Dah Casino,** 777 Ariz. 260 (✆ **800/929-8744** or 928/369-0299; www.hon-dah.com), owned and operated by the White Mountain Apache Tribe. It's open daily round-the-clock and is at the junction of Ariz. 73 and Ariz. 260, about 4 miles east of Pinetop-Lakeside.

Where to Stay

Hon-Dah Resort Casino & Conference Center ★ This hotel, adjacent to the Hon-Dah Casino a few miles east of Pinetop-Lakeside, is the largest and most luxurious lodging in the White Mountains. As with most casino hotels, it was designed to impress. The portico is big enough to hold a basketball court, and inside the front door is an artificial rock wall upon which are mounted stuffed animals, including a cougar, a bobcat, a bear, ducks, and even a bugling elk. Guest rooms are, for the most part, very spacious.

777 Ariz. 260 (at junction with Ariz. 73), Pinetop, AZ 85935. www.hon-dah.com. ✆ **800/929-8744** or 928/369-0299. Fax 928/369-0382. 128 units. $99–$119 double; $160–$190 suite. AE, DC, DISC, MC, V. **Amenities:** Restaurant; 2 lounges; Jacuzzi; year-round outdoor pool; room service; sauna. *In room:* A/C, TV, fridge, hair dryer, free Wi-Fi.

Lake of the Woods ☺ Set on its own private lake right on Ariz. 260, Lake of the Woods is a rustic mountain resort that caters primarily to families. Cabins and houses range from tiny to huge, with rustic and modern side by side. The smallest sleep two or three, while the largest can take up to 20; all have kitchens and fireplaces. Some are on the edge of the lake, while others are tucked away under the pines; be sure to request a location away from the busy highway and ask for a newer cabin, as the accommodations vary considerably in quality. Kids, in particular, love this place: They can fish in the lake, row a boat, or play in the snow.

2244 W. White Mountain Blvd. (P.O. Box 777), Lakeside, AZ 85929. www.lakeofthewoodsaz.com. ✆ **928/368-5353.** 33 units. $79–$249 cabin for 2 people. 3- to 4-night minimum stay in summer and on some holidays. Children 1 and under stay free in parent's cabin. MC, V. Pets accepted. **Amenities:** 2 Jacuzzis; sauna; watersports equipment/rentals. *In room:* TV, kitchen, no phone.

CAMPGROUNDS

There are numerous campgrounds in the Pinetop-Lakeside area, including Fool Hollow, Lewis Canyon, and Lakeside. Of these, **Fool Hollow Lake Recreation Area,** 1500 N. Fool Hollow Lake Rd., Show Low (www.azstateparks.com; ✆ **928/537-3680**), is the nicest. There are numerous campgrounds nearby on the Fort Apache Indian Reservation. For information about these campgrounds, contact the **White Mountain Apache Tribe Wildlife and Outdoor Recreation Division,** 100 W. Fatco Rd., Whiteriver (www.wmatoutdoors.org; ✆ **928/338-4385**), or the **White Mountain Apache Tribe Office of Tourism** (http://wmat.us/tourism.shtml; ✆ **877/338-9628**).

Where to Eat

Charlie Clark's Steak House AMERICAN Charlie Clark's, the oldest steakhouse in the White Mountains, has been serving up thick, juicy steaks since 1938 (before that, during Prohibition, the building was used as a sort of backwoods speak-easy). Mesquite-broiled steaks and chicken, as well as seafood and prime rib, fill the menu.

1701 E. White Mountain Blvd., Pinetop. ✆ **888/333-0259** or 928/367-4900. www.charlieclarks.com. Reservations not accepted. Main courses $10–$20 lunch, $16–$40 dinner. AE, DISC, MC, V. Sun–Thurs 11am–9pm; Fri–Sat 11am–10pm.

GREER & SUNRISE PARK ★

51 miles SE of Show Low; 98 miles SE of Holbrook; 222 miles NE of Phoenix

The tiny community of Greer, set in the lush meadows on either side of the Little Colorado River and surrounded by forests, is by far the most picturesque mountain community in Arizona. The elevation of 8,525 feet usually ensures plenty of snow in winter and pleasantly cool temperatures in summer, and together these two factors have turned Greer into something of an upscale mountain getaway that's popular among lowlanders with an eye for aesthetics. Modern log homes are springing up all over the valley, but Greer is still free of the sort of strip-mall developments that have forever changed the character of Payson and Pinetop-Lakeside.

The Little Colorado River, which flows through the middle of Greer on its way to the Grand Canyon, is little more than a babbling brook up here. Still, it's known for its trout fishing, one of the main draws in these parts. In winter, cross-country skiing is popular. Greer is also the closest community to Sunrise Park ski area, which is what gives the village its ski-resort atmosphere.

Essentials

GETTING THERE From Phoenix, take U.S. 87 N. to Payson and then go east on Ariz. 260, or take U.S. 60 east from Phoenix through Globe and Show Low to Ariz. 260. Greer is just a few miles south of Ariz. 260 on Ariz. 373.

VISITOR INFORMATION Online, contact the **Business Council of Greer** (www.greerarizona.com).

Outdoor Pursuits

Winter is one of the busiest seasons in Greer because the town is so close to the **Sunrise Park Resort** ski area (✆ **800/772-7669** or 928/735-7669; www.sunriseskipark.com). Located just off Ariz. 260 on Ariz. 273, this ski area, the largest and most popular in Arizona, is operated by the White Mountain Apache Tribe. It usually opens in November, but thaws and long stretches without snow can make winters a bit unreliable. Although there are some good advanced runs, beginner and intermediate skiers will be in heaven. I've rarely seen so many green runs starting from the uppermost lifts of a ski area, which makes this a very family-oriented place. The ski area encompasses three mountains, including 11,000-foot-tall Apache Peak. A ski school offers a variety of lessons. Lift tickets cost $49 for adults, $42 for youths, and $28 for children 12 and under. Ski rentals are available here and at numerous shops in Pinetop-Lakeside.

More than 13 miles of groomed cross-country ski trails wind their way through forests of ponderosa pines and across high snow-covered meadows at Sunrise. These trails begin at the **Sunrise General Store** (✆ **928/735-7669,** ext. 2180), located at the turnoff for the downhill area. All-day trail passes are $7 for adults and $4 for children ages 10 to 14, and rental equipment is available. When there is enough snow, there are also good opportunities for cross-country skiing in Greer. At 8,500 feet, the alpine scenery in this area is quiet and serene.

Come summer, the ski slopes and cross-country ski trails become **mountain-biking trails** and, when combined with the nearby **Pole Knoll trail system** (14 miles west of Springerville/Eagar on Ariz. 260), provide mountain bikers with 35 miles of trails of varying degrees of difficulty. In the summer, mountain bikers can get an all-day lift pass for $20. If you aren't mountain biking and just want to ride the lift to the top of the mountain, the charge is $10 for adults and $5 for seniors and children 12 and under.

This area offers some of the finest mountain hiking in Arizona, and my favorite area trail is up 11,590-foot **Mount Baldy ★**, the second-highest peak in Arizona. This peak lies on the edge of the Fort Apache Indian Reservation and is sacred to the Apaches. Consequently, the summit is off-limits to non-Apaches. There are two trail heads for the hike. The **West Baldy Trail,** the most popular and scenic route, begins 6 miles south of Sunrise Park ski area (off the gravel extension of Ariz. 273) and follows the West Fork of the Little Colorado River. This trail climbs roughly 2,000 feet and is moderately strenuous, although the high elevation often leaves lowland hikers gasping for breath.

Some of the best mountain hiking in the state is at Mount Baldy.

For an easier hike, try the **Butler Canyon Trail,** a 1-mile nature trail through Butler Canyon, which is at the north end of Greer. To reach the trail head, take East Fork Road, which is 4 miles south of Ariz. 260. From the south end of Greer, the **East Fork Trail** eventually leads to Mount Baldy. This trail starts with a

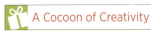

A Cocoon of Creativity

The **Butterfly Lodge Museum** (✆ **928/735-7514;** www.azcama.com/museums/butterflylodge.html), located just off Ariz. 373 between Ariz. 260 and Greer, is a restored historic cabin built in 1914. Built by James Willard Schultz (a writer) and his son Hart Merriam Schultz (a painter), the museum is a memorial to these two unusual and creative individuals who once called Greer home. It's open Memorial Day to Labor Day Thursday through Sunday (and holidays) from 10am to 5pm. Admission is $2 for adults and $1 for youths 12 to 17.

steep 600-foot climb but then becomes a much easier ascent. Another good choice for a day hike is the **West Fork Trail,** which begins north of Greer on Osborne Road and meanders through forests and meadows. The turnoff for the trail head is 4¼ miles south of Ariz. 260.

Horseback riding in Greer can be arranged through **Wiltbank Trail Rides,** 38735 Ariz. 373, Greer (✆ **928/735-7454;** www.wiltbankstables.com), which charges $30 for a 1-hour ride, $50 for a 2-hour ride, and $70 for a 3-hour ride. In winter, sleigh rides are available.

The three Greer Lakes on the outskirts of town—Bunch, River, and Tunnel reservoirs—are popular fishing spots. All three hold brown and rainbow trout. On **River Reservoir,** try the shallows at the south end. On **Tunnel Reservoir,** you can often do well from shore, especially if you're fly-fishing, though there is a boat launch. However, **Big Lake,** south of Greer, has the best fishing reputation here. Fishing is also good on **Sunrise Lake;** be sure to get a Fort Apache Indian Reservation fishing license ($7 per day for adults, available at the Sunrise General Store).

Where to Stay

Amberian Peaks Lodge and Restaurant ★ Set on a hillside at the upper end of the valley, this luxurious lodge is just a few steps away from the waters of the Little Colorado River, which at this point is little more than a creek. The lodge, with its two-story stone fireplace, log beams above the lobby, and wide expanse of decks, is a great place to soak up Greer's mountain-getaway atmosphere. There's a wide range of accommodations, from rooms (most of which are huge) and suites in the main lodge to spacious cabins. Throughout the lodge, the emphasis is on comfort and tranquillity. The restaurant is one of your best bets in Greer for a reliable meal. Many of the cabins rented by the lodge are not right on this property but elsewhere around the village of Greer.

1 Main St. (P.O. Box 1), Greer, AZ 85927. www.peaksaz.com. ✆ **800/556-9997** or 928/735-9977. 25 units. $135–$195 double; $215–$295 suite; $98–$325 cabin. Children 2 and under stay free in parent's room. 2-night minimum on weekends, 3-night minimum on holidays. AE, DISC, MC, V. Closed Nov 1–21 and Apr 1–May 1. Pets accepted in 2 cabins ($50 fee). **Amenities:** Restaurant; lounge; concierge; exercise room; 2 Jacuzzis; room service; sauna; spa. *In room:* TV/VCR/DVD, fridge, hair dryer, free Wi-Fi.

Hidden Meadow Ranch ★★ Although this luxurious guest ranch isn't located right in Greer, it is far and away the best place to stay in the region. Set on 150 acres of pine forests, the ranch offers accommodations in large, modern log cabins that are rustic yet elegant and have wood-burning fireplaces, slate-tiled bathrooms, soaking tubs, and loft bedrooms. The dining room here, which might be featuring elk tenderloin when you visit, serves the best food in the White Mountains. In summer, horseback riding and fly-fishing are the most popular activities, while in winter there are sleigh rides and cross-country skiing. Elk, deer, and wild turkeys are all regular visitors to the meadows here.

P.O. Box 300, Greer, AZ 85927. www.hiddenmeadow.com. ✆ **866/333-4080** or 928/333-1000. Fax 928/333-1010. 12 units. $525–$600 double. Rates include all meals and ranch activities. Children 3 and under stay free in parent's room. AE, DISC, MC, V. Pets accepted ($20). **Amenities:** Restaurant; bikes; children's programs; concierge; Jacuzzi; room service; watersports equipment/rentals. *In room:* CD player, hair dryer, kitchen, free Wi-Fi.

Snowy Mountain Inn ☺ Set back from the main road down a long gravel driveway and shaded by tall pines, the Snowy Mountain Inn has a remote yet comfortable feel about it. The modern cabins, although a bit cramped, are great for family vacations; they come equipped with gas fireplaces, porches, and sleeping lofts, and all but one have outdoor hot tubs. Surrounding the log cabins and main lodge are 10 acres of private forest, so guests have plenty of room to roam. There's a trout pond and, for the kids, a playground. The lodge's restaurant is a sports bar.

38721 Rte. 373, Greer, AZ 85927. www.snowymountaininn.com. ✆ **888/766-9971** or 928/735-7576. Fax 928/735-7705. 8 units. $175–$225 cabin. AE, DISC, MC, V. Pets accepted ($15 per day). **Amenities:** Restaurant; lounge. *In room:* TV/VCR, kitchen, no phone.

CAMPGROUNDS

In the immediate vicinity of Greer are a couple of nice campgrounds in Apache and Sitgreaves National Forests. Contact the **National Recreation Reservation Service** (✆ **877/444-6777** or 518/885-3639; www.recreation.gov) to make reservations for both the **Rolfe C. Hoyer Campground** ($14–$16 per night), 1 mile north of Greer on Ariz. 373, and the **Winn Campground** ($12–$14 per night), 12 miles southwest of Greer on Ariz. 273 (the road past Sunrise Park Resort). Because of its proximity to Greer and the Greer Lakes, Rolfe C. Hoyer is your best choice in the area. There are also several campgrounds nearby on the Fort Apache Indian Reservation (no reservations accepted).

Where to Eat

For filling breakfasts and delicious sweet rolls and cobbler, rendezvous at the **Rendezvous Diner,** 117 Main St. (✆ **928/735-7483**), which is housed in a log cabin that dates back to 1909. The diner is open Wednesday through Monday from 7am to 4pm (7am–3pm in winter).

Molly Butler Lodge AMERICAN Although it may not look it, this restaurant has been in business since 1910 and is one of the oldest restaurants in the state. However, the Molly Butler has been much updated over the years and now sports a mountain-rustic look. While the menu sticks to simple fare, it's the most reliable menu in town. The steaks are your best choices, but the chili's good, too. The bar here is a favorite après-fishing hangout and has live music on Friday and Saturday nights.

109 Main St. ✆ **928/735-7226.** www.mollybutlerlodge.com. Reservations recommended. Main courses $14–$26. AE, DISC, MC, V. May–Sept daily 11am–9:15pm; Oct–Apr Thurs–Sun 5–9pm.

SPRINGERVILLE & EAGAR

56 miles E of Show Low; 82 miles SE of Holbrook; 227 miles NE of Phoenix

Together the adjacent towns of Springerville and Eagar constitute the northeastern gateway to the White Mountains. Although the towns themselves are at the foot of the mountains, the vistas from around Springerville and Eagar take in all the area's peaks. The two towns also like to play up their Wild West backgrounds—in fact, John Wayne liked the area so much that he had a ranch along the Little Colorado River just west of Eagar. Today, large ranches still run their cattle on the windswept plains north of the twin towns.

Volcanic activity between 300,000 and 700,000 years ago left the land north of the twin towns dotted with cinder cones and gave the land its distinctive character. Containing 405 extinct volcanic vents, the area known as the Springerville Volcanic Field covers an area bigger than the state of Rhode Island and is the third-largest volcanic field of its kind in the continental United States. Only the San Francisco Field near Flagstaff and the Medicine Lake Field in California are larger. For a brochure outlining a tour of the volcanic field, contact the Springerville-Eagar Regional Chamber of Commerce (see "Visitor Information," below).

Essentials

GETTING THERE Springerville and Eagar are in the northeast corner of the White Mountains at the junction of U.S. 60, U.S. 180/191, and Ariz. 260. From Phoenix, there are two routes: Ariz. 87 N. to Payson and then east on Ariz. 260, or U.S. 60 east to Globe and then north to Show Low and on to Springerville (or you can take Ariz. 260 from Show Low to Springerville). From Holbrook, take U.S. 180 southeast to St. Johns and U.S. 180/191 south to Springerville. From southern Arizona, U.S. 191 is very slow but very scenic.

VISITOR INFORMATION For information on the Springerville and Eagar areas, contact the **Springerville-Eagar Regional Chamber of Commerce** (✆ **928/333-2123;** www.springerville-eagarchamber.com).

Indian Ruins

Casa Malpais Archaeological Park and Museum ★ 🎁 The Casa Malpais ruins are unique in Arizona in that the pueblo, which was constructed around 1250 and was occupied until about 1400, was built to take advantage of existing caves. Many of these caves form a system of catacomb-like rooms under the pueblo. The only way to visit the ruin is on guided tours that leave from the Casa Malpais museum, which is located in downtown Springerville. At the museum, you'll find exhibits on both the Mogollon people and dinosaurs that once roamed this region.

418 E. Main St., Springerville. ✆ **928/333-5375.** Guided tours $8 adults, $6 seniors, $5 children. Museum Tues–Sat 8am–4pm. Tours daily 9 and 11am and 2pm (weather permitting). Closed New Year's Day, Thanksgiving, and Christmas.

Lyman Lake State Park Although this state park is most popular with anglers and water-skiers, it also contains both petroglyphs that date back thousands of years and the ruins of an early Ancestral Puebloan village called Rattlesnake Point Pueblo. Some of the petroglyphs are accessible only by boat, and in the past, there have been guided tours both to petroglyphs and the ruins during the summer. ***Note:*** In 2011, this park remained closed for budgetary reasons.

Casa Malpais Archaeological Park.

However, by the time you visit, it may have reopened. If visiting here is important to you, please contact them before your visit to confirm they're open.

On U.S. 180/191, 18 miles north of Springerville. ✆ **928/337-4441.** www.azstateparks.com.

Museums

A couple of small museums are worth a look if you have the time. The **Reneé Cushman Art Museum** is housed in the LDS (Mormon) Church in Springerville. It consists of one woman's personal collection of European art and antiques. Among the works are an etching attributed to Rembrandt and three pen-and-ink drawings by Tiepolo. The antique furniture dates back to the Renaissance. The museum is open by appointment only. Contact the **Springerville-Eagar Regional Chamber of Commerce** (✆ **928/333-2123;** www.springerville-eagarchamber.com) for information on arranging a visit.

Local history and old automated musical instruments are the focus of the X Diamond Ranch's **Little House Museum** (✆ **928/333-2286;** www.xdiamond ranch.com), 7 miles west of Eagar on South Fork Road, off Ariz. 260. Tales of colorful Wild West characters as told by the guide are as much a part of the museum as the displays themselves. Museum visits are by reservation only and cost $10 for adults and $4 for children 11 and under. The X Diamond Ranch also has a Native American archaeological site that is open to the public. Combination museum and archaeological site tours are $12 for adults and $6 for children.

Outdoor Pursuits

Alternatively, you can head out to the **X Diamond Ranch** (✆ **928/333-2286;** www.xdiamondranch.com), off Ariz. 260 between Eagar and Greer (take C.R. 4124). The ranch maintains a section of the Little Colorado River as a fly-fishing stream. The half-day fishing rate is $35, while a full day costs $45. Horseback rides are also available, with options ranging from 1 hour ($25) to a full day ($150).

For a chance to see pronghorn antelope, elk, and mule deer, head south of Eagar to the **Sipe White Mountain Wildlife Area.** This grassy valley at the foot of the White Mountains was once a cattle ranch, and today the old ranch house serves as a visitor center that's open daily from 8am to 5pm between mid-May and mid-October. Several miles of hiking trails wind through forest and pasture and past lakes and ponds. There's good bird-watching here, too. Sipe is 5 miles down a gravel road that begins 2 miles south of Eagar off U.S. 180/191. For more information, contact the **Arizona Game & Fish Department,** Pinetop Regional Office, 2878 E. White Mountain Blvd., Pinetop (✆ **928/367-4281;** www.gf.state.az.us).

Where to Stay

X Diamond Ranch Well known in the area for its Little House Museum (see above) and trout fishing on the Little Colorado River, this ranch off Ariz. 260 between Eagar and Greer also rents a variety of cabins. Activities include fishing, horseback riding, and touring the ranch's museum and archaeological site ($12 for a combination tour). There's no restaurant on the premises, but cabins have full kitchens.

P.O. Box 113, Greer, AZ 85927. www.xdiamondranch.com. ✆ **928/333-2286.** 7 units. Apr–Oct $110–$175 double; Nov–Mar $95–$155 double. Children 1 and under stay free in parent's room. AE, DISC, MC, V. *In room:* TV, kitchen, no phone (in some units).

Where to Eat

Even in Springerville, you can now get a good espresso. Head to **Java Blues Coffee Bar & Bistro,** 341 E. Main St. (✆ **928/333-5282**), which also serves sandwiches, quiche, salads, and desserts. It's open Monday through Saturday from 6am to 9pm and Sunday from 7am to 3pm.

Los Dos Molinos NEW MEXICAN With restaurants in Phoenix and Mesa, Los Dos Molinos is legendary for its fiery New Mexican food. So, let me warn you up front, if you can't stand the heat, stay out of Los Dos Molinos. The *adovada* ribs (pork marinated in chili sauce) are the meal to have here. You get a huge portion of off-the-bone rib meat in a spicy red sauce accompanied by chili beans and a house-made tortilla. If your appetite isn't very big, try the *carne adovada* burrito instead. The margaritas aren't nearly as good as the ribs, so I advise washing down your meal with a beer.

900 E. Main St., Springerville. ✆ **928/333-4846.** www.losdosmolinosaz.com. Reservations recommended. Main courses $3.25–$9.25. No credit cards. Tues–Fri 11am–2:30pm and 5–9pm; Sat 11am–9pm.

THE CORONADO TRAIL ★

Alpine: 28 miles S of Springerville; 75 miles E of Pinetop-Lakeside; 95 miles N of Clifton

Winding southward from the Springerville-Eagar area to Clifton and Morenci, the Coronado Trail (U.S. 191) is one of the most remote and little-traveled paved roads in the state. Because this road is so narrow and winding, it's slow going—meant for people who aren't in a hurry to get anywhere anytime soon. If you are *not* prone to carsickness, you may want to take a leisurely drive down this scenic stretch of asphalt.

The Coronado Trail is named for the Spanish explorer Francisco Vásquez de Coronado, who came to Arizona in search of gold in the early 1540s. Although he never found it, his party did make it as far north as the Hopi pueblos and would have traveled through this region on their march northward from Mexico. Centuries later, the discovery of huge copper reserves would make the fortunes of the towns of Clifton and Morenci, at the southern end of the Coronado Trail.

Alpine, at the northern end of the Coronado Trail, is the main base for today's explorers, who tend to be outdoor types in search of uncrowded trails and streams where the trout are biting. Located near the New Mexico state line, Alpine offers a few basic lodges and restaurants, plus easy access to the region's many trails.

This area is known as the Alps of Arizona, and Alpine's picturesque setting in the middle of a wide grassy valley at 8,030 feet certainly lives up to this image. Alpine is surrounded by the Apache and Sitgreaves National Forests, which together have miles of trails and numerous campgrounds. In spring, wildflowers abound and the trout fishing is excellent. In summer, there's hiking and mountain biking on forest trails. In autumn, the aspens in the Golden Bowl on the mountainside above Alpine turn a brilliant yellow, and in winter, visitors come for the cross-country skiing, snowmobiling, and ice-fishing.

Essentials

GETTING THERE Alpine is 28 miles south of Springerville and Eagar at the junction of U.S. 191, which continues south to Clifton and Morenci, and U.S. 180, which leads east into New Mexico.

VISITOR INFORMATION For more information on the region, contact the **Alpine Area Chamber of Commerce,** P.O. Box 410, Alpine, AZ 85920 (✆ **928/339-4656;** www.alpinearizona.com). For outdoor information, contact the Apache and Sitgreaves National Forests' **Alpine Ranger District,** P.O. Box 469, Alpine, AZ 85920 (✆ **928/339-5000;** www.fs.fed.us/r3/asnf).

Outdoor Pursuits

Fall, when the aspens turn the mountainside gold, is one of the most popular times of year in this area—there are only a few places in Arizona where the fall color is worth a drive, and this is one of them.

Not far outside Alpine, there's cross-country skiing at the **Williams Valley Winter Recreation Area,** which doubles as a mountain-biking trail system in summer.

Alpine serves as a base for outdoor explorers.

If you're looking to fish, try **Luna Lake,** east of Alpine off U.S. 180. Here at the lake, you'll also find some easy-to-moderate mountain-bike trails that usually offer good wildlife-viewing opportunities. The best hike in the area is the trail up **Escudilla Mountain,** just outside Alpine, where you'll see some of the best autumn displays of aspens. The Escudilla National Recreation Trail leads 3 miles to the summit of the mountain (6-mile round-trip) and involves more than 1,300 feet of elevation gain.

Summer or winter, **Hannagan Meadows,** 23 miles south of Alpine, is the place to be. Here you'll find excellent hiking, mountain biking, and cross-country ski trails. Hannagan Meadows also provides access to the **Blue Range Primitive Area,** which is popular with hikers.

A Mexican gray wolf recovery project has been under way here in the remote wilderness for more than a decade. The reintroduction has so far met with mixed success, as wolves have been killed by cars, people, disease, and even mountain lions. Some wolves have had to be recaptured because they strayed out of the area set aside for them or because they had encounters with humans.

Where to Stay & Eat

Between Springerville-Eagar and Clifton-Morenci, there are nearly a dozen National Forest Service campgrounds. If fishing and boating interest you, head to **Luna Lake Campground,** just east of Alpine on U.S. 180, where the daily campsite fee is $12. Reserve a Luna Lake campsite through the **National Recreation Reservation Service** (✆ **877/444-6777** or 518/885-3639; www.recreation.gov). For a more tranquil forest setting, try the free **Hannagan Campground** (reservations not accepted), which makes a good base for exploring the Coronado Trail. For information on these campgrounds, contact the **Alpine Ranger District** (✆ **928/339-5000**).

If you're looking for someplace to eat, Alpine has a couple of basic restaurants.

Hannagan Meadow Lodge Located 22 miles south of Alpine at an elevation of 9,100 feet, this rustic lodge dates back to 1926 and is set amid cool forests on the winding route of the Coronado Trail. With both rustic pine-paneled cabins and lodge rooms done up primarily with pastel-colored quilts and wrought-iron beds, this place offers comfortable, if dated, accommodations and is a good spot for a quiet getaway or a family vacation. In summer, the lodge is a base for exploring the hundreds of miles of hiking trails in the area, and offers horseback riding. In winter the lodge rents cross-country skis and snowshoes to its guests.

HC 61 (P.O. Box 335), Alpine, AZ 85920. www.hannaganmeadow.com. ✆ **928/339-4370.** 17 units. $55–$115 double; $90–$200 cabin. Children stay free in parent's room. DISC, MC, V. Pets accepted in cabins ($20 fee). **Amenities:** Restaurant; free Wi-Fi. *In room:* No phone.

Tal-Wi-Wi Lodge Located 4 miles north of Alpine on U.S. 191, Tal-Wi-Wi Lodge is nothing fancy—just a rustic lodge popular with anglers and hunters—but it's the best choice in the area. The deluxe rooms come with a hot tub or woodstove (one unit has both), heat sources that are well appreciated on cold winter nights (Alpine is often the coldest town in Arizona). The furnishings are rustic yet comfortable, and the wood-paneled walls and large front porches give the lodge a classic country flavor. The dining room serves country breakfasts and dinners.

U.S. 191 (P.O. Box 169), Alpine, AZ 85920. www.talwiwilodge.com. ✆ **928/339-4319.** Fax 928/339-1962. 20 units. $60–$110 double. 2-night minimum stay on summer holiday weekends. MC, V. Pets accepted ($10 per day). **Amenities:** Restaurant; lounge. *In room:* No phone, free Wi-Fi.

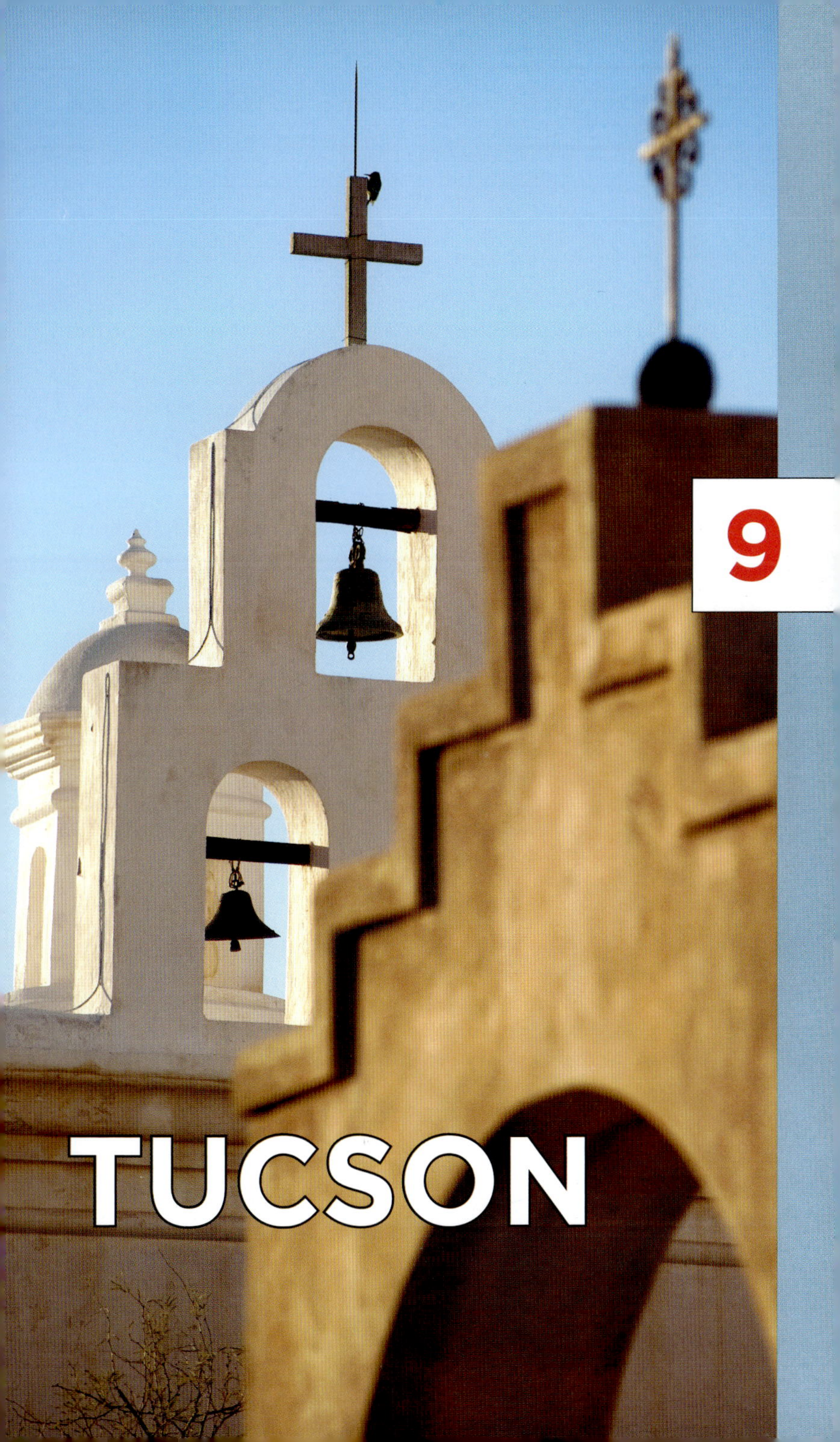

9

TUCSON

Encircled by mountain ranges and bookended by the two units of Saguaro National Park, Tucson is Arizona's second-largest city, and, for the vacationer, it has everything that Phoenix has to offer, plus a bit more. There are world-class golf resorts, excellent restaurants, art museums and galleries, an active cultural life, and, of course, plenty of great weather. Tucson also has a long history that melds Native American, Hispanic, and Anglo roots. And with a national park, a national forest, and other natural areas just beyond the city limits, Tucson is a city that celebrates its Sonoran Desert setting.

At Saguaro National Park, you can marvel at the massive cacti that have come to symbolize the desert Southwest, while at the Arizona–Sonora Desert Museum (actually a zoo), you can acquaint yourself with the flora and fauna of this region. Take a hike or a horseback ride up one of the trails that leads into the wilderness from the edge of the city, and you may even meet up with a few desert denizens on their own turf. Look beyond the saguaros and prickly pears, and you can find a desert oasis, complete with waterfalls and swimming holes, and, a short drive from the city, a pine forest that's home to the southernmost ski area in the country.

Founded by the Spanish in 1775, Tucson was built on the site of a much older Native American village. The city's name comes from the Pima Indian word *chukeson,* which means "spring at the base of black mountain," a reference to the peak now known simply as "A Mountain," because of the large letter A on its slopes. From 1867 to 1877, Tucson was the territorial capital of Arizona, but eventually the capital was moved to Phoenix. Consequently, Tucson did not develop as quickly as Phoenix and still holds on to some of its Hispanic and Western heritage.

Tucson has a history of valuing quality of life over development, which sets it apart from the Phoenix area. Back in the days of urban renewal, its citizens turned back the bulldozers and managed to preserve at least some of the city's old Mexican character. Likewise, today, in the face of the sort of sprawl that has given Phoenix the feel of a landlocked Los Angeles, advocates for controlled growth are fighting hard to preserve both Tucson's desert environment and the city's unique character. However, the inevitable sprawl has now ringed much of Tucson with vast suburbs, though as yet, the city is far from becoming another Phoenix.

The struggle to retain an identity distinct from other Southwestern cities is ongoing, and despite long, drawn-out attempts to breathe life into the city's core, downtown Tucson has little to offer visitors other than an art museum, a convention center, a couple of historic neighborhoods, and a few good restaurants.

Despite this minor shortcoming, Tucson remains Arizona's most beautiful and most livable city. With the Santa Catalina Mountains for a backdrop, Tucson boasts one of the most dramatic settings in the Southwest, and whether you're taking in the mountain vistas from the tee box of the 12th hole, the saddle of a palomino, or a table for two, I'm sure you'll agree that Tucson makes a memorable vacation destination.

PREVIOUS PAGE: **Mission San Xavier del Bac.**

ORIENTATION

Not nearly as large and spread out as Phoenix and the Valley of the Sun, Tucson is small enough to be convenient, yet large enough to be sophisticated. The mountains ringing Tucson are bigger and closer to town than those in Phoenix, which gives Tucson a more dramatic skyline, and the desert here is closer and more easily accessed than in Phoenix.

Arriving

BY PLANE Located 6 miles south of downtown, **Tucson International Airport,** 7250 S. Tucson Blvd. (✆ 520/573-8100; www.tucsonairport.org), is served by the following major airlines: **Alaska Airlines/Horizon Air** (✆ 800/252-7522; www.alaskaair.com), **American** (✆ 800/433-7300; www.aa.com), **Continental** (✆ 800/523-3273; www.continental.com), **Delta** (✆ 800/221-1212; www.delta.com), **Frontier** (✆ 800/432-1359; www.flyfrontier.com), **Southwest** (✆ 800/435-9792; www.southwest.com), **United** (✆ 800/864-8331; www.ual.com), and **US Airways** (✆ 800/428-4322; www.usairways.com).

Visitor centers in both baggage-claim areas can give you brochures and reserve a hotel room if you haven't done so already.

Many resorts and hotels in Tucson provide a free or competitively priced airport shuttle service. **Arizona Stagecoach** (✆ **877/782-4355** or 520/889-1000; www.azstagecoach.com) operates 24-hour van service to downtown Tucson and the foothills resorts. Fares to foothills resorts are around $42 one-way and $78 round-trip ($49 and $92 for a couple). It takes between 45 minutes and 1 hour to reach the foothills resorts. To return to the airport, it's best to call at least a day before your scheduled departure.

You'll also find taxis waiting outside baggage claim, or you can call **Yellow Cab** (✆ **520/624-6611;** www.yellowcabtucson.com) or **VIP Taxi** (✆ **520/847-8294**). The flag-drop rate at the airport is $4.50, and then $2.50 per mile. A taxi to downtown costs around $25, to the foothills resorts about $30 to $50.

One of the many decorated bus stops in downtown Tucson.

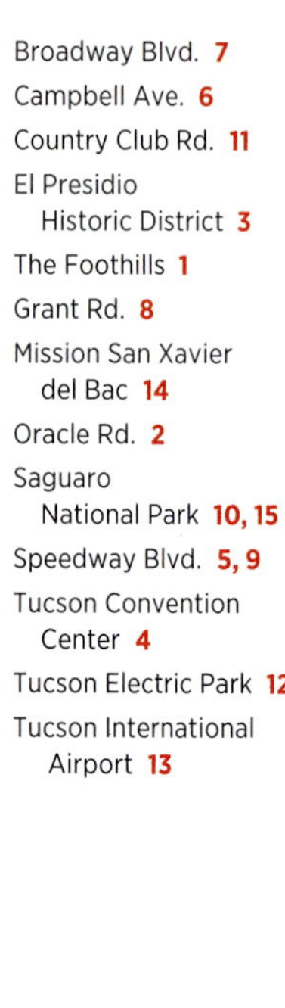

Broadway Blvd. **7**
Campbell Ave. **6**
Country Club Rd. **11**
El Presidio Historic District **3**
The Foothills **1**
Grant Rd. **8**
Mission San Xavier del Bac **14**
Oracle Rd. **2**
Saguaro National Park **10, 15**
Speedway Blvd. **5, 9**
Tucson Convention Center **4**
Tucson Electric Park **12**
Tucson International Airport **13**

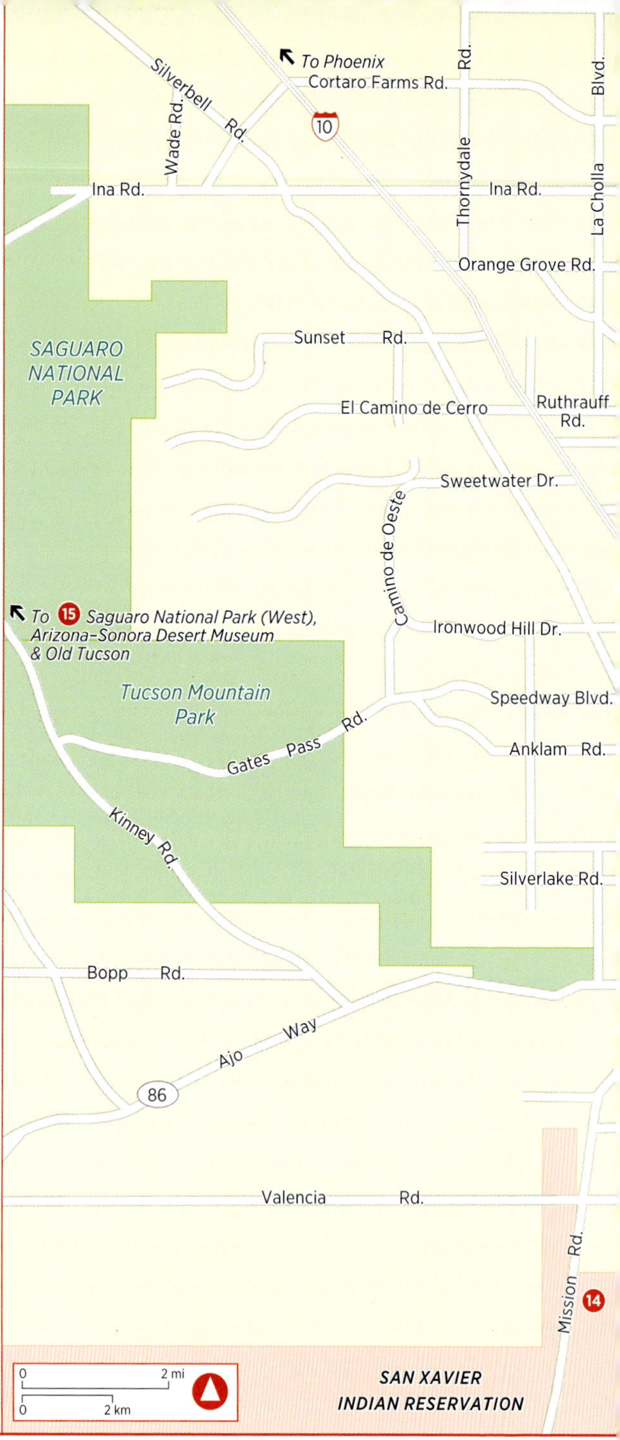

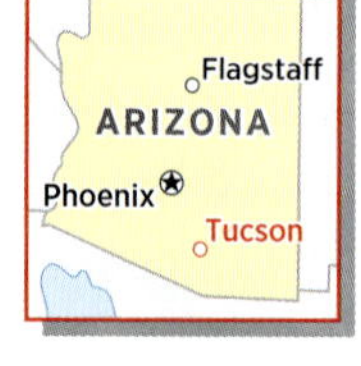

To Phoenix
Cortaro Farms Rd.
Silverbell Rd.
Wade Rd.
10
Thornydale Rd.
La Cholla Blvd.
Ina Rd.
Ina Rd.
Orange Grove Rd.
Sunset Rd.
SAGUARO NATIONAL PARK
El Camino de Cerro
Ruthrauff Rd.
Sweetwater Dr.
Camino de Oeste
To 15 Saguaro National Park (West), Arizona-Sonora Desert Museum & Old Tucson
Ironwood Hill Dr.
Tucson Mountain Park
Speedway Blvd.
Gates Pass Rd.
Anklam Rd.
Kinney Rd.
Silverlake Rd.
Bopp Rd.
Ajo Way
86
Valencia Rd.
Mission Rd.
14
0 2 mi
0 2 km
SAN XAVIER INDIAN RESERVATION

Flagstaff
ARIZONA
Phoenix
Tucson

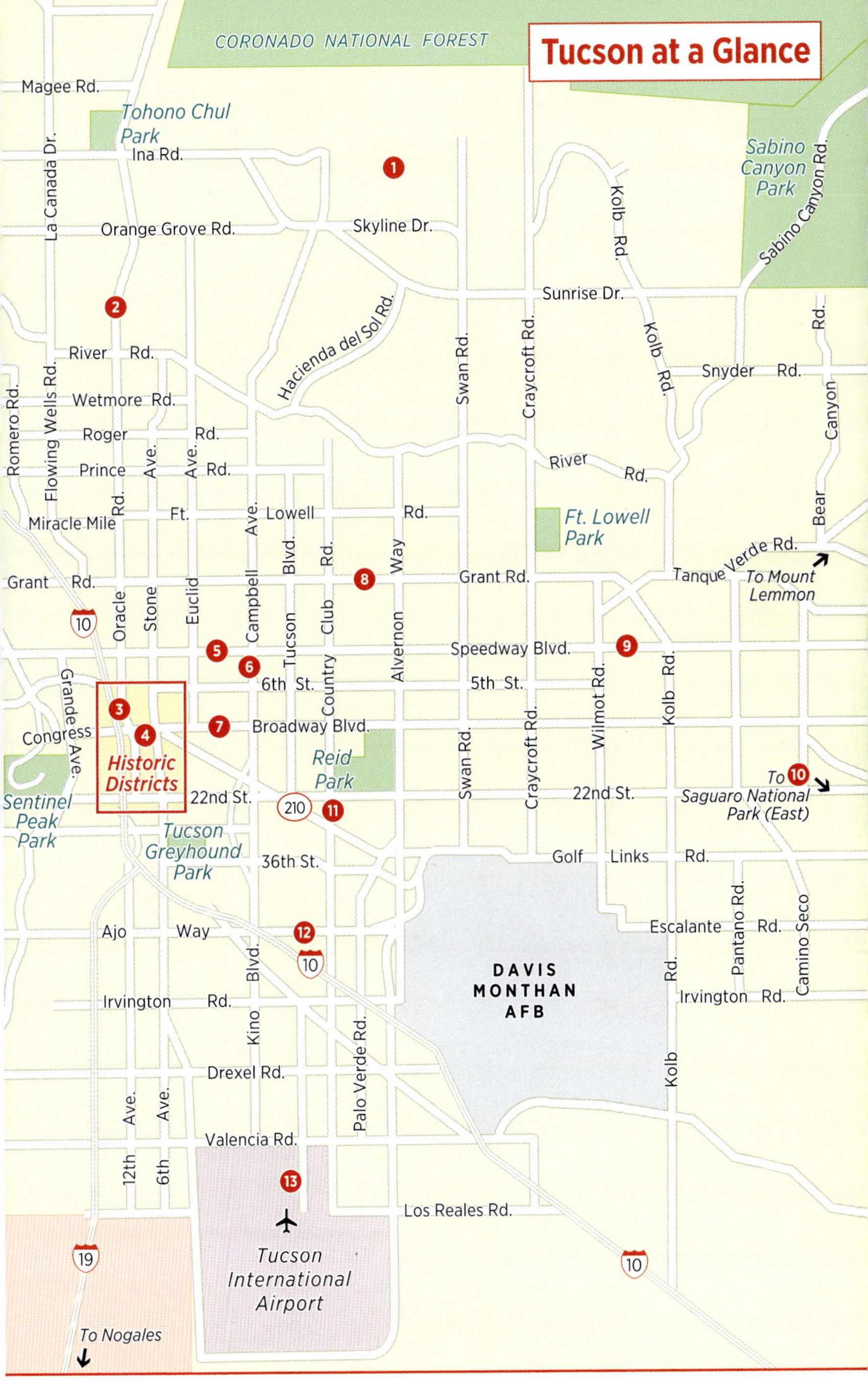
Tucson at a Glance
CORONADO NATIONAL FOREST
Magee Rd.
Tohono Chul Park
Ina Rd.
La Canada Dr.
Orange Grove Rd.
Skyline Dr.
Sabino Canyon Park
Sabino Canyon Rd.
Kolb Rd.
Sunrise Dr.
Hacienda del Sol Rd.
River Rd.
Wetmore Rd.
Roger Rd.
Prince Rd.
Romero Rd.
Flowing Wells Rd.
Swan Rd.
Craycroft Rd.
Snyder Rd.
Bear Canyon Rd.
River Rd.
Miracle Mile
Ft. Lowell Rd.
Ft. Lowell Park
Tanque Verde Rd.
To Mount Lemmon
Grant Rd.
Grant Rd.
Oracle Rd.
Stone Ave.
Euclid Ave.
Campbell Ave.
Tucson Blvd.
Country Club Rd.
Alvernon Way
Speedway Blvd.
6th St.
5th St.
Wilmot Rd.
Kolb Rd.
Grande Ave.
Congress
Broadway Blvd.
Historic Districts
Reid Park
Sentinel Peak Park
22nd St.
22nd St.
To Saguaro National Park (East)
Tucson Greyhound Park
36th St.
Golf Links Rd.
Escalante Rd.
Pantano Rd.
Camino Seco
Ajo Way
Kino Blvd.
DAVIS MONTHAN AFB
Irvington Rd.
Irvington Rd.
Palo Verde Rd.
Drexel Rd.
Valencia Rd.
12th Ave.
6th Ave.
Los Reales Rd.
Tucson International Airport
To Nogales
10
19
210
1
2
3
4
5
6
7
8
9
10
11
12
13

Sun Tran (✆ **520/792-9222;** www.suntran.com), the local public transit system, operates bus service to and from the airport. The fare is $1.25. Route no. 6, to downtown, runs Monday through Friday from about 4:30am to 10:50pm, Saturday from about 6:15am to 8:15pm, and Sunday from about 6:15am to 7:15pm. Departures are mostly every 30 to 60 minutes on weekdays and every hour on weekends. It takes 40 to 50 minutes to reach downtown. Route no. 11 operates on a similar schedule and travels along Alvernon Road to the midtown area.

BY CAR **I-10,** the main east-west interstate across the southern United States, passes through Tucson and connects to Phoenix. **I-19** connects Tucson with the Mexican border at Nogales. **Ariz. 86** heads southwest into the Tohono O'odham Indian Reservation, and **Ariz. 79** leads north toward Florence and eventually connects with **U.S. 60** into Phoenix.

If you're headed downtown, take the Congress Street exit off I-10. If you're coming from the north and going to one of the foothills resorts north of downtown, you'll probably want to take the Ina Road exit off I-10.

BY TRAIN Tucson is served by **Amtrak** (✆ **800/872-7245;** www.amtrak.com) passenger rail service. The *Sunset Limited,* which runs between New Orleans and Los Angeles, stops in Tucson, as does the *Texas Eagle,* which runs between Los Angeles and Chicago. The **train station** is at 400 N. Toole Ave., in the heart of downtown and within walking distance of the Tucson Convention Center, El Presidio Historic District, and a few hotels. You'll see taxis waiting to meet the train; see "Getting Around," below, for more info.

BY BUS **Greyhound** (✆ **800/231-2222** or 520/792-3475; www.greyhound.com) connects Tucson to the rest of the United States through its extensive system. The bus station is at 471 W. Congress St.

Visitor Information

The **Metropolitan Tucson Convention & Visitors Bureau (MTCVB),** 100 S. Church Ave. (at Broadway; ✆ **800/638-8350** or 520/624-1817; www.visittucson.org), is an excellent source of information on Tucson and its environs. The visitor center is open Monday through Friday from 9am to 5pm, Saturday and Sunday from 9am to 4pm.

City Layout

MAIN ARTERIES & STREETS Tucson is laid out on a grid that's fairly regular in the downtown areas but becomes less orderly the farther you go from the city center. In the flatlands, major thoroughfares are spaced at 1-mile intervals, with smaller streets filling in the squares created by the major roads. In the foothills, where Tucson's most recent growth has occurred, the grid system breaks down completely because of the hilly terrain.

The main **east-west roads** are (from south to north) 22nd Street, Broadway Boulevard, Speedway Boulevard, Grant Road (with Tanque Verde Rd. as an extension), and Ina Road/Skyline Drive/Sunrise Road. The main **north-south roads** are (from west to east) Miracle Mile/Oracle Road, Stone/Sixth Avenue, Campbell Avenue, Country Club Road, Alvernon Road, and Swan Road. **I-10** cuts diagonally across the Tucson metropolitan area from northwest to southeast.

In **downtown Tucson,** Congress Street and Broadway Boulevard are the main east-west streets; Stone Avenue, Sixth Avenue, and Fourth Avenue are the main north-south streets.

FINDING AN ADDRESS Because Tucson is laid out on a grid, finding an address is relatively easy. The zero (or starting) point for all Tucson addresses is the corner of Stone Avenue, which runs north and south, and Congress Street, which runs east and west. From this point, streets are designated either north, south, east, or west. Addresses usually, but not always, increase by 100 with each block, so an address of 4321 E. Broadway Blvd. should be 43 blocks east of Stone Avenue. In the downtown area, many of the streets and avenues are numbered, with numbered streets running east and west, and numbered avenues running north and south.

STREET MAPS The best way to find your way around Tucson is to pick up a free map at the visitor center at the airport or at the MTCVB (see "Visitor Information," above). The maps handed out by car-rental agencies are not very detailed but will do for some purposes. Local gas stations and convenience stores also sell detailed maps.

Neighborhoods in Brief

DOWNTOWN This is Tucson's main business district, and though it incorporates parts of two historic districts, it has little to offer visitors who aren't in town for an event at the Tucson Convention Center, which dominates much of downtown. There are a few art galleries and a couple of good restaurants in the area, but for the most part, downtown is a 9-to-5 business district. The main reason most visitors find themselves in downtown is to stop in at the Metropolitan Tucson Convention & Visitors Bureau visitor center or to visit the Tucson Museum of Art in the adjacent Presidio Historic District.

EL PRESIDIO HISTORIC DISTRICT Named for the Spanish military garrison that once stood here, this neighborhood is bounded by Alameda Street on the south, Main Avenue on the west, Franklin Street on the north, and Church Avenue on the east. El Presidio was the city's most affluent neighborhood in the 1880s, and most of the large homes from that period have been restored. The Tucson Museum of Art anchors the neighborhood.

BARRIO HISTÓRICO DISTRICT Another 19th-century neighborhood, the Barrio Histórico is bounded on the north by Cushing Street, on the west by railroad tracks, on the south by 18th Street, and on the east by Stone Avenue. The Barrio Histórico is characterized by Sonoran-style adobe row houses that directly abut the street with no yards, a style typical in Mexican towns. A few restaurants dot the neighborhood, but most restored buildings serve as offices and private residences. This remains a borderline neighborhood where restoration is a slow, ongoing process, so try to avoid it late at night.

FOURTH AVENUE Running from University Boulevard in the north to Ninth Street in the south, Fourth Avenue is the favored shopping district of cash-strapped college students. Shops specialize primarily in ethnic and used/vintage clothing, as well as handcrafted items from around the world. Twice a year, in March or April and December, the street is closed to traffic for a street fair. Plenty of restaurants, bars, and clubs also make this the city's favorite college nightlife district.

UNIVERSITY DISTRICT/MIDTOWN Northeast of downtown Tucson, this part of the city is actually a collection of different neighborhoods surrounding the University of Arizona. Just to the west of the university campus, you'll find the sort of shops and restaurants you'd expect adjacent to a university. On the east side, you'll find neighborhoods that are home to the historic Arizona Inn and a few other hotels. Stretching north from the university is Campbell Avenue, which has city's the greatest concentrations of interesting budget restaurants.

EAST TUCSON This part of the city includes pretty much everything east of the University District all the way to the eastern unit of Saguaro National Park. Within east Tucson you'll find lots of hotels, including several all-suites properties, plenty of good restaurants, and both the national park and Sabino Canyon Recreation Area. Be prepared to spend quite a bit of time in your car as you drive this sprawling section of the city.

WEST TUCSON This sprawling area of town is where you'll find some of the city's top attractions, including the Arizona–Sonora Desert Museum, Old Tucson Studios, and the west unit of Saguaro National Park. However, there aren't very many places to stay in this area, nor are there very many recommendable restaurants.

ORO VALLEY & MARANA These two cities northwest of Tucson are vast suburbs that are where all the city's recent development has taken place. It is in this area that you'll find the posh Ritz-Carlton Dove Mountain resort and several good restaurants. The views of the west slopes of the Santa Catalina Mountains from this area are stupendous, and there's access to the mountains at Catalina State Park.

FROM TOP: **Mexican-style adobe houses in the Barrio Histórico District; Tucson is home to the University of Arizona.**

THE FOOTHILLS This huge area in northern Tucson houses the city's most affluent neighborhoods. Elegant shopping plazas, modern malls, world-class resorts, golf courses, and expensive residential neighborhoods are surrounded by hilly desert at the foot of the Santa Catalina Mountains.

GETTING AROUND

By Car

Unless you plan to stay by the pool or on the golf course, you'll want to rent a car. Luckily, rates are a little lower than rates in Phoenix. At press time, Alamo was charging around $250 per week ($325 with taxes and surcharges included) during high season for a compact car with unlimited mileage in Tucson. See "Getting Around," in chapter 12, for general tips on car rentals in Arizona.

The following agencies have offices at or near Tucson International Airport as well as other locations in the area. Because taxes and surcharges add up to around 30% on car rentals at the airport, you may want to consider renting at some other location, where you can avoid paying some of these fees. Among the Tucson car-rental agencies are **Advantage** (✆ 800/777-5500 or 520/294-4028; www.advantage.com), **Alamo** (✆ 877/222-9075 or 520/573-4740; www.alamo.com), **Avis** (✆ 800/331-1212 or 520/294-1494; www.avis.com), **Budget** (✆ 800/527-0700 or 520/889-8800; www.budget.com), **Dollar** (✆ 800/800-3665 or 866/434-2226; www.dollar.com), **Enterprise** (✆ 800/261-7331 or 520/573-5250; www.enterprise.com), **Hertz** (✆ 800/654-3131 or 520/573-5201; www.hertz.com), **National** (✆ 877/222-9058 or 520/573-8050; www.nationalcar.com), and **Thrifty** (✆ 800/847-4389 or 877/283-0898; www.thrifty.com).

Downtown Tucson is still a relatively easy place to find a parking space, and parking fees are low. There are two huge parking lots on the south side of the Tucson Convention Center, a couple of small lots on either side of the Tucson Museum of Art (one at Main Ave. and Paseo Redondo, south of El Presidio Historic District, and one at the corner of Council St. and Court Ave.), and parking garages beneath the main library (101 N. Stone Ave.) and El Presidio Park (on Alameda St.). You'll find plenty of metered parking on the smaller downtown streets. Almost all Tucson hotels and resorts provide free parking.

Lanes on several major avenues in Tucson change direction at rush hour to facilitate traffic flow, so pay attention to signs that tell you the time and direction of traffic.

By Public Transportation

BY BUS Covering much of the Tucson metropolitan area, **Sun Tran** (✆ **520/792-9222;** www.suntran.com) public buses are $1.25 for adults and students, 40¢ for seniors, and free for children 5 and under. Day passes are available on buses for $3.

Downtown Tucson's **Ronstadt Transit Center,** 215 E. Congress St., is served by about 30 regular and express bus routes to all parts of Tucson. The bus system does *not* extend to such tourist attractions as the Arizona–Sonora Desert Museum, Old Tucson, Saguaro National Park, or the foothills resorts, and thus is of limited use to visitors.

BY TROLLEY Although they don't go very far, the restored electric streetcars of **Old Pueblo Trolley** (✆ **520/792-1802;** www.oldpueblotrolley.org) are a fun way to get from the downtown to the University of Arizona via the Fourth Avenue shopping district. The trolleys operate on Friday from 6 to 10pm, Saturday from noon to midnight, and Sunday from noon to 6pm. The fare is $1.25 for adults and 75¢ for children 6 to 12. The fare on Sunday is only 25¢ for all riders. Friday and Saturday all-day passes are $3 for adults and $2 for children.

By Taxi

If you need a taxi, you'll have to phone for one. **Yellow Cab** (✆ **520/624-6611;** www.yellowcabtucson.com) and **Discount Cab** (✆ **520/388-9000;** www.discountcab.com) provide service throughout the city. The flag-drop rate is between $2.50 and $2.95, and after that it's $1.95 to $2 per mile. Although distances in Tucson are not as great as those in Phoenix, it's still a good 10 or more miles from the foothills resorts to downtown Tucson, so expect to pay at least $15 to $20 for a taxi. Most resorts have shuttle vans or can arrange taxi service to major attractions.

On Foot

Downtown Tucson is compact and easily explored on foot, and many old streets in the downtown historic neighborhoods are narrow and much easier to appreciate if you leave your car in a parking lot. Also, although several major attractions—including the Arizona–Sonora Desert Museum, Old Tucson Studios, Saguaro National Park, and Sabino Canyon—can be reached only by car, they require quite a bit of walking once you arrive. These attractions often have uneven footing, so be sure to bring a good pair of walking shoes.

[Fast FACTS] TUCSON

Car Rentals See "Getting Around," above.

Dentist Call the **Arizona Dental Association** (✆ **800/866-2732;** www.azda.org) for a referral.

Doctor For a doctor referral, ask at your hotel, or call the **Northwest Medical Center** (✆ **866/694-9355;** www.northwestmedicalcenter.com).

Emergencies For fire, police, or medical emergencies, phone ✆ **911.**

Eyeglass Repair **Alvernon Optical** (www.alvernonoptical.com) has several stores around town where you can have your glasses repaired or replaced. Locations include 440 N. Alvernon Way (✆ **520/327-6211**), 6987 N. Oracle Rd. (✆ **520/297-2501**), and 7123 E. Tanque Verde Rd. (✆ **520/296-4157**).

Hospitals The **Tucson Medical Center** is at 5301 E. Grant Rd. (✆ **520/327-5461;** www.tmcaz.com). The **University Medical Center** is at 1501 N. Campbell Ave. (✆ **520/694-0111;** www.umcarizona.org).

Information See "Visitor Information" in "Orientation," above.

Internet Access Internet access is free at downtown's **Joel D. Valdez Main Library,** 101 N. Stone Ave. (✆ **520/594-5500;** www.library.pima.gov/locations/main). Also, try FedEx Office locations around the city.

Lost Property If you lose something at the airport, call ✆ **520/573-8156** or ✆ **520/746-8474** if you lost something at a TSA checkpoint. If you lose something on a Sun Tran bus, call ✆ **520/792-9222.**

Newspapers & Magazines The *Arizona Daily Star* is Tucson's morning daily. The *Tucson Weekly* is the city's news-and-arts journal, published on Thursday.

Pharmacies Contact **Walgreens** (✆ **800/925-4733;** www.walgreens.com) for the Walgreens pharmacy that's nearest you; some are open 24 hours a day.

Police In case of an emergency, phone ✆ **911.**

Post Office There's a post office in downtown Tucson at 141 S. Sixth Ave. (✆ **800/275-8777** or 520/903-1958; www.usps.com); it's open Monday through Friday from 9am to 5pm.

Safety Tucson is surprisingly safe for a city of its size. However, downtown isn't all that lively after dark and attracts a lot of street people and panhandlers. Be particularly alert if you're down here for a performance of some sort. Just to the south of downtown lies a poorer section of the city that's best avoided after dark unless you are certain of where you're going. Take the same precautions you would in any other city.

When driving, be aware that many streets in the Tucson area are subject to flooding when it rains. Heed warnings about possible flooded areas and don't try to cross a low area that has become flooded. Find an alternate route instead.

Taxes In addition to the 6.6% sales tax levied by the state, Tucson levies a 2% city sales tax and there is also a 0.5% county sales tax for a total of 9.1% sales tax in Tucson. Car-rental taxes, surcharges, and fees add up to around 30% on weekly rentals at the Tucson International Airport. The hotel tax in the Tucson area is approximately 13%.

Taxis See "Getting Around," above.

Weather For the local weather forecast, call the **National Weather Service** (✆ **520/881-3333**).

WHERE TO STAY

Although Phoenix still holds the title of Resort Capital of Arizona, Tucson is not far behind, and this city's resorts boast much more spectacular settings than most comparable properties in Phoenix and Scottsdale. As far as nonresort accommodations go, Tucson has a wider variety than Phoenix—partly because there are numerous bed-and-breakfast inns both in historic neighborhoods and in the desert on the outskirts of the city. The presence of two guest ranches within a 20-minute drive of Tucson also adds to the city's diversity of accommodations. Business and budget travelers are well served with all-suite and conference hotels, as well as plenty of budget chain motels.

At the more expensive hotels and resorts, summer rates, usually in effect from May to September, are often less than half what they are in winter. Surprisingly, temperatures usually aren't unbearable in May or September, which makes these good times to visit if you're looking to save money. When making late-spring or early-fall reservations, always be sure to ask when rates are scheduled to go up or down. If you aren't coming to Tucson specifically for the winter gem and mineral shows, then you'll save quite a bit if you avoid the last week in January and the first 2 weeks in February, when hotels around town generally charge exorbitant rates.

BED & BREAKFASTS If you're looking to stay in a B&B, several agencies can help. The **Arizona Association of Bed & Breakfast Inns** (www.arizona-bed-breakfast.com) has several members in Tucson. **Mi Casa Su Casa** (✆ **800/456-0682** or 480/990-0682; www.azres.com) can book you into one of its many B&Bs and homestays in the Tucson area or elsewhere in the state, as will **Arizona Trails Travel Services** (✆ **888/799-4284** or 480/837-4284; www.arizonatrails.com), which also books tour and hotel reservations.

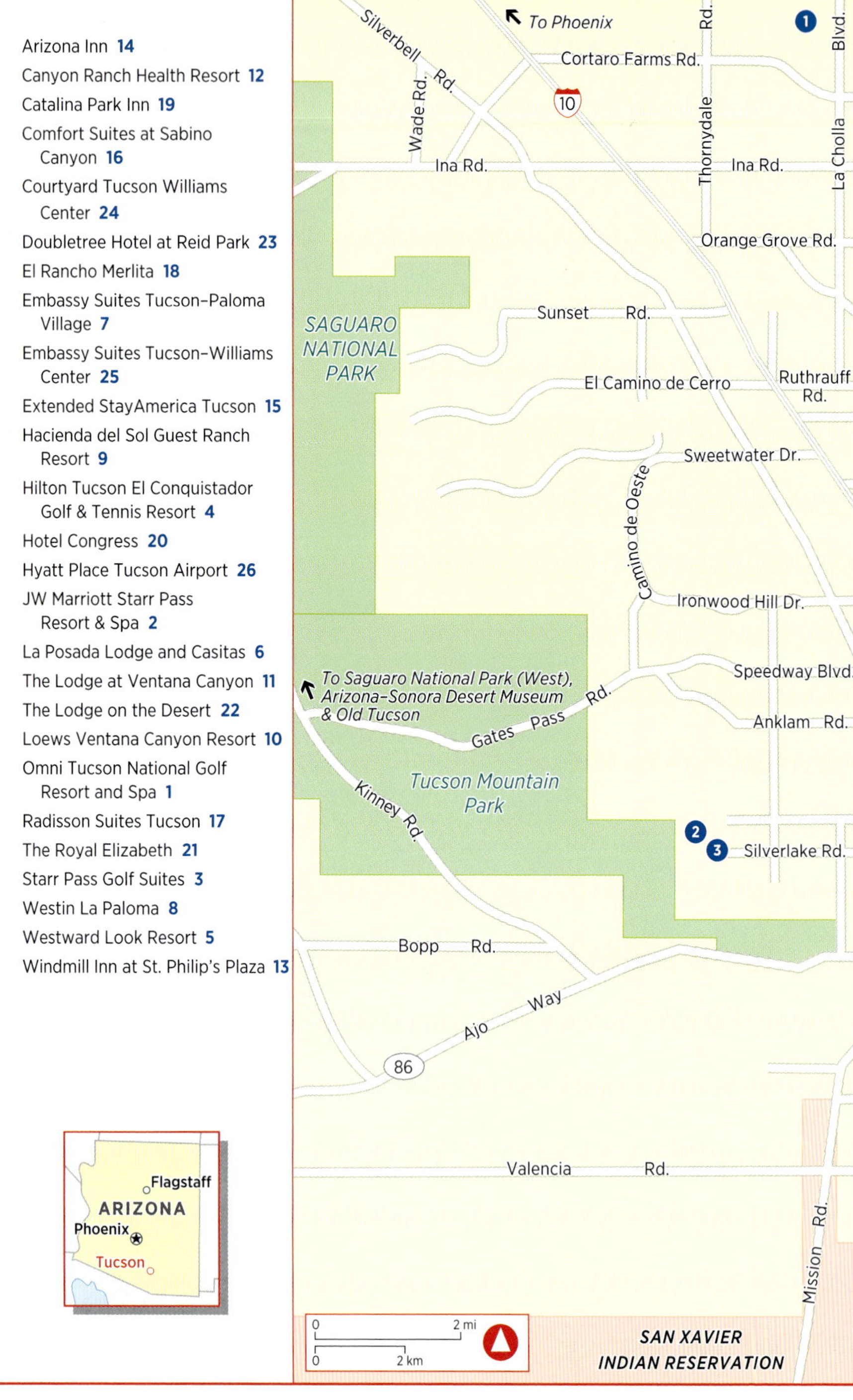

Arizona Inn 14
Canyon Ranch Health Resort 12
Catalina Park Inn 19
Comfort Suites at Sabino Canyon 16
Courtyard Tucson Williams Center 24
Doubletree Hotel at Reid Park 23
El Rancho Merlita 18
Embassy Suites Tucson-Paloma Village 7
Embassy Suites Tucson-Williams Center 25
Extended StayAmerica Tucson 15
Hacienda del Sol Guest Ranch Resort 9
Hilton Tucson El Conquistador Golf & Tennis Resort 4
Hotel Congress 20
Hyatt Place Tucson Airport 26
JW Marriott Starr Pass Resort & Spa 2
La Posada Lodge and Casitas 6
The Lodge at Ventana Canyon 11
The Lodge on the Desert 22
Loews Ventana Canyon Resort 10
Omni Tucson National Golf Resort and Spa 1
Radisson Suites Tucson 17
The Royal Elizabeth 21
Starr Pass Golf Suites 3
Westin La Paloma 8
Westward Look Resort 5
Windmill Inn at St. Philip's Plaza 13
To Phoenix
Silverbell Rd.
Cortaro Farms Rd.
Thornydale Rd.
La Cholla Blvd.
10
Wade Rd.
Ina Rd.
Ina Rd.
Orange Grove Rd.
SAGUARO NATIONAL PARK
Sunset Rd.
El Camino de Cerro
Ruthrauff Rd.
Sweetwater Dr.
Camino de Oeste
Ironwood Hill Dr.
To Saguaro National Park (West), Arizona-Sonora Desert Museum & Old Tucson
Speedway Blvd.
Gates Pass Rd.
Anklam Rd.
Tucson Mountain Park
Kinney Rd.
Silverlake Rd.
Bopp Rd.
Ajo Way
86
Valencia Rd.
Mission Rd.
0 2 mi
0 2 km
SAN XAVIER INDIAN RESERVATION
Flagstaff
ARIZONA
Phoenix
Tucson

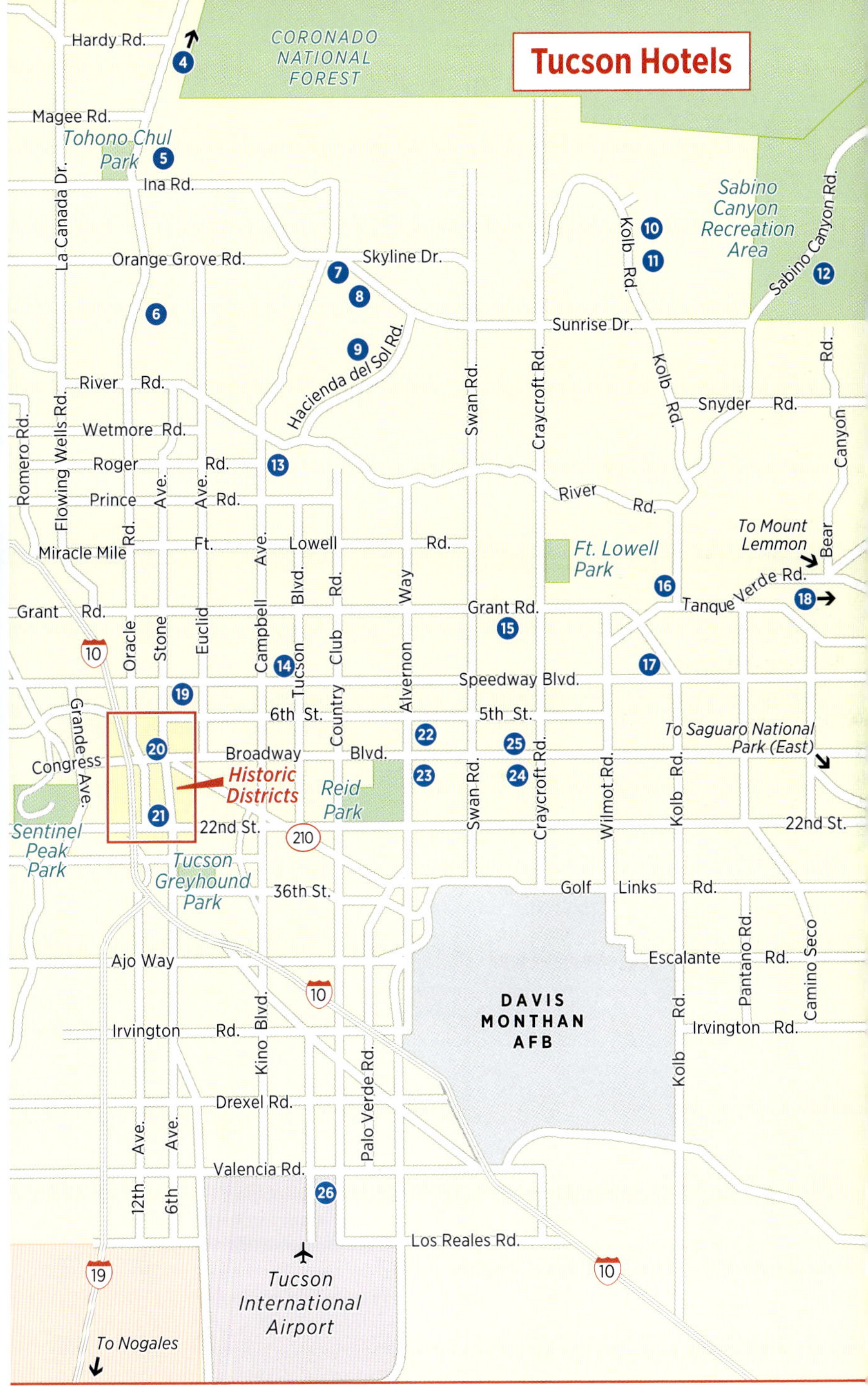
Tucson Hotels
CORONADO NATIONAL FOREST
Hardy Rd.
Magee Rd.
Tohono Chul Park
Ina Rd.
Orange Grove Rd.
Skyline Dr.
Sunrise Dr.
Hacienda del Sol Rd.
Sabino Canyon Recreation Area
Sabino Canyon Rd.
Kolb Rd.
River Rd.
Wetmore Rd.
Roger Rd.
Prince Rd.
Miracle Mile
Ft. Lowell Rd.
Snyder Rd.
Ft. Lowell Park
To Mount Lemmon
Bear Canyon Rd.
Tanque Verde Rd.
Grant Rd.
Speedway Blvd.
6th St.
5th St.
Broadway Blvd.
Congress
Grande Ave.
Historic Districts
Reid Park
To Saguaro National Park (East)
22nd St.
Sentinel Peak Park
Tucson Greyhound Park
36th St.
Golf Links Rd.
Escalante Rd.
Ajo Way
Irvington Rd.
Drexel Rd.
Valencia Rd.
Los Reales Rd.
DAVIS MONTHAN AFB
Tucson International Airport
To Nogales
Romero Rd.
Flowing Wells Rd.
La Canada Dr.
Oracle Rd.
Stone Ave.
Euclid Ave.
Campbell Ave.
Tucson Blvd.
Country Club Rd.
Alvernon Way
Swan Rd.
Craycroft Rd.
Wilmot Rd.
Pantano Rd.
Camino Seco
Kino Blvd.
Palo Verde Rd.
12th Ave.
6th Ave.
10
19
210
1
2
3
4
5
6
7
8
9
10
11
12
13
14
15
16
17
18
19
20
21
22
23
24
25
26

Downtown & the University Area

VERY EXPENSIVE

Arizona Inn ★★★ ☺ With its pink-stucco buildings and immaculately tended flower gardens, the Arizona Inn is an oasis of tranquillity. Gracious and welcoming, it's an unforgettable place to spend a vacation. Opened in 1930 by Isabella Greenway, Arizona's first congresswoman, the inn is still family-owned and -operated, and is imbued with Old Arizona charm. Playing a game of croquet, taking high tea in the library, or lounging by the pool, I always feel as if this were my second home. Guest rooms vary in size and decor, but most have a mix of reproduction antiques and original pieces made for the inn years ago by World War I veterans with disabilities. Some units have gas fireplaces, and most suites have private patios or enclosed sun porches. The inn's Main Dining Room (p. 419) is a casually elegant space. Fragrant flowering trees and vines surround the small pool.

2200 E. Elm St., Tucson, AZ 85719. www.arizonainn.com. ✆ **800/933-1093** or 520/325-1541. Fax 520/881-5830. 95 units. Mid-Jan to mid-Apr from $329 double, from $459 suite; mid-Apr to May from $219 double, from $369 suite; June to mid-Sept from $149 double, from $289 suite; mid-Sept to mid-Dec from $219 double, from $369 suite; mid-Dec to mid-Jan $259 double, from $359 suite. Children 12 and under stay free in parent's room. AE, MC, V. **Amenities:** 3 restaurants, including the Main Dining Room (review, p. 419); 2 lounges; babysitting; bikes; concierge; exercise room; heated outdoor pool; room service; saunas; 2 Har-Tru clay tennis courts. *In room:* A/C, TV/DVD, fridge, hair dryer, free Wi-Fi.

EXPENSIVE

Doubletree Hotel Tucson at Reid Park ★ This in-town high-rise hotel, with its pleasant orange-tree-shaded pool area, is midway between the airport and downtown Tucson, and is something of an in-town budget resort (the Randolph Park municipal golf course is right across the street). Guest rooms boast bright colors and bold contemporary designs, and there's a big exercise room by the pool. Although the hotel does a lot of convention business and sometimes feels crowded, the gardens, with their citrus trees (feel free to pick the fruit) and lawns, are always tranquil. Guest rooms are divided between a nine-story tower that offers views of the valley (even-numbered rooms face the pool, odd-numbered rooms face the mountains) and a two-story building with patio rooms overlooking the garden and pool area.

445 S. Alvernon Way, Tucson, AZ 85711. www.dtreidpark.com. ✆ **800/222-8733** or 520/881-4200. Fax 520/323-5225. 295 units. Jan–May $119–$329 double, $189–$429 suite; June–Aug $79–$139 double, $179–$299 suite; Sept–Dec $119–$259 double, $179–$359 suite. Children 17 and under stay free in parent's room. AE, DC, DISC, MC, V. Pets accepted ($50 fee). **Amenities:** 2 restaurants; 2 lounges; concierge; exercise room; Jacuzzi; outdoor pool; room service; 3 tennis courts. *In room:* A/C, TV, fridge, hair dryer, MP3 docking station, Wi-Fi ($10 per day).

MODERATE

Catalina Park Inn ★★ Close to downtown and overlooking a shady park, this 1927 home has been lovingly restored by owners Mark Hall and Paul Richard. From the outside, the inn has the look of a Mediterranean villa, while many interesting and playful touches enliven the classic interior. The huge Catalina Room in the basement is one of my favorites. Not only does it conjure up the inside of an adobe, but it also has a whirlpool tub in a former cedar closet. Two upstairs rooms have balconies, while two units in a separate cottage across the garden offer more contemporary styling than the rooms in the main house.

309 E. 1st St., Tucson, AZ 85705. www.catalinaparkinn.com. ✆ **800/792-4885** or 520/792-4541. 6 units. $119–$189 double. Children 10 and under stay free in parent's room. Rates include full breakfast. AE, DISC, MC, V. Pets accepted ($20 fee). **Amenities:** Concierge. *In room:* A/C, TV/DVD, CD player, hair dryer, MP3 docking station, free Wi-Fi.

Lodge on the Desert ★ Dating from 1936 and set amid neatly manicured lawns and gardens, the Lodge on the Desert is a classic old Arizona resort that was completely remodeled and expanded in 2009. The relaxing retreat looks a bit like a Mexican village, with narrow pathways winding between buildings. Guest rooms are in both hacienda-style adobe buildings tucked amid cacti and orange trees and newly constructed adobe-style two-story buildings. Rooms feature a mix of contemporary and Southwestern furnishings; many units have beamed ceilings or fireplaces, and some have patios and tile floors. The small pool has a good view of the Catalinas. The new casitas are definitely the nicest rooms here.

306 N. Alvernon Way, Tucson, AZ 85711-2855. www.lodgeonthedesert.com. ✆ **877/498-6776** or 520/320-2000. Fax 520/327-5834. 103 units. Jan to late May $139–$309 double, $179–$349 suite; late May to mid-Sept $99–$219 double, $139–$259 suite; mid-Sept to Dec $119–$269 double, $159–$309 suite. Children 17 and under stay free in parent's room. AE, DC, DISC, MC, V. Pets accepted ($50 deposit plus $25 per night). **Amenities:** Restaurant; lounge; Jacuzzi; outdoor pool; room service. *In room:* A/C, TV, fridge, hair dryer, free Wi-Fi.

The Royal Elizabeth ★★ Located downtown and just a block from the Temple of Music and Art, the Royal Elizabeth is an 1878 Victorian adobe mansion that features an unusual combination of architectural styles that makes for a uniquely Southwestern-style inn. In classic 19th-century Tucson fashion, the old home looks thoroughly unpretentious from the outside, but inside you'll find beautiful woodwork and gorgeous Victorian-era antique furnishings. Guest rooms (which are as gorgeous as the rest of the house, with high ceilings, beautiful antiques, and hardwood floors) open off a large, high-ceilinged central hall. The immediate neighborhood doesn't have a lot to offer, but art galleries, the Tucson Museum of Art, and several good restaurants are within walking distance.

204 S. Scott Ave., Tucson, AZ 85701. www.royalelizabeth.com. ✆ **877/670-9022** or 520/670-9022. Fax 928/833-9974. 6 units. $159–$219 double. Rates include full breakfast. Children 9 and under stay free in parent's room. AE, DISC, MC, V. **Amenities:** Concierge; access to nearby health club; Jacuzzi; outdoor heated pool. *In room:* A/C, TV/VCR/DVD, CD player, fridge, hair dryer, free Wi-Fi.

INEXPENSIVE

Hotel Congress Located in the heart of downtown Tucson, the Hotel Congress, built in 1919 to serve railroad passengers, once hosted John Dillinger. Today, it operates as a budget hotel and youth hostel and attracts young globetrotters. Although the place is utterly basic, the lobby has loads of Southwestern elegance. Guest rooms remain true to their historical character, with antique telephones and old radios, so don't expect anything fancy (such as TVs). Most bathrooms have tubs or showers, but a few have both. The classic little Cup Cafe is just off the lobby (think Edward Hopper meets Gen X), as is the tiny Tap Room bar. At night, the hotel's Club Congress (p. 460) is a popular (and loud) dance club (pick up earplugs at the front desk).

311 E. Congress St., Tucson, AZ 85701. www.hotelcongress.com. ✆ **800/722-8848** or 520/622-8848. Fax 520/792-6366. 40 units. $79–$119 double (lower rates in summer). AE, DISC, MC, V. Pets accepted ($10 per night). **Amenities:** Restaurant; bar; nightclub. *In room:* Free Wi-Fi.

East Tucson

EXPENSIVE

Courtyard Tucson Williams Center ★ Set a block off busy E. Broadway Boulevard amid tall palm trees, this modern business hotel is in such a pretty setting that it makes a good choice for vacationers as well as business travelers. Rooms are large and modern (I prefer the king rooms), but it's the courtyard with its pond, small waterfall, and pleasant pool area, that really makes this an enjoyable place to stay. Because this is a business hotel, rates are lower on weekends. 201 S. Williams Blvd., Tucson, AZ 85711. www.marriott.com/tusce. ✆ **800/321-2211** or 520/745-6000. Fax 520/745-2393. 153 units. $99–$259 double; $119–$279 suite. Children 17 and under stay free in parent's room. AE, DC, DISC, MC, V. **Amenities:** Restaurant; lounge; exercise room; Jacuzzi; outdoor pool; free Wi-Fi. *In room:* A/C, TV, hair dryer, free Internet.

El Rancho Merlita ★★ Once the winter home of cosmetics queen Merle Norman, this spacious east-side B&B is a sprawling brick ranch house set behind wide lawns. The views of the Santa Catalina Mountains from the long veranda are superb, so don't miss an opportunity to watch the sunset from this patio. When the home opened as an inn, it was used as a designer show house, so every room is full of luxurious modern touches. Rooms vary in size, but for a splurge, it's impossible to beat the Merle Norman Suite, which has a huge bathroom with a steam shower and soaking tub. This room also has its own private patio. In back of the house, you'll find a game cottage, a horseshoe pit, massage cottage, and a meditation labyrinth. Note that four of the rooms are in a separate building just outside the grounds of the main house.

1924 N. Corte El Rancho Merlita, Tucson, AZ 85715. www.ranchomerlita.com. ✆ **888/218-8418** or 520/495-0071. 8 units. $75–$235 double; $175–$275 suite. Rates include full breakfast. AE, DISC, MC, V. No children 11 or under. **Amenities:** Concierge; Jacuzzi; seasonal outdoor pool. *In room:* A/C, TV/DVD, CD player, fridge, hair dryer, free Wi-Fi.

MODERATE

Embassy Suites Tucson–Williams Center ★ ☺ With its red-tile roof, cactus gardens, and colonial Mexican furniture in the lobby, this all-suite hotel feels as if it could be in Mexico, which makes it one of my favorite east Tucson lodgings. You'll surely feel like you're on vacation when you're here, even if you are in the middle of a business district. Guest rooms are two-room suites, which makes this place great for families, and the courtyard pool area, although not very large, provides plenty of opportunities for soaking up the sun on warm days.

5335 E. Broadway Blvd., Tucson, AZ 85711. www.tucsonwilliamscenter.embassysuites.com. ✆ **800/362-2779** or 520/745-2700. Fax 520/790-9232. 142 units. Sept–May $129–$209 double; June–Aug $109–$119 double. Rates include full breakfast and evening social hour. Children 17 and under stay free in parent's room. AE, DC, DISC, MC, V. **Amenities:** Exercise room; Jacuzzi; outdoor pool; room service. *In room:* A/C, TV, fridge, hair dryer, Wi-Fi ($10 fee).

Radisson Suites Tucson ★★ With large and very attractive rooms, this all-suite hotel is a good choice for both those who need plenty of space and those who want to be in the east-side business corridor. The five-story brick building is arranged around two long garden courtyards, one of which has a large pool and whirlpool. In fact, the pool and gardens are among the nicest at any nonresort hotel in Tucson and are the best reasons to stay here. Some rooms have Sleep Number® beds, and rooms on the fourth and fifth floors on the east side have nice mountain views.

6555 E. Speedway Blvd., Tucson, AZ 85710. www.radissontucson.com. ✆ **800/333-3333** or 520/721-7100. Fax 520/721-1991. 299 suites. Oct–May $114–$209 double; June–Sept $109–$129 double. Children 17 and under stay free in parent's room. AE, DC, DISC, MC, V. Pets accepted ($25 fee). **Amenities:** Restaurant; lounge; concierge; exercise room; Jacuzzi; outdoor pool; room service. *In room:* A/C, TV, fridge, hair dryer, free Wi-Fi.

INEXPENSIVE

Comfort Suites at Sabino Canyon Although it looks rather stark from the outside and shares a parking lot with a shopping center, this Comfort Suites is surprisingly pleasant inside, and is built around four tranquil and lushly planted garden courtyards. Most of the rooms are quite large, and some have kitchenettes. This is a good economical choice close to Sabino Canyon, the Mount Lemmon Highway, and Saguaro National Park's east unit.

7007 E. Tanque Verde Rd., Tucson, AZ 85715. www.choicehotels.com. ✆ **800/424-6423** or 520/298-2300. Fax 520/298-6756. 90 units. $65–$150 double. Rates include full breakfast and evening social hour. Children 17 and under stay free in parent's room. AE, DC, DISC, MC, V. Pets accepted ($25 per night). **Amenities:** Access to nearby health club; Jacuzzi; small outdoor pool. *In room:* A/C, TV, fridge, hair dryer, free Wi-Fi.

Extended StayAmerica Tucson With no pool or exercise room and maid service only if you pay extra ($5–$10) or stay for more than a week, this east-side hotel is pretty basic, but the rooms are clean and the rates are low. Guest rooms also have full kitchens, so you can save even more money on your Tucson stay by doing a little cooking in your room.

5050 E. Grant Rd., Tucson, AZ 85712. www.extendedstayamerica.com. ✆ **800/804-3724** or 520/795-9510. Fax 520/795-9504. 120 units. $57–$157 double (lower weekly rates). Children 17 and under stay free in parent's room. AE, DC, DISC, MC, V. Pets accepted ($25 per night, $150 maximum). *In room:* A/C, TV, kitchen, Wi-Fi ($5 fee).

The Foothills

VERY EXPENSIVE

The Lodge at Ventana Canyon ★★ This boutique golf resort shares the same two Tom Fazio–designed golf courses as Loews Ventana Canyon Resort. Stay here, though, and you'll get more personal service. The Lodge at Ventana Canyon is part of a gated country club community at the base of the Santa Catalina Mountains, so when you stay here you feel more like a resident than just another hotel guest. Because this is such a small resort, it has a more relaxed feel than the Hilton Tucson El Conquistador Resort or the Omni Tucson National Resort. Accommodations are in spacious suites, most of which have mission-style furnishings, small kitchens, large bathrooms with oversize tubs, and walls of windows facing the mountains. A few units have balconies, cathedral ceilings, and spiral stairs that lead to sleeping lofts. The third hole of the resort's Mountain Course is one of Tucson's most photographed holes.

6200 N. Clubhouse Lane, Tucson, AZ 85750. www.thelodgeatventanacanyon.com. ✆ **800/828-5701** or 520/577-1400. Fax 520/577-4065. 50 units. Jan to early Apr $289–$599 1-bedroom suite, $459–$739 2-bedroom suite; early Apr to mid-May $189–$419 1-bedroom suite, $359–$619 2-bedroom suite; mid-May to early Sept $109–$175 1-bedroom suite, $189–$275 2-bedroom suite; early Sept to Dec $179–$399 1-bedroom suite, $349–$599 2-bedroom suite. Rates do not include $24 nightly service charge. Children 11 and under stay free in parent's room. AE, DC, DISC, MC, V. Pets accepted ($50 fee). **Amenities:** Restaurant; snack bar; lounge; children's programs;

concierge; two acclaimed 18-hole golf courses; exercise room; 2 Jacuzzis; outdoor pool; room service; full-service spa; 11 tennis courts. *In room:* A/C, TV, hair dryer, kitchen, Wi-Fi (included in service fee).

Loews Ventana Canyon Resort ★★★ ☺ With two fabled desert-style golf courses out the front door and a national forest trail out the back, this luxurious resort is a great choice for both golfers and hikers. The craggy peaks of the Santa Catalina Mountains rise behind the property, and the distinctive architecture and flagstone floors in the lobby lend a rugged but luxurious character. Guest rooms have balconies that overlook city lights or mountains. Bathrooms include tubs for two, and some rooms have fireplaces. The lobby lounge serves afternoon tea before becoming an evening piano bar. In addition to numerous other amenities, the resort has a nature trail with a waterfall and lots to keep the kids busy, including a playground.

7000 N. Resort Dr., Tucson, AZ 85750. www.loewshotels.com/hotels/tucson. ✆ **800/234-5117** or 520/299-2020. Fax 520/299-6832. 398 units. Early Jan to late May $179–$369 double, from $529 suite; late May to early Sept $119–$229 double, from $289 suite; early Sept to early Jan from $159–$319 double, from $399 suite. Children 17 and under stay free in parent's room. AE, DC, DISC, MC, V. Valet parking $9. Pets accepted ($25 fee). **Amenities:** 4 restaurants, including Flying V Bar & Grill (review, p. 424); 3 lounges; babysitting; bikes; children's programs; concierge; two acclaimed 18-hole golf courses; exercise room and access to nearby health club; 2 Jacuzzis; 2 outdoor pools; room service; full-service spa; 3 tennis courts. *In room:* A/C, TV, hair dryer, Internet ($11), minibar, MP3 docking station.

The Westin La Paloma Resort & Spa ★★★ ☺ If grand scale is what you're looking for, this is the place. Everything about the Westin La Paloma is big—big portico, big lobby, big pool area—and from the resort's sunset-pink mission-revival buildings, there are big views. While adults will appreciate the resort's tennis courts, exercise facilities, and poolside lounge chairs, kids will love the 177-foot water slide. Guest rooms are in 27 low-rise buildings surrounded by desert landscaping. Couples should opt for the king rooms (ask for a mountain or golf-course view if you don't mind spending a bit more). French-inspired Southwestern cuisine is the specialty at the on-site restaurant Janos (p. 424), which is one of Tucson's finest restaurants. The resort's spa is a Red Door Spa by Elizabeth Arden.

3800 E. Sunrise Dr., Tucson, AZ 85718. www.westinlapalomaresort.com. ✆ **800/937-8461** or 520/742-6000. Fax 520/577-5878. 487 units. Jan to late May $249–$479 double, from $445 suite; late May to mid-Sept $119–$169 double, from $245 suite; mid-Sept to Dec $209–$279 double, from $375 suite. Rates do not include $15 daily service fee. Children 17 and under stay free in parent's room. AE, DC, DISC, MC, V. Valet parking $15. Pets accepted. **Amenities:** 5 restaurants, including Janos (review, p. 424); 2 lounges; babysitting; children's programs; concierge; 27-hole golf course; health club and full-service spa; 4 Jacuzzis; 5 pools (1 for adults only); room service; 10 tennis courts. *In room:* A/C, TV, fridge, hair dryer, Wi-Fi ($13 per night).

EXPENSIVE

Embassy Suites Tucson–Paloma Village ★ ☺ Situated at the intersection of Skyline Drive and Campbell Road, this hotel is surrounded by upscale shopping centers and is close to some of Tucson's best restaurants. Although the suites here are small by Embassy Suites standards, you will still get two rooms, which makes this hotel a good choice for families on a budget. Some suites have mountain views, while others overlook the dense desert vegetation of a dry wash.

The pool area has limited mountain views. The full breakfast and afternoon snacks and drinks can help you save on meal costs.

3110 E. Skyline Dr., Tucson, AZ 85718. www.tucsonpalomavillage.embassysuites.com. **800/362-2779** or 520/352-4000. Fax 520/352-4001. 119 units. Jan–Apr $169–$260 double; May and Sept–Dec $139–$180 double; June–Aug $89–$140 double. Rates include full breakfast and evening social hour. Children 17 and under stay free in parent's room. AE, DC, DISC, MC, V. **Amenities:** Exercise room; Jacuzzi; outdoor pool; room service; free Wi-Fi. *In room:* A/C, TV, fridge, hair dryer, Internet ($10 per night).

Hacienda del Sol Guest Ranch Resort ★★ With its colorful Southwest styling, historical character, mature cactus gardens, and ridge-top setting, Hacienda del Sol is one of Tucson's most distinctive getaways. The lodge's basic rooms, set around flower-filled courtyards, are evocative of old Mexican inns and have a rustic and colorful character, with a decidedly artistic flair. If you prefer more modern, spacious accommodations, ask for a suite; if you want loads of space and the chance to stay where Katharine Hepburn and Spencer Tracy may have stayed, ask for the casita grande. With large terraces for alfresco dining, the Grill (p. 424) is one of Tucson's best restaurants. During the day, you can lounge by the small pool, get a spa treatment, or go for a horseback ride.

5501 N. Hacienda del Sol Rd., Tucson, AZ 85718. www.haciendadelsol.com. **800/728-6514** or 520/299-1501. 30 units. Early Jan to May $175–$280 double, $345–$355 suite, $415–$425 casita; June–Sept $79–$164 double, $200–$355 suite, $295–$400 casita; Oct to early Jan $99–$260 double, $330–$340 suite, $370–$495 casita. Children 12 and under stay free in parent's room. AE, DC, DISC, MC, V. Pets accepted ($50 fee). **Amenities:** 2 restaurants, including the Grill (review, p. 424); lounge; concierge; access to nearby health club; Jacuzzi; small outdoor pool; room service; spa. *In room:* A/C, TV, fridge, hair dryer, minibar, MP3 docking station, free Wi-Fi.

Westward Look Resort ★★ This reasonably priced resort, which underwent a $14-million renovation in 2009, has the desert at its doorstep and is a favorite of mine. Built in 1912 as a private estate, Westward Look is the oldest resort in Tucson, and although it doesn't have a golf course, it has horseback-riding stables, a nature trail, an excellent spa, and plenty of tennis courts. The large guest rooms have a Southwestern flavor and private patios or balconies with city views. For the ultimate in Southwest luxury, opt for one of the stargazer spa suites, which have outdoor hot tubs. GOLD, the resort's main restaurant, utilizes herbs and vegetables grown on-site. If you aren't a golfer but do enjoy resort amenities, this is one of your best bets in Tucson.

245 E. Ina Rd., Tucson, AZ 85704. www.westwardlook.com. **800/722-2500** or 520/297-1151. Fax 520/297-9023. 244 units. Jan–Apr $179–$395 double; May $149–$199 double; June–Sept $89–$189 double; Oct–Dec $169–$295 double. Rates do not include $15 daily resort fee. Children 17 and under stay free in parent's room. AE, DC, DISC, MC, V. Pets accepted. **Amenities:** 2 restaurants; 2 lounges; bikes; children's programs; concierge; exercise room; 3 Jacuzzis; 3 pools; room service; full-service spa; 8 tennis courts. *In room:* A/C, TV, CD player, fridge, hair dryer, Wi-Fi (included in resort fee).

MODERATE

Windmill Suites at St. Philip's Plaza Located on the edge of the foothills in the St. Philip's Plaza shopping center, this hotel offers both a great location and a good value. Best of all, you can walk to several restaurants and upscale shops right across the parking lot. Bikes are available to guests, and out the hotel's back door is a paved pathway along the Rillito River (which, by the way, is usually bone-dry). Accommodations are spacious and have double vanities, wet bars, and two TVs—basically, everything you need for a long, comfortable stay.

4250 N. Campbell Ave., Tucson, AZ 85718. www.windmillinns.com. ✆ **800/547-4747** or 520/577-0007. Fax 520/577-0045. 122 units. Oct–May $138–$199 double; June–Sept $119–$143 double. Rates include continental breakfast. Children 17 and under stay free in parent's room. AE, DC, DISC, MC, V. Pets accepted. **Amenities:** Bikes; exercise room and access to nearby health club; Jacuzzi; outdoor pool. *In room:* A/C, TV, fridge, hair dryer, free Wi-Fi.

INEXPENSIVE

La Posada Lodge and Casitas ★ Although this hotel fronts busy Oracle Road, once you check in and park yourself on your patio overlooking the pool or the grassy courtyard, you'll forget all about the traffic out front. There are several different types of rooms here, but my favorites are the "Western"-style rooms, which have a sort of retro south-of-the-border decor that includes headboards painted with classic Mexican scenes. Casitas, which are the largest and most expensive rooms here, have a similar decor. There are also some fun rooms with a 1950s retro feel. The attractive rooms, pleasant pool area, and on-site Mexican restaurant together make this an excellent and economical choice.

5900 N. Oracle Rd., Tucson, AZ 85704. www.laposadalodge.com. ✆ **800/810-2808** or 520/887-4800. Fax 520/293-7543. 72 units. $79–$179 double. Rates include full breakfast. Children 17 and under stay free in parent's room. AE, DC, DISC, MC, V. Pets accepted ($25 fee). **Amenities:** Restaurant; lounge; exercise room; Jacuzzi; outdoor pool. *In room:* A/C, TV, fridge, hair dryer, free Wi-Fi.

West Tucson, Oro Valley & Marana

VERY EXPENSIVE

JW Marriott Starr Pass Resort & Spa ★ Set on the edge of Tucson Mountain Park, on the far west side of Tucson, this sprawling resort is a favorite of golfers, but also makes a good choice for families and outdoors enthusiasts. Kids will love the great family-friendly pool area, while hikers and mountain bikers have access to miles of trails through the adjacent park. With its many restaurants, this resort is designed to be a destination, and you could very easily spend several days just hanging out and never venturing out to see Tucson's sights. Unfortunately, low-flying fighter jets from nearby Davis-Monthan Air Force Base often disturb the tranquillity of the resort. Then again, you can always retreat to the plush bed in your room.

3800 W. Starr Pass Blvd., Tucson, AZ 85745. www.jwmarriottstarrpass.com. ✆ **888/527-8989** or 520/792-3500. Fax 520/792-3351. 575 units. Mid-Oct to May $249–$289 double, from $349 suite; June to mid-Oct $169 double, from $269 suite. Children 17 and under stay free in parent's room. AE, DC, DISC, MC, V. Valet parking $20; self-parking $10. **Amenities:** 5 restaurants; 4 lounges; espresso bar; children's programs; concierge; exercise room; 2 Jacuzzis; 3 outdoor pools; room service; full-service spa. *In room:* A/C, TV, CD player, fridge, hair dryer, minibar, Wi-Fi ($13 per day).

The Ritz-Carlton, Dove Mountain ★★★ Set amid saguaro-covered hills 45 minutes northwest of Tucson, this luxury resort, which opened in late 2009, is in such a beautiful desert setting that it feels as if it's in a national park. Desert landscaping along the resort's entrance road even manages to hide Dove Mountain's world-class golf course. Grand in design and painted to blend in with the surrounding hills, the resort conjures images of Wild West ranches, though cattle ranches were never so luxurious. Guest rooms have balconies and large bathrooms with soaking tubs and separate showers. With hiking trails, horseback riding, pools for both kids and grown-ups, excellent restaurants, and a bar with Arizona's largest whiskey selection, the Ritz-Carlton is a world unto itself. Sure, it's a bit of a drive from Tucson's many attractions, but if you're like me, you might just want to stay put.

15000 N. Secret Springs Dr., Marana, AZ 85658. www.ritzcarlton.com/dovemountain. ✆ **800/241-3333** or 520/572-3000. Fax 520/572-3001. 253 units. Mid-Sept to mid-May from $259 double, from $359 suite; mid-May to mid-Sept from $189 double, from $289 suite. Children 18 and under stay free in parent's room. AE, DC, DISC, MC, V. Valet parking $20. Pets accepted ($125 fee). **Amenities:** 4 restaurants; 4 lounges; bikes; children's programs; concierge; executive-level rooms; 27-hole golf course; health club and spa; 4 Jacuzzis; 3 outdoor pools; room service; 4 tennis courts. *In room:* A/C, TV/DVD, CD player, hair dryer, minibar, MP3 docking station, Wi-Fi ($10–$20 per day).

EXPENSIVE

Hilton Tucson El Conquistador Golf & Tennis Resort ★★ ☺ Although El Conquistador is a bit out of the way, the view of the Santa Catalina Mountains rising behind the property makes this northern foothills resort one of my favorites in Tucson. Sunsets are truly spectacular! Most guest rooms are built around a central courtyard with manicured lawns and a large oasis of swimming pools, one of which has a long water slide. The pool area and the nearby horseback-riding stables make the Hilton an excellent choice for families. All rooms feature Southwestern-influenced contemporary furniture, spacious marble bathrooms, and balconies or patios. Be sure to ask for a mountain-view room. Golf on the resort's three courses is the favorite pastime here, but this is not so exclusively a golf resort as such places as the Lodge at Ventana Canyon or the Omni Tucson National Resort.

10000 N. Oracle Rd., Tucson, AZ 85704. www.hiltonelconquistador.com. ✆ **800/325-7832** or 520/544-5000. Fax 520/544-1222. 428 units. Jan to late May $139–$239 double, from $279 suite; late May to early Sept $99–$199 double, from $179 suite; early Sept to Dec $119–$209 double, from $239 suite. Children 18 and under stay free in parent's room. AE, DC, DISC, MC, V. Valet parking $11. Pets accepted ($50 fee). **Amenities:** 4 restaurants; 2 lounges; seasonal children's programs; concierge; 1 9-hole and two 18-hole golf courses; health club and spa; 3 Jacuzzis; 4 pools; room service; saunas; 31 tennis courts. *In room:* A/C, TV, hair dryer, minibar, Wi-Fi ($10 per day).

Omni Tucson National Resort ★★ Golf is the name of the game at this boutique resort, which, though a bit out of the resort mainstream, is looking good after a major makeover a few years back. The spacious rooms here, with their warm contemporary styling and balconies or patios, are some of the finest and most luxurious in town, and most cling to the edges of the golf course. The golf course here is far more forgiving than those shared by the Lodge at Ventana Canyon and Loews Ventana Canyon, which makes this a good choice for golfers not up to the challenge of desert-style golf courses.

2727 W. Club Dr. (off Magee Rd.), Tucson, AZ 85742. www.omnihotels.com. ✆ **800/843-6664** or 520/297-2271. Fax 520/297-7544. 128 units. Jan–Apr $199–$479 double; May $119–$329 double; June–Aug $99–$329 double; Sept–Dec $139–$409 double. Rates do not include $14 nightly resort fee. Children 17 and under stay free in parent's room. AE, DC, DISC, MC, V. Pets accepted ($50 fee). **Amenities:** 3 restaurants; lounge; concierge; two 18-hole golf courses; health club and full-service spa; 2 Jacuzzis; 2 pools; room service; sauna; 4 tennis courts; Wi-Fi (free). *In room:* A/C, TV, CD player (in some), hair dryer, Internet (included in resort fee).

MODERATE

Casa Tierra Adobe Bed & Breakfast Inn ★ If you've come to Tucson to be in the desert, then this secluded B&B west of Saguaro National Park is another good choice. Built to look as if it has been here since Spanish colonial days, the modern adobe home is surrounded by cactus and paloverde trees. There are great views across a landscape full of saguaros to the mountains, and sunsets are enough to take your breath away. Guest rooms, which have wrought-iron sleigh beds, open onto a central courtyard surrounded by a covered seating area. The two outdoor hot tubs make perfect stargazing spots, and there's a telescope on the property.

11155 W. Calle Pima, Tucson, AZ 85743. www.casatierratucson.com. ✆ **866/254-0006** or 520/578-3058. 4 units. Nov–Apr $165–$195 double, $215–$285 suite; May and Oct $150–$175 double, $195–$265 suite; June–Sept $135–$150 double, $165–$225 suite. Rates include full breakfast. 2-night minimum stay. AE, DISC, MC, V. Closed June 15–Aug 16. **Amenities:** Concierge; exercise room; Jacuzzi. *In room:* A/C, CD player, fridge, hair dryer, free Wi-Fi.

Paca de Paja Bed & Breakfast ★ Although this inn has only one suite and is 30 minutes west of Tucson, it's a great choice for anyone who is coming to Arizona to experience the desert. The inn is a very energy-efficient straw-bale house, which means that the walls are constructed of straw that is then covered with stucco. Owner/innkeeper Caroline Wilson also harvests rainwater to irrigate her garden, which is designed to minimize water usage. A nature trail on the property meanders through a dense cactus forest, and lots of other opportunities to explore the desert are within a 30-minute drive. The guest suite has both a sitting room full of natural-history books and an outdoor living area, which gives guests loads of room to enjoy. Birds and other wildlife are plentiful.

16242 Pinacate Ave., Tucson, AZ 85736. www.pacadepaja.com. ✆ **888/326-4588** or 520/822-2065. 1 unit. Jan–Apr $160 double ($130 per night for 2 or more nights); May–Dec $150 double ($120 per night for 2 or more nights). Rates include full breakfast. Children 2 and under stay free in parent's room. No credit cards. **Amenities:** Bikes. *In room:* TV/DVD, fridge, hair dryer, free Wi-Fi.

INEXPENSIVE

Starr Pass Golf Suites ★ Located 3 miles west of I-10, Starr Pass is the most economically priced golf resort in the city. It's a condominium resort, however, which means you shouldn't expect the sort of service you get at other resorts. Accommodations are in privately owned Santa Fe–style casitas rented as two-bedroom units, master suites, or standard hotel-style rooms. The small hotel-style rooms are a bit cramped and not nearly as lavishly appointed as the master suites, which are more comfortable and have fireplaces, full kitchens, balconies, and a Southwestern style throughout. The desert-style 27-hole golf course is one of the best courses in the city. There are also hiking/biking trails on the property.

3645 W. Starr Pass Blvd., Tucson, AZ 85745. www.shellhospitality.com. ✆ **800/503-2898** or 520/670-0500. Fax 520/670-0427. 80 units. $69–$109 double, $119–$169 suite, $159–$259 casita. Children 17 and under stay free in parent's room. AE, DC, DISC, MC, V. **Amenities:** Restaurant; lounge; bikes; 27-hole golf course; exercise room; Jacuzzi; outdoor pool; 2 tennis courts; free Wi-Fi. *In room:* A/C, TV/DVD/VCR, CD player, fridge, hair dryer, free Internet.

Near the Airport

MODERATE

Hyatt Place Tucson Airport Okay, I know the airport location is none too appealing and that this is primarily a business-travelers' hotel, but the Hyatt

Place is just so pretty and well-designed that you should consider it. The suites all have separate sitting and sleeping areas, with 42-inch flat-panel TVs that can be angled to either area. Unusual features include electronic self-service check-in kiosks, continental (free) or hot (charge) breakfasts, and a tiny lounge area to one side of the lobby. You can even get a light meal here if you don't feel like going out to a restaurant for dinner. Another reason to stay here? It's close to the Pima Air & Space Museum and Mission San Xavier del Bac.

6885 S. Tucson Blvd., Tucson, AZ 85756. www.hyattplace.com. ✆ **800/492-8847** or 520/295-0405. Fax 520/295-9140. 120 units. $79–$249 double. Rates include continental breakfast. Children 17 and under stay free in parent's room. AE, DC, DISC, MC, V. **Amenities:** Restaurant; lounge; free airport transfers; exercise room; outdoor pool. *In room:* A/C, TV, fridge, hair dryer, free Wi-Fi (most rooms).

Outlying Areas

NORTH OF TUCSON

Across the Creek at Aravaipa Farms ★★ Located 60 miles north of Tucson on Aravaipa Creek, this B&B is a romantic getaway near one of the state's most spectacular desert-wilderness areas. Because the inn is 3 miles up a gravel road and then across a stream (high-clearance vehicles recommended), it's a long way to a restaurant. Consequently, innkeeper Carol Steele provides all meals. Guests entertain themselves hiking in the Aravaipa Canyon Wilderness, bird-watching, and cooling off in the creek. The casitas are eclectically decorated with a mix of folk art and rustic Mexican furnishings, and have tile floors, stone-walled showers, and shady verandas. For a romantic weekend or a vigorous vacation, this inn makes an ideal base. Carol also rents out a three-bedroom house that sleeps up to six people.

89395 E. Aravaipa Rd., Winkelman, AZ 85292. www.aravaipafarms.com. ✆ **520/357-6901.** 5 units. Oct–May $345 double, $750 house; June–Sept $250 double, $600 house. Rates include all meals. 2-night minimum stay weekends and holidays. AE, DISC, MC, V. Children by prior arrangement. **Amenities:** Dining room; outdoor pool. *In room:* Fridge, no phone.

SOUTH OF TUCSON

Chuparosa Inn ★ Tucked amid the shady trees of Madera Canyon, this rustic inn is built of stone and wood, and, with its tower at the front entrance, looks a bit like a miniature castle or a chalet. In other words, this place is beautiful and is a delightful place to stay if you have come up the canyon to do some bird-watching, which is the objective of many of the inn's guests. By the way, the inn's name is a Spanish term for "hummingbirds," and if you visit in the warmer months, you're likely to see plenty of the colorful little birds (14 species have been spotted here). There are also regularly scheduled hummingbird banding programs here.

1300 W. Madera Canyon Rd., Madera Canyon, AZ 85614. www.chuparosainn.com. ✆ **520/393-7370.** 4 units. $150 double; $175–$200 suite. Rates include continental breakfast. 2-night minimum on weekends, holidays, and Mar–May. MC, V. Children 12 and over are welcome. *In room:* A/C, hair dryer, kitchenette, no phone.

Santa Rita Lodge Nature Resort This lodge in the shady depths of Madera Canyon is used primarily by bird-watchers and hikers, and although the rooms are not as nice as those at the Chuparosa Inn, the birding is as good as it gets. The rooms and cabins are large, comfortable, and simply furnished, and all have kitchenettes in which you can do a bit of light cooking. So, because the nearest restaurants are 13 miles away, I recommend bringing food for your stay.

1218 S. Madera Canyon Rd., Madera Canyon, AZ 85614. www.santaritalodge.com. ✆ **520/625-8746.** Fax 520/625-1956. 12 units. $105–$125 double. MC, V. Pets accepted ($25 per night). *In room:* A/C, TV/DVD, kitchen.

Spa Resorts

Canyon Ranch Health Resort ★★★ Canyon Ranch, one of America's premier health spas, offers the sort of complete spa experience that's available at only a handful of places around the country (and then only if you have both money and fat to burn). On staff are doctors, nurses, life-management therapists, exercise physiologists, massage therapists, and tennis and golf pros. Services offered include health and fitness assessments; health, nutrition, exercise, and stress-management evaluations; fitness classes; massage therapy; therapeutic body treatments; facials, manicures, pedicures, and haircuts; makeup consultations; cooking demonstrations; and art classes. Guests stay in a variety of spacious and very comfortable accommodations. Three gourmet, low-calorie meals are served daily. If you're serious about getting healthy or leading a more fulfilled life, this is your place in the sun.

8600 E. Rockcliff Rd., Tucson, AZ 85750. www.canyonranch.com. ✆ **800/742-9000** or 520/749-9000. Fax 520/239-8535. 185 units. Oct to mid-June 4-night packages from $3,910 double; mid-June to mid-Sept 4-night packages from $2,860 double. Rates include all meals, classes, and allowances for a variety of spa and wellness services. AE, DC, DISC, MC, V. Pets accepted ($50–$150 fee). No children 13 or under (with exception of infants in the care of personal nannies). **Amenities:** 2 dining rooms; free airport transfers; bikes; concierge; 7 exercise rooms; 8 Jacuzzis; 3 outdoor pools and 11,000-sq.-ft. aquatic center; room service; saunas; spa complex; 7 tennis courts. *In room:* A/C, TV/DVD, CD player, hair dryer, fridge, kitchenette (some rooms), MP3 docking station, free Wi-Fi.

Miraval Arizona ★★★ Miraval, Tucson's other world-class destination spa, emphasizes stress management, self-discovery, and relaxation. To this end, activities at the all-inclusive resort include meditation, yoga, art classes, and a variety of confidence-building activities; more active types can go hiking, mountain biking, and rock climbing. Of course, there are also plenty of more traditional spa offerings such as massages, wraps, scrubs, facials, manicures, and pedicures. The spa also offers a variety of lifestyle-management workshops, fitness/nutrition consultations, exercise classes, and an "equine experience" program. The spa's main pool is a gorgeous three-tiered leisure pool surrounded by waterfalls and desert landscaping. Guest rooms, many of which have views of the Santa Catalina Mountains, are done up in a Southwestern style. Miraval has LEED-certified sustainable rooms, and its dining room uses local and organic ingredients as much as possible.

5000 E. Via Estancia Miraval, Tucson, AZ 85739. www.miravalresorts.com. ✆ **800/232-3969.** Fax 520/825-5163. 116 units. From $850 double. Rates do not include 18.5% service charge. Rates include all meals, classes, and a $130 per-person per-day credit for spa service, a round of golf, or private session. AE, DC, DISC, MC, V. No children. **Amenities:** Restaurant; snack bar; lounge; free airport transfers; bikes; concierge; executive-level rooms; superbly equipped exercise room; 5 Jacuzzis; 5 pools; room service; saunas; one of the most extensive spas in Arizona; 2 tennis courts. *In room:* A/C, TV/DVD, CD player, fridge, hair dryer, free Wi-Fi.

Guest Ranches

Tanque Verde Ranch ★★ Want to spend long days in the saddle but don't want to give up resort luxuries? Then Tanque Verde Ranch, which was founded in 1868 and still has some of its original buildings, is for you. This is far and away the most luxurious guest ranch in Tucson. With Saguaro National Park and the Coronado National Forest bordering the ranch, there's plenty of room for horseback riding. There are also nature trails and a nature center, and at the end of the day, the spa provides ample opportunities to recover from too many hours in the saddle. Guest rooms are spacious and comfortable, with fireplaces and patios in many units. Some of the large casitas are among the most luxurious accommodations in the state. The dining room, which overlooks the Rincon Mountains, sets impressive buffets.

14301 E. Speedway Blvd., Tucson, AZ 85748. www.tanqueverderanch.com. ✆ **800/234-3833** or 520/296-6275. Fax 520/721-9426. 76 units. $390–$790 double. Rates include all meals and ranch activities. Children 3 and under stay free in parent's room. AE, DC, DISC, MC, V. **Amenities:** Dining room; lounge; free airport transfers w/4-night stay; bikes; children's programs; exercise room and access to nearby health club; 2 Jacuzzis; 2 pools (indoor and outdoor); small spa; 5 tennis courts. *In room:* A/C, hair dryer, free Wi-Fi.

White Stallion Ranch ★ ☺ Set on 3,000 acres of desert, the White Stallion Ranch is perfect for those who crave wide-open spaces. Operated since 1965 by the True family, this spread has a more authentic feel than any other guest ranch in the area. A variety of horseback rides are offered, and a petting zoo keeps kids entertained. There are also nature trails, guided nature walks and hikes, hayrides, weekly rodeos, and team cattle penning. Guest rooms vary considerably in size and comfort, from tiny, spartan single units to deluxe two-bedroom suites. Renovated rooms are worth requesting.

9251 W. Twin Peaks Rd., Tucson, AZ 85743. www.whitestallion.com. ✆ **888/977-2624** or 520/297-0252. Fax 520/744-2786. 42 units. Early Oct to mid-Dec, early Jan to mid-Feb, and May to mid-June $332–$408 double, $410–$496 suite; mid-Dec to early Jan and mid-Feb to Apr $395–$494 double, $498–$600 suite; June to early Oct $264–$322 double, $328–$390 suite. Rates do not include 15% service charge. Rates include all meals. 4- to 6-night minimum stay in winter. Children 2 and under stay free in parent's room. AE, DISC, MC, V. **Amenities:** Dining room; lounge; free airport transfers with minimum 4-night stay; concierge; exercise room; Jacuzzi; small outdoor pool; sauna; tennis court. *In room:* A/C, fridge, hair dryer, no phone, free Wi-Fi.

WHERE TO EAT

Variety, they say, is the spice of life, and Tucson certainly dishes up plenty of variety (and spice) when it comes to eating out. Tucson is a city that lives for spice, and in the realm of fiery foods, Mexican reigns supreme. There's historical Mexican at both El Charro Café and El Minuto Cafe, *nuevo* Mexican at Café Poca Cosa and J Bar, and family-style Mexican at El Minuto. So if you like Mexican food, you'll find plenty of places in Tucson to get all fired up.

On the other hand, if Mexican leaves you cold, don't despair—there are plenty of other restaurants serving everything from the finest French cuisine to innovative American, Italian, and Southwestern food. The last of these is almost as prevalent in Tucson as Mexican food, and you should be sure to dine at a Southwestern restaurant early in your visit. This cuisine can be brilliantly creative, and after trying it, you may want *all* your meals to be Southwestern.

The Abbey Eat + Drink **20**
Anthony's in the Catalinas **15**
Arizona Inn – Main Dining Room **36**
Beyond Bread **34**
Blanco Tacos + Tequila **14**
Bluefin Seafood Bistro **11**
Blue Willow **27**
Brooklyn Pizza Company **6**
Brushfire BBQ **29**
Café à la C'Art **1**
Café Poca Cosa **4**
The Dish Bistro & Wine Bar **43**
Downtown Kitchen + Cocktails **3**
El Charro Café **2**, **19**, **46**
El Corral Restaurant **21**
El Guero Canelo **30**
El Minuto Cafe **33**
Feast **42**
Flying V Bar & Grill **18**
Frankie's South Philly Cheesesteaks **28**
Ghini's French Café **24**
The Grill **17**
HiFalutin Rapid Fire Western Grill **10**
Janos **16**
JAX Kitchen **9**
J Bar **16**
Kingfisher Bar & Grill **37**
Little Anthony's Diner **45**
Lovin' Spoonfuls **26**
Mariscos Chihuahua **31**
Maynard's Market & Kitchen **5**
McMahon's Prime Steakhouse **39**
Miguel's **12**
Pastiche Modern Eatery **25**
Pat's Drive-In **32**
Pinnacle Peak Steakhouse **40**
Teresa's Mosaic Café **7**
Tohono Chul Tea Room **8**
Tucson Tamale Company **44**
Vero Amore **38**
Vivace Restaurant **23**
Wildflower **11**
Yoshimatsu Healthy Japanese Eatery **35**
Zinburger Wine & Burger Bar **22**
Zona 78 **13**, **41**

Downtown Tucson

University Blvd.
N. 6th Ave.
N. 4th Ave.
N. Stone Ave.
6th St.
N. Euclid Ave.
La Cholla Blvd.
N. Court Ave.
N. Main St.
Granada Ave.
10
Toole Ave.
Alameda St.
E. 9th St.
S. Scott Ave.
E. Congress St.
E. Broadway Blvd.
1
2
3
4
5
6
To Phoenix
Sweetwater Dr.
10
SAGUARO NATIONAL PARK
Camino de Oeste
Silverbell Rd.
7
To Saguaro National Park (West), Arizona-Sonora Desert Museum & Old Tucson
Ironwood Hill Dr.
Tucson Mountain Park
Speedway Blvd.
Gates Pass Rd.
Anklam Rd.
Kinney Rd.
Silverlake Rd.
Bopp Rd.
Ajo Way
86
Valencia Rd.
Mission Rd.
0 2 mi
0 2 km
SAN XAVIER INDIAN RESERVATION

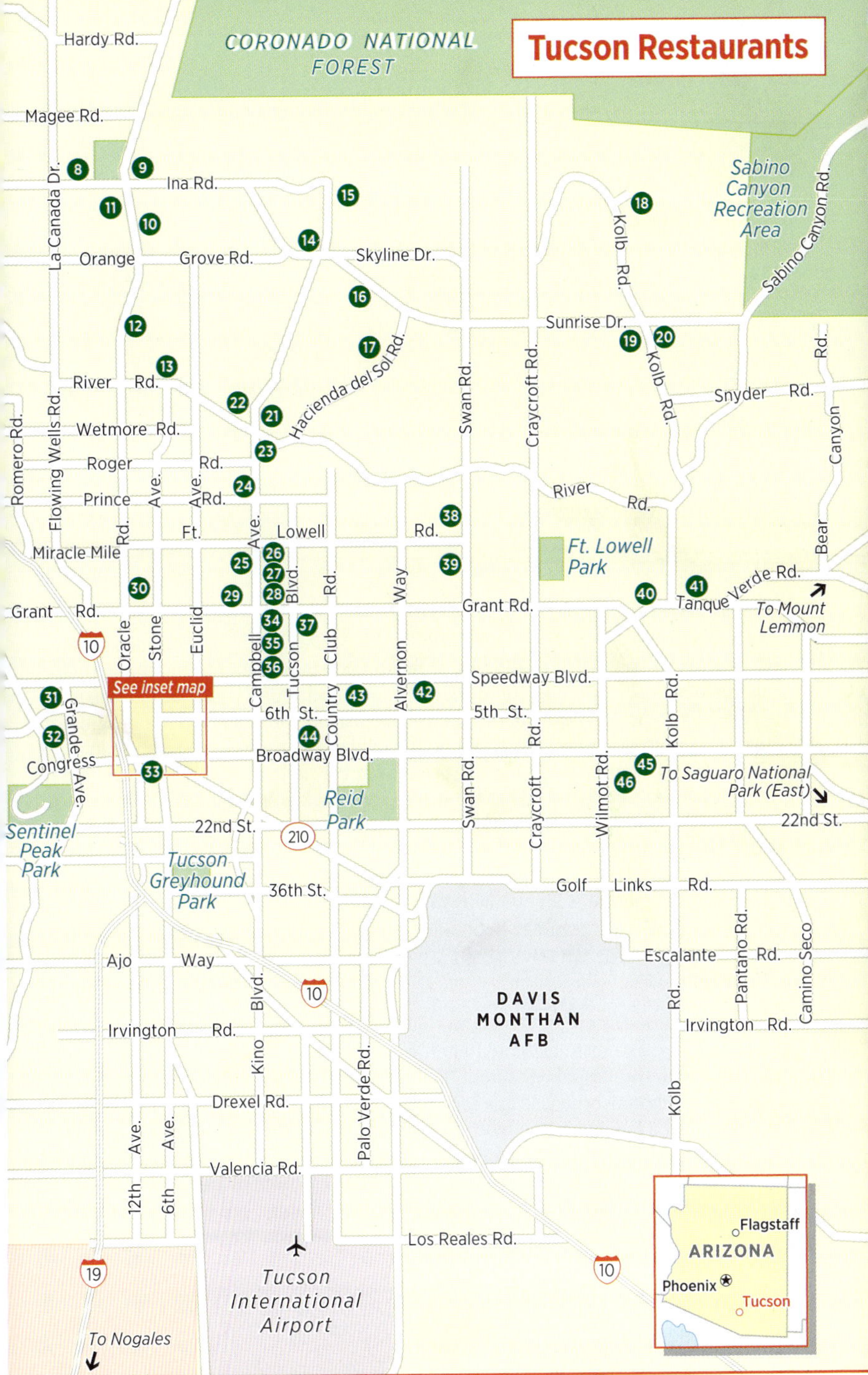
Tucson Restaurants
CORONADO NATIONAL FOREST
Sabino Canyon Recreation Area
Hardy Rd.
Magee Rd.
Ina Rd.
La Canada Dr.
Orange
Grove Rd.
Skyline Dr.
Kolb Rd.
Sabino Canyon Rd.
Sunrise Dr.
Hacienda del Sol Rd.
River Rd.
Wetmore Rd.
Roger Rd.
Prince Rd.
Romero Rd.
Flowing Wells Rd.
Swan Rd.
Craycroft Rd.
Snyder Rd.
Bear Canyon Rd.
River Rd.
Ft. Lowell Rd.
Miracle Mile
Ft. Lowell Park
Tanque Verde Rd.
To Mount Lemmon
Grant Rd.
Oracle Rd.
Stone Ave.
Euclid Ave.
Campbell Ave.
Tucson Blvd.
Country Club Rd.
Alvernon Way
Speedway Blvd.
5th St.
6th St.
See inset map
Grande Ave.
Congress
Broadway Blvd.
Kolb Rd.
Wilmot Rd.
Craycroft Rd.
Swan Rd.
To Saguaro National Park (East)
Reid Park
22nd St.
Sentinel Peak Park
Tucson Greyhound Park
36th St.
Golf Links Rd.
Escalante Rd.
Pantano Rd.
Camino Seco
Ajo Way
Kino Blvd.
DAVIS MONTHAN AFB
Irvington Rd.
Drexel Rd.
Palo Verde Rd.
Kolb Rd.
12th Ave.
6th Ave.
Valencia Rd.
Los Reales Rd.
Tucson International Airport
To Nogales
ARIZONA
Flagstaff
Phoenix
Tucson

Foodies fond of the latest culinary trends will find plenty of spots to satisfy their cravings. On the other hand, if you're on a tight dining budget, look for early-bird dinners, which are quite popular with retirees.

Downtown

EXPENSIVE

Maynard's Market & Kitchen ★★ NEW AMERICAN At this restaurant in Tucson's restored downtown train station, a railroad theme prevails throughout, with old trolley track used for a foot rail at the bar and railroad spikes turned into table lamps. I've had good pizza here, and the cassoulet is some of the best I've had anywhere. I know not everyone loves Mexican food as much as I do, so, if you're more the soup-and-sandwich or pizza-and-calzone type, Maynard's makes a great downtown lunch option. There's also a little market here where you can grab some gourmet-to-go food or a bottle of wine for your dinner in the dining room. As much as possible ingredients are organic, local, or sustainably produced. The restaurant garden even includes a citrus grove.

400 N. Toole Ave. ✆ **520/545-0577.** www.maynardsmarkettucson.com. Reservations highly recommended. Main courses $9–$14 lunch, $14–$28 dinner. AE, DISC, MC, V. Sun–Thurs 11am–10pm; Fri–Sat 11am–midnight.

MODERATE

Café Poca Cosa ★★ CONTEMPORARY MEXICAN The cuisine served at this stylish downtown restaurant is the creation of owner/chef Suzana Davila and has been compared to the dishes dreamed up in *Like Water for Chocolate*. Although ostensibly Mexican, this food is not just *any* Mexican food; it's imaginative and different and is served in a bold and angular space that belies the location on the ground floor of a parking garage. Expect such creations as grilled beef with a jalapeño chili and tomatillo sauce, and chicken with a dark *mole* sauce made with Kahlúa, chocolate, almonds, and chilies. The menu is posted on portable blackboards, so you never know what you might find on any given day. However, I always opt for the *plato* Poca Cosa, a trio of dishes chosen by the chef. This lively restaurant is an excellent value.

110 E. Pennington St. ✆ **520/622-6400.** www.cafepocacosatucson.com. Reservations highly recommended. Main courses $14–$15 lunch, $20–$26 dinner. DISC, MC, V. Tues–Thurs 11am–9pm; Fri–Sat 11am–10pm.

Downtown Kitchen + Cocktails MODERN AMERICAN Chef Janos Wilder, Tucson's most celebrated chef, got his start in downtown Tucson years ago, and with this casual restaurant he has returned to his roots, at least as far as the location is concerned. While his original restaurant, which is now located at the Westin La Paloma in the foothills, served a blend of French and Southwestern cuisines, Downtown has an eclectic menu that draws on influences from all over the world. The appetizers menu has become a favorite of locals, so consider making a meal of several small plates such as the flavor-packed Laotian chicken-and-papaya salad and the beet carpaccio with avocado mousse. Imaginative cocktails are a highlight.

135 S. Sixth Ave. ✆ **520/623-7700.** www.downtownkitchen.com. Reservations recommended. Main courses $10–$20 lunch, $13–$28 dinner. AE, MC, V. Mon–Fri 11am–9 or 9:30pm; Sat 4–9 or 9:30pm; Sun 4–9pm.

El Charro Café ★ SONORAN MEXICAN El Charro, housed in an old stone building in El Presidio Historic District, is Tucson's oldest family-operated Mexican restaurant and is legendary around these parts for its unusual *carne seca,* a traditional air-dried beef that is a bit like shredded beef jerky. To see how they make *carne seca,* just glance up at the restaurant's roof as you approach. The large metal cage up there is filled with beef drying in the desert sun. You'll rarely find *carne seca* on a Mexican menu outside of Tucson, so indulge while you're here.

The adjacent **¡Toma!** (p. 462), a colorful bar/cantina, is under the same ownership. There are other El Charro locations at 6310 E. Broadway (© **520/745-1922**), 6910 E. Sunrise Dr. (© **520/514-1922**), and 7725 N. Oracle Rd., Oro Valley (© **520/229-1922**).

311 N. Court Ave. © **520/622-1922.** www.elcharrocafe.com. Reservations recommended for dinner. Main courses $7–$20. AE, DISC, MC, V. Daily 11am–9pm.

INEXPENSIVE

Café à la C'Art LIGHT FARE Located in the courtyard on the grounds of the Tucson Museum of Art, this cafe serves up tasty sandwiches and makes a good lunch spot if you're downtown wandering the Presidio neighborhood or touring the museum. Try the gingered apricot-almond chicken-salad croissant or the Cuban sandwich, which is made with roasted pork and ham. Wash it all down with some fresh lemonade, and be sure to save room for dessert.

150 N. Main Ave. © **520/628-8533.** www.cafealacarttucson.com. Reservations not accepted. Sandwiches and salads $8.50–$11. AE, DISC, MC, V. Mon–Fri 7–10am and 11am–3pm.

El Minuto Cafe MEXICAN El Minuto, located downtown at the edge of the Barrio Histórico next to El Tiradito shrine, is a meeting ground for both Anglos and Latinos who come for the lively atmosphere and Mexican home-cooking. In business since 1936, this establishment is a neighborhood landmark and a prototype that other Mexican restaurants often try to emulate. Cheese crisps (that is, Mexican pizzas) are a specialty, and the enchiladas, especially *carne seca* (dried meat), are tasty. The chili con carne is another local favorite. This is a fun place for people-watching—you'll find all types, from kids to businessmen in suits.

354 S. Main Ave. © **520/882-4145.** www.elminutocafe.com. Reservations not accepted. Main courses $4.50–$15. AE, DISC, MC, V. Mon–Thurs 11am–10pm; Fri–Sat 11am–11pm.

Central Tucson & the University Area

EXPENSIVE

Arizona Inn—Main Dining Room ★ FRENCH/AMERICAN The dining room at the Arizona Inn, one of the state's first resorts, is consistently excellent. The pink-stucco pueblo-style buildings are surrounded by neatly manicured gardens that have matured gracefully, and the courtyard and the bar patio overlooking the colorful gardens make for romantic dining spots. The menu changes regularly, but includes plenty of classic dishes such as vichyssoise, bouillabaisse, and boeuf bourguignon and a handful of Southwestern-inspired offerings. Presentation is artistic, and fresh ingredients are emphasized. The homemade ice creams are fabulous.

2200 E. Elm St. © **520/325-1541.** www.arizonainn.com. Reservations recommended. Main courses $12–$24 lunch, $30–$44 dinner; tasting menu $50–$65 ($65–$85 with wine). AE, MC, V. Daily 6:30–10:30am, 11:30am–2pm, and 5:30–10pm.

The Dish Bistro & Wine Bar ★★ NEW AMERICAN Located inside the RumRunner wine-and-spirits shop, this tiny, minimalist restaurant is brimming with urban chic. On a busy night, the space could be construed as either cozy or crowded, so if you like it more on the quiet side, come early or late. The chef has a well-deserved reputation for artfully presented dishes that can be both creative and comforting at the same time. Beef ribs might be braised in a Sicilian style and come served with chipotle yam fries, while pork medallions might be wrapped in bacon and served with truffled edamame and rhubarb jam. Check for weeknight meal specials in the bar. Naturally, because this place is associated with a wine shop, the wine list is great. Despite what the address says, the Dish is right on Speedway Boulevard.

3131 E. 1st St. ✆ **520/326-1714.** www.dishbistro.com. Reservations recommended. Main courses $19–$34. AE, DISC, MC, V. Tues–Thurs 5–9pm; Fri–Sat 5–10pm.

MODERATE

Kingfisher Bar & Grill ★ SEAFOOD If you're serious about seafood, Kingfisher is definitely one of your best bets for a memorable meal in Tucson. The freshest seafood, artfully blended with bright flavors and imaginative ingredients, is deftly prepared as appetizers, sandwiches, and main dishes. You may have difficulty deciding whether to begin with oysters, house-smoked trout, or ceviche—so why not tackle them all and call it a meal? By the way, the warm cabbage salad is a must—delicious! The atmosphere is upscale and lively and the bar and late-night menu are a hit with night owls. You'll hear live jazz and blues on Monday and Saturday nights.

2564 E. Grant Rd. ✆ **520/323-7739.** www.kingfishertucson.com. Reservations recommended. Main courses $10–$15 lunch, $16–$29 dinner. AE, DC, DISC, MC, V. Mon–Fri 11am–3pm and 5pm–midnight; Sat–Sun 5pm–midnight. Closed July 1–15.

Pastiche Modern Eatery ★ NEW AMERICAN Located in a little shopping plaza that has lots of Tucson character, this high-energy bistro serves such an eclectic variety of dishes that it has long been a Tucson favorite. The colorful artwork and vibrant contemporary food fairly shout *trendy,* but the restaurant manages to appeal to a broad spectrum of the population. From a Southwest burger to thyme-crusted sea bass, there's enough here to keep everyone at the table happy. Light eaters can get half-orders of many entrees. The crowded bar is a popular watering hole that turns out tasty margaritas. There's also an adjacent wine shop.

3025 N. Campbell Ave. ✆ **520/325-3333.** www.pasticheme.com. Reservations recommended. Main courses $12–$27. AE, DC, DISC, MC, V. Tues–Fri 11:30am–midnight; Sat–Sun 4:30pm–midnight.

INEXPENSIVE

Beyond Bread AMERICAN/BAKERY Although ostensibly a bakery, this place is really a bustling sandwich shop that also sells great breads and pastries. You can even get hot breakfasts here, but in the morning, I much prefer a latte and a selection from the pastry case. The sandwich list is long, with both hot and cold varieties, and they all come on the great bread that's baked on the premises. Most of the sandwiches are so big that you could split them between two people if you weren't too hungry.

Other locations are on the east side of town at Monterey Village, 6260 E. Speedway Blvd. (✆ **520/747-7477**), and in the foothills at 421 W. Ina Rd. (✆ **520/461-1111**).

3026 N. Campbell Ave. ✆ **520/322-9965.** www.beyondbread.com. Reservations not accepted. Main courses $5–$11. AE, MC, V. Mon–Fri 6:30am–8pm; Sat 7am–8pm; Sun 7am–6pm.

Blue Willow AMERICAN The crowds of people waiting on the front patio for a table on weekend mornings should be a clue that this place does great breakfasts. Better yet, the breakfasts are massive and they're available all day long. The Blue Willow Special—made with scrambled eggs, green chilies, tomatoes, chopped corn tortillas, cheddar cheese, salsa, and sour cream—is my favorite breakfast here, but the chorizo scramble is another Mexican-inspired dish worth trying. Be sure to peruse the shelves in the little gift shop at the front of the restaurant; it has a wonderfully eclectic selection.

2616 N. Campbell Ave. ✆ **520/327-7577.** www.bluewillowtucson.com. Reservations not accepted for weekend breakfast or lunch. Main courses $7–$17. AE, DISC, MC, V. Mon–Fri 7am–9pm; Sat–Sun 8am–9pm.

Brooklyn Pizza Company PIZZA Solar-powered pizza? That's what the sign says, and if you look on the roof of the building housing this little pizza joint, you'll see dozens of photovoltaic panels. While the pizzas themselves are baked in a gas-fired oven, everything else in the restaurant runs on the power of the sun. Now that's eco-friendly! There are lunch, late-night, and happy-hour specials, plus house-made gelatos.

534 N. 4th Ave. ✆ **520/622-6868.** www.brooklynpizzacompany.com. Reservations not accepted. Main courses $6–$17. AE, MC, V. Mon–Sat 11am–11pm; Sun noon–10pm.

Brushfire BBQ Co. BARBECUE At this tiny barbecue joint, you pick the size of your meal (regular or hungry), the type of sauce you want (they've got six flavors), and what sides you'd like (be sure to get the flavored slaw of the day). I know these are a lot of choices to make on an empty stomach, but once you've made all these difficult decisions, just sit back and wait for some of the best barbecue in Tucson. Oh, and I almost forgot, be sure to get an order of messy fries topped with hot sauce, cheese, and pork, brisket, or sausage.

2745 N. Campbell Ave. ✆ **520/624-3223.** www.brushfirebbq.com. Reservations not accepted. Main courses $7–$20. AE, DISC, MC, V. Daily 11am–9pm.

El Guero Canelo 🎁 MEXICAN The first time I stopped in at El Guero Canelo for one of their famous Sonoran hot dogs, a teenage mariachi band started playing *La Bamba* just as I ordered my meal. It was a Sunday afternoon, and the place was packed with local Hispanic families. The sun was shining in through the 20-foot-tall walls of glass, and just about everything in the restaurant was painted in the colors of the Mexican flag (green, white, and red). The hot dog, wrapped in bacon and slathered with beans and salsa, was good, but it wasn't nearly as memorable as the restaurant scene itself. For a slice of authentic Tucson culture, this place is not to be missed. The original El Guero Canelo is at 5201 S. 12th Ave. (✆ **520/295-9005**).

2480 N. Oracle Rd. ✆ **520/882-8977.** www.elguerocanelo.com. Reservations not accepted. Main courses $2.50–$6.75. AE, DISC, MC, V. Mon–Sat 7am–midnight; Sun 7:30am–midnight.

Frankie's South Philly Cheesesteaks LIGHT FARE Frankie Santos, owner of this casual fast-food joint, is originally from south Philly, and to say that he is obsessive about his cheesesteak sandwiches is an understatement. The rolls are from Amoroso's bakery in Philadelphia, the steaks (certified angus beef) are chopped, not sliced (but that's an entire discussion on its own), and you can get American cheese, provolone, or, of course, Cheez Whiz. You can also get a variety of toppings, including mushrooms and a variety of different peppers. There are even chicken cheesesteaks and veggie cheesesteaks.

2574 N. Campbell Ave. ✆ **520/795-2665.** www.frankiescheesesteaks.com. Reservations not accepted. Main courses $5.50–$9.50. AE, DISC, MC, V. Mon–Sat 11am–8pm; Sun 11am–5pm.

Ghini's French Caffe 🎁 FRENCH A French cafe and breakfast spot in the middle of Tucson? *Mais oui!* This casual little spot is a real gem. The owner is from Marseille and reproduces plenty of favorites from the home country. At breakfast, there are flaky croissants, a Marseille-style omelet made with anchovies, and wonderful Provençal-style fried eggs with tomatoes, garlic, and thyme. Lunchtime brings interesting salads, sandwiches made with baguettes, and a good range of simple pastas. Everything is available to go.

1803 E. Prince Rd. ✆ **520/326-9095.** www.ghiniscafe.com. Reservations not accepted. Sandwiches and pastas $7.50–$13. AE, DISC, MC, V. Tues 6:30am–3pm and 5–7pm; Wed–Sat 6:30am–3pm; Sun 8am–2pm.

Lovin' Spoonfuls VEGAN Chili dogs, turkey sandwiches, tuna melts, bacon cheeseburgers. The menu at this casual little place may not sound too interesting until you realize that not one of those dishes actually has meat in it. This is a vegan restaurant, so there are no eggs or dairy products to be seen (or tasted). If you're already a vegetarian or vegan, you may not want to eat anywhere else while you're in Tucson. Oh, and there are organic beers and wines to accompany your meal.

2990 N. Campbell Ave. ✆ **520/325-7766.** www.lovinspoonfuls.com. Main courses $5.25–$8.25 lunch, $8–$11 dinner. DISC, MC, V. Mon–Sat 9:30am–9pm; Sun 10am–3pm.

Tucson Tamale Company 🎁 MEXICAN Tamales, stuffed cornmeal dumplings steamed in corn husks, are a staple among the Southwest's Hispanic population, but the owners of this restaurant are taking tamales to a broader audience. To that end, the tamales here are made without lard and sometimes include some very nontraditional ingredients. There are vegan tamales (one with spinach and mushrooms), as well as a Wisconsin grilled cheese tamale. However, my favorites are the more traditional offerings made with pork loin and green chilies, chicken and tomatillos, and beef sirloin and chipotle peppers.

2545 E. Broadway. ✆ **520/305-4760.** www.tucsontamalecompany.com. Reservations not accepted. Main courses $3–$6.50. AE, DISC, MC, V. Mon–Sat 10am–7pm.

Yoshimatsu Healthy Japanese Eatery ★ JAPANESE I found out about this unusual place from a friend who had recently been to Japan and raved about this restaurant's authenticity. However, that's only part of the story. Not only is there a long menu of health-conscious Japanese dishes, but the decor in this ultracasual place is also truly outrageous, with little glass cases displaying all manner of Japanese toys and action figures. The *okonomiyaki,* sort of a Japanese pizza, is one of my favorite dishes here. My wife, on the other hand, adores the green-tea milkshake. A stylish little sushi bar is attached to the restaurant.

2660 N. Campbell Ave. ✆ **520/320-1574.** www.yoshimatsuaz.com. Reservations not accepted. Main courses $7.50–$17. AE, MC, V. Sun–Thurs 11:30am–2:30pm and 5–9pm; Fri–Sat 11:30am–2:30pm and 5–10pm.

East Tucson

INEXPENSIVE

Feast ★ INTERNATIONAL Feast is not only a casual sit-down restaurant, but also a highly creative gourmet to-go place, which makes it the perfect spot to pick up food for a sunset picnic dinner at Sabino Canyon Recreation Area or Saguaro National Park. The menu changes monthly, but you may find spice-brined pork belly confit with roasted turnips, autumn vegetable salad, crawfish étouffée, or duck tamales with *huitlacoche* (Mexican corn fungus) cream sauce.

4122 E. Speedway Blvd. ✆ **520/326-9363** or 520/326-6500. www.eatatfeast.com. Reservations recommended. Main courses $8.75–$18. AE, DISC, MC, V. Tues–Sun 11am–9pm.

Little Anthony's Diner ☺ AMERICAN This place is primarily for kids, although lots of big kids enjoy the 1950s music and decor. The menu includes such offerings as a Jailhouse Rock burger and Chubby Checker triple-decker club sandwich. Daily specials and bottomless soft drinks make feeding the family fairly inexpensive, and a video-game room will keep your kids entertained while you finish your milkshake. If you want to make a night of it (and you make a reservation far enough in advance), you can take in an old-fashioned melodrama next door at the Gaslight Theatre. Together, these two places make for a fun night out with the family.

7010 E. Broadway Blvd. (in back of the Gaslight Plaza). ✆ **520/296-0456.** www.littleanthonysdiner.com. Burgers and sandwiches $5.50–$9.50. MC, V. Mon 11am–9pm; Tues–Thurs 11am–10pm; Fri 11am–11pm; Sat 7:30am–11pm; Sun 7:30am–9pm.

Vero Amore ★ ITALIAN Everyone loves pizza, but some people are absolutely fanatical about it. The owners of this cozy little east Tucson pizza place are solidly in the fanatics category. Vero Amore adheres to the rigid Neapolitan (Italian) pizza-making standards that require pizzas to have thin crusts and be made with Italian flour and Italian tomatoes. The pizzas also have to be baked in a very hot wood-fired oven. Put this all together and you get pizzas that are simple in presentation yet packed with flavor. Small and casual, Vero Amore is a good lunch choice if you find yourself on the east side of the city in the middle of the day.

There's a second location in Marana at 12130 N. Dove Mountain Blvd., Ste. 104 (✆ **520/579-2292**).

3305 N. Swan Rd., Ste. 105. ✆ **520/325-4122.** www.veroamorepizza.com. Reservations not accepted. Main courses $8–$13. AE, DISC, MC, V. Sun–Thurs 11am–9pm; Fri–Sat 11am–10pm.

Zona 78 ★ PIZZA I'm a sucker for good pizza, and I think the pizza here is the best in Tucson. Maybe it's the big stone oven they use or maybe it's all the locally grown organic produce, but whatever it is, this place does it right. Try the Tuscany, which is covered with Italian sausage, mozzarella, kalamata olives, fennel, roasted garlic, onions, mushrooms, and fresh basil. This pie is just bursting with flavors. To really get the most out of a visit to Zona 78, you need to bring enough people so that you can order the big antipasti plate.

There's a second Zona 78 on the west side at 78 W. River Rd. (✆ **520/888-7878**).

7301 E. Tanque Verde Rd. ✆ **520/296-7878.** www.zona78.com. Reservations recommended. Main courses $9–$17. AE, DISC, MC, V. Daily 11am–10pm.

The Foothills

EXPENSIVE

Anthony's in the Catalinas ★★ NEW AMERICAN/CONTINENTAL Housed in a modern Italianate building overlooking the city, this restaurant is as traditional as it gets, with tuxedoed waiters, valet parking, and such classic fine-dining dishes as escargots, French onion soup, Caesar salad prepared tableside, chateaubriand, and filet mignon with béarnaise sauce. Such a timeless experience appeals primarily to an older foothills cigars-and-single-malt set. In such a rarefied atmosphere, you'd expect only the finest meal and service, and that's exactly what you get. Wine is not just an accompaniment, but also a reason for dining out at Anthony's; with more than 1,700 wines, the wine list is one of the most extensive in the city.

6440 N. Campbell Ave. ✆ **520/299-1771.** www.anthonyscatalinas.com. Reservations highly recommended. Main courses $30–$41. DC, DISC, MC, V. Daily 5:30–9pm.

Flying V Bar & Grill ★ SOUTHWESTERN Creative Southwestern dishes that emphasize local ingredients, some even sourced from the local Tohono O'odham tribe, make this restaurant at the Loews Ventana Canyon Resort a good bet for anyone wanting to sample some regional flavors. While there are well-prepared standards such as guacamole (prepared tableside), I can't resist the duck-confit flautas and the bison-burger with blue cheese and onions. Keep an eye out for any dish with the local tepary beans, which come from the nearby Tohono O'odham Reservation. You might find them made into a vegan stew or served as an accompaniment to a veal chop. With lots of shareable small plates, this is a great place for grazing.

At Loews Ventana Canyon Resort, 7000 N. Resort Dr. ✆ **520/299-2020.** www.loewshotels.com. Reservations recommended. Main courses $13–$33. AE, DC, DISC, MC, V. Sun–Thurs 5:30–9pm; Fri–Sat 5:30–10pm.

The Grill ★★ REGIONAL AMERICAN Great food, historical Southwest character, views, live jazz—this place has it all. Located in a 1920s hacienda-style building at a former foothills guest ranch, the Grill is one of Tucson's best restaurants, so don't leave town without having at least one meal here. The menu changes regularly and always manages to keep up with the latest culinary trends. For a starter, you might be able to have artichoke hearts stuffed with housemade lamb sausage or gazpacho made with crab meat. Despite the price, the New York strip steak is deservedly the most popular entree on the menu and is big enough for two people to share. Sunday brunch here is a real treat. The main patio overlooks the Catalinas and the fairways of the adjacent golf course.

At the Hacienda del Sol Guest Ranch Resort, 5501 N. Hacienda del Sol Rd. ✆ **520/529-3500.** www.haciendadelsol.com. Reservations recommended. Main courses $24–$42; Sun brunch $32. AE, DC, DISC, MC, V. Daily 5:30–10pm; Sun brunch 9:30am–2pm.

Janos ★★★ SOUTHWESTERN/REGIONAL AMERICAN Janos Wilder, Tucson's most celebrated chef, is not only a world-class chef, but a real sweetheart, too. Should you happen to bump into him while dining here, he'll make you feel as though you've been a regular at his restaurant for years. It is this conviviality—which spills over into all aspects of a meal here—that makes this one of my favorite restaurants in the state. Consequently, this luxuriously appointed restaurant, which is just outside the front door of the Westin La Paloma (p. 408), is my top choice for a special-occasion dinner while in Tucson. The menu changes both daily and seasonally, but always features complex dishes that seamlessly meld Southwestern flavors with classic culinary traditions. No other restaurant in Tucson does as much to promote local and indigenous ingredients as Janos.

At the Westin La Paloma, 3770 E. Sunrise Dr. ✆ **520/615-6100.** www.janos.com. Reservations highly recommended. Main courses $28–$50; multicourse tasting menus $60 ($95 with wine). AE, MC, V. Mon–Thurs 5:30–9pm; Fri–Sat 5:30–9:30pm (May–Sept closed Mon).

McMahon's Prime Steakhouse ★ STEAK/SEAFOOD If a perfectly done steak is what you're craving, then McMahon's is the place. This restaurant serves some of the best steaks in Tucson, and with a decidedly modern opulence, McMahon's boasts an atmosphere calculated to impress (a large glass-walled wine room dominates the main dining room). You can drop a bundle on dinner here, but no more than you'd spend at other high-end restaurants around town. The main difference is that your choices at McMahon's are simpler: steak, seafood, or steak and seafood. You'd be wasting a night out, though, if you didn't order a steak.

2959 N. Swan Rd. ✆ **520/327-7463.** www.metrorestaurants.com. Reservations recommended. Main courses $9–$18 lunch, $24–$55 dinner. AE, DISC, MC, V. Mon–Thurs 11:30am–10pm; Fri 11:30am–10:30pm; Sat 5–10:30pm; Sun 4–9pm.

Miguel's ★ NUEVO LATINO If you're staying at one of the foothills resorts and just can't get enough Mexican food, this is another good bet for upscale south-of-the-border cuisine on the north side of the city. Be sure to start your meal with the guacamole. The grilled pork chop with orange-ancho-chili sauce is a favorite of mine, but there are also flavorful steaks and lots of seafood dishes. The tequila selection here is one of the best in Tucson, and the margaritas are delicious. If you can, eat before the sun goes down, as there are views of the Santa Catalinas and the city.

At La Posada, 5900 N. Oracle Rd. ✆ **520/887-3777.** www.miguelstucson.com. Reservations recommended. Main courses $17–$28. AE, DISC, MC, V. Daily 5–10pm.

MODERATE

The Abbey Eat + Drink AMERICAN After a day of hiking at Sabino Canyon, this is a fun place to refuel. The decor is modern, though not so stylish that you won't feel comfortable in jeans, and the atmosphere is as lively as at many bars around town. If breakfast is one of your favorite meals of the day, you should be sure to try the "breakfast for dinner" entree. It's sort of like having your cake and eating it, too. Likewise, the Abbey burger, served on an English muffin and topped with bacon jam, aioli, caramelized onions, and cheddar cheese is hard to beat. By the way, the Abbey is affiliated with Jax Kitchen way over on the west side of the foothills.

6960 E. Sunrise Dr. ✆ **520/299-3132.** www.theabbeytucson.com. Reservations recommended. Main courses $11–$22. AE, DISC, MC, V. Tues–Sun 5–10pm.

Blanco Tacos + Tequila ★ MEXICAN The retro Swedish-modern decor at this restaurant is about as far as you can get from the usual perpetual-fiesta styling of most Mexican restaurants. However, Blanco, from the same restaurant group responsible for Wildflower, another of my favorite Tucson restaurants, is far from an average Mexican restaurant. The food here doesn't break any new ground, but the fish tacos are some of the best in Tucson. Dishes are made with fresh ingredients, and even the rice and vegetables that come with meals are well done. Service is friendly and there are great views from the deck. There's a great tequila list, and the bar makes some fun cocktails.

In La Encantada Center, 2905 E. Skyline Dr., Ste. 246. ✆ **520/232-1007.** www.foxrc.com. Reservations not accepted. Main courses $9–$19. AE, DISC, MC, V. Sun–Thurs 11am–10pm; Fri–Sat 11am–11pm.

Bluefin Seafood Bistro ★ SEAFOOD Sure, this is the middle of the desert, but there's only so much beef you can eat on a week's vacation. If you've had enough steak to start your own ranch and are craving a nice bouillabaisse, this is a good choice. Adopting a sort of New Orleans styling, Bluefin is a sister restaurant to the ever-popular and always-reliable Kingfisher in central Tucson (p. 420). The menu is extensive; in addition to that bouillabaisse, you can get oysters Rockefeller, a classic New England lobster roll, or cashew-crusted mahimahi. There's live music on Friday and Saturday nights.

In Casas Adobes Plaza, 7053 N. Oracle Rd. ✆ **520/531-8500.** www.bluefintucson.com. Reservations recommended. Main courses $9.50–$15 lunch, $14–$29 dinner. AE, DC, DISC, MC, V. Sun–Thurs 11am–9pm; Fri–Sat 11am–10pm.

JAX Kitchen ★ NEW AMERICAN JAX Kitchen is something of a French bistro gone global, with dishes showing the influence of cuisines from around the world. The salmon might be tandoori style, while the duck confit might be served in a salad with beets, apples, pears, blue cheese, and pickled-cranberry vinaigrette. However, despite the global influences, the menu also contains some wonderful comfort foods, including a whole salt-crusted roast chicken, which takes an hour to prepare and is the ultimate comfort food. Order it as soon as you walk in. There's a good selection of wines by the glass, and prices tend to be reasonable.

7286 N. Oracle Rd. ✆ **520/219-1235.** www.jaxkitchen.com. Reservations recommended. Main courses $13–$22. AE, DISC, MC, V. Sun and Tues–Thurs 5–9pm; Fri–Sat 5–10pm.

J Bar ★★★ SOUTHWESTERN The mouthwatering culinary creations of celebrity chef Janos Wilder at half-price? Sounds impossible, but that's pretty much what you'll find at this casual bar and grill adjacent to the famed foothills restaurant. Ask for a seat out on the heated patio, and with the lights of Tucson twinkling in the distance, dig into the best nachos you'll ever taste—here made with chorizo sausage, smoked poblano peppers, chili con queso, and fresh salsa. No matter what you order, you'll likely find that the ingredients and flavor combinations are most memorable. Who can forget spicy jerked pork with cranberry-habanero chutney or Yucatán-style plantain-crusted chicken with green coconut-milk curry? You won't want to miss sampling one of the *postres* (desserts). The dark-chocolate–jalapeño sundae may sound unusual, but it's delicious.

At the Westin La Paloma, 3770 E. Sunrise Dr. ✆ **520/615-6100.** www.janos.com. Reservations highly recommended. Main courses $13–$19. AE, DC, MC, V. Daily 5–9:30pm.

Vivace Restaurant ★★ NORTHERN ITALIAN In a beautiful Tuscan-inspired setting, this restaurant serves reasonably priced, creative Italian dishes. The atmosphere is lively and the food down-to-earth. For starters, consider indulging in the luscious antipasto platter for two; it has marinated vegetables, prosciutto, roasted red peppers, grilled asparagus, and herbed goat-cheese mousse. Pasta dishes, such as penne with sausage and red pepper–tomato sauce, come nicely presented and in generous portions. But it's the crab-filled chicken breast that is most memorable. The wine list has plenty of selections.

At St. Philip's Plaza, 4310 N. Campbell Ave. ✆ **520/795-7221.** www.vivacetucson.com. Reservations recommended. Main courses $9.50–$16 lunch, $16–$33 dinner. AE, DC, DISC, MC, V. Mon–Thurs 11:30am–9pm; Fri–Sat 11:30am–10pm.

Market Timing

Saturday and Sunday mornings are great times to stop by St. Philip's Plaza. No, this isn't a church, it's a shopping center, and on weekend mornings, there is a wonderful little farmers' market here. You can pick up organic bread, prickly pear cactus juice and jelly, homemade tamales, Mexican cheeses, and plenty of produce. Stock up here and then head to Sabino Canyon Recreation Area for a picnic.

Wildflower ★ NEW AMERICAN Stylish comfort food in large portions is the order of the day at this chic and casually elegant north-Tucson bistro. Interior decor, calculated to appeal to the local ladies-who-lunch crowd, is a blend of boudoir and patio. The heaping plate of fried calamari with *mizuna* greens is a good bet for a starter, and entrees run the gamut from a comforting cheeseburger with white cheddar to miso-glazed black cod to herb-crusted rack of lamb. Both pasta and salmon also show up in reliable guises.

At Casas Adobes Shopping Plaza, 7037 N. Oracle Rd. (at Ina Rd.). ✆ **520/219-4230.** www.foxrc.com. Reservations recommended. Main courses $9–$18 lunch, $12–$29 dinner. AE, DC, DISC, MC, V. Sun–Thurs 11am–9pm; Fri–Sat 11am–10pm.

INEXPENSIVE

HiFalutin Rapid Fire Western Grill AMERICAN Tired of highfalutin steakhouses with highfalutin prices? Me, too. The only thing highfalutin at this casual restaurant is the name, and that's why it's one of my favorite Tucson restaurants. This place has loads of Southwest character and knows how to set the mood. It also comes through with reasonably priced tasty comfort food with a Western twist. Get anything with the marinated flank steak, and you won't be disappointed. You can get it tossed with pasta, in a salad, or just plain straight up. Wash it all down with one of the great margaritas they serve, and you'll definitely have a highfalutin kind of meal.

6780 N. Oracle Rd. ✆ **520/297-0518.** www.hifalutintucson.com. Reservations recommended. Main courses $8.50–$25. AE, DISC, MC, V. Sun–Thurs 11am–9pm; Fri–Sat 11am–10pm.

Tohono Chul Tea Room REGIONAL AMERICAN Located in a brick territorial-style building in Tohono Chul Park (p. 444), this is one of the most tranquil restaurants in the city, and the garden setting provides a wonderful opportunity to experience the desert. As often as possible, ingredients are local and organic, and before or after lunching on *posole* (a Mexican stew), lobster macaroni and cheese, or a Sonoran BLT, you can wander through the park and admire the many species of cacti. Be sure to ask for a table on the patio, which is surrounded by gardens that attract numerous bird species. Unfortunately, because service here can be frustratingly slow, you might spend more time bird-watching than you had anticipated.

7366 N. Paseo del Norte (1 block west of the corner of Ina and Oracle rds. in Tohono Chul Park). ✆ **520/797-1222.** www.tohonochulpark.org. Reservations accepted only for parties of 6 or more. Main courses $7–$14. AE, MC, V. Daily 8am–5pm.

Zinburger Wine & Burger Bar ★ AMERICAN I have to admit, I was resistant to the whole concept of this restaurant for the longest time. Burgers and beer? Yes. Burgers and wine? Maybe, but not wine in a stemmed wine glass, not with fingers dripping burger juices. Oh well, I haven't dropped a glass yet, and the burgers are fabulous. The wine list is pretty good, too. Although you're welcome to bring the kids, who will be happy with the burgers, fries, and root beer floats, this place has more the feel of a hip bar. Think burger joint for grown-ups. Oh, and by the way, the turkey burger here is just about the best burger of any type I've ever had, and it goes well with red or white wine. Cheers.

In Joesler Village, 1865 E. River Rd. ✆ **520/299-7799.** www.foxrc.com. Reservations not accepted. Main courses $8–$14. AE, DISC, MC, V. Sun–Thurs 11am–10pm; Fri–Sat 11am–11pm.

West Tucson, Oro Valley & Marana

EXPENSIVE

Harvest Restaurant ★★ NEW AMERICAN This restaurant, affiliated with both the Grill at Hacienda del Sol and Tucson's two Zona 78s, emphasizes fresh, local, seasonal ingredients and is an excellent choice if you're staying in the northwest foothills area. The empanadas, which have a lusciously flaky crust and come with a tangy *chimichurri* sauce, are the best I've ever had. Likewise, if you want a great burger, this is the place. Keep an eye out for unusual fish entrees such as ling cod with tomato-olive relish. The attention to ingredients also extends to the cocktail menu, which features seasonal drinks made with fresh-squeezed juices.

10355 N. La Cañada Dr., Oro Valley. ✆ **520/731-1100.** www.marketrg.com. Reservations recommended. Main courses $9–$14 lunch, $14–$25 dinner. AE, DISC, MC, V. Sun–Thurs 11:30am–9pm; Fri 11:30am–10pm.

McClintock's ★★ NEW AMERICAN For classic Western ranch atmosphere, there simply is no place else in Arizona to compare with this restaurant inside the exclusive Saguaro Ranch housing development. When you arrive at the development gate, you'll even be escorted to the restaurant. Be sure to make a reservation that will let you sit on the restaurant's veranda and watch the sun go down over the rugged saguaro-covered hills; the view is gorgeous. As often as possible, dishes are made with natural or organic ingredients, and the pastas and steaks are highlights. I've also had a great calamari appetizer here. You'll find McClintock's at the north end of Thornydale Road (north of Tangerine Rd.).

In Saguaro Ranch, 3755 W. Conrads Way, Marana. ✆ **520/579-2100.** www.mcclintocks-restaurant.com. Reservations required. Main courses $18–$46; Sun brunch $30. AE, DISC, MC, V. Mon–Sat 5–10pm; Sun 11am–2pm and 5–10pm.

MODERATE

Teresa's Mosaic Café ★ 🎁 MEXICAN A mile or so west of I-10, this casual Mexican restaurant, with colorful mosaic tile tables, mirror frames, and a kitchen counter, is hidden behind a McDonald's on the corner of Grant and Silverbell roads but is well worth finding for breakfast or lunch. Try the legendary *huevos rancheros, chilaquiles* (another popular Mexican breakfast dish), or chorizo and eggs for breakfast, and don't pass up the fresh lemonade or *horchata* (spiced rice milk). This is an especially good spot for a meal if you're on your way to the Arizona–Sonora Desert Museum, Old Tucson, or Saguaro National Park's west unit.

2455 N. Silverbell Rd. ✆ **520/624-4512.** www.mosaiccafes.com. Reservations recommended on weekends. Main courses $5–$16. AE, DISC, MC, V. Mon–Sat 7:30am–9pm; Sun 7:30am–2pm.

INEXPENSIVE

Mariscos Chihuahua MEXICAN In the dining room of this funky little westside Mexican joint, a life-size marlin leaps out of a wall that has been painted with a mural of the open ocean. This unusual decor should give you a hint about what they serve here—seafood, Mexican seafood. Fish, shrimp, and octopus, prepared in numerous styles, are the specialty here. You can start with a delicious ceviche tostada and then have spicy shrimp *endiablados* or a *culichi*-style fish filet (made with a creamy green-pepper sauce). Wash your meal down with an inexpensive margarita or a *michelada,* a popular Mexican drink that mixes beer and tomato juice. You'll find Mariscos Chihuahua just south of Speedway Boulevard west of I-10 and downtown Tucson.

1009 N. Grande Ave. ✆ **520/623-3563.** www.mariscoschihuahua.com. Reservations not accepted. Main courses $9–$19. AE, DISC, MC, V. Daily 9am–9pm.

Pat's Drive-In AMERICAN In business for more than 40 years, this old-fashioned drive-in, with its distinctive red-and-white striped paint job, is famous in Tucson for its chili dogs. The dogs come in both mild and spicy versions and should be accompanied by some of the great french fries. Be forewarned, these dogs are messy. You'll find Pat's just south of Speedway west of I-10.

1202 W. Niagara St. ✆ **520/624-0891.** Main dishes $1.50–$6. No credit cards. Sun–Thurs 11am–9pm; Fri–Sat 11am–10pm.

Cowboy Steakhouses

El Corral Restaurant ☺ STEAK El Corral is another of Tucson's fun, inexpensive, and atmospheric steakhouses. Good prime rib and cheap prices have made this place hugely popular with retirees and families. The restaurant doesn't accept reservations, so expect long lines or come before or after regular dinner hours. Inside, the hacienda building has a genuine old-timey feeling, with flagstone floors and wood paneling that make it dark and cozy. In keeping with the name, there's a traditional corral fence of mesquite branches around the restaurant parking lot. Prime rib is the house specialty, but you can also get steaks, chicken, pork ribs, and burgers.

2201 E. River Rd. ✆ **520/299-6092.** www.elcorraltucson.com. Reservations not accepted. Main courses $9–$20. AE, DC, DISC, MC, V. Mon–Thurs 5–9pm; Fri–Sat 4:30–10pm; Sun 4:30–9pm.

Pinnacle Peak Steakhouse ★ ☺ STEAK Located in Trail Dust Town (see the "Especially for Kids" section in "Seeing the Sights," below), a Wild West–themed shopping, dining, and family entertainment center, the Pinnacle Peak Steakhouse specializes in family dining in a fun cowboy atmosphere. Stroll the wooden sidewalks past the opera house and saloon to the grand old dining rooms of the restaurant. Once through the doors, you'll be surprised at the authenticity of the place, which really does resemble a dining room in old Tombstone. Be prepared for crowds—this place is very popular with tour buses. Oh, and by the way, wear a necktie into this place, and you'll have it cut off! Actually, lots of people wear ties just so they can have them added to the collection tacked to the ceiling.

6541 E. Tanque Verde Rd. ✆ **520/296-0911.** www.pinnaclepeaktucson.com. Reservations not accepted. Main courses $8–$22. AE, DC, DISC, MC, V. Mon–Fri 5–10pm; Sat–Sun 4:30–10pm.

Late-Night Noshing

If your movie didn't let out until 10pm and the popcorn wasn't enough to fill you up, where do you go to satisfy your hunger? Try **Kingfisher,** 2564 E. Grant Rd. (✆ **520/323-7739;** www.kingfishertucson.com), which stays open until midnight every night, or **Pastiche Modern Eatery,** 3025 N. Campbell Ave. (✆ **520/325-3333;** www.pasticheme.com), which stays open until midnight

Tuesday through Sunday. (For more information, see the reviews of Kingfisher and Pastiche earlier in this chapter.)

Bakeries, Cafes & Quick Bites

For some of the best espresso in Tucson, head to **Raging Sage Coffee Roasters,** 2458 N. Campbell Ave. (✆ **520/320-5203;** www.ragingsage.com); prices are high, but the espresso here sure is tasty. **Avenue Coffee,** 2502 N. Campbell Ave. (✆ **520/225-0437;** www.avenuecoffee.com), just up the street from Raging Sage, is another strong contender. If you've been visiting the museums on the University of Arizona campus and need a pick-me-up, try **Caffe Luce,** 943 E. University Blvd., no. 191 (✆ **520/207-5504;** www.caffeluce.com), which is directly across the street from the campus. If you're a tea person, be sure to check out **Seven Cups,** 2516 E. Sixth St. (✆ **520/881-4072;** www.sevencups.com), a traditional Chinese tearoom in a hip residential neighborhood near the University of Arizona.

If you find yourself craving a cupcake, head over to the university area to **Red Velvet Cupcakery,** 943 E. University Blvd., Ste. 165 (✆ **520/829-7780;** www.redvelvetcupcakery.com). For eight-layer cakes and light food in an edgy atmosphere, I like to stop in at the **Cup Cafe,** at Hotel Congress, 311 E. Congress St. (✆ **520/798-1618;** www.hotelcongress.com). At **La Baguette Bakery,** 1797 E. Prince Rd. (✆ **520/322-6297;** www.ghiniscafe.com/page.cfm/bakery), which is affiliated with Ghini's French Caffe (p. 422), you can get all kinds of delicious French pastries. **AJ's Fine Foods,** 2805 E. Skyline Dr. (✆ **520/232-6340;** www.ajsfinefoods.com), a gourmet supermarket in La Encantada shopping center at the northwest corner of Skyline Drive and Campbell Avenue, is another good place to grab a pastry. If it's a hot day, head to **Frost, A Gelato Shoppe,** 7131 N. Oracle Rd., Ste. 101 (✆ **520/797-0188;** www.frostgelato.com), a great little gelateria in the Casas Adobes shopping center. Other Frosts can be found at 7301 E. Tanque Verde Rd. (✆ **520/886-0354**), which is conveniently close to Sabino Canyon, and at 2905 E. Skyline Dr., Ste. 286 (✆ **520/299-0315**), in La Encantada shopping center. Alternatively, chill out with gelato at **Café Italiano,** 2485 N. Swan Rd., Ste. 141 (✆ **520/393-3396;** www.cafeitalianoaz.com), which is in the Cornerstone Plaza on the northwest corner of Grant and Swan roads.

If you need a quick lunch, head for the nearest **Baggins Gourmet Sandwiches** (www.bagginsgourmet.com) for a delicious sandwich. Baggins has several locations, including 7201 E. Speedway Blvd. at Kolb Road (✆ **520/290-9383**), 1800 E. Fort Lowell Rd. at Campbell Avenue (✆ **520/327-1611**), and downtown at 33 N. Stone Ave. at Church and Pennington streets (✆ **520/792-1344**). Good pizza can be had at **Magpies Gourmet Pizza** (www.magpiespizza.com) downtown at 605 N. Fourth Ave. (✆ **520/628-1661**), 4654 E. Speedway Blvd. (✆ **520/795-5977**), 105 S. Houghton Rd. (✆ **520/751-9949**), and 7315 N. Oracle Rd. (✆ **520/297-2712**). **Whole Foods Market** is a good place to get picnic supplies: organic fruit, delicious baked goods, cheese, meats, and wine. Locations are at 3360 E. Speedway Blvd. (✆ **520/795-9844**) and 7133 N. Oracle Rd. (✆ **520/297-5394**).

SEEING THE SIGHTS

Go west, young man (and woman). That's what you'll need to do if you're visiting Tucson and want to immerse yourself in the desert Southwest or the cinematic

Wild West. Out past the western outskirts of Tucson, where the cactus grows and the tumbleweed blows, you'll find not only the west unit of Saguaro National Park (with the biggest and best stands of saguaro cactus), but also the Arizona–Sonora Desert Museum (one of the nation's top zoological parks) and Old Tucson Studios (film site over the years for hundreds of Westerns). Put these three attractions together for one long day of getting to know Tucson, and you have the city's best family outing (and you can bet the kids will be beat by the end of the day).

The Tucson Area's (Mostly) Natural Wonders

Arizona-Sonora Desert Museum ★★★ ☺ Don't be fooled by the name. This is a zoo, and it's one of the best in the country. The Sonoran Desert of central and southern Arizona and parts of northern Mexico contains within its boundaries not only arid lands, but also forested mountains, springs, rivers, and streams. To reflect this diversity, exhibits here encompass the full spectrum of Sonoran Desert life—from plants and insects to fish, reptiles, and mammals—and all are on display in very natural settings. Coyotes and javelinas (peccaries) seem very much at home in their compounds, which are surrounded by fences that are nearly invisible and that make it seem as though there is nothing between you and the animals. You'll also see black bears and mountain lions, tarantulas and scorpions, and prairie dogs and desert bighorn sheep. My favorite exhibit, however, is the walk-in hummingbird aviary.

The grounds here are quite extensive, so wear good walking shoes; a sun hat of some sort is also advisable. Don't be surprised if you end up staying here hours longer than you had intended. If you get hungry, there are two excellent dining options—the cafeteria-style Ironwood Terraces and the more upscale Ocotillo Café. You'll find this zoological park 14 miles west of downtown.

2021 N. Kinney Rd. ✆ **520/883-2702.** www.desertmuseum.org. Admission Sept–May $15 adults, $4.50 children 6–12; June–Aug $12 adults, $3 children 6–12. Oct–Feb daily 8:30am–5pm; Mar–May and Sept daily 7:30am–5pm; June–Aug Sun–Fri 7am–4:30pm, Sat 7am–10pm. From downtown Tucson, go west on Speedway Blvd., which becomes Gates Pass Rd., and follow the signs.

Rattlesnake Crossing

Generally speaking, rattlesnakes should not be crossed, but there is one Tucson rattler that should not be avoided. I am referring here to the city's unusual **Diamondback Bridge,** a snake-shaped pedestrian bridge that spans E. Broadway Boulevard just east of downtown Tucson. From the north end, you enter through the giant vipers open mouth (watch out for the fangs). At the south end of the bridge, a giant rattle is raised in the air, and if you're lucky you just might hear it buzzing as you pass. The bridge is best accessed from the south end of the Fourth Avenue shopping district. Just walk east on E. Ninth Street, turn right on N. Third Avenue, and then follow the bike path through Iron Horse Park. You can also visit this local landmark on a Segway personal-transporter tour with **Segway of Tucson** (✆ **520/749-5325;** www.tucsonsegway.com), which charges $70 for its 2¼-hour tours of the neighborhood. Also, if you've ever been accused of being lower than a snake's belly (hopefully you haven't), you can live up to the aspersion by driving under this bridge.

Arizona Historical Society Downtown Museum **7**

Arizona History Museum **21**

Arizona State Museum **22**

Arizona-Sonora Desert Museum **1**

Center for Creative Photography **19**

De Grazia Gallery in the Sun **12**

El Tiradito **8**

Flandrau: The UA Science Center **18**

Fort Lowell Museum **15**

Gadsden-Pacific Division Toy Train Operating Museum **10**

Golf n' Stuff **17**

The International Wildlife Museum **9**

The Mini-Time Machine Museum of Miniatures **14**

Mission San Xavier del Bac **27**

Old Tucson Studios **2**

Pima Air & Space Museum **28**

Presidio San Agustin del Tucson **4**

Reid Park Zoo **25**

Sabino Canyon Recreation Area **13**

Southern Arizona Transportation Museum **6**

Steward Observatory Mirror Lab **23**

Tohono Chul Park **11**

Trail Dust Town **16**

Tucson Botanical Gardens **24**

Tucson Children's Museum **7**

Tucson Museum of Art & Historic Block **3**

Tucson Rodeo Parade Museum **26**

The University of Arizona Museum of Art **20**

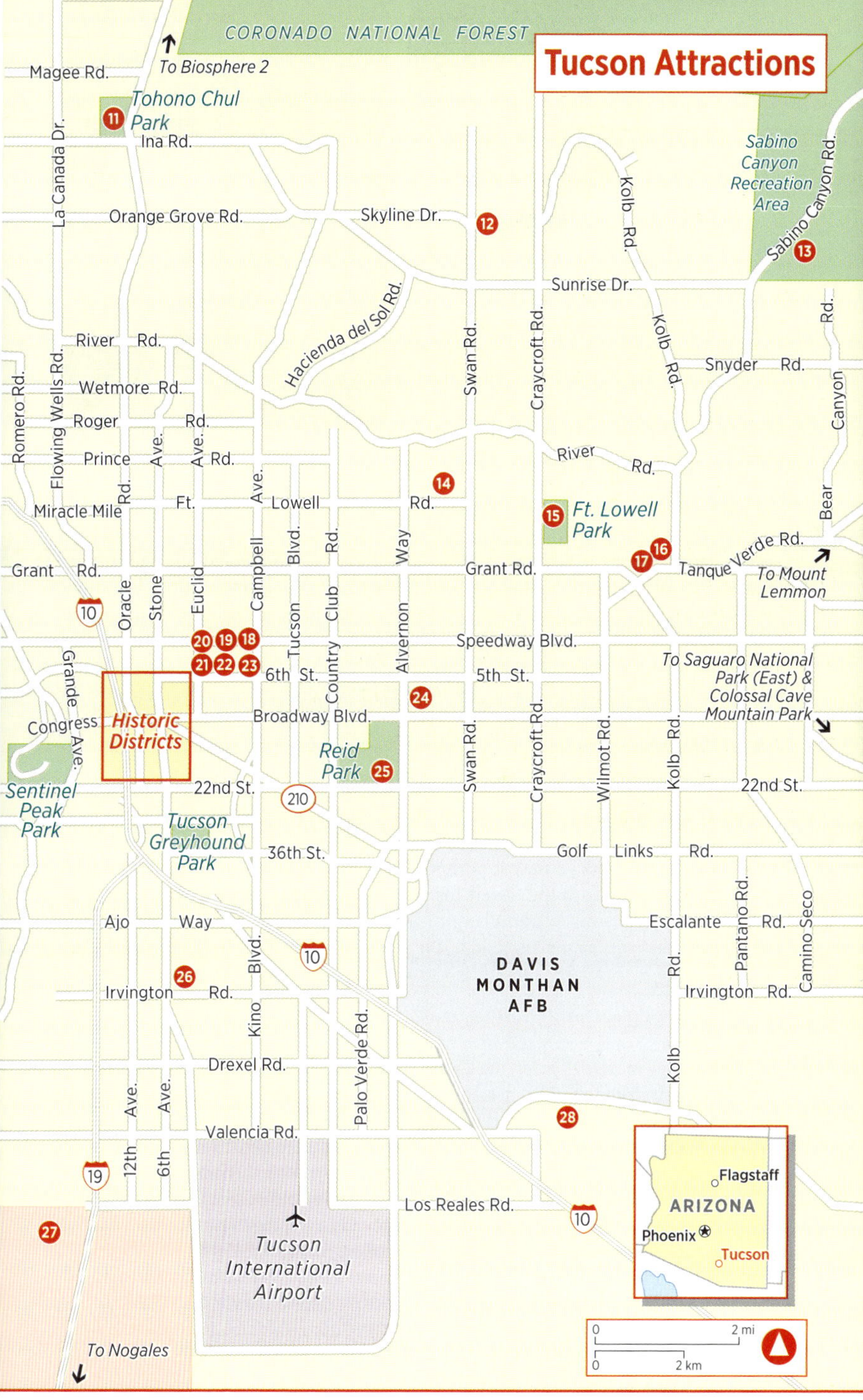
Tucson Attractions
CORONADO NATIONAL FOREST
To Biosphere 2
Magee Rd.
Tohono Chul Park
Ina Rd.
La Canada Dr.
Orange Grove Rd.
Skyline Dr.
Sabino Canyon Recreation Area
Sabino Canyon Rd.
Kolb Rd.
Sunrise Dr.
Hacienda del Sol Rd.
Swan Rd.
Craycroft Rd.
River Rd.
Wetmore Rd.
Roger Rd.
Prince Rd.
Romero Rd.
Flowing Wells Rd.
Snyder Rd.
Bear Canyon Rd.
Miracle Mile
Ft. Lowell Rd.
Ft. Lowell Park
Grant Rd.
Tanque Verde Rd.
To Mount Lemmon
Oracle Rd.
Stone Ave.
Euclid Ave.
Campbell Ave.
Tucson Blvd.
Country Club Rd.
Alvernon Way
Speedway Blvd.
6th St.
5th St.
To Saguaro National Park (East) & Colossal Cave Mountain Park
Grande Ave.
Congress
Historic Districts
Broadway Blvd.
Reid Park
Sentinel Peak Park
22nd St.
Wilmot Rd.
Tucson Greyhound Park
36th St.
Golf Links Rd.
Escalante Rd.
Pantano Rd.
Camino Seco
Ajo Way
Irvington Rd.
Kino Blvd.
DAVIS MONTHAN AFB
Drexel Rd.
Palo Verde Rd.
12th Ave.
6th Ave.
Valencia Rd.
Los Reales Rd.
Tucson International Airport
To Nogales
Flagstaff
ARIZONA
Phoenix
Tucson
0 2 mi
0 2 km
10
19
210
11 12 13 14 15 16 17 18 19 20 21 22 23 24 25 26 27 28

FROM LEFT: **The hummingbird aviary at the Arizona-Sonora Desert Museum; Sabino Canyon Recreation Area.**

Colossal Cave Mountain Park ☺ It seems nearly every cave in the Southwest has its legends of bandits and buried loot, and Colossal Cave is no exception. A tour through this cavern, which isn't exactly colossal but is certainly impressive, combines a bit of Western lore with a bit of geology for an experience that both kids and adults will enjoy. Although there was much damage to the formations here before the cave was protected, the narrow passageways and dramatic lighting keep the 45-minute tours interesting. For more adventurous types, there are tours into little-visited parts of the cave. This private park also offers horseback riding ($27 for a 1-hr. ride) and has a small museum and picnic areas as well as snack bars.

16721 E. Old Spanish Trail Rd., Vail. ✆ **520/647-7275.** www.colossalcave.com. Cave tours $11 adults, $6 children 5–12, in addition to $5 per car for park entry. Mar 16–Sept 15 daily 8am–5pm; Sept 16–Mar 15 daily 9am–5pm. Take Old Spanish Trail southeast from east Tucson, or take I-10 and get off at the Vail exit.

Sabino Canyon Recreation Area ★★ At the base of the Santa Catalina Mountains on the northeastern edge of the city, Sabino Canyon is a desert oasis and, with its impressive desert scenery, hiking trails, and stream, is a fabulous place to commune with the desert for a morning or an afternoon. The chance to splash in the canyon's waterfalls and swim in natural pools (water conditions permitting) attracts many visitors, but it is just as enjoyable simply to gaze at the

Driving the Catalina Highway

Within a span of only 25 miles, the Catalina Highway climbs roughly 1 mile in elevation from the lowland desert landscape of cacti and ocotillo bushes to forests of ponderosa pines. Passing through several different life zones, this route is the equivalent of driving from Mexico to Canada. When you look at it this way, the $5 use fee for stopping at overlooks along this highway is small compared to what a flight to Canada would cost (and that fee will also get you into Sabino Canyon). Along the way, there are numerous overlooks, some of which are nauseatingly vertiginous. Other spots are particularly popular with rock climbers. There are numerous hiking trails, picnic areas, and campgrounds along the route. For more information, contact the **Coronado National Forest Santa Catalina Ranger District,** 5700 N. Sabino Canyon Rd. (✆ **520/749-8700;** www.fs.fed.us/r3/coronado).

beauty of crystal-clear water flowing through a rocky canyon guarded by saguaro cacti. There are numerous picnic tables in the canyon, and many miles of hiking trails wind their way into the mountains from here, making it one of the best places in the city for a day hike.

A narrated tram shuttles visitors up and down the lower canyon throughout the day, and between April and November (but not July or Aug), there are moonlight tram rides three times each month (usually the nights before the full moon). The Bear Canyon tram is used by hikers heading to the picturesque Seven Falls, which are at the end of a 2.5-mile trail and are my favorite destination within this recreation area.

Another good way to experience the park is by bicycling up the paved road during the limited hours when bikes are allowed: Sunday through Tuesday, Thursday, and Friday before 9am and after 5pm. This is a strenuous uphill ride for most of the way, but the scenery is beautiful.

5900 N. Sabino Canyon Rd. ✆ **520/749-8700,** 749-2861 for shuttle information, or 749-2327 for moonlight shuttle reservations. www.fs.fed.us/r3/coronado or www.sabinocanyon.com. Parking $5 (also good for driving the Catalina Hwy.). Sabino Canyon tram ride $8 adults, $4 children 3–12; Bear Canyon tram ride $3 adults, $1 children 3–12. Park daily dawn–dusk. Sabino Canyon tram rides daily 9am–4:30pm (July to mid-Dec Mon–Fri 9am–4pm, Sat–Sun and holidays 9am–4:30pm). Bear Canyon tram rides daily 9am–4:30pm. Take Grant Rd. east to Tanque Verde Rd., continuing east; at Sabino Canyon Rd., turn north and watch for the sign.

Saguaro National Park ★★★ Saguaro cacti are the quintessential symbol of the American desert and occur naturally only here in the Sonoran Desert. Sensitive to fire and frost, and exceedingly slow to mature, these massive, treelike cacti grow in great profusion around Tucson but have long been threatened by both development and plant collectors. In 1933, to protect these desert giants, the federal government set aside two large tracts of land as a saguaro preserve. This preserve eventually became Saguaro National Park. The two units of the park, one on the east side of the city (Rincon Mountain District) and one on the west (Tucson Mountain District), preserve not only dense stands of saguaros, but also the many other wild inhabitants of this part of the Sonoran Desert. Both units have loop roads, nature trails, hiking trails, and picnic grounds.

Sunset on Signal Hill

A hike to Signal Hill, located off the Bajada Loop Drive in Saguaro National Park's west unit and only a quarter-mile walk from the parking area, will reward you with not only a grand sunset vista away from the crowds at Gates Pass, but also the sight of dozens of petroglyphs.

The west unit of the park, because of its proximity to both the Arizona–Sonora Desert Museum and Old Tucson Studios, is the more popular area to visit (and your best choice if you're trying to do a lot in a short amount of time). This also happens to be where you'll see the most impressive stands of saguaros. Be sure to take the scenic Bajada Loop Drive, where you'll find good views and several hiking trails (the Hugh Morris Trail involves a long, steep climb, but great views are the reward). To reach the west unit of the park, follow Speedway Boulevard west from downtown Tucson (it becomes Gates Pass Blvd.).

The east section of the park contains an older area of saguaro "forest" at the foot of the Rincon Mountains. This section is popular with hikers because most of it has no roads. It has a visitor center, a loop scenic drive, a picnic area, and a trail open to mountain bikes (the paved loop drive is a great road-bike ride). To reach the east unit of the park, take Speedway Boulevard east, then head south on Freeman Road to Old Spanish Trail.

Rincon Mountain District visitor center: 3693 S. Old Spanish Trail. ✆ **520/733-5153.** Tucson Mountain District visitor center: 2700 N. Kinney Rd. ✆ **520/733-5158.** www.nps.gov/sagu. Entry fee $10 per car, $5 per hiker or biker. Daily 7am–sunset; visitor centers daily 9am–5pm; open to hikers 24 hr. a day. Visitor centers closed Christmas.

Historic Attractions Both Real & Reel

Mission San Xavier del Bac ★★★ Called the White Dove of the Desert, Mission San Xavier del Bac, an active Roman Catholic church serving the San Xavier Indian Reservation, is a blindingly white adobe building that rises from a sere, brown landscape. Considered the finest example of mission architecture in the Southwest, the beautiful church was built between 1783 and 1797, and incorporates Moorish, Byzantine, and Mexican Renaissance architectural styles. The church, however, was never actually completed, which becomes apparent only when the two bell towers are compared. One is topped with a dome, while the other has none.

Colorful murals cover the interior walls, and behind the altar are elaborate decorations. To the left of the main altar, in a glass sarcophagus, is a statue of St. Francis Xavier, the mission's patron saint, who is believed to answer the prayers of the faithful. A visit to San Xavier's little museum provides a bit of historical perspective and a chance to explore more of the mission. To the east of the church, atop a small hill, you'll find not only an interesting view of the church, but also a replica of the famous grotto in Lourdes, France. There are often food stalls selling fry bread in the parking lot in front of the church.

1950 W. San Xavier Rd. ✆ **520/294-2624.** www.sanxaviermission.org. Free admission; donations accepted. Daily 7am–5pm. Take I-19 south 9 miles to exit 92 and turn right.

Colorful murals cover the interior of the Mission San Xavier del Bac.

Seeing It All from "A Mountain"

The best way to get a feel for the geography of the Tucson area is to drive to the top of a mountain—but not just any mountain. "A Mountain" (officially called Sentinel Peak) rises just to the west of downtown Tucson on the far side of I-10. The peak gets its common name from the giant whitewashed letter *A* (for University of Arizona) near the summit. To get here, drive west to the end of Congress Street and turn left on Sentinel Peak Road. The park is open Monday through Saturday from 8am to 8pm and Sunday from 8am to 6pm.

Old Tucson Studios ★ ☺ Despite the name, this is not the historical location of the old city of Tucson—it's a Western town originally built as the set for the 1939 movie *Arizona.* In the years since, Old Tucson has been used during the filming of John Wayne's *Rio Lobo, Rio Bravo,* and *El Dorado;* Clint Eastwood's *The Outlaw Josey Wales;* Kirk Douglas's *Gunfight at the O.K. Corral;* Paul Newman's *The Life and Times of Judge Roy Bean;* and, more recently, *Tombstone* and *Geronimo.*

Today, however, Old Tucson is far more than just a movie set. In addition to serving as a site for film, TV, and advertising productions (call ahead to find out if any filming is scheduled), it has become a Wild West theme park with diverse family-oriented activities and entertainment. Throughout the day, there are staged shootouts in the streets, stunt demonstrations, a cancan musical revue, and other performances. Train and kiddie rides, restaurants, and gift shops round out the experience. Currently, the studios are open on a limited basis on Tuesday and Wednesday and are open for tours only.

201 S. Kinney Rd. ✆ **520/883-0100.** www.oldtucson.com. Admission $17 adults, $11 children 4–11 (Tues–Wed $8.75 adults, $5 children ages 4–11). Daily 10am–4pm to 6pm (seasonal; contact for hours). Closed Thanksgiving, Dec 24–25, and occasional special events. Take Speedway Blvd. west, continuing in the same direction when it becomes Gates Pass Blvd., and turn left on S. Kinney Rd.

Art Museums

Center for Creative Photography Have you ever wished you could see an original Ansel Adams print up close, or perhaps an Edward Weston or a Richard Avedon? You can at the Center for Creative Photography. Originally conceived by Ansel Adams, the center now holds more than 80,000 master prints by more than 2,000 of the world's best photographers, making it one of the best and largest collections in the world. The center mounts fascinating exhibits year-round and is also a research facility that preserves the photographic archives of more than 50 photographers, including Adams. While the main gallery is open on a regular basis, you must make an appointment to view images from the archives.

University of Arizona campus, 1030 N. Olive Rd. (east of Park Ave. and Speedway Blvd.). ✆ **520/621-7968.** www.creativephotography.org. Admission by donation. Mon–Fri 9am–5pm; Sat–Sun 1–4pm. Closed major holidays. Bus: 1, 4, 5, or 6.

De Grazia Gallery in the Sun Southwestern artist Ettore "Ted" De Grazia was a Tucson favorite son, and his home, a sprawling, funky adobe building in the foothills, is a city landmark and now serves as a museum for this prolific artist. De Grazia is said to be the most reproduced artist in the world because many of his images of big-eyed children were used as greeting cards during the 1950s and 1960s. Today De Grazia's images seem trite and maudlin, but in his day he was a

The Palice Pavilion—Art of the Americas exhibit at the Tucson Museum of Art.

The pottery at the Arizona State Museum spans 2,000 years.

very successful artist. This gallery is packed with original paintings, so it may surprise you to learn that, near the end of his life, De Grazia burned several hundred thousand dollars' worth of his paintings in a protest of IRS inheritance taxes. The gift shop has lots of reproductions and other objects with De Grazia images. 6300 N. Swan Rd. ✆ **800/545-2185** or 520/299-9191. www.degrazia.org. Free admission. Daily 10am–4pm. Closed New Year's Day, Easter, Thanksgiving, and Christmas.

Tucson Museum of Art & Historic Block ★ This museum complex includes galleries housed in historic adobe homes, a courtyard frequently used to display sculptures, and a large modern building that often mounts the most interesting exhibits in town. The Palice Pavilion—Art of the Americas exhibit, which consists of a large collection of pre-Columbian art that represents 3,000 years of life in Mexico and Central and South America, is a highlight of the museum. This collection is housed in the historic Stevens/Duffield House, which also contains Spanish colonial artifacts and Latin American folk art. The noteworthy Goodman Pavilion of Western Art comprises an extensive collection that depicts cowboys, horses, and the wide-open spaces of the American West. The museum has preserved a total of five historic homes on this same block, and all are open to the public. See "History Museums & Landmark Buildings," below, for details.

Art in the Open Air

Although it isn't very big, the **Jewish Community Center Sculpture Park,** 3800 E. River Rd. (✆ **520/299-3000;** www.tucsonjcc.org/arts/sculpture-garden), manages to exhibit some excellent sculptures and is well worth wandering through. Because it is just off the Rillito River Park path, you can combine a visit to the sculpture park with a walk or bike ride along the dry river bed. You'll find the community center at the north end of North Dodge Boulevard.

140 N. Main Ave. ✆ **520/624-2333.** www.tucsonmuseumofart.org. Admission $8 adults, $6 seniors, $3 students, free for children 12 and under; free on 1st Sun of each month. Tues-Sat 10am-5pm; Sun noon-5pm. Closed Thanksgiving, Christmas. Bus: All downtown-bound buses.

The University of Arizona Museum of Art ★★ With European and American works dating from the Renaissance up to the 20th century, the art collections at this museum are even more extensive and diverse than those of the Tucson Museum of Art. Tintoretto, Rembrandt, Picasso, O'Keeffe, Warhol, and Rothko are all represented. Another attraction, the *Retablo of Ciudad Rodrigo,* consists of 26 paintings from 15th-century Spain that were originally placed above a cathedral altar. The museum also has an extensive collection of 20th-century sculpture that includes more than 60 clay and plaster models and sketches by Jacques Lipchitz.

University of Arizona campus, 1031 N. Olive Rd. (at Park Ave. and Speedway Blvd.). ✆ **520/621-7567.** www.artmuseum.arizona.edu. Admission $5 adults, free for students and children. Tues-Fri 9am-5pm; Sat-Sun noon-4pm. Closed major holidays. Bus: 1, 4, 5, or 6.

History Museums & Landmark Buildings

Among the more interesting buildings are those maintained by the Tucson Museum of Art and located on the block surrounding the museum. These restored homes date from 1850 to 1907, and are all built on the former site of the Tucson presidio. A map and brochures are available at the museum's front desk, and October through April, guided tours of the historic block and Corbett House are available (free with museum admission).

Arizona Historical Society Downtown History Museum If you want to learn more about the history of Tucson, this is the museum to visit. Exhibits cover Spanish presidio days, American army days, merchants, and schools. Through the use of artifacts and old photos, these exhibits help bring the city's past to life. One of the most curious exhibits focuses on the gangster John Dillinger, who was arrested here in Tucson.

140 N. Stone Ave. ✆ **520/770-1473.** www.arizonahistoricalsociety.org. Admission $3 adults, $2 seniors and students ages 12-18, free for children 11 and under; free on 1st Fri of each month. Tues-Fri 10am-4pm. Closed major holidays. Bus: All downtown-bound buses.

Arizona History Museum As the state's oldest historical museum, this repository of all things Arizonan is a treasure-trove for the history buff. If you've never explored a real mine, you can do the next best thing by exploring the museum's full-scale reproduction of an underground mine tunnel. You'll see an assayer's office, miner's tent, stamp mill, and blacksmith's shop in the mining exhibit. A transportation exhibit displays stagecoaches and the horseless carriages that revolutionized life in the Southwest, while a range of temporary exhibits give a pretty good idea of what it was like back then.

949 E. 2nd St. ✆ **520/628-5774.** www.arizonahistoricalsociety.org. Admission $5 adults, $4 seniors and students ages 12-18, free for children 11 and under; free for all 1st Sat of each month. Mon-Sat 10am-4pm. Closed major holidays. Bus: 1, 4, 5, or 6.

Arizona State Museum This museum, which is the oldest anthropological museum in the Southwest, houses Paths of Life: American Indians of the Southwest, one of the state's most interesting exhibits on prehistoric and contemporary Native American cultures of the Southwest. The exhibit focuses on 10 different tribes from around the Southwest and northern Mexico, not only displaying a wide range of artifacts, but also exploring the lifestyles and cultural traditions of Indians living in the region today. In addition, the museum showcases a collection of some 20,000 ceramic pieces. This pottery spans 2,000 years of life in the desert Southwest.

University of Arizona campus, 1013 E. University Blvd. at Park Ave. ✆ **520/621-6302.** www.statemuseum.arizona.edu. Admission $5 adults, free for children 17 and under. Mon–Sat 10am–5pm. Closed major holidays. Bus: 1, 4, 5, or 6.

THE shrine THAT STOPPED A FREEWAY

The southern Arizona landscape is dotted with roadside shrines, symbols of the region's Hispanic and Roman Catholic heritage. Most are simple crosses decorated with plastic flowers and dedicated to people who have been killed in auto accidents. One shrine, however, stands out from all the rest. It is Tucson's **El Tiradito** (the Castaway), which is dedicated to a sinner. Not only does this crumbling shrine attract the devout, but it once also stopped a freeway.

El Tiradito, on South Granada Avenue at West Cushing Street, is the only shrine in the United States dedicated to a sinner buried in unconsecrated soil. Several stories tell of how this shrine came to be, but the most popularly accepted one tells of a young shepherd who fell in love with his mother-in-law sometime in the 1880s. When the father-in-law found his wife in the arms of this young man, he shot the son-in-law. The young shepherd stumbled from his in-laws' house and fell dead beside the dusty street. Because he had been caught in the act of adultery and died without confessing his sins, his body could not be interred in the church cemetery, so he was buried where he fell.

The people of the neighborhood soon began burning candles on the spot to try to save the soul of the young man, and eventually people began burning candles in hopes that their own wishes would come true. They believed that if the candle burned through the night, their prayers would be answered. The shrine eventually grew into a substantial little structure, and in 1927 was dedicated by its owner to the city of Tucson. In 1940, the shrine became an official Tucson monument.

However, such status was not enough to protect the shrine from urban renewal, and when the federal government announced that it would level the shrine when it built a new freeway through the center of Tucson, the city's citizens were outraged. Their activities and protests led the shrine to be named to the National Register of Historic Places, and, subsequently, the freeway was moved a few hundred yards to the west.

To this day, devout Catholics from the surrounding neighborhood still burn candles at the shrine that stopped a freeway. A visit after dark, perhaps in conjunction with dinner next door at El Minuto (p. 419), a popular Mexican restaurant, is a somber experience that will easily convince you of how important this shrine is to the neighborhood.

Passport to Tucson

The Tucson Attractions Passport is a great way to save money on admissions to many of the city's top attractions. The passport, available at the downtown Visitors Center, 100 S. Church Ave. (✆ 800/638-8350 or 520/624-1817; www.tucsonpassport.com), costs $15 and gets you two-for-one admissions to the Arizona-Sonora Desert Museum, Old Tucson Studios, Biosphere 2, the Pima Air & Space Museum, Tohono Chul Park, the Tucson Museum of Art, Kartchner Caverns State Park, and many other attractions in Tucson and across southern Arizona.

Fort Lowell Museum Located in Fort Lowell Park, this museum is on the site of a cavalry outpost that was in operation between 1873 and 1891. The museum chronicles the history of life at the fort, and some of the ruins of the original fort can still be seen. Before it was a fort, this site was a Hohokam village, and artifacts uncovered from archaeological digs are also on display. Renowned medical researcher Walter Reed, who discovered how yellow fever is transmitted, served as base surgeon here in 1876. A display focusing on medical facilities at the fort explains that, despite Hollywood's version of history, illness, not injury from Indian attacks, was the biggest medical problem during the wars with the Apaches.

2900 N. Craycroft Rd. ✆ **520/885-3832.** www.arizonahistoricalsociety.org. Admission $3 adults, $2 seniors and students ages 12–18, free for children 11 and under; free for all 1st Sat of each month. Fri–Sat 10am–4pm. Closed major holidays. Bus: 34.

Presidio San Agustin del Tucson This reconstruction of part of the Spanish fort that was the birthplace of Tucson is the best place to start a tour of downtown or to learn about the early history of this city. The presidio (fort) is built of adobe blocks, and within the walls and in an adjacent adobe building, you'll find displays on the early history of Tucson. Most months between fall and spring, there is a Saturday living-history event here.

133 W. Washington St. ✆ **520/791-4873.** http://cms3.tucsonaz.gov/parksandrec/el-presidio. Free admission. Wed–Sun 9am–4:30pm. Bus: All downtown-bound buses.

Southern Arizona Transportation Museum Housed in a building adjacent to the former Southern Pacific Railroad Depot, which was built in 1941, this little museum is worth a visit as much for the opportunity to wander around the depot grounds as to see the museum's exhibits, which focus on the history of the railroad in southern Arizona. On the grounds are an old steam engine (open to the public Sat 10am–1pm) and a statue of Doc Holliday and Wyatt Earp.

414 N. Toole Ave. ✆ **520/623-2223.** www.tucsonhistoricdepot.org. Free admission. Tues–Thurs 11am–3pm; Fri–Sat 10am–4pm; Sun 11am–3pm. Bus: All downtown-bound buses.

Tucson Rodeo Parade Museum A parade must be pretty special to warrant its own museum, and Tucson's Fiesta de los Vaqueros Rodeo Parade is indeed special. It's the longest nonmotorized parade in the country and includes all manner of horse-drawn carriages, buggies, and wagons. If you aren't in town for the rodeo, you can still see lots of those old horse-drawn vehicles at this museum. Included in the collection is the original surrey with the fringe on top that was used in the filming of *Oklahoma!* (which was shot not in Oklahoma but in southern Arizona near the town of Patagonia). There's also a beautiful carriage that was used by Ava Gardner during the filming of *The Life and Times of Judge Roy Bean.* There are more than 150 vehicles on display here, as well as a wide variety of other displays focusing on the early history of Tucson. The only drawback of this fascinating museum is that it's open for only a couple of months each year (early Jan to mid-Mar).

4823 S. 6th Ave. ✆ **520/294-3636.** www.tucsonrodeoparade.com. Admission $10 adults, $2 children 15 and under. Mon–Sat 9:30am–3:30pm (11am–1pm during rodeo week). Closed mid-Apr to early Jan, and certain days during rodeo week (late Feb). Bus: 6, 8, 11, or 26.

Science & Technology Museums

Biosphere 2 For 2 years, beginning in September 1991, four men and four women were locked inside this airtight, 3-acre greenhouse in the desert 35 miles north of Tucson near the town of Oracle. During their tenure in Biosphere 2 (earth is considered Biosphere 1), they conducted experiments on how the earth, basically a giant greenhouse, manages to support all the planet's life forms. Today there are no longer any people living in Biosphere 2, and the former research facility is operated more as a tourist attraction than as a science center. Tours take visitors inside the giant greenhouse and into the mechanisms that helped keep this sealed environment going for 2 years. The strangest sight is the giant "lung" that allowed for the expansion and contraction of the air within Biosphere 2. Although the building, which is in the middle of desert hill country, is an impressive sight, the tours are something of a letdown.

32540 S. Biosphere Rd., Oracle (off Ariz. 77 at mile marker 96.5). ✆ **520/838-6200.** www.b2science.org. Admission $20 adults, $18 seniors, $13 children 6–12. Daily 9am–4pm. Closed Thanksgiving and Christmas. Take Oracle Rd. north out of Tucson and continue north on Ariz. 77 until you see the sign.

Flandrau: The UA Science Center Located on the University of Arizona campus, Flandrau is the most convenient place in Arizona to do a little stargazing through a professional telescope. On clear nights, astronomers train the science center's 16-inch telescope on whatever objects in the night sky are most interesting. You might get a close-up look at the craters of the moon or the rings of Saturn. The science center also has a large mineral collection, and there are laser-light shows Thursday through Saturday evenings.

University of Arizona campus, 1601 E. University Blvd., at Cherry Ave. ✆ **520/621-7827.** www.flandrau.org. $7.50 adults, $5 children 4–15, free for children 4 and under; telescope viewing free. Mon–Tues 10am–3pm; Wed 10am–3pm and 7–10pm; Thurs–Fri 10am–3pm and 6–10pm; Sat 10am–10pm; Sun 1–4pm. Telescope viewing (weather permitting) Wed–Sat 7–10pm. Closed major holidays. Bus: 1, 3, 4, 5, 6, 9, 15, or 20.

The International Wildlife Museum This castlelike building (modeled after a French Foreign Legion fort), located on the road that leads to the Arizona–Sonora Desert Museum, is a natural-history museum filled with stuffed animals in lifelike poses and surroundings. Animals from all over the world are displayed, and there are exhibits of extinct animals, including the Irish elk and the woolly mammoth. Among the more lifelike displays are the predator-and-prey exhibits. There are also fascinating exhibits of butterflies and other unusual insects.

4800 W. Gates Pass Rd. ✆ **520/629-0100.** www.thewildlifemuseum.org. Admission $8 adults, $6 seniors, $3 children 4–12. Mon–Fri 9am–5pm; Sat–Sun 9am–6pm. Closed Thanksgiving and Christmas. Take Speedway Blvd. west, continuing in the same direction when it becomes Gates Pass Blvd. The museum is 5 miles west of I-10.

Pima Air & Space Museum ★ Located just south of Davis-Monthan Air Force Base, the Pima Air & Space Museum houses one of the largest collections of

historic aircraft in the world. On display are more than 275 aircraft, including a mock-up of an X-15A-2 (the world's fastest aircraft), an SR-71 Blackbird, several Russian MIGs, a "Superguppy," and a B-17G "Flying Fortress." Tours are available.

The museum also offers guided tours of Davis-Monthan's AMARG (Arizona Maintenance and Regeneration Group) facility, which goes by the name of the Boneyard. Here, thousands of mothballed military planes are lined up in neat rows under the Arizona sun. Tours, offered Monday through Friday, last about 90 minutes and cost $7 for adults and $4 for children 12 and under.

6000 E. Valencia Rd. ✆ **520/574-0462.** www.pimaair.org. Admission Nov–May $16 adults, $13 seniors and military, $9 children 7–12; June–Oct $14 adults, $12 seniors and military, $8 children 7–12. Daily 9am–5pm. Closed Thanksgiving and Christmas. Take the Valencia Rd. exit from I-10 and drive east 2 miles to the museum.

FROM TOP: **Titan Missile Museum; the Tohono Chul Park blooms with wildflowers in spring.**

Titan Missile Museum ★ If you've ever wondered what it would be like to have your finger on the button of a nuclear missile, here's your opportunity to find out. This deactivated intercontinental ballistic missile (ICBM) silo is now a museum—and is the only museum in the country that allows visitors to descend into a former missile silo. There's a huge Titan missile on display, and, even without its nuclear warhead, it is a terrifying sight. The guided tours do a great job of explaining not only the ICBM system, but also what life was like for the people who worked here. Operated by the Pima Air & Space Museum, this museum is located 25 miles south of Tucson near the community of Green Valley. On the

Mirror, Mirror in the Hall

The mountaintops of southern Arizona are dotted with astronomical observatories, and one thing many of these have in common is that they use massive glass mirrors to reflect the light of distant stars. At the University of Arizona's Steward Observatory Mirror Lab (✆ 520/626-8792; http://mirrorlab.as.arizona.edu), you can tour a facility that has made mirrors for telescopes all over the world. Keep in mind that some of these mirrors are more than 25 feet in diameter. The mirrors are cast and polished inside a facility *under* the east wing of the UA football stadium (not actually a hall). Tuesday through Friday at 1 and 3pm, there are 90-minute tours of the mirror lab ($15 adults; $8 children and students 8–22). Reservations are required.

first and third Saturday of each month, there are Beyond the Blast Door tours, which take visitors into areas not on the normal tour. There are also Top to Bottom Tours on certain weekends and Moonlight Madness Tours in summer.

1580 W. Duval Mine Rd., Sahuarita (exit 69 off I-19). ✆ **520/625-7736.** www.titanmissilemuseum.org. Admission $9.50 adults, $8.50 seniors, $6 children 7–12; Beyond the Blast Door Tour $18 adults, $16 seniors, $10 children 8–12. Daily 8:45am–5:30pm. Closed Thanksgiving and Christmas. Take I-19 south to Green Valley; take exit 69 west a half-mile to main entrance.

Parks, Gardens & Zoos

See "The Tucson Area's (Mostly) Natural Wonders," earlier in this chapter, for details on the Arizona–Sonora Desert Museum, the region's premier zoo.

Reid Park Zoo ☺ Although small and overshadowed by the Arizona–Sonora Desert Museum, the Reid Park Zoo makes a fun in-town destination if you have the kids along. The zoo has good Africa, Asia, and South America enclosures that include African and Asian elephants, white rhinoceroses, giraffes, anteaters, capybaras (the largest rodents in the world), and rheas (sort of like ostriches). Get here early, when the animals are more active and before the crowds hit. If you've got the kids along, there's a good playground in the adjacent park.

1100 S. Randolph Way (at 22nd St. btw. Country Club Rd. and Alvernon Way). ✆ **520/791-4022.** www.tucsonzoo.org. Admission $7 adults, $5 seniors, $3 children 2–14. Daily 9am–4pm. Closed Thanksgiving and Christmas. Bus: 7.

Tohono Chul Park ★ Although this park covers fewer than 50 acres, it provides an excellent introduction to the plant and animal life of the desert. You'll see a forest of cholla cacti as well as a garden of small pincushion cacti. From mid-February to April, the wildflower displays here are gorgeous (if enough rain has fallen in the previous months). The park also includes an ethnobotanical garden; a garden for children that encourages them to touch, listen, and smell; a demonstration garden; natural areas; an exhibit house for art displays; a tearoom that's great for breakfast, lunch, or afternoon tea; and two very good gift shops. Park docents lead guided tours throughout the day. Special events take place throughout the cooler months of the year.

7366 N. Paseo del Norte (off Ina Rd. west of the intersection with Oracle Rd.). ✆ **520/742-6455.** www.tohonochulpark.org. Admission $7 adults, $5 seniors, $3 students, $2 children ages 5–12. Grounds daily 8am–5pm. Exhibit house daily 9am–5pm. Tearoom daily 8am–5pm. Buildings closed New Year's Day, July 4th, Thanksgiving, and Christmas (free admission to grounds on these days).

Tucson Botanical Gardens ☺ Set amid residential neighborhoods in midtown Tucson, these gardens are an oasis of greenery and, though small, are well worth a visit if you're interested in desert plant life, landscaping, or gardening. On the 5½-acre grounds, there are a dozen different gardens that not only have visual appeal, but also are educational. You can learn about creating a garden for birds or for butterflies, and then see what sort of crops the Native Americans of this region have traditionally grown. A sensory garden stimulates all five senses. A toy train layout and a tropical butterfly house (open fall through spring) make this a surprisingly good place to bring the kids.

2150 N. Alvernon Way. ✆ **520/326-9686.** www.tucsonbotanical.org. Admission $8 adults, $4 children 4–12. Daily 8:30am–4:30pm. Closed New Year's Day, July 4th, Thanksgiving, and Dec 24–25. Bus: 9 or 11.

Especially for Kids

In addition to the museums listed below, two of the greatest places to take kids in the Tucson area are the Arizona–Sonora Desert Museum and Old Tucson Studios. Kids will also get a kick out of the Sabino Canyon tram ride, the Reid Park Zoo, Flandrau Science Center & Planetarium, and the Pima Air & Space Museum. All are described in detail earlier in this chapter.

They'll also enjoy **Trail Dust Town,** 6541 E. Tanque Verde Rd. (✆ **520/296-4551;** www.traildusttown.com), a Wild West–themed shopping and dining center. It has a full-size carousel, a miniature train to ride, the Museum of the Horse Soldier (open daily 1–7pm; $2 admission), shootout shows, and a family steakhouse. Basically, it's a sort of scaled-down Old Tucson. If the kids are into miniature golf, take them to **Golf n' Stuff,** 6503 E. Tanque Verde Rd. (✆ **520/296-2366;** www.golfnstuff.com), which is right next door to Trail Dust Town. Not only are there two miniature-golf courses, but there are also bumper boats, go-karts, batting cages, laser tag, a climbing wall, and a video-game arcade. Between these two side-by-side attractions, you've got plenty to keep the family entertained for hours.

All Aboard!

If you've got kids who idolize Thomas the Tank Engine, then you'd better schedule your Tucson visit for the second or fourth Sunday of the month. On those days (with a few exceptions), the **Gadsden-Pacific Division Toy Train Operating Museum,** 3975 N. Miller Ave. (✆ **520/888-2222;** www.gpdtoytrainmuseum.com/toytrains), sends out little engines that think they can. The trains chug around a variety of layouts built in different model-railroad gauges. On the 2 days each month that it is open, the museum's hours are from 12:30 to 4:30pm. Admission is free. In July and August, the museum is closed.

Breakers Water Park If your family vacation plans have you visiting Tucson in the summer, don't despair that you'll be stuck inside air-conditioned buildings the whole time. Keep cool at this water park. Breakers has the largest wave pool in Arizona. There are also lots of water slides and a water-play area for toddlers.

8555 W. Tangerine Rd., Marana. ✆ **520/682-2304.** www.breakerswaterpark.com. Admission $20 ages 12 and older, $14 children 4–11, $10 seniors. After 3pm, $12 general admission. Tues–Sun 10am–6pm. Closed early Sept to late May.

Children's Museum Tucson This museum, in the historic Carnegie Library in downtown Tucson, is filled with fun and educational hands-on activities. Exhibits include a music room, a room where kids can paint with light, an enchanted rainforest, an ocean discovery center, and an electricity gallery. Expect to find such perennial kid favorites as a firetruck, a toy train, and dinosaur sculptures. Activities are featured daily.

200 S. 6th Ave. ✆ **520/792-9985.** www.tucsonchildrensmuseum.org. Admission $8 adults, $6 seniors and children 2–18. Tues–Fri 9am–5pm; Sat–Sun 10am–5pm. Closed Easter, Thanksgiving, and Christmas. Bus: All downtown-bound buses.

The Mini-Time Machine Museum of Miniatures Okay, so maybe adults will like this museum as much, or more, than kids. Still, a museum full of dollhouses seems like a museum for children, even if one of the dollhouses is 200 years old. This private museum is filled with more than 200 miniature houses, including a rococo palace, an old English pub, and a Craftsman bungalow patterned after Pasadena's famous Gamble house, which was designed by architects Charles and Henry Greene. There are miniature houses from all over the world, including a Mexican cantina and Thai spirit houses. One wing of the museum is devoted to haunted and enchanted houses that are full of witches and fairies. Keep an eye out for the miniature violin-maker's studio inside an actual violin.

4455 E. Camp Lowell Dr. ✆ **520/881-0606.** www.theminitimemachine.org. Admission $7 adults, $6 seniors, $5 children 4–17. Tues–Sat 9am–4pm. Closed major holidays. Bus: 34.

ORGANIZED TOURS

With desert mountain ranges encircling the city, Tucson is a great place for a rugged off-road adventure. To explore some rugged sections of the Sonoran Desert, contact **Black Diamond Hummer Tours** (✆ **520/907-1061;** www.bdhummertours.com). Owner Dolores Zimmerman is a former NASCAR stock-car racer, and she loves to show off both the desert and the capabilities of her company's Hummers.

If you're more interested in the history of Tucson, join a walking tour of the Old Pueblo. Between late October and mid-April, the **Arizona Historical Society** (✆ **520/770-1473;** www.arizonahistoricalsociety.org/education) offers a variety of 2-hour tours around some of the city's historic districts. Tours begin at the Arizona Historical Society Downtown History Museum and cost $10 for adults (children 10 and under are free). Tours of downtown Tucson are also offered several times each week by local historian Ken Scoville of **Old Pueblo Walking tours** (✆ **520/358-850**), who charges $15 per person for his tours.

For a look at a completely different sort of excavation, head 15 miles south of Tucson to the **ASARCO Mineral Discovery Center,** 1421 W. Pima Mine Rd., Sahuarita (✆ **520/625-7513;** www.mineraldiscovery.com), where you can tour a huge open-pit copper mine and learn about copper mining past and present. The center is open Tuesday through Saturday from 9am to 5pm; admission is free. The 1-hour mine tours are offered four times a day (call for summer days and hours). These tours cost $8 for adults, $6 for seniors, and $5 for children 5 to 12. To get here, drive south from Tucson on I-19 and take exit 80. You might want to combine this tour with a visit to the nearby Titan Missile Museum.

Learning Expeditions, a program run by the **Arizona State Museum,** occasionally offers scholar-led archaeological tours. For information, contact the marketing department at the museum (✆ **520/626-8381;** www.statemuseum.arizona.edu).

OUTDOOR PURSUITS

BICYCLING Tucson is one of the best bicycling cities in the country, and the dirt roads and trails of the surrounding national forest and desert are perfect for mountain biking. At **Fair Wheel Bikes,** 1110 E. Sixth St. (✆ **520/884-9018;** www.fairwheelbikes.com), bikes rent for $45 to $65 per day.

If you'd rather confine your pedaling to paved surfaces, there are some great options around town. The number-one choice in town for cyclists in halfway decent shape is the road up **Sabino Canyon** (p. 434). Keep in mind, however, that bicycles are allowed on this road only 5 days a week and then only before 9am and after 5pm (the road is closed to bikes all day Wed and Sat). For a much easier ride, try the **Rillito River Park path,** which is paved for 12 miles between Craycroft Road and I-10. The trail parallels River Road and the usually dry bed of the Rillito River.

There are lots of great mountain-bike rides in the Tucson area, too. For an easy and very scenic dirt-road loop through forests of saguaros, head to the west unit of Saguaro National Park (p. 435) and ride the 6-mile **Bajada Loop Drive.** You can turn this into a 12-mile ride (half on paved road) by starting at the Red Hills Visitor Center.

BIRD-WATCHING Southern Arizona has some of the best bird-watching in the country, and although the best spots are south of Tucson, there are a few places around the city that birders will enjoy seeking out. Call the **Tucson Audubon Society's Rare Bird Alert** (✆ **520/629-0510;** www.tucsonaudubon.org) to find out which birds have been spotted in the area lately.

For the best bird-watching in the area, head to Madera Canyon.

The city's premier birding spot is the **Sweetwater Wetland,** a man-made wetland just west of I-10 and north of Prince Road. These wetlands were created as part of a wastewater treatment facility and now have an extensive network of trails that wind past numerous ponds and canals. There are several viewing platforms and enough different types of wildlife habitat that the area attracts a wide variety of bird species. To find the wetlands, take I-10 south to the Prince Road exit, and at the end of the exit ramp, turn right onto Sweetwater Drive. If you're driving west on Prince Road, go to the end of the road, turn right on Business Center Drive, turn left on River Park Road (which becomes Commerce Dr.), take the first left (probably unmarked), and then turn left again on Sweetwater Drive.

Roy P. Drachman Agua Caliente Regional Park, 12325 E. Roger Rd. (off N. Soldier Trail), in the northeast corner of the city, is another great place to do some birding. The year-round warm springs here are a magnet for dozens of species, including waterfowl, great blue herons, black phoebes, soras, and vermilion flycatchers. To find the park, follow Tanque Verde Road east 6 miles from the intersection with Sabino Canyon Road and turn left onto Soldier Trail. Watch for signs.

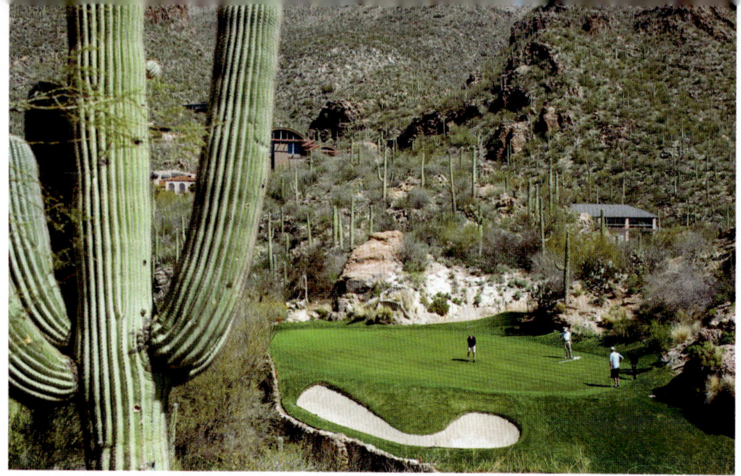

The famous 3rd hole at Ventana Canyon Golf and Racquet Club.

Other good places include **Sabino Canyon Recreation Area** (p. 434), the path to the waterfall at **Loews Ventana Canyon Resort** (p. 408), and the **Rillito River path** between Craycroft and Swan roads.

The best bird-watching in the immediate Tucson area is at **Madera Canyon ★**, which is in **Coronado National Forest** (✆ **520/281-2296;** www.fs.fed.us/r3/coronado), about 40 miles south of the city. Because of the year-round water here, Madera Canyon attracts a surprising variety of bird life. Avid birders from around the country flock to this canyon in hopes of spotting more than a dozen species of hummingbirds and an equal number of flycatchers, warblers, tanagers, buntings, grosbeaks, and many rare birds not found in any other state. However, before birding became a hot activity, this canyon was popular with families looking to escape the heat down in Tucson, and the shady picnic areas and trails still get a lot of use by those who don't carry binoculars. If you're heading out for the day, arrive early—parking is very limited. To reach Madera Canyon, take the Continental Road/Madera Canyon exit off I-19; from the exit, it's another 12 miles southeast. The canyon is open daily from dawn to dusk for day use; there is a $5 day-use fee. There's also a campground (Bog Springs Campground; $10 per night; reservations not accepted). For information on the canyon's Santa Rita Lodge and Chuparosa Inn, see p. 413.

GOLF Although there aren't quite as many golf courses in Tucson as in Phoenix, this is still a golfer's town. For last-minute tee-time reservations, contact **Standby Golf** (✆ **800/655-5345** or 480/874-3133; www.discountteetimes.com). No fee is charged for this service.

In addition to public and municipal links, numerous resort courses allow nonguests to play. Perhaps the most famous of these are the two 18-hole courses at **Ventana Canyon Golf and Racquet Club ★★**, 6200 N. Clubhouse Lane (✆ **520/577-4015;** www.ventanacanyonclub.com). These Tom Fazio–designed courses offer challenging desert-style target play that is nearly legendary. The 3rd hole on the Mountain Course is one of the most photographed holes in the West. In winter, the greens fee is $159 ($99 for twilight play). You'll spend a bit less if you're staying at Loews Ventana Canyon Resort or the Lodge at Ventana Canyon.

As famous as the Ventana Canyon courses is the 27-hole **Omni Tucson National Resort ★**, 2727 W. Club Dr. (✆ **520/575-7540** or 520/297-2271; www.tucsonnational.com), a traditional course that is perhaps more familiar to golfers due to the fact that it was for many years the site of the annual Tucson Open. One of the 9-hole courses here is a desert-style target course, which makes this a good place for an introduction to desert golfing. If you are not staying at the resort, the greens fee is $188 in winter ($102 after 2pm).

El Conquistador Country Club, 10555 N. La Cañada Dr., Oro Valley (✆ **520/544-1801;** www.elconquistadorcc.com), with two 18-hole courses and a 9-hole course, offers stunning (and very distracting) views of the Santa Catalina Mountains. Greens fees are $79 to $99 in winter.

At the 27-hole Arnold Palmer–designed course at **Starr Pass Tucson Golf Club,** 3645 W. Starr Pass Blvd. (✆ **520/670-0400;** www.jwmarriottstarrpass.com/Arizona-Golf-Resort/Starr-Pass-4.html), the fairways play up to the narrow Starr Pass, which was once a stagecoach route. The greens fee is $215 in winter ($120 for twilight play).

There are many public courses around town. The **Arizona National,** 9777 E. Sabino Greens Dr. (✆ **520/749-3636;** www.arizonanationalgolfclub.com), incorporates stands of cacti and rocky outcroppings into the course layout. Greens fees are $79 to $89 in winter. The **Golf Club at Vistoso,** 955 W. Vistoso Highlands Dr. (✆ **520/797-9900;** www.vistosogolf.com), has a championship desert course, with fees of $79 to $89 in winter ($49 for twilight play). **Heritage Highlands at Dove Mountain,** 4949B W. Heritage Club Blvd., Marana (✆ **520/579-7000;** www.heritagehighlands.com), is a championship desert course at the foot of the Tortolita Mountains; greens fee is $71 in winter.

Tucson Parks and Recreation operates five municipal golf courses, of which the **Randolph** and **Dell Urich,** 600 S. Alvernon Way (✆ **520/791-4161**), are the premier courses. The former has been the site of Tucson's LPGA tournament. Greens fees for 18 holes at these two courses are $56 to $80 in winter. Other municipal courses include **El Rio,** 1400 W. Speedway Blvd. (✆ **520/791-4229**); **Silverbell,** 3600 N. Silverbell Rd. (✆ **520/791-5235**); and **Fred Enke,** 8251 E. Irvington Rd. (✆ **520/791-2539**). This latter course is the city's only desert-style golf course. Greens fees for 18 holes at these three courses are $36 to $52 in winter. For general information and tee-time reservations for any of the municipal courses, visit **www.tucsoncitygolf.com**.

HIKING Tucson is one of the country's premier hiking destinations. The city is nearly surrounded by mountains, most of which are protected as city and state parks, national forest, or national park, and within these public areas are hundreds of miles of hiking trails.

Saguaro National Park (✆ **520/733-5153** for the east unit or 520/733-5158 for the west unit; www.nps.gov/sagu) flanks Tucson on both the east and the west, with units accessible off Old Spanish Trail east of Tucson and past the end of Speedway Boulevard west of the city. In these areas, you can observe Sonoran Desert vegetation and wildlife, and hike among the huge saguaro cacti for which the park is named. For saguaro-spotting, the west unit is the better choice. See p. 435 for details.

Hiking Pima Canyon Trail.

Tucson Mountain Park, at the west end of Speedway Boulevard, is adjacent to Saguaro National Park and preserves a similar landscape. The parking area at Gates Pass, on Speedway, is a favorite sunset spot.

Sabino Canyon (p. 434), off Sabino Canyon Road, is one of Tucson's best hiking areas, but is also the city's most popular recreation area. A cold mountain stream here cascades over waterfalls and forms pools that make great swimming holes. The 5-mile round-trip **Seven Falls Trail ★**, which follows Bear Canyon deep into the mountains, is the most popular hike in the recreation area. You can take a tram to the trail head or add extra miles by hiking from the main parking lot.

With the city limits pushing right to the boundary of the Coronado National Forest, there are some convenient hiking options in Tucson's northern foothills. The **Ventana Canyon Trail** begins at a parking area adjacent to the Loews Ventana Canyon Resort (off Sunrise Dr. west of Sabino Canyon Rd.) and leads into the Ventana Canyon Wilderness. A few miles west, there's the **Finger Rock Trail,** which starts at the top of the section of Alvernon Road accessed from Skyline Drive. There are actually a couple of trails starting here, so you can hike for miles into the desert. Over near the Westward Look Resort is the **Pima Canyon Trail ★**, which leads into the Ventana Canyon Wilderness and is reached off Ina Road just east of Oracle Road. Both of these trails provide classic desert canyon hikes of whatever length you feel like (a dam at 3 miles on the latter trail makes a good turnaround point). Just south of the Hilton Tucson El Conquistador Golf & Tennis Resort, you'll find the **Linda Vista Trail,** which begins just off Oracle Road on Linda Vista Boulevard. This trail lies at the foot of Pusch Ridge and winds up through dense stands of prickly pear cactus. Higher up on the trail, there are some large saguaros. Because this trail is shaded by Pusch Ridge in the morning, it's a good choice for a morning hike on a day that's going to be hot.

Catalina State Park, 11570 N. Oracle Rd. (✆ **520/628-5798;** www.azstateparks.com/Parks/CATA/index.html), is on the rugged northwest face of the Santa Catalina Mountains, between 2,500 and 3,000 feet in elevation. Hiking trails here lead into the Pusch Ridge Wilderness; however, the park's best day hike is the 5.5-mile round-trip to **Romero Pools,** where small natural pools of water set amid the rocks are a refreshing destination on a hot day (expect plenty of other people on a weekend). This hike involves about 1,000 feet of elevation gain. Admission to the park is $7 per vehicle. Within the park is a Hohokam ruin. On winter weekends there are free guided hikes here.

One of the reasons Tucson is such a livable city is the presence of the cool (and, in winter, snow-covered) pine forests of 8,250-foot Mount

Lemmon. Within the **Mount Lemmon Recreation Area,** at the end of the Catalina Highway, are many miles of trails, and the hearty hiker can even set out from down in the lowland desert and hike up into the alpine forests (although it's easier to hike from the top down). For a more leisurely excursion, drive up onto the mountain to start your hike. However, be aware that in winter, there can be snow atop Mount Lemmon. There is a $5-per-vehicle charge to use most of the sites within this recreation area, so you'll need to stop at the roadside ticket kiosk at the base of the mountain and pay your fee. For more information, contact the **Coronado National Forest Santa Catalina Ranger District,** 5700 N. Sabino Canyon Rd. (✆ **520/749-8700;** www.fs.fed.us/r3/coronado).

HORSEBACK RIDING If you want to play cowboy or cowgirl, there are plenty of stables around Tucson where you can saddle up. In addition to providing guided trail rides, some of the stables below offer sunset rides with cookouts. Although reservations are not always required, they're a good idea. You can also opt to stay at a guest ranch and do as much riding as your muscles can stand.

Pusch Ridge Stables, 13700 N. Oracle Rd. (✆ **520/825-1664;** www.puschridgestables.com), is adjacent to Catalina State Park and Coronado National Forest. Rates are $37 for 1 hour, $57 for 2 hours, and $47 for a sunset ride.

Slightly more convenient are the rides offered at the Westward Look Resort by **Spanish Trail Outfitters** (✆ **520/631-3787;** www.spanishtrailoutfitters.com). Rates are $35 for a 1-hour ride, $45 for a 1½-hour ride, $50 for a sunset ride, and $65 for a 2½-hour ride.

HOT-AIR BALLOONING The ballooning season in Tucson runs October to April or May. **Balloon America** (✆ **520/299-7744;** www.balloonridesusa.com) offers flights over the foothills of the Santa Catalina Mountains ($349–$399 per person). Check the website for discounts. **Fleur de Tucson Balloon Tours** (✆ **520/403-8547;** www.fleurdetucson.net) offers rides over the Tucson Mountains and Saguaro National Park. Rates are $225 per person, including brunch and a champagne toast.

SKIING Located 35 miles from Tucson (a 1-hr. drive), **Mount Lemmon Ski Valley,** 10300 Ski Run Rd. (✆ **520/576-1321;** www.skithelemmon.com), is the southernmost ski area in the United States and offers 22 runs for experienced downhill skiers as well as beginners. The season here isn't very reliable, so be sure to call first to make sure it's open. Locals recommend not using your own skis or snowboard (too many exposed rocks). The ski area often opens only after a new dump of snow, so be sure to call the road-condition information line (✆ **520/547-7510**) before driving up. An all-day lift pass is $37 for adults, $30 for seniors, and $20 for children. In a good year, the season runs from mid-December to April.

TENNIS The **Reffkin Tennis Center,** 50 S. Alvernon Way (✆ **520/791-4896;** www.reffkintenniscenter.com), convenient to downtown, is the Southwest's largest public tennis facility and offers 25 lighted courts. During the day, court time is $2.50 per person for 1½ hours; at night, it's $10 per court. Many of the city's hotels and resorts also provide courts for guest use.

WILDFLOWER VIEWING Bloom time varies from year to year, but April and May are good times to view native wildflowers in the Tucson area. While the crowns of white blossoms worn by saguaro cacti are among the most visible blooms in the area, other cacti are far more colorful. **Saguaro National Park** (p. 435) and **Sabino Canyon** (p. 434) are among the best local spots to see saguaros, other cactus species, and various wildflowers in bloom. If you feel like heading farther afield, the wildflower displays at **Picacho Peak State Park** (p. 195), between Tucson and Casa Grande, are the most impressive in the state.

SPECTATOR SPORTS

FOOTBALL The **University of Arizona Wildcats** (✆ **800/452-2287** or 520/621-2287; www.arizonaathletics.com), a Pac-10 team, play at UA's Arizona Stadium. Most tickets cost between $20 and $60.

GOLF TOURNAMENTS The **World Golf Championships–Accenture Match Play Championship** (✆ **520/207-0595;** www.pgatour.com), Tucson's main PGA tournament, is held in late February at the Ritz-Carlton Golf Club at Dove Mountain. Daily tickets are $25 to $55.

HORSE/GREYHOUND RACING **Rillito Park Race Track,** 4502 N. First Ave. (✆ **520/293-5011;** www.rillitodowns.com), the birthplace of both the photo finish and organized quarter horse and Arabian racing, hosts quarter horse and thoroughbred racing for 6 weeks each winter. The ponies run on weekends in January and February, and admission is free to $5.

Greyhounds race year-round at **Tucson Greyhound Park,** 2601 S. Third Ave. (✆ **520/884-7576;** www.tucsongreyhound.com). Admission is free. Races are held Monday through Saturday evenings. To reach the track, take exit 261 off I-10.

SPAS

If you'd prefer a massage to a round on the links, you'll want to spend a few hours at one of Tucson's world-class spas. While full-service health spas can cost $400 to $500 or more per day, for under $100 you can avail yourself of a spa treatment or two (massages, facials, seaweed wraps, salt scrubs, and the like) and maybe even get to spend the day lounging by the pool at some exclusive resort. Spas are also great places (for both men and women) to while away an afternoon if you couldn't get a tee time at that golf course you wanted to play or if it happens to be raining.

The **Elizabeth Arden Red Door Spa ★**, at the Westin La Paloma Resort & Spa, 3666 E. Sunrise Dr. (✆ **866/733-3667** or 520/742-7866; www.reddoorspas.com), focuses on skin-care services, but plenty of body wraps and massages are available as well. With a 50-minute treatment (mostly $120–$150), you can use the spa's facilities for the day. However, unlike other spas in town, the Red Door is more about relaxation than staying fit, so you won't find aerobics classes here. Spa packages range in price from $99 to $490.

For a variety of services and a gorgeous location, you just can't beat the **Lakeside Spa at Loews Ventana Canyon Resort,** 7000 N. Resort Dr. (✆ **520/529-7830;** www.loewslakesidespa.com), which is wedged between the rugged Santa Catalinas and the manicured fairways of one of the most fabled golf courses in the state. Soothed by the scent of aromatherapy, you can treat yourself to herbal wraps, mud treatments, massages, facials, complete salon services, and much more. Fifty-minute treatments run $105 to $140. With any 50-minute

More than 50 shops, galleries, and restaurants make up the Fourth Avenue historic shopping and entertainment district.

body treatment, you get use of the spa's facilities and pool and can attend any fitness classes being held that day.

With five locations around the Tucson area, **Gadabout Salon Spas** (www.gadabout.com) offers the opportunity to slip a relaxing visit to a spa into a busy schedule. Mud baths, facials, and massages as well as hair and nail services are available, and body treatments and massages start at $60 for a 50-minute massage. You'll find Gadabout at the following locations: St. Philip's Plaza, 1990 E. River Rd. (✆ **520/577-2000**); 6393 E. Grant Rd. (✆ **520/885-0000**); 3207 E. Speedway Blvd. (✆ **520/325-0000**); 6960 E. Sunrise Dr. (✆ **520/615-9700**); and 8303 N. Oracle Rd. (✆ **520/742-0000**).

SHOPPING

Although the Tucson shopping scene is overshadowed by that of Scottsdale and Phoenix, Tucson does provide a respectable diversity of merchants. Tucsonans have a strong sense of their place in the Southwest, and this is reflected in the city's shopping opportunities. Southwestern clothing, food, crafts, furniture, and art abound (and often at reasonable prices), as do shopping centers built in a Southwestern architectural style.

The city's population center continues to move steadily northward, so it is in the northern foothills that you'll find most of the city's large enclosed shopping malls as well as the more tasteful small shopping plazas full of boutiques and galleries.

Along Fourth Avenue between Congress Street and Speedway Boulevard (just north of downtown Tucson), more than 50 shops, galleries, and restaurants make up the **Fourth Avenue historic shopping and entertainment district.** The buildings here were constructed in the early 1900s, and the proximity to the University of Arizona helps keep this district bustling. Many of the shops cater primarily to student needs and interests.

El Presidio Historic District, around the Tucson Museum of Art, is the city's center for crafts shops. This area is home to Old Town Artisans and the Tucson Museum of Art shop. The city's **"Lost Barrio"** district, on the corner of Southwest Park Avenue and 12th Street (a block off Broadway), is a good place to look for Mexican imports and Southwestern-style home furnishings at good prices.

Antiques & Collectibles

Eric Firestone Gallery ★★ Collectors of Stickley and other Arts and Crafts furniture will not want to miss this impressive gallery, which is located in one of the historic buildings at Joesler Village shopping plaza. In addition to the furniture, there are period paintings and accessories. At Joesler Village, 4425 N. Campbell Ave. ✆ **520/577-7711.** www.ericfirestonegallery.com.

Michael D. Higgins & Son Located next door to the Eric Firestone Gallery, this little shop specializes in pre-Columbian artifacts but also carries African, Asian, and even ancient Greek and Roman pieces. At Joesler Village, 4429 N. Campbell Ave. ✆ **520/577-8330.** www.mhiggins.com.

Morning Star Antiques In a shop that adjoins Morning Star Traders (see "Native American Art, Crafts & Jewelry," below), Morning Star Antiques carries an excellent selection of antique Spanish and Mexican furniture, as well as other unusual and rustic pieces. 2020 E. Speedway Blvd. ✆ **520/881-2112.** www.morningstartraders.com.

Art

Tucson's gallery scene is not as concentrated as that in many other cities. Tucson's galleries are scattered across the foothills and other more affluent suburbs. One art hot spot is the corner of Campbell Avenue and Skyline Drive, where you'll find **Gallery Row,** a stylishly modern Southwestern shopping plaza that has several contemporary art galleries. Behind this complex, at 6420 N. Campbell Ave., is a small courtyard complex that is home to **Sanders Galleries** (✆ **520/299-1763;** www.sandersgalleries.com) and **Settlers West Galleries** (✆ **520/299-2607;** www.settlerswest.com), both of which specialize in Western art, as well as **Gallery West** (✆ **520/529-7002;** www.indianartwest.com), which specializes in American Indian art.

Davis Dominguez Gallery Located just a couple of blocks off Fourth Avenue in downtown Tucson, this huge gallery features some of the best and most creative contemporary art in the city. 154 E. 6th St. ✆ **866/629-9759** or 520/629-9759. www.davisdominguez.com.

Etherton Gallery For more than 25 years, this gallery has been presenting some of the most distinctive art to be found in Tucson, including contemporary and historical photographs. A favorite of museums and serious collectors, Etherton Gallery isn't afraid to present work with strong themes. A smaller location is at the Temple of Music and Art, 330 S. Scott Ave. (✆ **520/624-7370**). 135 S. 6th Ave. ✆ **520/624-7370.** www.ethertongallery.com.

Jane Hamilton Fine Art This gallery's boldly colored contemporary art really stands out, and much of the artwork reflects a desert aesthetic. At Plaza Colonial Center, 2890 E. Skyline Dr., Ste. 180. ✆ **520/529-4886.** www.janehamiltonfineart.com.

Medicine Man Gallery/Mark Sublette Modern ★★★ This gallery has the finest and most tasteful traditional Western art you'll find just about anywhere in Arizona. Artists represented include Ed Mell, Maynard Dixon, and Howard Post, and most of the gallery's artists have received national attention. There's an excellent selection of Native American crafts as well; see "Native American Art, Crafts & Jewelry," below, for more details. The gallery also houses a small Maynard Dixon Museum. At Santa Fe Square, 7000 E. Tanque Verde Rd. ✆ **800/422-9382** or 520/722-7798. www.medicinemangallery.com.

Philabaum Contemporary Art Glass For almost 30 years, this gallery has been exposing Tucson to the latest trends in contemporary glass art. The gallery is full of lovely and colorful pieces by Tucson's own Tom Philabaum and more than 100 other artists from around the country. 711 S. 6th Ave. ✆ **520/884-7404.** www.philabaumglass.com.

Books

Chain bookstores in the Tucson area include **Barnes & Noble,** 5130 E. Broadway Blvd. (✆ **520/512-1166**), and 7325 N. La Cholla Blvd., Ste. 100, in the Foothills Mall (✆ **520/742-6402**).

Bookmans This big bookstore, housed in a former supermarket, is crammed full of used books and recordings, and has long been a favorite of Tucsonans. There are other Bookmans stores at 6230 E. Speedway Blvd. (✆ **520/748-9555**) and 3733 W. Ina Rd. (✆ **520/579-0303**). 1930 E. Grant Rd. ✆ **520/325-5767.** www.bookmans.com.

Clues Unlimited If you forgot to pack your vacation reading, drop by this fun little store. Not only can you shop for the latest Carl Hiaasen or other mystery, but you can also say hi to Sophie and Emily, the resident potbellied pigs. 3146 E. Fort Lowell Rd. ✆ **520/326-8533.** www.cluesunlimited.com.

Crafts

Details Art & Design If you enjoy highly imaginative and colorful crafts with a sense of humor, you'll get a kick out of this place. Unexpected objets d'art turn up in the forms of clocks, ceramics, glass, and other media. At Gallery Row, 3001 E. Skyline Dr., Ste. 103. ✆ **520/577-1995.** www.detailsart.com.

Obsidian Gallery Contemporary crafts by nationally recognized artists fill this gallery. You'll find luminous glass art, unique and daring jewelry, imaginative ceramics, and much more. At St. Philip's Plaza, 4320 N. Campbell Ave., Ste. 130 (at River Rd.). ✆ **520/577-3598.** www.obsidian-gallery.com.

Old Town Artisans ★ Housed in a restored 1850s adobe building covering an entire city block in El Presidio Historic District, this unique shopping plaza houses several shops brimming with traditional and contemporary Southwestern designs. There's also free Wi-Fi in the courtyard here. 201 N. Court Ave. ✆ **800/782-8072** or 520/623-6024. www.oldtownartisans.com.

Skyline Gallery I'm a sucker for bright colors, and at this fine-crafts gallery, you'll find display cases full of gorgeous, colorful jewelry, art glass, and ceramics. There are also exquisite works in wood. In Paloma Village Center, 6360 N. Campbell Ave., Ste. 150. ✆ **520/615-3800.** www.skylinegallerytucson.com.

Tucson Museum of Art Shop The Tucson Museum's gift shop offers a colorful and changing selection of Southwestern crafts, mostly by local and regional artists. 140 N. Main Ave. ✆ **520/624-2333.** www.tucsonarts.com.

Fashion

See also the listing for the Beth Friedman Collection under "Jewelry," below. For cowboy and cowgirl attire, see "Western Wear," below.

Dark Star Leather If you're in the market for a distinctive leather jacket, belt, or purse, be sure to stop by this little locally owned shop in Plaza Palomino.

Exotic leathers are used in the one-of-a-kind designs. You can sometimes find great deals on sale items. At Plaza Palomino, 2940 N. Swan Rd., Ste. 129. ✆ **520/881-4700.** www.darkstarleather.com.

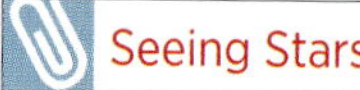

Seeing Stars

Amateur astronomers, take note. Because of all the great star-viewing opportunities in southern Arizona, Tucson has a large number of stargazers, and they all shop at Stellar Vision Astronomy Shop, 3721 E. 37th St. (✆ 520/571-0877; www.stellarvision tucson.com). This store is packed with telescopes of all shapes and sizes, as well as books and star charts.

Maya Palace This shop features ethnic-inspired but sophisticated women's clothing in natural fabrics. The friendly staff helps customers of all ages put together a Southwestern chic look, from casual to dressy. A second shop can be found at El Mercado, 6332 E. Broadway Blvd. (✆ 520/748-0817). At Casas Adobes Plaza, 7057 N. Oracle Rd. ✆ **520/575-8028.** www.mayapalacetucson.com.

Rochelle K Fine Women's Apparel With everything from the latest in the little black dress to drapey silks and casual linens, Rochelle K attracts a well-heeled clientele. You'll also find beautiful accessories and jewelry here. At Casas Adobes Plaza, 7039 N. Oracle Rd. ✆ **520/797-2279.** www.rochellek.com.

Gifts & Souvenirs

B&B Cactus Farm This plant nursery is devoted exclusively to cacti and succulents, and is worth a visit just to see the amazing variety on display. It's a good place to stop on the way to or from Saguaro National Park East. The store can pack your purchase for traveling or ship it anywhere in the United States. 11550 E. Speedway Blvd. ✆ **520/721-4687.** www.bandbcactus.com.

DAH Rock Shop If you can't make it to Tucson for the annual gem and mineral shows, don't despair. At this cluttered shop, you can pick through shelves crammed with all manner of rare minerals and exotic stones. 3401 N. Dodge Blvd. ✆ **520/323-0781.**

Native Seeds/SEARCH ★★ Gardeners, cooks, and just about anyone in search of an unusual gift will likely be fascinated by this shop, which is operated by a nonprofit organization dedicated to preserving the biodiversity offered by native Southwest seeds. The shelves are full of heirloom beans, corn, chilies, and other seeds from a wide variety of native desert plants. In addition, you'll also find gourds and inexpensive Tarahumara Indian baskets, bottled sauces and salsas made from native plants, and books about native agriculture. 3061 N. Campbell Ave. ✆ **866/622-5561** or 520/622-5561. www.nativeseeds.org.

Picánte Designs The plethora of Hispanic-themed icons and accessories here include *milagros,* Day of the Dead skeletons, Mexican crosses, jewelry, greeting cards, and folk art from around the world. This is a great place to shop for distinctive south-of-the-border kitschy gifts. 2932 E. Broadway. ✆ **520/320-5699.** www.picantetucson.com.

Tohono Chul Museum Shops ★ The two shops here are packed with Mexican folk art, nature-themed toys, household items, T-shirts, and books. These shops are an absolute must after a visit to surrounding Tohono Chul Park, which is landscaped with desert plants. Add a meal at the park's tearoom, and you've got a good afternoon's outing. For a description of the park, see p. 444. 7366 N. Paseo del Norte (1 block west of the corner of Ina and Oracle roads in Tohono Chul Park). ✆ **520/742-6455.** www.tohonochulpark.org.

UN Center/UNICEF If your tastes run to ethnic imports, be sure to check out this great little gift shop. Not only is there a lot of cool stuff from all over the world, but when you buy something here, you'll also be helping underprivileged children. Monterey Village, 6242 E. Speedway Blvd. ✆ **520/881-7060.** www.untucson.org.

Jewelry

In addition to the store mentioned below, see the listing for the Obsidian Gallery under "Crafts," above.

Beth Friedman Collection This shop sells a well-chosen collection of jewelry by Native American craftspeople and international designers. It also carries some extravagant cowgirl get-ups in velvet and lace, as well as contemporary women's fashions. At Joesler Village, 1865 E. River Rd., Ste. 121. ✆ **520/577-6858.** www.bethfriedman.com.

Malls & Shopping Centers

Casas Adobes Plaza With some of the best boutiques in Tucson, a great Southwestern crafts shop, and several good restaurants, this little hacienda-style shopping center in the foothills is a great place to spend an afternoon shopping. 7001–7153 N. Oracle Rd. ✆ **520/299-2610.** www.casasadobesplaza.com.

Foothills Mall This large factory-outlet mall and discount shopping center has, among many other stores, a Nike Factory Store, Saks Fifth Avenue Off 5th, and Barnes & Noble, as well as a brewpub and a couple of good restaurants. 7401 N. La Cholla Blvd. (at Ina Rd.). ✆ **520/219-0650.** www.shopfoothillsmall.com.

Plaza Palomino Built in the style of a Spanish hacienda with a courtyard and fountains, this little shopping center is home to some of Tucson's most interesting specialty shops, as well as galleries and restaurants. There's a farmers' market here on Saturday mornings. 2900–2990 N. Swan Rd. (at the southeast corner of N. Swan and Fort Lowell rds.). ✆ **520/323-1005.** www.plazapalomino.com.

St. Philip's Plaza This upscale Southwestern-style shopping center contains a couple of good restaurants, a beauty salon/day spa, and numerous shops and galleries. On Saturday and Sunday mornings, there is a farmers' market. Makes a great one-stop Tucson shopping outing. 4280 N. Campbell Ave. (at River Rd.). ✆ **520/529-2775.** www.stphilipsplaza.com.

Tucson Mall The foothills of northern Tucson have become shopping-center central, and this is the largest of the malls. You'll find more than 200 retailers in this busy, two-story skylit complex. 4500 N. Oracle Rd. ✆ **520/293-7331.** www.shoptucsonmall.com.

Mexican & Latin American Imports

In addition to the shop mentioned below, the **"Lost Barrio,"** on the corner of Southwest Park Avenue and 12th Street (a block south of Broadway), is a good place to look for Mexican imports and Southwestern-style home furnishings at good prices.

Antigua de Mexico This warehouselike shop is absolutely packed with crafts from Mexico—oversize ceramics and painted plates, wooden and wrought-iron furniture, and punched-metal frames and framed mirrors. Smaller items include crucifixes and candlesticks. 3235 W. Orange Grove Rd. ✆ **520/742-7114.** www.antiguademexico.us.

Native American Art, Crafts & Jewelry

Bahti Indian Arts Family-owned for more than 50 years, this store sells exquisitely made Native American crafts—jewelry, baskets, sculpture, paintings, books, weavings, kachina dolls, Zuni fetishes, and much more. At St. Philip's Plaza, 4330 N. Campbell Ave., Ste. 73. ✆ **520/577-0290.** www.bahti.com.

Gallery West Located right below Anthony's in the Catalinas restaurant, this tiny shop specializes in very expensive Native American artifacts (mostly pre-1940s) such as New Mexico Pueblo pots, Apache and Pima baskets, 19th-century Plains Indian beadwork, Navajo weavings, and kachinas. Also for sale is plenty of both contemporary and vintage jewelry. 6420 N. Campbell Ave. (at Skyline Dr.). ✆ **520/529-7002.** www.indianartwest.com.

Medicine Man Gallery/Mark Sublette Modern This shop has the best and biggest selection of old Navajo rugs in the city. There are also Mexican and other Hispanic textiles, Acoma pottery, basketry, and other Indian crafts, as well as artwork by cowboy artists. At Santa Fe Square, 7000 E. Tanque Verde Rd., Ste. 16. ✆ **800/422-9382** or 520/722-7798. www.medicinemangallery.com.

Morning Star Traders ★★★ With hardwood floors and a museumlike atmosphere, this store features Native American crafts of the highest quality, including antique Navajo rugs, kachinas, furniture, and a huge selection of old Native American jewelry. This just may be the best store of its type in the entire state. An adjoining shop, Morning Star Antiques, carries an impressive selection of antique furniture (see "Antiques & Collectibles," above). 2020 E. Speedway Blvd. ✆ **520/881-2112.** www.morningstartraders.com.

Western Wear

Arizona Hatters Arizona Hatters carries the best names in cowboy hats, from Stetson to Bailey to Resistol, and the shop specializes in custom-fitting hats to the customer's head and face. 2790 N. Campbell Ave. ✆ **520/292-1320.** www.arizonahatters.com.

Boot Barn If you want to put together your Western-wear ensemble under one roof, this is the place. It's the largest such store in Tucson and can outfit you and your kids in the latest cowboy fashions, including hats and boots. In Northwest Plaza, 3719 N. Oracle Rd. (at Prince Rd.). ✆ **520/888-1161.** www.bootbarn.com.

J. Gilbert Footwear The old West and the new West come together at this foothills shoe store. You can buy both men's and women's Lucchese cowboy boots, as well as lots of other gorgeous shoes from a range of designers from around the world. Of course, there's also plenty of Western wear to go with your new shoes. At Casas Adobes Plaza, 7041 N. Oracle Rd. ✆ **520/531-8385.** www.jgilbertfootwear.com.

Stewart Boot Manufacturing Co. Boots that fit so well you don't even need socks. That's how a Tucson friend described the custom-made cowboy boots turned out by this South Tucson boot maker. You'll have to wait for your boots, though, because all the boots sold here are made to order. 30 W. 28th St. ✆ **520/622-2706.**

TUCSON AFTER DARK

Tucson after dark is a much easier landscape to negotiate than the vast cultural sprawl of the Phoenix area. Rather than having numerous performing-arts centers all over the suburbs as in the Valley of the Sun, Tucson has a more concentrated nightlife scene. The **Downtown Arts District** is the center of the action, with the Temple of Music and Art, the Tucson Convention Center Music Hall, and several nightclubs. The **University of Arizona campus,** a mile away, is another entertainment nexus.

The free *Tucson Weekly* contains thorough listings of concerts, theater and dance performances, and club offerings. The entertainment section of the *Arizona Daily Star* ("Caliente") comes out each Thursday and is a good source of information for what's going on around town.

The Club & Music Scene

COMEDY

Laffs Comedy Caffé This stand-up comedy club features local and professional comedians from around the country Thursday through Saturday nights. A full bar and a limited menu are available. At the Village, 2900 E. Broadway Blvd., Ste. 154. ✆ **520/323-8669.** www.laffscomedyclub.com. Cover free Thurs, $10–$15 Fri–Sat.

COUNTRY

Cactus Moon Café A 20- to 40-something crowd frequents this large and glitzy nightclub, which features primarily country music (with dance lessons several nights each week). Keep in mind, though, that rock instead of country may be played on some nights. Check the schedule before putting on your boots. 5470 E. Broadway Blvd. (at Craycroft Rd.). ✆ **520/748-0049.** www.cactusmoon.net. No cover to $5.

The Maverick The Maverick, in different incarnations and different locations around town, has been Tucson's favorite country-music dance club since 1962. Currently it's located in a modern space out in east Tucson and is open Tuesday through Saturday nights, with live country music every night. 6622 E. Tanque Verde Rd. ✆ **520/298-0430.** www.tucsonmaverick.com. No cover to $5.

DANCE CLUB

El Parador Restaurant Tropical decor sets the mood for live Latin dance music and salsa lessons on Friday nights. The music starts at 10pm and dance lessons start at 10:15pm. Customers of this club range from 20- to 60-somethings. 2744 E. Broadway. ✆ **520/881-2744.** www.elparadortucson.com. Cover $7.

JAZZ

To find out what's happening on the local jazz scene, contact the **Tucson Jazz Society** (✆ **520/903-1265;** www.tucsonjazz.org). This organization's website lists various jazz nights at restaurants all over Tucson, including **Old Pueblo Grill Alvernon,** 60 N. Alvernon Way (✆ **520/326-6000;** www.metrorestaurants.com), with live jazz on Sunday nights.

The Grill/Terraza Garden Patio & Lounge ★★ No other jazz venue in Tucson has more flavor of the Southwest than this restaurant/lounge perched high on a ridge top overlooking the city. There are live bands (jazz, blues, flamenco) Friday and Saturday nights, and a pianist on other nights. At Hacienda del Sol Guest Ranch Resort, 5501 N. Hacienda del Sol Rd. ✆ **520/529-3500.** www.haciendadelsol.com.

MARIACHI

Tucson is the mariachi capital of the United States, and no one should visit without spending at least one evening listening to some of these strolling musicians. At the **St. Augustine Cathedral,** 192 S. Stone Ave. (✆ **520/623-6351;** www.staugustinecathedral.com), there is even a mariachi Mass every Sunday at 8am.

Sample mariachi and Mexican food at La Fuente.

Guadalajara Grill Located just west of North Campbell Avenue, this large Mexican restaurant is convenient to several of the foothills resorts, which makes it a great place to catch an evening of lively mariachi music. The musicians perform Sunday through Thursday from 6 to 9pm and Friday and Saturday from 6 to 10pm. 1220 E. Prince Rd. ✆ **520/323-1022.** www.ggrill.com.

La Fuente ★ La Fuente is one of the largest Mexican restaurants in Tucson and serves up good food, but what really draws the crowds is the live mariachi music. If you just want to listen and not have dinner, you can hang out in the lounge. The mariachis perform Thursday through Sunday. 1749 N. Oracle Rd. ✆ **520/623-8659.** www.lafuenterestaurant.com.

ROCK, BLUES & REGGAE

Chicago Bar Transplanted Chicagoans love to watch their home teams on the TVs at this neighborhood bar, but there's also live music nightly. Sure, blues gets played a lot, but so do reggae and rock and about everything in between. 5954 E. Speedway Blvd. ✆ **520/748-8169.** www.chicagobartucson.com. No cover to $5.

Club Congress Just off the lobby of the restored Hotel Congress (now a budget hotel catering to younger travelers), Club Congress is Tucson's main alternative-music venue. There are usually several nights of live music each week, and over the years such bands as Nirvana, Dick Dale, and the Goo Goo Dolls have played here, although more recently, the club has tended to book primarily local and regional acts. 311 E. Congress St. ✆ **520/622-8848.** www.hotelcongress.com. No cover to $25.

The Rialto Theatre This renovated 1919 vaudeville theater, although not a nightclub, is now Tucson's main venue for performances by bands that are too big to play across the street at Club Congress. 318 E. Congress St. ✆ **520/740-1000.** www.rialtotheatre.com. Tickets $3–$32.

The Bar, Lounge & Pub Scene

Armitage Wine Lounge If you're a wine lover and are staying at a foothills resort, be sure to check out this stylish wine bar at the corner of Skyline and Campbell. In addition to having more than 30 wines available by the glass, they also have a long cocktail menu. In La Encantada shopping center, 2905 E. Skyline Dr., Ste. 168. ✆ **520/682-9740.** www.armitagewine.com.

Audubon Bar If you're looking for a quiet, comfortable scene, the piano music in this classic lounge at the Arizona Inn is sure to soothe your soul. The Audubon has a timeless feel, and before or after drinks, you can stroll the resort's beautiful gardens. 2200 E. Elm St. ✆ **520/325-1541.** www.arizonainn.com.

Barrio Brewing Co. Located in a warehouse district southeast of downtown and a few blocks south of Broadway, this big brewpub, which is affiliated with Gentle Ben's Brewing Co., isn't easy to find, but it is definitely worth searching out. Grab a seat on the loading-dock patio and sip a stout as the sun goes down. 800 E. 16th St. (at E. Euclid Ave. and Toole St.). ✆ **520/791-2739.** www.barriobrewing.com.

The Canyon's Crown It's so cool and dark and appropriately atmospheric inside this eastside English pub that you'd never know that sunshine and blue skies lurk just outside the door. This is a great place to stop for a pint after hiking at Sabino Canyon. 6958 E. Tanque Verde Rd. ✆ **520/885-8277.** www.canyonscrown.com.

Cascade Tucson Lounge ★ This is Tucson's ultimate piano bar. With a view of the Catalinas, the plush lounge is perfect for romance or relaxation at the start or end of a night on the town. Sunday through Thursday nights, there's live piano music or a jazz band, and on Fridays and Saturdays, there's a live band and dancing. At Loews Ventana Canyon Resort, 7000 N. Resort Dr. ✆ **520/299-2020.** www.loewshotels.com.

Cushing Street Bar & Restaurant Located on the edge of the Barrio Histórico district just south of the Tucson Convention Center, this restaurant/bar is in a historic 1860s adobe building and has loads of old Tucson character. There's also live jazz on Saturday nights and occasionally other nights in the month. 198 W. Cushing St. ✆ **520/622-7984.** www.cushingstreet.com.

Famous Sam's With 10 branches around the city, Famous Sam's keeps a lot of Tucson's sports fans happy with its cheap prices and large portions. Other locations include 7930 E. Speedway Blvd., no. 170 (✆ **520/290-9666**), and 2320 N. Silverbell Rd. (✆ **520/884-7267**). 1830 E. Broadway Blvd., no. 106. ✆ **520/884-0119.** www.famoussams.net.

Gentle Ben's Brewing Co. Located just off the UA campus, Gentle Ben's, a big, modern place with plenty of outdoor seating, is Tucson's favorite microbrewery and, not surprisingly, attracts primarily a college crowd. 865 E. University Blvd. ✆ **520/624-4177.** www.gentlebens.com.

The Kon Tiki With a Polynesian luau theme, this joint is not some modern-day designer's idea of what the 1950s were like; this is the real thing. Tiki lovers rejoice, but be careful, those sweet tropical cocktails can pack a Hawaiian punch! 4625 E. Broadway Blvd. ✆ **520/323-7193.** www.kontikitucson.com.

Nimbus Brewing ★ Located in a warehouse district on the south side of Tucson, this brewpub is basically the front room of Nimbus's brewing and bottling facility. The beer is good, and there's live blues, rock, folk, and reggae on a regular basis. Hard to find, and definitely a local scene. There's a second Nimbus at 6464 E. Tanque Verde Rd. (✆ **520/733-1111**). 3850 E. 44th St. (2 blocks east of Palo Verde Rd.). ✆ **520/745-9175.** www.nimbusbeer.com.

The Shelter Housed in an unusual round building that supposedly was once a fallout shelter (thus the name of the bar), this place is totally retro, with lots of JFK memorabilia on the walls. There are even vintage pinball machines. Fun and funky. 4155 E. Grant Rd. ✆ **520/326-1345.**

Sky Bar Taking the night sky as its theme, this bar has telescopes set up on the patio at night, projects images from space on screens around the room, and has regularly scheduled astronomy lectures and presentations. As if this astronomical orientation isn't cool enough, the Sky Bar is also solar powered, utilizing power from a photovoltaic array on the roof. 536 N. Fourth Ave. ✆ **520/622-4300.** www.skybartucson.com.

Thunder Canyon Brewery Although I usually prefer the beers at Nimbus Brewing, this big brewpub is way more convenient if you're staying at a foothills resort. There are always plenty of different brews on tap, and some of them can be both unusual and tasty. At Foothills Mall, 7401 N. La Cholla Blvd. (at Ina Rd.). ✆ **520/797-2652.** www.thundercanyonbrewery.com.

¡Toma! ★ This bar, in El Presidio Historic District and owned by the family that operates El Charro Café next door, has a fun and festive atmosphere complete with a Mexican hat fountain/sculpture in the courtyard. Drop by for half-price margaritas and appetizers during happy hour (Mon–Fri 3–6pm). 311 N. Court Ave. ✆ **520/622-1922.**

GAY & LESBIAN BARS & CLUBS

To find out about other gay bars around town, keep an eye out for the *Observer* (✆ **520/622-7176;** www.tucsonobserver.com), Tucson's newspaper for the gay, lesbian, and bisexual community. You'll find it at **Antigone Books,** 411 N. Fourth Ave. (✆ **520/792-3715;** www.antigonebooks.com), as well as at the bars listed here.

Ain't Nobody's Bizness Located in a small shopping plaza in midtown, this bar has long been *the* lesbian gathering spot in Tucson. This bar also has nights for gay men as well, so check the schedule. 2900 E. Broadway Blvd., Ste. 118. ✆ **520/318-4838.** www.thebiztuc.com.

IBT's Located on funky Fourth Avenue, IBT's has long been the most popular gay men's dance bar in town. The music ranges from 1980s retro to hip-hop, and regular drag shows add to the fun. There's always an interesting crowd. 616 N. 4th Ave. ✆ **520/882-3053.**

The Performing Arts

Tucson's performing arts scene is just as lively as Phoenix's, and three of Tucson's major companies—the Arizona Opera Company, Ballet Arizona, and the Arizona Theatre Company—spend half their time in Phoenix. This means that whatever gets staged in Phoenix also gets staged in Tucson. Tucson also has its own symphony and manages to sustain a diversified theater scene. Usually, the best way to purchase tickets is directly from the company's box office. Tickets to Tucson Convention Center events (but not the symphony or the opera) and other venues around town may be available by calling **Ticketmaster** (✆ **800/745-3000** or 866/448-7849; www.ticketmaster.com) or by stopping by the **TCC box office,** 260 S. Church Ave. (✆ **520/791-4101;** www.cityoftucson.org/tcc).

PERFORMING ARTS CENTERS & CONCERT HALLS

Tucson's largest performance venue is the **Tucson Convention Center (TCC) Music Hall,** 260 S. Church Ave. (✆ **520/791-4101;** www.cityoftucson.org/tcc). It's the home of the Tucson Symphony Orchestra and where the Arizona Opera Company usually performs when it's in town. This hall also hosts many touring companies. The box office is open Monday through Friday from 10:30am to 5:30pm.

The centerpiece of the Tucson theater scene is the **Temple of Music and Art,** 330 S. Scott Ave. (✆ **520/622-2823**), a restored historic theater dating from 1927. The 605-seat Alice Holsclaw Theatre is the Temple's main stage, but there's also the 90-seat Cabaret Theatre. Call for box office hours.

University of Arizona Centennial Hall, 1020 E. University Blvd. at Park Avenue (✆ **520/621-3341;** www.uapresents.org), on the UA campus, is Tucson's other main performance hall. It stages Broadway shows and performances by national and international musical acts. A big stage and excellent sound system permit large-scale productions. The box office is open Monday through Friday from 10am to 6pm, and September to May Saturday from noon to 5pm and Sunday from noon to 4pm.

Originally opened in 1930, downtown Tucson's **Fox Theatre,** 17 W. Congress St. (✆ **520/624-1515** or 520/547-3040; www.foxtucsontheatre.org), is a restored movie palace that is now the city's most beautiful place to catch live music, a play, or even a classic or independent film. The box office is open Tuesday through Friday from 11am to 6pm and on performance Saturdays and Sundays from 2 hours before showtime.

The **Center for the Arts Proscenium Theatre,** Pima Community College (West Campus), 2202 W. Anklam Rd. (✆ **520/206-6986;** www.pima.edu/cfa), is another good place to check for classical music performances. It offers a wide variety of shows.

OUTDOOR VENUES & SERIES

Weather permitting, Tucsonans head to Reid Park's **DeMeester Outdoor Performance Center,** at Country Club Road and East 22nd Street (✆ **520/791-4873**), for performances under the stars. This amphitheater stages live theater performances, as well as frequent concerts (many of which are free).

The **Tucson Jazz Society** (✆ **520/903-1265;** www.tucsonjazz.org), which manages to book a few well-known jazz musicians each year, sponsors different series at various locations around the city. Tickets are usually between $15 and $35.

CLASSICAL MUSIC, OPERA & DANCE

Both the **Tucson Symphony Orchestra** (✆ **520/882-8585** or 520/792-9155; www.tucsonsymphony.org), which is the oldest continuously performing symphony in the Southwest, and the **Arizona Opera Company** (✆ **520/293-4336;** www.azopera.org), the state's premier opera company, perform at the Tucson Convention Center Music Hall. Symphony tickets run mostly $36 to $60; opera tickets are $15 to $99. If you want to catch some economical classical music, check out the schedule at the **University of Arizona College of Fine Arts School of Music** (✆ **520/621-1162;** www.music.arizona.edu). Performances include classical music and opera held in the Music Building's Crowder and Holsclaw halls, both of which are near the intersection of Speedway Boulevard and Park Avenue on the UA campus. Equally worthwhile are the performances by the UA Dance Ensemble, which are staged in the **Stevie Eller Dance Theatre,** a little jewel box of a building. The bold contemporary architecture of this building makes seeing a performance here a double treat. Call the above number for information on performances.

THEATER

Tucson doesn't have a lot of theater companies, but what few it does have stage a surprisingly diverse sampling of both classic and contemporary plays. **Arizona Theatre Company** (✆ **520/622-2823;** www.aztheatreco.org), which performs at the Temple of Music and Art, splits its time between Tucson and Phoenix, and is the state's top professional theater company. Each season sees a mix of comedy,

Stevie Eller Dance Theatre stages performances by the UA Dance Ensemble.

drama, and Broadway-style musical shows; tickets cost $31 to $55. The **Invisible Theatre,** 1400 N. First Ave. (✆ **520/882-9721;** www.invisibletheatre.com), a tiny theater in a converted laundry building, has been home to Tucson's most experimental theater for more than 40 years (it does off-Broadway shows). Tickets run about $18 to $42.

The West just wouldn't be the West without good old-fashioned melodramas, and the **Gaslight Theatre,** 7010 E. Broadway Blvd. (✆ **520/886-9428;** www.thegaslighttheatre.com), is where evil villains, stalwart heroes, and defenseless heroines pound the boards. You can boo and hiss, cheer and sigh as the predictable stories unfold on stage. It's great fun for kids and adults, with plenty of pop-culture references. Tickets are $18 for adults, $16 for students and seniors, and $8 for kids 12 and under. Performances are held nightly, with two shows on Friday and Saturday nights, plus a Sunday matinee. Tickets often sell out a month in advance.

Casinos

Casino del Sol Located 15 miles southwest of Tucson off I-19 (take the Valencia Rd. exit and drive west) and operated by the Pascua Yaqui tribe, this is one of the two largest casinos in southern Arizona. There are plenty of slot machines, plus keno, bingo, and a card room. 5655 W. Valencia Rd. ✆ **800/344-9435.** www.casinodelsol.com.

Desert Diamond Casino Operated by the Tohono O'odham tribe and just off I-19 south of Tucson, this casino offers the same variety of slot and video poker machines found at other casinos in the state. A card room, bingo, and keno round out the options. 1100 W. Pima Mine Rd., Sahuarita (take exit 80 off I-19). ✆ **866/332-9467** or 520/294-7777. www.desertdiamondcasino.com.

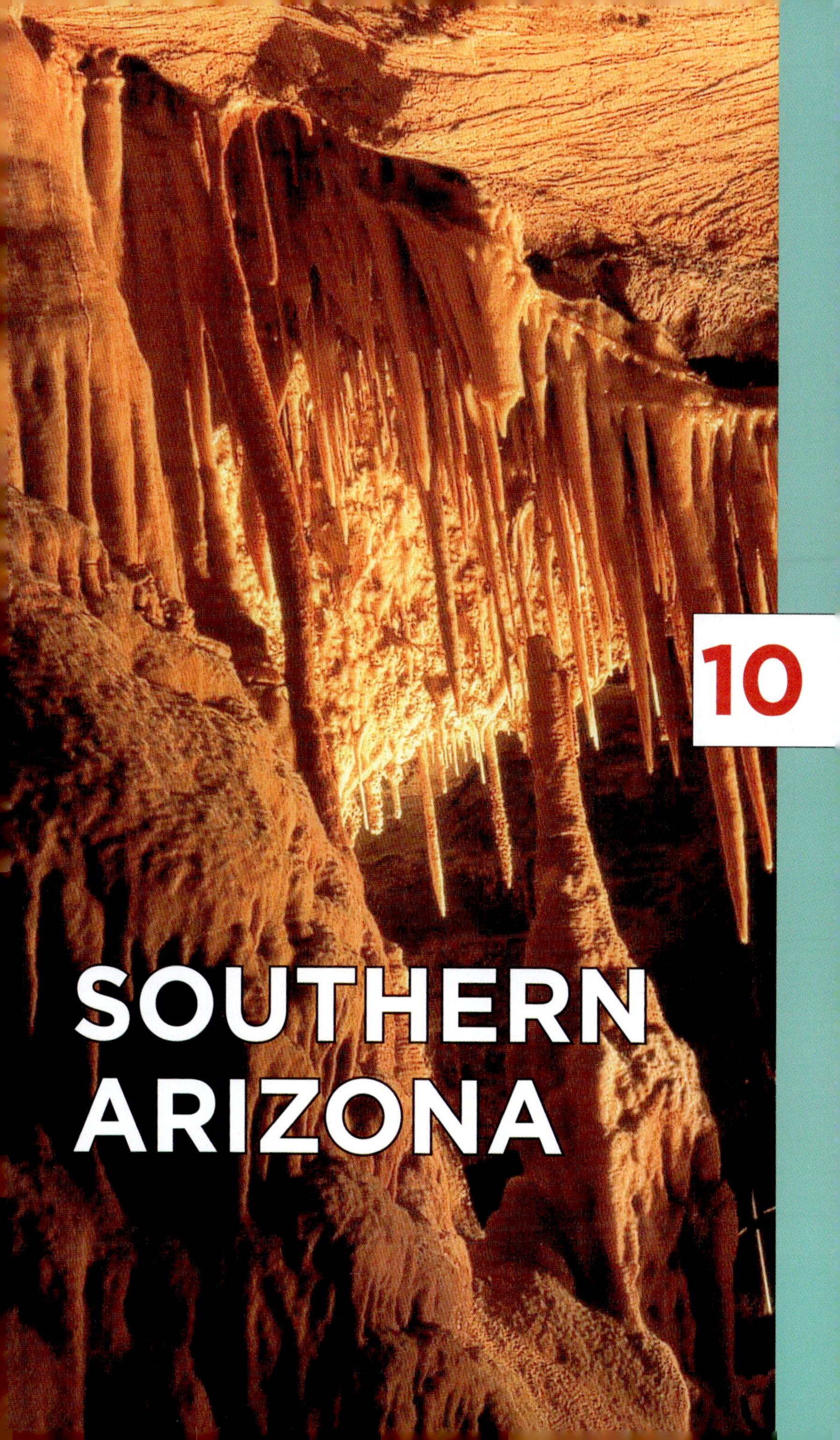

10

SOUTHERN ARIZONA

Although southern Arizona has its share of prickly pears and saguaros, much of this region has more in common with the Texas plains than it does with the Sonoran Desert. In the southeastern corner of the state, mile-high grasslands, punctuated by forested mountain ranges, have long supported vast ranches where cattle range across wide-open plains. It was here that some of America's most legendary Western history took place—Wyatt Earp and the Clantons shot it out at Tombstone's O.K. Corral; Doc Holliday played his cards; and Cochise and Geronimo staged the last Indian rebellions.

Long before the prospectors and outlaws arrived, this region had gained historical importance as the first part of the Southwest explored by the Spanish. As early as 1540, a Spanish expedition led by Francisco Vásquez de Coronado passed through this region, and today a national memorial near Hereford commemorates Coronado's journey.

Nearly 150 years later, Father Eusebio Francisco Kino founded a string of Jesuit missions across the region the Spanish called the Pimeria Alta, an area that would later become northern Mexico and eventually southern Arizona. Converting the Indians and building mission churches, Father Kino left a long-lasting mark on this region. Two of the missions he founded—San Xavier del Bac (p. 436), 9 miles south of present-day Tucson, and San José de Tumacácori, south of Tubac (see the listing for Tumacácori National Historical Park, below)—still stand.

More than 450 years after Coronado marched through this region, the valley of the San Pedro River is undergoing something of a population explosion, especially in the city of Sierra Vista, where retirement communities sprawl across the landscape. Nearby, in the once nearly abandoned copper-mining town of Bisbee, urban refugees and artists have taken up residence and opened numerous galleries and B&Bs, making this one of the most interesting small towns in the state.

The combination of low deserts, high plains, and even higher mountains has given this region a fascinating diversity of landscapes. Giant saguaros cover the slopes of the Sonoran Desert throughout much of southern Arizona, and in the western parts of this region, organ pipe cacti reach the northern limit of their range. In the cool mountains, cacti give way to pines, and passing clouds bring snow and rain. Narrow canyons and broad valleys, fed by the rain and snowmelt, provide habitat for hundreds of species of birds and other wildlife. For many birds usually found only south of the border, this is the northernmost limit of their range. Consequently, southeastern Arizona has become one of the nation's most important bird-watching spots.

The region's mild climate has also given rise to a small wine industry. Touring the handful of wineries and vineyards in southeastern Arizona is a favorite

PREVIOUS PAGE: **Kartchner Caverns State Park®.**

weekend excursion for residents of Tucson and Phoenix. When planning a trip through southern Arizona, it's well worth mapping out a route that will let you stop at a winery or two.

ORGAN PIPE CACTUS NATIONAL MONUMENT ★★

135 miles S of Phoenix; 140 miles W of Tucson; 185 miles SE of Yuma

Located roughly midway between Yuma and Tucson, Organ Pipe Cactus National Monument is a preserve for the rare cactus for which the monument is named. The organ pipe cactus resembles the saguaro cactus in many ways, but instead of forming a single main trunk, organ pipes have many trunks, some 20 feet tall, that resemble—you guessed it—organ pipes.

This is a rugged region with few towns or services. To the west lie the inaccessible Cabeza Prieta National Wildlife Refuge and the Barry M. Goldwater Air Force Range (a bombing range), and to the east is the large Tohono O'odham Indian Reservation. The only motels in the area are in the small town of Ajo, a former company town that was built to house copper-mine workers. The downtown plaza, with its tall palm trees, covered walkways, and arches, has the look and feel of a Mexican town square. Be sure to gas up your car before leaving Ajo.

Essentials

GETTING THERE From Tucson, take Ariz. 86 west to Why and turn south on Ariz. 85. From Yuma, take I-8 east to Gila Bend and drive south on Ariz. 85.

FEES The park entry fee is $8 per car.

VISITOR INFORMATION For information, contact **Organ Pipe Cactus National Monument** (✆ **520/387-6849;** www.nps.gov/orpi). The Kris Eggle Visitor Center is open daily from 8am to 5pm, although the park itself is open 24 hours a day. The visitor center is closed Thanksgiving and Christmas.

Organ pipe cactus can have trunks as high as 20 feet.

Exploring the Monument

Two well-graded gravel roads lead through different sections of this large national monument, and many visitors are content to just drive through this unusual landscape. For the best scenery in the park, follow Ajo Mountain Drive, a 21-mile one-way loop that meanders through the rugged foothills of the Ajo Mountains. Along this route, you can get out and hike the Arch Canyon, Estes Canyon, or Bull Pasture trails. Alternatively, if you are short on time, take Puerto Blanco Drive, a 5-mile route leading to the Pinkley Peak picnic area.

Guides available at the park's visitor center explain natural features of the landscape along both drives. In the winter, there are guided van tours of Ajo Mountain Drive, as well as guided hikes. Much of the monument is now closed to the public due to safety concerns about the use of this area by illegal immigrants crossing the border from Mexico. Be sure to check with the national monument before planning any hikes.

Where to Stay

There are two campgrounds within the park. Campsites are $8 in primitive **Alamo Campground** and $12 in the more developed **Twin Peaks Campground.** The nearest lodgings are in Ajo, with several old and very basic motels as well as a B&B. There are also plenty of budget chain motels in the town of Gila Bend, 70 miles north of the monument.

Guest House Inn Bed & Breakfast Built in 1925 as a guesthouse for mining executives, this B&B has attractive gardens in the front yard, a mesquite thicket off to one side, and a modern Southwestern feel to its interior decor. Guest rooms are simply furnished with reproduction antique and Southwestern furnishings. There are sunrooms on both the north and the south sides of the house.

700 Guest House Rd., Ajo, AZ 85321. www.guesthouseinn.biz. ✆ **520/387-6133.** 4 units. $89 double. Rates include full breakfast. MC, V. *In room:* A/C, fridge, hair dryer, free Wi-Fi.

En Route to Tucson

If you're on your way from Organ Pipe Cactus National Monument to Tucson via Ariz. 86, you will pass through the large Tohono O'odham Indian Reservation. To learn more about this tribe, stop at the **Tohono O'odham Nation Cultural Center & Museum,** Fresnal Canyon Road, Topawa (✆ **520/383-0201;** www.tonation-nsn.gov/cultural_center_museum.aspx), south of the community of Sells. The museum is in a beautiful modern building with attractive gardens, and, although displays are designed primarily for tribal members, there is also plenty to interest anyone not from the reservation. A gift shop sells baskets, native wild foods, and other interesting gift items. The museum is open Monday through Saturday from 10am to 4pm; admission is free. To find the museum, drive 9 miles south from Sells on Indian Rte. 19 and watch for a water tower. Turn left here onto Fresnal Canyon Road and drive ¼ mile.

Farther east on Ariz. 86, be sure to stop at **Coyote Store,** Ariz. 86, Milepost 140 (✆ **520/383-5555**), where you can shop for Tohono O'odham baskets, as well as silver jewelry. You'll find this trading post east of the turnoff for Kitt Peak National Observatory (p. 477), which is a must-visit spot along this route.

WHERE TO EAT

Desert Rain Café NATIVE AMERICAN Despite the many Indian reservations in Arizona, there are very few restaurants in the state that serve traditional Native American meals. This little cafe an hour west of Tucson on the Tohono O'odham reservation is one of the few I've found, and it is well worth a stop. The cafe serves simple dishes made with traditional ingredients such as tepary beans, cholla cactus buds, and prickly-pear syrup. If you happen to be passing through the area, Desert Rain should not be missed. A small gallery adjacent to the cafe sells traditional Tohono O'odham crafts and cooking ingredients.

Tohono Plaza, Main St. (Indian Rte. 19), Sells. ✆ **520/383-4918.** www.desertraincafe.com. MC, V. Main courses $5–$7. Mon–Fri 6:30am–3pm.

Southern Arizona
0
15 mi
0
15 km
Amerind Foundation Museum 8
Chiricahua National Monument 11
Cochise Stronghold 9
Coronado National Memorial 6
Fort Bowie National Historic Site 10
Kartchner Caverns State Park 4
Patagonia–Sonoita Creek Preserve 3
Ramsey Canyon Preserve 5
San Pedro Riparian Nat'l Conservation Area 7
Tubac Presidio State Historic Park 1
Tumacácori National Historical Park 2
Flagstaff
ARIZONA
Phoenix
Tucson
Area of detail
To Phoenix
Tucson
SAGUARO NATIONAL PARK
CORONADO NATIONAL FOREST
San Pedro River
To Organ Pipe Cactus National Monument
Green Valley
Santa Cruz River
Arivaca Junction
Amado
To Arivaca, Sasabe and Buenos Aires Nat'l Wildlife Refuge
Tubac
Tumacacori
Patagonia Lake State Park
Mt. Wrightson
Sonoita
Patagonia
Elgin
Benson
St. David
Presidio Santa Cruz de Terrenate
Fairbank
Huachuca City
Fort Huachuca
Sierra Vista
Huachuca Peak
Miller Peak
Murray Springs Clovis Site
Tombstone
Hereford
Palominas
Bisbee
Nogales
MEXICO
Willcox
Cochise
Mt. Glenn
Sunsites
Pearce
Gleeson
Sunizona
Elfrida
McNeal
Douglas
Agua Prieta
To Portal
Bowie
Dos Cabezas

TUBAC ★★ & BUENOS AIRES NATIONAL WILDLIFE REFUGE ★

45 miles S of Tucson; 21 miles N of Nogales; 84 miles W of Sierra Vista

Located in the fertile valley of the Santa Cruz River 45 miles south of Tucson, Tubac is one of Arizona's largest arts communities and home to a large retirement community. Because the town's old buildings also house more than 80 shops selling fine arts, crafts, unusual gifts, and lots of Southwest souvenirs, Tubac is one of southern Arizona's most popular destinations.

In 1691, Father Eusebio Francisco Kino established Tumacácori as one of the first Spanish missions in what would eventually become Arizona. At that time, Tubac was a Pima Indian village, but by the 1730s, the Spanish had begun settling here in the region they called Pimeria Alta. After a Pima uprising in 1751, Spanish forces were sent into the area to protect the settlers, and in 1752 Tubac became a presidio (fort).

While the European history of this area dates back more than 300 years, human habitation of the region dates far back into prehistory. Archaeologists have found evidence that there have been people living along the Santa Cruz River for nearly 10,000 years. The Hohokam lived in the area from about A.D. 300 until their mysterious disappearance around 1500, and when the Spanish arrived some 200 years later, they found the Pima people inhabiting this region.

Tubac's other claim to fame is as the site from which Juan Bautista de Anza III, the second commander of the presidio, set out in 1775 to find an overland route to California. De Anza led 240 settlers and more than 1,000 head of cattle on this grueling expedition, and when the group finally reached the coast of California, they founded the settlement of San Francisco. A year after de Anza's journey to the Pacific, the garrison was moved from Tubac to Tucson, and, with no protection from marauding Apaches, Tubac's settlers soon moved away from the area. Soldiers were once again stationed here beginning in 1787, but lack of funds later caused the closure of the presidio when, in 1821, Mexican independence brought Tubac under a new flag. It was not until this region became U.S. territory that settlers returned, and by 1860, Tubac was the largest town in Arizona.

After visiting Tubac Presidio State Historic Park and Tumacácori National Historical Park to learn about the area's history, you'll probably want to spend some time browsing through the shops. If you happen to be visiting between June and September, keep in mind that many of the local artists leave town during the summer and local shops tend to close on weekdays. During the busy season from October to May, however, shops are open daily.

Essentials

GETTING THERE The Santa Cruz Valley towns of Amado, Tubac, and Tumacácori are all due south of Tucson on I-19.

Spanish explorer Juan Bautista de Anza III.

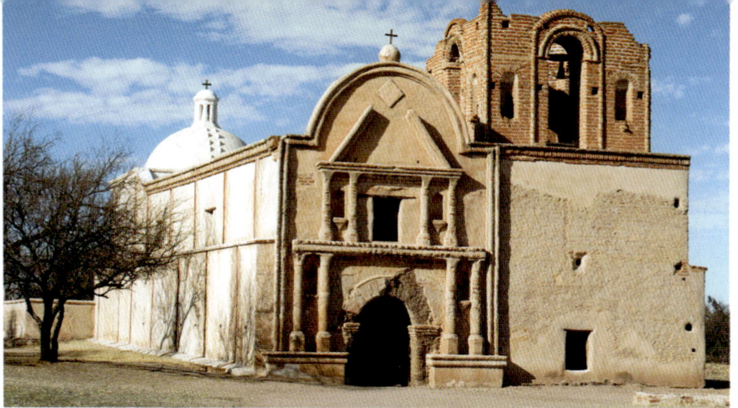

Tumacácori National Historical Park.

VISITOR INFORMATION For information on Tubac and Tumacácori, contact the **Tubac Chamber of Commerce,** 2 Tubac Rd. (✆ **520/398-2704;** www.tubacaz.com).

SPECIAL EVENTS Each year in February, artists from all over the country participate in the **Tubac Festival of the Arts.** On the third weekend in October, the **Anza Day Celebration** commemorates Capt. Juan Bautista de Anza's 1775 westward trek that led to the founding of San Francisco.

Art & History in the Santa Cruz Valley

Tubac Center of the Arts ★ Tubac is an arts community, and this Spanish colonial building serves as its center for cultural activities. Throughout the season, the center features workshops, traveling exhibitions, juried shows, an annual crafts show, and theater and music performances. The quality of the art at these shows is generally better than what's found in most of the surrounding stores. There is also a good little gift shop here.

9 Plaza Rd. ✆ **520/398-2371.** www.tubacarts.org. Admission by donation. Mon–Sat 10am–4:30pm; Sun 1–4:30pm. Closed major holidays and Mon–Wed in summer.

Tubac Presidio State Historic Park Although little remains of the old presidio (fort) other than buried foundation walls, this small park does a good job of presenting the region's Spanish colonial history. Park exhibits focus on the Spanish soldiers, Native Americans, religion, and contemporary Hispanic culture in southern Arizona. Also on the grounds is the old Tubac School, built in 1885 and the oldest schoolhouse in the state. Living-history presentations are staged October through March on the first and third Fridays of the month between noon and 3:30pm. Among the characters you'll meet are Spanish soldiers, settlers, and friars.

1 Burruel St. ✆ **520/398-2252.** www.azstateparks.com. Admission $4 adults, $2 children 7–13, free for children 6 and under. Daily 9am–5pm. Closed Christmas.

Tumacácori National Historical Park ★ Founded in 1691 by Jesuit missionary and explorer Father Eusebio Francisco Kino, San José de Tumacácori mission was one of the first Anglo settlements in what is today Arizona. Father Kino's mission was to convert the Pima Indians, and for the first 60 years, the mission was successful. However, in 1751, during the Pima Revolt, the mission was destroyed. For the next 70 years, this mission struggled to survive, but during the 1820s, an adobe mission church was constructed. Today, the mission ruins are a silent and haunting reminder of the role that Spanish missionaries played in settling the Southwest. Much of the old adobe mission church still stands, and the Spanish architectural influences can readily be seen. A small museum contains exhibits on mission life and the history of the region. On weekends between January and April, Native American and Mexican craftspeople give demonstrations of indigenous crafts. January through April, there are also tours to the nearby mission ruins of Calabazas and Guevavi. These tours are by reservation and cost $20 per person. **La Fiesta de Tumacácori,** a celebration of Indian, Hispanic, and Anglo cultures, is held the first weekend of December.

1891 E. Frontage Rd. ✆ **520/398-2341.** www.nps.gov/tuma. Admission $3 adults, free for children 15 and under. Daily 9am–5pm. Closed Thanksgiving and Christmas. Take I-19 to exit 29; Tumacácori is 3 miles south of Tubac.

Shopping

While tourist brochures like to tout Tubac as an artists' community, the town is more of a Southwest souvenir mecca. There are a few genuine art galleries here, but you have to look hard amid the many tourist shops to find the real gems.

Some of the better fine art in the area is at the **Karin Newby Gallery,** Mercado de Baca, 19 Tubac Rd. (✆ **888/398-9662** or 520/398-9662; www.karinnewbygallery.com), which also has a large sculpture garden. For traditional Western art, some by members of the prestigious Cowboy Artists of America, visit **Big Horn Galleries,** 37 Tubac Rd. (✆ **520/398-9209;** www.bighorngalleries.com).

If you want to take the flavor of the area home, stop in at the **Santa Cruz Chili & Spice Company** ★, 1868 E. Frontage Rd. (✆ **520/398-2591;** www.santacruzchili.com). At this combination store and packing plant near Tumacácori National Historical Park, you'll find all things hot (chilies, hot sauces, salsas) arranged on the shelves of one of the more genuine Tubac-area institutions. There's an amazing assortment of familiar and obscure spices for sale. In back, you can see various herbs being prepared and packaged. The shop is open Monday through Friday from 8am to 5pm and Saturday from 10am to 5pm (until 3pm in summer).

Going Nuts in Sahuarita

As you drive south from Tucson to Tubac, you pass through the town of Sahuarita, which is home to one of the largest pecan farms in the country. More than 6,000 acres surrounding Sahuarita are planted with pecan trees. At the **Pecan Store,** 1625 E. Sahuarita Rd., Sahuarita (✆ **800/327-3226** or 520/791-2062; www.pecanstore.com), you can go "nuts" stocking up on everything from fresh pecans to chocolate toffee pecans to mesquite-spiced pecans (my personal favorite). The store is open Monday through Saturday from 9am to 5pm and Sunday from 10am to 4pm.

Buenos Aires National Wildlife Refuge ★

If you're a bird-watcher, you'll definitely want to make the trip to **Buenos Aires National Wildlife Refuge** (✆ **520/823-4251;** www.fws.gov/southwest/refuges/arizona/buenosaires/index.html), about 28 miles from Tubac. To get here, head north from Tubac on I-19 to Arivaca Junction, then drive west on a winding two-lane road. The refuge begins just outside the small community of Arivaca.

Bird-watchers shouldn't miss Buenos Aires National Wildlife Refuge.

Your first stop should be **Arivaca Cienega,** a quarter of a mile east of Arivaca. *Cienega* is Spanish for "marsh," and that is exactly what you'll find here. A boardwalk leads across this marsh, which is fed by seven springs that provide year-round water and consequently attract a wide variety of bird life. Vermilion flycatchers are quite common here, and this is one of the few places in the United States where you can see a gray hawk. Other good birding spots within the refuge include **Arivaca Creek,** 2 miles west of Arivaca, and **Aguirre Lake,** a seasonal lake a half-mile north of the refuge headquarters and visitor center, which is off Ariz. 286 north of Sasabe.

The **visitor center** is a good place to spot one of the refuge's rarest birds, the masked bobwhite quail. These quail disappeared from Arizona in the late 19th century, but have been reintroduced in the refuge. Other birds you might spot outside the visitor center include Bendire's thrashers, Chihuahuan ravens, canyon towhees, and green-tailed towhees. The visitor center is open daily from 7:30am to 4pm (closed New Year's Day, Thanksgiving, Christmas, and summer weekends).

Other wildlife in the refuge includes pronghorn antelopes, javelinas, coatimundis, white-tailed deer, mule deer, and coyotes. Guided birding walks are offered Saturday mornings at 8am from November through April. During these same months, on the second and fourth Saturdays of the month, there are 5-mile guided hikes in Brown Canyon. Reservations are required for these latter hikes. There is primitive **camping** at nearly 100 designated spots along rough gravel roads. Look for the brown campsite signs along the road, and bring your own water.

These roads also offer good mountain biking. If you're looking for a strenuous hike, try the **Mustang Trail,** which has its trail head 2 miles west of Arivaca. The trail climbs from Arivaca Creek into the surrounding dry hills and makes for a 5-mile round-trip hike.

Other Outdoor Pursuits

The 8-mile **de Anza Trail,** which passes through forests and grasslands and follows the Santa Cruz River for much of its route, links Tubac with Tumacácori. This trail is part of the **Juan Bautista de Anza National Historic Trail,** which stretches from Nogales to San Francisco and commemorates the overland journey of the Spanish captain who, in 1775 and 1776, led a small band of colonists overland to California. These settlers founded what is now the city of San Francisco. Today, bird-watching is the most popular activity along the trail. History buffs will also get to see an excavation of part of the Spanish colonial settlement of Tubac. The most convenient trail head is beside Tubac Presidio State Historic Park. **Rex Ranch** (✆ **520/398-2914;** www.rexranch.com) offers horseback rides starting at $40 per hour.

If golf is more your speed, you can play a round at the **Tubac Golf Resort & Spa** (✆ **520/398-2021;** www.tubacgolfresort.com), just north of Tubac off East Frontage Road. Greens fees range from $99 to $109 in the winter ($79–$89 after 12:30pm).

The Ruby Road

If you enjoy scenic drives and don't mind gravel roads, you won't want to pass up the opportunity to drive the Ruby Road from Arivaca through Coronado National Forest to Peña Blanca Lake and Nogales. This road winds its way through the mountains just north of the Mexican border, passing Arivaca Lake before reaching picturesque Peña Blanca Lake, where the pavement resumes. Along the way, you'll pass the privately owned ghost town of Ruby (✆ **520/744-4471**), which is open to the public Thursday through Sunday from dawn to dusk (admission $12). Call first to make sure the caretaker is available.

Where to Stay

IN AMADO

Amado Territory Inn ★ This modern inn, just off I-19 at the crossroads of Amado, is built in the territorial style and has a bit of the feel of an old Arizona ranch house. Guest rooms are outfitted in a mix of Mexican rustic furnishings and reproduction antiques, much like homes would have been furnished in Arizona more than 100 years ago. Rooms on the second floor feature balconies with views across the farm fields of the Santa Cruz Valley, while those on the ground floor have patios.

3001 E. Frontage Rd. (P.O. Box 81), Amado, AZ 85645. www.amadoterritoryinn.com. ✆ **888/398-8684** or 520/398-8684. Fax 520/398-8186. 14 units. Nov–June $130–$165 double, $250 suite; July–Oct $105–$130 double, $220 suite. Rates include full breakfast. AE, DISC, MC, V. Children 13 and over welcome. Pets accepted. **Amenities:** Restaurant; spa services. *In room:* A/C, hair dryer, no phone, free Wi-Fi.

The Rex Ranch ★ With its classic Southwestern styling and location adjacent to the de Anza Trail, this place is truly a hidden getaway. Just getting to the remote property is something of an adventure, because you have to drive *through* the Santa Cruz River to reach the ranch. When you see the pink-walled mission-revival building in the middle of the desert, you'll know you've arrived someplace distinctly different. Although not all of the guest rooms are as attractively decorated as the public areas, the new rooms and the more recently renovated rooms are quite comfortable. Primarily a conference center, the ranch offers horseback riding and a wide variety of economical spa treatments and massages.

131 Amado Montosa Rd. (P.O. Box 636), Amado, AZ 85645. www.rexranch.com. ✆ **520/398-2914.** 30 units. Oct to mid-Dec $135 double, $160 suite; mid-Dec to May $150 double, $205 suite; June–Sept $115 double, $125 suite. 2-night minimum stay. AE, DISC, MC, V. **Amenities:** Restaurant; bikes; concierge; Jacuzzi; outdoor pool; spa. *In room:* A/C, fridge, no phone, free Wi-Fi.

IN TUBAC

Tubac Golf Resort & Spa ★★ This economical golf resort is built on the Otero Ranch, which dates back to 1789 and is the oldest Spanish land-grant ranch in the Southwest. Today, with its green fairways, the resort is a lush oasis amid the dry hills of the Santa Cruz Valley and is luxurious enough to compete with many of Tucson's resorts. However, the Tubac Golf Resort has more a classic Southwestern ambience than most of the Tucson golf resorts, and because it is fairly small, it has a low-key feel that I like. The red-tile roofs and brick archways throughout the resort conjure its Spanish heritage, while guest rooms are spacious and modern and set amid expansive lawns. Casitas have patios, beamed ceilings, and beehive fireplaces; newer rooms are worth requesting.

1 Otero Rd. (P.O. Box 1297), Tubac, AZ 85646. www.tubacgolfresort.com. ✆ **800/848-7893** or 520/398-2211. Fax 520/398-9261. 98 units. $99–$279 double; $239–$339 suite. Children 12 and under stay free in parent's room. AE, DC, DISC, MC, V. Pets accepted ($25 fee). **Amenities:** 3 restaurants; 2 lounges; babysitting; bikes; concierge; 27-hole golf course; exercise room; 2 Jacuzzis; outdoor pool; room service; full-service spa; tennis court. *In room:* A/C, TV/DVD, CD player, fridge, hair dryer, free Wi-Fi.

Where to Eat

In addition to the restaurants mentioned below, **Stables,** at the Tubac Golf Resort & Spa, serves good steaks, as does **Cantina Romantica,** at the Rex Ranch.

IN TUBAC & TUMACÁCORI

If you need a latte while you're in town, stop by the **Tubac Deli & Coffee Co.,** 6 Plaza Rd. (✆ **520/398-3330;** www.tubacdeli.com).

Dos Silos ★ MEXICAN Set amid the green lawns and gardens of the Tubac Golf Resort, this restaurant takes its name from the two old silos that tower over the patio. Good Mexican food and a fun atmosphere make this my favorite area restaurant. I always order the fish tacos and a margarita when I eat here; both are excellent. There's also decent guacamole, and the ceviche is another good bet.

Tubac Golf Resort, 1 Otero Rd., Tubac. ✆ **520/398-3787.** Reservations recommended. Main courses $12–$25 dinner. AE, DISC, MC, V. Daily 4:30–9pm.

Elvira's Restaurant ★ MEXICAN This Mexican restaurant, its ceiling decorated with hundreds of unusual glass "teardrop" ornaments, was originally south of the border in Nogales, Mexico, where it was a popular dinner destination for gringos. Because safety concerns and passport requirements have been keeping Americans from crossing the border into Mexico, Elvira's has moved north, making it much easier to enjoy the restaurant's complex and flavorful *mole* dishes and the unusual flank-steak *molcajete* that is served in a stone dish traditionally used for grinding guacamole. The margaritas here are notoriously strong.

2221 E. Frontage Rd., Ste. A101–102. ✆ **520/398-9421.** www.elvirasrestaurant.com. Reservations recommended. Main courses $12–$26. AE, DISC, MC, V. Tues–Thurs 11am–9pm; Fri–Sat 11am–10pm; Sun 11am–3pm.

Wisdom's Cafe 🎁 MEXICAN Located between Tubac and Tumacácori (look for the giant chicken statues out front), this roadside diner is a Santa Cruz Valley institution, in business since 1944. With a cement floor and walls hung with old cowboy stuff, it feels a bit like a cross between a cave and an old barn. The menu is short but includes some twists on standard Mexican fare, including tostadas, tacos, and enchiladas made with turkey. Don't eat too much, though, or you won't have room for this restaurant's main draw—huge fruit burritos that are basically Mexican fruit pies.

1931 E. Frontage Rd., Tumacácori. ✆ **520/398-2397.** www.wisdomscafe.com. Reservations not necessary. Main courses $5.25–$16. AE, DISC, MC, V. Mon–Sat 11am–3pm and 5–8pm.

STARRY, STARRY nights

Southern Arizona's clear skies and the absence of lights in the surrounding desert make the night sky here as brilliant as anywhere on earth. This fact has not gone unnoticed by the world's astronomers, and consequently, southern Arizona has come to be known as the Astronomy Capital of the World.

Many observatories are open to the public, but you'll need to make tour reservations well in advance. In addition to the ones listed below, the **Flandrau: The UA Science Center** (p. 442) in Tucson offers public viewings. In Flagstaff, there are public viewing programs at the **Lowell Observatory** (p. 298). Flagstaff is also home to the **Shooting Star Inn,** 27948 N. Shooting Star Lane, Flagstaff, AZ 86001 (✆ **928/606-8070;** www.shootingstarinn.com), an off-the-grid inn where you can gaze through the owner's impressive array of telescopes (p. 302).

The **Mount Lemmon Sky Center** (✆ **520/626-8122;** http://skycenter.arizona.edu), 27 miles from Tucson near the summit of Mount Lemmon, is affiliated with the University of Arizona and is the most convenient place to attend a night-sky viewing program. This facility has a 24-inch telescope, and celestial objects you'll see during one of these programs include binary stars, star clusters, nebulae, galaxies, planets, and the moon. These SkyNights programs cost $48, last 4 to 5 hours, and include a light dinner. Allow 90 minutes to drive to the center from midtown Tucson.

The **Fred Lawrence Whipple Observatory** (✆ **520/670-5707;** www.cfa.harvard.edu/facilities/flwo), atop 8,550-foot Mount Hopkins, is the largest observatory operated by the Smithsonian Astrophysical Observatory. Six-hour tours of the observatory are offered mid-March through November on Monday, Wednesday, and Friday, and cost $7 for adults, $2.50 for children 6 to 12; no children 5 or under are allowed. Reservations are required and should be made 4 to 6 weeks in advance. No food is available here, so bring a picnic lunch. The observatory's visitor center (Mon–Fri 8:30am–4:30pm; closed federal holidays) is reached by taking I-19 south from Tucson to the Canoa exit (exit 56); go under the freeway and then turn right on E. Frontage Road and drive south 3 miles, and turn left on Elephant Head Road and then right on Mount Hopkins Road.

NOGALES

63 miles S of Tucson; 175 miles S of Phoenix; 65 miles W of Sierra Vista

Situated on the Mexican border, the twin towns of Nogales, Arizona, and Nogales, Sonora, Mexico (known jointly as Ambos Nogales), form a bustling border community. All day long, U.S. citizens cross into Mexico to shop for bargains on Mexican handicrafts, pharmaceuticals, tequila, and Kahlúa, while Mexican citizens cross into the United States to buy products not available in their country.

Essentials

GETTING THERE Nogales is the last town on I-19 before the Mexican border. Ariz. 82 leads northeast from town toward Sonoita and Sierra Vista.

VISITOR INFORMATION Contact the **Nogales Chamber of Commerce,** 123 W. Kino Park Way (✆ **520/287-3685;** www.nogaleschamber.com).

Located in the Quinlan Mountains atop 6,875-foot Kitt Peak, **Kitt Peak National Observatory** ★ (✆ **520/318-8726;** www.noao.edu/kpno) is the largest and most famous astronomical observatory in the region and is the site of the world's largest collection of optical telescopes. This is the region's only major observatory to offer public nighttime viewing. Day visitors can stop in at the observatory's visitor center (daily 9am–3:45pm), explore a museum, and take a guided tour. Tours are held at 10am, 11:30am, and 1:30pm. Admission to the visitor center is free; tours are $5.75 to $7.75 for adults ($7.75–$9.75 for all three tours) and $3 to $4 for children ages 7 to 12 ($3.25–$4.25 for all three tours). The observatory is 56 miles southwest of Tucson off Ariz. 86 (allow 90 min. for the drive). Nighttime stargazing (reservations required, call 2–4 weeks in advance) costs $48 for adults; $44 for students and seniors. The visitor center is closed New Year's Day, Thanksgiving, and Christmas.

The **Mount Graham International Observatory** near the town of Safford offers 7-hour tours that include lunch but do not include viewing through the observatory's telescopes. Tours are arranged through **Eastern Arizona College's Discovery Park Campus,** 1651 W. Discovery Park Blvd., Safford (✆ **928/428-6260;** www.eac.edu/discoverypark). The tours operate from May through October and cost $40 (reservations are required).

Exploring North & South of the Border

Most people who visit Nogales, Arizona, are here to cross the border to Nogales, Mexico. The favorable exchange rate makes shopping in Mexico very popular with Americans, although many of the items for sale in Mexico can sometimes be found at lower prices in Tucson. Many people now cross the border specifically to purchase prescription drugs, and pharmacies line the streets near the border crossing.

Nogales, Mexico, is a typical border town filled with tiny shops selling crafts and souvenirs. Some of the better deals are on wool rugs, which cost a fraction of what a Navajo rug costs but are not nearly as well made. Pottery is another popular buy. My personal favorites are the ceramic sinks and hand-blown glass tumblers and pitchers. Dozens of restaurants serve simple Mexican food and cheap margaritas.

Plenty of shops and restaurants in Nogales, Mexico, are within walking distance of the border, so unless you plan to continue farther into Mexico, it's not a good idea to take your car. There are numerous pay parking lots and garages on

These Boots Were Made for Ridin'

Cowboys and cowgirls in search of the ultimate pair of boots should be sure to schedule a visit to Nogales's **Paul Bond Boot Company,** 915 W. Paul Bond Dr. (✆ **520/281-0512;** www.paulbondboots.com), where you can shop for cowboy boots that are both functional and works of art. These boots can sell for $1,200 or more, although you can also get boots for as little as $550. This boot maker has been in business in Nogales since the 1950s. Take exit 4 (Mariposa Rd.) off I-19 and drive west.

the U.S. side of the border where your vehicle will be secure for the day. If you should take your car into Mexico, be sure to get Mexican auto insurance beforehand—your U.S. auto insurance will not be valid. If you are a member of the American Automobile Association, you can get Mexican auto insurance through the AAA office in Tucson. You can also get insurance through **Sanborn's** (✆ **800/222-0158;** www.sanbornsinsurance.com).

Most businesses in Nogales, Mexico, accept U.S. dollars. You may bring back $800 worth of merchandise duty-free, including 1 liter of liquor (if you are 21 or older). You now need either a passport, a passport card, a Trusted Traveler Card, or some other U.S. government–accepted identification document to cross the border into Mexico and return to the U.S. Be sure to verify that you have appropriate documentation before entering Mexico; visit www.travel.state.gov for more info.

Note: Nogales has had a high crime rate in recent years, but tourists have not been targeted. Still, it's advisable to check the current situation before crossing the border.

Where to Stay & Eat

Esplendor Resort at Rio Rico ★★ Just a few miles north of Nogales, Esplendor is a secluded hilltop golf resort with great views across the Santa Cruz Valley and amenities that are similar to what you'll find at many Tucson resorts. Rooms are done up in a very tasteful Spanish colonial decor, have attractive tile work in the bathrooms, and are some of the prettiest in southern Arizona. The only drawback is that the resort's Robert Trent Jones golf course is a short drive away on the far side of the freeway. The dining room serves good food and has very nice views. The resort is a good place to get away from it all, but it also makes a good base for exploring east to Patagonia and west to Buenos Aires National Wildlife Refuge.

1069 Camino Caralampi, Rio Rico, AZ 85648. www.esplendor-resort.com. ✆ **800/288-4746** or 520/281-1901. Fax 520/281-7132. 180 units. $109–$179 double; $199–$450 suite. Children 12 and under stay free in parent's room. AE, DC, DISC, MC, V. Pets accepted ($25 fee). **Amenities:** 2 restaurants; 2 lounges; 18-hole golf course; exercise room; Jacuzzi; Olympic-size outdoor pool; room service; sauna; 4 tennis courts. *In room:* A/C, TV, fridge, hair dryer, free Wi-Fi.

Hacienda Corona de Guevavi ★ Few lodging places anywhere in Arizona capture the character of the state better than this historic hilltop ranch house outside of Nogales. Originally the headquarters of the Guevavi Ranch, the sprawling home was once a favorite getaway for John Wayne and had been abandoned when Phil and Wendy Stover bought the hacienda and embarked on a major restoration. Today the inn, which is built around courtyards and quiet gardens, has five very tastefully decorated guest rooms, all but one of which reflect the inn's Southwestern heritage (La Patrona is my favorite room). The one room that does not have a Southwestern flavor has the feel of a room at an African safari lodge. There are also several casitas (guesthouses) available for families. Dinners and horseback riding can be arranged.

348 S. River Rd., Nogales, AZ 85628. www.haciendacorona.com. ✆ **520/287-6503.** Fax 520/287-9312. 8 units. $189–$249 double. Rates include full breakfast and evening hors d'oeuvres. DISC, MC, V. No children 5 or under in main house but young children accepted in casitas. Pets accepted ($100 refundable deposit, plus $5 per night). **Amenities:** Concierge; outdoor pool; free Wi-Fi. *In room:* A/C, fridge, hair dryer, no phone.

PATAGONIA ★★ & SONOITA ★

Patagonia: 18 miles NW of Nogales; 60 miles SE of Tucson; 171 miles SE of Phoenix; 50 miles SW of Tombstone

A mild climate, a few good restaurants, bed-and-breakfast inns, and a handful of wineries have turned the small communities of Patagonia and Sonoita into a favorite weekend getaway for Tucsonans. Sonoita Creek, one of the only perennial streams in southern Arizona, attracts an amazing variety of bird life and, consequently, this area also attracts flocks of bird-watchers from all over the country.

Patagonia and Sonoita are only about 12 miles apart, but they have decidedly different characters. Patagonia is a sleepy little hamlet with tree-shaded streets, quite a few old adobe buildings, and a big park in the middle of town. The town's main draw, especially for bird-watchers, is the Nature Conservancy preserve on the western edge of town. Sonoita, on the other hand, sits out on the windswept high plains and is really a highway crossroads, not a town. The landscape around Sonoita, however, is filled with expensive new homes on small ranches, and not far away are the vineyards of one of Arizona's main wine regions.

Essentials

GETTING THERE Sonoita is at the junction of Ariz. 83 and Ariz. 82. Patagonia is 12 miles southwest of Sonoita on Ariz. 82.

VISITOR INFORMATION The **Patagonia Area Business Association Tourist Information Center,** 317 McKeown Ave. (✆ **888/794-0060;** www.patagoniaaz.com), is open Monday through Saturday from 10am to 5pm and Sunday from 10am to 4pm.

Bird-Watching, Wine Tasting & Other Area Activities

Patagonia, 18 miles northwest of Nogales on Ariz. 82, is a historic mining and ranching town that is surrounded by the Patagonia Mountains. If the scenery here leaves you with a sense of déjà vu, that is probably because you've seen this landscape in numerous movies and television shows. Over the years, this area has been a backdrop for such films as *Oklahoma!*, *Red River*, *A Star Is Born*, and *David and Bathsheba*, and such TV programs as *Little House on the Prairie* and *The Young Riders*. Today, however, bird-watching and tranquillity draw most people to this remote town.

FROM TOP: **Patagonia–Sonoita Creek Preserve; Nesting red-tailed hawks in the Patagonia–Sonoita Creek Preserve.**

The **Patagonia–Sonoita Creek Preserve** (✆ **520/394-2400;** www.nature.org) is owned by the Nature Conservancy and protects 2 miles of Sonoita Creek riparian (riverside) habitat, which is important to migratory birds. More than 300 species of birds have been spotted at the preserve, which makes it a popular destination with birders from all over the country. Among the rare birds that can be seen are 22 species of flycatchers, kingbirds, and phoebes, plus the Montezuma quail. A forest of cottonwood trees, some more than 100 feet tall, lines the creek. At one time, such forests grew along all the rivers in the region, but today, this is one of southern Arizona's best remaining examples of a cottonwood-willow riparian forest. To reach the sanctuary, which is just outside Patagonia on a dirt road that parallels Ariz. 82, turn west on Fourth Avenue and then south on Pennsylvania Street, drive through the creek, and continue about 1 mile. From April to September, hours are Wednesday through Sunday from 6:30am to 4pm; from October to March, hours are Wednesday through Sunday from 7:30am to 4pm. Admission is $5 ($3 for Nature Conservancy members). On Saturday at 9am, there are naturalist-guided walks through the preserve; reservations are not required.

On your way to or from the Nature Conservancy Preserve, be sure to drop by **Paton's Birder's Haven.** Numerous hummingbird feeders and a variety of other feeders attract an amazing range of birds to the yard, making this a favorite stop of avid birders who are touring the region. If you're heading out to the Nature Conservancy preserve, watch for the BIRDER'S HAVEN sign at 477 Pennsylvania Rd. after you cross the creek.

Another required birders' stop in the area is at the **Patagonia Roadside Rest Area,** 4¼ miles south of Patagonia on Ariz. 82. This pull-off is a good place to look for rose-throated becards, varied buntings, and zone-tailed hawks.

Avid birders will also want to visit **Las Cienegas National Conservation Area** (✆ **520/258-7200;** www.blm.gov/az), which has grasslands, wetlands, and oak forests. This is a good place to look for the rarely seen gray hawk. Access is off the east side of Ariz. 83, about 7 miles north of Sonoita.

Patagonia Lake State Park (✆ **520/287-6965;** www.azstateparks.com), about 7 miles south of Patagonia off Ariz. 82, is a popular boating and fishing lake that was formed by the damming of Sonoita Creek. The lake is 2½ miles long and stocked in winter with rainbow trout. Other times of the year, people fish for bass, crappie, bluegill, and catfish. Park facilities include a picnic ground, campground, and swimming beach. Adjacent to the state park, you'll find the **Sonoita Creek State Natural Area** (✆ **520/287-2791**), a 5,000-acre preserve along the banks of Sonoita Creek. This natural area is known for its excellent bird-watching, and guided birding walks are offered on a regular basis. Elegant trogons, which are among the most beautiful of southern Arizona's rare birds, are often spotted here. The park day-use fee is $10. Campsites are $17 to $25; reservations are not accepted.

If you'd like to have a local birding guide take you out and help you identify the area's many species of flycatchers, contact Matt Brown at the **Patagonia Birding & Butterfly Co.** (✆ **520/604-6300;** www.lifebirds.com). For two people, the charge is $30 per hour. If you want to do some horseback riding while you're in the area, contact **Arizona Horseback Experience** (✆ **520/455-5696;** www.horsebackexperience.com), and book a trail ride through the area's grasslands. A 3-hour ride is $95 and a wine-tasting ride to a local winery is $180.

While in Patagonia, be sure to check out the interesting shops and galleries around town. You'll find interesting books and gifts at **Mariposa Books,** 317 McKeown Ave. (✆ **520/394-9186**). **Mesquite Grove Gallery,** 371 McKeown Ave. (✆ **520/394-2356**), has a good selection of works by area artists. At **Global Arts Gallery,** 315 McKeown Ave. (✆ **520/394-0077;** www.globalartsgallery.com), you'll find a wide range of ethnic arts, fine art, jewelry, and women's clothing. Also be sure to visit **La Galeria Dia de los Muertos,** 266 Naugle Ave. (✆ **520/394-2035**). This little cottage, associated with Grayce's Gift and Candle Shop, was the creation of Grayce Arnold, who assembled a collection of hundreds of Mexican skeleton figures that were created for Mexico's Dia de los Muertos (Day of the Dead) celebration. The gallery is usually open on weekends, call ahead on weekdays.

Sonoita is little more than a crossroads with a few shops and restaurants, but surrounding the community are miles of rolling grasslands that are a mix of luxury-home "ranchettes" and actual cattle ranches, all of which have spectacular big-sky views. Out on those high plains, more than just deer and antelope play. Oenophiles roam, as well. With nine wineries between Sonoita and Elgin, this is Arizona's biggest little wine country (there are also concentrations of wineries to the east of here near Willcox and in the Sedona area of central Arizona). Most of the wineries are located in or near the village of Elgin, which is 10 miles east of Sonoita. The following are my favorite area wineries. If you want to try some of the other wineries in the area, pick up a map at any of these wineries. Also, remember that most area wineries will give you a discount on your tasting if you bring a glass from another area winery.

Right in Sonoita, you'll find **Dos Cabezas WineWorks,** 3248 Ariz. 82 (✆ **520/841-1193;** www.

Navajo Rugs

If you happen to be in the market for a Navajo rug, get in touch with Steve Getzwiller at **Nizhoni Ranch Gallery** (✆ **520/455-5020;** www.navajorug.com), which is located outside Sonoita. Here you'll find one of Arizona's best selections of contemporary and old Navajo rugs.

See the collection of hundreds of skeleton figures at La Galeria Dia de los Muertos.

Callaghan Vineyards produces the best wines in the region.

doscabezaswinery.com), which is located in the middle of town. The winery's tasting room is open Thursday through Sunday from 10:30am to 4:30pm ($7 tasting fee). Five miles south of Sonoita, you'll find **Lightning Ridge Cellars,** 2368 Ariz. 83 (✆ **520/455-5383;** www.lightningridgecellars.com), which makes several surprisingly good red wines, primarily from estate-grown grapes. The tasting room is open Friday through Sunday from 11am to 4pm, and the tasting fee is $7. Just west of Elgin, you'll find **Callaghan Vineyards ★**, 336 Elgin Rd. (✆ **520/455-5322;** www.callaghanvineyards.com), which is open for tastings Friday through Sunday from 11am to 3pm ($7 tasting fee). This winery produces by far the best wines in the region and, arguably, the best wines in the state. Next door to Callaghan is **Canelo Hills Vineyard & Winery,** 342 Elgin Rd. (✆ **520/455-5499;** www.canelohillswinery.com), a small winery with a casual tasting room in the winery itself. Owners Joan and Tim Mueller produce some excellent wines in the $20 to $30 range. The tasting room is open Friday through Sunday from 11am to 4pm ($5 tasting fee). Next door to this winery is **Kief-Joshua Vineyards,** 370 Elgin Rd. (✆ **520/455-5582;** www.kj-vineyards.com), which boasts the most ostentatious tasting room in the area. It's open daily from 11am to 5pm ($5 tasting fee).

Where to Stay

IN PATAGONIA

Circle Z Ranch ★ In business since 1926, this is the oldest continuously operating guest ranch in Arizona. Over the years, it has served as a backdrop for numerous movies and TV shows, including *Gunsmoke* and John Wayne's *Red River*. The 6,500-acre ranch on the banks of Sonoita Creek is bordered by the Nature Conservancy's Patagonia–Sonoita Creek Sanctuary, Patagonia State Park, and the Coronado National Forest. More than 165 miles of nearby trails ensure that everyone gets in plenty of riding in a variety of terrain, from desert hills to grasslands to the riparian forest along the creek. The adobe cottages provide an authentic ranch feel that's appreciated by guests hoping to find a genuine bit of the Old West.

Ariz. 82 (btw. Nogales and Patagonia), P.O. Box 194, Patagonia, AZ 85624. www.circlez.com. ✆ **888/854-2525** or 520/394-2525. Fax 520/394-2058. 24 units. $2,440–$3,920 double per week. Rates do not include 15% service charge. Lower rates for children 15 and under. Nightly rates sometimes available, with 3-night minimum. Rates include all meals and horseback riding. MC, V. Closed early May to late Oct. **Amenities:** Dining room; BYOB lounge; outdoor pool; tennis court. *In room:* No phone.

Duquesne House B&B ★ This historic adobe building 1 block off Patagonia's main street was built in 1898 as a boarding house for miners. Today the little adobe building, with its shady front porch, is your best choice for overnight accommodations in Patagonia. Each of the three suites has its own entrance, sitting room, and bedroom, and is decorated in an eclectic Southwestern style. The studio apartment has its own kitchenette. My favorite room has an ornate woodstove and claw-foot tub. At the back of the house, an enclosed porch overlooks the large garden.

357 Duquesne Ave. (P.O. Box 162), Patagonia, AZ 85624. www.theduquesnehouse.com. ✆ **520/394-2732.** 4 units. Thurs–Mon $125 double (rate includes full breakfast); Tues–Wed $110 double (rate does not include breakfast). No credit cards. *In room:* A/C, CD player, hair dryer, no phone, free Wi-Fi.

IN SONOITA

Xanadu Ranch GetAway To "B" or not to "B," that is the question at Xanadu Ranch, which calls itself a hybrid B&B. What this means is that you can opt for a breakfast basket or not, your choice. You can also opt to bring your own horse with you if you wish, since this place is also a "horse motel." The ranch owners, Bernie and Karen Kauk, don't offer horseback riding, but they can put you in touch with people who do. Rooms are spacious and comfortable, and the setting, on a hill south of town, provides great views and awesome sunsets. Despite the name, the Bunkhouse is both the nicest (and newest) room on the ranch. This makes a good base both for touring the wine country and bird-watching.

92 S. Los Encinos Rd. (P.O. Box 1291), Sonoita, AZ 85637. www.xanaduranchgetaway.com. ✆ **520/455-0050.** 4 units. $99–$129 double (lower rates for longer stays). AE, DC, DISC, MC, V. Pets accepted ($10 per night). *In room:* AC, TV/DVD, CD player, fridge, hair dryer, kitchen (in some), free Wi-Fi.

Where to Eat

IN PATAGONIA

For good coffee and pastries, check out **Gathering Grounds,** 319 McKeown Ave. (✆ **520/394-2009**), which also serves ice cream and has a deli.

Velvet Elvis Pizza Company ITALIAN This casual hangout sums up the unusual character of Patagonia's residents. Faux-finished walls ooze artiness, while paeans to pop culture include shrines to both the Virgin Mary and Elvis. The menu features a variety of pizzas heaped with veggies, cheeses, and meats, but if you can remember to plan a day in advance, you should call in an order for the Inca pizza (made with a quinoa-flour crust). Add an organic salad and accompany it with some fresh juice, microbrew, espresso, or wine.

292 Naugle Ave. ✆ **520/394-2102.** www.velvetelvispizza.com. Reservations accepted for parties of 6 or more. Pizzas $12–$45; other dishes $7.50–$10. MC, V. Thurs–Sun 11:30am–8:30pm.

IN SONOITA

Grab good breads and pastries, hot breakfasts, and sandwiches at the **Grasslands Bakery & Café,** 3119 Ariz. 83 (✆ **520/455-4770;** www.grasslandsbakery.com), which is an outpost of organic foods. There are even tastings of organic wines and loads of house-made salsas, jams, and other items for sale. The bakery is open Thursday through Saturday from 10am to 3pm and Sunday from 8am to 3pm.

Canela ★★ SOUTHWESTERN This little restaurant at the crossroads of Sonoita is the most upscale restaurant between Tucson and Bisbee and is an absolute must if you are in the area for a wine-country getaway. The menu changes frequently to take advantage of what's fresh and seasonal, but may include sunchoke soup garnished with paprika and sunchoke chips; crispy sweetbreads with local spinach, black olives, cream, and grilled lemon; roasted Churro (heirloom) leg of lamb; or Arizona beef hanger steak with local cress and honey-thyme mashed sweet potatoes, and *chimichurri* sauce. This is the quintessential Arizona wine-country restaurant. The Sunday brunch is a great way to begin an afternoon of wine tasting at area wineries.

3252 Ariz. 82. ✆ **520/455-5873.** www.canelabistro.com. Reservations recommended. Main courses $17–$24. AE, DISC, MC, V. Thurs–Sat 3–9pm; Sun 10am–3pm. Closed July–Aug.

The Steak Out STEAK This is ranch country, and this big barn of a place is where the ranchers and everyone else for miles around head when they want a good steak. A classic cowboy atmosphere prevails—there's even a mounted steer head just inside the front door. The restaurant's name and the scent of a mesquite fire should be all the hints you need about what to order—a grilled steak, preferably the exceedingly tender filet mignon. Wash it down with a beer, and you've got the perfect cowboy dinner.

3200 S. Sonoita Hwy. (at intersection of Ariz. 82 and Ariz. 83). ✆ **520/455-5205.** www.azsteakout.com. Reservations recommended. Main courses $8–$36. AE, DISC, MC, V. Mon–Thurs 5–9pm; Fri 5–10pm; Sat 11am–10pm; Sun 11am–9pm.

SIERRA VISTA & THE SAN PEDRO VALLEY ★

70 miles SE of Tucson; 189 miles SE of Phoenix; 33 miles SW of Tombstone; 33 miles W of Bisbee

At an elevation of 4,620 feet above sea level, Sierra Vista is blessed with the perfect climate—never too hot, never too cold. This fact more than anything else has contributed to Sierra Vista becoming one of the fastest-growing cities in Arizona. Although the city itself is a modern, sprawling community outside the gates of the U.S. Army's Fort Huachuca, it is wedged between the Huachuca Mountains and the valley of the San Pedro River. Consequently, Sierra Vista makes a good base for exploring the region's natural attractions.

Within a few miles' drive of town are the San Pedro Riparian National Conservation Area, Coronado National Memorial, and the Nature Conservancy's Ramsey Canyon Preserve. No other area of the United States attracts more attention from birders, who come in hopes of spotting some of the 300 bird species that have been sighted in southeastern Arizona. About 25 miles north of town is Kartchner Caverns State Park®, the region's biggest attraction.

Essentials

GETTING THERE Sierra Vista is at the junction of Ariz. 90 and Ariz. 92 about 35 miles south of I-10.

VISITOR INFORMATION The **Sierra Vista Convention & Visitors Bureau,** 3020 Tacoma St. (✆ **800/288-3861** or 520/417-6960; www.visitsierravista.com), can provide information on the area. To find the visitor center if you're coming from the north, take the Ariz. 90 Bypass, turn right on Coronado Drive, turn left on Tacoma Street, and continue to the Oscar Yrun Community Center.

SPECIAL EVENTS In February, cowboy poets, singers, and musicians come together at the **Cochise Cowboy Poetry & Music Gathering** (www.cowboypoets.com).

Attractions Around Benson

Tucson may have Old Tucson Studios, but Benson has **Mescal** (✆ **520/883-0100**). This Western-town movie set is operated by Old Tucson Studios and has been used for years in the making of Westerns, as well as TV shows and commercials. Hour-long walking tours of Mescal are offered and provide a feel for the many movies that have been shot here. While Old Tucson Studios feels like an amusement park, this place seems like an old ghost town. For fans of old Westerns, this is a must. Tours are available on Saturday between 10am and 2pm, and cost $9 per person. Roughly 35 miles east of Tucson, take Exit 297 off I-10, then head north for 3 miles on Mescal Road. When the pavement ends, head west for ½ mile on the dirt road to the town, which is visible on the hill ahead.

While Kartchner Caverns® is the main draw in the Benson area, you may also want to visit the remarkable **Singing Wind Bookshop** (✆ **520/586-2425**), on a ranch down a dirt road north of town. The store has been in business more than 30 years and started out with just a couple of shelves of books. Now the inventory is well into the thousands, with an emphasis on the Southwest, natural sciences, and children's literature. To get here, take exit 304 from I-10 in Benson. Drive north 2¼ miles and take a right (east) at the sign that says SINGING WIND ROAD. Drive to the end, opening and closing the gate. The store is open daily from 9am to 5pm.

Kartchner Caverns State Park®.

Kartchner Caverns State Park® ★★ These caverns are among the largest and most beautiful in the country, and because they are wet caverns, stalactites, stalagmites, soda straws, and other cave formations are still growing. Within the caverns are two huge rooms, each larger than a football field with ceilings more than 100 feet high. These two rooms can be visited on two separate tours. On the shorter Rotunda/Throne Room Tour, you'll see, in the Rotunda Room, thousands of delicate soda straws. The highlight, though, is the Throne Room, at the center of which is a 58-foot-tall column. The second, and longer, tour visits the Big Room and leads past many strange and rare cave formations. Within the park are several miles of aboveground hiking trails. A campground ($25 per night) provides a convenient place to stay in the area.

Because the caverns are a popular attraction and tours are limited, try to make a reservation in advance, especially if you want to visit on a weekend. However, it is sometimes possible to get same-day tickets.

Off Ariz. 90, 9 miles south of Benson. ✆ **520/586-2283** for reservations or 520/586-4100 for information. www.azstateparks.com. Admission $6 per car (up to 4 adults). Tours $23 adults, $13 children 7–13, children 6 or under not allowed on Big Room Tour. Park 8:30am–5:30pm. Closed Christmas; no Big Room Tours mid-Apr to mid-Oct.

Attractions Around Sierra Vista

Arizona Folklore Preserve Set beneath the shady cottonwoods and sycamores of Ramsey Canyon, the Arizona Folklore Preserve is the brainchild of Dolan Ellis, Arizona's official state balladeer, and his wife, Rose. Ellis was first appointed state balladeer back in 1966 and has been writing songs about Arizona for more than 45 years. He performs most weekends and often welcomes musical guests to the stage of this performance hall.

56 E. Folklore Trail. ✆ **520/378-6165.** www.arizonafolklore.com. Admission $15 adults, $6 students 17 and under. Showtime Sat–Sun 2pm. Reservations recommended. Take Ariz. 92 south from Sierra Vista and turn right onto Ramsey Canyon Rd.

Fort Huachuca Museum Fort Huachuca, an army base at the mouth of Huachuca Canyon just west of Sierra Vista, was established in 1877. The buildings of the old post have been declared a National Historic Landmark, and one is now a museum dedicated to the many forts that dotted the Southwest in the latter part of the 19th century. Interesting aspects of the exhibits include quotes by soldiers that give an idea of what it was like to serve back then. The associated **U.S. Army Intelligence Museum,** at Hungerford and Cristi streets, has displays on early code machines, surveillance drones, and other pieces of equipment formerly used for intelligence gathering.

At the Fort Huachuca U.S. Army base, Grierson Rd., Sierra Vista. ✆ **520/533-5736.** Admission by donation. Mon–Fri 9am–4pm; Sat–Sun 1–4pm. Closed all federal holidays.

Birding Hot Spots & Other Natural Areas

Bird-watching is big business in these parts, with birders' B&Bs, bird refuges, and even birding festivals. The **Southwest Wings Birding and Nature Festival** (www.swwings.org), one of southern Arizona's biggest annual birding events, is held each year in early August in Sierra Vista.

If you'd like to join a guided bird walk along the San Pedro River or up Miller Canyon in the Huachuca Mountains, an owl-watching night hike, or a hummingbird banding session, contact the **Southeastern Arizona Bird Observatory** (✆ **520/432-1388;** www.sabo.org), which also has a public bird-viewing area at its headquarters 2 miles north of the Mule Mountain Tunnel on Ariz. 80 north of Bisbee (watch for Hidden Meadow Lane). Most activities cost $10 to $20, although there are also half-day trips for $45 and day trips for $70. Workshops and tours are also offered.

Serious birders who want to be sure to add lots of rare birds to their life lists might want to visit this area on a guided tour. Your best bet is **Mark Pretti Nature Tours** (✆ **520/803-6889;** www.markprettinaturetours.com), run by the former resident naturalist at Ramsey Canyon Preserve. A half-day birding tour costs $120 and a full-day tour costs $200 to $220. Three-day ($625) and 7- to 8-day ($1,300–$1,400) trips are also offered. Melody Kehl's of **Melody's Birding Adventures** (✆ **520/245-4085;** www.ebiz.netopia.com/outdoor) is another reliable local guide; her rates start at $25 per hour. **High Lonesome**

Hummingbird Heaven

If it's summer and you're looking to add as many hummingbirds to your life list as possible, take a drive up Miller Canyon (south of Ramsey Canyon) to **Beatty's Guest Ranch and Orchard,** 2173 E. Miller Canyon Rd., Hereford (✆ **520/378-2728;** www.beattysguestranch.com), where a public hummingbird-viewing area is set up. A total of 15 species of hummers have been sighted here, and several times, 14 species have been seen in 1 day.

Birdtours (✆ **443/838-6589;** www.hilonesome.com), another local tour company, charges $2,450 per person for a 7-day birding trip.

South of Ramsey Canyon off Ariz. 92, you'll find **Carr Canyon,** which has a road that climbs up through the canyon to some of the higher elevations in the Huachuca Mountains. Keep your eyes open for buff-breasted flycatchers, red crossbills, and red-faced warblers. The one-lane road is narrow and winding (usually navigable by passenger car), and not for the acrophobic. It climbs 5 miles up into the mountains to the old mining camp of Reef Townsite.

The **Environmental Operations Park,** 3 miles east of Ariz. 92 on Ariz. 90, is a grasslands and wetlands restoration site at Sierra Vista's sewage treatment facility, and is a good place to see yellow-headed blackbirds, ducks, peregrines, and harriers from fall to spring. For more information, contact the City of Sierra Vista (✆ **520/458-3315**) or the Southeast Arizona Bird Observatory (✆ **520/432-1388**).

Coronado National Memorial About 20 miles south of Sierra Vista is a 5,000-acre preserve dedicated to Francisco Vásquez de Coronado, the first European to explore this region. In 1540, Coronado, leading more than 700 people, left Compostela, Mexico, in search of the fabled Seven Cities of Cíbola, said to be rich in gold and jewels. Sometime between 1540 and 1542, Coronado led his band of weary men and women up the valley of the San Pedro River, which this monument overlooks. At the visitor center, you can learn about Coronado's fruitless quest for riches and check out the wildlife observation area. A quarter-mile from the visitor center, a trail leads three-quarters of a mile to 600-foot-long Coronado Cave. (You'll need to bring your own flashlight.) After stopping at the visitor center, drive up to 6,575-foot Montezuma Pass, which is in the center of the memorial and provides far-reaching views of Sonora, Mexico, to the south, the San Pedro River to the east, and several mountain ranges and valleys to the west. Along the .8-mile round-trip Coronado Peak Trail, you'll also have good views of the valley and can read quotations from the journals of Coronado's followers. There are also some longer trails where you'll see few other hikers.

4101 E. Montezuma Canyon Rd., Hereford. ✆ **520/366-5515.** www.nps.gov/coro. Free admission. Visitor center daily 8am–4pm; memorial daily dawn–dusk. Closed Thanksgiving and Christmas. Take Ariz. 92 south from Sierra Vista to S. Coronado Memorial Dr. and continue 5 miles to the visitor center.

Ramsey Canyon Preserve ★ Each year, beginning in late spring, a buzzing fills the air in Ramsey Canyon, but instead of reaching for the bug repellant, visitors reach for their binoculars. It's not the buzzing of bees or mosquitoes that fills the air, but rather the buzzing of hummingbirds. Over the years, 14 species of hummingbirds have been sighted here, and it is the whirring of these diminutive birds' wings that fills the air. Because Ramsey Creek, which flows through the canyon, is a year-round stream, it attracts a wide variety of wildlife, including bears, bobcats, and more than 170 species of birds. A short nature trail leads through the canyon, and a second trail leads higher up the canyon. April and May are the busiest times here, while May and August are the best times to see hummingbirds. Between March and October, guided walks are offered Tuesday, Thursday, and Saturday at 9am.

Ramsey Creek attracts a variety of wildlife.

27 Ramsey Canyon Rd., off Ariz. 92, 5 miles south of Sierra Vista. ✆ **520/378-2785.** www.nature.org. Admission $5 ($3 for Nature Conservancy members); free on 1st Sat of each month. Mar–Aug daily 8am–5pm; Sept–Feb Thurs–Mon 8am–5pm. Closed New Year's Day, Thanksgiving, and Christmas.

San Pedro Riparian National Conservation Area ★ Over the past century, roughly 90% of Arizona's free-flowing year-round rivers and streams have disappeared due to human use of desert waters. These rivers and streams once supported riparian areas that provided water, food, and protection to myriad plants, animals, and even humans. You can get an idea of what such riparian areas were like by visiting this sprawling preserve, which is located 8 miles east of Sierra Vista. Fossil findings from this area indicate that people were living along this river as much as 13,000 years ago. At that time, this area was a swamp, not a desert. Today, the San Pedro River is all that remains of this ancient wetland, and, due to an earthquake a century ago, much of the San Pedro's water now flows underground. Don't expect a wide, rushing river when you visit the San Pedro; what you'll see here would be called a creek anywhere but Arizona. Still, the water attracts wildlife, especially birds, and the conservation area is very popular with birders, who have a chance of spotting more than 350 species here.

Also within the riparian area is the **Murray Springs Clovis Site,** where 16 spear points and the remains of a 13,000-year-old mammoth kill were found in the 1960s. Although there isn't much to see other than some trenches, there are numerous interpretive signs along the short trail through the site. It's just north of Ariz. 90 about 5 miles east of Sierra Vista.

For a glimpse of the region's Spanish history, visit the ruins of the **Presidio Santa Cruz de Terrenate,** about 20 miles northeast of Sierra Vista off Ariz. 82 near the ghost town of Fairbank. This military outpost was established in 1775 or 1776 but was never completed due to the constant attacks by Apaches. Today

A Holy Bird Sanctuary

In the community of St. David, 5 miles south of Benson on Ariz. 80, you'll find the Holy Trinity Monastery (✆ 520/720-4016; www.holytrinitymonastery.org), which is near the banks of the San Pedro River and has a 1.3-mile birding trail.

San Pedro Riparian National Conservation Area.

only decaying adobe walls remain. To reach this site, take Ariz. 82 east from U.S. 90 and drive north 1¾ miles on Ironhorse Ranch Road, which is at milepost 60. It's a 1.3-mile hike to the site.

To visit **Fairbank** ghost town, drive Ariz. 82 to the bridge over the San Pedro River. Here you'll find the remains of several buildings from the heyday of this former railroad town. Fairbank, which was founded in the 1880s to serve nearby silver-mining towns, once had a population of nearly 15,000 people. Today, only one of the old buildings has been restored and opened to the public. The old Fairbank School is now the **Fairbank Schoolhouse Museum and Store** (✆ **520/457-3062**) and is open Friday through Sunday from 9:30am to 4:30pm; admission is free. From Fairbank, several miles of hiking trails lead along the San Pedro River. You can walk to two other ghost towns, Millville and Charleston, but there is very little to see at either of these old town sites. It is also possible to walk from Fairbank to the ruins of the Presidio Santa Cruz de Terrenate.

For bird-watching, the best place is the system of trails at the Ariz. 90 crossing of the San Pedro. Here you'll find the **San Pedro House,** a 1930s ranch that is operated as a visitor center and bookstore. It's open daily from 9:30am to 4:30pm and has information on guided walks and hikes, bird walks, bird-banding sessions, and other events that are scheduled throughout the year. Outside the old ranch house, there's a huge old cottonwood tree.

Ariz. 90. ✆ **520/439-6400.** www.blm.gov/az/st/en/prog/blm_special_areas/ncarea/sprnca.html. Free admission. Parking areas sunrise–sunset.

Other Outdoor Pursuits

Hikers will find numerous trails in the Huachuca Mountains west of Sierra Vista. There are trails at Garden Canyon on Fort Huachuca, at Ramsey Canyon Preserve, at Carr Canyon in Coronado National Forest, and within Coronado National Memorial. See "Birding Hot Spots & Other Natural Areas," above, for details. For information on hiking in the Coronado National Forest, contact the **Sierra Vista Ranger District,** 5990 S. Hwy. 92 (✆ **520/378-0311;** www.fs.fed.us/r3/coronado), 8 miles south of Sierra Vista.

Where to Stay

IN BENSON

Desert Rose Inn If you're looking for lodging close to Kartchner Caverns®, try this off-ramp budget hotel in Benson. The hotel's lobby is done in Santa Fe style with flagstone floors and rustic Southwestern furniture. Guest rooms are strictly hotel modern, but they are roomy and reliable.

630 S. Village Loop, Benson, AZ 85602. www.desertroseinnaz.com. ✆ **866/943-4970.** Fax 520/586-1370. 62 units. $92–$162 double. Rates include continental breakfast. Children 19 and under stay free in parent's room. AE, DC, DISC, MC, V. **Amenities:** Exercise room; outdoor pool. *In room:* A/C, TV, fridge, hair dryer, free Wi-Fi.

IN SIERRA VISTA

Lazy Dog Ranch This small B&B is located within the San Pedro Riparian National Conservation Area, with the river flowing past the edge of the property. Consequently, the inn is an excellent choice for bird-watchers. Accommodations are both quite large, and are decorated with Southwestern style. One unit is a cottage just off the courtyard, and the other unit has a kitchenette. In that courtyard you'll find both a fire pit (for cool nights) and a swimming pool (for warm days). There are hiking trails nearby. Around the inn, you'll find lots of art and artifacts from owners Michael and Catherine McCormack's world travels, and, yes, there are lazy dogs in residence.

3123 N. Thistle Rd., Sierra Vista, AZ 85635. www.lazydogranch.net. ✆ **520/458-5583.** 2 units. $125 double. 2-night minimum on weekends. Rates include continental breakfast. Children 10 and under stay free in parent's room. AE, DC, DISC, MC, V. Pets accepted ($10 per night). **Amenities:** Seasonal outdoor pool. *In room:* Fridge, free Wi-Fi.

IN HEREFORD

Ash Canyon Bed & Breakfast ★ With a single casita (little house), this secluded birders' B&B may be small, but if you're serious about birds, this is *the* place to stay in the area. People come from all over the country to sit on owner/innkeeper Mary Jo Ballator's back patio watching rare birds, many of which never make it much farther north than right here. Stay in the cute little cottage, and you'll be able to catch all the bird activity at sunrise and sunset. By the way, the casita is built from straw bales and consequently is very energy efficient.

5255 Spring Rd., Hereford, AZ 85615-9029. www.ashcanyonbandb.com. ✆ **520/378-0773.** 1 unit. $140 double (discounts for longer stays). Sept 15–Feb 15 and June 2-night minimum; other months 3-night minimum. Rates include full breakfast. Children 2 and under stay free in parent's room. No credit cards. *In room:* CD player, hair dryer, kitchen, free Wi-Fi.

Casa de San Pedro ★ Built with bird-watching tour groups in mind, this modern inn is set on the west side of the San Pedro River on 10 acres of land. The inn is built in the territorial style around a courtyard garden and has large, comfortable hotel-style guest rooms and a large common room where birders gather to swap tales of the day's sightings. The inn also offers birding, cultural, and history tours. This is by far the most upscale inn in the region and is my favorite.

8933 S. Yell Lane, Hereford, AZ 85615. www.bedandbirds.com. ✆ **888/257-2050** or 520/366-1300. Fax 520/366-0701. 10 units. $169–$179 double. Rates include full breakfast. AE, DISC, MC, V. No children 11 or under. **Amenities:** Concierge; Jacuzzi; outdoor pool. *In room:* A/C, CD player, hair dryer, free Wi-Fi.

Ramsey Canyon Inn Bed & Breakfast Adjacent to the Nature Conservancy's Ramsey Canyon Preserve, this inn is the most convenient choice in the area for avid birders who are here to see the canyon's famous hummingbirds. The property straddles Ramsey Creek, with guest rooms in the main house and housekeeping suites reached by a footbridge over the creek. In addition to the large gourmet breakfast, you'll also get pie in the afternoon. Book early during the birding season. With its on-demand water heaters, gray-water irrigation of the inn's orchard, and use of organic ingredients as often as possible, this inn is doing quite a bit to be eco-friendly.

29 Ramsey Canyon Dr., Hereford, AZ 85615. www.ramseycanyoninn.com. ✆ **520/378-3010.** 9 units. $135–$150 double; $150–$225 suite. Room rates include full breakfast (except in housekeeping suites). DISC, MC, V. No children 15 or under in inn, but children are accepted in suites. **Amenities:** Free Wi-Fi. *In room:* A/C (in some), no phone.

CAMPGROUNDS

There are two Coronado National Forest campgrounds—14-site **Reef Townsite** and 8-site **Ramsey Vista**—up winding Carr Canyon Road south of Sierra Vista off Ariz. 92. Both charge $10 per night. For information, contact the Coronado National Forest Sierra Vista Ranger District, 5990 S. Hwy. 92, Hereford, AZ 85615 (✆ **520/378-0311;** www.fs.fed.us/r3/coronado).

Where to Eat

In addition to the restaurants below, Sierra Vista supports quite a number of Asian restaurants, with an emphasis on Chinese, Japanese, and Korean cuisine.

Hana Tokyo ★ JAPANESE Surprisingly upscale for Sierra Vista, this large Japanese restaurant has tatami rooms, a sushi bar, and hibachi (*teppanyaki*) tables where chefs entertain you as they cook right at your table. The menu is equally diverse, so whether you're in the mood for a steak or sushi, you'll find something. At night, there's even a lively bar here, although if you're here to birdwatch, you're probably an early-to-bed type. You'll find Hana on the south side of town not far from Ramsey Canyon.

1633 S. Ariz. 92. ✆ **520/458-1993.** Reservations recommended. Main courses $7–$30; sushi $1.50–$13. AE, DISC, MC, V. Mon–Sat 11am–2:30pm and 4:30–10pm; Sun noon–9:30pm.

The Mesquite Tree STEAK This casual steakhouse south of town (and not far from the mouth of Ramsey Canyon) has long been a favorite of locals. It's funky and dark, and the prices can't be beat. Although you can get chicken and fish dishes done in a variety of traditional Continental styles, most people come here for the steaks. Try the Vargas rib-eye, which is smothered with green chilies, jack cheese, and enchilada sauce—a real border-country original. When the weather is warm, try to get a seat on the patio.

S. Ariz. 92 and Carr Canyon Rd. ✆ **520/378-2758.** Reservations recommended. Main courses $13–$25. AE, DC, DISC, MC, V. Tues–Sat 5–9pm; Sun 5–8pm.

Sophia's Italian Ristorante ★★ 🎁 ITALIAN If I didn't tell you that Sophia's is one of the best restaurants in southern Arizona and should not be missed, you might never give this place a second glance. It's in a nondescript strip mall in the middle of Sierra Vista and is easily overlooked, but the meals served here are unforgettable. You should be sure to start with the house-made mozzarella rolled around basil and tomatoes, and be sure to keep an eye out for any dish with whipped goat cheese (yum!). The lobster ravioli with creamy pistachio pesto is a good bet as is the seared sea bass with leek-potato puree. Sophia's could hold its own in Tucson or Scottsdale and feels like a genuine discovery.

1630 E. Fry Blvd. ✆ **520/452-0622.** www.sophias-italian.com. Reservations highly recommended. Main courses $8–$10 lunch, $16–$27 dinner. DISC, MC, V. Tues–Fri 11am–2pm and 5–9pm; Sat 5–9pm.

TOMBSTONE ★

70 miles SE of Tucson; 181 miles SE of Phoenix; 24 miles N of Bisbee

All it took was a brief blaze of gunfire more than 125 years ago to seal the fate of this former silver-mining boomtown. On these very streets, outside a livery stable known as the O.K. Corral, Wyatt Earp, his brothers Virgil and Morgan, and their friend Doc Holliday took on the outlaws Ike Clanton and Frank and Tom McLaury on October 26, 1881. Today, Tombstone, "the town too tough to die," is one of Arizona's most popular attractions, but I'll leave it up to you to decide whether it is more of a tacky tourist trap or a genuine historical attraction.

Tombstone was named by Ed Schieffelin, a silver prospector who ventured into this area at a time when the region's Apaches were fighting to preserve their way of life. Schieffelin was warned that all he would find here was his own tombstone, so when he discovered silver, he named the strike Tombstone. Within a few years, the town of Tombstone was larger than San Francisco, and between 1880 and 1887, an estimated $37 million worth of silver was mined here. Such wealth created a sturdy little town, and as the Cochise County seat of the time, Tombstone boasted a number of imposing buildings, including the county courthouse, which is now a state park. In 1887, underground water flooded the silver mines, and despite attempts to pump the water out, the mines were never reopened. With the demise of the mines, the boom came to an end and the population rapidly dwindled.

Today, Tombstone's historic district consists of both original buildings that went up after a fire in 1882 destroyed much of the town and newer structures built in keeping with the architectural styles of the late 19th century. Most house souvenir shops and restaurants, but adults raised on Louis L'Amour, John Wayne, and the outlaw aesthetic seem to love the town.

Essentials

GETTING THERE From Tucson, take I-10 east to Benson and then Ariz. 80 south to Tombstone. From Sierra Vista, take Ariz. 90 north to Ariz. 82, heading east.

VISITOR INFORMATION For more information once you hit town, stop by the **Tombstone Chamber of Commerce Visitor Center,** 395 E. Allen St. (© **888/457-3929** or 520/457-3929; www.tombstonechamber.com).

SPECIAL EVENTS Tombstone's biggest annual celebrations are **Wyatt Earp Days** (www.wyattearpdays.com), which is held in late May and includes an 1880s fashion show and plenty of gunfights, and, on the third weekend in October, **Helldorado Days** (www.wyattearpdays.com), which commemorates the gunfight at the O.K. Corral and includes countless shootouts in the streets, mock hangings, and a parade.

Gunslingers & Saloons: In Search of the Wild West

As portrayed in novels, movies, and TV shows, the shootout has come to epitomize the Wild West, and nowhere is this great American phenomenon more glorified than in Tombstone, where the star attraction is the famous **O.K. Corral,** 308 E. Allen St. (© **520/457-3456;** www.ok-corral.com), site of a 30-second gun battle that has taken on mythic proportions over the years. Inside the corral, you'll find not only displays on the shootout, but also an exhibit focusing on local photographer C. S. Fly, who ran the boardinghouse where Doc Holliday was staying at the time of the shootout. Next door is **Tombstone's Historama,** a kitschy multimedia affair that rehashes the well-known history of Tombstone's "bad old days" and has a recorded narration by Vincent Price. The O.K. Corral and Tombstone's Historama are open daily from 9am to 5pm, and admission is $6 (free for kids 5 and under); for $10, you can visit both attractions and take in a shootout reenactment almost on the very site of the original gunfight.

If you aren't able to catch one of the staged shootouts at the O.K. Corral (daily at 2pm), don't despair—there are plenty of other shootouts staged regularly in Tombstone (usually btw. noon–4pm). Expect to pay $6 for adults, $4 for seniors, and $3 for children at any of these shows. For a little fun and games, try to catch the Tombstone Cowboys shootout at **Helldorado Town,** Fourth and Toughnut streets (no phone). These shootouts, which are staged two to three times a day, are more hysterical than historical.

When the smoke cleared in 1881, three men lay dead. They were later carted off to the **Boot Hill Graveyard,** 408 N. Ariz. 80 (© **520/457-3300**), on the north edge of town. The graves of Clanton and the McLaury brothers, as well as those of others who died in gunfights or by hanging, are well marked. Entertaining epitaphs grace the grave markers; among the most famous is that of Lester Moore—"Here lies Lester Moore, 4 slugs from a 44, No Les, no more." The cemetery is open to the public daily 8am to dusk. Enter through a gift shop on Ariz. 80.

When the residents of Tombstone weren't shooting each other in the streets, they were likely to be found in the saloons and bawdy houses that lined Allen Street. Most famous was the **Bird Cage Theatre,** Allen and Sixth streets (© **800/457-3423** or 520/457-3421; www.tombstonebirdcage.com), so named for the cagelike cribs (what most people would think of as box seats) suspended from the ceiling. These velvet-draped cages were used by prostitutes to ply their trade. For old Tombstone atmosphere, this place is hard to beat. Admission is $10 for adults, $9 for seniors, $8 for children 8 to 18; the theater is open daily from 8am to 6pm.

Wyatt Earp.

A historic poster from the Bird Cage Theatre.

When it's time for a cold beer, Tombstone has a couple of very lively old saloons. The **Crystal Palace Saloon,** 436 E. Allen St. (✆ **520/457-3611;** www.crystalpalacesaloon.com), was built in 1879 and has been completely restored. This is one of the favorite hangouts of the town's costumed actors and other would-be cowboys and cowgirls. **Big Nose Kate's,** 417 E. Allen St. (✆ **520/457-3107;** www.bignosekate.com), is an equally entertaining spot full of Wild West character and characters.

Tombstone has long been a tourist town, and its streets are lined with souvenir shops selling wind chimes, dream catchers, and loads of cowboy souvenirs, and, of course, there are places where you can dress up in old-fashioned clothes and get your picture taken. However, there are also several interesting little museums around town. At the **Rose Tree Inn Museum,** at Fourth and Toughnut streets (✆ **520/457-3326**), you can see the world's largest rose tree. Inside are antique furnishings from Tombstone's heyday in the 1880s. The museum is open daily from 9am to 5pm (closed Thanksgiving and Christmas). Admission is $5 (free for children 13 and under).

Tombstone Courthouse State Park, 223 Toughnut St. (✆ **520/457-3311;** www.azstateparks.com), is the most imposing building in town and provides a much less sensationalized version of local history. Built in 1882, the courthouse is now a state historic park and museum containing artifacts, photos, and newspaper clippings that chronicle Tombstone's lively past. In the courtyard, you can still see the gallows that once ended the lives of outlaws. The park is open daily from 9am to 5pm (closed on Christmas); the entrance fee is $5 for adults and $2 for children 7 to 13.

At the **Tombstone Epitaph Museum,** Fifth Street between Allen and Fremont streets (✆ **520/457-2211;** www.tombstone-epitaph.com), you can inspect the office of the town's old newspaper and learn about John Clum, the original editor of the paper. The museum is open daily from 9:30am to 5pm; admission is free.

The **Tombstone Western Heritage Museum ★**, Fremont (Ariz. 80) and Sixth streets (✆ **520/457-3800;** www.thetombstonemuseum.com), a privately owned museum, holds the town's most fascinating collection of Tombstone artifacts and ephemera and should not be missed. Included in this impressive collection are artifacts that once belonged to Wyatt and Virgil Earp, rare photos of the Earps and the outlaws of Tombstone, and all kinds of original documents that date to the days of the shootout at the O.K. Corral. The museum is open Monday, Tuesday, and Thursday through Saturday from 9am to 6pm and Sunday from 12:30 to 6pm; admission is $5 for adults and $3 for children 12 to 18 ($13 for families).

For more Tombstone history, stop by the **Wyatt Earp House & Gallery,** 102 E. Fremont St. (✆ **520/457-3111;** www.wyattearphouse.com), a tiny adobe house that may once have been the home of Wyatt Earp and was lovingly restored a few years ago. The old house now serves as a small art gallery.

Tombstone Western Heritage Museum.

Andrea's Museum of Victorian Fashions, Third and Toughnut streets (✆ **520/457-2387**), is a tiny private museum exhibit with displays of gorgeous gowns from Victorian times. There are also displays of men's and children's clothes from the period. The museum is usually open daily from 9am to 5pm, and admission is free.

To further immerse yourself in Tombstone's Wild West history, take a walk around town with a guide from **Tombstone Walking Tour** (✆ **520/457-9876;** www.tombstonewalkingtours.com). Tours cost $15 for 1 hour and $25 for 2 hours. Alternatively, take a 20-minute stagecoach ride around the town's historic district ($10 for adults; $5 for children). Stagecoaches leave from in front of the O.K. Corral, which is also where you buy tickets for the **Tombstone Ghost Hunters Tour** (✆ **520/457-3456;** www.spiritsoftombstone.com). These tours of haunted Tombstone are offered on Friday and Saturday nights at 8pm and cost $8. With all the outlaws and lawmen who were gunned down on these streets, it's not surprising that ghost tours are popular.

To see some of the landscapes once roamed by the Earps and the Clantons, get out of town on a Jeep tour. Tours are offered by **Guided Discovery Tours** (✆ **330/819-1041;** www.guideddiscoverytours.com) and **Into the West Jeep Tours** (✆ **520/559-2151** or 520/559-2228; wwwintothewestjeeptours.com). Expect to pay $75 to $100 for a tour (two-person minimum).

Where to Stay

Apache Spirit Ranch ★ Down a gravel road on the outskirts of Tombstone, this guest ranch is built to resemble an old Western cow town. What with the false-fronted buildings and the wind whistling in the mesquite, you can't help but want to walk bowlegged up "Main Street" with a six-gun strapped to your hip. While other guest ranches strive to feel like working cattle operations, this place goes for the Hollywood Western look. The dining room is a saloon that looks as if it could have been frequented by Wyatt Earp, while guest rooms are spacious enough and attractive enough to have kept Mrs. Earp happy. Horseback rides, campfires, an Apache "camp," Native American presentations, line dancing, and live country music all add up to good times and a Wild West feel.

895 W. Monument Rd., Tombstone, AZ 85638. www.apachespiritranch.com. ✆ **877/404-7262** or 520/457-7299. 17 units. 5-night package $1,850–$2,100 double; $2,400 suite. Rates do not include a 15% gratuity. Rates include all meals and horseback riding. AE, DC, DISC, MC, V. **Amenities:** Restaurant; lounge; free airport transfer w/7-night stay; Jacuzzi; outdoor pool. *In room:* A/C, TV, hair dryer, MP3 docking station, free Wi-Fi.

Best Western Lookout Lodge This comfortable motel is a mile north of town overlooking the Dragoon Mountains. Stone walls, porcelain doorknobs, Mexican tiles in the bathrooms, and old-fashioned "gas" lamps give the spacious guest rooms an Old West feel. Ask for a room with a view of the mountains.

781 N. Hwy. 80 W. (P.O. Box 787), Tombstone, AZ 85638. www.bestwesterntombstone.com. ✆ **877/652-6772** or 520/457-2223. Fax 520/457-3870. 40 units. $103–$113 double. Rates include full breakfast. Children 13 and under stay free in parent's room. AE, DC, DISC, MC, V. Pets accepted ($20 per night). **Amenities:** Restaurant; lounge; seasonal outdoor pool. *In room:* A/C, TV, fridge, hair dryer, free Wi-Fi.

Holiday Inn Express Tombstone On the northern outskirts of Tombstone, right next door to the older but slightly nicer Best Western, this is the newest hotel in Tombstone. The decor draws on a bit of Southwestern and Spanish colonial styling, but basically this is just a modern chain motel.

580 W. Randolph Way, Tombstone, AZ 85638. www.hitombstone.com. ✆ **800/315-2621** or 520/457-9507. Fax 520/457-9506. 60 units. $95–$125 double. Rates include continental breakfast. Children 19 and under stay free in parent's room. AE, DC, DISC, MC, V. **Amenities:** Jacuzzi; outdoor pool. *In room:* A/C, TV, hair dryer, free Wi-Fi.

Where to Eat

Unless you're absolutely famished, do not eat in Tombstone. Hold out for Bisbee or even Sierra Vista. Restaurants in Tombstone cater exclusively to tourists, and both food and service are reliably disappointing. Sure there are a couple of bars and a restaurant in historic buildings, but plastic chairs and burger baskets long ago supplanted historic character.

Big Nose Kate's Saloon AMERICAN The food here isn't all that memorable, but the atmosphere sure is. Big Nose Kate's dates back to 1880 and is primarily a saloon. As such, it stays packed with visitors who have come to revel in Tombstone's outlaw past. While you sip your beer, why not order a sandwich and call it lunch? You might even catch some live country music.

417 E. Allen St. ✆ **520/457-3107.** www.bignosekate.com. Reservations not accepted. Sandwiches $7.50–$10; pizzas $13–$20. AE, MC, V. Daily 11am–8pm.

Crystal Palace AMERICAN Okay, so the food here isn't particularly memorable, but the setting sure is. The bar is a fairly authentic reproduction of the original, and the wood floors have been pounded by countless cowboy boots. While you sip your beer and munch your buffalo burger, you can entertain yourself by trying to spot bullet holes in the pressed tin ceiling.

436 E. Allen St. ✆ **520/457-3611.** www.crystalpalacesaloon.com. Reservations not accepted. Main courses $4.50–$17. AE, DISC, MC, V. Daily 11am–8pm.

BISBEE ★★

94 miles SE of Tucson; 205 miles SE of Phoenix; 24 miles NW of Douglas

Arizona has a wealth of ghost towns that boomed on mining profits and then quickly went bust when the mines played out, but none is as impressive as Bisbee, which is built into the steep slopes of Tombstone Canyon on the south side of the Mule Mountains. Between 1880 and 1975, Bisbee's mines produced more than $6 billion worth of metals. When the Phelps Dodge Company shut down its copper mines here, Bisbee nearly went the way of other abandoned mining towns, but because it's the Cochise County seat, it was saved from disappearing into the desert dust.

Bisbee's glory days date from 100 years ago, and because the town stopped growing in the early part of the 20th century, it is now one of the best-preserved historic towns in the Southwest. Old brick buildings line narrow winding streets, and miners' shacks sprawl across the hillsides above downtown. Television and movie producers discovered these well-preserved streets years ago, and since then, Bisbee has doubled as New York, Spain, Greece, Italy, and, of course, the Old West.

The rumor of silver in "them thar hills" is what first attracted prospectors in 1877, and within a few years the diggings attracted the interest of some San

Bisbee is buzzing with bikers most weekends.

Francisco investors, among them Judge DeWitt Bisbee, for whom the town is named. However, it was copper and other less-than-precious metals that would make Bisbee's fortune. With the help of outside financing, large-scale mining operations were begun in 1881 by the Phelps Dodge Company. By 1910, the population had climbed to 25,000, and Bisbee was the largest city between New Orleans and San Francisco. The town boasted that it was the liveliest spot between El Paso and San Francisco—and the presence of nearly 50 saloons and bordellos along Brewery Gulch backed up that claim.

Tucked into a narrow valley surrounded by red hills, Bisbee today has a funky cosmopolitan air. Many artists call the town home, and aging hippies and other urban refugees have for many years been dropping out of the rat race to restore Bisbee's old buildings and open small inns, restaurants, and galleries. Between the rough edges left over from its mining days and this new fringe-culture atmosphere, Bisbee is one of Arizona's most interesting towns. However, be aware that Bisbee is not for everyone. It appeals mostly to young, hip travelers in search of economical, and often somewhat eclectic, accommodations. On weekends, the rumble of motorcycles is a constant on Bisbee's streets.

Essentials

GETTING THERE Bisbee is on Ariz. 80, which begins at I-10 in the town of Benson, 45 miles east of Tucson.

VISITOR INFORMATION Contact the **Bisbee Visitor Center,** 2 Copper Queen Plaza (✆ **866/224-7233** or 520/432-3554; www.discoverbisbee.com).

SPECIAL EVENTS Bisbee puts on **coaster races** (similar to a soap-box derby) on the Fourth of July. September's **Brewery Gulch Daze,** a celebration of Bisbee's bawdy past, includes live music, an art-car show, and a pet parade. In October, there is the **Bisbee 1000: The Great Stair Climb,** a race up and down the town's many public stairways.

Exploring the Town

At the Bisbee Visitor Center, in the middle of town, pick up walking-tour brochures that guide you past the town's most important historic buildings and sites. On the second floor of the **Copper Queen Library,** 6 Main St. (✆ **520/432-4232**), which is the oldest public library in Arizona, old photographs give a good idea of what the town looked like in the past century.

Don't miss the **Bisbee Mining & Historical Museum ★**, 5 Copper Queen Plaza (✆ **520/432-7071;** www.bisbeemuseum.org), housed in the 1897 Copper Queen Consolidated Mining Company office building. This small but comprehensive museum features exhibits on the history of Bisbee. It's open daily from 10am to 4pm; admission is $7.50 for adults, $6.50 for seniors, and $3 children 15 and under.

For another look at early life in Bisbee, visit the **Muheim Heritage House Museum,** 207 Youngblood Hill (✆ **520/432-7698;** www.bisbeemuseum.org), which is reached by walking up Brewery Gulch. The house was built between 1898 and 1915 and has an unusual semicircular porch. The interior is decorated with period furniture. It's open Friday through Tuesday from 10am to 4pm; admission is $4.

O.K. Street, which parallels Brewery Gulch but is high on the hill on the southern edge of town, is a good place to walk for views of Bisbee. At the top of O.K. Street is a path that takes you up to a hill above town for an even better panorama of Bisbee's jumble of old buildings. Atop this hill are numerous small, colorfully painted shrines that are built into the rocks and filled with candles, plastic flowers, and pictures of the Virgin Mary. It's a steep climb on a rocky, very uneven path, but the views and the fascinating little shrines make it worth the effort.

Mining made this town what it is, so you should be sure to take an underground mine tour to find out what it was like to be a miner here in Bisbee. **Queen Mine Tours ★** (✆ **866/432-2071** or 520/432-2071; www.queenminetour.com) takes visitors down into one of the town's old copper mines. Tours are offered daily between 9am and 3:30pm and cost $13 for adults and $5.50 for children 4 to 12. The ticket office and mine are just south of the Old Bisbee business district at the Ariz. 80 interchange.

For an exploration of some of the steeper and narrower streets of Bisbee, take a 90-minute tour ($40) of old Bisbee with **Lavender Jeep Tours** (✆ **520/432-5369;** www.lavenderjeeptours.com). Several other tours are also available. For a walk on the dark side, sign up for the **Old Bisbee Ghost Tour** (✆ **520/432-3308;** www.oldbisbeeghosttour.com). These 90-minute tours are offered Friday through Sunday nights at 7pm and cost $13 for adults and $9 for children 11 and under.

Bisbee has lots of interesting stores and galleries, and shopping is the main recreational activity here. Because turquoise is associated with copper mines, and Bisbee's mines once produced some of the most famous turquoise in the country, you'll see quite a bit of turquoise jewelry around town. To get a look at some of the quality jewelry created from minerals mined in the area, stop by **Czar Jewelry,** 13 Main St. (✆ **520/432-3027**). In **Jewelry Designs by Owen,** 45 Main St. (✆ **520/432-4400;** www.jewelrydesignsbyowen.com), you'll find lots of beautiful jewelry in a wide range of styles. Across the street, at the **Gold Shop,** 46 Main St. (✆ **520/432-4557**), you'll find lots of turquoise set in gold instead of silver, which is much more common. **Uptown Tribal,** 2 Copper Queen Plaza (✆ **520/432-7818;** www.katedrew-wilkinson.com), in the same building that houses Bisbee's visitor center, is another jewelry store worth checking out.

If it's art you're after, you've got lots of good galleries to visit

A Golfer's Nightmare

Beware the Bogeyman at the **Turquoise Valley Golf & RV Park,** 1794 W. Newell St. (✆ **520/432-3091;** www.turquoisevalley.com), in nearby Naco. This little public course dates to 1908, is the oldest golf course in Arizona, and boasts one of the few par-6 holes in the world. The hole, called the Rattler, stretches for 747 yards and is every golfer's nightmare. A round of golf here will run you between $35 and $45.

You'll find vintage bikes at Bisbee Bicycle Brothel.

here in Bisbee. You'll find fanciful kinetic sculptures and colorful paintings at **Sam Poe Gallery,** 24 Main St. (✆ **520/432-5338;** www.sampoegallery.com). Right next door is **PanTerra Gallery,** 22 Main St. (✆ **520/432-3320;** www.panterragallery.com), which sells both the photographs of co-owner Charles Feil and gorgeous women's fashions and jewelry selected by his wife, co-owner Maralyce Ferree. At **Belleza Gallery,** 27 Main St. (✆ **520/432-5877;** www.bellezagallery.org), your art purchase will go to a good cause. The gallery is operated by a nonprofit organization that helps homeless women in a substance-abuse treatment program. The **55 Main Gallery,** 55 Main St. (✆ **520/432-4694;** www.55maingallery.com), featuring contemporary art, jewelry, furniture, and women's fashions, is another of my favorite galleries in town.

Bicyclists should be sure to drop by the **Bisbee Bicycle Brothel,** 43 Brewery Ave. (✆ **520/432-3339;** www.bisbeebicyclebrothel.com), where cycling enthusiast Ken Wallace has a shop full of vintage road bikes, primarily from England and Italy. There are also some interesting modern bikes as well.

To protect your face from the burning rays of the sun (and make a fashion statement), visit **Optimo Custom Hat Works,** 47 Main St. (✆ **520/432-4544;** www.optimohatworks.com), where owner Grant Sergot will custom-fit your felt fedora, cowboy hat, or Panama straw hat. (By the way, Panama hats actually come from Ecuador.)

Where to Stay

MODERATE

Copper City Inn ★ Operated by Fred Miller (bartender at Bisbee's Cafe Roka for 17 years) and his wife, Anita Fox, this inn boasts some of the most attractive rooms in Bisbee. One room is done up with French antiques, and another, dedicated to early-20th-century hotel designer Mary Jane Colter, has a modern Art Deco styling. One suite has modern mission-style furnishings and a full kitchen, while another has two bedrooms, two bathrooms, and a mix of modern and antique furniture. All the rooms have balconies overlooking Bisbee. There's allergy-barrier bedding, and "green" cleaning products are used. Whichever room you reserve, you'll receive a complimentary bottle of wine upon check-in. The Copper City Inn is a "self-service" sort of place; when you make your reservation, you'll be given the key code for the door to your room.

99 Main St., Bisbee, AZ 85603. www.coppercityinn.com. ✆ **520/432-1418** or 520/456-4254. 5 units. $110 double; $135–$250 suite. Rates include continental breakfast. Children 10 and under

stay free in parent's room. AE, DC, DISC, MC, V. **Amenities:** Access to nearby health club. *In room:* A/C, TV/DVD, CD player, fridge, hair dryer, no phone, free Wi-Fi.

Letson Loft Hotel ★★ Located up a flight of stairs, the Letson Loft Hotel feels a bit like an old Italian villa and has some of the prettiest rooms in town. High ceilings, original wood floors, antique furnishings, and plush beds with great linens all add up to comforts and class rarely seen in this funky town. Book one of the front rooms and you'll have a front-row seat for watching the Main Street action through bay windows. If you're a light sleeper, ask for a room at the back of the hotel or avail yourself of the bedside earplugs; Bisbee can be a bit noisy at times. One of my favorite rooms has a huge skylight and another has a claw-foot tub. There's even a suite with a kitchen.

26 Main St. (P.O. Box 623), Bisbee, AZ 85603. www.letsonlofthotel.com. ✆ **877/432-3210** or 520/432-3210. 8 units. $95–$175 double; $125–$185 suite. Rates include continental breakfast. AE, DISC, MC, V. No children 11 or under. **Amenities:** Concierge. *In room:* A/C, TV/DVD, CD player, hair dryer, free Wi-Fi.

INEXPENSIVE

Canyon Rose Suites Located on the second floor of a commercial building just off Bisbee's main street, this property offers spacious suites with full kitchens, which makes it a good bet for longer stays. All units have hardwood floors and high ceilings, and the works by local artists and the mix of contemporary and rustic furnishings give the place plenty of Bisbee character. Constructed on a steep, narrow street, the building housing this lodging has an unusual covered sidewalk, making it one of the more distinctive commercial buildings in town.

27 Subway at Shearer St. (P.O. Box 1915), Bisbee, AZ 85603. www.canyonrose.com. ✆ **866/296-7673** or 520/432-5098. 7 units. $99–$210 double. Children 12 and under stay free in parent's room. AE, DISC, MC, V. *In room:* A/C, TV/DVD, hair dryer, kitchen, free Wi-Fi.

Copper Queen Hotel Built in 1902 by the Copper Queen Mining Company and right in the center of town, this is the oldest continuously operating hotel in Arizona. While the hotel is historic, it has not had a thorough restoration, so it feels more like an old hotel than a historic hotel. The atmosphere is casual yet quite authentic with rooms opening off spacious hallways. Unfortunately, the rooms vary considerably in size, and the smallest are so cramped that they really aren't comfortable for two people. Rooms also vary considerably in the quality of the furnishings, so you should be sure to ask for a renovated room. The restaurant's food can be uneven, but out front is a pleasant terrace for alfresco dining. And what would a mining-town hotel be without its saloon or ghosts (yes, they say this place is haunted)?

11 Howell Ave. (P.O. Drawer CQ), Bisbee, AZ 85603. www.copperqueen.com. ✆ **520/432-2216.** Fax 520/432-3819. 53 units. $89–$197 double. Children 17 and under stay free in parent's room. AE, MC, V. **Amenities:** Restaurant; lounge; small outdoor pool. *In room:* A/C, TV, free Wi-Fi.

Shady Dell Trailer Court Yes, this really is a trailer court, but you'll find neither shade nor dell at the Shady Dell's roadside location just south of the Lavender Pit mine. What you will find are 10 vintage trailers, a 1947 Airporter bus done in retro-Tiki style, and a 1947 Chris Craft yacht, all of which have been lovingly restored. Although some of the trailers don't have their own private bathrooms (a bathhouse is in the middle of the property), they do have all kinds of vintage decor and furnishings—even tapes and records of period music and radio shows. In trailers that have vintage TVs, there are DVDs of old movies. Make reservations far in advance. There's also a 1957 vintage diner on-site.

1 Old Douglas Rd., Bisbee, AZ 85603. www.theshadydell.com. ✆ **520/432-3567.** 11 units. $55–$145 per trailer (for 1–2 people). DISC, MC, V. No children 10 or under. **Amenities:** Restaurant. *In room:* A/C, kitchen, no phone.

Where to Eat

Café Cornucopia, 14 Main St. (✆ **520/432-4820**), offers fresh juices, smoothies, and sandwiches. It's open Tuesday through Sunday from 11am to 5pm. For good coffee and a mining theme (there's an old mining cart and photos of miners on the walls), check out the **Bisbee Coffee Co.,** Copper Queen Plaza, Main Street (✆ **520/432-7879;** www.bisbeecoffee.com). For gourmet picnic supplies, peruse the shelves of the **High Desert Market and Café,** 203 Tombstone Canyon Rd. (✆ **520/432-6775;** www.highdesertmarket.net), which has organic produce, imported cheeses, wine, and other assorted goodies for a great picnic. There is also a cafe here that is a great place for breakfast or lunch. If you're a chocolate lover, do not miss **Chocoláte,** 134 Tombstone Canyon Rd. (✆ **520/432-3011;** www.spiritedchocolate.com; open seasonally, call ahead), a shop that makes chocolate bars and chocolate confections from cacao beans it roasts right here in Bisbee. Be sure to try the Madagascar chocolate; it has a unique flavor that may ruin you for any other chocolate. If chocolate just isn't enough to satisfy your sweet tooth, how about some honey? The **Killer Bee Guy,** 20 Main St. (✆ **877/227-9338;** www.killerbeeguy.com), is full of honeys and honey products.

Bisbee Breakfast Club ★ AMERICAN In the Lowell district on the far side of the Lavender Pit from old Bisbee, this huge diner is a locals' favorite. Big breakfasts (served all day) are the specialty here, and the cinnamon rolls are legendary around town. At lunch, try the coffee-charred breast of chicken salad; it'll really wake up your taste buds.

75 Erie St. ✆ **520/432-5885.** www.bisbeebreakfastclub.com. Reservations not accepted. Main courses $5.50–$8.50. AE, MC, V. Thurs–Mon 7am–3pm.

Bisbee Grille REGIONAL AMERICAN Located in the Art Deco Copper Queen Plaza building at the bottom of Main Street, this is one of Bisbee's best casual restaurants. Not only is the food decent, but there are also large photographs of old Bisbee that give the place a lot of historic character. At lunch or dinner, the buffalo burger is a good bet, as is the Caesar salad. Reliable dinner entrees include several steaks and a variety of pasta dishes. Grab a seat by the window for great people-watching.

2 Copper Queen Plaza. ✆ **520/432-6788.** www.thebisbeegrille.blogspot.com. Reservations accepted for parties of 6 or more. Main course $8–$24. AE, DISC, MC, V. Daily 11am–9pm.

Cafe Roka ★★ NEW AMERICAN The food at Cafe Roka is so good that it is reason enough for a visit to Bisbee. Casual and hip, this place is a real find in such an out-of-the-way town and offers good value as well as delicious and imaginatively prepared food. All meals include, for one fixed price, salad, soup, sorbet intermezzo, and your choice of entree (different entrees are priced differently). The grilled salmon with a Gorgonzola-dill crust and artichoke-and-portobello lasagna are two of my favorites. The flourless chocolate cake with raspberry sauce is an exquisite ending. Local artists display their works, and on Friday nights there is live jazz.

35 Main St. ✆ **520/432-5153.** www.caferoka.com. Reservations highly recommended. Main courses $17–$27. MC, V. Thurs–Sat 5–9pm (closed Wed in summer; call to confirm).

Santiago's MEXICAN Repeat after me: "Fish tacos and a margarita, please." That's all you need to know or say when dining at Santiago's. Order this perfect pairing, and you'll almost certainly leave the restaurant *muy contento.* This is a casual place, but don't be surprised if, on a weekend night, someone sits down in the corner and starts playing classical guitar music. You'll find Santiago's a couple of doors down from the Copper Queen Hotel at the start of Brewery Gulch.

1 Howell Ave. ✆ **520/432-1910.** www.santiagosbisbee.com. Reservations accepted for parties of 6 or more. Main courses $8.50–$16. AE, DISC, MC, V. Daily 5–10pm.

Bisbee After Dark

For more than a century, Bisbee's Brewery Gulch has been known for its many bars. Although there aren't nearly as many drinking establishments today as there were 100 years ago, a few dive bars remain especially popular with the weekend Harley-riding crowd from Tucson. For local microbrews, stop in at **Old Bisbee Brewing Company,** 200 Review Alley (✆ **520/432-2739;** www.oldbisbeebrewingcompany.com), a tiny place wedged into a cramped little space in Brewery Gulch. They have a very good assortment of beers.

EXPLORING THE REST OF COCHISE COUNTY ★

Willcox: 81 miles E of Tucson; 192 miles SE of Phoenix; 74 miles N of Douglas

Although the towns of Bisbee, Tombstone, and Sierra Vista all lie within Cochise County, much of the county is taken up by the vast Sulphur Springs Valley, which is bounded by several mountain ranges. It is across this wide-open landscape that Apache chiefs Cochise and Geronimo once rode. Gazing out across this country today, it is easy to understand why the Apaches fought so hard to keep white settlers out.

The Apaches first moved into this region of southern Arizona sometime in the early 16th century. They pursued a hunting-and-gathering lifestyle that was supplemented by raiding neighboring tribes for food and other booty. When the Spanish arrived in the area, the Apaches acquired horses and became even more efficient raiders. They attacked Spanish, Mexican, and eventually American settlers, and despite repeated attempts to convince them to give up their hostile way of life, the Apaches refused to change. Not long after the Gadsden Purchase of 1848 made Arizona U.S. soil, more people than ever began settling in the region. The new settlers immediately became the object of Apache raids, and eventually the U.S. Army was called in to put an end to the attacks; by the mid-1880s, the army was embroiled in a war with Cochise, Geronimo, and the Chiricahua Apaches.

Sulphur Springs Valley.

Although the Chiricahua and Dragoon mountains, which flank the Sulphur Springs Valley on the east and west, respectively, are relatively unknown outside the region, they offer some of the Southwest's most spectacular scenery. Massive boulders litter the mountainsides, creating fascinating landscapes. The Chiricahua Mountains are also a favorite destination of bird-watchers, for it is here that the colorfully plumed elegant trogon reaches the northern limit of its range.

In the southern part of this region lies the town of Douglas, an important gateway to Mexico. Unless you're heading to Mexico, though, there aren't many reasons to visit. Yet if you do find yourself passing through Douglas, be sure to stop at the historic Gadsden Hotel (see "Where to Stay," below); the Slaughter Ranch is also worth a visit.

Essentials

GETTING THERE Willcox is on I-10, with Ariz. 186 heading southeast toward Chiricahua National Monument.

VISITOR INFORMATION The **Willcox Chamber of Commerce and Agriculture,** 1500 N. Circle I Rd. (✆ **800/200-2272** or 520/384-2272; www.willcoxchamber.com), can provide information.

SPECIAL EVENTS **Wings Over Willcox** (✆ **800/200-2272;** www.wingsoverwillcox.com), a festival celebrating the annual return to the area of more than 40,000 sandhill cranes, takes place in January.

Willcox

Railroad Avenue in downtown Willcox is something of a little historic district. Here you'll find the Rex Allen Museum, plus the restored **Southern Pacific Willcox Train Depot,** 101 S. Railroad Ave., a redwood depot built in 1880. Inside the old depot is a small display of historical Willcox photos. Also worth checking out is the **Willcox Commercial,** 180 N. Railroad Ave. (✆ **520/384-2448**), a general store that has been around since the days of Geronimo.

Downtown Willcox is also becoming something of a wine-touring destination. Currently, there are two tasting rooms in downtown Willcox. These are in addition to several wineries outside of town. My favorite local winery is **Keeling-Schaefer Vineyards Tasting Room,** 154 N. Railroad Ave. (✆ **520/824-2500;** www.keelingschaefervineyards.com), which has its tasting room in town and its vineyards and winery southeast of town at the foot of the Chiricahua Mountains. Keeling-Schaefer produces excellent syrah and grenache from estate-grown grapes, and also does chardonnay and a rosé. The tasting room is open Thursday through Sunday from 11am to 4pm, and the tasting fee is $5. Also here in town, you'll find the tasting room of **Carlson Creek Vineyard,** 115 Railview Ave. (✆ **520/766-3000;** www.carlsoncreek.com), which is across the railroad tracks from the Keeling-Schaefer tasting room and produces primarily Rhone varietals. Currently, Eric Glomski, one of my favorite Arizona winemakers, is making the wines for this little winery. The tasting room is open Tuesday through Sunday from 11am to 5pm, and tastings cost $6. In the town of Bowie, 25 miles east of Willcox, you'll find the tasting room of **Fort Bowie Vineyards,** 156 N. Jefferson St. (✆ **888/299-5951;** www.fortbowievineyards.net). This winery sells some very drinkable, inexpensive wines. It also produces an unusual pecan-flavored sparkling wine and sells locally grown pecans, pistachios, walnuts, and peaches. The tasting room is open daily from 8am to 4pm.

Rex Allen Arizona Cowboy Museum If you grew up in the days of singing cowboys, then you're probably familiar with Willcox's favorite hometown star: Rex Allen, who made famous the song "Streets of Laredo." Allen died in 1999, but his legend lives on here in Willcox. At the small museum dedicated to him, you'll find plenty of Allen memorabilia, as well as a Cowboy Hall of Fame exhibit. The town celebrates Rex Allen Days every October. Next door to this museum, you'll find the small **Friends of Marty Robbins Museum,** 156 N. Railroad Ave. (✆ **520/766-1404;** www.friendsofmartyrobbins.org), which is open Monday through Saturday from 10am to 4pm.

150 N. Railroad Ave. ✆ **877/234-4111** or 520/384-4583. www.rexallenmuseum.org. Admission $2 per person, $3 per couple, $5 per family. Daily 10am–4pm. Closed New Year's Day, Thanksgiving, and Christmas.

Southwest of Willcox

SCENIC LANDSCAPES

While Chiricahua National Monument claims the most spectacular scenery in this corner of the state, a couple of areas southwest of Willcox in the Dragoon Mountains are almost as impressive. The first of these, **Texas Canyon,** lies right along I-10 between Benson and Willcox, and can really only be enjoyed from the comfort of a speeding car. Huge boulders are scattered across this rolling desert landscape.

South of the community of Dragoon, which is known for its pistachio farms, lies a much less accessible area of the Dragoon Mountains known as **Cochise Stronghold** ★ (www.cochisestronghold.com). During the Apache uprisings of the late 19th century, the Apache leader Cochise used this rugged section of the Dragoon Mountains as his hideout and managed to elude capture for years. The granite boulders and pine forests made it impossible for the army to track him and his followers. Cochise eventually died and was buried at an unknown spot somewhere within the area. This rugged jumble of giant boulders is reached by a rough gravel road, at the end of which you'll find a campground, a picnic area, and hiking trails. For a short, easy walk, follow the .4-mile Nature Trail. For a longer and more strenuous hike, head up the Cochise Trail. The Stronghold Divide makes a good destination for a 6-mile round-trip hike. For more info, contact the **Coronado National Forest Douglas Ranger District,** 1192 W. Saddleview Rd., Douglas (✆ **520/364-3468;** www.fs.fed.us/r3/coronado).

A MEMORABLE MUSEUM IN AN UNLIKELY LOCALE

Amerind Foundation Museum ★★ It may be out-of-the-way and difficult to find, but this museum is well worth seeking out. Established in 1937, the Amerind Foundation is dedicated to the study, preservation, and interpretation of prehistoric and historical Indian cultures. To that end, the foundation has compiled the nation's finest private collection of archaeological artifacts and contemporary pieces. There are exhibits on the dances and religious ceremonies of the major Southwestern tribes and cases full of archaeological artifacts amassed from the numerous Amerind Foundation excavations over the years. Fascinating ethnology exhibits include amazingly intricate beadwork from the Plains tribes, old Zuni fetishes, Pima willow baskets, old kachina dolls, 100 years of Southwestern tribal pottery, and Navajo weavings. The art gallery displays works by 19th- and 20th-century American artists, such as Frederic Remington, whose paintings focused on the West. The small museum store has a surprisingly good selection of books and Native American crafts.

Chiricahua National Monument.

2100 N. Amerind Rd., Dragoon. ✆ **520/586-3666.** www.amerind.org. Admission $8 adults, $7 seniors, $5 college students and children 12–18, free for children 11 and under. Tues–Sun 10am–4pm. Closed major holidays. Located 64 miles east of Tucson btw. Benson and Willcox; take the Dragoon Rd. exit (exit 318) from I-10 and continue 1 mile east.

East of Willcox

If you'd like to explore the Chiricahua Mountains from the back of a horse, **Blue Sky Ranches** (✆ **520/824-1660** or 818/726-5430; www.blueskyranches.com) offers trail rides of anything from 1 hour ($40) to all day ($125).

Chiricahua National Monument ★★ Sea Captain, China Boy, Duck on a Rock, Punch and Judy—these may not seem like appropriate names for landscape features, but this is no ordinary landscape. These gravity-defying rock formations—called "the land of the standing-up rocks" by the Apache and the "wonderland of rocks" by the pioneers—are the equal of any of Arizona's many amazing rocky landmarks. Rank upon rank of monolithic giants seem to have been turned to stone as they marched across the forested Chiricahua Mountains. Some of these rocks, including Big Balanced Rock and Pinnacle Balanced Rock, seem ready to come crashing down at any moment. Formed about 25 million years ago by a massive volcanic eruption, these rhyolite badlands were once the stronghold of renegade Apaches. If you look closely at Cochise Head peak, you can even see the famous chief's profile. If you're in good physical condition, don't miss the chance to hike the 7.5-mile round-trip **Heart of Rocks Trail ★★**, which can be accessed from the visitor center or the Echo Canyon or Massai Point parking areas. This trail leads through the most spectacular scenery in the monument. A shorter loop is also possible. Within the monument are a visitor center, a campground, a picnic area, miles of hiking trails, and a scenic drive with views of many of the most unusual rock formations.

12856 E. Rhyolite Creek Rd. (off Ariz. 186). ✆ **520/824-3560.** www.nps.gov/chir. Admission $5 adults. Visitor center daily 8am–4:30pm. Closed Thanksgiving and Christmas. From Willcox, drive southeast on Ariz. 186 for 36 miles.

Fort Bowie National Historic Site ★ The Butterfield Stage, which carried mail, passengers, and freight across the Southwest in the mid-1800s, followed a route that climbed up and over Apache Pass, in the heart of the Chiricahua Mountains' Apache territory. In 1862, Fort Bowie was established near the mile-high pass to ensure the passage of the slow-moving stage as it traversed this difficult region. The fort was also used to protect the water source for cavalry going east to fight the Confederate army in New Mexico. Later, federal troops stationed at Fort Bowie battled Geronimo until, in 1886, the Apache chief finally surrendered. Today, little more than Fort Bowie's crumbling adobe walls remain, but the hike along the old stage route to the ruins conjures the ghosts of Geronimo and the Indian Wars.

3203 S. Old Fort Bowie Rd. (off Ariz. 186). ✆ **520/847-2500.** www.nps.gov/fobo. Free admission. Visitor center daily 8am–4:30pm; grounds daily dawn–dusk. Closed Thanksgiving and Christmas. From Willcox, drive southeast on Ariz. 186; after about 20 miles, watch for signs; it's another 8 miles up a dirt road to the trail head. Alternatively, drive east from Willcox to Bowie and go 13 miles south on Apache Pass Rd. From the trail head, it's a 1.5-mile hike to the fort.

Douglas & Environs

The town of Douglas abounds in old buildings, and although not many are restored, they hint at the diverse character of this community. Just across the border from Douglas is Agua Prieta, in Sonora, Mexico, where Pancho Villa lost his first battle. In Agua Prieta, whitewashed adobe buildings, old churches, and sunny plazas provide a contrast to Douglas. At the **Douglas Visitor Center,** 345 E. 16th St. (✆ **800/315-9999** or 520/364-2478; www.visitdouglas.com), pick up a map to the town's historic buildings, as well as a rough map of Agua Prieta.

Slaughter Ranch Museum ★ Down a dusty gravel road outside Douglas lies a little-known Southwestern landmark: the Slaughter Ranch. If you're old enough, you may remember a Walt Disney TV show called *Texas John Slaughter.* This was his spread. In 1884, former Texas Ranger John Slaughter bought the San Bernardino Valley and turned it into one of the finest cattle ranches in the West. Slaughter later went on to become the sheriff of Cochise County and helped rid the region of the unsavory characters who had flocked to the many mining towns of this remote part of the state. Today, the ranch is a National Historic Landmark and has been restored to its late-19th-century appearance. Wide lawns surround the ranch buildings and a large pond attracts a variety of birds, making this one of Arizona's best winter birding spots. For the-way-it-was tranquillity, this old ranch can't be beat.

6153 Geronimo Trail, about 14 miles east of Douglas. ✆ **520/558-2474.** www.slaughterranch.com. Admission $8 adults, free for children 13 and under. Wed–Sun 10am–3pm. Closed New Year's Day and Christmas. From Douglas, go east on 15th St., which runs into Geronimo Trail; continue east 14 miles.

Birding Hot Spots

At the **Willcox Chamber of Commerce,** 1500 N. Circle I Rd. (✆ **800/200-2272** or 520/384-2272; www.willcoxchamber.com), you can pick up several birding maps and checklists for the region.

To the east of Chiricahua National Monument, on the far side of the Chiricahuas, lies **Cave Creek Canyon,** one of the most important bird-watching spots in the United States. It's here that the colorful elegant trogon reaches the northern limit of its range. Other rare birds that have been spotted here include sulfur-bellied flycatchers, and Lucy's, Virginia's, and black-throated gray warblers. Stop by the visitor center for information on the best birding spots in the area. Cave Creek Canyon is just outside the community of Portal. In summer,

Wings Over Willcox celebrates the masses of sandhill cranes that gather in the Sulphur Springs Valley.

the canyon can be reached from the national monument by driving over the Chiricahuas on graded gravel roads. In winter, you'll likely have to drive around the mountains, which entails going south to Douglas and then 60 miles north to Portal or north to I-10, and then south 35 miles to Portal.

The **Cochise Lakes** (actually, the Willcox sewage ponds) are another great bird-watching spot. Birders can see a wide variety of waterfowl and shorebirds, including avocets and ibises. To find the ponds, head south out of Willcox on Ariz. 186, turn right onto Rex Allen, Jr. Drive at the sign for the Twin Lakes golf course, and go past the golf course.

Between October and March, as many as 40,000 sandhill cranes gather in the Sulphur Springs Valley south of Willcox, and in January, the town holds the **Wings Over Willcox** festival (www.wingsoverwillcox.com), a celebration of these majestic birds. There are a couple of good places in the area to see sandhill cranes during the winter. Southwest of Willcox on U.S. 191 near the community of Cochise and the Apache Generating Station electricity-generating plant, you'll find the **Apache Station Wildlife Viewing Area.** About 60 miles south of Willcox, off U.S. 191 near the town of Elfrida, is the **Whitewater Draw Wildlife Area.** To reach this latter area, go south from Elfrida on Central Highway, turn right on Davis Road, and in another 2½ miles, turn left on Coffman Road and continue 2 miles. The last 2 miles are on a dirt road that should be avoided after rainfall. The Sulphur Springs Valley is also well known for its large wintering population of raptors, including ferruginous hawks and prairie falcons.

Near Douglas, the **Slaughter Ranch,** which has a large pond, and the adjacent **San Bernardino National Wildlife Refuge** are good birding spots in both summer and winter. (See the description of the Slaughter Ranch Museum, above, for directions.)

North of Willcox, at the end of a 30-mile gravel road, lies the **Muleshoe Ranch Cooperative Management Area** (✆ **520/212-4295;** www.nature.org), a 49,000-acre Nature Conservancy preserve that contains seven perennial streams. These streams support endangered aquatic life as well as riparian zones that attract a large number of bird species. To get here, take exit 340 off I-10 and go south; turn right on Bisbee Avenue and then right again onto Airport Road. After 15 miles, watch for a fork in the road and take the right fork. If the road is dry, it is usually passable in a passenger car. In May and from September to February, the headquarters, which includes the visitor center, is open Thursday through Monday from 8am to 5pm (Mar–Apr daily and June–Aug Sat–Sun only). From late September through May, overnight accommodations in casitas

($180–$195 double) are available by reservation (2-night minimum, 3-night minimum on holidays). Casita guests have access to hot springs on the grounds.

Where to Stay

IN & NEAR WILLCOX

Cochise Stronghold B&B ★★ Set on 5 acres of private land within Coronado National Forest's Cochise Stronghold area, this remote and beautiful B&B is one of my favorites in the state. The inn is an energy-efficient, passive solar home with two housekeeping suites. It makes a superb base for hikes amid the area's fascinating rock formations and for excursions farther afield in Cochise County. Innkeeper Nancy Yates is a great source of information both on solar-home design and on the preservation of desert. In-room breakfast options include Southwestern dishes such as mesquite-cornmeal pancakes that are made with flour produced by grinding mesquite-bean pods. For a luxury camping experience, stay in the inn's yurt. This inn is a great choice for bird-watching trips.

2126 W. Windancer Trail (P.O. Box 232), Pearce, AZ 85625. www.cochisestrongholdbb.com. ✆ **877/426-4141** or 520/826-4141. $179–$209 double; $129 yurt. Rates include full breakfast. 2-night minimum stay. AE, DC, DISC, MC, V. **Amenities:** Jacuzzi. *In room (but not in yurt):* A/C, TV/VCR, kitchenette, free Wi-Fi.

IN DOUGLAS

Gadsden Hotel Built in 1907, the Gadsden is listed on the National Register of Historic Places. The marble lobby, though dark, is a classic. Vaulted stained-glass skylights run the length of the ceiling, and above the landing of the Italian marble stairway is a genuine Tiffany window. Although the carpets in the halls are well-worn and rooms aren't always spotless, many units have been renovated and refurnished. The bathrooms are, however, a bit worse for wear. The lounge is a popular local hangout, with more than 200 cattle brands painted on the walls.

1046 G Ave., Douglas, AZ 85607. www.hotelgadsden.com. ✆ **520/364-4481.** Fax 520/364-4005. 160 units. $60–$85 double; $100–$150 suite. AE, DISC, MC, V. Pets accepted ($15 per night). **Amenities:** Restaurant; lounge; room service. *In room:* A/C, TV, free Wi-Fi.

IN PORTAL

Portal Peak Lodge, Portal Store & Cafe This motel-like lodge, located behind the general store/cafe in the hamlet of Portal, has fairly modern guest rooms that face one another across a wooden deck. Meals are available in the adjacent cafe. If you're seeking predictable accommodations in a remote location, you'll find them here.

2358 S. Rock House Rd., Portal, AZ 85632. www.portalpeaklodge.com. ✆ **520/558-2223.** Fax 520/558-2473. 16 units. $75–$85 double. AE, DISC, MC, V. **Amenities:** Restaurant. *In room:* A/C, TV, no phone.

Southwestern Research Station, The American Museum of Natural History Located in Cave Creek Canyon, this is a field research station that takes guests when the accommodations are not filled by scientists doing research. As such, it is the best place in the area for serious bird-watchers, who will find the company of researchers a fascinating addition to a visit. Guests stay in simply furnished cabins scattered around the research center. Spring and fall are the easiest times to get reservations and the best times for bird-watching.

P.O. Box 16553, Portal, AZ 85632. www.research.amnh.org/swrs. ✆ **520/558-2396.** Fax 520/558-2018. 12 units. Mar–Oct $170–$190 double (rate includes all meals); Nov–Feb $60–$80 double (no meals provided). Children 3 and under stay free in parent's room. DISC, MC, V. **Amenities:** Dining room; outdoor pool; free Wi-Fi. *In room:* Kitchen (in some), no phone.

AREA GUEST RANCHES

Grapevine Canyon Ranch About 35 miles southwest of Willcox, in the foothills of the Dragoon Mountains adjacent to Cochise Stronghold, this guest ranch can be either a quiet hideaway where you can enjoy the natural setting, or a place to experience traditional ranch life—horseback riding, team penning, or rounding up cattle. The landscape of mesquite, yucca, and oaks conjures images of the high chaparral, and a variety of rides are offered. If you don't care to go horseback riding, sightseeing excursions can be arranged, and there is a pool and hot tub. The small cabins (with shower-only bathrooms) and larger casitas are set under groves of manzanita and oak trees; you can view wildlife and the night sky from the decks.

P.O. Box 302, Pearce, AZ 85625. www.gcranch.com. ✆ **800/245-9202** or 520/826-3185. Fax 520/826-3636. 12 units. $296–$456 double. Rates do not include 15% gratuity. Rates include all meals. 3-night minimum stay. DISC, MC, V. No children 11 or under. **Amenities:** Dining room; lounge; concierge; 2 Jacuzzis; outdoor pool. *In room:* A/C, fridge, hair dryer, minibar, no phone.

Price Canyon Ranch ★ Despite the address listed below, this ranch is in Arizona, although just barely. Price Canyon is northeast of Douglas off U.S. 80 and down a 7½-mile dirt road. Can you say remote? If you're looking to get away from it all and do some cowboying (or cowgirling), this is your best bet in the area. The ranch guest rooms have a luxurious, modern rancho-deluxe feel with the sort of furnishings you might expect to find in Scottsdale or Tucson. Set in the southern foothills of the Chiricahua Mountains, Price Canyon Ranch is a mix of grasslands and forests that provides loads of great horseback-riding opportunities. Whether you just want to head out on an easy trail ride or join the ranch cowboys checking on the herd and riding fences, you've got plenty of options here. Guests can even help with monthly cattle drives.

P.O. Box 39, Rodeo, NM 88056. www.pricecanyon.com. ✆ **800/727-0065** or 520/558-2383. 10 units. $460 double (10% discount for 7-night stays). Rates do not include 15% gratuity. Rates include all meals and horseback riding. 2-night minimum (3-night minimum Oct and Apr). AE, DC, DISC, MC, V. Closed Dec–Feb 15 and June–Aug 15. No children 11 or under. **Amenities:** Dining room; Jacuzzi; outdoor pool. *In room:* A/C, CD player, fridge, hair dryer, no phone, free Wi-Fi.

Sunglow Guest Ranch ★★ Located in the western foothills of the Chiricahua Mountains, roughly 40 miles southeast of Willcox, this remote ranch is surrounded by Coronado National Forest and is one of the most idyllic spots in the state. Guests can ride mountain bikes, paddle a canoe on a small lake, and hike the ranch's trails. There's also great bird-watching both on the ranch and in the nearby hills. Horseback riding can also be arranged for an additional charge. The guest rooms are quite large, and decor includes rustic Mexican furnishings. More than half the units have wood-burning fireplaces. The beautiful little dining hall/cafe here, built in classic Western-ranch style, serves some of the best food in this corner of the state. The ranch has also made numerous changes in the past few years to be more eco-friendly.

14066 S. Sunglow Rd., Pearce, AZ 85625. www.sunglowranch.com. ✆ **866/786-4569** or 520/824-3334. 9 units. $270–$375 double. Rates include breakfast and dinner. Children 5 and under stay free in parent's room. 2-night minimum. AE, DC, DISC, MC, V. Pets accepted ($10 per night). **Amenities:** Dining room; babysitting; bikes; exercise room; Jacuzzi; outdoor pool; room service. *In room:* Fridge, hair dryer, no phone, free Wi-Fi.

CAMPGROUNDS

The 22-site Bonita Canyon Campground in **Chiricahua National Monument** (described above), on Ariz. 186 (✆ **520/824-3560**), charges $12 per night. Along the road to Portal not far from the national monument, there are several small national forest campgrounds. Some are free and some charge $10 for a site. At **Cochise Stronghold,** 35 miles southwest of Willcox off U.S. 191, a 10-site campground charges $10 per night. For information on the national forest campgrounds, contact the Coronado National Forest Douglas Ranger District, 1192 W. Saddleview Rd., Douglas, AZ 85607 (✆ **520/364-3468;** www.fs.fed.us/r3/coronado). Reservations are not accepted for these campgrounds.

Where to Eat

IN WILLCOX

Right across the parking lot from the Willcox Chamber of Commerce (off I-10 at exit 340), you'll find **Stout's Cider Mill ★**, 1510 N. Circle I Rd. (✆ **520/384-3696;** www.cidermill.com), which makes delicious concoctions with apples. You can get cider, cider floats, "cidersicles," apple cake, and the biggest apple pie in the world. It's open Monday through Saturday from 9am to 5pm and Sunday from 1 to 5pm.

Rodney's 🎁 BARBECUE Willcox doesn't have much in the way of good restaurants, but if you're a fan of barbecue, you'll want to schedule a stop at Rodney's. This hole in the wall near the Rex Allen Museum is so nondescript that you can easily miss it. Inside, you'll find Rodney Brown, beaming with personality and dishing up lip-smackin' barbecued pork sandwiches and plates of ribs, shrimp, and catfish. Be sure to ask Rodney about the park across the street, which he looked after for many years.

118 N. Railroad Ave. ✆ **520/507-1516.** Main courses $4.25–$12. No credit cards. Tues–Sun 11am–8pm.

North Toward Phoenix: The Safford Area & Mount Graham

Roughly 50 miles north of Willcox, off U.S. 191 in a unit of Coronado National Forest, rise the Pinaleño Mountains and 10,717-foot **Mount Graham,** a favorite summer-vacation spot for desert dwellers. Here you'll find campgrounds, hiking trails, and an astronomical observatory (see the box "Starry, Starry Nights," earlier in this chapter). This observatory, funded partly by the University of Arizona and partly by the Vatican, was built despite concerns that the mountaintop was the last remaining habitat of 400 endangered Mount Graham red squirrels.

To the northwest of Mount Graham, at the end of a 45-mile gravel road, is the **Aravaipa Canyon Wilderness,** through which flows the perennial Aravaipa Creek. This scenic canyon is bordered on both ends by the Nature Conservancy's **Aravaipa Canyon Preserve.** Together these natural areas protect Arizona's healthiest population of native desert fish species, as well as cougars, desert bighorn sheep, bobcats, and 200 species of birds. Permits, which are required for hiking in the canyon, can be requested from the **Bureau of Land Management,** Safford Field Office, 711 14th Ave., Safford, AZ 85546 (✆ **928/348-4400;** www.blm.gov/az/st/en/arolrsmain/aravaipa.html), 13 weeks in advance of your visit (spring and fall are the most difficult times to get reservations).

Not far from the turnoff for Mount Graham and just south of Safford, you'll find **Roper Lake State Park** (✆ **928/428-6760;** www.azstateparks.com), which has a hot spring, a campground, rustic rental cabins ($55 per night), and a lake with a swimming beach. The day-use fee is $7 per car; camping costs $15 to $23. There's good bird-watching here and at the nearby Dankworth Pond (where you'll find a nature trail and an outdoor exhibit on the various Native American cultures that used this site in centuries past). The state park is off U.S. 191, about 6 miles south of Safford; the Dankworth Pond site is another 3 miles south.

In this same area is the **Kachina Hot Springs Mineral Spa,** 1155 W. Cactus Rd. (✆ **928/428-7212;** www.kachinaspa.com), 6 miles south of Safford. Visitors can soak in hot mineral waters, enjoy a sweat wrap, and get a massage. A 30-minute soak costs $10; treatments range from $45 for a 15-minute soak, foot reflexology, and a 30-minute wrap to $95 for a soak, wrap, foot reflexology, and 1-hour massage. Just around the corner is **Essence of Tranquility,** 6074 S. Lebanon Loop (✆ **928/428-9312;** www.azhotmineralspring.com), a more rustic establishment that has cement-lined hot tubs and offers similar services. Use of tubs is $5 per person for 1 hour; 1-hour massages go for $65. Tubs are available Monday from 2 to 9pm, Tuesday through Saturday from 8am to 9pm, and Sunday from 8am to 7pm.

Just south of Safford off U.S. 191, you'll find **Eastern Arizona College's Discovery Park Campus,** 1651 W. Discovery Park Blvd. (✆ **928/428-6260;** www.eac.edu/discoverypark), an interesting stop for both kids and adults. This science park includes the Gov Aker Observatory, which is home to one of the world's largest camera obscuras (a dark room inside of which views of the outdoors can be seen projected on a wall). The observatory also has a 20-inch telescope that is available for public use and a space-flight simulator ride that is one of the park's top attractions. A marsh offers good birding opportunities. The park is open Monday through Friday from 8am to 5pm and Saturday from 4 to 9:30pm; admission is free.

Twenty miles northeast of Safford off U.S. 70, you'll come to the **Gila Box Riparian National Conservation Area** (www.blm.gov/az/st/en/prog/blm_special_areas/ncarea/gbox.html), a popular hiking area on BLM land. As at Aravaipa Canyon, this area preserves the landscape around a perennial stream, in this case the upper reaches of the Gila River. There is no fee to hike the area.

For more information on the Safford area, contact the **Graham County Chamber of Commerce,** 1111 Thatcher Blvd., Safford, AZ 85546 (✆ **888/837-1841** or 928/428-2511; www.graham-chamber.com), or the **Bureau of Land Management,** Safford Field Office, 711 14th Ave., Safford, AZ 85546 (✆ **928/348-4400;** www.blm.gov/az/st/en/fo/safford_field_office.html).

11

ARIZONA'S "WEST COAST"

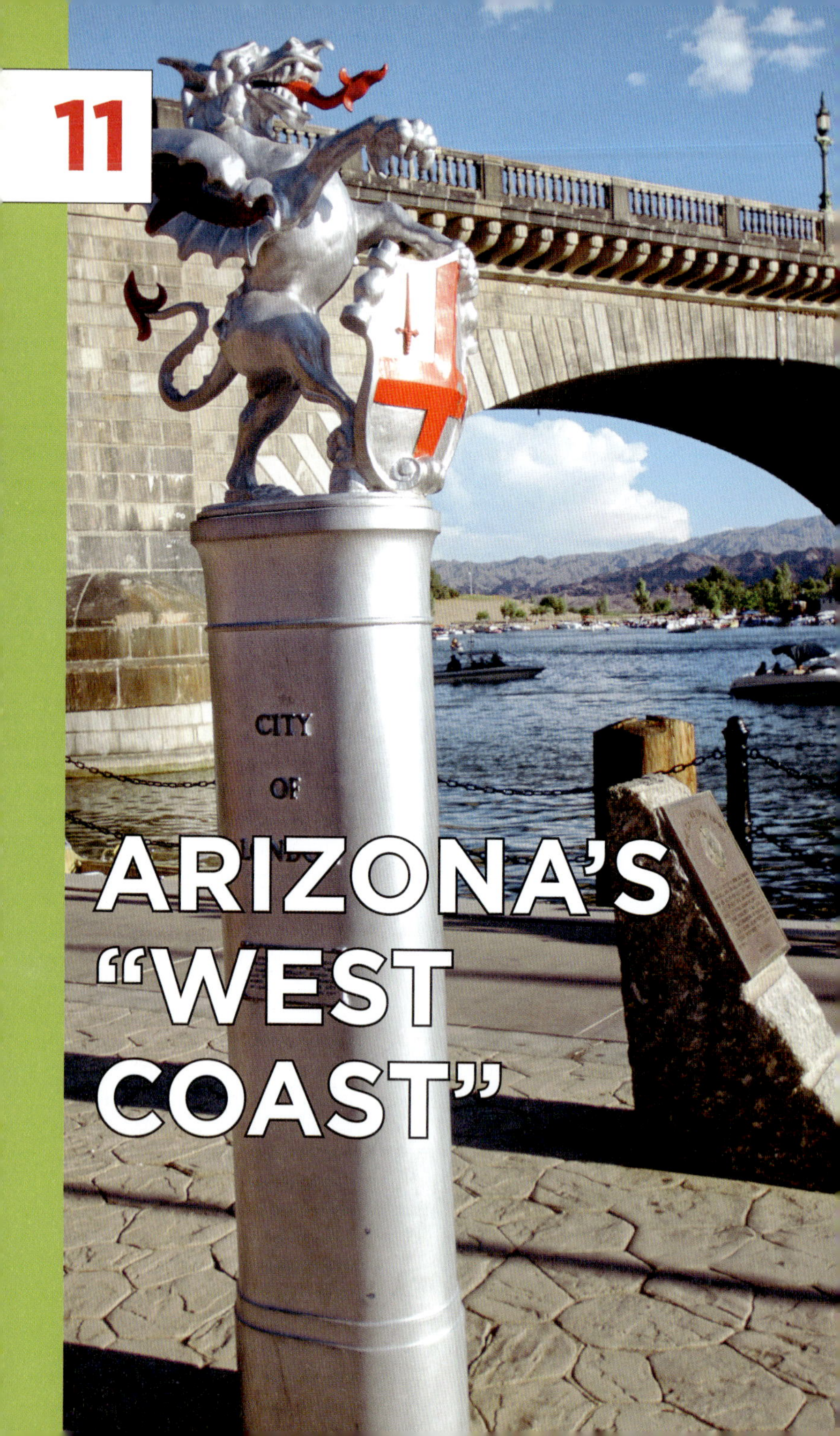

I bet you thought the West Coast was over there by Los Angeles and San Diego. Well, that may be true, but Arizona also has a "west coast," or at least that's how Arizonans see it. However, Arizona's west coast is formed not by the Pacific Ocean, but by the Colorado River. Separating Arizona from California and Nevada are 340 miles of Colorado River waters, most of which are impounded in three huge reservoirs—Lake Mead, Lake Mohave, and Lake Havasu—that provide water and electricity to such sprawling Southwest boomtowns as Phoenix and Las Vegas.

It is because of all this water that the region has come to be known as Arizona's West Coast, and it is to the waters of this inland "coast" that boaters, water-skiers, and anglers head throughout the year.

In some ways, Arizona's West Coast is superior to California's Pacific coastline. Although there aren't many waves on this stretch of the Colorado River, both the weather and the water are warmer than California's. Consequently, watersports of all types are extremely popular, and the fishing is some of the best in the country. Due to convolutions in the landscape, Lake Havasu, Lake Mohave, and Lake Mead also offer thousands of miles of shoreline.

While the Colorado River has always been the lifeblood of this rugged region, it was not water that first attracted settlers. A hundred years ago, prospectors ventured into this sun-baked landscape hoping to find gold in the mountains flanking the river. Some actually hit pay dirt, and mining towns sprang up overnight, only to be abandoned a few years later when the gold ran out. Today, Oatman (see chapter 6) is the most famous of these mining boomtowns, but it has too many people and wild burros to be called a ghost town.

People are still venturing into this region in hopes of striking it rich, but now they head across the river from Bullhead City, Arizona, to the casinos in Laughlin, Nevada, where a miniature version of Las Vegas has grown up on the banks of the Colorado.

Laughlin and Bullhead City aren't the only towns in this area with an abundance of waterfront accommodations. As with any warm coastline, Arizona's West Coast is lined with lakefront resorts, hotels, RV parks, and campgrounds. For the most part, it's a destination for desert residents, so you won't find any hotels or resorts even remotely as upscale or expensive as those in Phoenix, Tucson, or Sedona. There are, however, plenty of houseboats for rent. These floating vacation homes are immensely popular with families and groups. With a houseboat, you can get away from the crowds, dropping anchor and kicking back when you find a remote cove, the best fishing, or the most spectacular views. You can even houseboat to London Bridge, which is no longer falling down, but rather bridges a backwater of Lake Havasu and is now one of Arizona's biggest tourist attractions.

FACING PAGE: **Arizona's London Bridge.**

LAKE MEAD NATIONAL RECREATION AREA

70 miles NW of Kingman; 256 miles NW of Phoenix; 30 miles SE of Las Vegas, NV

Lake Mead National Recreation Area, which includes Lake Mead, Lake Mohave, and a scenic, free-flowing stretch of the Colorado River, straddles the border between Arizona and Nevada and is a vast watersports playground. Throughout the year, anglers fish for striped bass, rainbow trout, channel catfish, and other sport fish, while during the hot summer months, Lake Mead and Lake Mohave attract tens of thousands of water-skiers and personal watercraft riders. Due to its proximity to Las Vegas and the fact that there are more facilities on the Nevada side of Lake Mead, the recreation area tends to be more popular with Nevadans than with Arizonans.

Lake Mead, the larger of the two reservoirs, was created by Hoover Dam, which was built between 1931 and 1935 and was the first major dam on the Colorado River. By supplying huge amounts of electricity and water to Arizona and California, it set the stage for the phenomenal growth the region experienced in the latter half of the 20th century. Today, with water levels in Lake Mead at all-time lows, the cities that depend on the lake's water have finally begun to address the issue of water conservation. Rest assured, though, that there is still plenty of water left in the lakes to float your boat.

Essentials

GETTING THERE U.S. 93, which runs between Las Vegas and Kingman and long ran across the top of Hoover Dam, connects Nevada and Arizona via the Colorado River Dam, which opened in late 2010. On either side of the river, small secondary roads lead to various marinas on Lake Mead, and there are also many miles of unpaved roads within the recreation area. If you have a high-clearance or four-wheel-drive vehicle, these roads can take you to some of the least visited shores of the two lakes.

Hoover Dam.

Western Arizona
0
30 mi
0
30 km
Las Vegas
Temple Bar
Lake Mead
GRAND CANYON NATIONAL PARK
Colorado River
Meadview
Hoover Dam
Lake Mead National Recreation Area
Grand Canyon West
NEVADA
93
Dolan Springs
HUALAPAI INDIAN RESERVATION
Peach Springs
95
Lake Mohave
Chloride
Valentine
66
Katherine Landing
66
Hackberry
Seligman
To Flagstaff
68
40
Kingman
Ash Fork
Laughlin
Bullhead City
Oatman
Yucca
89
95
40
Needles
PRESCOTT NATIONAL FOREST
Wikieup
93
Lake Havasu
Flagstaff
ARIZONA
Area of detail
Phoenix
Tucson
Prescott
Lake Havasu City
Bill Williams NWR
Alamo Lake State Park
Yarnell
Parker
93
Buckskin Mountain State Park
Congress
71
Wickenburg
CALIFORNIA
River
Bouse
Aguila
95
72
Bouse Fisherman
60
Wenden
60
Colorado
Quartzsite
Hope
Ehrenberg
10
Sun City
Palm Canyon
To Phoenix
Cibola NWR
Kofa National Wildlife Refuge
Wintersburg
95
Buckeye
Arlington
85
Imperial NWR
Painted Rocks Petroglyph Site
GILA RIVER INDIAN RESERVATION
Gila Bend
Sentinel
Dateland
85
To Tucson
Tacna
8
Yuma
To Organ Pipe Cactus National Monument
San Luis
BARRY M. GOLDWATER AIR FORCE RANGE
Ajo
MEXICO

VISITOR INFORMATION For information, contact the **Lake Mead National Recreation Area,** 601 Nevada Way, Boulder City, NV 89005 (✆ **702/293-8906;** www.nps.gov/lame), or stop by the **Alan Bible Visitor Center** (✆ **702/293-8990**), between Hoover Dam and Boulder City. The visitor center is open daily from 8:30am to 4:30pm (closed New Year's Day, Thanksgiving, and Christmas).

Dam, Lake & River Tours

Standing 726 feet tall, from bedrock to the roadway atop it, and tapering from a thickness of 660 feet at its base to only 45 feet at the top, **Hoover Dam** (✆ **866/730-9097** or 702/494-2517; www.usbr.gov/lc/hooverdam) is the tallest concrete dam in the Western Hemisphere. Behind this massive dam lie the waters of **Lake Mead,** which at 110 miles long and with a shoreline of more than 550 miles is the largest artificial lake in the United States. To learn about the construction of Hoover Dam, stop in at the visitor center, which is beside the dam on U.S. 94 and is open daily from 9am to 6pm in summer and until 5pm in other months (closed Thanksgiving and Christmas). Admission is $8 for anyone over age 3, and guided tours of the dam cost $11 for adults, $9 for seniors and children 4 to 16. Tickets, which include visitor center admission, can be purchased online. More extensive tours of the dam cost $30, and are offered only on a nonreservation basis. Parking is an additional $7. Including a tour, it takes about 2 hours to visit the dam.

If you'd like to tour the lake, call **Lake Mead Cruises** (✆ **702/293-6180;** www.lakemeadcruises.com) to book passage on the *Desert Princess* paddlewheeler. These cruises leave from Lake Mead Cruises Landing, off Lakeshore Road on the Nevada side of Hoover Dam. Day tours, which go to the dam, last 1½ hours and cost $24 for adults and $12 for children 2 to 11. Other options include dinner cruises ($49 for adults, $25 for children) and brunch cruises ($39 for adults, $18 for children).

One of the most interesting ways to see remote parts of Lake Mohave is by sea kayak. **Desert River Outfitters** (✆ **888/529-2533;** www.desertriveroutfitters.com) will rent you a boat and shuttle you and your gear to and from put-ins and take-outs. The trip through Black Canyon ($60 per person with a four-person minimum) starts at the base of Hoover Dam and is the most interesting route. (***Note:*** This trip requires advance planning because a permit is necessary.) You can also paddle past the casinos in Laughlin ($35), through the Topock Gorge ($50), or around Lake Mohave ($35). Raft trips through Black Canyon are offered by **Black Canyon River Adventures** (✆ **800/455-3490;** www.blackcanyonadventures.com). The 1-day rafting trips, on big motorized rafts, are an easy float through a scenic canyon and cost $86 for adults, $83 for children ages 13 to 15, and $54 for children ages 5 to 12. If you're not a paddler, this is a great way to see this remote stretch of river—it's definitely a highlight of a visit to this corner of the state.

Outdoor Pursuits

As you would expect, swimming, fishing, water-skiing, sailing, windsurfing, and powerboating are the most popular activities in Lake Mead National Recreation Area. On Arizona shores, there are swimming beaches at Lake Mohave's Katherine Landing (outside Bullhead City) and Lake Mead's Temple Bar (north of Kingman off U.S. 93). Picnic areas can be found at these two areas, as well as at Willow Beach on Lake Mohave and at more than half a dozen spots on the Nevada side of Lake Mead.

Fishing for monster striped bass (up to 50 lb.) is one of the most popular activities on Lake Mead, and while Lake Mohave's striped bass may not reach these awesome proportions, fish in the 25-pound range are not uncommon. Largemouth bass and even rainbow trout are plentiful in the national recreation area's waters due to the diversity of habitats. Try for big rainbows in the cold waters that flow out from Hoover Dam through Black Canyon and into Lake Mohave. To fish from shore, you'll need a license from either Arizona or Nevada (depending on which shore you're fishing from). To fish from a boat, you'll need a license from one state and a special-use stamp from the other. Most Lake Mead marinas sell both licenses and stamps.

The season for striped bass starts around the beginning of April, when the water begins to warm up. If you don't have your own boat, try fishing from the shore of Lake Mohave near Davis Dam, where the water is deep. Anchovy pieces work well as bait, but put some shot on your line to get it down to the depths where the fish are feeding. You can get bait, tackle, licenses, and fishing tips at the **Lake Mohave Resort and Marina,** 2690 E. Katherine Spur Rd. (✆ **928/754-3245;** www.sevencrown.com), at Katherine Landing, which is near Bullhead City.

In Arizona, marinas can be found at Katherine Landing on Lake Mohave (just outside Bullhead City), near the north end of Lake Mohave at Willow Beach (best access for trout angling), and at Temple Bar on Lake Mead. There's also a boat ramp at South Cove, north of the community of Meadview at the east end of Lake Mead. This latter boat ramp is the closest to the Grand Canyon end of Lake Mead. On the Nevada side of Lake Mohave, there's a marina at Cottonwood Cove, and on the Nevada side of Lake Mead, you'll find marinas at Boulder Beach, Las Vegas Bay, Callville Bay, and Echo Bay. These marinas offer motels, restaurants, general stores, campgrounds, and boat rentals. At **Temple Bar Resort & Marina** (✆ **800/255-5561** or 928/767-3211; www.templebarlakemead.com), you can rent speedboats, fishing boats, and patio boats for $210 to $525 per day and a personal watercraft for $350 per day. At **Lake Mohave Resort** (✆ **800/752-9669** or 928/754-3245), you can rent ski boats, fishing boats, and patio boats for between $90 and $260 per day and a personal watercraft for $360 per day.

Unlike these other two marinas, **Willow Beach Marina,** Willow Beach Road (✆ **928/767-4747;** www.willowbeachharbor.com), 14 miles south of Hoover Dam (56 miles north of Kingman), is on a free-flowing stretch of the Colorado River downstream from Black Canyon. The river here is bounded by rugged, rocky slopes and canyon walls and is one of the prettiest stretches of the Colorado between Hoover Dam and Yuma. If you want to explore this scenic stretch of river on your own, you can rent a canoe ($15 per hour), kayak ($10 to $20 per hour), or motorboat ($25 to $50 per hour). On Sundays and Mondays throughout the year, motorboats are prohibited on this stretch of the river.

Despite the area's decidedly watery orientation, there's quite a bit of mountainous desert here that's home to bighorn sheep, roadrunners, and other wildlife. This land was also once home to several indigenous tribes, and petroglyphs scratched into rocks are reminders of the people who lived here before the first European settlers arrived. The best place to see petroglyphs is Grapevine Canyon, due west of Laughlin, Nevada, in the southwest corner of the National Recreation Area. To reach Grapevine Canyon, take Nev. 163 west from Laughlin to milepost 13 and turn right on the marked dirt road. From the highway, it's about 2 miles to the turnoff for the parking area. From the trail head, it's less than a quarter-mile to the petroglyph-covered jumble of rocks at the mouth of

Grapevine Canyon. Covering the boulders are thousands of cryptic symbols, as well as ancient illustrations of bighorn sheep. To see these petroglyphs, you'll have to do a lot of scrambling, so wear sturdy shoes (preferably hiking boots).

For information on other hikes, contact **Lake Mead National Recreation Area** (✆ **702/293-8906** or 702/293-8990; www.nps.gov/lame).

Where to Stay

HOUSEBOATS

Seven Crown Resorts ★ ☺ Why pay extra for a lakeview room when you can rent a houseboat that always has a 360-degree water view? There's no better way to explore Lake Mohave than on one of these floating vacation homes. You can cruise for miles, tie up at a deserted cove, and enjoy a wilderness adventure with all the comforts of home. Houseboats come complete with full kitchens, air-conditioning, and space to sleep up to 13 people. Bear in mind that the scenery here on Lake Mohave isn't nearly as spectacular as that on Lake Powell, Arizona's other major houseboating lake.

P.O. Box 16247, Irvine, CA 92623-6247. www.sevencrown.com. ✆ **800/752-9669.** $1,250–$4,250 per week. DISC, MC, V. Pets accepted. *In room:* A/C, kitchen, no phone.

MOTELS

Lake Mohave Resort ☺ Just up Lake Mohave from Davis Dam and only a few minutes outside Bullhead City, the Lake Mohave Resort is an older motel, but the huge rooms are good for families. Most have some sort of view of the lake, which is across the road, and some have kitchenettes. Just across the road are the resort's nautical-theme restaurant and lounge, which overlook the marina. The resort also has a convenience store and a bait-and-tackle store.

Katherine Landing, 2690 E. Katherine Spur Rd., Bullhead City, AZ 86429. www.sevencrown.com. ✆ **800/752-9669** or 928/754-3245. 51 units. Late Apr to mid-Sept $95–$115 double, $125–$250 suite; mid-Sept to late Apr $60–$80 double, $90–$250 suite. Children 5 and under stay free in parent's room. DISC, MC, V. Pets accepted ($50 deposit plus $10 per night). **Amenities:** Restaurant; lounge; watersports equipment/rentals. *In room:* A/C, TV.

Temple Bar Marina Although basically just a motel, the Temple Bar Marina has a wonderfully remote setting that will have you thinking you're on vacation in Baja, California. With a beach right in front, great fishing nearby, and 40 miles of prime skiing waters extending from the resort, this place makes a good budget getaway for anyone into watersports. A restaurant and lounge overlook the lake and provide economical meals. The resort offers houseboat and powerboat rentals and has a convenience store.

1 Main St., Temple Bar, AZ 86443. www.templebarlakemead.com. ✆ **800/255-5561** or 928/767-3211. 22 units. Apr–Oct $90–$115 double, $130 suite; Nov–Mar $77–$98 double, $111 suite. Children 5 and under stay free in parent's room. AE, DISC, MC, V. Pets accepted ($50 deposit plus $10 per night). **Amenities:** Restaurant; lounge; watersports equipment/rentals. *In room:* A/C, TV.

CAMPGROUNDS

In Arizona, there are campgrounds at Katherine Landing on Lake Mohave and at Temple Bar on Lake Mead. Both of these campgrounds have been heavily planted with trees, so they provide some semblance of shade during the hot, but popular, summer months. In Nevada, you'll find campgrounds at Cottonwood Cove on Lake Mohave and at Boulder Beach, Las Vegas Bay, Callville Bay, and

Echo Bay on Lake Mead. Campsites at all campgrounds are $10 per night. For more information, contact **Lake Mead National Recreation Area** (✆ **702/293-8906** or 702/293-8990; www.nps.gov/lame).

BULLHEAD CITY & LAUGHLIN, NEVADA

30 miles W of Kingman; 60 miles N of Lake Havasu City; 216 miles NW of Phoenix

You may find it difficult at first to understand why anyone would ever want to live in Bullhead City. This is one of the hottest places in North America, with temperatures regularly topping 120°F (49°C) in summer. However, to understand this town's attraction, you need only gaze across the Colorado River at the gambling mecca of Laughlin, Nevada, where the slot machines are always in action and the gaming tables are nearly as hot as the air outside. Laughlin is the southernmost town in Nevada and, before the advent of Indian casinos in Arizona, was the closest place to Phoenix to do any gambling. The 10 large casino hotels across the river in Nevada still make Bullhead City one of Arizona's busiest little towns.

Laughlin is a perfect miniature Las Vegas. High-rise hotels loom above the desert like glass mesas, miles of neon lights turn night into day, and acres of asphalt are always covered with cars and RVs as hordes of hopeful gamblers go searching for Lady Luck. Cheap rooms and meals lure people into spending on the slot machines what they save on a bed and dinner. It's a formula that works well.

Essentials

GETTING THERE From Phoenix, take U.S. 60, which becomes U.S. 93, northwest to I-40. From Kingman, take Ariz. 68 west to Bullhead City. From Las Vegas, take U.S. 95 south.

Shuttle-bus service between Laughlin and the Las Vegas McCarran Airport is operated by **Tri-State Super Shuttle** (✆ **800/801-8687** or 928/704-9000; www.tristateshuttle.net), which charges $50 each way and $90 round-trip.

Laughlin is a miniversion of Las Vegas.

VISITOR INFORMATION For information on Bullhead City and Laughlin, contact the **Bullhead Area Chamber of Commerce,** 1251 Hwy. 95, Bullhead City (✆ **928/754-4121;** www.bullheadchamber.com). In Laughlin, stop by the **Laughlin Visitor Information Center,** 1555 Casino Dr. (✆ **800/452-8445** or 702/298-3321; www.visitlaughlin.com).

GETTING AROUND For car rentals in the area, contact **Avis** (✆ **800/331-1212** or 928/754-4686), **Enterprise** (✆ **800/261-7331** or 928/754-2700), or **Hertz** (✆ **800/654-3131** or 928/754-4111). The **Southern Nevada Transit Coalition** (✆ **702/298-4435;** www.sntc.net) provides public bus service in Laughlin. The fare is $2 for adults and $1 for seniors and youths age 6 to 17. There are also ferries that shuttle to and from parking lots on the Arizona side of the river and water taxis that go from casino to casino.

Casinos & Other Indoor Pursuits

The casinos of Laughlin, Nevada, just across the Colorado River from Bullhead City, Arizona, are known for having liberal slots—that is, the slot machines pay off frequently. Consequently, Laughlin is a very popular weekend destination for Phoenicians and other Arizonans. In addition to the slot machines, there is keno, blackjack, poker, craps, off-track betting, and sports betting. All the hotels in Laughlin offer live entertainment of some sort, including an occasional headliner, but gambling is still the main event.

If you'd like to learn more about the history of this area, visit the **Colorado River Museum,** 355 Hwy. 95, Bullhead City (✆ **928/754-3399**), a half-mile north of the Laughlin Bridge. It's open Tuesday through Saturday from 10am to 4pm (closed June–Aug). Admission is by $2 suggested donation.

Boat Tours

If you'd like to see a bit of the Colorado River, daily paddle-wheeler cruises are available through **Laughlin River Tours** (✆ **800/228-9825** or 702/298-1047; www.laughlinrivertours.com) at the Aquarius Casino Resort (see "Where to Stay,"

London Bridge Jet Boat Tours.

below). These cruises cost $10 for adults and $5 for children 3 to 12; dinner cruises ($40) are also available. At **Riverside Resort Hotel & Casino,** 1650 S. Casino Dr., Laughlin (✆ **800/227-3849** or 702/298-2535; www.riversideresort.com), you can take a tour on the 65-foot USS *Riverside* to Davis Dam. These excursions last 80 minutes and cost $10 for adults and $6 for children ages 3 to 12.

If you'd rather look at natural surroundings than casino towers, consider booking a 6-hour jet-boat tour to the London Bridge with **London Bridge Jet Boat Tours** (✆ **888/505-3545** or 702/298-5498; www.jetboattour.com). On the way, the boat passes through scenic Topock Gorge. These powerful boats cruise at up to 40 mph and make the 58-mile one-way trip in 2 hours. Tours cost $66 for adults, $60 for seniors, and $46 for children ages 12 and under. Tours don't operate in December or January.

Outdoor Pursuits

Desert River Outfitters, 1034 U.S. 95, Bullhead City (✆ **888/529-2533;** www.desertriveroutfitters.com), will rent you a boat and shuttle you and your gear to and from put-ins and take-outs. The least expensive trip is down the Colorado River past the casinos in Laughlin ($35 for adults, $15 for children 6 to 15).

For information on fishing in nearby Lake Mohave, see the section on Lake Mead National Recreation Area, earlier in this chapter. If you'd rather just feed the fish, look for the carp that hang out at the dock behind the Edgewater Hotel & Casino. There are machines dispensing carp chow so that you can feed these piscine vacuums.

In Laughlin, golfers can play a round at the **Mojave Resort Golf Club,** 9905 Aha Macav Pkwy. (✆ **702/535-4653;** www.mojaveresortgolfclub.com), adjacent to the Avi Resort & Casino. Carved out of dense thickets of desert vegetation, this course has wide, user-friendly fairways and charges greens fees of $89 to $109 during the cooler months (lower rates for guests of Avi Resort & Casino). In Bullhead City, try the **Desert Lakes Golf Course,** 5835 Desert Lakes Dr., Fort Mohave (✆ **928/768-1000;** www.desertlakesgc.com), 15 miles south of town off Ariz. 95. Greens fee is around $39 in the cooler months. Rates after 1 or 2pm are usually lower at these courses.

Bird-watching is excellent in **Havasu National Wildlife Refuge** (✆ **760/326-3853;** www.fws.gov/southwest/refuges/Arizona/havasu), a wintering area for many species of waterfowl. However, much of this refuge lies within the scenic Topock Gorge and is accessible only by boat. The most accessible birding areas are along the marshes in the vicinity of the communities of Golden Shores and Topock, which are both north of the I-40 bridge over the Colorado. Topock Gorge, one of the most scenic stretches of the lower Colorado River, is a 15-mile stretch of river bordered by multicolored cliffs.

Where to Stay

IN LAUGHLIN, NEVADA

Laughlin, Nevada, currently has 10 huge hotel-and-casino complexes, 8 of which are on the west bank of the Colorado River (the 9th is across the street from the river, and the 10th is on the river but several miles south of town). All offer cheap rooms (often under $30 on weeknights) to lure potential gamblers. In addition to huge casinos with hundreds of slot machines and every sort of gaming table, these hotels all have several restaurants (with ridiculously low prices in at least one restaurant, which usually has long lines), bars and lounges (usually with live country or pop music nightly), swimming pools, video arcades, ferry service to parking lots on the Arizona side of the river, valet parking, room service, car-rental desks, airport shuttles, gift shops, and gaming classes. The only real difference between most of these places is the theme each has adopted for its decor.

Should you wish to stay at one of these hotels, here's the information you'll need:

- **Aquarius Casino Resort,** 1900 S. Casino Dr., Laughlin, NV 89029 (www.aquariuscasinoresort.com; ✆ 800/662-5825 or 702/298-5111)
- **Avi Resort & Casino ★,** 10000 Aha Macav Pkwy., Laughlin, NV 89029 (www.avicasino.com; ✆ 800/284-2946 or 702/535-5555)
- **Colorado Belle Hotel & Casino,** 2100 S. Casino Dr., Laughlin, NV 89029 (www.coloradobelle.com; ✆ 866/352-3553 or 702/298-4000)
- **Edgewater Hotel & Casino,** 2020 S. Casino Dr., Laughlin, NV 89029 (www.edgewater-casino.com; ✆ 866/352-3553 or 702/298-2453)
- **Golden Nugget Laughlin,** 2300 S. Casino Dr., Laughlin, NV 89028 (www.goldennugget.com/laughlin; ✆ 800/950-7700 or 702/298-7111)
- **Harrah's Laughlin ★,** 2900 S. Casino Dr., Laughlin, NV 89029 (www.harrahs.com; ✆ 800/221-1306 or 702/298-4600)
- **Pioneer Hotel & Gambling Hall,** 2200 S. Casino Dr., Laughlin, NV 89029 (www.pioneerlaughlin.com; ✆ 800/634-3469 or 702/298-2442)
- **River Palms Resort & Casino,** 2700 S. Casino Dr., Laughlin, NV 89029 (www.river-palms.com; ✆ 800/835-7904)
- **Riverside Resort Hotel & Casino,** 1650 S. Casino Dr., Laughlin, NV 89029 (www.riversideresort.com; ✆ 800/227-3849, 702/298-2535, or 928/763-7070)
- **Tropicana Express Hotel & Casino,** 2121 S. Casino Dr., Laughlin, NV 89029 (www.tropicanax.com; ✆ 800/243-6846 or 702/298-4200)

Where to Eat

The dozens of inexpensive casino-hotel restaurants in the area are usually the top choice of visitors to Laughlin and Bullhead City. Cheap steaks, prime rib, and all-you-can-eat buffets are the specialties of these places.

LAKE HAVASU & THE LONDON BRIDGE

60 miles S of Bullhead City; 150 miles S of Las Vegas, NV; 200 miles NW of Phoenix

"London Bridge is falling down, falling down, falling down." Well, not anymore it isn't. There once was a time when the London Bridge really was falling down, but that was before Robert McCulloch, founder of Lake Havasu City, hit upon the brilliant idea of buying the bridge and having it shipped to his undertouristed little planned community in the Arizona desert. That was almost 40 years ago, and today the London Bridge is still standing and still attracting tourists by the millions. An unlikely place for a bit of British heritage, true, but the London Bridge has turned Lake Havasu City into one of Arizona's most popular tourist destinations.

Lake Havasu was formed in 1938 by the building of the Parker Dam, but it wasn't until 1963 that McCulloch founded the town of Lake Havasu City. In the town's early years, not too many people were keen on spending time in this remote corner of the desert, where summer temperatures are often more than 110°F (43°C). Despite its name, Lake Havasu City at the time was little more than an expanse of desert with a few mobile homes on it. It was then that McCulloch began looking for ways to attract more people to his little "city" on the lake. His solution proved to be a stroke of genius.

Today, Lake Havasu City attracts an odd mix of visitors. In winter, the town is filled with retirees, and you'll rarely see anyone under the age of 60. On weekends, during the summer, and over spring break, however, Lake Havasu City is popular with Arizona college students. In fact, the city has become something of a Fort Lauderdale or Cancún in the desert, and many businesses now cater primarily to young partyers. Expect a lot of noise if you're here on a weekend or a holiday. Summers bring out the water-ski and personal-watercraft crowds.

Essentials

GETTING THERE From Phoenix, take I-10 west to Ariz. 95 north. From Las Vegas, take U.S. 95 south to I-40, then east to Ariz. 95 south.

The **Havasu/Vegas Express** (✆ **800/459-4884** or 928/453-4884; www.havasuvegasexpress.com) operates a shuttle van between Lake Havasu City and Las Vegas. Fares are $58 one-way and $104 round-trip ($53 and $95 for seniors).

VISITOR INFORMATION For more information on this area, contact the **Lake Havasu Convention & Visitors Bureau,** 314 London Bridge Rd. (✆ **800/242-8278** or 928/453-3444; www.golakehavasu.com), which has its Visitor Information Center, 420 English Village, at the foot of the London Bridge. This visitor center is open daily from 9am to 5pm.

GETTING AROUND For car rentals, try **Avis** (✆ **800/331-1212** or 928/764-3001), **Enterprise** (✆ **800/261-7331** or 928/453-0033), or **Hertz** (✆ **800/654-3131** or 928/764-3994).

London Bridge

Back in the mid-1960s, when London Bridge was indeed falling down—or, more correctly, sinking—into the Thames River due to heavy car and truck traffic, the British government decided to sell the bridge. Robert McCulloch and his partner paid nearly $2.5 million for the famous bridge; had it shipped 10,000 miles to Long Beach, California; and then trucked it to Lake Havasu City. Reconstruction of the bridge began in 1968, and the grand reopening was held in 1971. Oddly enough, the 900-foot-long bridge was not built over water; it just connected desert to more desert on a peninsula jutting into Lake Havasu. It wasn't until after the bridge was rebuilt that a mile-long channel was dredged through the base of the peninsula, thus creating an island offshore from Lake Havasu City.

Although the bridge that now stands in Arizona is not very old by British standards, the London Bridge has a long history. The first bridge over the Thames River in London was probably a wooden bridge built by the Romans in A.D. 43. In 1176, the first stone bridge over the Thames was built. They just don't build 'em like that one anymore—it lasted for more than 600 years but was eventually replaced in 1824 by the bridge that now stands in Lake Havasu City.

London Bridge was shipped from the U.K. to Arizona in the mid-1960s.

Boats traverse the waters of Lake Havasu during summer.

At the base of the bridge sits **English Village,** which is done up in proper English style and has a few shops, some casual restaurants, and Lake Havasu's main visitor center. There is also a waterfront promenade, along which you'll find several cruise boats and boat-rental docks.

Unfortunately, the London Bridge is not very impressive as bridges go, and the tacky commercialization of its surroundings makes it something of a letdown for many visitors. On top of that, over the years the jolly Olde England styling that once predominated around here has been supplanted by a Mexican beach-bar aesthetic designed to appeal to partying college students on spring break.

Land, Lake & River Tours

Several companies offer different types of boat tours on Lake Havasu. **Bluewater Jet Boat Tours** (✆ **888/855-7171** or 928/855-7171; www.coloradoriverjetboattours.com) runs jet-boat tours that leave from the London Bridge and spend 2½ hours cruising up the Colorado River to the Topock Gorge, a scenic area 25 miles from Lake Havasu City. The cost is $38 for adults, $35 for seniors, and $20 for children 5 to 12. You can also go out on the ***Dixie Belle*** (✆ **866/332-9231** or 928/453-6776), a small replica paddle-wheel riverboat, or the even smaller ***Kontiki.*** Cruises range from $20 to $30 for adults and $8 to $15 for children 4 to 12. The *Kontiki* goes to Copper Canyon, the narrow cliff-ringed cove that is the destination for college-age partyers each year during spring break.

In addition to tours on the water, there are also tours *over* the water. **Lake Havasu Parasail** (✆ **928/302-0683;** www.lakehavasuparasail.com) will strap you into a parasail and tow you behind a speedboat as you soar 600 feet over the lake. These short flights cost $45 to $55. Don't want to get wet? Try **Lake Havasu Seaplane** (✆ **928/855-4472** or 928/486-6997; www.lakehavasuseaplane.com), which starts out on the water but soon takes to the skies in its floatplane. A 30-minute air tour costs $175 and a 1-hour tour costs $250. Want a classic aerial experience? **Edgewater Aviation** (✆ **928/764-1044;** www.biplanerides.net) offers tours in a restored Stearman biplane. Air tours run from $99 for a 15-minute flight to $265 for a 45-minute flight. Looking for something a bit quieter and slower paced? Book a hot-air balloon ride with **Wanderlust Balloons** (✆ **928/486-1075;** www.wanderlustballoons.com), which charges $185 per person ($125 for children under 100 lb.).

Watersports

While the London Bridge is what made Lake Havasu City, these days watersports on 45-mile-long Lake Havasu are the area's real draw. Whether you want to go for a swim, take a leisurely pedal-boat ride, try parasailing, or spend the day water-skiing, there are plenty of places to get wet. Lake Havasu is also known as the Jet Ski Capital of the World, so don't expect much peace and quiet when you're out on the water.

London Bridge Beach is the best in-town beach and is located in a county park off West McCulloch Boulevard behind the Island Inn. This park has a sandy beach, lots of palm trees, and views of both the London Bridge and the distant desert mountains. There are also picnic tables and a snack bar. Just south of the London Bridge on the "mainland" side, you'll find the large **Rotary Community Park,** which is connected to the bridge by a paved waterside path. Adjacent to the park is the **Lake Havasu Aquatic Center,** 100 Park Ave. (✆ **928/453-2687**), which has an indoor wave pool, 254-foot water slide, and lots of other facilities. There are more beaches at **Lake Havasu State Park** (✆ **928/855-2784;** www.azstateparks.com), 2 miles north of the London Bridge, and at **Cattail Cove State Park** (✆ **928/855-1223;** www.azstateparks.com), 15 miles south of Lake Havasu City. Both state parks charge a $10 day-use fee ($15 Fri–Sun and state holidays).

You can rent boats from **Fun Time Boat Rentals,** 1685 Industrial Blvd. (✆ **800/680-1003** or 928/680-1003; www.funtimeboatrentals.com). Pontoon boats and ski boats equipped with water skis or knee boards both rent for $285 per day. If you're interested in kayaking or canoeing, contact **Western Arizona Canoe and Kayak Outfitter** (✆ **888/881-5038** or 928/855-6414; www.azwacko.com), which charges $25 to $40 per day for canoes and kayaks.

If your main reason for getting out on the water is to catch some fish, you'll likely come away from a visit to Lake Havasu with plenty of fish stories to tell. Striped bass, also known as stripers, are the favorite quarry of anglers here. These fish have been known to weigh in at more than 60 pounds in these waters, so be sure to bring the heavy tackle. Largemouth bass in the 2- to 4-pound range are

CANOEING THE colorado

Paddling down a desert river is a fascinating experience. Rugged rock walls, prickly cacti, and thickets of water-loving plants drift by on shore as the cool water rushes past your boat. If you're interested in a scenic canoe tour, there are a couple of outfitters in the area. Both provide boats, paddles, life jackets, maps, and shuttles to put-in and take-out points, but usually no guide. **Western Arizona Canoe and Kayak Outfitters** (✆ **888/881-5038** or 928/855-6414; www.azwacko.com) offers self-guided kayak or canoe trips through the beautiful and rugged Topock Gorge, where you can see ancient petroglyphs and possibly bighorn sheep. Trips take 5 to 6 hours, and the cost is $48 per person, which includes the use of a kayak or canoe, paddles, life jackets, dry bags, coolers, and, most important, the shuttle service to the put-in point and back from the take-out point. **Jerkwater Canoe Company** (✆ **800/421-7803** or 928/768-7753; www.jerkwatercanoe.com) offers a similar Topock Gorge excursion and also arranges other canoe and kayak trips of varying lengths. Jerkwater's Topock Gorge self-guided 5- to 6-hour trip is $46 per person. There is a two-person minimum.

also fairly common, and giant channel catfish of up to 35 pounds have been caught in Topock Marsh. The best fishing starts in spring, when the water begins to warm up, but there is also good winter fishing.

Golf

Lake Havasu City has three courses that are open to the public. Panoramic views are to be had from each of the courses here, and there's enough variety to accommodate golfers of any skill level.

London Bridge Golf Club, 2400 Clubhouse Dr. (✆ **928/855-2719;** www.londonbridgegc.com), with two 18-hole courses, is the area's premier course. High-season greens fees (with cart) on either the Olde London course or the Nassau course are $49 to $59. The **Havasu Island Golf Course,** 1040 McCulloch Blvd. (✆ **928/855-5585**), is a 4,012-yard, par-61 executive course with lots of water hazards. Greens fees are $26 to $32 if you walk and $35 to $43 if you ride. The 9-hole **Bridgewater Links,** 1477 Queens Bay Rd. (✆ **928/855-4777;** www.londonbridgeresort.com), at the London Bridge Resort, is the most accessible and easiest of the area courses. Greens fees for 9 holes are $9 to $18 if you walk and $15 to $24 if you ride.

Golfers won't want to miss the **Emerald Canyon Golf Course ★★**, 7351 Riverside Dr., Parker (✆ **928/667-3366;** www.emeraldcanyongolf.com), about 30 miles south of Lake Havasu City. This municipal course is the most spectacular in the region and plays through rugged canyons and past red-rock cliffs, from which there are views of the Colorado River. One hole even has you hitting your ball off a cliff to a green 200 feet below! Greens fees are $55 to $65 in the cooler months ($50 after 1pm), and tee-time reservations can be made a week in advance (further out if you pay $10 per player). Also in Parker is the golf course at the **Havasu Springs Resort,** 2581 Ariz. 95 (✆ **928/667-3361**), which

Emerald Canyon Golf Course.

Seeing the Light

Lighthouses may seem as out of place in the desert as the London Bridge, but there are now 19 lighthouses along the shores of Lake Havasu. The lights are replicas of famous navigation beacons from around the country and are roughly one-third the size of the originals. The lighthouses were built by the **Lake Havasu Lighthouse Club** (www.lh-lighthouseclub.org), and several of the lighthouses can be seen in the parks flanking the London Bridge.

some people claim is the hardest little 9-hole, par-3 course in the state. It's atop a rocky outcropping with steep drop-offs all around. If you aren't staying here, greens fees are only $12 for 9 holes and $18 for 18 holes.

Where to Stay

Heat Hotel ★ Located at the foot of the London Bridge, this surprisingly stylish boutique hotel is by far the hippest hotel between Scottsdale and Las Vegas. Guest rooms are reminiscent of those at W hotels, although here you get much more room at a much lower price. Rooms are large and have balconies, and most overlook the bridge or the water. Platform beds, stylish lamps, and a sort of Scandinavian-modern aesthetic make this the most distinctive hotel on this side of the state. The Inferno Suites, with their Tempur-Pedic beds and Jacuzzi tubs, are my favorite rooms here. ***One caveat:*** The open-air bar directly across the channels plays loud music until 2am on warm nights (especially during spring break).

1420 McCulloch Blvd. N., Lake Havasu City, AZ 86403. www.heathotel.com. ✆ **888/898-4328.** Fax 928/854-1130. 25 units. $99–$239 double; $169–$389 suite. Children 18 and under stay free in parent's room. AE, DC, DISC, MC, V. Pets accepted ($50 fee). **Amenities:** 2 bars; concierge. *In room:* A/C, TV/DVD, hair dryer, minibar, free Wi-Fi.

London Bridge Resort & Convention Center ★ Merry Olde England was once the theme at this timeshare resort, and Tudor half-timbers are jumbled up with towers, ramparts, and crenellations. However, England has given way to the tropics and the desert as the resort strives to please its young, partying clientele (who tend to make a lot of noise and leave the hotel looking much the worse for wear). Although the bridge is just out the hotel's back door, and a replica of Britain's gold state coach is inside the lobby, guests are more interested in the three pools and the tropical-theme outdoor nightclub. The one- and two-bedroom units are spacious, comfortable, and attractive, and those on the ground floor have double whirlpool tubs.

1477 Queens Bay, Lake Havasu City, AZ 86403. www.londonbridgeresort.com. ✆ **866/331-9231** or 928/855-0888. Fax 928/855-5404. 122 units. $69–$139 studio condo; $109–$239 1-bedroom condo. AE, DC, DISC, MC, V. **Amenities:** Restaurant; 2 lounges; 9-hole golf course; exercise room and access to nearby health club; Jacuzzi; 3 pools; spa; tennis court; watersports equipment/rentals. *In room:* A/C, TV, hair dryer, kitchenette, free Wi-Fi.

CAMPGROUNDS

There are two state park campgrounds in the Lake Havasu City area. **Lake Havasu State Park** (✆ **928/855-2784;** www.azstateparks.com) is 2 miles north of the London Bridge on London Bridge Road, while **Cattail Cove State Park** (✆ **928/855-1223;** www.azstateparks.com) is 15 miles south of Lake Havasu City off Ariz. 95. The former campground charges $18 per night per vehicle, while the latter charges $20 to $26 per site. Reservations are not accepted.

Where to Eat

Cha-Bones ★ AMERICAN Move over Scottsdale, Lake Havasu City is gettin' hip and crowdin' your turf. Well, sort of. This very stylish restaurant a few blocks north of the London Bridge could hold its own in the big city, at least as far as the decor goes. The menu, on the other hand, sticks to familiar mesquite-grilled steaks, barbecued ribs, build-your-own burgers, and a few designer pizzas. Granted, the menu doesn't break any new ground, but the setting is so unlike anything else in town that this is my favorite Lake Havasu City restaurant.

112 London Bridge Rd. ✆ **928/854-5554.** www.chabones.com. Reservations not accepted. Main courses $6–$16 lunch, $10–$39 dinner. AE, DC, DISC, MC, V. Oct–Apr Sun–Thurs 11am–9pm, Fri–Sat 11am–10pm; May–Sept Sun–Thurs 11am–10pm, Fri–Sat 11am–11pm.

Javelina Cantina MEXICAN Located at the foot of the London Bridge on the island side, this large, modern Mexican restaurant is affiliated with Shugrue's on the other side of the street. As at Shugrue's, there is a great view of the bridge. In this case, it is from a large patio area that is kept heated during the cooler winter months. The bar has an excellent selection of tequilas, and margaritas are a specialty here. Accompany your libations with tortilla soup, fish tacos, or a salad made with blackened scallops, papaya, pecans, and blue cheese.

1420 McCulloch Blvd. ✆ **928/855-8226.** www.javelinacantina.com. Reservations recommended. Main courses $9–$17. AE, DISC, MC, V. Sun–Thurs 11am–8 or 9pm; Fri–Sat 11am–9 or 10pm.

Mudshark Brewing Company SOUTHWESTERN/INTERNATIONAL At this big, boisterous brewpub a few blocks south of the London Bridge, you'll find excellent brews that go especially well with the pizzas, pastas, and other more substantial dishes on the menu. There's a movie theater right next door, which makes this a good spot for a night out.

210 Swanson Ave. ✆ **928/453-2981.** www.mudsharkbrewing.com. Reservations not necessary. Main courses $9–$22. AE, MC, V. Sun–Thurs 11am–9pm; Fri–Sat 11am–10pm.

Shugrue's ☺ AMERICAN Just across the London Bridge from the English Village shopping complex, Shugrue's seems to be popular as much for its view of the bridge as for its food. Offerings include seafood, steaks, and prime rib at dinner and burgers, sandwiches, and a short list of pastas at lunch. This place is a favorite of vacationing retirees and families. The adjacent affiliated Barley Brothers Brewpub has the same good view of the bridge and serves a menu calculated to appeal to a younger clientele.

At the Island Mall, 1425 McCulloch Blvd. ✆ **928/453-1400.** www.shugrues.com. Reservations recommended. Main courses $8–$12 lunch, $12–$32 dinner. AE, DISC, MC, V. Daily 11am–9pm.

Lake Havasu City After Dark

Lake Havasu City has two brewpubs. I prefer Mudshark Brewing Company (see above), but if you want a brew with a view of the London Bridge, head to **Barley Brothers Brewery & Grill,** 1425 McCulloch Blvd. (✆ **928/505-7837;** www.barleybrothers.com). If you're staying at the Heat Hotel and have eaten at Cha-Bones, then you'll want to do your drinking at the swanky **Martini Bay,** 1477 Queens Bay (✆ **928/855-0888;** www.londonbridgeresort.com), a stylish lounge at the London Bridge Resort. You can also do some gambling across Lake Havasu at the **Havasu Landing Resort and Casino** (✆ **800/307-3610;** www.havasulanding.com), which is located in California and is operated by the Chemehuevi Indian Tribe. A ferry operates from the Island Mall beside the London Bridge.

The Desert Bar

Set on the site of an abandoned mine, the **Desert Bar** (www.thedesertbar.com), which is officially known as the **Nellie E Saloon,** makes use of salvaged parts and scrap metal left over from the mining days. A covered footbridge leads to the saloon, and out in the parking lot, there's a steel "church" with a copper-roofed steeple. The bar is open Labor Day to Memorial Day, Saturday and Sunday from high noon until sunset. Expect live music and lots of retirees. To reach the Desert Bar, drive 4 miles north from Parker or 5 miles south from Buckskin Mountain State Park, and turn east on Cienega Springs Road. Continue 5 miles down a gravel road to the bar.

En Route to Yuma

THE PARKER AREA

About 16 miles south of Lake Havasu City stands the **Parker Dam,** which holds back the waters of Lake Havasu and is said to be the deepest dam in the world because 73% of its 320-foot height is below the riverbed. Beginning just above the dam and stretching south to the town of Parker is one of the most beautiful stretches of the lower Colorado River. Just before you reach the dam, you'll come to the **Bill Williams River National Wildlife Refuge** (✆ **928/667-4144;** http://southwest.fws.gov/refuges/arizona/billwill.html), which preserves the lower reaches of the Bill Williams River. This refuge offers some of the best bird-watching in western Arizona. Keep your eyes open for vermilion flycatchers, Yuma clapper rails, soras, Swainson's hawks, and white-faced ibises.

Continuing south, you'll reach a dam overlook and the Take-Off Point boat launch, where you can do some fishing from shore. Below the dam, the river becomes narrow and red-rock canyon walls close in. Although this narrow gorge is lined with mobile-home parks, the most beautiful sections have been preserved in two state parks: **Buckskin Mountain State Park** (✆ **928/667-3231;** www.azstateparks.com) and **River Island State Park** (✆ **928/667-3386;** www.azstateparks.com). Both parks have campgrounds ($25–$28 for campsites or cabanas at Buckskin Mountain; $23 for campsites at River Island), and a few of the campsites can be reserved. There are also day-use areas that include river beaches and hiking trails leading into the Buckskin Mountains. The day-use fee is $10 per vehicle at either park. In this area you'll also find the spectacular Emerald Canyon Golf Course (see "Golf," above, for details).

Where to Stay

Blue Water Resort and Casino ★★ Located 37 miles south of Lake Havasu City, this riverside casino resort is western Arizona's most impressive hotel. Even if you aren't interested in spending your time at the slot machines, you'll find something here that appeals to you. There's a marina, a mile of riverfront land, a miniature-golf course, a theater for live entertainment, a movie theater, and a big indoor pool complex (with water slide) that's designed to resemble ancient ruins. Guest rooms are all close to the water, which means nice river views but also traffic noise from the ski boats. Furnishings are standard motel modern.

11300 Resort Dr., Parker, AZ 85344. www.bluewaterfun.com. ✆ **888/243-3360** or 928/669-7000. 200 units. $60–$140 double; $140–$220 suite. AE, DISC, MC, V. **Amenities:** 3 restaurants; snack bars; 2 lounges; exercise room; Jacuzzi; 4 pools; room service. *In room:* A/C, TV, hair dryer.

THE QUARTZSITE AREA

For much of the year, the community of **Quartzsite** is little more than a few truck stops at an interstate off-ramp. But the population explodes with the annual influx of winter visitors (also known as snowbirds), and from early January to mid-February it's the site of numerous gem-and-mineral shows that together attract hordes of rockhounds. Among these shows is the **QIA Pow Wow** (✆ **928/927-6325;** www.qiaaz.org), which is held in late January and is one of the largest gem-and-mineral shows in the country. During the winter months, Quartzsite sprouts thousands of vendor stalls, as flea markets and the like are erected along the town's main streets. A variety of interesting food makes it a good place to stop for lunch or dinner.

For information on parking your RV in the desert outside Quartzsite, contact the **Bureau of Land Management,** Yuma Field Office, 2555 E. Gila Ridge Rd., Yuma (✆ **928/317-3200;** www.blm.gov/az/st/en/fo/yuma_field_office.html). Alternatively, you can get information and camping permits at the La Posa Long-Term Visitor Area entrance stations just south of Quartzsite on U.S. 95. The season here runs from September 15 to April 15, with permits going for $180 for the season and $40 for 14 consecutive days.

There are only three places in Arizona where palm trees grow wild, and one of those spots is 27 miles south of Quartzsite off U.S. 95 (watch for the turnoff 18 miles south of Quartzsite). Palm Canyon lies within the boundaries of the **Kofa National Wildlife Refuge,** which was formed primarily to protect the desert bighorn sheep that live here in the rugged Kofa Mountains. The palms are 9 miles off U.S. 95 in a narrow canyon a short walk from the end of the well-graded gravel road, and although there are fewer than 100 palm trees, the hike to see them provides an opportunity to experience these mountains up close. Keep your eyes peeled for desert bighorn sheep. Incidentally, the Kofa Mountains took their name from the King of Arizona Mine. For maps and more information, contact the Kofa National Wildlife Refuge, 9300 E. 28th St., Yuma (✆ **928/783-7861;** www.fws.gov/southwest/refuges/arizona/kofa).

Back in the 19th century, the mountains of this region were pockmarked with mines. To get an idea of what life was like in the mining boomtowns, make a detour to **Castle Dome City Mines Museum** (✆ **928/920-3062**), a reconstructed mining town in the middle of the desert. To find this place, turn east at

The Bouse Fisherman

If ancient rock art interests you, be sure to watch for Plomosa Road as you travel between Parker and Quartzsite. Off this road, you'll find a 30-foot intaglio (or geoglyph) known as the **Bouse Fisherman.** This primitive image of a person spearing fish was formed by scratching away the rocky crust of the desert soil. Its origin and age are unknown, but it is believed to have been created centuries ago by native peoples and may depict the god Kumastamo, who created the Colorado River by thrusting a spear into the ground. To find it, drive 8 miles up Plomosa Road, which is approximately 6 miles north of Quartzsite, and watch for a wide parking area on the north side of the road. From here, follow the trail for a quarter of a mile over a small hill.

the Castle Dome turnoff near milepost 55 and continue another 10 miles (only 3 miles are paved). In winter, the museum/ghost town is open daily from 10am to 5pm (closed Mon in spring and fall; in summer, open by appointment only), and admission is $6 for adults and $3 for children (free for children 6 and under). It's also possible to do a separate self-guided walking tour of the mining district for an additional $6 ($3 for children). If you do both tours, the charge is $10 for adults and $5 for children.

YUMA

180 miles SW of Phoenix; 240 miles W of Tucson; 180 miles E of San Diego, CA

According to the *Guinness Book of World Records,* Yuma is the sunniest place on earth. Of the possible 4,456 hours of daylight each year, the sun shines in Yuma for roughly 4,050 hours, or about 90% of the time. Combine all that sunshine with the warmest winter weather in the country, and you've got a destination guaranteed to attract sun worshipers and other refugees from colder climes. In fact, each winter, tens of thousands of snowbirds (retired winter visitors) drive their RVs to Yuma from as far away as Canada. However, by late spring, all those RVers head north to escape the steadily rising temperatures, and by high summer, Yuma starts posting furnacelike high temperatures that make this one of the hottest cities in the country.

Way back in the middle of the 19th century, long before RVers discovered Yuma, this was one of the most important towns in the region and was known as the Rome of the Southwest because all roads led to Yuma Crossing—the shallow spot along the Colorado River where this town was founded. Despite its location in the middle of the desert, Yuma became a busy port town during the 1850s as shallow-draft steamboats traveled up the Colorado River from the Gulf of California. Later, when the railroad pushed westward into California in the 1870s, it, too, passed through Yuma. Today, it is I-8, which connects San Diego with Tucson (and Phoenix via I-10), that brings travelers to Yuma and across the Colorado River.

However, despite having more than a dozen golf courses and two important historic sites, Yuma constantly struggles to attract visitors (blame it on the lure of San Diego, which is just a few hours away). In the hopes of luring more travelers off the interstate, Yuma has upgraded and restored some of its downtown historic buildings and restored its natural setting on the Colorado River. A visual arts center downtown rivals galleries in Scottsdale, and an adjacent historic movie theater has been restored to its former glory and now serves as a performing arts center. However, despite all these attempts at resuscitation, Yuma continues to be known primarily as a warm place to escape the cold and snows up north. For some people that is enough, but personally, I'd spend my time someplace with more charm and more to do.

Essentials

GETTING THERE Yuma is on I-8, which runs from San Diego, California, to Casa Grande, Arizona. **Amtrak** (© **800/872-7245**) runs passenger service to Yuma on its Sunset Limited route, which runs between Los Angeles and Orlando. The station is at 281 Gila St.

The Yuma International Airport (YUM), 2191 E. 32nd St. (✆ **928/726-5882;** www.yumaairport.com), is served from Phoenix by **US Airways** (✆ **800/428-4322**) and from Los Angeles by **United Express** (✆ **800/864-8331**).

VISITOR INFORMATION Contact the **Yuma Convention and Visitors Bureau,** 201 N. Fourth Ave. (✆ **800/293-0071** or 928/783-0071; www.visityuma.com). The visitor center, which is at the Yuma Quartermaster Depot State Historic Park, is open daily from 9am to 5pm (June–Aug, closed on Sun).

GETTING AROUND Rental cars are available from **Avis** (✆ **800/331-1212** or 928/726-5737), **Budget** (✆ **800/527-0700** or 928/344-1822), **Enterprise** (✆ **800/261-7331** or 928/726-9923), and **Hertz** (✆ **800/654-3131** or 928/726-5160).

SPECIAL EVENTS The Yuma area is a major producer of lettuce, and celebrates this during **Yuma Lettuce Days** (www.yumalettucedays.com) in mid-March. The **Yuma Birding & Nature Festival** (✆ **928/783-0071;** www.yumabirding.com), held each year in mid-April, is the city's other major festival.

Historic Sites

Arizona Historical Society Sanguinetti House Museum If you'd like to find out more about pioneer life in Yuma, stop by this territorial-period home, which is full of historical photographs and artifacts and is surrounded by lush gardens and aviaries containing exotic birds. Adjacent to the museum is the Garden Cafe, a wonderful alfresco breakfast and lunch spot (see "Where to Eat," below).

240 S. Madison Ave. ✆ **928/782-1841.** www.arizonahistoricalsociety.org. Admission $3 adults, $2 seniors and students 12–18, free for children 11 and under; free 1st Sat of each month. Tues–Sat 10am–4pm.

Yuma Quartermaster Depot State Historic Park ★ In 1865, Yuma Crossing, the narrow spot on the Colorado River where the town of Yuma sprang up, became the site of the military's Quartermaster Depot. Yuma was a busy river port during this time, and after supplies shipped from California were unloaded, they went to military posts throughout the region. When the railroad arrived in Yuma in 1877, the Quartermaster Depot began to lose its importance in the regional supply network, and by 1883, the depot was closed. Today, the depot's large wooden buildings have been restored, and although they're set back from the current channel of the Colorado River, it's easy to imagine being stationed at this hot and dusty outpost in the days before air-conditioning. Exhibits tell the story of those who lived and worked at Yuma Crossing.

201 N. 4th Ave. (at the Colorado River). ✆ **928/783-0071.** www.azstateparks.com. Free admission. Daily 9am–5pm. Closed Christmas.

Yuma Territorial Prison State Historic Park ★ If you've ever wondered where they really locked up the bad guys in the Wild West, check out this fortresslike prison on a bluff above the Colorado River. This prison opened for business in 1876 and, despite the thick stone walls and iron bars, was considered a model penal institution in its day. It even had its own electricity-generating plant and ventilation system. The prison museum has some interesting displays, including photos of many of the men and women who were incarcerated here.

1 Prison Hill Rd. ✆ **928/783-4771.** www.azstateparks.com. Admission $5 adults, $2 children 7–13, free for children 6 and under. Sept–May daily 9am–5pm; June–Aug Thurs–Mon 8am–3pm. Closed Christmas.

Downtown Yuma

While Yuma may not seem at first like the sort of place to find cutting-edge contemporary art, that's just what you sometimes encounter at the **Yuma Art Center and Galleries,** 254 S. Main St. (✆ **928/329-6607;** www.yumafinearts.org), which is next door to the Historic Yuma Theatre and is a gorgeous gallery that could hold its own in Scottsdale. Don't leave town without stopping by to see what's on view. The center is open Tuesday through Thursday from 10am to 6pm, Friday from 10am to 7pm (until 9pm the last Fri of each month), and Saturday from 10am to 5pm. Admission is by donation. The **Yuma Symposium** (✆ **928/782-1934;** www.yumasymposium.org), held here each year in February, brings in talented artists from all over the country.

Historic downtown Yuma isn't exactly a bustling place, and it doesn't exactly abound in historical flavor. Funky and inexpensive crafts and antiques shops occupy an occasional storefront, and down a landscaped alleyway off Main Street (at 224 Main St., across from Lutes Casino), there's a potpourri of small tourist-oriented stores. Just off Main Street, you'll also find two pottery studios/galleries: **Tomkins Pottery,** 78 W. Second St. (✆ **928/782-1934;** www.claystuff.com), and **Colorado River Pottery,** 67 W. Second St. (✆ **888/410-2689** or 928/343-0413; www.coloradoriverpottery.com).

Yuma Territorial Prison State Historic Park.

Desert Touring

While you're in a Middle Eastern mood (or if you've got the kids with you), consider spending some time at the **Camel Farm,** 15672 S. Ave. 1E (✆ **928/920-7281**), which is on the east side of Yuma at the corner of County 16th Road (call for directions). Here at the farm you can get to know the resident camels and the other 25 species of exotic animals. The farm is open Tuesday through Sunday from 9am to 5pm, and admission is $4 ($3 for seniors), free for children 3 and under. Closed in summer.

The Colorado River has been the lifeblood of the Southwestern desert for centuries, and today there's a wealth of history along its banks. **Yuma River Tours** (✆ **928/783-4400;** www.yumarivertours.com) operates narrated jet-boat tours from Yuma to the **Imperial National Wildlife Refuge** (see below) and a 48-mile trip upriver to Draper. Along the way, you'll learn about the homesteaders, boatmen, Native Americans, and miners who once relied on the Colorado River. Tours cost $48 to $95. This company also does tours in a paddle-wheeler. Three-hour tours are $48 ($57 with lunch), and 2-hour sunset dinner cruises are $63. During the warmer months (early May through mid-Oct), you can also float a stretch of the Colorado River in an inner tube. **Yuma River Tubing** (✆ **928/750-0247;** www.letsgotubing.com) rents inner tubes and operates a shuttle from West Wetlands Park, 350 N. 12th Ave. You can float the river for as little as an hour or as long as half a day.

If you're a bird-watcher, an angler, or a canoeist, you'll want to spend some time along the Colorado River north of Yuma. Here you'll find the Imperial and Cibola national wildlife refuges, which preserve marshes and shallow lakes along the river. Plenty of bird species and good fishing and canoeing make it a popular area. For more information, contact the **Imperial National Wildlife Refuge** (✆ **928/783-3371;** www.fws.gov/southwest/refuges/arizona/imperial/index.html) or the **Cibola National Wildlife Refuge** (✆ **928/857-3253;** www.fws.gov/southwest/refuges/cibolanwr/index.html).

One of the best ways to explore the Imperial National Wildlife Refuge is by canoe. You can rent one from **Martinez Lake Resort** (✆ **800/876-7004;** www.martinezlake.com) for $20 a day and paddle around Martinez Lake. Multiday canoe trips are offered by **Yuma River Tours** (✆ **928/783-4400;** www.yumarivertours.com) along this stretch of the lower Colorado, which features rugged, colorful mountains and quiet backwater areas.

Bird-watchers will want to head out to **Betty's Kitchen Watchable Wildlife Area** ($10 day-use fee per vehicle) and the adjacent **Mittry Lake Wildlife Area.** To get there, take U.S. 95 east out of town, turn north on Avenue 7E (Laguna Dam Rd.), and continue 9 miles, at which point the road turns to gravel. Turn left in a quarter of a mile to reach Betty's Kitchen; continue straight to reach Mittry Lake. Fall and spring migrations are some of the best times of year for birding at these spots; many waterfowl winter in the area as well. For information on Betty's Kitchen and Mittry Lake, contact the **Bureau of Land Management,** Yuma Field Office, 2555 E. Gila Ridge Rd., Yuma (✆ **928/317-3200;** www.blm.gov/az/st/en/fo/yuma_field_office.html).

Golf

While Yuma's golf courses are not nearly as impressive as those at the resorts in Phoenix and Tucson, there are certainly plenty of them, and you can't beat the winter climate. The **Mesa del Sol Golf Club,** 12213 Calle del Cid

(✆ **928/342-1283;** www.mesadelsolgolf.com), off I-8 at the Fortuna Road exit, is the most challenging local course open to the public. Greens fee is $50 during the cooler months ($41 for twilight play). On the other hand, the **Desert Hills Golf Course,** 1245 Desert Hills Dr. (✆ **928/344-4653;** www.deserthillsgc.com), has been rated one of the best municipal courses in the state. Greens fees range from $35 to $48 during the cooler months.

Where to Stay

MODERATE

Best Western Coronado Motor Hotel With its red-tile roofs, whitewashed walls, and archways, this mission-revival building on the edge of downtown is the picture of a mid-20th-century motel—but rooms, all recently remodeled, are as up-to-date as you would expect from a major chain. The convenient location puts you within walking distance of a couple of good restaurants, Yuma Quartermaster Depot State Historic Park, and the Arizona Historical Society Sanguinetti House Museum.

233 S. 4th Ave., Yuma, AZ 85364. www.bwcoronado.com. ✆ **877/234-5567** or 928/783-4453. Fax 928/782-7847. 126 units. $93–$130 double; $100–$150 suite. Rates include full breakfast. Children 12 and under stay free in parent's room. AE, DC, DISC, MC, V. Pets accepted ($50 deposit). **Amenities:** Restaurant; lounge; exercise room; Jacuzzi; 2 outdoor pools, free Wi-Fi. *In room:* A/C, TV, fridge, hair dryer, free Internet.

Best Western InnSuites Hotel & Suites Located just off I-8, this modern hotel offers an attractive setting and spacious accommodations at reasonable rates. Although not all the rooms are full suites, all are quite large and have loads of amenities and nice decorative touches. The pool, though small, is in a pleasant courtyard.

1450 S. Castle Dome Ave., Yuma, AZ 85365. http://yuma.innsuites.com. ✆ **800/922-2034** or 928/783-8341. Fax 928/783-1349. 166 units. $79–$123 double. Rates include full breakfast and evening social hour. Children 17 and under stay free in parent's room. AE, DC, DISC, MC, V. Pets accepted ($25 fee). **Amenities:** Free airport transfers; exercise room; Jacuzzi; outdoor pool; 2 tennis courts. *In room:* A/C, TV, hair dryer, kitchenette, MP3 docking station, free Wi-Fi.

Hilton Garden Inn Yuma/Pivot Point ★ This is the best hotel in Yuma and boasts the best location as well. The property backs up to both Yuma Quartermaster Depot State Historic Park and the city's downtown riverfront park on the Colorado River. A paved walking and biking path also runs past the hotel. Rooms are large and have great beds and bathrooms with granite counters. While the hotel is designed primarily for business travelers (there's a small convention center across the parking lot), it also makes a good choice for vacationers looking to explore downtown Yuma.

310 N. Madison Ave., Yuma, AZ 85364. http://hiltongardeninn.hilton.com. ✆ **877/782-9444** or 928/783-1500. Fax 928/783-1540. 150 units. $89–$149 double. Children 18 and under stay free in parent's room. AE, DC, DISC, MC, V. **Amenities:** Restaurant; lounge; babysitting; exercise room; Jacuzzi; outdoor pool; room service. *In room:* A/C, TV, fridge, hair dryer, MP3 docking station, free Wi-Fi.

La Fuente Inn & Suites Conveniently just off the interstate, this appealing hotel is done in Spanish colonial style with a red-tile roof, pink-stucco walls, and a fountain out front. Lush landscaping and a sort of tropical colonial decor in the lobby lend the hotel a somewhat exotic, tropical feel. Definitely not what you'd expect from a hotel just off the interstate. French doors open from the lobby onto the pool terrace and a large courtyard, around which the guest rooms are arranged. Standard units feature modern motel furnishings, while the well-designed suites offer much more space. The Spanish/tropical styling and pleasant courtyard pool area make this a good place for a sunny winter getaway.

1513 E. 16th St., Yuma, AZ 85365. www.lafuenteinn.com. ✆ **800/841-1814** or 928/329-1814. Fax 928/343-2671. 96 units. $89–$109 double. Rates include full breakfast and evening happy hour. Children 9 and under stay free in parent's room. AE, DC, DISC, MC, V. **Amenities:** Free airport transfers; exercise room and access to nearby health club; Jacuzzi; pool. *In room:* A/C, TV/VCR, fridge, hair dryer, free Internet.

Where to Eat

The Garden Cafe ★★ LIGHT FARE In back of the Arizona Historical Society Sanguinetti House Museum is Yuma's favorite breakfast and lunch spot (it's particularly popular with local retirees). Set amid quiet terraced gardens and large aviaries full of singing birds, the Garden Cafe provides a welcome respite from Yuma's heat. On the hottest days, misters spray the air with a gentle fog that keeps the gardens cool. There's also an indoor dining area. The menu consists of various delicious sandwiches, daily special quiches, salads, and rich desserts. Pancakes with lingonberry sauce are a breakfast specialty. On Sunday, there's a brunch buffet.

250 S. Madison Ave. ✆ **928/783-1491.** Reservations not accepted. Main courses $9–$12. AE, MC, V. Tues–Fri 9–10:45am and 11am–2:30pm; Sat 8–10:45am and 11am–2:30pm; Sun 8am–2:30pm. Closed June to Sept.

Lutes Casino ☺ AMERICAN Lutes, in business since the 1920s, is a dark and cavernous restaurant known for serving the best hamburgers in town and for having the strangest decor, too. You don't need to see a menu—just walk in and ask for a special, or *especial* (this is a bilingual joint). What you'll get is a cheeseburger/hot dog combo. Then cover your special with Lutes's own secret-recipe hot sauce to make it truly special. Don't bother looking for slot machines or poker tables at Lutes Casino; they've been gone for years.

221 S. Main St. ✆ **928/782-2192.** www.lutescasino.com. Reservations not accepted. Sandwiches and burgers $2.50–$6.50. MC, V. Mon–Thurs 10am–8pm; Fri–Sat 10am–9pm; Sun 10am–6pm.

River City Grill ★ INTERNATIONAL With its hip, big-city decor and innovative menu, this restaurant is something of a novelty in Yuma. Although you can get a steak at dinner and a burger at lunch, seafood dominates the menu. The crab-and-salmon cakes with spicy Thai peanut sauce are a must for a starter. Flavor combinations range all over the globe: Vietnamese spring rolls, Mediterranean salad, pad Thai, and Jamaican jerked chicken. The owners of this restaurant also operate **Ciao Bella,** 2255 S. Fourth Ave. (✆ **928/783-3900**), an upscale Italian restaurant.

600 W. 3rd St. ✆ **928/782-7988.** www.rivercitygrillyuma.com. Reservations recommended. Main courses $8–$11 lunch, $14–$26 dinner. AE, DISC, MC, V. Mon–Fri 11:30am–2pm and 5–10pm; Sat–Sun 5–10pm.

Yuma After Dark

In most small towns across Arizona, you'll find an old downtown movie theater. Most of them are boarded up and abandoned. Not so with Yuma's old theater.

Historic Yuma Theatre.

The renovated and updated **Historic Yuma Theatre,** 254 S. Main St. (✆ **928/373-5202;** www.ci.yuma.az.us/4753.htm), is now host to live theater productions and touring musical groups. Originally opened in 1912, the theater has been restored to the way it looked in the 1930s, when it sported a distinctive Art Deco decor.

Looking for something else to do after dark in Yuma? You can try your luck at the **Paradise Casinos,** 450 Quechan Dr. (✆ **888/777-4946;** www.paradise-casinos.com), across the Colorado River on the Quechan Indian Reservation, or at the **Cocopah Casino,** 15318 S. Ave. B, Somerton (✆ **800/237-5687;** www.cocopahresort.com/casino), 15 minutes south of Yuma.

East Toward Tucson

It's a long stretch of desert from Yuma east to Tucson, and there's not much to break up the monotony of the drive. However, keep an eye out for exit 67, the Dateland exit. Although **Dateland Date Gardens** (✆ **928/454-2772;** www.dateland.com) is little more than a gift shop and diner, it is well known for its thick and creamy date shakes (on a hot afternoon, nothing tastes better).

The next exit to watch for is exit 102 (Painted Rock Dam Rd.). Getting off at this exit will lead you north to an impressive collection of petroglyphs at the Bureau of Land Management's **Painted Rock Petroglyph Site.** To find this ancient rock art, drive north on Painted Rock Dam Road for 11 miles to a left turn onto dirt Rocky Point Road. Continue another ½ mile to the parking area. There is a $2 day-use fee here. For more information, contact the BLM Lower Sonoran Field Office, 21605 N. Seventh Ave., Phoenix (✆ **623/580-5500;** www.blm.gov/az/st/en/fo/lower_sonoran_field.html).

West Toward San Diego

West of Yuma, I-8 heads out across the California desert toward San Diego, soon passing through barren, windswept sand dunes that Hollywood has long used to represent the Sahara. This region may seem like it's a long way from anywhere, but if you pull off the freeway 9 miles west of Yuma at exit 164 (Sidewinder Rd.), you'll find yourself in the "town" of **Felicity** (✆ **760/572-0100;** www.felicityusa.com), which, according to town founder Jacques-Andres Istel, is the center of the world. Actually, it was a dragon in a fairy tale that claimed that Felicity was the center of the world, and who's going to argue with a dragon? The fact that Istel wrote the fairy tale shouldn't matter. Make a pilgrimage to this unusual attraction, and you can stand inside a pyramid at the "exact" center of the world. As an added bonus, you can admire Istel's monument to the history of French aviation and marvel at his granite remembrance walls. The Official Center of the World is open for tours from Thanksgiving to Easter.

12

PLANNING YOUR TRIP TO ARIZONA

No matter what your plans are when you arrive in Arizona, you'll need to do some planning in advance to make the most of your visit. This chapter gives you the information to help plan your trip and to point you toward some additional resources.

GETTING THERE

By Plane

Arizona is served by numerous airlines flying to both Phoenix (Code: PHX) and Tucson (Code: TUS) from cities around the U.S. and Canada. Phoenix is the more centrally located of the two airports and is closer to the Grand Canyon. However, if you plan to explore the southern part of the state or are going to visit both Phoenix and Tucson, I recommend flying into Tucson, which is a smaller airport and charges lower taxes on its car rentals. The only drawback is that your plane will probably stop in Phoenix on its way to Tucson. If a trip to the Grand Canyon is your only reason for visiting Arizona, consider flying into Las Vegas, which sometimes has lower airfares and better car-rental rates.

Alaska Airlines often has low fares to Arizona. Also, be sure to check the fares at Southwest Airlines, which does not list its fares on big travel search engines. Phoenix and Tucson are both served by most of the major U.S. airlines and also a handful of international airlines. To find out which airlines travel to Arizona, please see "Airline Websites," p. 555.

By Car

Arizona is bordered on the west by California and Nevada, on the north by Utah, on the east by New Mexico, and on the south by Mexico. I-40 runs east-west across the state connecting to Los Angeles (via I-15) and to Albuquerque. I-10 also passes through the state connecting to Los Angeles in the west and all the way to Jacksonville, Florida, in the east. I-8 connects Casa Grande with San Diego. I-17 is the state's only north-south interstate highway; it links Flagstaff with Mexico at Nogales. Using the interstate highways, you can travel between Phoenix and Tucson in a little more than 1½ hours. From Phoenix to Flagstaff takes about 2½ hours (add another 1½ hours to get to the Grand Canyon). For information on car rentals, gasoline, and driving rules in Arizona, see "By Car" under "Getting Around" below.

By Train

Amtrak (✆ **800/872-7245;** www.amtrak.com) provides service aboard the Southwest Chief between Flagstaff (for the Grand Canyon) and Los Angeles, also connecting with Albuquerque, Kansas City, and Chicago. The Sunset Limited connects Tucson with Orlando, New Orleans, Houston, San Antonio, El Paso, and Los Angeles. At press time, the fare from Los Angeles to Flagstaff was $61 one-way and $122 round-trip. There is no rail service to Phoenix, but Amtrak

PREVIOUS PAGE: **Arizona is home to one of the longest stretches of Route 66.**

will sell you a ticket and then put you on a bus from either Tucson or Flagstaff to Phoenix. Book early for lower fares.

By Bus

Greyhound (✆ **800/231-2222** in the U.S.; 001/214/849-8100 outside the U.S.; www.greyhound.com) is the sole nationwide bus line. International visitors can obtain information about the **Greyhound North American Discovery Pass.** The pass, which offers unlimited travel and stopovers in the U.S. and Canada, can be obtained outside the United States from travel agents or through www.discoverypass.com.

GETTING AROUND

By Car

Arizona is a big state (the sixth largest), and because many of the state's top attractions are national parks, national monuments, and other natural areas, a car is almost a necessity for getting the most out of a visit to the state. Unfortunately, car-rental rates are surprisingly high, and while gasoline is less expensive than in most parts of the world, the distances that must be covered while exploring Arizona mean that you'll need to factor fuel costs into your vacation budget. At the time of this writing, gasoline was selling for around $3.60 to $3.70 per gallon throughout much of Arizona. For this reason, I tend to rent compact, fuel-efficient cars whenever I explore the state in a rental car. That said, with Arizona's abundant sunshine, convertibles are very popular rental cars, as are SUVs.

Because Phoenix and Tucson are major resort destinations, both have numerous car-rental agencies, including such major rental-car companies as Advantage, Alamo, Avis, Budget, Dollar, Enterprise, Hertz, National, Payless, and Thrifty. **Fox Rent a Car** (✆ **800/225-4369** or 310/641-3838; www.foxrentacar.com) is a small regional rental-car company that has a rental office at Phoenix Sky Harbor Airport. Rental rates in Tucson are usually lower than in Phoenix, as are the many taxes and surcharges that are tacked onto car-rental rates. In Phoenix, taxes and surcharges add as much as 50% to the price of a rental car if you rent at the airport. In Tucson, expect to pay around 30% in taxes and surcharges for airport rentals.

Rates for rental cars vary considerably among companies and with the model you want to rent, the dates you rent, and your pickup and drop-off points. If you contact the same company three times to check rates on the same model car, you may get three different quotes, depending on current availability of vehicles. It pays to shop early and ask lots of questions. At press time, a compact car with unlimited mileage was renting in Phoenix for $250 to $400 per week ($400–$600 including taxes and surcharges) during the winter high season. In Tucson for the same time period, compact cars were renting for $250 ($325 with taxes and surcharges) per week.

You can sometimes save money by renting at a location away from the airport, though many rental-car companies raise the rates at these off-airport offices effectively negating any potential savings. If you will be staying at a hotel that offers a free airport shuttle, you can check in and then have an off-airport rental-car location pick you up and drive you to its office. However, if you have to pay for a shuttle or taxi to either your hotel or the off-airport rental-car office, you may wipe out any potential savings you might have realized by renting away from the airport. Be sure to weigh all the costs carefully. Also, before making a reservation, be sure to ask about the tax and the loss-damage waiver (LDW) if you want to know what your total rental cost will be.

In the U.S., virtually all rental cars have automatic transmissions. If you're visiting from abroad and plan to rent a car in the United States, keep in mind that foreign driver's licenses are usually recognized in the U.S., but you may want to consider obtaining an international driver's license. International visitors should also note that insurance and taxes are generally not included in quoted rental car rates in the U.S. Be sure to ask your rental agency about additional fees for these. They can add a significant cost to your car rental. At gas (petrol) stations, taxes are already included in the printed price. One U.S. gallon equals 3.8 liters or .85 imperial gallons.

For information on major routes into Phoenix and Tucson, see chapters 4 and 9. For driving times between destinations, see specific sections in regional chapters.

In Arizona, a right turn on a red light is permitted after a complete stop. Seat belts are required for the driver and for all passengers. Children 4 and under, or who weigh 40 pounds or less, must be in a child's car seat. General speed limits are 25 to 35 mph in towns and cities, 15 mph in school zones, and 55 to 65 mph on two-lane highways. On rural interstate highways, the speed limit ranges from 65 to 75 mph.

Always be sure to keep your gas tank topped off. In many parts of the state, it's not unusual to drive 60 miles without seeing a gas station. ***Note:*** A breakdown in the desert can be more than just an inconvenience—it can be dangerous. Always carry drinking water with you while driving through the desert, and if you plan to head off on back roads, carry extra water for the car's radiator as well.

By Plane

Arizona is a big state (the sixth largest), so if your time is short, you may want to consider flying between cities. **US Airways** (✆ **800/428-4322;** www.usairways.com) serves Phoenix, Tucson, Flagstaff, and Yuma. **Great Lakes Airlines** (✆ **800/554-5111** or 307/433-2899; www.flygreatlakes.com) flies between Page/Lake Powell and Phoenix.

Attention visitors to the U.S. from abroad: Some major airlines offer transatlantic or transpacific passengers special discount tickets under the name **Visit USA,** which allows mostly one-way travel from one U.S. destination to another at very low prices. Unavailable in the U.S., these discount tickets must be purchased abroad in conjunction with your international fare. This system is the easiest, fastest, cheapest way to see the country. Inquire with your air carrier.

By Train

International visitors can buy a **USA Rail Pass,** good for 15, 30, or 45 days of unlimited travel on **Amtrak** (✆ **800/USA-RAIL** in the U.S. or Canada; **001/215-856-7953** outside the U.S.; www.amtrak.com). The pass is available online or through many overseas travel agents. See Amtrak's website for the cost of travel within the western, eastern, or northwestern United States. Reservations are generally required and should be made as early as possible. Regional rail passes are also available.

The train is not really a viable way of getting around much of Arizona because there is no north-south Amtrak service between Grand Canyon/Flagstaff and Phoenix or between Tucson and Phoenix. However, Amtrak will sell you a ticket to Phoenix, which includes a shuttle-bus ride from Flagstaff or Tucson. You can also get to the town of Williams, 30 miles west of Flagstaff, on Amtrak, and in Williams transfer to the Grand Canyon Railway excursion train, which runs to Grand Canyon Village at the South Rim of the Grand Canyon (see chapter 6 for details). Be aware, however, that the Williams stop is on the outskirts of town; you'll have to arrange in advance to be picked up.

By Bus

Greyhound (✆ **800/231-2222** in the U.S.; ✆ **001/214/849-8100** outside the U.S.; www.greyhound.com) has service to 18 cities across the state. Shuttle bus service between Phoenix, Flagstaff, Williams, and Grand Canyon National Park is available through **Arizona Shuttle** (✆ **877/226-8060** or 928/226-8060; www.arizonashuttle.com). These shuttles are more useful than Greyhound if you are trying to get around the state without a car.

TIPS ON ACCOMMODATIONS

When making hotel reservations for late spring or early fall, find out when hotel rates drop for the summer or go up for the fall so that you can, if possible, schedule your trip for right after the rates go down (or just before they go back up). Many resorts also have a short discounted season right before Christmas (just think, you can do your holiday shopping in Arizona).

As if winter resort rates in Arizona aren't high enough, you can expect to also pay a resort fee at most resorts around the state. These fees, which are generally around $15 to $20, cover such things as local calls and toll-free phone number access, daily newspaper delivery, and exercise-room use. Of course, if you're like me, you think all those things should be included in the regular room rates.

Remember, if you don't absolutely need all the amenities of a big resort, there are dozens of chain-motel options in the Phoenix and Tucson areas. Alternatively, you can get a bit more for your money if you head to such smaller towns as Wickenburg, Bullhead City, Lake Havasu City, and Yuma. If you must stay in the Phoenix or Tucson area, head for the suburbs. The farther you drive from the resort areas, the more you can save.

Most hotels offer special packages, weekend rates, various discounts (such as for AARP or AAA members), and free accommodations for children, so it helps to ask when you reserve. Nearly all hotels in the state have smoke-free and wheelchair-accessible rooms.

If you like to stay at B&Bs, there are a few helpful resources you should know about. **Mi Casa Su Casa** (✆ **800/456-0682** or 480/990-0682; www.azres.com) can book you into hundreds of homes across the state, as can **Arizona Trails Travel Services** (✆ **888/799-4284** or 480/837-4284; www.arizonatrails.com), which also books tour and hotel reservations. For a list of some of the best B&Bs in the state, contact the **Arizona Association of Bed & Breakfast Inns** (www.arizona-bed-breakfast.com).

If you'll be traveling by RV or with a tent, you've got loads of camping options all across Arizona. However, be aware that campgrounds at and near Grand Canyon National Park, the state's top camping destination, fill up nightly during the summer and often in spring and fall as well. If you can, make a campsite reservation as far in advance as possible. To make campsite reservations at national park and national forest campgrounds, contact the **National Recreation Reservation Service** (✆ **877/444-6777** or 518/885-3639; www.recreation.gov). To find out about campsites in state parks, contact **Arizona State Parks,** 1300 W. Washington St., Phoenix, AZ 85007 (✆ **602/542-4174;** www.azstateparks.com).

If you want to rent an RV, try **Cruise America** (✆ **800/671-8042;** www.cruiseamerica.com), which has offices in Phoenix, Tucson, and Flagstaff. Expect to pay between $400 and $1,300 per week (plus taxes) depending on the time of year and size of the RV you rent. RVs can also be rented in Phoenix from **El Monte RV,** 3020 E. Bell Rd. (✆ **888/337-2214;** www.elmonterv.com). Rental rates here range from around $660 to $1,200 per week.

[Fast FACTS] ARIZONA

Area Codes The area code in Phoenix is 602. In Scottsdale, Tempe, Mesa, and the east valley, it's 480. In Glendale and the west valley, it's 623. The area code for Tucson and southeastern Arizona is 520. The rest of the state is area code 928.

Business Hours The following are general hours; specific establishments' hours may vary. Banks are open Monday through Friday from 9am to 5pm (some also Sat 9am–noon). Stores are open Monday through Saturday from 10am to 6pm, and Sunday from noon to 5pm (malls usually stay open until 9pm Mon–Sat). Bars are legally allowed to be open until 2am.

Car Rental See "By Car" under "Getting Around," earlier in this chapter.

Cellphones See "Mobile Phones," later in this section.

Crime See "Safety," later in this section.

Customs Every visitor 21 years of age or older may bring in, free of duty, the following: (1) 1 liter of alcohol; (2) 200 cigarettes, 100 cigars (but not from Cuba); and (3) $100 worth of gifts. These exemptions are offered to travelers who spend at least 72 hours in the United States and who have not claimed them within the preceding 6 months. It is forbidden to bring into the country almost any meat products (including canned, fresh, and dried meat products, such as bouillon and soup mixes). Generally, condiments including vinegars, oils, pickled goods, spices, coffee, tea, and some cheeses and baked goods are permitted. Avoid rice products, as rice can often harbor insects. Bringing fruits and vegetables is prohibited since they may harbor pests or disease. International visitors may carry in or out up to $10,000 in U.S. or foreign currency with no formalities; larger sums must be declared to U.S. Customs on entering or leaving, which includes filing form FinCEN 105. For details regarding U.S. Customs and Border Protection, consult your nearest U.S. embassy or consulate, or **U.S. Customs** (www.customs.gov).

Disabled Travelers Most disabilities shouldn't stop anyone from traveling in the U.S. Thanks to provisions in the Americans with Disabilities Act, most public places are required to comply with disability-friendly regulations. Almost all public establishments (including hotels, restaurants, museums, and such, but not including certain National Historic Landmarks) and at least some modes of public transportation provide accessible entrances and other facilities for those with disabilities.

If you have no intention of letting your disability prevent you from having the adventure of a lifetime, contact **Arizona River Runners,** P.O. Box 47788, Phoenix, AZ 85068 (✆ **800/477-7238;** www.raftarizona.com), or **Arizona Raft Adventures,** 4050 E. Huntington Dr., Flagstaff, AZ 86004 (✆ **800/786-7238;** www.azraft.com), both of which offer Grand Canyon rafting trips for people with disabilities. In the northwest corner of the state, **Stagecoach Trails Guest Ranch,** P.O. Box 580, Yucca, AZ 86438 (✆ **866/444-4471** or 928/727-8270; www.stagecoachtrailsranch.com), is a guest ranch that was designed with the needs of persons with disabilities in mind. All the ranch buildings are accessible, and there are horseback riding programs for persons with disabilities.

The **America the Beautiful—National Park and Federal Recreational Lands Pass—Access Pass** gives travelers with visual impairments or those with permanent disabilities (regardless of age) free lifetime entrance to federal recreation sites administered by the National Park Service, including the Fish and Wildlife Service, the Forest Service, the Bureau of Land Management, and the Bureau of Reclamation. This includes national parks, monuments, historic sites, recreation areas, and national wildlife refuges.

The America the Beautiful Access Pass can only be obtained in person at a National Park Service facility that charges an entrance fee, such as Grand Canyon National Park, Saguaro National Park, Petrified Forest National Park, Organ Pipe Cactus National Monument, Montezuma Castle National Monument, Wupatki National Monument, Casa Grande Ruins National Monument, Tonto National Monument, and Tumacácori National Historical Park. You need to show proof of a medically determined disability. Besides free entry, the pass also offers a 50% discount on some federal-use fees charged for such facilities as camping, swimming, parking, boat launching, and tours. For more information, go to www.nps.gov/fees_passes.htm, or call the United States Geological Survey/USGS (✆ **888/275-8747;** www.usgs.gov), which issues the passes.

Doctors To find a doctor, check with the front desk or concierge at your hotel or look in the yellow pages of the local telephone book under "Physician." Also see the "Doctor" and "Hospitals" listings in the "Fast Facts" sections of the Phoenix and Tucson chapters (chapters 4 and 9).

Drinking Laws The legal age for purchase and consumption of alcoholic beverages is 21; proof of age is required and often requested at bars, nightclubs, and restaurants, so it's always a good idea to bring ID when you go out. In Arizona, liquor is sold at supermarkets. Do not carry open containers of alcohol in your car or any public area that isn't zoned for alcohol consumption. The police can fine you on the spot. Don't even think about driving while intoxicated.

Driving Rules See "Getting Around," earlier in this chapter.

Electricity Like Canada, the United States uses 110 to 120 volts AC (60 cycles), compared to 220 to 240 volts AC (50 cycles) in most of Europe, Australia, and New Zealand. Downward converters that change 220–240 volts to 110–120 volts are difficult to find in the United States, so bring one with you.

Embassies & Consulates All embassies are in the nation's capital, Washington, D.C. Some consulates are in major U.S. cities, and most nations have a mission to the United Nations in New York City. If your country isn't listed below, call for directory information in Washington, D.C. (✆ **202/555-1212**) or check **www.embassy.org/embassies**.

The embassy of **Australia** is at 1601 Massachusetts Ave. NW, Washington, DC 20036 (✆ **202/797-3000;** www.usa.embassy.gov.au). Consulates are in New York, Honolulu, Houston, Los Angeles, and San Francisco.

The embassy of **Canada** is at 501 Pennsylvania Ave. NW, Washington, DC 20001 (✆ **202/682-1740;** www.canadainternational.gc.ca/washington). Other Canadian consulates are in Buffalo (New York), Detroit, Los Angeles, New York, and Seattle.

The embassy of **Ireland** is at 2234 Massachusetts Ave. NW, Washington, DC 20008 (✆ **202/462-3939;** www.embassyofireland.org). Irish consulates are in Boston, Chicago, New York, San Francisco, and other cities. See website for complete listing.

The embassy of **New Zealand** is at 37 Observatory Circle NW, Washington, DC 20008 (✆ **202/328-4800;** www.nzembassy.com). New Zealand consulates are in Los Angeles, Salt Lake City, San Francisco, and Seattle.

The embassy of the **United Kingdom** is at 3100 Massachusetts Ave. NW, Washington, DC 20008 (✆ **202/588-6500;** http://ukinusa.fco.gov.uk). Other British consulates are in Atlanta, Boston, Chicago, Cleveland, Houston, Los Angeles, New York, San Francisco, and Seattle.

Emergencies Call ✆ **911** to report a fire, call the police, or get an ambulance anywhere in the U.S. This is a toll-free call. (No coins are required at public telephones.)

Family Travel With its sunshine, swimming pools, guest ranches, and baseball spring-training camps, Arizona is a popular spring-break destination for families from around the country, especially those from cold, snowy northern states. Likewise, in summer, the state is popular for its many natural wonders, foremost of which is the Grand Canyon. If you plan to take in the canyon on a road trip that also takes in the canyon country of southern Utah, keep in mind that distances are great out here. Don't expect to find someplace to eat whenever the kids are hungry; pack food before heading out on a long drive. Also bring plenty to entertain the kids as you drive for hours through uninteresting scenery.

For recommendations of kid-friendly activities, see "The Best Family Experiences" in chapter 1, and for family-oriented resorts, see "The Best Family Resorts," also in chapter 1. To locate accommodations, restaurants, and attractions that are particularly kid-friendly, see the "Kids" icon throughout this guide. Also, check out the "Especially for Kids" sections of the Phoenix and Tucson chapters (chapters 4 and 9). Many of the resorts in Phoenix and Tucson offer children's programs, though these programs may only be available during spring break and the hot summer months. In the absence of children's programs, many hotel and resort concierges throughout the state can recommend babysitters.

Gasoline Please see "By Car" under "Getting Around," earlier in this chapter.

Health If you've never been to the desert, be sure to prepare yourself for this harsh environment. No matter what time of year it is, the desert sun is strong and bright. Use sunscreen when outdoors—particularly if you're up in the mountains, where the altitude makes sunburn more likely. The bright sun also makes sunglasses a necessity. Also, in the desert, even when you don't feel hot, the dry air steals moisture from your body, so drink plenty of fluids. You may want to use a body lotion as well; skin dries out quickly in the desert.

Bugs, Bites & Other Wildlife Concerns It's not only the sun that makes the desert a harsh environment. Poisonous creatures are out there, too, but with a little common sense and some precautions, you can avoid them. Rattlesnakes are common, but your chances of meeting one are slight—they tend not to come out in the heat of the day. Still, you should never stick your hand into holes among the rocks in the desert, and always look to see where you're going to step before putting your foot down. Arizona is also home to a large poisonous lizard called the Gila monster. These black-and-orange lizards are far less common than rattlesnakes, and your chances of meeting one are very slight. Although the tarantula has developed a nasty reputation, the tiny black widow is more likely to cause illness. Scorpions are another danger of the desert. Be extra careful when turning over rocks or logs that might harbor either black widows or scorpions.

Respiratory & Desert Illnesses Valley fever, a fungal infection of the lungs, is common in the desert Southwest, although it generally affects only long-term residents of the desert. The fungus is carried on dust particles, which are carried by dust storms and winds blowing across farms and construction sites. Symptoms include fever, chest pain, fatigue, headaches, and rashes. By the way, if you happen to be atop a mountain in Phoenix and can't see across the Valley, blame it on the smog, which is as bad as that in Los Angeles.

If you plan to do any camping or backcountry travel in the Four Corners region, which is where the Navajo and Hopi Indian reservations are located, you should be aware of hantavirus. This virus is spread by mice and is often fatal. Symptoms include fatigue, fever, and muscle aches; should you come down with any such symptoms within 1 to 5 weeks of traveling through the Four Corners area, see a doctor and mention that you have been in an area where hantavirus is known to occur.

High-Altitude Hazards Both the South Rim of the Grand Canyon and the canyon gateway city of Flagstaff are at around 7,000 feet (2,133 meters) in elevation and the North Rim of the Grand Canyon is at 8,000 feet (2,438 meters). While these elevations are generally not high enough to cause altitude sickness even in the most sensitive, they are high enough to cause shortness of breath after even moderate exercise if you are from lower elevations. Take it slow, and remember that if you hike down into the Grand Canyon, you'll really feel the elevation when you turn around and start hiking back out.

Sun/Elements/Extreme Weather Exposure "It's a dry heat" is a mantra in the lowland deserts of Arizona. What this means is that, in the absence of humidity, the air always seems quite a bit cooler than it does on a hot day in, say, Atlanta, Houston, or Miami. Trust me. When it's hot here, it's hot. Drink lots of fluids, and wear plenty of sunscreen. In fact, it is so sunny in Arizona most of the time (even in the winter), that you should be sure to wear sunscreen whenever you're outdoors here. If you should happen to be visiting during the late summer monsoon season, be alert for flash floods. Do not ignore signs on roadways warning motorists not to enter flooded areas. The monsoon season also brings impressive thunderstorms, and should you encounter a thunderstorm at the Grand Canyon, seek cover immediately (cars are among the safest places to be).

Insurance For information on traveler's insurance, trip cancellation insurance, and medical insurance while traveling, please visit www.frommers.com/planning.

Internet & Wi-Fi Nearly anywhere you go in Arizona, even on Indian reservations, you can find some way to connect to the Internet. Among the more common places to get access to the Internet are cybercafes, public libraries, and in hotel lobbies where computers are often available for guests' use. See "Fast Facts" in chapters 4 (p. 96) and 9 (p. 400) for details on Internet access in the Phoenix and Tucson areas.

Legal Aid While driving, if you are pulled over for a minor infraction (such as speeding), never attempt to pay the fine directly to a police officer; this could be construed as attempted bribery, a much more serious crime. Pay fines by mail, or directly into the hands of the clerk of the court. If accused of a more serious offense, say and do nothing before consulting a lawyer. In the U.S., the burden is on the state to prove a person's guilt beyond a reasonable doubt, and everyone has the right to remain silent, whether he or she is suspected of a crime or actually arrested. Once arrested, a person can make one telephone call to a party of his or her choice. The international visitor should call his or her embassy or consulate.

LGBT Travelers As elsewhere in the U.S., the major cities in Arizona (Phoenix and Tucson) are large enough to support businesses and organizations catering specifically to the gay and lesbian communities. At gay bars around Phoenix and Tucson, you can pick up various gay-oriented local publications, including ***Echo Magazine*** (✆ **888/324-6624** or 602/266-0550; www.echomag.com).

For information on gay- and lesbian-friendly businesses in the Phoenix metro area, contact the **Greater Phoenix Gay & Lesbian Chamber of Commerce** (✆ **602/266-5055;** www.gpglcc.org). **Wingspan,** 430 E. 7th St., Tucson (✆ **520/624-1779;** www.wingspan.org), is southern Arizona's lesbian, gay, bisexual, and transgender community center. The ***Tucson Observer*** (✆ **520/622-7176;** www.tucsonobserver.com) is a local Tucson gay newspaper available at both Wingspan and **Antigone Bookstore,** 411 N. 4th Ave. (✆ **520/792-3715;** www.antigonebooks.com).

Mail At press time, domestic postage rates were 28¢ for a postcard and 44¢ for a letter. For international mail, a first-class letter of up to 1 ounce costs 98¢ (75¢ to Canada and 79¢ to Mexico); a first-class postcard costs the same as a letter. For more information go to **www.usps.com**.

If you aren't sure what your address will be in the United States, mail can be sent to you, in your name, c/o General Delivery at the main post office of the city or region where you expect to be. (Call ✆ **800/275-8777** for information on the nearest post office.) The addressee must pick up mail in person and must produce proof of identity (driver's license, passport, or the like). Most post offices will hold mail for up to 1 month, and are open Monday to Friday from 8am to 6pm, and Saturday from 9am to 3pm.

Always include zip codes when mailing items in the U.S. If you don't know your zip code, visit www.usps.com/zip4.

Medical Requirements Unless you're arriving from an area known to be suffering from an epidemic (particularly cholera or yellow fever), inoculations or vaccinations are not required for entry into the United States. Also see "Health."

Mobile Phones Just because your cellphone works at home doesn't mean it'll work everywhere in the U.S. (thanks to the fragmented cellphone system in the United States). If you live in the U.S., it's a good bet that your phone will work in Arizona's major cities, but take a look at your wireless company's coverage map on its website before heading out; T-Mobile, Sprint, and Nextel are particularly weak in rural areas. (To see where GSM phones work in the U.S., check out www.t-mobile.com/coverage.) If you're visiting from another country, be sure to find out about international calling rates and roaming charges before using your phone in the United States. You could ring up a huge phone bill with just a few calls.

Options for staying connected in the U.S. include renting a mobile phone from a company such as **Roberts Rent-A-Phone** (✆ **800/964-2468;** www.roberts-rent-a-phone.com). However, you can also buy an inexpensive phone and prepaid minutes from such companies as **TracFone** (www.tracfone.com). These phones are readily available in such stores as Wal-Mart and Target and usually cost less than $20. Prepaid minutes might cost $20 for 60 minutes, though double-minute plans can lower this cost. Another alternative if you are traveling with your laptop computer or have a smartphone is to install **Skype** (www.skype.com), a VoIP (voice-over Internet protocol) program/app that allows you to use your computer or smartphone as an Internet-based telephone. Doing this allows you to call other Skype users at no charge.

If you're heading down into the Grand Canyon and want to rent a satellite phone, contact **World Communications Center** (✆ **800/221-2575** or 480/857-6656; www.wcclp.com).

Money & Costs Frommer's lists exact prices in the local currency. The currency conversions quoted below were correct at press time. However, rates fluctuate, so before departing consult a currency exchange website such as **www.oanda.com/currency/converter** to check up-to-the-minute rates.

THE VALUE OF THE U.S. DOLLAR VS. OTHER POPULAR CURRENCIES

US$	Aus$	Can$	Euro (€)	NZ$	UK£
1	0.98715	0.98122	0.72503	1.33264	0.62049

What will a vacation in Arizona cost? That depends on your comfort needs. If you drive an RV or carry a tent, you can get by very inexpensively and find a place to stay almost anywhere in the state. If you don't mind staying in motels that date from the 1940s and can sleep just fine on a sagging mattress, you can stay for less money in Arizona than almost anyplace else in the U.S. (under $40 a night for a double in some places). On the other hand, you can easily spend several hundred dollars a day on a room at one of the state's world-class resorts. Expect to pay around $200 per day for a room at a midlevel resort in Phoenix or Tucson. Rooms in Sedona and at the Grand Canyon are also at a premium, so plan on spending between $150 and $200 for a mid-level room. If you're looking to stay in clean, modern motels at interstate highway offramps, expect to pay $45 to $65 a night for a double room in most places (a little bit more in Phoenix and Tucson).

WHAT THINGS COST IN ARIZONA	$US
Taxi from the airport to downtown Scottsdale	21.00–36.00
Double room, moderate	150.00–200.00
Double room, inexpensive	65.00–100.00
Three-course dinner for one without wine, moderate	20.00–35.00
Bottle of beer	2.50–3.50
Cup of coffee	1.50–2.00
1 gallon/1 liter of premium gas	3.30/0.87
Admission to most museums	5.00–10.00
Admission to Grand Canyon National Park	25.00

In Arizona, you'll find ATMs at banks in even the smallest towns. You can also usually find them at gas station minimarts, although these machines usually charge a slightly higher fee than banks. You can sometimes avoid a fee by searching out a small community bank, a savings and loan, or a credit union ATM. To avoid fees, you can also go into a grocery store, make a purchase, and ask for cash back on your debit card. Four-digit PINs work fine in Arizona.

For help with currency conversions, tip calculations, and more, download Frommer's convenient Travel Tools app for your mobile device. Go to www.frommers.com/go/mobile and click on the Travel Tools icon.

Newspapers & Magazines The *Arizona Republic* is Arizona's largest daily newspaper and can be found throughout central and northern Arizona. In the southern part of the state, you are more likely to find Tucson's *Arizona Daily Star,* a morning daily. *Arizona Highways* is a beautiful and informative photo-driven monthly magazine published by the Arizona Department of Transportation. Both Phoenix and Tucson have a number of glossy monthly lifestyle magazines that are worth picking up for their monthly events listings.

Packing Arizona is hot, hot, hot. Everyone knows that, but did you also know that from the fall through the spring temperatures at higher elevations (for instance, the Grand Canyon) can fall well below freezing? Sure, you need to bring shorts and sandals for a spring-break vacation in Phoenix or Tucson, but if you have any plans to visit the Grand Canyon, Flagstaff, or just about any place else in northern Arizona from October to April, you better bring some warm clothes, too. In fact, while this state has a reputation for its sunny weather, December and January can even bring chilly temperatures to Phoenix and Tucson. For more helpful information on packing for your trip, download our convenient Travel Tools app for your mobile device. Go to www.frommers.com/go/mobile and click on the Travel Tools icon.

Passports Virtually every air traveler entering the U.S. is required to show a passport. All persons, including U.S. citizens, traveling by air between the United States and Canada, Mexico, Central and South America, the Caribbean, and Bermuda are required to present a valid passport. ***Note:*** U.S. and Canadian citizens entering the U.S. at land and sea ports of entry from within the western hemisphere must now also present a passport or other documents compliant with the Western Hemisphere Travel Initiative (WHTI; see www.getyouhome.gov for details). Children 15 and under may continue entering with only a U.S. birth certificate, or other proof of U.S. citizenship.

Australia **Australian Passport Information Service** (✆ **131-232;** www.passports.gov.au).

Canada **Passport Office,** Department of Foreign Affairs and International Trade, Ottawa, ON K1A 0G3 (✆ **800/567-6868;** www.ppt.gc.ca).

Ireland **Passport Office,** Setanta Centre, Molesworth Street, Dublin 2 (✆ **01/671-1633;** www.foreignaffairs.gov.ie).

New Zealand **Passports Office,** Department of Internal Affairs, 47 Boulcott St., Wellington, 6011 (✆ **0800/225-050** in New Zealand or 04/474-8100; www.passports.govt.nz).

United Kingdom Visit your nearest passport office, major post office, or travel agency or contact the **Identity and Passport Service (IPS),** 89 Eccleston Sq., London, SW1V 1PN (✆ **0300/222-0000;** www.ips.gov.uk).

United States To find your regional passport office, check the U.S. State Department website (http://travel.state.gov/passport) or call the **National Passport Information Center** (✆ **877/487-2778**) for automated information.

Petrol Please see "By Car" under "Getting Around," earlier in this chapter.

Police In most places in Arizona, phone ✆ **911** for emergencies. A few small towns have not adopted this emergency phone number, so if 911 doesn't work, dial 0 (zero) for the operator and state your reason for calling.

Safety Over the past few years, problems along Arizona's border with Mexico have repeatedly garnered national media attention. If you believed everything you heard, you probably now assume that Arizona is a war zone as dangerous as Afghanistan or Iraq. Well, it's not. Arizona is as safe for travelers as any other state. However, you can expect to encounter U.S. Border Patrol checkpoints in the southern part of the state, and, if driving after dark close to the border, you might even encounter illegal immigrants walking along the road. Do not stop for them.

Far more important to remember is that when driving long distances, always carry plenty of drinking water and, if you're heading off onto dirt roads, extra water for your car's radiator as well. When hiking or walking in the desert, keep an eye out for rattlesnakes; these poisonous snakes are not normally aggressive unless provoked, so give them a wide berth. Also be sure to give cactus a wide berth, especially cholla cactus, which has particularly painful spines that often break off in your skin and must be removed with tweezers.

Don't leave valuables, especially purses, wallets, or cameras, in view in your car when going for a hike or wandering off to take pictures at a scenic overlook in Canyon de Chelly National Monument, or anywhere for that matter.

Senior Travel With its abundant sunshine and lack of cold, icy, snowy winters, Arizona has long been a favorite vacation and retirement destination with seniors. The state goes out of its way to accommodate senior travelers with discounts on accommodations and attractions, discounted "early-bird" dinners at many restaurants, and economical places to park RVs. Seniors should be sure to get an **America the Beautiful—National Park and Federal Recreational Lands Pass—Senior Pass.** Issued by the U.S. National Park Service, these passes give seniors 62 years or older lifetime entrance to all properties administered by the National Park Service—national parks, monuments, historic sites, recreation areas, and national wildlife refuges—for a one-time processing fee of $10. Besides free entry, the America the Beautiful Senior Pass also offers a 50% discount on some federal-use fees charged for such facilities as camping, swimming, parking, boat launching, and tours. For more information, see the "Disabled Travelers" section above.

Smoking With the exception of buildings on tribal lands and at tobacco retailers, smoking is prohibited in public indoor spaces throughout Arizona. This regulation applies to restaurants and bars, although such establishments can have outdoor patios where smoking is permitted. Consequently, you may not find the fresh desert air you were expecting if you ask for an outdoor table at a restaurant.

Student Travel Student travel in Arizona usually means one of two things: spring break at Lake Havasu or a summer visit to the Grand Canyon. In either case, you might want to check out the **International Student Travel Confederation** (**ISTC;** www.istc.org) website for comprehensive travel services information and details on how to get an **International Student Identity Card (ISIC),** which qualifies students for substantial savings on rail passes, plane tickets, entrance fees, and more. The card is valid for a maximum of 16 months. You can apply for the card online or in person at **STA Travel** (✆ **800/781-4040** in North America, 134-782 in Australia, 0871/230-0040 in the U.K.; www.statravel.com), the biggest student travel agency in the world; check out the website to locate STA Travel offices worldwide. If you're no longer a student but are still 25 or under, you can get an **International Youth Travel Card (IYTC)** from the same people, which entitles you to some discounts. **Travel CUTS** (✆ **866/246-9762;** www.travelcuts.com) offers similar services for Canadian residents. Irish students may prefer to turn to **USIT** (✆ **01/602-1906;** www.usit.ie), an Ireland-based specialist in student, youth, and independent travel.

Taxes The United States has no value-added tax (VAT) or other indirect tax at the national level. Every state, county, and city may levy its own local tax on all purchases, including hotel and restaurant checks and airline tickets. These taxes will not appear on price tags.

In Arizona, the state, counties, and communities can all levy a sales tax (officially called a transaction privilege tax). In most places, you'll pay 9% or more. On car rentals at Phoenix Sky Harbor Airport, expect to pay 50% or more in taxes and surcharges; at Tucson Airport, you'll pay around 30%. You can sometimes save 10% or so on surcharges if you rent outside the airports, but sometimes the rental rates are higher outside of the airport, which negates the tax savings. Hotel room taxes range from around 9% to 17%. There is no sales tax at museum and other nonprofit gift shops.

Telephones Many convenience groceries and packaging services sell **prepaid calling cards** in denominations up to $50. Many public pay phones at airports now accept American Express, MasterCard, and Visa. **Local calls** made from most pay phones cost either 25¢ or 35¢. Most long-distance and international calls can be dialed directly from any phone. **To make calls within the United States and to Canada,** dial 1 followed by the area code and the seven-digit number. **For other international calls,** dial 011 followed by the country code, city code, and the number you are calling.

Calls to area codes **800, 888, 877,** and **866** are toll-free. However, calls to area codes **700** and **900** (chat lines, bulletin boards, "dating" services, and so on) can be expensive—charges of 95¢ to $3 or more per minute. Some numbers have minimum charges that can run $15 or more.

For **reversed-charge or collect calls,** and for person-to-person calls, dial the number 0 then the area code and number; an operator will come on the line, and you should specify whether you are calling collect, person-to-person, or both. If your operator-assisted call is international, ask for the overseas operator.

For **directory assistance** ("Information"), dial 411 for local numbers and national numbers in the U.S. and Canada. For dedicated long-distance information, dial 1, then the appropriate area code plus 555-1212.

Time The continental United States is divided into **four time zones:** Eastern Standard Time (EST), Central Standard Time (CST), Mountain Standard Time (MST), and Pacific Standard Time (PST). Alaska and Hawaii have their own zones. For example, when it's 9am in Los Angeles (PST), it's 7am in Honolulu (HST), 10am in Denver (MST), 11am in Chicago (CST), noon in New York City (EST), 5pm in London (GMT), and 2am the next day in Sydney.

Daylight saving time (summer time) is in effect from 1am on the second Sunday in March to 1am on the first Sunday in November, except in Arizona, Hawaii, the U.S. Virgin Islands, and Puerto Rico. Daylight saving time moves the clock 1 hour ahead of standard time.

Arizona is in the Mountain Time zone, but it does *not* observe daylight saving time. From the second Sunday in March until the first Sunday in November, there is no time difference between Arizona and California and other states on the West Coast. There is an exception, though—the Navajo Reservation observes daylight saving time. (However, the Hopi Reservation does not.)

For help with time translations, and more, download our convenient Travel Tools app for your mobile device. Go to www.frommers.com/go/mobile and click on the Travel Tools icon.

Tipping In hotels, tip **bellhops** at least $1 per bag ($2–$3 if you have a lot of luggage) and tip the **chamber staff** $1 to $2 per day (more if you've left a big mess for him or her to clean up). Tip the **doorman** or **concierge** only if he or she has provided you with some specific service (for example, calling a cab for you or obtaining difficult-to-get theater tickets). Tip the **valet-parking attendant** $1 every time you get your car.

In restaurants, bars, and nightclubs, tip **service staff** and **bartenders** 15% to 20% of the check, tip **checkroom attendants** $1 per garment, and tip **valet-parking attendants** $1 per vehicle.

As for other service personnel, tip **cab drivers** 15% of the fare; tip **skycaps** at airports at least $1 per bag ($2–$3 if you have a lot of luggage); and tip **hairdressers** and **barbers** 15% to 20%.

For help with tip calculations, currency conversions, and more, download our convenient Travel Tools app for your mobile device. Go to www.frommers.com/go/mobile and click on the Travel Tools icon.

Toilets You won't find public toilets or "restrooms" on the streets in most U.S. cities but they can be found in hotel lobbies, bars, restaurants, museums, department stores, railway and bus stations, and service stations. Large hotels and fast-food restaurants are often the best bet for clean facilities. Restaurants and bars in resorts or heavily visited areas may reserve their restrooms for patrons.

VAT See "Taxes," earlier in this section.

Visas The U.S. State Department has a **Visa Waiver Program (VWP)** allowing citizens of the following countries to enter the United States without a visa for stays of up to 90 days: Andorra, Australia, Austria, Belgium, Brunei, Czech Republic, Denmark, Estonia, Finland, France, Germany, Greece, Hungary, Iceland, Ireland, Italy, Japan, Latvia, Liechtenstein, Lithuania, Luxembourg, Malta, Monaco, the Netherlands, New Zealand, Norway, Portugal, San Marino, Singapore, Slovakia, Slovenia, South Korea, Spain, Sweden, Switzerland, and the United Kingdom. (***Note:*** This list was accurate at press time; for the most up-to-date list of countries in the VWP, consult http://travel.state.gov/visa.) Even though a visa isn't necessary, in an effort to help U.S. officials check travelers against terror watch lists before they arrive at U.S. borders, visitors from VWP countries must register online through the Electronic System for Travel Authorization (ESTA) before boarding a plane or a boat to the U.S. Travelers must complete an electronic application providing basic personal and travel eligibility information. The Department of Homeland Security recommends filling out the form at least 3 days before traveling. Authorizations will be valid for up to 2 years or until the traveler's passport expires, whichever comes first. Currently, there is one US$14 fee for the online application. Existing ESTA registrations remain valid through their expiration dates. ***Note:*** Any passport issued on or after October 26, 2006, by a VWP country must be an **e-Passport** for VWP travelers to be eligible to enter the U.S. without a visa. Citizens of these nations also need to present a round-trip air or cruise ticket upon arrival. E-Passports contain computer chips capable of storing biometric information, such as the required digital photograph of the holder. If your passport doesn't have this feature, you can still travel without a visa if the valid passport was issued before October 26, 2005, and includes a machine-readable zone; or if the valid passport was issued between October 26, 2005, and October 25, 2006, and includes a digital photograph. For more information, go to http://travel.state.gov/visa. Canadian citizens may enter the United States without visas, but will need to show passports and proof of residence.

Citizens of all other countries must have (1) a valid passport that expires at least 6 months later than the scheduled end of their visit to the U.S.; and (2) a tourist visa. For information about U.S. visas go to http://travel.state.gov and click on "Visas." Or go to one of the following websites:

Australian citizens can obtain up-to-date visa information from the **U.S. Embassy Canberra,** Moonah Place, Yarralumla, ACT 2600 (✆ **02/6214-5600**), or by checking the U.S. Diplomatic Mission's website at http://canberra.usembassy.gov/visas.html.

British subjects can obtain up-to-date visa information by calling the **U.S. Embassy Visa Information Line** (✆ **09042-450-100** from within the U.K. at £1.20 per minute, or ✆ **866/382-3589** from within the U.S. at a flat rate of $16 that is payable by credit card only) or by visiting the "Visas to the U.S." section of the American Embassy London's website at http://london.usembassy.gov/visas.html.

Irish citizens can obtain up-to-date visa information through the **U.S. Embassy Dublin,** 42 Elgin Rd., Ballsbridge, Dublin 4 (✆ **1580-47-VISA** [8472] from within the Republic of Ireland at €2.40 per minute; http://dublin.usembassy.gov).

Citizens of **New Zealand** can obtain up-to-date visa information by contacting the **U.S. Embassy New Zealand,** 29 Fitzherbert Terrace, Thorndon, Wellington (✆ **644/462-6000;** http://newzealand.usembassy.gov).

Visitor Information For statewide travel information, contact the **Arizona Office of Tourism** (✆ **866/275-5816;** www.arizonaguide.com). Nearly every city and town in Arizona has a tourism office or a chamber of commerce that can also provide information. See the individual chapters for details on how to contact these sources. For some suggested driving tours along Arizona's scenic roads, also check out the Arizona Office of Tourism's site, www.arizonascenicroads.com.

If you want to load up your smartphone with Arizona-specific apps, I recommend the following. For news and entertainment/event information go to www.azcentral.com (the website for the *Arizona Republic,* Phoenix's daily newspaper). For making restaurant reservations, the **OpenTable** app, available from the iTunes app store, is invaluable. You can also find a list of Frommer's travel apps at www.frommers.com/go/mobile.

Water While tap water throughout Arizona is safe to drink, the water in the Phoenix and Tucson areas tends to have an unpleasant flavor due to the fact that it travels long distances in open canals before being treated. For this reason, local residents tend to drink bottled water.

Wi-Fi See "Internet & Wi-Fi," earlier in this section.

AIRLINE WEBSITES

MAJOR AIRLINES

Aeromexico
www.aeromexico.com

Air Canada
www.aircanada.com

Alaska Airlines
www.alaskaair.com

American Airlines
www.aa.com

British Airways
www.britishairways.com

Continental Airlines
www.continental.com

Delta Air Lines
www.delta.com

Hawaiian Airlines
www.hawaiianair.com

United Airlines
www.united.com

US Airways
www.usairways.com

BUDGET AIRLINES

AirTran Airways
www.airtranairways.com

Frontier Airlines
www.frontierairlines.com

Great Lakes Airlines
www.flygreatlakes.com

JetBlue Airways
www.jetblue.com

Southwest Airlines
www.southwest.com

Sun Country Airlines
www.suncountry.com

WestJet
www.westjet.com

Index

C

D

E

F

I

J

K

L

M

N

Q

R

S

U

V

W

X

Y

Z

Photo Credits

p. i: © John Cancalosi / Alamy; p. iii-v: © Kevin Moloney / Aurora Photos; p. vii: © Mike Coffey; p. 1: © Ron Niebrugge / Alamy; p. 3, left: © James S. Wood; p. 3, right: © James S. Wood; p. 4: © Josh Biggs; p. 5: © Josh Biggs; p. 6, top: © Mark Newman / Prisma / AGE Fotostock; p. 6, bottom: © Robert Shantz / Alamy; p. 7: © Josh Biggs; p. 8: © James S. Wood; p. 9: © James S. Wood; p. 10: © Tony Roberts / Corbis; p. 11, left: © James S. Wood; p. 11, right: © Gavriel Jecan / Corbis; p. 12, top: © Josh Biggs; p. 12, right: © James S. Wood; p. 14: © James S. Wood; p. 15: © James S. Wood; p. 16: © Josh Biggs; p. 17: © James S. Wood; p. 18, left: © Josh Biggs; p. 18, right: © James S. Wood; p. 19: © Courtesy of Enchantment Resort; p. 21: © Courtesy of La Posada Hotel, photo by Dan Lutzick; p. 23: © Courtesy of Hyatt Regency Scottsdale; p. 24: © James S. Wood; p. 25: © James S. Wood; p. 26: © Kirk Mastin / Aurora Photos / Alamy; p. 28: © Josh Biggs; p. 29: © James S. Wood; p. 33: © Underwood & Underwood / Corbis; p. 34: © Look and Learn / The Bridgeman Art Library; p. 36: © Underwood & Underwood / Corbis; p. 37: © Jim West / Alamy; p. 42: © James S. Wood; p. 48: © Josh Biggs; p. 49: © A. T. Willett / Alamy; p. 51, left: © James S. Wood; p. 51, right: © James S. Wood; p. 52: © James S. Wood; p. 65: © S Tauqueur / Flonline / AGE Fotostock; p. 67: © Josh Biggs; p. 70: © Ron Niebrugge / Alamy; p. 71: © Josh Biggs; p. 72: © Josh Biggs; p. 74: © Cindy Miller Hopkins / Danita Delimont Stock Photography; p. 75, left: © James S. Wood; p. 75, right: © Josh Biggs; p. 77: © Josh Biggs; p. 78, left: © Courtesy Arizona State Parks, Photo by Noelle Wilson; p. 78, right: © Josh Biggs; p. 80: © James S. Wood; p. 81: © James S. Wood; p. 82: © Josh Biggs; p. 84: © Peter McBride / Aurora Photos; p. 86: © James S. Wood; p. 87: © James S. Wood; p. 89: © James S. Wood; p. 90: © James S. Wood; p. 93, left: © James S. Wood; p. 93, right: © James S. Wood; p. 140: © James S. Wood; p. 141: © James S. Wood; p. 142: © James S. Wood; p. 143: © James S. Wood; p. 144: © James S. Wood; p. 145: © James S. Wood; p. 147: © James S. Wood; p. 148: © James S. Wood; p. 149, top: © James S. Wood; p. 149, right: © James S. Wood; p. 151: © James S. Wood; p. 153: © James S. Wood; p. 154: © James S. Wood; p. 157: © James S. Wood; p. 158: © James S. Wood; p. 161: © Buddy Mays / Alamy; p. 162: © Niebrugge Images / Alamy; p. 166: © James S. Wood; p. 168: © Dave and Les Jacobs / Blend / Aurora Photos; p. 172, left: © Christian Petersen / Getty Images; p. 172, right: © James S. Wood; p. 179: © James S. Wood; p. 182: © Courtesy of Evening Entertainment Group; p. 183, left: © Courtesy of Evening Entertainment Group; p. 183, right: © James S. Wood; p. 185: © James S. Wood; p. 187: © Courtesy of Sanctuary Camelback Mountain Resort & Spa; p. 188: © Courtesy of The Phoenix Symphony, Photo by Tim Trumble; p. 189: © James S. Wood; p. 192, left: © James S. Wood; p. 192, right: © Skip Higgins of Raskal Photography / Alamy; p. 194, left: © James S. Wood; p. 194, right: © James S. Wood; p. 195: © James S. Wood; p. 196: © Josh Biggs; p. 198: © Josh Biggs; p. 200: © Richard Cummins / SuperStock; p. 203: © Richard Cummins / SuperStock; p. 204: © Tom Bean / Alamy; p. 205: © Courtesy of Kay El Bar Ranch; p. 208, left: © Josh Biggs; p. 208, right: © Josh Biggs; p. 209: © Josh Biggs; p. 210: © Josh Biggs; p. 211: © Josh Biggs; p. 215: © Josh Biggs; p. 217: © Josh Biggs; p. 218, left: © Josh Biggs; p. 218, right: © Josh Biggs; p. 221: © Josh Biggs; p. 223: © Josh Biggs; p. 224: © Josh Biggs; p. 226: © Josh Biggs; p. 230: © Josh Biggs; p. 231: © Josh Biggs; p. 232, left: © Josh Biggs; p. 232, right: © Josh Biggs; p. 237: © Josh Biggs; p. 240: © Josh Biggs; p. 254: © Dan Barba / Stock Connection / Alamy; p. 256: © Josh Biggs; p. 258: © US Geological Survey / Time Life Pictures / Getty Images; p. 259: © Josh Biggs; p. 260: © Josh Biggs; p. 264: © Josh Biggs; p. 266: © Tom Bean / Alamy; p. 268, top: © Josh Biggs; p. 268, right: © Josh Biggs; p. 270: © Josh Biggs; p. 271: © Josh Biggs; p. 272: © Josh Biggs; p. 274, top: © Josh Biggs; p. 274, right: © Michael DeYoung / Corbis; p. 276: © Josh Biggs; p. 278: © Carol Barrington / Aurora Photos; p. 279: © Josh Biggs; p. 287: © Douglas Peebles / Danita Delimont Stock Photography; p. 289, top: © National Geographic / SuperStock; p. 289, left: © Josh Biggs; p. 290: © Josh Biggs; p. 296: © Josh Biggs; p. 297, left: © Josh Biggs; p. 297, right: © Josh Biggs; p. 298: © Josh Biggs; p. 300: © Don Smetzer / Alamy; p. 301: © Dennis MacDonald / Alamy; p. 308: © Josh Biggs; p. 309: © Josh Biggs; p. 313: © Josh Biggs; p. 314: © Julie Quarry / Alamy; p. 317: © Michael Dwyer / Alamy; p. 319: © Brian Barnes / Alamy; p. 321: © David Ball / Alamy; p. 323: © offiwent.com / Alamy; p. 324: © Nicholas Pitt / Alamy; p. 326: © Francisco González / AGE Fotostock; p. 328: © Josh Biggs; p. 329: © Josh Biggs; p. 332: © Underwood & Underwood / Corbis; p. 335, right: © Chuck Place / Alamy; p. 335, bottom: © Bettmann / Corbis; p. 337: © Antonello Lanzellotto / TIPS Italia / Photolibrary; p. 339: © Bob Rowan / Progressive Image / Corbis; p. 341: © Josh Biggs; p. 342: © Josh Biggs; p. 345, left: © Cindy Miller Hopkins / Danita Delimont Stock Photography; p. 345, right: © Cindy Miller Hopkins / Danita Delimont Stock Photography; p. 348: © Della Huff / Alamy; p. 349: © Cindy Miller

Hopkins / DanitaDelimont.com / Alamy; p. 350, left: © Tom Benoit / SuperStock; p. 350, right: © Mediacolor's / Alamy; p. 353: © Kevin Moloney / Aurora Photos; p. 357: © SERDAR / Alamy; p. 362: © Josh Biggs; p. 363: © Sal Maimone / SuperStock; p. 364: © Josh Biggs; p. 365: © Josh Biggs; p. 367: © Josh Biggs; p. 373: © James Bearden / Alamy; p. 374: © Underwood & Underwood / Corbis; p. 376: © Brian Green / Alamy; p. 378: © Josh Biggs; p. 383: © Laurent Baig / Alamy; p. 387: © Marek Zuk / Alamy; p. 389: © Robert Shantz / Alamy; p. 391: © James S. Wood; p. 393: © James S. Wood; p. 398, right: © James S. Wood; p. 398, bottom: © James S. Wood; p. 434, left: © James S. Wood; p. 434, right: © James S. Wood; p. 436: © James S. Wood; p. 438, left: © James S. Wood; p. 438, right: © James S. Wood; p. 440: © James S. Wood; p. 443, top: © James S. Wood; p. 443, right: © James S. Wood; p. 447: © Rolf Nussbaumer / Imagebroker / Photolibrary; p. 448: © James S. Wood; p. 450: © James S. Wood; p. 453: © James S. Wood; p. 460: © James S. Wood; p. 464: © James S. Wood; p. 465: © Courtesy Arizona State Parks, Photo by Noelle Wilson; p. 467: © Werner Bollmann / AGE Fotostock; p. 470: © Bettmann / Corbis; p. 471: © Richard Cummins / AGE Fotostock; p. 473: © Robert Shantz / Alamy; p. 477: © Susan E. Degginger / Alamy; p. 480, top: © Genevieve Vallee / Alamy; p. 480, right: © National Geographic Image Collection / Alamy; p. 482, left: © James S. Wood; p. 482, right: © James S. Wood; p. 485: © Courtesy Arizona State Parks, Photo by Noelle Wilson; p. 488: © John Cancalosi / Alamy; p. 489: © Bob Gibbons / Alamy; p. 493, left: © Pictorial Parade / Getty Images; p. 493, right: © James S. Wood; p. 494: © James S. Wood; p. 497: © James S. Wood; p. 499: © James S. Wood; p. 502: © Science Faction / SuperStock; p. 505: © Phil Degginger / Alamy; p. 507: © Robert Shantz / Alamy; p. 512: © Mike Goldwater / Alamy; p. 514: © Damian Davies / AGE Fotostock; p. 519: © John Elk III / Alamy; p. 520: © Jenny Fitch; p. 524, left: © Jeremy Edmanson / World Pictures / Photoshot; p. 524, right: © Mike Goldwater / Alamy; p. 526: © Courtesy of Emerald Canyon Golf Course; p. 533: © Randy Bradley / Alamy Images; p. 537: © Courtesy of City of Yuma Arts and Culture Division; p. 539: © Peter Brouillet / Alamy